Praise for
The Dancing Dialogue

D1556963

"This book has exceptional originality and power. It cl
to read the nuances of movement and nonverbal expression in order to guide
assessment and intervention. A major strength is its unique and creative use
of observation. I highly recommend *The Dancing Dialogue* for practitioners
working in the fields of early childhood development and early intervention."
> —**G. Gordon Williamson, Ph.D., OTR,** Associate Clinical Professor of
> Occupational Therapy, College of Physicians and Surgeons, Columbia
> University

"Absolutely the most comprehensive and lucid explanation of what is so often
a mysterious process: how to observe and intervene in the dance of learning,
the dance of interaction, the dance of expression, the dance of healing, and the
dance of being human. Suzi Tortora's book is a must for anyone who deals with
how we humans grow and learn."
> —**Karen Bradley,** Director of Graduate Studies in Dance, University of
> Maryland, College Park

"A truly unique and engaging text for everyone interested in the health and
well-being of young children. Dr. Suzi Tortora demonstrates unusual skill in
rendering academic and specialized concepts easily understandable. From the
many descriptions of her actual work with children and parents to the photographs and tools included throughout the book, this is a complete and author-
itative volume on the power of movement to inspire communication and
growth. *The Dancing Dialogue* is a huge achievement and will most certainly
become a classic text for dance/movement therapists, educators, clinicians,
and parents who care for the welfare of young children."
> —**Robyn Flaum Cruz, Ph.D., ADTR,** Lesley University; Editor-in-
> Chief, *The Arts in Psychotherapy*; Vice President, American Dance Therapy
> Association

"A treasury of information on observing and assessing nonverbal communication unlike any that I have seen. Weaving together interdisciplinary theories
on movement and development with new 'ways of seeing' all children as com-
municators, Tortora provides useful strategies to help professionals across disciplines move beyond the limits of our usual assessment tools. Her stories
bring children to life on the page, reflecting her expertise in enacting the ideas
described in *The Dancing Dialogue* and making it a pleasure to read."
> —**Susan L. Recchia, Ph.D.,** Associate Professor and Coordinator,
> Program in Early Childhood Special Education; Faculty Co-Director, Rita
> Gold Early Childhood Center, Teachers College, Columbia University

"This comprehensive volume will enhance enormously therapists', educators', caregivers', and parents' understanding of the 'whole child.' Through practical guidelines woven together with current interdisciplinary child development theory and research, Dr. Tortora creatively decodes children's nonverbal communication. A wide array of vibrant clinical vignettes with children greatly illuminates Tortora's integrative model. Over and over we learn how movement is the point of entry for interaction and communication. Each chapter is packed full of useful information."

—**Susan Loman, M.A., ADTR, NCC,** Director, M.A. Program in Dance/ Movement Therapy; Professor and Associate Chair, Department of Applied Psychology, Antioch New England Graduate School

"A much-needed resource for all persons who work with young children, especially children with developmental challenges. In so many cases, nonverbal cues are the richest form of communication for these children. *The Dancing Dialogue* is rich in information on both accessing and responding to these cues. Its seamless blend of anecdotes, theoretical perspectives, and specific strategies delivers this information in an enjoyable and reader-friendly way. I will recommend it to everyone I know!"

—**Isaura Barrera, Ph.D.,** Associate Professor, Special Education Department, University of New Mexico

"In this remarkable book, Suzi Tortora shows us, by examples and by systematically described techniques, how to enter, understand, and engage in a realm of communication with young children that spoken language can never reach. This 'new way of seeing' has important therapeutic implications that she describes with clarity, imagination, and practicality."

—**Myron A. Hofer, M.D.,** Sackler Institute Professor of Developmental Psychobiology, Department of Psychiatry, Columbia University

"Nothing less than a tour de force . . . . Remarkably, layers of nonverbal, experiential, and movement 'knowing' literally dance to life through the inspired *words* Tortora has selected . . . . They leap off the pages into imagination and idea in this large, satisfying volume. Indeed, this is a thorough, exhaustive, well-organized, yet unique account by a pioneer, a creator of infant and child relationship-based movement therapy, who motivates us to see how she thinks, understand the ways she knows, and to dare to dance in our own work and lives, as well."

—**Rebecca Shahmoon Shanok, LCSW, Ph.D.,** Institute for Infants, Children and Families, Jewish Board of Family and Children's Services

the DANCING
DIALOGUE

the DANCING DIALOGUE

Using the Communicative Power
of Movement with Young Children

by

Suzi Tortora, Ed.D., ADTR, CMA

·P·A·U·L·H·
BROOKES
PUBLISHING CO. ®

Baltimore • London • Sydney

Paul H. Brookes Publishing Co.
Post Office Box 10624
Baltimore, Maryland 21285-0624
www.brookespublishing.com

Typeset by Auburn Associates, Inc., Baltimore, Maryland.
Manufactured in the United States of America by Versa Press, East Peoria, Illinois.

The vignettes in this book are composites based on the author's actual experiences. In most instances, names and identifying details have been changed to protect confidentiality. Actual names and identifying details are used by permission of the individuals or their parents/guardians. All photographs in this book are used by permission of the individuals pictured or their parents and/guardians.

Library of Congress Cataloging-in-Publication Data

Tortora, Suzi.
   The dancing dialogue : using the communicative power of movement with young children / Suzi Tortora.
      p.   cm.
   Includes bibliographical references and index.
   ISBN-13: 978-1-55766-834-9 (pbk.)
   ISBN-10: 1-55766-834-5 (pbk.)
      1. Movement education.   2. Needs assessment.   3. Dance therapy for children.
I. Title.

GV452. T676 2006
372.86'8—dc22   2005025312

British Library Cataloguing in Publication data are available from the British Library.

Contents

About the Author

Suzi Tortora, Ed.D., ADTR, CMA, 80 East 11th Street, Suite 307, New York, NY 10003; The Carriage House, 8 Marion Avenue, Suite 1, Cold Spring, NY 10516

Suzi Tortora has a clinical dance movement psychotherapy practice in New York City and in the Hudson Valley region of upstate New York. She received her doctorate from Teachers College, Columbia University, with a specialization in infancy; her master's degree in dance therapy from New York University; and her bachelor of arts degree in child development, psychology, and education with teaching certification for typical and special needs early childhood and elementary education from the Elliot Pearson Department of Tufts University. A dancer, gymnast, and athlete since childhood, Dr. Tortora has spent a lifetime exploring all of the ways the body, movement, movement meditation, yoga, and dance can be tools of nonverbal expression and personal growth. The philosophy of her work uses movement and dance-based activities to encourage each person's creativity, self-expression, and individuality while developing physical, social, emotional, communicative, and cognitive skills. She has had more than 20 years of clinical experience in designing wellness, preventative, and therapeutic mental health programs for people of all ages—from infants to older adults.

Dr. Tortora developed the dance movement therapy program for the Integrative Medicine Service for pediatric patients at Memorial Sloan-Kettering Cancer Center in New York City, sponsored by the Andrea Rizzo Foundation, where she is currently creating a multisensory technique to support pain management for infants and young children undergoing painful medical procedures. Dr. Tortora trains allied professionals and lectures about her dance therapy work with infants and families at national and international professional meetings and universities. She is on the faculties of the Infant–Parent Study Center of the Institute for Infants, Children, and Families at the Jewish Board of Family and Children's Services (JBFCS), and the dance therapy master's program at Pratt Institute, both in New York City. She has been featured on ABC's *Good Morning America* and has twice been guest editor for the *Zero to Three* journal.

Dr. Tortora's programs are applicable to patients of all ages along the spectrum from wellness/prevention/creative self-expression to psychotherapeutic treatment, including patients with physical and mental health challenges and those recovering from injuries or adapting to chronic illnesses. In children, these challenges include autism spectrum disorders, developmental delays, adoption, parent–child relationship concerns, and behavioral problems. Dr. Tortora's adult work includes patients with anxiety; depression; eating disorders; arthritis; chronic fatigue; fibromyalgia; migraine headaches; chronic low back, neck, and shoulder pain; and other chronic painful conditions.

Preface

The field of early childhood development and intervention in the 21st century is about opening, sharing, blending, and learning across boundaries that were once separated according to distinct disciplines. Such a description elicits a very physical image for me as a dance movement psychotherapist participating in the field. In this image, I envision a dance that begins with individual dancers, of varying shapes, sizes, genders, and ethnicities, one by one entering the stage to perform a solo. Each dancer's dance is unique, fascinating, and separate and independent from the dances of the other dancing members. Each soloist has his or her own style, rhythm, and tempo and each traverses the stage creating singular spatial floor patterns. At this early stage of the dance, the soloists realize that they are dancing on a stage with other dancers, but they do not experience themselves as dialoguing members of one dance—rather, they maintain the qualitative aspects of their dances that make them each unique. However, as they dance simultaneously on one stage, the dancers find it difficult not to become attracted to or distracted by the other participants.

One by one, the dancers are drawn to an aspect of another's dance. One dancer hears a strong beat, which causes her to almost unconsciously add more weight to her rhythm. Another dancer is visually taken by the gliding pathway of a dancer crisscrossing through his marching, linear path. And as he watches, his own lines begin to sway. One dancer brushes up against another, and they smile at the unexpected contact. Two others collide with force—and so the dance continues, with solos becoming duets and duets becoming ensembles until the stage is filled with this community of dancers. The experience of opening, sharing, blending, and learning from one another has enabled each dancer to expand his or her personal movement repertoire, providing an entrance into new ways of exploring, engaging, and mingling with self and others.

Early childhood development and intervention in the 21st century has gone through an experience similar to the one the dancing image describes. A surge of new infancy development and brain research, clinical practice, and policy making has created a pathway across disciplines, and each discipline's uniqueness and expertise can

support and inform other disciplines. As a result, the potential for dialoguing, sharing, and blending across fields that were once separated
according to discrete practices is enormous. It is an exciting time filled
with much promise for children, their families, and those of us working with them.

The dance image previously described also illustrates a clinical
approach taken in working with children with disabilities and their
families. Many of the ideas presented in this book have come from my
clinical practice as a dance movement psychotherapist working with
individuals, groups, children, and families for more than 20 years. One
of the purposes of this book is to introduce dance movement therapy
and nonverbal observation (through the principles of Laban Movement Analysis) to demonstrate how they can facilitate early childhood
intervention and complement the more traditional methods of special
education. In my clinical practice I have repeatedly witnessed the positive results of introducing dance movement therapy to the traditional
roster of therapeutic and special education interventions, frequently in
cases in which there had been a cessation of progress and growth.

Over the years I have developed a program called the *Ways of
Seeing* approach that encompasses a full intervention spectrum, from
observation/assessment to intervention to educational programming.
The components of this approach combine the two nonverbally oriented processes mentioned above—dance movement therapy and
Laban Movement Analysis. The *Ways of Seeing* approach has evolved as
I sought a systematic way to organize and codify the most useful tools
and theoretical foundations from the fields of dance movement therapy, psychology, and child development.

During the past 2 decades, I have had opportunities to work with
a diverse population of families and children. The children vary in age
from a few months to the preteen years and have a wide variety of
diagnoses, including failure to thrive, pervasive developmental disorders and autism spectrum disorders, hyperactivity, communication disorders, Rett syndrome, agenesis of the corpus callosum, emotional or
physical trauma, adoption issues, physical disabilities, anxiety, sensory
integration dysfunction, regulatory dysfunction, and attachment disorders. I also have worked with pregnant women and then, after the
baby's birth, with the mother–child dyad. The parent–child dyadic
work has included issues of goodness of fit between parent and child
that affects the developing bond and issues of parenting.

I have found that the most consistent reason a family has sought intervention is the parents' belief that aspects of their child's condition have not been addressed in their current forms of intervention, and the parents have felt a need to investigate other ways of working with their child. Often the child has been seen by an assortment of practitioners—pediatricians, occupational therapists, physical therapists, special educators, early intervention specialists, psychiatrists, and neurologists—and has particular difficulties that do not easily fit into a specific diagnosis. He may frequently demonstrate peculiar or problematic styles in relating, and his parents may feel rejected and/or inadequate in their ability to understand their child's needs.

During the initial interviews, I focus on *my* experience of the children before I gather too much information from outside sources. The children often appear angry and uncomfortable. They seem to be desperately striving to control and regulate their environments. Frequently they either shut down—limiting their engagement with their surroundings—or they draw attention to themselves through extreme fussiness. I regularly wonder if these behaviors result from the children's not being understood, from not having their emotional needs met, or from having been pushed to perform beyond their ability or comfort level. Could the behaviors represent their efforts to get someone to understand what they need? I am continually amazed at the extreme exertions of these little ones. Despite their often-limited motoric, communicative, cognitive, social, and emotional abilities, they seem to be striving to preserve themselves.

Taking this perspective, my first task is to establish rapport with the child through nonverbal, movement-oriented dialogues. My goal is to acknowledge a child's effort by entering into his world, exemplified by nonverbal actions and expressions. From this place of relating and communicating, the child often seems relieved to be listened to rather than asked to perform. Once this rapport is established through continued dance-play, I incorporate skill development into our growing social interactions. Through this work, individual children have shown improvement in their ability to relate and express themselves.

When I begin working with a child, I pay close attention to my initial reaction to her and her family. Often when a family first enters my office, I am taken by a sensation of deep resentment and sadness from the parents as well as the child. There are complex issues at hand. The child is uneasy and angry and the parents are worried and depressed about their child's condition and the fact that she doesn't seem to be progressing enough. They are losing hope that something can be done for their child.

During the initial stages of my work, the child seems to be performing solos that are so unique it is questionable whether she can—or will—create relationships between herself and others. By observing her nonverbal movement styles and paying close attention to the specific qualities of her nonverbal expressions, however, I enter into her world, following her cues as a way to literally start a dancing dialogue. By trying on the child's rhythms, tempos, and even the stillness within her body, I pay particular attention to the precise qualities of her movement repertoire. Giving attention to qualitative aspects provides a window into the child even when she has difficulty communicating. In this way, a dance of relating begins among the child, the child's family, and myself. Through this process, using movement, music, body awareness, and touch, the child's experience transforms from a solo to a duet, to a complete ensemble, and she is encouraged to explore and express herself in the surrounding world.

As emphasized throughout this book, all activities in a *Ways of Seeing* dance therapy session, whether undertaken to enhance body awareness, emotional expression, or skill ability, occur within the primary context of relating socially. This relating shares characteristics that are similar to a dancer's experience moving with a partner. Such a mutual dancing dialogue emphasizes the body and involves touching and holding, balancing the whole body and body parts to provide a stable or mobile container for the partner, shifting placement and weight of the body, being aware of body tone and tension, using strength and lightness and mutual gaze, moving toward and away from each other, feeling and playing with each other's energy levels and tempos, and regarding movement interactions as phrases of ongoing communication.

Although the principles discussed in this book may be applied to any population, the emphasis here is on early childhood development and early intervention. This is due to the paramount role nonverbal communication plays in all levels of development of self during these primary years. The main audiences for this book are professionals in multiple disciplines, including pediatricians, physical therapists, occupational therapists, child care providers, educators and special educators, nurses, social workers, psychologists, creative arts therapists, students, and others in the fields of early childhood and early intervention.

Acknowledgments

I wrote this book with much support from my family, friends, colleagues, and the staff at Paul H. Brookes Publishing Co. But a special acknowledgment must go to the children and parents with whom I have had the honor to explore my ideas over the last 20 years. Many of these family members grace the pages of this book through words and through photographs—spontaneous snapshots taken during my creative dance classes by a parent or a teacher who was moved by the spirit and energy of the dancing dialogue.

I thank the staff at Brookes Publishing for including me in the details of the publishing process. I am grateful to have been given the opportunity to write this book and am especially indebted to my editors Heather Shrestha, Kathy Thurlow, and Trish Byrnes for their clarity, patience, expertise, and unending support.

I appreciate the many colleagues who have supported my ideas in numerous ways—for example, by stimulating conversations; by inviting me to write for their publications; by inviting me to speak to their organizations, universities, staff, and intervention centers; and by referring to me the families with whom I was able to work collaboratively. I thank Nancy Beardall, my first dance therapy mentor, lifelong friend, and confidante, who continually converses with me on all matters personal and professional. I am grateful to my dance therapy colleague and valued friend Jane Wilson Cathcart for the spaces we share both in thought and in physical structure. I am beholden to Martha Eddy, also a dear friend and movement colleague, whom I consider to be our walking encyclopedia on all historic matters in the realm of nonverbal body–mind theory.

I am indebted to Emily Fenichel, who many years ago was the first person in the field of early childhood to encourage me to find a way to write about the treatment that uses the elusive qualities of dance and movement as a healing agent. I thank G. Gordon Williamson for his continual support of my effort from its earliest stages, which is especially meaningful since he has been such an inspiration. I thank Myron and Lynne Hofer, both of whom have engaged in meaningful exchanges with me throughout the development of my work. I also deeply appreciate the support Beatrice Beebe has given me; I have learned much from her. And I am very much beholden to Gil Foley for our engaging theoretical discussions and clinical collaborations.

The foundation of my work in understanding how a body communicates has come from an in-depth study of the body in motion. Several women who were pioneers in the exploration of the body and movement have influenced my work greatly. It is the power of the unspoken word that first captured them—through the universal language of the dance. Among these women are my early teachers Janet Adler, Miriam Roskin Berger, Bonnie Bainbridge Cohen, Robyn Flaum Cruz, Irene Dowd, and Susan Loman. Although I did not actually meet Irmgard Bartenieff, for her passing occurred just weeks before I began my Laban Movement Analyst training, her presence was greatly felt through her protégés, most notably Jane Wilson Cathcart and Martha Eddy, mentioned above, and Virginia Reed. Each of these women directed her interest in dance into other professions including dance therapy, occupational therapy, physical therapy, professional management training, and neuromuscular reeducation. A similar relationship with women in the field of education also occurred with Annette Axtmann, Lori Custodero, Celia Genishi, and Susan Recchia, all at Teachers College, Columbia University, who encouraged me to continue my investigation into relationships among dance, expression, communication, early childhood development, education, and intervention. I am indebted to each of these strong and creative women who have danced with me in partnership, greatly adding to my continuing choreography, which has evolved into the presenting material in this book.

And last, for they make up the home base from which everything else has been built, I give my heartfelt thanks to my adored son Bryce for his willingness to join in the dance with the children and for his love, trust, and belief in his mother, even when writing this book took precious time away from him; and to Paul, my 24-hour on-call fix-it, edit-it, read-it, electronic wizard, who keeps everything humming smoothly with tireless patience and kindness.

To my family (with whom I share the dance):

my mother Lucille, who first introduced me to the dance

my father Antonio, who supported the dance—even when he didn't have a clue what it was about!

my son Bryce, with whom I have been honored to dance the dance of life between mother and child

and Michele, with whom I learned the dance of sisterhood

And to Paul, my dancing partner

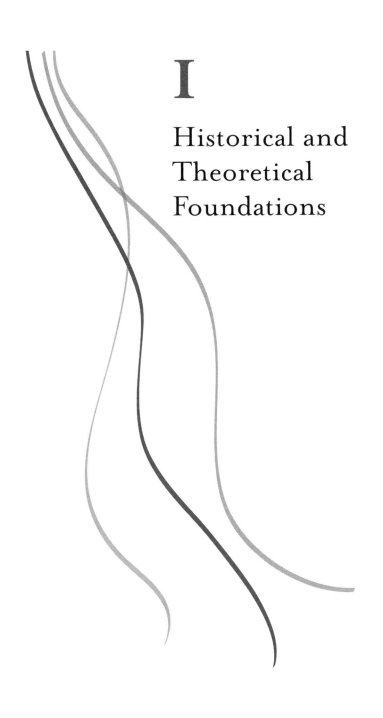

I

Historical and Theoretical Foundations

1

Introduction

Lisa enters the studio for the first time giving me a blank stare. "Lisa, can you take off your shoes?" "Shoes," she says in a soft high-pitched voice. "Would you like to dance?" "Dance," she responds, again with softness and again with no real expression, her eyes seeming to almost look through me. I put out my hand and it is met with her light touch. I respond with gentleness and eagerness. I don't want to lose this connection so I forgo the music and begin our dance with walking—simple, slow, walking steps, holding hands. We walk up and down the room. "Walking," I say. "Walking," she replies. Do I detect a slight increase in her speed? I try it out, increasing the tempo of our gait. She follows. Soon we are traversing the room in high speed, holding hands. She feels the breeze across her face and glances over at me. Did I see a flicker of excitement, I wonder? The lightness of her step and the gentleness of her grasp encourage me to turn our run into a skip. I know this requires a more advanced coordination, but I just have to try. Without missing a step, she follows the skip. I feel as if I have a gentle bobbing butterfly in the palm of my outstretched hand. "Skip," I say. "Skip," she repeats, and this time, there is a smile and a slight exclamation of glee. Now her blue eyes maintain their steady gaze at me, but they are accompanied by a fixed smile. We try gallops, glides, side steps, and prances. As with her echolalic speech, she is able to repeat my actions. We progress to the grapevine—crossing the right leg in front, stepping with the left leg to the side, crossing the right leg to the back, and repeating. At first she gets confused with front and back crossings, but with a little hands-on guidance, she masters this quickly too. Actually she is a master of following, repeating, and copying. But where is she underneath all of this? What does she feel? What does she think? These questions immediately sprint through my mind as I experience Lisa.

Experiencing is a key word in dance movement psychotherapy, the therapeutic technique discussed throughout this book. Experiencing involves gaining an awareness of the infant or child with whom you are working by following her[1] lead and actually trying on her actions. Experiencing also involves paying attention to your own reactions and questions as you engage in this process. Dance movement psychotherapy can be defined as the psychotherapeutic use of movement, body awareness, dance, and relaxation techniques to facilitate changes on all developmental levels: social, emotional, physical, cognitive, and communicative. Just as important as these techniques is the foundational principle that creating a social-emotional relationship with the child is the essential initial goal that makes all further growth possible.

Using dance and movement in a therapeutic way has evolved over the past 60 years into a specialized field of practice. The concepts and tools of dance movement psychotherapy, however, can be useful for a variety of professionals working with infants, children, and families— and for parents as well. Under these circumstances, the primary use of dance and movement is to encourage self-expression and understanding of nonverbal communication rather than to promote proficiency in formal dance techniques. All movements—from a crawl, to a run, to a waltz—and even standing still are included in the vocabulary of dance movement because they all have the capability of becoming communicative. Most parents, teachers, therapists, and other professionals already apply, perhaps unknowingly, many dance movement therapeutic concepts as they strive to read and respond to the unspoken cues of an infant or child's behaviors. All movements have the potential to communicate, regardless of how distracting or idiosyncratic they may appear at first. Movement and the observation of movements are the primary tools emphasized in this treatment approach, which succeeds even with the most difficult-to-reach children.

The concepts of dance, dance choreography, creativity, spontaneity, and play are explained in detail for readers who are unfamiliar with dance, to provide new insights into the power and universality of the body as a medium for understanding social-emotional expression. The discussions and vignettes in this book are drawn largely from the author's clinical practice. Recent developments in early childhood development, psychology, nonverbal communication, and brain research are included to explain how the concepts of dance

[1]To be fair to both genders in describing children in this book, pronouns will be alternated.

movement psychotherapy can be placed within the context of current therapeutic interventions. The goal of this book is twofold—to demonstrate how dance movement psychotherapy is a valuable modality to the intervention/educational team, and to educate those who work with infants and children to better understand how nonverbal communication and movement-based activities can become valuable tools that support their interactions.

A DIALOGUE BETWEEN THE ARTS AND SCIENCES

Research in early childhood development and psychology places a great value on nonverbal expressions and interactions, as shown by studies discussed in Chapter 2 and elsewhere throughout this book. Although the role that a dance-based therapeutic program can play in childhood development and psychology may not be readily apparent, there has been a longstanding dialogue in which scholars from the arts, movement, and the sciences have examined one another's works in the study of human emotions. These references include the 19th-century works of Jaques-Dalcroze, the founder of the Eurhythmics music education system (Jaques-Dalcroze, 1918, 1976, 2003), and Delsarte, the French philosopher and teacher of dramatic expression (1892). Related studies of the 20th century include the early work on movement expression and individual differences by psychologists Allport and Vernon (1933) and the analysis of body language, nonverbal communication, and social order, including family interactions, by Scheflen (1965, 1972, 1973, 1976; Davis, personal communication, 2005). The connection between emotions and movement in the behavioral sciences include Darwin's study of emotional expressions in man and animals (2002) and Ekman and Friesen's studies of facial expressions (1976; Davis, personal communication, 2005). The use of dance and movement as conduits for nonverbal expression—so essential a concept in the dance world—has proven to be a prevailing concept that supports the conversation between the arts and sciences in this book.

Dance therapy was founded in the 1940s and expanded on in the 1950s during the modern dance movement by dancers who wanted to use their understanding of the body as a therapeutic tool to express the deepest emotions of self, self and other, and the universality of life's experiences (Bartenieff, 1957). A dancer's training, involving extensive exploration into how the body regulates and organizes its movements, requires keen proprioceptive and kinesthetic awareness to be used in the service of emotional expression. Dance training creates an experiential knowing of how body and emotions interrelate through nonverbal expression.

Literature in fields unrelated to the arts also addresses nonverbal expression, especially in regard to the observation and study of children. This scientific research investigates nonverbal expression by examining how infants and young children experience motor development, how they learn about self in relation to others, and how their early preverbal experiences influence communication and cognition. The book discusses and demonstrates how and why nonverbal expression can be such a powerful element in intervention, underlying all observations, interactions, communications, and treatments.

Using the *Ways of Seeing* approach described later in more detail, the therapist's[2] experiential knowing is always guided by detailed observations. These observations continually remind the therapist to consider both how an infant or child might be experiencing an interaction and at the same time how this interpretation of the experience may be influencing the interaction. Following careful observation, the therapist attunes and mirrors the infant or child's nonverbal actions in an effort to create a dancing dialogue. Finally, the therapist creates experiences for infants and children using dance, movement, play, and improvisation to follow their leads and to extend their communication and interactions. Therapists encourage the growth of social-emotional relationships when they pay close attention to the infant or child's nonverbal actions and then choose movements that match or complement specific details.

Dance movement psychotherapy is a branch of creative arts therapy. Throughout history and in all cultures, one of the most essential and universal roles of the arts is their ability to tap into otherwise unexpressed avenues of the self. The graphic arts, music, drama, poetry, and dance can all be used within the traditional therapeutic relationship as tools for expression and self-discovery and as constructs within a therapeutic philosophy.

Dance movement psychotherapy reveals how a person's expression of self and experience of the world are conveyed through the media of the body and the body in motion. The body, movement, and dance become part of a methodology that plays an important role in

---

[2]This book generally uses the word *therapist,* although the *Ways of Seeing* approach can be useful to any adult who works with children.

learning how an infant or child understands and experiences the surrounding world. One of the key gifts that dance movement psychotherapy brings to the therapeutic milieu is its link to nonverbal expression. It enables a therapist to gain access to information that may not be readily available through verbal processing for a variety of reasons. In the youngest population—infants and toddlers—verbalization and symbolic realms of understanding are not fully developed; nonverbal, sensory, and sensorimotor processing dominate how they create their experience of the world. In older children and adults, understanding nonverbal expression can uncover experiences that are not easily tapped into through words. Finally, for children and adults who have difficulties in expressive or receptive communicative processing, the nonverbal methods advocated in this book can have a powerful effect on both the individuals and their families. The *Ways of Seeing* approach can provide an avenue for expression and deeper understanding that often leads to improved relationships.

THE DANCING DIALOGUE

The word *dance* is often used metaphorically to describe the give and take of social interactions and emotional expressions. We "dance around issues" in an effort to avoid exposure or conflict with others; we "are dancing as fast as we can" to keep going under pressure; and we use the "dance of intimacy" to describe the complexities of intimate personal engagement. Indeed, social-emotional interactions are essential parts of a true dance duet. To dance with another, both dancing members must be aware of their own and their partner's individual styles of moving, as well as the overall feeling tone created as they move together and their individual qualities combine. Designing an engaging dancing duet involves paying close attention to each dancer's energy level and range of movement repertoire. Each dancer must know when and how to apply just the right amount of strength or softness to support his or her partner's movement. Both must have the ability to move through a series of actions in synchrony, harmony, and opposition to keep the dancing interchange going. They must learn to balance their bodies in numerous positions to provide a stable or mobile container for their partners who are sharing and traversing the space with them. The proper timing of approach, initiation, and withdrawal of contact becomes essential to create an affable experience. An awareness of the elements of tempo and phrasing within the context of the dancing story line must always be maintained to support the expressiveness of the dancing conversation—the dancing dialogue.

The Dancing Dialogue has been chosen as the title of this book to bring together the metaphoric use of the word *dance* and the nature of its truest application. Dance enables the viewer and the mover[3] alike to experience life through physical expression. To see interactions with others as a dance, through a deeper understanding of dance as an art form, enhances the appreciation of nonverbal communication—perhaps the most elusive element of social exchange.

Reading Nonverbal Cues

⁓ *Xavier, age 2½, comes running helter-skelter down the hall, suddenly crossing in front of his mom as if he doesn't notice her and then just as suddenly running behind her all the way to the classroom. He seems to be gazing everywhere and nowhere all at the same time. But just as they approach the classroom door, his energy spike ends as Xavier drops his body and becomes a heavy log, refusing to move. His mom gives his arm a few tugs, shrugs her shoulders, and steps over him to enter the classroom. A few moments later he picks himself up with a start, darts into the room, and abruptly stops again at the two-way mirror on the wall near the entrance. Is he gazing at his image, the teachers wonder? It is hard to tell what his eyes are registering because without warning, he is off again! This time his fleeting body makes traversing pathways through the classroom, only stopping when he gets to a solid surface such as the wall or the floor. When he comes to one of these stable places, he bumps into it, pauses for a while, and seems to look around. When his teacher approaches him, his eye contact is only fleeting. A typical school day for Xavier has begun.* ⁓

Xavier's teachers have come to know and expect this "solo entrance dance" because his nonverbal cues have become familiar to them. By reading and experiencing these behaviors again and again, they interpret that transitions are difficult for him. Xavier needs time to settle in and does not respond well to being approached directly—it only sets him off running again. The teachers cue into his nonverbal expressions and use these cues to inform themselves how to help him adjust to his classroom routines. Such observations are taken one step

---

[3]The word *mover* is used here and elsewhere to refer to the person who is moving and whose movements are being observed.

further as the dance movement therapist begins her interactions with Xavier.

I stay back and watch as Xavier runs from place to place bumping and falling into the wall or the floor. I begin to collect a few ideas: It seems as though these surfaces enable him to stop; each of these locations is on the outskirts of the room, and counter to everyone's impressions, there does seem to be a pattern to his path—he keeps coming to the same spots! I am curious to feel this pathway, so I join him. I want to respect his personal space, so I decide to follow his path, stopping in each place he does after he has just left it, and I gently call out "IIi, Xavier!" when I get there. Pretty soon he catches on. He looks at me as if to ask, "What is this lady doing?" but he is excited. Each time he gets to his next place, he turns around to look at me rather than falling into the spot. After a little of this follow-the-leader dance, I take a chance—I quickly sprint to his spot while he is still there and give him a brief but firm squeeze hello. He giggles, and a new dance begins. Now he purposely waits for me at each place. Our dance of relating has begun.

This was Xavier's first dance movement psychotherapy session, taking place in an infant–toddler child care setting. As the year continues, this follow-the-leader dance develops into a close relationship. Xavier's limited movement repertoire becomes a source of social exchange as the therapist first mirrors and next incorporates his actions, adding them into her own movements, which Xavier then imitates. Soon Xavier and the therapist do not need to traverse the whole room in order to interact. As they start to play in one area of the room, the therapist is able to add a verbal component to their movement exchange. She begins to label the actions, emphasizing Xavier's involvement in the dance-play.

"Oh! Xavier is jumping! I will jump too! It feels good to jump so quickly like Xavier. Jump! Jump! JUMP! Oh, now it is my turn. I will stamp my feet strong! Oh look! Xavier is stamping too! Look how strong you are stamping. I can hear your stamping feet. Stamp. Stamp. STAMP! You are a good stamper. You are a good follower. What would you like to add to our dance now?" Xavier watches with gleeful stillness as I follow and describe his actions. When I stop, Xavier begins to jump again, looking closely to see if I will follow him. He responds joyfully again when I repeat his action.

Xavier begins to learn about the give and take and sharing of social interactions and to explore the more complex aspects of relating through movement and simple verbal dialogue. With the therapist acting as catalyst, Xavier becomes able to participate in group creative dance classes by following the actions and sharing his own movement ideas—although at first always staying on the outskirts of the room. Through continued individual and group-movement interactions, Xavier's ability to relate to those around him increases. Slowly, Xavier inches his way closer and closer into the dance circle, until by the end of the year, by his own initiative, he is playing and dancing with his classmates throughout the day.

This vignette exemplifies how a therapist can take a child's initial observable behaviors and build on them as a way of creating a relationship. In this "dancing duet," Xavier and the dance movement therapist learn about each other by exploring and sharing their individual movement styles through playful interactions. These interactions enable free expression of feelings and emotions as their individual movements co-construct their dance-play. The spontaneous, improvisational nature of their interactions keeps the dialogue alive. The decision to begin the movement exchange within Xavier's expressive repertoire, later supplemented by dance-play initiated by the therapist and eventually by his classmates, enables Xavier to experience socializing. From the comfort and stability of his familiar repertoire, Xavier becomes able to reach out into a larger social circle. Using movement, music, touch, and body awareness, actions are transformed from a solo, to a duet, and ultimately to a complete ensemble, which encourages him to explore and express himself in the surrounding world.

THE *WAYS OF SEEING* APPROACH

The *Ways of Seeing* approach combines the principles of dance movement psychotherapy, the discipline of the Authentic Movement program, and the Laban Movement Analysis (LMA) nonverbal movement observation system to create a complete assessment, intervention, and educational approach for infants, children, and their families. This program successfully illustrates how nonverbal behaviors are meaningful communications that can be used to create a bridge from observation and assessment to intervention and education. The name *Ways of Seeing* emphasizes the many different ways there are to look, assess, and receive information. Therapists are asked to raise their awareness through observation and interaction of how nonverbal and multisensory experiences may be influencing an individual's experience. The term *individual* here represents the therapists themselves, the infants and children being treated, and other family members involved in the intervention or educational program.

The *Ways of Seeing* model was inspired by two concepts. The first is the dance movement psychotherapy principle that everyone has a need to be "seen." The term *seeing* refers to each individual's need to be acknowledged and understood for his or her own uniqueness. The second concept is taken from the work of writer and provocative thinker, John Berger (1977), who uses words and images from the fine arts to stimulate people into questioning their own personal process of seeing. Using art as the subject of inquiry, Berger's work continually reflects on the multitude of ways that people absorb and express visual information.

A basic principle of the *Ways of Seeing* approach is that every individual creates a nonverbal movement style or profile composed of a unique combination of movement qualities that can be observed by a trained eye. These movement styles reveal aspects of the individual's experience with the surroundings. This book instructs readers how to detect these nonverbal cues and develop movement profiles of themselves, others, and parent–child dyads. Movement profiles can next be used to analyze behaviors and interaction styles to decide whether they are complementary, compatible, or conflicting. Readers can then use this information to create tools for interventions that will improve interactions and promote creative expression. Although the principles discussed may be applied to any population, early childhood development and early intervention/education are stressed for two reasons: 1) to highlight the significant role nonverbal communication plays in all levels of self-development established during the primary years and 2) to support the conviction that early intervention provides the strongest potential for change. Despite this emphasis, it is the author's belief based on years of experience as a dance movement psychotherapist, that there is no age range or specific population limitation to the *Ways of Seeing* approach.

This program expands the notion of kinesthetic learning and emphasizes its applicability in the creation of collaborative goals and treatment strategies across disciplines. The program also underscores the impact of nonverbal communication during interactions. Focusing on the qualities of expression defines nonverbal components of affect and affective sharing, and their influence on the development of creativity and healing. Using dance, movement, and music enables people to express themselves and to enjoy their bodies even under circumstances in which there are significant delays, disabilities, or other difficulties. Ultimately, because the *Ways of Seeing* method uses the body, movement, and nonverbal expression simultaneously, it is an integrative approach that crosses multiple developmental levels and facilitates growth in all domains.

Why Look at Individual Movement Styles?

The *Ways of Seeing* approach does not initially focus on skill or developmental levels, but rather on the qualities of children's nonverbal behaviors. These qualities are the children's expressive/communicative styles, regardless of how unconventional or atypical those styles might be. Even severe movement limitations have a qualitative element to them—it may be in the level of tension in musculature, the position the body habitually takes, or the frequency or infrequency of eye contact. Moreover, the expression of these qualities creates a sensation, attitude, or response from the individuals to those in the environment. In return, the observers of these behaviors have a reaction, based on their own experiences. It is this action–reaction that influences the developing social-emotional relationships and affects therapeutic and educational interventions.

An example of this phenomenon can be seen in the simple action of a child's swaying—an everyday occurrence. The action of swaying the body is innocuous in and of itself; still, its effect and expressive impact is dependent on how the sway is executed. A child's gentle sway, created by shifting weight from foot to foot, such as the child might do while he is standing in line to return from recess, might go virtually unnoticed by the

Dance and music help children to express themselves.

teacher. If the child increases the speed of that sway, however, pulsing from side to side, the teacher may ask him to stop moving and to wait more patiently in line. If the child has trouble with impulse control, this suggestion might have the opposite effect, causing him not only to increase his speed further but also to lose spatial awareness—so that now the child is bumping into his classmates nearby. Thus, this initially harmless sway has spun out of control as the child's ability to maintain physical and mental attention diminishes. This example shows that it is not just the specific action but the particular manner in which the action is performed that creates its feeling tone. At this point the teacher's comments and attitude toward the child most likely will be influenced by the child's inability to respond to the teacher's directives. The children who are disturbed by him might also have a negative response to his behavior. If such behavior becomes a repeated pattern, it will permanently affect how his teacher and classmates view the child. This in turn will influence how the child feels about himself and how he continues to interact with those around him. Ultimately, this not-so-simple act of swaying might significantly affect how the child forms social relationships.

From a dance movement therapist's perspective, how movement actions are executed is the qualitative aspect that is of special interest to the nonverbal movement analysis. A dance movement therapist pays attention to both the specific action and how the action is performed in determining an individual's personal movement style. In fact, the manner in which the movement is brought together is the qualitative piece that makes each individual's movement style unique.

This emphasis on the qualitative elements of an individual's movement style demonstrates the complex yet invaluable contribution an awareness of nonverbal movement expression can provide to the analysis of children's behaviors. A therapist can determine how a child feels about himself emotionally by observing how he interacts socially and how he communicates with others. The child's cognitive understanding of his surroundings also influences his behaviors. Because all of these aspects of behavior are observable, paying attention to the qualitative elements of an infant or child's actions can facilitate a deeper understanding of his unique social, emotional, physical, cognitive, and communicative developmental history and style. A therapist's awareness of a child's movement style thus provides significant and valuable information about how best to support the child's growth in developmental areas through therapeutic and educational systems.

Why Study Nonverbal Movement Qualities?

As explained above, the nonverbal qualitative elements of an individual's movement style reveal how that person is relating and interacting with the surrounding world. Relating and interacting not only include emotional and social engagement but also encompass how a person's unique ways of absorbing and processing information from the surroundings affect his or her learning styles. Qualitative elements—that is, the specific descriptive components of physical actions—provide information about *how* an action is performed, *which* specific body parts execute the action, and *where* the action occurs in reference to others and the surrounding environment. Such details color a person's experiences and affect nonverbal expression. Observation and analysis of the qualitative elements of a person's nonverbal languages of movement can provide a window into a fuller understanding of the person's expression and style of interaction.

The qualitative elements are the key features of a person's movement repertoire that are unique. Although actions may require similar executions, the elements used to perform an action can differ vastly from person to person. Thus, these specific qualitative elements provide self-expression. For example, walking requires a weight shift from one foot to the other. How this weight is shifted (e.g., whether a heavy step *or* a light step is used); how different body parts participate in this walk (e.g., whether both arms alternately swing and the head leans forward to lead in front of the hips, *or* both arms are held tightly at the sides and the body is upright); and the speed in which the walk occurs (e.g., whether fast *or* slow) create a different feeling and mood, thus presenting a different interpretation. Each particular nuance of a movement—conscious or unconsciously chosen—reflects a personal choice. There are an infinite number of qualitative ways that an action can be performed, and even the slightest variation expresses something different about a person's feelings, expressions, and interactions. These variations provide information about every person's unique ways of relating to the surroundings.

Individuality and Uniqueness   Acknowledging each person's uniqueness is especially significant when decoding nonverbal actions in the process of interpreting behaviors. As emphasized throughout this book, the process of interpreting the qualitative aspects of a body action is not a dictionary system so structured or defined that each gesture or movement quality has a codified universal meaning; nor can the process be based on a predetermined vocabulary of body language.

Movement qualities cannot be viewed in isolation; therefore, an observer must take into consideration how specific movement qualities relate to each other within the context of a mover's style, history, and environment. Compare the following description of two toddlers who are both observed in postures that initially involve crossing their arms in front of their chests:

Taylor stands with his back to the child care room, holding his body stiff and straight. His arms are pressed tightly across his chest, causing his shoulders to lift. With his brow firmly furrowed and his lower lip extended, he buries his chin into his chest and stands frozen for a long time, avoiding contact with his sympathetic teacher. Mom has just dropped him off at child care, and he doesn't want to be there. He has been having a difficult time these first 2 weeks, transitioning into this new setting. Across the room, Bobby is also standing tall with his arms crossed tightly, shoulders lifted, and head bowed in his chest. Suddenly his arms burst open, and he lifts his head with a broad smile, swiftly turning his head from side to side as he begins to dart around the room. He bends down to look under the table, and then runs over to the pillow pile, haphazardly casting the pillows off to the side. It soon becomes clear that he is searching for Amanda, with whom he is playing Hide-and-Seek. He stops and points, gleefully giggling, when he discovers her under the pillows.

It is not just actions that communicate a movement's meaning. Instead, it is how an action's qualitative elements are clustered together—along with the context of the individual child's attitude—that allows correct interpretation. Taylor's crossed arms, tight body, and dropped head can be read as angry and anguished due to his accompanying facial expression, the length of time he stays frozen in this position, and his refusal to respond to his teacher. The observer's knowledge that Taylor is a new student provides additional insight. Most likely, the observer will reserve immediate serious concern about the child's behavior due to the new setting. If Taylor's behavior persists for many months and is displayed throughout the day whenever he gets upset, this posture will take on added meaning, eliciting more cause for concern.

Although Bobby's posture is initially similar to Taylor's, the difference in how the qualities of his actions unfold soon makes it obvious that he is having a very different experience. The exuberance of his smile, the suddenness of his postural changes, the speed and gaiety of his gestures, and the control he demonstrates in his ability to quickly stop his searching actions, all suggest a light, playful attitude. Any observer should be able to sense the difference between these two boys' behaviors but may not be able to explain what qualitative elements underlie the difference. A trained observer, however, can detect and articulate exactly what makes the actions different and explain how and why each child's experience is distinct. Understanding qualitative aspects of movement provides a therapist with added information to decipher the deeper meaning of what is influencing a child's behaviors.

A therapist must always strive to understand how a child's way of relating and moving shapes the child's experience. Finding and then using the child's unique style to highlight her individuality allows the therapist to create an intervention program that supports growth across developmental areas. All work must begin by following the child's lead. Trying on a child's rhythms, tempos, and even stillness is often the ideal way for a therapist to determine the precise qualities of a child's movement repertoire. This can even provide a window into understanding a child who has difficulties communicating. Through this method a child becomes an active participant and creator of the therapeutic/educational activities, rather than a passive recipient of exercises and skills done to him. Most important, following the child's lead is the way to create a dance of relating between the child and the therapist.

Movement Messages We give two messages when we communicate with others—the message that our words relay and also the message that our body movements reveal. Picture in your mind a child whose eyelids are drooping heavily, his body sliding down in a chair, who then insists that he is not tired and attempts to refuse to be put down for a nap. An adult's perception of the situation most often prevails, and the exhausted child takes his nap. But a person's mismatched movement and verbal messages can be much more complex and can have serious implications, as was revealed in Tronick and Gianino's (1986) classic research on the impact that depressed mothers have on their babies. This study showed how the deadpan expression; monotone voice; flattened affect; and the slow, listless qualities that often accompany the actions of a truly depressed person deeply influence the way that a baby reacts to a depressed mother. After a period of time in which the baby unsuccessfully attempts to arouse the mother's eye contact through active vocalizations and movements, the baby may show signs of distress and disengagement, such as shutting down, looking away, and becoming listless or irritable. Similarly, despite a parent's attempt to hide behavior by saying, "Everything is fine," the forced smile and rigid actions of an anxious parent do not go unnoticed by a child who relies on this person for comfort. Such situations disorient communication and confuse the child's understanding of her immediate experience. The source of this confusion is the discrepancy between the message of the words and the quality of the actions. A person's true meaning can only be discovered by paying attention to both the quality of the spoken words and the quality of the movements—conscious and unconscious.

Ideally, we aim for our verbal messages to match our nonverbal messages, but too often our words say one thing and our bodies say another. Perhaps the old axiom "Do as I say, not as I do" should be changed to "Do as I say *and* as I do," to remind adults of the importance of sending a single coherent message to children. Children are reading both messages—but perhaps they are learning even more from body language than from spoken words when the messages are inconsistent.

Requiring people to match the meaning of their words with their actions is not an easy task because it demands a greater awareness of nonverbal messages. Take the example of a therapist who has worked with a baby on a particular skill and now wants to demonstrate this achievement to the baby's parent. The therapist is understandably nervous in the parent's company. When alone with the baby, the therapist's pace of instruction was slow and calm, but in the parent's presence the therapist's actions become more animated and tense. When the therapist adds an extra push of enthusiastic encouragement, the baby's reaction is to stop his performance and start to cry instead. He knows that something has changed, and he doesn't like it. Although the therapist's words and actions are the same, the atmosphere is different. The quality of the therapist's actions has intensified, and despite the therapist's attempts to act calm, the therapist's musculature exudes tension. This relays a mixed message that will push any baby with a sensitive sensory system over the top!

Children often do not know the complex innuendoes of language, and these complexities can be even more difficult for children with special challenges. Such children respond to how experiences make them feel. They call the shots as they experience and see them. In truth, everyone responds much more to nonverbal cues than is often acknowledged. A teacher—without bothering to look up—often recognizes which child is entering a classroom by the rhythm and speed of the footsteps. Taking this example one step further, as students become better known, the teacher may be able to recognize more sub-tle shifts in style, such as increased energy or lethargy, that provide clues about the children's moods. Noticing the qualitative elements of particular movement styles enables the teacher—and other perceptive adults—to get to know children more deeply.

A *Ways of Seeing* therapist can use LMA to take these observations yet another step further, by noticing the body parts that are used to exe-cute a particular movement, the shapes that the body makes to create this movement, the manner that these movements are performed, and where these movements are made in space. A *Ways of Seeing* therapist can then use this nonverbal information to decide how to approach and to work with children and their families, always striving to use these nonverbal elements to help children reach their maximum potentials. An example of this method can be seen in the following vignette:

⌒ *Brianna, age 25 months, lies on her back and stares off into space without direct eye focus. Brianna can spend extended periods of time disen-gaged visually. When she is not physically or emotionally engaged, her extreme hypotonic condition leaves her body limp, with her arms and legs spread out wide at her sides. I reach into her visual field with the back of my hand, careful to use the qualities of lightness and directness so as not to sud-denly intrude on, but instead to gently enter into her state. I pause my hand in the air within her view, without touching her. Brianna begins to gently roll her body side to side, initiating the action with her head, turning toward me, making a soft sound, but still not giving or maintaining eye contact. This rocking is a common action in her movement repertoire, but she has initiated it just as I have entered her intimate space. Could this be a response to my action, I wonder? I again reach my hand out, but this time I add quickness to the light, direct gesture, and briefly touch her. I strive to make my desire to connect with her more definite. Brianna stops rocking, and rolls over toward me, reaching her right arm out with a quick, light, sweeping gesture, and makes eye contact. I take this as a cue—yes, perhaps she is extending her attention to me! I begin to mirror her head and body roll. Again, with an extreme light quality to her action, Brianna pulls her legs and arms up, enclosing her torso as she continues to watch me. Mirroring her, I add her reaching arm action to my movements. In addition, I slow down my rocking roll as I enter closer into her kinesphere (that is, the space immediately sur-rounding her that is within reach of her limbs). I enclose my body like hers, limbs at my chest, as we lie face to face, with hands touching, eyes softly gaz-ing at each other for an extended time.* ⌒

Brianna has a medical condition called *agenesis of the corpus callosum*, a rare congenital abnormality in which there is a partial or complete absence of the brain area that connects the left and right cerebral hemispheres. Although asymptomatic in some individuals, it can also cause impairments in mental and physical development, visual and auditory memory, and hand–eye coordination. At the time of this vignette, Brianna demonstrates a 1- to 2-year delay in all areas of development, most often functioning at a 4- to 6-month developmental age.

A detailed analysis of her videotaped *Ways of Seeing* sessions reveals that Brianna actually pays attention to and participates in her surroundings far more than her parents and therapist initially believed. Brianna communicates nonverbally by rocking, gliding, or pushing her legs, hands, or head, attuned to the movement rhythms of the adult with whom she is working. Despite her limited movement repertoire, in her own way Brianna often initiates further communicative engagements with adults.

In the terminology of LMA (Laban 1975, 1976), Brianna uses spoking and arcing actions of her limbs directed outward in an attempt to engage with her surroundings. When interpreted as Brianna's efforts to reach out into space and connect with the people in her surroundings and the environment itself, these actions are called *directional movements*. In contrast, *shaping* movements require a more intricate level of engagement in which the mover molds body actions around objects or others in the surroundings. *Shape-flow* movements involve undulations of the torso and reveal an inner connectedness or focus toward one's self. Brianna's hypotonia prevents her from being able to employ shape flow movements because she does not yet have sufficient muscular strength or body awareness.

After analyzing their movement exchanges, the *Ways of Seeing* therapist ponders how Brianna's experience of her body might contribute to her difficulties in developing more complex social relationships. Her lack of muscular strength prevents Brianna from feeling in control of herself or her body. The directional movements that she performs often involve sudden bursts of initiation that too soon dissipate into passivity. Such dissipated actions, which simply melt away or wind down, do not create in Brianna a sense of closure or completion to her experience. The dance movement therapist becomes aware on reflection that when she tries on Brianna's current movement phrasing style and low muscle tone, she experiences only a primitive sense of agency in relating. While experimenting with relating in this way during sessions, she is struck by her inability to articulate and pay attention to the fine details usually involved both in self-expression and in understanding others. She realizes that the ability to concentrate on such details is an integral part of more complex socializing.

This recognition influences how the therapist structures subsequent sessions. Because Brianna's experiences of self are largely through her body, incorporating actions that use shaping and shape flow movements of the torso becomes the targeted goal. LMA regards shaping movements as actions that foster relationships between self and other, whereas shape flow movements support deeper physical experiences of self. The therapist chooses movement experiences that contain both of these qualities in the hope of facilitating a more effective development of Brianna's sense of self in relation to others.

Because movement and body awareness are the tools that the therapist uses to improve communications and relationships during her sessions, an increase in Brianna's motor function also occurs. Moreover, without a task focus, Brianna has the freedom to direct and explore her movements, and that, in turn, naturally leads to her development of innate motor patterns. Perhaps most important, Brianna's parents provide a key role in their daughter's growth: They have learned during the sessions how they can play with Brianna at home, observing and responding to her nonverbal cues with increased perceptiveness and understanding.

COMPONENTS OF THE
WAYS OF SEEING APPROACH

The *Ways of Seeing* approach is composed of three components:

1. An underlying belief system in which nonverbal movement qualities reveal information about an individual's social, emotional, physical, cognitive, and communicative development. This belief system guides all observations and interventions with a child and family. This information is gathered informally during interactions in natural, school-based, and intervention-based environments.

2. The nonverbal observational assessment, called the Movement Signature Impressions (MSI) Checklist, which looks at the specific qualitative elements that provide information about an individual's personal movement repertoire. The MSI Checklist (see Ap-

pendix A), described in greater detail in Chapter 5, is used to formally process these observations and experiences to create a more tangible image of how a child's movement qualities, the therapist's self-observations, and nonverbal interactions interweave to form a picture of the whole child.

3. Application of the information gleaned from the MSI Checklist to the continuum of assessment, intervention, and education. The information derived from the sessions and the MSI Checklist are used to design continued work with a child and family through their incorporation into the child's total educational and intervention plan.

Scope and Purpose of This Book

This book focuses on using the creative art of dance along with an understanding of nonverbal expression as a tool for the observation, assessment, interaction, intervention, and educational programming of infants and young children. The key to becoming aware of nonverbal expression involves observation: waiting, watching, and listening to children, as well as becoming aware of our own responses to children. This book provides instruction in how to gain information about children of all ages from their nonverbal expressions. The book also provides instruction in how to become aware of our own nonverbal reactions and interactions because self-observation, discussed in Chapter 7, is essential for parents and professionals working with children. Throughout this book, therapeutic and creative expression techniques are discussed that involve nonverbal communication as the primary tool for interactions and interventions.

This program is based on the premise that having an awareness of nonverbal expression supports communication by providing an alternative avenue of contact that is especially useful in reaching infants and children with diverse or delayed communicative, developmental, and learning styles. Adding nonverbal expression to social-emotional, motor, cognitive, and communicative development can greatly support a child's diverse abilities to learn and engage in the environment. Although many assessment, intervention, and educational programs exist to support the growth of children, none emphasize the qualitative nonverbal elements of expression. The enhanced awareness of nonverbal expression can augment the formation of meaningful relationships with young children with special needs and their families. This way of working fills a gap in existing assessment, intervention, and educational methods because it provides a way to reach even the youngest children with difficult or undefined challenges. The *Ways of Seeing* approach is not an alternative method, replacing other systems, but is designed instead to be an additional system easily integrated into other approaches.

For Whom Was This Book Written?

The *Ways of Seeing* approach can be used in both therapeutic and educational settings to provide professionals with additional tools to include in their observational techniques. Psychologists, mental health therapists, occupational and physical therapists, early childhood and elementary educators, child care workers and specialists, social workers, child life specialists, nurses, medical staff, parent educators, and even parents can benefit from the ideas provided in this book. A deeper understanding of the "whole child" has become a prevalent practice in many fields, as therapists have begun to assimilate concepts from other fields into their own. Occupational therapists are incorporating social-skill activities in group sensory integration classes, educators are integrating specialized learning tools into the standard curriculum to support all children's learning differences, and psychologists now consider the effects of specific foods on children's abilities to focus and attend. Every professional who deals with children can benefit from a better understanding of the essential role that nonverbal expression plays in a child's total functioning because such knowledge provides a truly comprehensive perspective of the whole child.

Education is moving toward the inclusion of children with diverse learning styles within the same educational milieu (Brantlinger, 1996; Darling-Hammond, 1997; Davis, Monda-Amaya, & Hammitte, 1996; Reinhiller, 1996). Children enter school with unique experiences based on their specific social, emotional, physical, cognitive, communicative, and ethnic/cultural make-up, which greatly affects their learning styles. The *Ways of Seeing* approach offers a useful component to supplement teachers' and therapists' existing observational skills by providing information about how individuals communicate through nonverbal expressions, how such nonverbal expressions influence interactions, and how this information can be used to maximize every child's learning potential.

The concepts in this book can be applied to children and families along a broad spectrum, ranging from those children who are developing as expected to those who are facing serious challenges in their functioning. The term *special needs* is used broadly to encompass children with issues in relating and communicating, developmental delays, learning challenges, and parent–child attachment disorders. This book will also show how an awareness of nonverbal communication can improve the parent–child and parent–child–therapist relationships. Throughout the book, the *Ways of Seeing* treatment approach is illustrated through case studies portraying a wide range of children, including those with autism spectrum disorders (ASD), Rett syndrome, pervasive developmental disorders (PDD), sensory integration dysfunction, attention-deficit/hyperactivity disorder (ADHD), communication and language delays, unspecified developmental delays, and issues associated with parent–child attachment, adoption, and trauma.

ORGANIZATION OF THIS BOOK

The first section of the book establishes a historical and theoretical framework relating dance, movement, and body-oriented theories; nonverbal communication research; and child developmental theories, within the context of the development of self, parent–child interaction, and early intervention. The chapters in this section establish the major goals of this book: to set the stage for collaboration across disciplines; to create a continuum from assessment to intervention to educational programming; to encourage professionals from diverse disciplines to appreciate the role nonverbal communication and movement play in relating; and to highlight how awareness of nonverbal communication can be used as a tool for observation, assessment, interaction, and intervention.

This introductory chapter explains the overall perspective of the book, and provides a brief overview of the theories, concepts, and history of dance movement therapy. The vignettes, examples, and discussions demonstrate how movements are nonverbal expressions that can be used as an added tool when working with families and children in intervention and educational settings.

Chapter 2, Communication without Words: Early Childhood Development and Interaction, discusses how somatic, sensorial, and nonverbal experiences influence the way an infant or young child perceives, engages in, and organizes herself in the surroundings. The *sense of body,* a term developed to describe this experiential level of processing, is described as it relates to a child's overall development. The man-

ner in which nonverbal communication occurs and can be interpreted
is highlighted within the context of early childhood theory. The chapter explains how an individual's early nonverbal experiences can
become established nonverbal communications that next develop into
a personal repertoire of actions that finally create an individual's
unique movement style. The chapter also traces how early communication influences the later development of attachment and relating
skills and how the primary principles of child development and movement analysis are connected. Finally, the chapter explains the important role that sensorimotor nonsymbolic representations play in the
development of an infant's nonverbal cuing; in the reading of nonverbal cues to establish patterns of interaction; in the acquisition of language; and, ultimately, in the quality of the attachment relationship.

Chapter 3, *Ways of Seeing:* Movement Development, Expression, and
Body Awareness, provides a comprehensive description of each component of the *Ways of Seeing* approach. This includes how to establish a relationship nonverbally, how to transform an action into a dialogue, how
to find the expressivity in difficult behaviors, how to identify the meaning of a specific movement, and how to understand a movement's relationship to the individual's personal movement repertoire. The chapter
also explains how children's movement metaphors develop into their
personal movement signatures and briefly describes the four Dynamic
Processes and their focuses. Finally, the chapter discusses the interrelationship between children's social-emotional development and their
movement development by correlating the physical and sensorial experiences they express through their movements with the social and emotional themes prevailing in each developmental stage.

Chapter 4, The Language of Movement: From Dysfunction to
Creative Expression, describes movement as a form of nonverbal communication and demonstrates how to decipher and to work with subtle, obscure, and difficult-to-read nonverbal cues. This includes a
discussion of the forces that influence communicative difficulties—
including such behaviors as repetitive idiosyncratic movements and
out-of-control actions—looked at from the perspective of sensory integration, regulatory dysfunction, neurological development and attachment, and relationship-based affect cuing issues. Weaving together the
arts, science, and child development with intervention, this chapter
demonstrates how nonverbal actions and experiential activities can be
used to support each child's development. The intent is to present new
ways of looking at movement disorders and to expand thinking about

methods of working with children exhibiting such movements, both through creative expression and improving movement functioning.

The second section of this book, Observation and Intervention, teaches the specific techniques involved in the *Ways of Seeing* approach. Chapter 5, Elements of Movement Observation, describes LMA and the MSI Checklist—the two major components that underlie the observational and assessment process of the *Ways of Seeing* approach. LMA instructs how to observe movement qualities and gives readers a method to characterize specific descriptive components that add the feeling tone to a physical action. The elements of the LMA system used in the *Ways of Seeing* approach—Body, Effort, Space, Shape, and Phrasing—provide information about how an action is performed, what body parts execute the action, and where the action occurs in relation to others and the surrounding environment. These provide a window into a fuller understanding of a child's personal expressions and style of interacting. Analyzing these elements is an essential step in creating a movement profile of a child and of significant people in the child's life.

Chapter 6, Nonverbal Observation in Context, presents five levels of nonverbal descriptive observation. Starting with a scene that uses only the most general of terms to depict a child's actions, the reader will learn about five different ways nonverbal information can be used to add more detail to a description. These five categories are general nonverbal descriptions, nonverbal intentional acts, physiologically based nonverbal responses, LMA descriptions, and potential nonverbal communications. This chapter illustrates through vignettes and discussions how nonverbal actions have the potential to become communications. A descriptive list of specific nonverbal cues is provided to assist the observer, and key points are outlined to help keep observations of a child's personal movement style and interactions with others as objective as possible.

Chapter 7, Witnessing, Kinesthetic Seeing, and Kinesthetic Empathy, asks the reader to reflect on his or her own personal responses to children's nonverbal styles and explains how self-reflection is an important component of the MSI Checklist. Self-observation deepens the understanding of the impact one's own nonverbal style has on interactions with children and their family members. Within the intervention continuum, it can provide therapists and other professionals with new, creative approaches to their treatment techniques. These self-observation techniques are divided into three descriptive categories:

1. Witnessing: The process in which an observer creates an objective, detailed "map" of the actions, while being aware of any personal historic experiences stimulated by the current child or situation being observed

2. Kinesthetic seeing: The process in which an observer becomes aware of any physical sensations that have arisen during the observation

3. Kinesthetic empathy: The process in which an observer discovers what personal emotional responses may be influencing the observations

A brief history of the discipline of Authentic Movement and its significance to the *Ways of Seeing* approach are also discussed. The end of the chapter contains exercises to promote development of self-observation skills and to encourage awareness of personal nonverbal styles.

Chapter 8, The *Ways of Seeing* Technique, explains the major principles of this program, using dance movement therapy practice as its foundation. Detailed information about the author's four-part therapeutic procedure is highlighted: 1) match and feel movement qualities through two styles of relating, attunement, and mirroring; 2) create a dialogue through use of these movements; 3) explore, expand, and develop these movements through interactive exchanges; and 4) move communication from nonverbal to verbal exchanges. These four procedures encourage children to develop self-awareness, social and emotional expressivity, and more effective ways to cope with personal difficulties and environmental demands. The elements of a typical *Ways of Seeing* session are described, including how to start a session; how to follow a child's lead to enter into the child's symbolic movement world; how to understand the importance of being "seen, held, and listened to"; and how to bring closure to a session.

Chapter 9, Movement and Dance-Based Tools, describes specific intervention tools and techniques, including starting where the child "is"; using awareness of the body's physical space and spatial placement in intervention; utilizing the body as a therapeutic tool; creating a sensorially enriched environment; using relaxation, visualization, and touch/massage techniques; including props in the treatment or educational setting; and choosing appropriate music for individual and group sessions. Dance and play activities are suggested, ranging from improvisation, choreography, finger-play songs, structured folk dances, singing movement games, dramatic story-plays, and exercises and yoga to a multitude of art activities.

The third section of the book, Movement as an Interdisciplinary Tool, provides strategies for integrating the *Ways of Seeing* approach across disciplines.

Chapter 10, Working with Parents, discusses how to include parents in the therapeutic session and what to look for in parent–child nonverbal relationships. Answers to specific questions and parent–child exercises that help parents learn more about their own and their children's nonverbal styles of relating are also included. Professionals across disciplines are instructed in how to observe, decode, and explore the nonverbal interactions between parents (or significant adults) and children as well as how to approach parents to discuss their nonverbal styles of relating to their children. Examples of working with parent–child dyads in cases of parental mental illness are also discussed.

Chapter 11, Focusing on the Child: From Nonverbal Assessment to Intervention to Educational Programming, supplies specific guidelines regarding how to obtain nonverbal movement observations within the classroom or group setting and how to apply this information to children's individual education and intervention plans. Through discussion and vignettes, this chapter elaborates on the concept that a continuum exists between assessment, intervention, and education. The *Ways of Seeing* approach creates this continuum by organizing knowledge within three areas of study: social-emotional experience, embodied experience, and cognitive experience. Guidelines for using the MSI Checklist for formal and informal assessment of nonverbal behavior are provided for home, clinical, and educational settings. Table 11.1 examines how to evaluate improvement in these three settings from a nonverbal perspective, based on five developmental areas—social, emotional, motor, cognitive and communicative. The chapter ends by demonstrating how a therapist using the *Ways of Seeing* approach can collaborate with a teacher to create an educational plan that supports a student's educational as well as nonverbal and sensory needs.

Chapter 12, Adding Nonverbal and Movement Awareness to the Classroom, describes how to effectively integrate body awareness, nonverbal observation, and creative dance activities into group care and educational settings. The reader will learn how to analyze and adjust curriculum to create an environment that has a rhythm and flow that supports different learning styles. A distinction is made between using movement observation and awareness to glean information about a particular child to create an effective intervention or educational program and using movement to introduce creative dance expression as a classroom activity. The chapter describes verbalizations that support each child's creative movement discovery and self-expression rather than prescribes directives for a child to follow. The emphasis is on the role that stories can play in encouraging self-expression and stimulating the young child's understandings of emotion and expression. The chapter includes a discussion about how to encourage the child's own dance imagery, play, and story creations. Specific guidelines about how to read the feeling tone and energy level of the class as a whole are provided.

Finally, Appendix A is a blank Movement Signature Impressions (MSI) Checklist. (A completed MSI Checklist as well as various blank forms and resources can be found at http:// www.brookespublishing. com/dancing.) Appendix B includes creative dance resources and a list of recommended children's stories and picture books that is divided into three categories: simple imagery, rhythm play, and imagination building. Appendix C is a glossary of key terms.

2

Communication without Words

Early Childhood Development and Interaction

Mother
　　　　　you made him little
　　　　　　　　　you started him
he was new to you
　　　　　and you arched
　　　　　　　　　the friendly world
over his new eyes
　　　　　and shut out
　　　　　　　　　the strange one.
Where, where
　　　　　are the years
　　　　　　　　　when your slender shape
was simply enough
　　　　　to block out
　　　　　　　　　waves of approaching chaos?
You hid so much from him this way
　　　　　rendering harmless
　　　　　　　　　the room that grew
suspicious at night
　　　　　and from the full
　　　　　　　　　sanctuary of your heart
you mixed something human
　　　　　into his nightspace.
　　　　　　　　　And you set the night-light
not in the darkness
　　　　　but in your nearness
　　　　　　　　　your presence
and it shone
　　　　　out of friendship.

　　　　　R.M. Rilke, *Duino Elegies* (1992, pp. 37–38)

29

When all goes right, an infant's initial experience of the world comes from within the protective confines of the primary meeting between infant and parent. This pairing is the infant's earliest experience of the dance—the nonverbal dance of relationship between self and other. Like two dancers, the infant–parent duet communicates through sensing, feeling, and touching. Each member uses his or her body to relate and express.

A baby looks out, under, and around his parents' watchful bodies—stationed in near proximity as they take on the role of guards, assessing what elements from the outside should be welcomed or shielded. During the initial stages, this is communicated and understood by the baby, primarily through implicit nonverbal means, originating in body and movement-based expression and articulated in qualities such as tone, rhythm, affect, and spatial placement. The infant experiences these qualitative elements of expressive interaction through physical means. Internal sensations, body contact, holding, touching, and the specific placement of an adult's comparatively large, physical self in proximity to his tiny shape all inform the baby's experience. It is the literal, bodily presence of others that the baby first experiences and watches. The infant's own body is the main avenue from which he can initially relate. Both the parent and the infant begin to learn about and get to know each other by paying attention to the unique styles of their nonverbal body cues.

The image in the Rilke poem exemplifies how the mere physical presence of a mother can be felt by an infant, conveying calmness and safety from the world yet unknown. This poem gracefully portrays several well-understood concepts in early childhood development literature. Infants first learn about their surroundings through sensorimotor experience (Piaget, 1962, 1970; Piaget & Inhelder, 1969). The primary caregivers in an infant's life assist the child in navigating through the world. Through these early experiences, the infant ventures out into the world, during which time she needs to develop her own sense of being, steering her own course when she encounters adversity. The poem depicts the budding infant–parent relationship that begins this journey, creating images that are physical and experiential. The focus of this chapter is on how these elements—the growth of the primary (attachment) relationship, and the physical sensation of such experiential events—are addressed in early childhood development literature. This will be explored by discussing the role body sensations play in the early development of self and attachment relationships. The discussion will reveal how the principles of child development, movement analysis, and early nonverbal expression play an important role in understanding the developing infant.

SENSE OF BODY

Many child development theorists have addressed the importance of the sensorial experience of the body during early development. Piaget (1962, 1970; Piaget & Inhelder, 1969) began development from sensorimotor awareness; Greenspan (1992, 1996) spoke of the necessity of body regulation of the senses to create a state of homeostasis; Mahler (Mahler, Pine, & Bergman, 1975) believed that the inner sensations occurring through bodily felt experiences are central in creating the feeling self; and Stern (1985) asserted that one of the earliest senses of self is the core self, which has a physical basis and enables a young infant to compare and differentiate experiences of self from other.

For this book, the author has adopted the model of a *sense of body* as the primary organizing principle from which all other experiences of self are formed. An infant's earliest experiences occur through his body and are initially registered on somatic, kinesthetic, and sensorial levels. These body-oriented experiences shape both how an infant begins to make sense of the world around him and how he begins to develop himself as a feeling, acting, moving, communicating, cognizant being in the world. It is through his body sensing—which includes sensing his own body as well as the body of another—that he first begins the *dance of relating.* The body and the interactional dance are continually intertwined, informing and developing one another. This chapter discusses the sense of body as it relates to an infant's own body experience, interpersonal relationships, and emergence of individuality, emphasizing the role somatic and nonverbally based early childhood experiences have in a young child's development.

Sense of Body as It Relates to
Early Child Development Literature

Infants become aware and develop an image of themselves as feeling, thinking individuals through the process of relating to others. How this self-concept and individuality arise and the role of the primary relationship between mother and baby in this development are widely discussed in the literature. For instance, attachment theory emphasizes the significance of an infant–mother relationship in forming both the infant's image of self and the quality of the growing individual's relationships with others (Ainsworth, 1978; Bowlby, 1969; Brazelton & Cramer, 1990). Mahler and colleagues (Mahler, Pine, & Bergman, 1975) contended that an infant is born in a state of merger or undifferentiation between self and mother, in contrast to Stern (1985), who believed that a newborn has a sense of self separate from mother that develops more fully through interactions with others. Stern (1985) used the term *sense of self* as his primary organizing principle to describe the interactions that enable a child to learn about self as being different from and yet still related to others.

In the *Ways of Seeing* approach, an infant enters the world with a sense of body as her organizing principle from which her understanding of self, relating to others, and the environment will emerge. This sense of body, created by bodily reactions and experiences, may even be present in utero, and follows a developmental progression in tandem with the sense of self discussed by Stern (1985). This is not to say that the sense of body replaces the sense of self or negates the importance of the mental representation of body defined in psychoanalytic literature as body image (Schilder, 1950). Rather, this sense of body concept suggests that body sensations significantly contribute to, inform, and continually influence one's experiences in the formation of the emotional, social, communicative, cognitive, and physical aspects of self.

This is readily observable within the first few weeks of a baby's birth into a family. Parents pay particular attention to their baby's physical signals—such as visual alertness, wake and sleep cycles, crying, eating patterns, and body/limb activity. These signals indicate the threshold of states, from awake to sleepy to fussy. Rituals of care begin to develop in an effort to best support the infant's presenting tendencies and to help him feel comfortable with his surroundings. The baby's nonverbal tendencies are often compared with those of older siblings, with parents' noting what is different and what is similar in each child's moods, sleep patterns, and activity levels. Predictions about the baby's personality begin to be formed. For instance, an older brother may have loved being swaddled tightly, calming immediately, whereas the newborn needs to be rocked in his mother's arms in order to relax. As these two siblings grow, the older brother may enjoy activities that include hiding and squeezing into tight places, whereas the younger brother may find pleasure in more energetic activities. The older brother may focus best through stillness, whereas the newborn may concentrate best by moving or adjusting his body freely.

During their earliest periods of development, infants do not have clear mental body images, but instead continually react and respond to their environments based on how the surroundings feel, very literally from a bodily sense. These bodily sensations become the reference points from which the infants will start to decode experiences during experiments with relating, interacting, and expressing themselves within their surroundings. In a sense, infants enter the world as all body, gradually creating, organizing, and making sense of their experiences as they take in information based on their physical reactions. Following the example in the previous paragraph, the older sibling who enjoyed being swaddled may have had difficultly as an infant relaxing with the baby sitter if the baby sitter did not follow this routine. The infant's fussiness and inability to calm with the sitter and his immediate calming as soon as his mother returned and swaddled him demonstrate his registration, on a body-sensing level, of the people and experiences that are familiar to him.

Mental representations will slowly emerge through experiences. Body-based experiences build knowledge about all aspects of self that become a reference point during the formation of self-concepts. Physical events involve sensations that confirm an infant's abilities. A baby's execution of a physical action creates a sense of "I do"; kinesthetic and external feedback of completed actions creates a sense of "I am able"; and "I am able" becomes "I am" as these actions and physical sensations become nonverbal movement styles that are repeated and codified into the child's personal movement signature. In this way, an infant's sense of body is a precursor to the emotional, mental, and symbolic body image that will evolve when cognitive processes come into play during the natural process of development.

The *Ways of Seeing* approach, which treats the body as the organizing principle from which all other self-references are derived, challenges the traditional notion that infants and young children do not have the ability to differentiate between self and other. This diverges from Mahler's concept of the "normal autistic" first stage of development, defined as the first few weeks of life, when the infant is in a state of primary narcissism and is not aware of the mother (Mahler, Pine, & Bergman, 1975). Instead, the *Ways of Seeing* approach describes how an initial sense of body creates a kinesthetic state that enables an infant to have an awareness of self—which informs a differentiation between self and other—through sensations that are physical and felt. In this earliest stage of development, differentiation does not and cannot occur on an emotional, mental, or cognitive level. Such levels of under-standing will take time and experience to develop. But this does not preclude a more primary, perhaps even primitive, way of knowing about self that significantly influences all aspects of development.

The sense of body concept offered by the *Ways of Seeing* approach enables a young child with special needs to be considered in a new way as well. A child's actual bodily experience, largely felt through sensory awareness and possibly influenced by developmental delays, sensory sensitivities, and/or neurological issues, substantially affects the child's way of being in the world. Some children with special needs continue to process the world primarily from this *felt* sense rather than ever developing their emotional, mental, and cognitive processing abilities.

The Qualitative Feeling of Body Experience

Babies first find out about the world and respond to it through their bodies, using their senses and movement sensations to explore. A newborn baby quickly settles when snuggled high up on the mother's shoulder. Just as quickly, many infants get upset, flexing and jerking their limbs in arrhythmic bursts, when their clothes are taken off, sud-denly exposing their skin to cool air. Without a verbal communication system in place, infants are first and foremost receiving information about the world through the stimulation of their senses. Movement and body sensations are among the primary modes from which babies receive information and communicate how they are experiencing this new world. Very young children pick up information and express themselves first through actions and then re*actions* to actions.

As experiences through repetition become familiar and consistent, an infant begins to develop a notion of cause and effect. Through physical exploration and similar sequences of events, a young infant slowly develops a mental representation of events. From early on, a baby is able to identify and turn toward the mother's voice when pre-sented with a variety of voices. A 3-month-old infant learns quickly that a smile draws a corresponding smile from the father, and this exchange leads to heightened enjoyable contact evidenced and felt in the infant's increased and excited arm and leg activity. This is why a baby never seems to tire of Peekaboo or the game of dropping a toy from the high chair, watching it fall, and hearing it clunk on the floor.

What at first is novel becomes familiar and predictable over time. Such experiences create the internal organization that enables an infant to learn about and differentiate self from other. Stern created a particularly clear image of this early "emergence of organization" that highlights body sensation and experience when he commented, "Infants are not 'lost at sea' in a wash of abstractable qualities of experience" (1985, p. 67). Instead, Stern described an infant's capacity to slowly and systematically order each component of experience into a "constellation" occurring "out of the experiential matrix," which enables the infant to establish a consistent sense of self in relation to, but different from, "other." These early accumulating events are the core from which thoughts, perceptions, actions, and verbalizations will evolve.

The *Ways of Seeing* approach accepts Stern's understanding of an infant's development of self and his premise that an infant enters the world with an existing and emerging self that becomes more fully formed through experience. Stern explained that an infant's first form of self, the *emergent self*, "concerns the body: its coherence, its actions, its inner feeling states, and the memory of all these." He added that the emergent self "is the experiential organization with which the sense of a core self is concerned" (1985, p. 46). This first stage is followed by the sense of *core self*, in which infants physically use their bodies to explore and learn about self-regulation and the regulation of external excitement caused by interaction with others. A simple example of this progression can be seen in an infant's earliest actions.

As a newborn sporadically flexes and extends her limbs and attempts to lift her head, she is discovering how it feels to move her body. Through continued exploration, she will gain more control and will soon be able to turn her head, move her torso, and change how she is flexing or extending her limbs in response to a stimulus in the environment. The manner in which she executes these body actions will affect her experience. She may occasionally arch her head back and flex her arms, pulling them toward her while bulging her chest forward. Physically this will cause a shortening between her head and shoulders. While exploring this movement by herself, the baby may appear to be experimenting with movement. If she continues this action but increases the tension in her limbs and torso and begins to rock her head rapidly from side to side, one might interpret this as a distress signal. If the mother immediately comes to comfort the baby, picking her up, and the baby softens into mother's arms, both the mother and the baby have a very particular physical and emotional experience. The baby's quick response demonstrates the baby's ability to be comforted by her mother. The success of mother's efforts exudes the mother's sense of knowing her baby. If the baby shifts into the arching-head, chest-bulging, arm-flexing position as the mother is attempting to playfully engage her with a smile, a very different set of experiences may occur, for both mother and baby. The baby's actions now suggest that she is not comforted by her mother's touch and physical presence, and the mother may feel inadequate in meeting her child's needs. Implications about a baby's response to her mother, the mother's response to her baby, and their growing relationship may be inferred by watching how nonverbal experiences like these unfold over a period of time. Questions arise: What might a baby's actions reveal about her current state? Is the mother able to read these actions and respond in a way that supports the baby's needs? Is this a continual pattern of interaction between this dyad, or is it a unique situation of the moment?

The qualitative elements of the experience also play an influential role in an infant's continually emerging understanding of self and other. The formation of self comes from both the sensed and the perceived feelings evoked from an experience because it is through a baby's early felt experiences on a physical level that his or her initial sense of self will develop. As addressed in the following chapters, the *Ways of Seeing* approach offers a systematic method for observing and analyzing how an experience is felt by a mover, how this felt experience may influence the unfolding of the experience, and how the actual feeling quality of these accumulating experiences affects the development of the child's understanding of self and others. This method reveals the quality of an experience by observing what is done *and* how it is executed, paying close attention to a baby's nonverbal actions while interacting with the surroundings. Attending to both what is done and how it is executed reveals the quality of an experience.

THE ROLE OF EXPERIENCE

An interplay exists between those innate bodily tendencies with which an infant enters the world and the external interactions the baby encounters. This interplay influences the actual course of individual development and is observable in how an infant interacts with the environment, including the unique nonverbal choices, executed through body movement. The philosopher Merleau-Ponty's (1964, 1981) phenomenological principles of perception influenced how experiences are regarded in the *Ways of Seeing* approach. He observed that the body is one's point of view of the world, and consciousness of the world is obtained through the direct bodily experience. Merleau-Ponty highlighted that we know we exist because we *experience* ourselves in existence. It is never just outside conditions that mold us, but rather, the way we as individuals take position in the outside environment that intersects with our relations with the external world. Our perceptions of existence develop from our experiences—past, present, and preexisting within the self.

This focus on experience is reinforced in childhood development literature as well. Piaget (1962, 1970; Piaget & Inhelder, 1969) emphasized a child's active role in seeking interactions with his environment and responding to these interactions through his personal interpretations of these experiences. He described how infants see others as "centers of force" with their own individual qualities that infants recognize and expect during interactions. Stern (1985) spoke of an infant having an experiential sense of self from birth, which the infant uses as a reference point to organize and understand external experiences. Mahler, Pine, and Bergman observed that "inner sensations form the core of the self" and are a central point in the "feeling self" (1975, p. 47).

Research on early brain development also has examined the dynamic role between biology, the environment, and experience (Schore, 2001a, 2001b). After researching the neurobehavior of other mammals to investigate how different social environments may influence the emotional brain, Panksepp (2001) believed that early emotional challenges greatly influence the development of a child's personality. He suggested the possibility that such events may actually change the "hardware" of the developing brain. His emerging findings seem to indicate that emotional strengths and weaknesses are greatly influenced by the child's lived emotional environments, therefore emphasizing the lifelong effects of early emotional experiences. Panksepp's final conclusion was that "during early development there is no sustained line of cognitive activity without a sustained line of emotional arousal" (p. 160).

The Role of Experience Evidenced in Personal Movement Styles

The *Ways of Seeing* approach describes how the unique ways that infants use their bodies to respond to their environment communicate how they are experiencing the environment. A 9-month-old baby visibly brightens when he sees a familiar face and stills his actions when seeing a stranger. A 20-month-old baby throws her bottle on the floor with vehemence, emphatically saying "No!" to protest going to sleep when she wants to keep playing. These examples are well known. They relate to language acquisition—the first-word period, when "what children do with objects is a manifestation of how they are thinking about the objects they act upon" (Lifter & Bloom, 1986, p. 4). This is the first step in the development of the expressive nature of an infant's personal movement style.

The next step in this natural progression is not frequently focused on or acknowledged. It is detectable only through careful and subtle nonverbal analysis, for it is more of a distillation of expressivity than a replication of experience. In this stage, a baby establishes repeated patterns of movement. These repeated patterns will begin to develop into a specific repertoire of movements—a personal movement style. Patterns will build on themselves as the baby continues to explore his surroundings, and variations will develop as he establishes particular and unique relationships with the significant people in his life. The child's growing organization of concepts of self in relation to his surroundings will be evident in the child's particular movement style. As mentioned previously, how a child is using his body to create movement responses to the environment tells how he is experiencing and learning about his body as a tool for understanding and communicating. By closely observing body movements, a great deal about how the young child is processing his experiences can be learned because body experiences of self are a precursor to mental representations of self.

A dramatic example can be seen in an infant who has witnessed the abrupt, violent actions characteristic of an abusive environment between her mother and father. With a limited vocabulary of movement available due to lack of muscular strength, the infant may develop a particular increased musculature tension level and a retreating head-turning action. The particular way in which the infant turns her head will be unique to her. Even when taken away from this environment, the baby might exhibit vigilance by responding with this specific tension and head-turning behavior whenever she senses any abrupt action in her surroundings. This kind of vigilance can greatly influence the young child's developing trust in the world and her personal sense of confidence, which can be observed in the way she approaches unfamiliar people and situations.

PARENT–CHILD INTERACTIONS

Our earliest experiences, especially with our most primary caregivers, greatly influence how we develop. Let us now take a closer look at how the primary relationship between infant and parent is portrayed through nonverbal interactions.

I am struck by 17-month-old Nikki's lack of movement away from the circle of physical support Mom creates as she places Nikki seated on the floor, in front of her crossed legs. Nikki is sitting vertically up, but with a slight slumping concavity in her chest, creating a sensation of passivity. As I roll the ball to Nikki, she watches it, but will only send it back to me with a gentle push if it comes within her nearest reach. If she has to shift her weight to reach for it farther away, she makes no attempt to get it. Noticing this, I lean forward to push the ball closer to her, and she visibly pulls her whole self back, into the safety of Mom's body. Mom reports that Nikki seems to be most comfortable in her arms and often cries when she puts her down.

Despite her mother's best efforts, her close proximity and caring touch cannot completely shield Nikki from the intricacies of her life. Diagnosed with Rett syndrome at 24 months, the multiple factors that affect Nikki's experience of her world are very complex. Quick observation of her movement style reveals that Nikki perceives movement out into the world as difficult and potentially dangerous. Immediately, many questions arise. What is life like for Nikki? What is her experience of the world? How do the innate characteristics of Nikki's condition influence how she experiences her surroundings? What roles do the significant people in her life play in this experience? Some possible responses will be addressed in this chapter (and Chapters 6, 7, and 8) as we follow Nikki's progress during 6 years of dance movement psychotherapy.

The Role of Parents and Significant Caregivers

Although child development research has most often looked at the mother–infant relationship, the more inclusive term of parents and significant caregivers is used in this discussion so as to include all of the prominent people who influence a young baby's life. The *Ways of Seeing* approach has worked effectively with each of these relationships.

Parents act as mediators, helping their young children navigate, interpret, and process their new experiences of the world. Winnicott

(1965, 1982, 1987) spoke about the mother providing a holding framework for the waxing and waning of the child's attention. As the mother learns to read the baby's nonverbal and vocal cues, she uses this information to regulate the amount of input from the outside world that the baby can manage at any particular time. In the poem that begins this chapter, Rilke's description of a mother's caring presence having the power to "arch" the "friendly world and shut out the strange one. . . . Rendering harmless/The room that grew/Suspicious at night" offers a clear image of the first relationship between parent and infant. Through the primary parent–child experience, an infant begins to safely explore and develop an understanding of the surroundings. In typical emotional development, these positive experiences within the safety of the "holding environment" will mature into a secure attachment (Brazelton, 1974), creating in the infant a sense of trust toward the primary parent. This will support the infant's development of a sense of trust in relationships with others and the world at large.

The process of developing a secure relationship grows out of multiple experiences between parents and their babies. A significant aspect of these interactions is that a parent and a baby are not always in continual synchrony with each other. It is important that a child and mother experience "mismatches and repairs" (a disruption of interaction followed by a reconnection) as a way for the infant to learn about temperamental differences in others, his ability to affect others, and his ability to regulate his own emotional needs (Tronick, 1989; Tronick & Gianino, 1986).

Through this process infants learn about self-regulation. *Self-regulation* includes both how infants learn to organize internal and external sensory input as well as how infants are affected by their own behaviors. Infants are keen observers of the world, continually absorbing

Parents help children process their new world.

and trying to put meaning to what they see, hear, smell, taste, and touch. Experiences happen to them first and foremost on a bodily level, and parents and caregivers become their initial interpreters of the world. It is the job of parents and caregivers to help explain, protect, and introduce children to all of the actions and experiences they are having in their surrounding world.

By watching babies, we can learn about how they are currently processing their experiences of their surroundings. Nikki's tendency to refrain from extending her physical self out into the far reaches of her space and her sudden gesture away from the therapist and toward her mother give the therapist insight into how dangerous the outside world feels to Nikki, and the important role her mother will play in the treatment program. The therapist's next actions provide additional useful information.

⁓ *I see that Nikki does not transition from her seated position. This suggests that she stays put wherever she is placed. There seems to be no spontaneous shifting of her weight through her pelvis to support her reaching her arms farther out into the surroundings—a necessary action to enable crawling, an activity she is not yet doing. As we all sit on the floor, I place Nikki between my straddled legs facing out toward her mom just 2–3 feet away. Noticing Nikki's soft muscle tone, I place my upright body close to hers to give her the tactile support of an extended torso and draw my legs closer into hers. I want to give her a sensation of my body hugging hers as I gently rock us together, as one unit, side to side, making sure my pelvis is lifting off the ground with each rock. I am using my body to give her the physical cues of an action she cannot create on her own. Nikki begins to cry. Okay. Well, of course, I am a stranger and this movement is not familiar and most likely uncomfortable. Unspoken questions about vestibular regulation flit across my mind as well—is the rocking sensation uncomfortable? I stop the action. Mom reaches out toward Nikki to take her in her arms. Nikki's response is very revealing. She visibly pulls her arms and torso away from her mother's arms coming through the surrounding space toward her!* ⁓

Through observation and physical interaction with Nikki, the therapist gains insight into how Nikki's experience of her body both reflects and influences her emotional experience. Nikki's pulling away action is so quick and tiny that it could have gone unnoticed. Keen observation of nonverbal behavior is the key. This pulling away action tells the therapist that she must be very careful about how she introduces activities and people into Nikki's world. Nikki's ability to receive and process stimuli is very fragile. If she is having this reaction in the carefully structured environment of the treatment room with her mother present, how must the unpredictable nature of the outside world affect her? Her mother's comment that Nikki is only comfortable in her arms begins to take on greater meaning. Since the primary approach in dance movement psychotherapy is to create a positive social-emotional environment from which all other therapeutic goals are built, two things become readily apparent. Extreme caution must be taken to support the activities that happen around and to Nikki, and her mother must be a significant participant in her therapy. Thus, Nikki is placed in her mother's lap instantly. The mother is instructed in how to perform this pelvic rocking action, and the therapist encourages her to practice this action at home as often as possible. This will help Nikki experience how her body can feel when it is moving, and, through kinesthetic exploration, teach her how to safely move out of her preferred stable sitting position.

The therapist wonders how Nikki's difficulties taking in and exploring the world around her have influenced her developing emotional sense of self. Nikki's inability at 17 months to move by crawling or walking is preventing her from feeling physical agency on a very basic bodily level. No wonder she instinctively seeks the comfort of her mother's arms. Her own body and body actions are not a source of achievement or serenity for her. Therefore, the next goal is to help Nikki feel the joy and satisfaction of moving her body through movement explorations that involve social interactions.

Nikki's spontaneous nonverbal actions—which would not typically be considered intentional nonverbal communications—are regarded as communicative and set the tone for the intervention process. This vignette shows both how babies first learn through their experiences, and how their significant relationships can dramatically influence their comfort with the larger world. These concepts will be elaborated on in the following section.

Nonverbal Cues Underlying Parent–Child Interactions

Through movement analysis a therapist can see if a parent and child's personal styles support positive interactions. The parent–child relationship can be revealed by analyzing the qualitative aspects of their nonverbal interactive behavior and determining whether their individual movement styles are similar, complementary, or incompatible. A parent's initial role is to offer a consistent and responsive presence as the baby's attention waxes and wanes. An infant will, over time, attempt to communicate needs, wants, and curiosities about the environment, not all of which will be immediately understood. The infant's need to repeat attempts should encourage her to explore making variations, which can expand her communicative repertoire. Through the process of mismatch (failed responses) and repair (successful response) the child will gain a sense of agency and accomplishment (Tronick, 1989; Tronick & Gianino, 1986).

Because a young child's communications originate as nonverbal expressions, this personal nonverbal *dance* is a reflection of inner experiences. The development of a personal movement style is derived from this dialogue between self and environment. An infant is at first dependent on significant adults to interpret his dance, so the compatibility between the infant and his significant adults is crucial. The type of match and mismatch experiences that an infant has during these early stages can greatly affect how he will navigate through development, and in turn how he feels about himself through this navigation. The compatibility and attraction between an adult and an infant can support, hinder, or encourage the infant's cumulative experiences.

Observing how interactions occur within the spatial domain can uncover significant information about styles of relating. For example, in one study, observations of mothers with their 4-month-old babies revealed that some mothers were spatially intrusive in that they displayed persistent physical "honing-in" on their babies (Beebe, 2004). These spatially intrusive actions included leaning very close to the baby and touching and poking the baby's body and face in an effort to gain or maintain his attention—even when the baby was forcibly turning his head or arching his body away. In Beebe's research this spatial element was one of the factors used to determine the quality of the mother–baby attachment relationship at 1 year of age.

The role of nonverbal communication is paramount during the first year of life because babies initially rely on sensations they experience and events they observe to communicate. Specifically, a baby will first recognize the qualities of a parent's nonverbal style. Over time, as these qualities are repeated in similar situations, the infant will begin to attach meaning and expectation to the unique way the parent combines specific movement qualities, which compose his or her individual movement style.

This explains why a very young baby who is crying as she is rocked in someone's arms can become immediately comforted when placed in her mother's arms. The feel of the mother's particular body, the manner in which she holds her arms, the tension of her muscles, the way she cocks her head as she gazes into her infant's eyes, and the tone of her voice all become signals representing a familiar place of comfort. Simultaneously, there is a reciprocal process happening for the mother. She becomes familiar with her baby's body signals, learning what each of her actions indicates about her needs, wants, preferences, and changing levels of attention. A nonverbal style of relating evolves as mother and child consciously and *unconsciously* learn to read the qualitative cues of each other's body signals. Unconsciously is emphasized to draw attention to those aspects of a movement style that are so innate they may at first go unnoticed, yet it is often the quality of these nonverbal stylistic elements that most need attention when analyzing differences in the dyadic interaction.

This also explains why some babies and their parents do not seem to be relating in a compatible way. Parents do not always read or know how to read their baby's cues effectively. A baby's nonverbal cuing style is not always easily discernible. In addition, the parent's nonverbal style and the baby's nonverbal style may not be a good fit. It is not necessary, of course, to read each of an infant's signals correctly all the time. It is normal for children to be misunderstood, and this gives infants the opportunity to try a variety of signaling approaches to get their needs met. This is a realistic and important part of the process that babies must experience while learning how to relate in our social world. What is important is how an infant's continued attempts to be understood get resolved. It is the accumulation of experiences with similar successful or unsuccessful resolutions that creates the nonverbal patterns of relating between a parent and a child. These experiences become the ongoing nonverbal dialogues that influence or set the template from which all other relationships to the surrounding world will occur.

Because infants learn through their experiences with others, it is important for adults to become aware of the impact that their own style of nonverbal interactions has on their infants. A primary caregiver's individual style can greatly influence an infant's cumulative experiences. Gaining knowledge about the effect of their actions can enable parents to have more thoughtful *responses* to their infants' needs, rather than simply *reactions* to their infants' *reactions*.

Mom comes back to the second session very excited. "Nikki is trying to move!" she exclaims. "You know, before, we just didn't know how to show her how to move. But playing with her to get her to rock her body really helped." She demonstrates how she and Nikki have begun to play with the pelvic rocking activity of last session. Through their movement play they have developed a new game! Nikki is placed on her belly and Mom sits in front of her just a few inches away calling her name. Nikki lifts her head up and rocks her whole body side to side, reaching her arms out to Mom. Mom grabs her hands and coos her name as she brings Nikki toward her. Great! Through their strong relationship, they have spontaneously found a way to motivate Nikki to use her body to explore her environment. So, can this skill be used to foster others?

By the next session, the continuation of this play has seemed to make Nikki a bit stronger in the upper body. She is able to hold her upper body and head up a little longer as she gazes at Mom, and her body rocks have a stronger quality to them. I ask Mom to sit just a bit farther out of Nikki's reach and wait a bit longer before she pulls Nikki toward her. Nikki begins to reach and rock toward Mom and is surprised when she is not picked up immediately. She begins to vocally protest. Mom responds by calling her name but does not pick her up. Nikki's vocal protest gets stronger, but so do her movements. She more vigorously rocks her weight side to side and reaches her arms out to Mom. Her efforts inch her forward! Nikki continues to protest but also continues to move forward in this ever so inch-by-inch way. When she gets to her mother's knee, Mom picks her up, and Nikki looks around in amazement. Her verbal protests have ceased! We are able to do this over and over again, and each time Nikki's perseverance prevails.

So much is learned from this experience. Nikki's determination and strong relationship to her mother are motivating factors that support her explorations. In this simple activity, two-way communication is explored as Nikki learns that if her first attempts are not successful, she can actually use her body—moving it through space—to get her needs met. Nikki's determination can be considered an expression of her inner experience. The therapist and mother rely on her nonverbal cues to understand this. They can tell by how she is rocking her body—with increased strength—that she can attempt this exploration. They can tell by the quality of her vocalizations and her movement actions that it is okay to delay her contact with her mother—she is not actually crying, and her actions become more vigorous, determined, and successful in moving herself forward. They also see that Nikki's mother had to subtly change her own nonverbal approach, stopping herself from immediately rescuing Nikki by picking her up whenever she first became uncomfortable.

Therapists who rely on nonverbal cues in gathering information obtain knowledge about the children and families with whom they work that can turn out to be of key importance to the intervention.

THE DISCUSSION OF NONVERBAL RESPONSES IN CHILD DEVELOPMENT LITERATURE

The *Ways of Seeing* approach considers nonverbal responses to include all externally observable body movement behaviors. Child development literature has focused attention in a variety of ways on how to use nonverbal behaviors to track emotional and social responses to the environment. The following summary of these approaches is included to provide an overview of other significant perspectives regarding nonverbal behavior.

One approach has been to study physiological reactions. Known as *psychophysiological responses,* these include heart-rate reactions, biological and culturally based differences and influences, critical analyses of genetic determinants on development, the role of reflexes as precursors for behaviors—including the smile and sucking—and a discussion of the anger response observable by noting the intensity of autonomic and withdrawal responses to unpleasant stimulation (Lipsitt, 1976).

Psychoneuroendocrinological responses have also been monitored during studies in brain development to analyze how infants react to stressors. Stressors are defined as anything actual or perceived that puts in jeopardy the optimal biological functioning (homoeostasis) of an individual (Gunnar & Cheatham, 2003; Sapolsky, 1992). These studies included measuring shifts in the hypothalamic-pituitary-adrenocortical (HPA) system, the part of the endocrine system whose main role is to aid and promote survival of the organism when faced with extreme environmental conditions (Gunnar & Cheatham, 2003), and looked at the development of an infant's stress-regulatory system as influenced by the environment (Gunnar, 1980, 1998; Gunnar, Brodersen, Krueger, & Rigatuso, 1996; Gunnar & Cheatham, 2003).

The work of Gunnar and her colleagues (1996) has studied a possible relationship between the ability of an infant (i.e., 2 months old) to clearly signal distress and the responsiveness of the caregiver. Consistent, sensitive responses by the caregiver at this early age, when an infant's regulatory system is becoming organized but is not yet fully self-regulated, may affect the reactivity and regulation of stress hormones and the development of particular brain structures. By the age of 6 months, young infants with experienced caregivers who respond supportively to stressful experiences seem to have more effective stress-regulatory systems, managed by the regulation that the parent–infant relationship creates and the quality of the mother's care (Nelson & Bosquet, 2000). In other words, optimal development of an infant's stress system is influenced by the transaction between the child and the quality of the mother's caregiving. Such research highlights the importance of a parent's skill in reading the nonverbal cues of an infant, and the infant's ability to provide clear cues. It seems that the caregiver's ability to mitigate the infant's responses to stress may affect the activity and production of stress hormones.

Brazelton and Cramer (1990) emphasized the neuromotor and psychophysiological characteristics necessary for nonverbal communication. They suggested that infants must possess a level of internal regulation and homeostasis in order to develop effective nonverbal communication skills. These include the ability to maintain an alert state in order to prolong attention to affective and cognitive cues of others, without getting overwhelmed by such stimuli.

Nonverbal cues also have been classified as actions and gestures that are performed by young children in the service of intentional communication. This means that children are purposefully using their bodies to communicate their responses to other persons. These actions include eye contact, head nodding, pointing and other hand gesturings, grasping people's hands to bring them to an object or activity, and using the body or head to turn or pull away from stimuli. They require a certain degree of understanding of communication in order to be performed by a child and have been viewed as precursors to the development of verbal language. Nonverbal actions that do not seem to have a communicative intent are usually not considered significant when analyzing communication.

All actions have the potential to be communicative, however, and the child does not necessarily have to be aware of the communicative potential of the act when it is first performed. The *Ways of Seeing* approach describes how to explore communication capabilities by analyzing the qualities of the action as well as the action itself. How and why this alternative way of viewing nonverbal action is effective will become evident in the following discussion about the role of nonverbal communication in the acquisition of language, the difficulties in acquiring language, and the development of an attachment relationship.

Nonverbal Communication in Language Acquisition

Development of verbal language naturally progresses from a preverbal or prelinguistic period, when a baby uses specific gestures and vocalizations to communicate, to a verbal period, when a young child has the cognitive capacity to use words as symbolic representations for communication. In studying the intentional communicative acts of preverbal to verbal children, researchers have found that gestural and vocal communications predominate in the prelinguistic and one-word stages of communication, whereas verbalizations predominate in the multiword stage (Wetherby, Cain, Yonclas, & Walker, 1988). Gestures are typically regarded as a nonverbal means of communication and a precursor and support for vocalizing and verbalizing. Once the ultimate goal is achieved—language acquisition—less focus is typically directed toward nonverbal acts of communication.

Nonverbal actions have also been considered to be presymbolic actions. Presymbolic actions have been studied in the development of the SCERTS™ Model (SCERTS stands for Social Communication, Emotional Regulation and Transactional Support; Prizant, Wetherby, & Rydell, 2000; Prizant, Wetherby, Rubin, Laurent, & Rydell, 2006a, 2006b) for intervention with children who have ASD. Linking communication with relationships, this method emphasizes that establishing a secure relationship is the foundation and product of successful communicative interactions with others. Emotional regulation—which requires a child to modulate emotional arousal—is believed to be a core developmental process that facilitates the building of secure relationships. However, emotional regulation involves the ability "to stay calm, and focused, to problem-solve, to maintain social engagement, to communicate effectively, and to benefit from the rich learning opportunities in everyday experiences" (Prizant et al., 2000, p. 211). Finding an emotionally regulated state is not easy for children within the autism spectrum. These children use sensorimotor and presymbolic actions—such as repetitive movements (spinning, rocking), averting eye gaze, or tactile and oral self-stimulation—as strategies to block off sensory input. Such actions are actually the child's attempt to strive for emotional regulation (Prizant et al., 2000, p. 211). The SCERTS™ Model explains how in this capacity these actions are serving a useful function and must be utilized in the initial stages of developing a relationship. The *Ways of Seeing* approach agrees that building a secure relationship is the essential element toward creating the child's desire to communicate, and that sensorimotor and presymbolic actions should be viewed as communications that can be used to establish a relationship.

Sensory Experiences, Communication, and the Development of Attachment

What role do nonverbal and sensory experiences play in communication and attachment during typical development? The communicative and relational power of nonverbal exchanges has been extensively studied by child development researchers who have used video and live analysis of mother–child interactions to ascertain the nature of the mother–infant attachment, early object experiences, and affect-sharing relationships (Beebe, Lachmann, & Jaffe, 1997; Beebe & Stern, 1977; Sander, 1962, 1980, 2000; Stern, 1977, 1985). These studies have used a variety of qualities specific to the nonverbal realm to examine the mother–child relationship.

Timing and rhythm, two important qualities in the *Ways of Seeing* approach, are referred to as the fundamental organizing principles of communication in a study of vocal rhythm coordination between mothers and their 4-month-old infants (Beebe, personal communication, 1999; Beebe, Jaffe, Lachmann, Feldstein, Crown, & Jasnow, 2000). This research found that the way an infant and mother coordinate the timing and rhythm of their vocal and nonverbal communicative exchanges reveals the organization of their social relatedness and the quality of their attachment. Using the classifications of attachment defined by Ainsworth (1978), other studies (Main, 1996; Main & Hesse, 1990; Main & Solomon, 1990) have cited the importance of flexible, midrange degrees of coordination when relating as a predictor of secure attachment between an infant and mother. Researchers conclude that not only is it unnecessary for the baby and mother to be in perfect coordination, but it is actually preferable that their nonverbal relating not always be exactly in tune. Instead, it is best if the mother and the baby demonstrate a range of ways to relate (Tronick, 1989; Tronick & Gianino, 1986).

Another study concluded that communication should be viewed as a process in which interactions are bidirectional in that the behavior of *each* member of the dyad contributes to the overall quality of the relationship (Beebe, personal communication, 1999, 2004). Such interactional exchanges are a result of unfolding behavior within the individual, known as self-regulation, in conjunction with modifications that are occurring simultaneously between the partners. These are a result of the concurrent and reciprocal influences each partner's behaviors have on the other, known as *interactive regulation* (Beebe, 2004; Fogel, 1992). Patterns of relating become anticipated, and how these experiences will be perceived by each member of the interaction is continually constructed and in process, rather than fixed.

Context is considered to play a critical role. The pattern of eye gaze and body movement activity between a mother and a baby helps to demonstrate the bidirectional and context-specific aspects of the relationship. As a self-regulating act, the baby may look away from the mother toward a nearby object, which causes the mother to look in the direction of her baby's gaze. The mother may then make a comment such as "Oooh! Look at the pretty kitty sitting on the couch!" drawing the baby's gaze back. When their eyes meet, they both burst into a smile, with the baby adding a flutter of arms and legs as the mother shakes her head from side to side, matching the rhythm of the baby's limbs. If this interaction begins when the baby is very tired, the eye gaze away from the mother may have been more of a signal of a sleepy state than a new visual focus. In this case, the mother's attempt to engage the baby's attention toward the cat might result in the baby becoming increasingly fussy. If the mother continually misreads the baby's nonverbal cues it may create difficulties in their communicative style that, if persistent, could escalate into difficult patterns of interaction. The mother's ability to read the baby's action as a signal of tiredness, cuing her to stay quiet rather than attempting to stimulate the baby, supports the communicative aspects of their growing relationship.

Researchers have also determined that change can only occur if sufficient variability exists—too much stability does not allow for exploration and the creation of new patterns (Thelen & Smith, 1994). Variability enables the exploration of new options, which leads to the development of new patterns. In one study, researchers encouraged an infant's capacity for exploration by first focusing on what the infant could do, had done, and was doing, and then slightly varying the context of the task to introduce and encourage variability (Thelen & Smith, 1994; Beebe et al., 2000). Nikki's and her mother's development of a new game in the previous vignette exemplifies this approach. Prior to treatment, Nikki was most comfortable in close proximity to her mother. Perceiving this, her mother was readily available physically to Nikki whenever possible. This built a trust that secured their relationship. Supporting this need for proximity, Nikki's mother then placed herself in reachable distance to Nikki, whom she placed on her belly on the floor. Nikki's striving to reach her mother, which caused her to rock her body from side to side, created a new physical sensation to explore. After meeting with the therapist, both Nikki and her mother were able to create further distance between them, delaying the physical reunion to encourage Nikki to extend her efforts. The success of these modifications demonstrates the flexibility and security of their relationship.

A number of studies have shown that an infant's ability to be flexible relates to a secure attachment between the infant and mother (Beebe et al., 2000; Beebe, Lachmann, & Jaffe, 1997). Beebe (personal communication, 1999) cited self-regulation research and interactive regulation research as finding that infant–mother dyads who have relationships that are bidirectionally coordinated within a mid-range— not too tightly or too loosely coordinated—have the most secure relationships and the ability to be flexible and variable. This is shown by the security of Nikki and her mother in their emotional relationship, which allowed room for some level of discomfort when a new movement strategy was explored. Secure relationships allow for adaptive behavior, which requires a balance between stability and change. This balance between stability and change is significant because if too much stability exists, new explorations and solutions will not be attempted. A balance enables the infant and the infant–mother dyad to be open to novelty and variation, representing a greater range of capabilities.

A too-tightly coupled dyad creates hypervigilance, anxiousness, and resistance (Beebe, personal communication, 1999, 2004). It is a problem if a mother and infant are too *hooked* into each other. An example of this type of relationship can be seen in a mother and baby who cannot be separated at all. The mother is too attentive, anticipating her baby's communications to the point that the baby is not given room to communicate them fully. The baby is so watchful of the mother that separation is intolerable, which minimizes the child's affective expressive range. Conversely, a too-loosely coupled dyad lacks coordination and coherence, inhibiting engagement (Beebe et al., 2000). In this type of relationship, the observer might notice patterns of interaction that involve a baby looking away at the same time that the mother is making efforts to engage the child, or the baby looking toward the mother when the mother is looking away.

Tronick's (1989; Tronick & Gianino, 1986) previously discussed "mismatch and repair" research supports this discussion about the need for flexibility. Mismatched relating provides infants with the opportunity to gain a sense of efficacy and mastery when they are able to repair the mismatch. In successful repairs, interactive coping strategies are developed that are internalized and able to be applied in relating to others.

This research explains why Nikki's ability to tentatively move away from her static position to begin exploring her surroundings is so encouraging. Her strong relationship with her mother enables her to take this next step and physically experiment, despite the limitations of her syndrome. The pelvic rock movements provide variability within a comfortable range of novelty. Moreover, both of their expressions have changed noticeably during the first 2 weeks, in which Nikki was seen six times. When they first entered treatment, there was a distinct tone of sadness, pain, and depression. Their presence was characterized by a foreboding, listless, and hesitant quality that is typical during the early stages of unknown infancy illness. But now, both are filled with eagerness and surprise, and they seem to be soaking up the notion of movement exploration.

It is our fourth session, and Nikki is watching me intently. I am mirroring her posture—sitting with my weight shifted toward my right hip, legs folded to my left, hands on my lap—about 10 feet away from her and Mom. As Nikki watches, I place both my hands on the floor in front of me, shifting my upper body weight onto them. In one smooth, gliding action, I swing my pelvis up so I am on all fours in a crawling position. Nikki never takes her eyes off of me. And then, ever so gently, she lifts her pelvis up too and attempts to mirror me, trying to bear weight on her extended arms and hands. Immediately they glide out from under her and she plops on her belly! But she maintains her eye contact and we are ALL elated. We exclaim with joy, and Nikki is all smiles. The sudden fall does not disturb her in the least. This is quite a feat for this young child who has only begun to mobilize within the last 8 days.

It now seems that Nikki's original static postures created too much stability. Her positive attachment to her mother, however, supported Nikki's trust to explore. She began treatment ready to move but didn't know how to begin. By observing and building on Nikki's very limited movement repertoire, the therapist guides Nikki into discovering a series of movement steps that transform her stable posture into a moving sequence. These experiences are carried out within the context of a shared social engagement. The events are two-way communications occurring through movement exchanges—*shared dance-play* in the *Ways of Seeing* vocabulary (see Chapters 3 and 8). Nikki is able to experience her actions as communicative social dialogue. The therapist's ability to regard Nikki's movements as nonverbal cues supports and encourages her to use her body to communicate. When Nikki spontaneously surprises everyone by taking the initiative to attempt to follow the therapist's movements, the therapist's and her mother's positive responses encourage her to continue to explore new ways to move her body and stay engaged. This experience also reveals that Nikki is a visual learner, and this knowledge becomes useful in Nikki's further treatment.

Becoming aware of Nikki's use of her visual sense is a very significant discovery because at this point in time Nikki is not using eye contact—the more typical signal of social connection—to maintain engagement. Nikki does not begin to make consistent eye contact for many months, and this lack of eye contact, hypotonia, and an inability to mobilize has greatly affected how her mother experiences and relates to her daughter. Later Nikki's mother recalls her first emotions while watching Nikki's behaviors in these early dance movement psychotherapy sessions.

Shock of recognition maybe. Realizing the issues can be defined and they were clear. . . . To me she was just this mush. You were breaking it down to specifics. You were showing me, look how Nikki is responding to this, look how she is not doing that. Let's try to work on this, this way. You were giving me guidance. Okay, I understand something here. I am feeling what Nikki is feeling . . . as a parent, with no experience with any of this . . . [I] didn't know a thing except that she wasn't moving!!

For Nikki, sustained social engagement initially occurs through this shared dance-play. Her ability to so readily respond to and sustain engagement through such play demonstrates the strength and security of her attachment to her mother. Her physical withdrawal when approached and her efforts to stay in her mother's close proximity can be seen in a new light. Perhaps these actions reflect Nikki's sense of insecurity in her environment rather than difficulties with engaging and creating relationships. Her extremely limiting communicative and motor abilities did not provide her with sufficient tools to help her express herself and connect to others in any easily identifiable way. Her listless faraway looks may have been a product of self-preservation, since a child can experience a lack of self-agency when the environment does not support or respond to the child's cues after repeated tries. Shutting down and withdrawing is a natural protective response to such an experience.

Nikki's mother's reflections about the role that nonverbal expression has played in her developing relationship with her daughter are poignant.

⌒ *I think nonverbal expression is an incredible way to communicate. Maybe if I didn't have Nikki, I wouldn't know or see it that much. . . . I think it's become an integral part of my life because Nikki communicates nonverbally—it's her movements and the way that she stands and the pace that she walks and the way that she bends her body or the way that she bends over that tells me so much about where she is at the moment and what she wants and needs. I'm dependent on that to know my daughter. . . . And she can communicate with us because we're listening to her nonverbal communication. Can you imagine understanding things and having no way to say it— the look on her face when you get it—when you know what she wants—is incredible. Yes, she has her computer and she can sometimes point and tell us when she's hungry. But all those finer things, you know, to be able to know that she's sad because of the way she is sitting on a chair or something and to be able to go to her and acknowledge that she's sad—it's so important.* ⌒

Sensorimotor Nonsymbolic Representation

The development from nonverbal to verbal communication in language acquisition follows a progression from having internally felt and sensorimotor experiences toward using words as symbolic representations to express these experiences. This progression begins with an individual processing experiences that are internally represented from a concrete sensorimotor and felt sense, but it eventually develops into the individual's using words as symbolic representations to express these experiences. Both forms of communication are necessary to support the development of social behavior.

Two distinct levels of representation organize social behavior: *symbolic* levels, which are discrete, categorical, and explicit, and *perception-*

action levels, which are nonsymbolic, continuous, procedural, and implicit (Beebe et al., 2000). Words and intentional nonverbal gestures are symbolic level representations. In contrast, perception-action levels are skill or action sequences that are sensorimotor "presymbolic representations," which are encoded nonsymbolically, become automatic with repeated practice, and influence the organizational processes that guide behavior. At this level, memory is implicit, procedural and emotionally based, and may be out-of-conscious awareness (Beebe et al., 2000). Perception-action levels of representation are dynamically created through an infant's experiential relationship with the environment that is continually being reorganized, moment to moment. The integration of these two levels of social behavior organization occurs when information from this perception-action system is represented symbolically (Beebe et al., 2000).

Bucci (1994) and Appelman (2000) emphasized the perception-action level of representation in their nonverbal communication research. They characterize it as being somatic, kinesthetic, sensorial, and visceral, developing through infants' experiences with their environment. Bucci delineated two modes of representation within the perception-action level: a continuous *subsymbolic* processing mode and a nonverbal *presymbolic categorical mode*. The *subsymbolic* mode is based on visceral, sensory, somatic experiences that have infinite gradations and variations. The *presymbolic* mode occurs before symbolization and is nonverbal but enables infants to categorize events, objects, and experiences into groups of discrete prototypic images. Appelman examines the caregiver's use of language in early infancy as it relates to attachment issues, paying particular attention to the significant role that nonverbal experience between infant and caregiver plays in the transformation and organization of experience into language. Citing Bucci, Appelman stated that these subsymbolic experiences, registered in multiple nonverbal modalities (e.g., sensory, kinesthetic, somatic), become organized into nonverbal *perceptual images*. These perceptual images become nonverbal symbols, independent of language, that become the basis from which nonverbal experiences connect to linguistic expression. She concluded, "These nonverbal symbols are the building blocks upon which the verbal system and the connections between the two systems are based" (2000, p. 198).

Nikki's mother illustrates these academic concepts in describing her impressions of Nikki's early experience in the *Ways of Seeing* approach.

~~~ *I think that she was aware that she could make something in her body happen. She was watching you. . . . She started to really watch you . . . very early on in therapy, to connect between what you were doing and that she could do it. You showing her movements and mimicking what she was doing and taking it a step forward. I loved that you would do exactly what she was doing and then take it a step. I guess because you were moving the way she was moving she was able to take that next step with you. So this whole dynamic started very soon, which was incredible for me to experience also.*

I think that's the beginning of communication. Imitation is the most basic form of communication. . . . I think that is where it started. . . . Knowing that we could help her learn and her knowing that she could learn. Somehow something clicked in there that she could learn. ~~~

Nikki's mother continues, sharing how what she and Nikki have learned in dance movement psychotherapy has affected Nikki's home life and who she is now.

~~~ *We all started working with her differently at home. Really trying to look at her movements and build on her movements to help her do more. It became a concept. . . . I always think that if I had had my older daughter after Nikki, I would have raised her totally differently because I would have brought this concept into just normal child development. It's such a natural way of teaching a child.* ~~~

The *Ways of Seeing* approach uses the nonsymbolic perception-action level of representation as a means of communicating. In this approach, the infant does not have to be at a symbolic representational level of communication to be able to communicate and relate. The first three procedural methods of the *Ways of Seeing* intervention described in Chapter 8 focus on interactions that utilize subsymbolic levels of representation, such as visceral and multisensory experiences. Infants repeatedly explore these experiences, thus creating patterns and variations on patterns of relatedness that become experiential presymbolic memories. In the fourth procedure of intervention, the first three methods of relating are linked to more symbolic, verbal levels of representation. Each of these four procedural methods creates and supports a child's emotional and social relationships, and nurtures each child's uniqueness.

NURTURING INDIVIDUALITY IN TREATMENT

Therapists should learn to observe even the smallest details of a child's individual movement style and use these observations to inform their understandings and draw out each child's individuality. When therapists use their observations to inform their understandings, they are allowing a child's experiences and expressions of experiences to shape and form the course of an intervention. The specific treatment protocol becomes directed by the child's input. Each case will follow its own path. Such a focus honors interplay between the individual and the environment. Each child's development occurs as an interactive process, rather than a linear progression, as the personal variations of each individual engages with the environment (Sander, 1962). Individuality emerges as individual differences are supported. Children are encouraged to learn about themselves by feeling and exploring their own existence from a physically and emotionally felt place. This method of working allows individual children to register experiences on a visceral, multisensory level, gaining knowledge about self as a personal sense of body develops, organizing these sensorially based events. Experiencing responses to their nonverbal actions enables children to begin to form clear images of self. Through nonverbal interactions with others, this initially experiential sensing of self eventually develops into more symbolic personal representations.

The Dance of Interaction

Nikki's story shows how the nonverbal dance of relating established early on through her strong relationship with her mother can be used as the basis from which a child can begin self-exploration. Nikki begins to discover herself by feeling her body's motions, which expands her way of being in her surroundings, first through actions with her mother, and then fueled by her own efforts. By becoming aware of her body actions and the movements of her mother and the therapist, Nikki learns new ways to relate as her actions become communications that further develop how others relate to her. Her body experiences and her nonverbal interactional dance with others continually interweave, informing and influencing each other. Her own individuality thrives. As the unique details of her style of relating become understood, Nikki's nonverbal actions enable her to maintain her relationships with her mother and therapist, even when she is not using typical nonverbal communications such as eye contact and head nodding. Instead, Nikki's relationships grow out of spontaneous, seemingly playful movement-based interactions.

The discovery that Nikki is able to maintain social engagement through her nonverbal actions demonstrates that all actions have the potential to be communicative. Viewing actions as *potential nonverbal communications* creates a new category within the realm of nonverbal communication. This category can be placed alongside *intentional nonverbal communications,* which require more advanced bodily control and regulation as well as higher communicative and cognitive skills involving symbolic understanding. Adult acknowledgment of nonverbal actions as potential communications helps a child with communication issues begin to experience more successful relationships.

Because the parent–child dyad does not need to always be in exact synchrony, Nikki's mother and therapist did not have to replicate Nikki's movements exactly to foster a positive social engagement. Instead, after analyzing the quality of the mother–child interactions, the therapist designed movement explorations that supported the parent–child relationship and developed new ways of nonverbally communicating. In addition, Nikki's movement vocabulary increased during her sessions as she spontaneously explored new dancing dialogues. These spontaneous movement explorations expanded Nikki's motor, cognitive, and emotional vocabulary. Stern's (1985) discussion of how a young child develops a sense of self through the experience of self and other is portrayed throughout these dance/movement-based activities.

Spontaneous explorations, often directed by the therapist and Nikki's mother attuning to Nikki's actions, reinforce the previously discussed research findings that emphasize the need and importance of flexibility within the dyadic relationship (Beebe et al., 1997; Thelen & Smith, 1994). Beebe emphasized that a secure attachment creates a balance between stability and change, enabling the young child to be open to novelty and variety. A child who can function in this manner has a greater range of capabilities. Thelen and Smith (1994) also discussed spontaneous explorations in terms of self-produced locomotion, stating that these experiences are foundationally significant for perceptual and cognitive development, and are also notably fundamental in social-emotional development. Beebe discussed this flexibility in the context of developing emotional and social interactional strength and security (Beebe et al., 1997; Beebe et al., 2000). The *Ways of Seeing* approach includes many improvisational explorations that positively affect children's development by fostering initiations and dialogues.

Using Sense of Body Concept in Intervention

The bodily sensations, reactions, expressions, and experiences of all children, with or without special needs, come from their keen physical receptivity to sensations. These are their initial experiences of self, and their body experiences define and continually inform them about who they are. Intervention and learning should focus on helping children to become aware of

- How their sense of body affects their experience

- How their body sensations—especially in the cases of children with special needs—sometimes overpower and distract their ability to fully utilize and develop other aspects of self, emotionally, socially, intellectually, and communicatively

- How to transform and elaborate on their existing sense of body to develop their personal styles into more complex and functionally adaptive systems

How the *Ways of Seeing* approach achieves these three goals unfolds through the next two chapters. Chapter 3 describes the key principles of the approach, providing the reader with new ways to view multisensory awareness, to identify meaning in a movement, to transform an action into a dancing dialogue, and to learn about the emotional themes that arise through movement and motor development. Chapter 4 focuses specifically on understanding and learning how to analyze nonverbal cues that are subtle, obscure, or difficult to understand.

3
Ways of Seeing

Movement Development, Expression, and Body Awareness

Seeing comes before words. The child looks and recognizes before it can speak. But there is also another sense in which seeing comes before words. It is seeing which establishes our place in the surrounding world; we explain that world with words, but words can never undo the fact that we are surrounded by it. . . . The relation between what we see and what we know is never settled. . . . The ways we see things is affected by what we know or what we believe. . . . Yet this seeing which comes before words, and can never be quite covered by them, is not a question of mechanically reacting to stimuli. . . . We only see what we look at. To look is a choice. As a result of this act, what we see is brought into our reach—though not necessarily within arm's reach.

J. Berger, *Ways of Seeing* (1977, pp. 7–8)

This quote uses the image of a young child's early development to emphasize the role our visual sense plays in how we learn about and interact with the world. It also suggests how our vision is influenced by other elements. Berger specifically notes that what we already know may affect how we look, what we choose to look at, and how we process that information through thoughts and words. Most significantly, Berger asserts that seeing and knowing are constantly changing events based on how we interact and make sense of our experiences. In essence, opportunities to "see" are always presenting themselves but may not enter our experience if they are not part of our current perspective or belief system. Sometimes, we must be guided to see in a different way, to see something that may have been in our surroundings all along—to take note of it and explore it in a manner that will create a new experience and a new way of knowing, relating, and making sense of our personal world.

Berger's quote reflects several key components of the *Ways of Seeing* approach—sensory experiences, experiential learning, perception, non-verbal observation, and the role relationships play in our development. These elements provide opportunities for growth on all developmental levels. Although these elements are always available, at times guidance may be needed to bring them into heightened awareness and to create a balance within a child's total functioning. The theoretical framework of the *Ways of Seeing* approach emphasizes the influential role that all multisensory, somatic, and nonverbal early childhood experiences play in a child's development. This framework is based on the belief that these experiences are held in the body and are revealed through an individual's physiology and nonverbal actions. This program investigates how infants and young children use their bodies through multisensory-based exploration to learn, communicate, and develop meaningful relationships in the world around them. Elements of experience become the actual tools of intervention. Therapists, parents, and caregivers can use these embodied experiences to create sensory and movement-based dialogues that support a child's healthy growth and development. In essence, the *Ways of Seeing* approach utilizes nonverbal movement observation, multisensory experience, dance, music, and play for the assessment, intervention, and education of children of all ages and their families.

To use nonverbal and multisensory movement-based experiences therapeutically may require a shift of perspective on the therapist's part. Becoming aware of the roles played by nonverbal experience and expression in all interactions might be a new way of looking at children's behaviors. Therapists must first become conscious of how to "look," assess, and read cues from children and families. Moreover, to discover this way of observing, interpreting, and interacting, therapists must first examine what influences their own perceptions. In this chapter, readers will be guided through this fresh awareness as the theoretical elements of the *Ways of Seeing* approach are described within the context of early childhood development.

The *Ways of Seeing* approach is helpful for a wide range of children, including those with ASD; Rett syndrome; PDD; sensory integration dysfunction; ADHD; communication and language delays; unspecified developmental delays; or issues associated with parent–child attachment, adoption, and trauma. Vignettes of children within this broad spectrum illustrate the *Ways of Seeing* concepts, both in this chapter and throughout the book. Finally, Chapter 8 describes the specific techniques employed to support the *Ways of Seeing* approach.

The following are the core principles of the *Ways of Seeing* approach:

- Our moving bodies tell stories, which speak of our experiences.

- All people, even children, create their own personal nonverbal movement styles composed of a unique combination of movement qualities.

- These movement qualities are their expressive communicative styles — regardless of how conventional or atypical these styles may be.

- Children's skills and developmental levels are best looked at within the context of the qualities of their nonverbal behaviors.

- Even severe movement limitations have a qualitative element — whether in the muscular tension level, the habitual body position, or the frequency or infrequency of eye contact.

- How these qualities are expressed creates a sensation, an attitude, or a response from the mover to those in the environment.

- In return, observers of these behaviors have reactions to these expressions based on their own personal experiences.

- It is this action–reaction that influences developing social-emotional relationships and affects therapeutic and educational interventions.

- Interventions are relationship-based, with the strength of emotional bonds being paramount and supporting all other areas of development.

SEEING WITH ALL THE SENSES

Ashley contracted spinal meningitis within the first 24 hours of her birth. Now 12 months old, she spends her days lying on her back. She cannot roll over onto her belly or transition to a vertical position. She cannot independently support herself to sit. She holds her body with extreme rigidity; sporadically flinging and swinging her arms out to her sides with intermittent bound and released muscular tension. In response to certain environmental stimuli, these actions of Ashley's often increase and are accompanied by her screeches. With this in mind, I choose to not touch her during our first few sessions. Instead, I let my presence be known by playing the same soft music from a portable CD player each time I sit next to her on the floor—at the edge of her arm-swinging reach. Watching closely and silently, I notice her arms swing more intently when she hears the music. It seems as if she is reaching out toward it. I place my arm in her swinging range—with my palm flat on the floor and my forearm perpendicular to it. This time, when Ashley flings her arm out she encounters my arm, a firm, warm, soft-skinned surface. She momentarily pauses. She swings her arm out again with the same result. She tries this over and over. After a while I change the position of my arm so that when she "reaches out" this time, she encounters my hand, and I give her a brief firm yet gentle squeeze that I soften before releasing her hand. This firmness matches the tension level of her musculature with a significant difference—the softening before the release adds a moment of relaxation from the tension before we disengage. She responds by increasing her contact, lingering longer in my grasp, turning her head toward me and calming her body down. Over the next few sessions, we slowly work this into an arm duet, gliding through the air with our hands clasped. This extended movement contact simultaneously increases the range of motion in her shoulder socket and creates a communicative social dance. Our dancing dialogue has begun. ～

Ashley relies on several senses to "see" and experience her surroundings. The dance movement psychotherapist guides Ashley to expand her experience by using her senses. Through the kinesthetic sense she feels her body tense and release. This kinesthetic sense becomes used in the service of her stimulated auditory sense to increase her swinging arm movements in response to the music. Her tactile senses are stimulated as she responds to the therapist's arm and hand. In the midst of these multiple sensory messages, Ashley adds visual awareness as she turns her head to gaze in the therapist's direction. Exploring each of her senses through this interactive experience enables Ashley to create new ways of seeing. Ashley and the therapist engage in shared dance-play.

This vignette also exemplifies a core concept in the *Ways of Seeing* approach. All of the senses are potential avenues to gain insight into how a child experiences the world, develops communicative bridges, and forms meaningful relationships. This perspective affects the implementation of the *Ways of Seeing* approach in two regards. It encourages a therapist to promote an emotional connection with a child by noticing seemingly incidental actions, gestures, and behaviors. Simultaneously, this perspective inspires the therapist to create an interactive relationship based on a child's existing style to encourage the child to explore the environment in a new way. As shown in Ashley's story, the therapist first perceives Ashley's reactions by watching them, taking particular note of which senses Ashley is utilizing to respond to her surroundings. The therapist then incorporates particular aspects of these actions to support Ashley's continued exploration of her environment.

Understanding *Ways of Seeing*

The *Ways of Seeing* approach is a philosophy and a method of relating. Its roots strongly derive from the practices of dance movement therapy. The American Dance Therapy Association defines dance movement therapy as "the psychotherapeutic use of movement as a process which furthers the emotional, cognitive, social and physical integration of the individual" (Loman & Tortora, 1999). The *Ways of Seeing* approach emphasizes the relational elements elicited by movement observations and interactions. A significant part of the program is the observation of the body in all of its states, running the spectrum from stillness to hyperactivity. Because the moving body and interpersonal relating—whether functional or dysfunctional—come into play in all forms of interaction, intervention, and educational practice, observation of body movements can provide additional insight into every therapist's methodology.

The *Ways of Seeing* approach applies the term *seeing* both literally and metaphorically. Used literally, *seeing*, or vision, is one of the senses we receive information from and communicate through. Observation is a key technique we employ to learn about self and others. Metaphorically, the term *seeing* is also based on the fundamental dance movement therapy principle that each of us has a need and desire to be seen and understood for who we really are—to be witnessed without prejudice. All seeing involves a subjective element, however, and is influenced by the viewer's own conscious and unconscious thoughts and experiences.

> We never look at just one thing; we are always looking at the relation between things and ourselves. Our vision is continually holding things in a circle around itself, constituting what is present to us as we are. (Berger, 1977, p. 9)

The viewer's experiences are encompassed in the *Ways of Seeing* approach through a specific self-observation process. This aspect of the approach, influenced by the discipline of Authentic Movement (Adler, 1987, 2002), involves a therapist's paying attention to personal thoughts, memory, and bodily reactions during observations and interactions with a child or family members. The *Ways of Seeing* process asks a therapist to monitor personal multisensory and nonverbal reactions in the following three ways:

1. Objectively mapping the details of the observed actions (*witnessing*)

2. Becoming aware of and reflecting on personal sensorially based reactions (*kinesthetic seeing*)

3. Becoming aware of and reflecting on personal emotional reactions being experienced and actually trying on the actions observed (*kinesthetic empathy*)

In this approach, a therapist takes a very active role during engagement with a child. The terms *witnessing, kinesthetic seeing,* and *kinesthetic empathy* used to describe this self-observation process are defined in detail in Chapter 7 of this book.

The *Ways of Seeing* approach also recognizes that certain uncontrollable environmental elements influence the interactional experience. Such elements cover a broad spectrum, from the time of day and location to the amount of furniture and noise level. Thus, experiences and observations of experiences involve input from both participants and the external environment. Moreover, each person's subjective experiences and interpretations constantly influence how these experiences are perceived.

Nonverbal Methods of Establishing Relationships

The first task of a *Ways of Seeing* therapist is to establish a rapport with a child by using whatever means possible to initiate a relationship. As seen in the previous vignette, the *Ways of Seeing* approach differs from traditional psychotherapies in that it does not initially use words as the primary tool of communication and interaction. Instead, nonverbal actions and interactions become the key source of information gathering, with words only later used to describe and interpret movement experiences. Three initial questions are asked when observing a child in the *Ways of Seeing* approach:

1. How does a child's way of relating and moving color the child's experience?

2. What does it feel like to experience the world through the child's particular expressive movement repertoire?

3. How can a therapeutic environment be structured to enable a child to experience a way of relating and functioning as a com-

municative tool, while simultaneously enabling the child to use the experience to explore new ways of interacting?

How Does a Child's Way of Relating and Moving Color the Child's Experience?   This question asks a therapist to think about how the child's unique balance among motor, sensorial, verbal-communicative, emotional, and cognitive levels of development influences how she perceives and responds to her surroundings. It prompts a therapist to keep in mind how a child is using her own unique internal structures to cope with, adapt, and respond to the environment. Consider the alternative scenarios of two toddlers—one of stocky and strong build and the other of slender and agile build—both wanting to get to their fathers, who have just entered their child care center. At this moment the pathways to their fathers are filled with toys, children, and other adults. The stocky child may make a beeline toward her father using her body as a block, bumping and stepping on people and objects, leaving them toppled in her wake. The slender toddler may use his agility to deftly weave through these obstacles, sailing into his father's arms. Both methods are effective!

In other words, examining nonverbal expression includes inquiring into how a child navigates through and subjectively experiences all levels of development. The distinctly individual ways a child approaches a situation affects how she perceives the specific experience. Moreover, the multisensory-based experience then affects how the child perceives her environment, which in turn influences how she expresses herself within her surroundings.

What Does It Feel Like to Experience the World Through the Child's Particular Expressive Movement Repertoire?   This is an experiential extension of the first question. It asks a therapist to imagine how all of the specific details of a child's movement style may influence the development of her perceptions and experiences. In the scenarios just described, each child experiences success. Yet, these very different visceral experiences may cause the children to encounter their surroundings differently—and then cause them to reach radically different conclusions about the best way to navigate through the world.

The experience of a young child who uses a wheelchair, for example, would undoubtedly be completely different from those of the two toddlers mentioned above. This child has never been able to physically mobilize his own body through space to draw people toward him. He must rely on other faculties such as verbal skills to gain attention. But how does his inability to simply walk up to anyone with whom he wants to talk influence how available the world feels to him? A movement-oriented therapist places extensive value in imagining how these different body-oriented experiences may influence a child's total functioning.

By initially imagining and then actually embodying elements of a child's nonverbal style, a therapist creates a dancing dialogue. Social-emotional relationships become established through these spontaneous dance and movement-based exchanges. A child gains a sense of agency by having his nonverbal expressions acknowledged. Such experiences build communication, foster a sense of relationship, and develop meaningful emotional ties. This is the initial step that enables a child to experience nonverbal actions as meaningful communications.

How Can a Therapeutic Environment Be Structured to Enable a Child to Experience a Way of Relating and Functioning to Communicate, as Well as to Explore New Ways of Interacting? This question highlights the concept that all activities provide children with opportunities for self-expression because nonverbal behaviors are expressions of self. Based on the conclusions reached from the first two questions, the therapist endeavors to create an environment that enables a child to feel that she is an effective communicator, even if her communications are nonverbal. At the same time, the therapist works to provide avenues that allow the child to expand, improve, or modulate her ways of functioning.

Each *Ways of Seeing* session unfolds as a therapist experiences a child's actions. These actions are the "words" from which the dancing dialogue must develop. Continuing with the example of the stocky toddler and the slender toddler, a therapist might introduce the element of time to the stocky toddler's repertoire. This could involve the creation of movement games that require the

Children may have totally different reactions to the same situation or event.

toddler to vary her timing as she stops and holds her position in front of obstacles that move or don't move at different rates of time. Some objects might require her to hold her body still for a moment while the object passes, whereas other objects might require her to move around or climb over them. Through these experiences the toddler learns to modulate her style to fit different settings. Once the toddler gains a better experiential sense of body control through her more effective use of timing, she may learn how to modulate her overall presence during interactions more easily.

Observations from this perspective can turn any child's actions into a dialogue by developing the movement into a two-way communication exchange. This occurs over time in multiple sessions, with the therapist first matching the child's actions and then transforming them into a reciprocal interchange by emphasizing and adding dynamic movement-related qualities.

Special Populations

The *Ways of Seeing* approach is especially useful with infants and young children who have difficulties with communication and who are unable to regulate themselves comfortably in their environments. Often their difficulties with self-regulation cause them to become preoccupied with their concerns, and relating to others becomes secondary.

When babies create such a focus early on, it can interfere with their establishment of secure emotional attachments to significant others. Often, such babies have a very limited expressive range of emotion, as is evidenced by their vocalizations and movement behaviors. For example, they may rely on crying to display frustration or distress or on making sounds of exclamation to gain attention. In the most extreme cases, they avoid vocalizing completely, creating a deep, unsettling silence. Examples of such babies' movement behaviors (discussed more extensively in Chapter 4) include averting eye gaze, contracting or pulling their bodies away from a stimulus, or holding their bodies still. They may engage in sporadic repetitive self-touch; flicking, rubbing, or picking at articles of clothing, blankets, or parts of their bodies in an effort at self-soothing; and turning their attention away from noxious stimuli. When these babies become mobile, they may run around seemingly aimlessly in any room where they find the environment uncomfortable. Alternatively, they may become very sedentary, controlling their environment by limiting free exploration. These babies may become rigid in their daily routines, constraining social engagement. Sometimes they become very content playing alone, and as they grow older, they may create simple or well-developed fantasy stories that support their solitary play. When this is occurring, these children do not elicit or welcome partners in their play, and they may turn away, protectively pulling their toys closer to their bodies. They may also stop playing if another child or adult tries to join them.

    ~~~ *Lindsay, 3½ years old, has been diagnosed with speech and language delays and sensory integration dysfunction. During our initial sessions, Lindsay seems to prefer playing in one place with toys rather than using large physical actions that move her through the room. Her play consists of placing animal figures in a semicircle in close proximity to herself. She sits with her legs in a "W" position, holding her upper torso with a slight concavity. She engages in solitary play, often whispering to the animal figures as she holds them up close to her eyes and placing them back down near her legs. It is as if Lindsay is using this posture and the toys to set up a barrier between her, the open space, and me. When I attempt to join in the play, Lindsay quickly draws the toys closer to her, becoming angry, tensing her body, and exclaiming in a tone that shows she is clearly upset, "No! Mine!" As the therapist, I feel shut out. I wonder about her muscular integrity, tactile defensiveness, and visual focus.* ~~~

Frequently these limited behaviors are a child's attempt to create regulation in what she perceives to be an intolerable environment. After observing this nonverbal environment set up by Lindsay, the therapist questions whether the young child's actions are a defense to her feelings of instability and danger as she moves through her environment. Her behaviors seem designed to protect her sensory vulnerabilities. Lindsay's visual system seems to play an especially significant role in her defensive behavior. If she does not visually process her world in an organized way, how can she freely move within it or comfortably interact with others? Moreover, Lindsay's desire to control all interactions seems a manifestation of her fear, frustration, and anger. Her demanding and controlling style of interaction combines with her lack of give-and-take during play to create a self-protective, defensive persona. Lindsay lacks the communication and processing skills to verbally express her concerns, but her nonverbal communication exposes her experience of vulnerability.

⁓ Through persistent physical, verbal, and social dialogue, I encourage Lindsay to include me in her play. I use my body to help Lindsay negotiate the social interaction by carefully yet purposefully placing myself just outside of her toy barrier, crouching down so I can glimpse at her eyes when she reaches for a toy. I verbalize my deep desire to be part of Lindsay's play and my interest in her ideas and friendship. Throughout our play, I encourage Lindsay to attempt to use words to explain her reactions to me. When she demonstrates her discomfort through screaming, hitting, or tensing her body, and turning herself away as she clutches a toy in her hands, I both mirror her actions and describe them verbally. I tell Lindsay about how these actions feel to me as a way of providing her with a vocabulary of possible feelings that her actions might be expressing. I am very consciously speaking with a firm tone while maintaining a calm, steady body attitude to provide Lindsay with an alternative behavioral model. As Lindsay looks over at me with interest, she attempts to adopt this style. Immediately I praise her and acknowledge her request by moving a little farther away. We begin a game of my moving closer and farther away based on her actions and verbal requests. A physical-social dialogue has begun. I develop this dialogue as I take a few toy figures with me, away from Lindsay's immediate reach. This requires Lindsay to track the toys—both visually and physically. Lindsay begins to crawl toward the toys. The social play is further extended when I suggest that Lindsay embody the animal movements. Lindsay's wonderful budding imagination is sparked by this suggestion. She immediately begins to create stories for this dance-play. By taking on the role of instructor and leader, Lindsay guides me to pretend that I am an animal on a journey, crawling, and climbing all over the room. She especially enjoys deciding when, how, and if I am allowed to play with her. ⁓

This dance-play provides Lindsay with a sense of controlling the comings and goings of others—an enjoyable but unfamiliar experience because she cannot completely control significant family members during her everyday life. These explorations allow Lindsay to be an active participant, both physically and emotionally taking charge of her surroundings. When she realizes she can participate in making choices, Lindsay's sensory issues begin to subside, and she becomes less controlling and more thoughtful. Through the use of sensory and movement-based expressions, the therapist's attempts to relate allow rapport to develop because Lindsay experiences—perhaps for the first time—a sense of control.

TRANSFORMING AN ACTION INTO A DIALOGUE

When a *Ways of Seeing* therapist uses a child's own actions as the initial points of interaction, the child's attempts at self-regulation become effective on an emotional level because they now support an interactive exchange. This contrasts with the more typical therapeutic response that attempts to redirect or correct a child's behaviors. Unfortunately, early attempts to redirect and correct behavior often cut off and shut down communication because they have the effect of telling a child to control his behavior—a request that must feel especially daunting if the behavior is in reaction to what is perceived to be a threatening environment. Using a child's limited behavioral movement and sensory-based vocabulary does not require the child to immediately adjust to the environment that caused the reactions in the first place. The use of his movements and vocabulary also sends the message that the therapist is interested in learning about a child's experiences as expressed in his actions.

Gaining Insight into the Expressivity of Difficult Behaviors

It is important to underscore that the *Ways of Seeing* approach does not exclude behavioral techniques that aim to help a child manage, attend to, and successfully accomplish tasks of everyday functioning. But the emphasis of many behavioral techniques is to gain control over inappropriate behaviors, whereas the emphasis of the *Ways of Seeing* approach is to gain insight into the expressive component of a full spectrum of a child's behaviors. The program's first goal is to help a child find ways to articulate his emotional and social experiences because it is through this articulation that ways to alleviate and develop more appropriate behaviors emerge.

The vignette that follows, which describes the first *Ways of Seeing* session with a 5-year-old child with ASD, exemplifies this focus. Bruce was referred for intervention because his mother believed that she did not know how to relate to or communicate with her child. Most often silent, he had seemed to be slipping even deeper into his own world recently, as evidenced by the following behaviors: wandering aimlessly through rooms; staring out into space; moving from blank stares to eerie laughs; and becoming absorbed in repeatedly turning, opening, closing, and spinning objects in a compulsive and methodical fashion.

As Bruce enters the studio, I am struck by his gentle manner. With his slight frame and glistening light-brown hair, he seems to float into the room. Without even a glance in my direction, he begins to survey the contents of the room, moving fluidly from one place to another. As he moves intermittently from the objects placed mostly along the walls to the large free open area in the center of the room, his floor pattern makes irregular, undulating pathways through the space. The rhythm of his actions creates soft phrases as he slightly accelerates and then pauses to gaze or to carefully manipulate an object. As I begin to glide cautiously through the room slightly behind and to his side, I feel as if I am moving to a Mozart adagio. Indeed, I find out later that his mom is a concert violinist and that Bruce tends to hum Mozart tunes.

Throughout this session I do not say a word, and I motion to Mom to stay silent as well. Following Bruce's actions has a mesmerizing effect on me. His subtle actions and silence cause the room to become quite serene. As we move through the room together I watch his gaze and at times assist him in his sensitive exploration of the objects to which he is drawn. When he wanders into the center of the room with a little acceleration that turns into a few prancing steps, I mirror his actions exactly. But I never require any verbal communication, nor do I produce any myself. I follow and respond purely by matching my body actions to his. A few moments before our session is over, Bruce slides down the wall and sits on the soft mound of pillows and blankets. I follow, sitting at his side, shoulder to shoulder. Gently, he turns to me for the first time in the session and looks me straight in the eye. His eyes have an inquisitive look to them. Just as gently, he lifts his hand and strokes my forehead, my cheeks, my nose, my chin, and my hair, all the while gazing at me. His expression is soft; his touch is kind. I respond with a warm smile but do not move, so as not to disturb his exploration. It feels as if he is assessing who I am through his touch—the same careful touching he has just done throughout the room for this past hour. I whisper that it is the end of the session and he willingly goes over to the door to put on his shoes. As he steps out of the door I am left alone in the room, still touched by his presence. I remain motionless, taken in by our shared experience—an hour of silence that seemed so filled with grace. I feel as if I have been given a gift. Bruce has showed me how copious and full his silent world can be.

By not requiring Bruce to speak or provide eye contact, the *Ways of Seeing* therapist adapts to Bruce's self-regulatory needs, modifying her own communicative style. Together they co-construct a means of relating through shared attention via their movements. As discussed in the previous chapter, such shared experiences change and affect their interaction, creating spontaneous exchanges that encourage Bruce to stay more engaged. Starting with his unique but limited means of connecting, their dance-play supports flexibility and novelty, providing expanded ways for Bruce to initiate further social contact.

Identifying the Meaning of a Movement

Bruce's story shows how a therapist can use movement and dance as tools to observe a child's explorations and to gain insight into his experiences and perceptions. To create activities to support expression, a therapist can begin by distinguishing the particular characteristics of a child's actions through a process of nonverbal movement analysis. The therapist identifies the individual qualities within each action before inferring the movement's meaning; the therapist also notices how each movement quality contributes and combines to make the overall action before determining the movement's feeling tone. These qualitative elements provide information about the attitude or motion factors of how the action is performed (known as *Effort*); what parts of the body execute the action (known as *Body*); and where the actions occur in reference to others and the surrounding spatial environment (known as *Space*). The terms *Effort, Body,* and *Space* are taken from the vocabulary of the LMA nonverbal movement analysis method that is discussed extensively in Chapters 5 and 6.

The initial identification of these qualities and the description of how this information can be used to derive meaning and create interaction are shown in the previous account of Bruce's first session. Bruce's slight, floating frame (Body); his soft, fluid movements that slightly accelerate and then pause when he gently touches an object (Effort); and the undulating floor pathways created as he explores the room (Space) lead the therapist to decide to relate to him without words. The success of this nonverbal approach is evident during the session's end when Bruce turns gently toward the therapist—thus acknowledging and including her in his explorations—and initiates and maintains expressive eye contact while stroking her face.

Qualitative movement elements—the specific details of an action that affect how the action is performed—can be used to construct a nonverbal language of movement. Moreover, how an action is specifically executed greatly affects how it feels on a personal body level, how successfully it supports the desired task or result, and how it looks to the observer. For example, if, on entering a room, Bruce would

throw his body on the floor, and then get up quickly and run in a haphazard manner from object to object, crashing into them and causing
them to fall, his actions would portray a very different type of child. In
this version of events, the feeling tone conveyed would be that of a
child who does not show modulation within his body or control
within his environment. The therapist would most likely need to use
stronger and more direct actions to define physical boundaries with
him. In addition, the child's inability to modulate his large body actions and his lack of fine motor movements under this scenario would
discourage the therapist from welcoming his touch on her face.

Almost every particular movement quality establishes its own
emotional tone. For example, to thread a needle, the hand holding the
thread must move with a direct, light, slow, and steady quality while
the hand holding the needle must be still. If the hand with the thread
attempts to push too hard, or if the hand holding the needle shakes,
the thread will not go into the needle. Repeated failure will eventually
cause frustration, which will most likely be revealed through some
qualitative change in the action. The person attempting to thread the
needle may increase speed or tension level, or even become so aggra-
vated that he or she might ultimately throw down the needle and
thread in irritation.

The quality of a movement colors an individual's experience, and
in turn, affects nonverbal expression. Therapists using the *Ways of
Seeing* perspective view all movements as meaningful expressions of
self. Therefore, a therapist's observation and analysis of this nonverbal
language can provide a window into a fuller understanding of an individual's expressions and style of interactions. To interpret a specific
movement's meaning, however, a therapist must look deeply at a
behavior and discern what feelings the movement is expressing. In this
sense, movement behaviors can be thought of as metaphors.

Understanding Movement
Repertoires, Signatures, and Metaphors

Over time every individual establishes a specific repertoire of movement qualities that is utilized in varying combinations. It is the qualitative aspects of these personal movement actions that enable us to
recognize a family member from afar. How people open doors, walk up
the steps, or use their facial muscles to display amusement make them
unique and endearing. In essence, we are always relying on reading

nonverbal qualitative elements in our interactions with others. The *Ways of Seeing* approach and nonverbal-movement analysis simply bring these natural tendencies into conscious awareness.

Based on the LMA system, this set of qualities is known as an individual's movement repertoire. A *movement repertoire* can be defined as the range of movement qualities and elements that a person uses to express himself or herself. A person's movement signature exists within his or her movement repertoire. As distinctive as a handwritten signature, a *movement signature* consists of the specific qualitative actions used most frequently in his or her repertoire; that is, the actions that most characterize or define his or her style of moving. The *Ways of Seeing* approach acknowledges that the development of a movement signature and repertoire originates during infancy, and that this development is influenced by both internal and external experiences: Internally, a baby's innate style and physical and biological makeup will greatly affect how she first explores and experiences her moving body—in fact, a baby's ability to create a physiological sense of homeostasis by organizing her sensory system will dominate the development of her movement repertoire. Externally, there are two influences that will have an impact on a baby's experiences—interactions with significant others and the specifics of the environment.

There are a significant number of studies investigating how parent–child interactions influence social-emotional development (Beebe et al., 2000; Jaffe, Larchmann, Feldstein, Crown, & Jasnow, 2000; Sander, 2000; Stern, 1985, 1995; Tronick, 1989; Tronick & Gianino, 1986). Research on the parent–child dyad has determined that each member's actions have an impact on the other member's responses so that a bidirectional system of relating develops. The *Ways of Seeing* approach recognizes that the early origins of a baby's qualitative movement style come from this bidirectional experience of interacting. If, for example, a baby is auditorially sensitive from birth, the specific ways that significant people approach him will have an impact on how the baby uses his body to nonverbally respond. Perhaps the mother's movement style is to approach the baby by quickly placing her whole body in close contact, firmly grasping his body while loudly exclaiming with cooing sounds. Such a sudden dramatic approach can be very startling for an auditorially sensitive infant. Because there is a limited movement repertoire in infancy, a baby may only be able to tense his musculature or to move away by turning his head. How long the baby actually holds this tensed musculature or physically averts his gaze will

will be determined by the continued actions of the mother. If she quickly and correctly reads the baby's nonverbal cues, the mother may soften her voice and loosen her grasp. The infant may respond by releasing tension and turning his gaze back to the mother. However, if the baby is having a difficult time with sensory system regulation, the infant may not know how to release muscular hold and may begin to cry instead. This escalates the situation, for now the mother must not only adjust her natural movement tendencies but also figure out how to help her baby calm down.

External environmental factors also affect this scenario. Perhaps this interaction is taking place in a location in which a television and siblings are nearby. Right at the point when the mother is attempting to soothe the baby, these other children make a noisy entrance and excitedly respond to some action drama on the television. The environmental situation will exacerbate the baby's discomfort. Attempting to shut down completely, the infant may maintain his adverted eyes and tensed body for several minutes even after he has been taken out of this immediate environment. If this incompatible style of interacting is repeated frequently, the baby will begin to internalize this nonverbal mode of response and create a defensive pattern of interaction. The infant may begin to tense and avert his eyes as soon as the mother's voice is heard. This will be very upsetting to the mother, who will likely feel rejected by her baby's negative response.

Over time, this reaction may become more subtle and generalized, shifting into what movement analysts call a *movement metaphor*. A movement metaphor is a specific, personally stylized nonverbal qualitative element, posture, or sequence of movements that frequently recurs within a person's repertoire. Developing from a specific experience or set of experiences, this movement becomes distilled into an idiosyncratic gesture or gestures that become so much a part of the person's repertoire that its origin may no longer be readily identifiable. When this metaphor is studied more deeply through nonverbal observation and exploration, however, its origin may become revealed. In the scenario described in the previous paragraph, the baby's tendency to tense and turn away when suddenly approached and confronted by loud sounds may develop into a specific stylized gesture. In response to any person or situation involving a sudden loud noise, the baby's gesture may evolve into a slight tensing of his musculature and a pulling back and sideways tilt of his head while gazing at the stimulus from the corner of his eyes. This gesture of the baby is a movement metaphor.

As is discussed in Chapter 10, the *Ways of Seeing* approach has a further distinction within the concept of movement metaphors—personal movement metaphors and relational movement metaphors. *Personal movement metaphors* are those uniquely stylized metaphors that are observable and occur as generalized qualities within the person's overall repertoire, as just described. *Relational movement metaphors* are the recurring nonverbal patterns that become established between two members of a dyadic relationship, are specific to the dynamics of this dyad, and often define the relational qualities of this dyad. These distinct patterns occur and are detectable (through close observation) within the dyadic interactions.

In the *Ways of Seeing* practice, a therapist first observes an infant's or young child's interactions between self and other (known as *spontaneous choreographies*) and then elaborates on these interactions within the therapeutic environment by creating extended movement explorations through both expressive movement improvisations and more choreographed movement, dance, and play-based activities. In doing this, the therapist should use the observed relational movement metaphors to improve relationships whenever possible. For example, the dynamics in the previous scenario could be described as a relational movement metaphor if the infant only tenses and turns away whenever the mother suddenly approaches and firmly grabs her baby's body. Observing this dynamic, the therapist might create a movement-based game along the lines of Peekaboo, in which the mother is instructed to pause and contain her voice and actions, watch the direction of the baby's gaze, and wait for the baby to return his gaze in the mother's direction before preceding. The therapist might also guide the mother to focus on her own breathing (e.g., inhaling and exhaling in a slow, even pace) to help her modulate her physical behavior as she waits for her baby's attention. When the baby finally returns the mother's gaze, the therapist might advise her to respond through facial expressions only, without using sound or touch.

Movement Metaphors, Early Infant Memory, and Sensory Photographs

Movement metaphors may play a role in early infant memory. Gaensbauer's study (2002, 2004) of the nature of an infant's internal experience during the preverbal period emphasized how multisensory experience relates to early childhood memory. His research suggested that even in early infancy an infant perceives and links affective and somatic experiences and develops a preverbal and sensory-based memory system that can be recalled when certain environmental qualities are present. In his case studies of very young children who had experienced trauma and abuse, Gaensbauer described each child's ability to register these events through multifaceted, multisensory modalities represented through the formation of "perceptual-cognitive-affective-sensory-motor schemata" (2004, p. 29).

The *Ways of Seeing* program uses the term *sensory photograph* to emphasize the felt-sense kinesthetic nature of memories. Sensory photographs are recorded on a multisensory level and may be revealed through the observation of a child's unique movement metaphors. During intervention a *Ways of Seeing* therapist will guide a child to become aware of such kinesthetic sensations by pausing, focusing inward, and registering these sensations, using the image of taking a photographic snapshot on a sensory level. Sensory photographs are taken both to register difficult and often previously unconscious sensations as well as to establish new, healing, and relaxing sensations. These sensory photographs can then be recalled and worked with throughout the course of the intervention. It is a way for the child to gain conscious awareness of difficult sensations and to feel control over these bodily felt impressions. It is also a way for the child to retrieve and recreate the positive sensory-based feelings felt when the snapshot was taken and a pleasing physical state had been achieved.

Relationship Between Movement and Emotional Development

In addition to the perceptual-cognitive-affective-sensory-motor impact of experiences, there is an innate movement and motor developmental progression that affects a child's emotional development. The *Ways of Seeing* linkage between movement development and emotional development is based on Piaget's notion that infants first experience the world through sensorimotor development (Piaget, 1970; Piaget & Inhelder, 1969), combined with Stern's (1985) hypothesis that each infant enters the world with an immediate sense of self that continues to unfold as the infant grows and interacts with others in the environment. Infants learn about the world through their use of their sensory and motor systems to explore and respond to their surroundings. Through early bodily and experientially based interactions, they develop understandings that will later on become symbolically represented through language as their cognitive abilities' progress. This "self" is influenced by their physical, social, verbal, and cognitive experiences, and many early experiences involve infants' becoming acquainted with how their bodies work and feel within the context of a world that continually stimulates all their senses. In the best possible scenario, a sense of homeostasis is created as infants learn how to regulate emotional and physiological systems through such explorations.

The development of an infant's innate qualities takes place within the context of the physical and social worlds. An infant's personal style evolves as a product of this dialogue between self and surroundings. As an infant matures into a young child, the ability to reach out into the world continues to revise this relationship between self and environment. The *Ways of Seeing* approach accepts that this developing sense of self is especially influenced by how a child is experiencing motor and movement development.

There is a distinction between motor development and movement development. *Motor development* refers to a child's progressive mastery of fine and gross motor skills following a developmental progression. *Movement development* is defined as a child's developmental process of acquiring different movement qualities involving muscular tension, strength, timing and spatial orientation (Bartenieff, 1980; Cohen, 1997; Kestenberg-Amighi, Loman, Lewis, & Sossin, 1999). Movement development addresses the qualitative aspects of the progression that support motor development. Together, motor development and movement development affect a child's orientations to the world.

A child's degree of body mastery will determine both the physical orientation and the ability to be dependent or independent in surroundings. From birth to age 3, life is experienced as a continuous cycle of frustration and triumph, as a child becomes aware of a desired physical task, and then works through the experience of trying to master it. Held back both by adult safety precautions and by personal failures, a child must continually struggle to balance eagerness against these limitations. How a child emotionally resolves this struggle through alternating feelings of frustration and triumph can greatly influence the development of his learning style.

The issues of control and independence/dependence are heightened during the years from birth to age 3 as a growing child expands motor and movement development and develops an ability to explore space. Therapists must keep in mind that a child is greatly influenced both by experiences of navigating through these early developmental tasks and by perceptions of support received from the early environment. These experiences and perceptions will also greatly influence the extent and the manner to which a therapist can interact and work with a particular child. Each child's way of navigating through these stages is unique, but can be observed by the therapist who uses the *Ways of Seeing* tools to analyze a child's movement repertoire.

Emotional Themes and Transitional Movement Awareness Through Each Age

Motor and movement development stages or levels influence how children learn to navigate their bodies in their surroundings. The relationship between preexisting developmental levels and a child's growth is dynamic—the term *dynamic* being defined as the nonlinear order that emerges from an interplay of influences (Smith & Thelen, 1993; Thelen & Smith, 1994). Each child's individual course of development is shaped as specific and unique elements of personal experiences interact with innate biological and physiological traits.

Table 3.1 and the descriptions that follow summarize the characteristic elements of each developmental level that influence children's experiences of moving. While reading through these descriptions, it is helpful for a reader to visualize specific children he or she has watched go through these stages. How each child maneuvers through these levels is unique and personal, and therefore the goal of considering a specific child is to identify the individuality within each child's style, rather than to fit each child into a category. It will be the qualitative aspects of style that depict each child's uniqueness and provide insight into that child's experience. The information gleaned from this type of understanding can become useful in future assessment, intervention, and educational programs.

Each level has broad and overlapping age ranges to highlight the dynamic nature of development and the fact that qualities of development coexist at all times. The particular qualities denoted depict the dominant qualities experienced through the specific movements of that stage. These qualities describe children's experiences of their moving bodies to explore specific actions in space. For example, when a baby begins to discover the transition from being primarily on the floor to standing, her spatial organization becomes vertical; as she stretches into the full length of her body, she begins to experience the qualitative (Effort) elements of weight—strength and lightness—as she feels

Table 3.1. Movement tasks, accomplishments, prominent movements, and emotional/body and spatial themes by age level

Movement tasks and accomplishments	Prominent movements	Emotional/body themes	Spatial themes
Birth to 3–6 months			
• **Free-bound tension flow fluctuations** • Stabilizing seven senses • Exploring new world through stimulation and stabilization of all senses • Quality of touch • Focus, attending, attention	• Breath flow • Flexion and extension • Muscular tension fluctuations	• Feeling body in world of gravity • Hard and soft surfaces versus floating fluidity of womb	• Inner space = body – self-regulation
3–12 months			
• **Space, horizontal dimension/plane** • **Budding mobility** • **Exploring space** • Taking in world and beginning to venture out • Early beginning of gaining more control of physical self, body	• First through eye gaze and focused attention, later actually venturing out through purposeful reaching of limbs out into space, and then increased exploration of space via whole body movement, rolling and pushing up	• Choosing to explore moving self and world around self • Awareness of quality of space, people, and things within space around self	• Horizontal orientation to world • Body weight most often in contact with full body surfaces prone, supine, side to side • Leads to crawling on all four limbs
9–24 months			
• **Weight, vertical dimension/plane** • **"Here I am"** • Balance, strength, lightness • Passive weight versus controlled use of weight • Falling, coming back up, recovering • Up-and-down movement	• Sensing length and use of spine • Feeling limbs as weight supports, develops into standing, balancing, falling, and recovering	• Budding self-will developing • Quality of weight, strength, and passivity	• Vertical orientation of body to surroundings, up and down

Table 3.1. (continued)

Movement tasks and accomplishments	Prominent movements	Emotional/body themes	Spatial themes
	18–36 months		
• **Time, sagittal dimension/ plane**	• Rising up onto toes	• Gaining control of self, body within surroundings, with others	• Sagittal forward/backward orientation
• **"Here I come"**	• Falling forward and catching self		
• **"On the go—coming and going"**	• Lifting feet off floor into jumping	• Use of quality of time for this control	
• Starting to become more aware of body part relationships	• Jumping forward, running, marching, galloping, leaping, turning		
	• Whole range of movements available to explore		
	• Able to attach symbolic meaning to movements		
	3–7 years		
• **Mastery and modulation** of all movement qualities above	• All of above available now		
	• Mastery, exploration, and development of own personal movement signature occurs		
• Able to explore variations and subtleties, not just extremes	• Clear differentiation of movement qualities and body parts occurs as defined sense of self develops		

83

and learns to maneuver her body weight to successfully balance. Her sense of success and safety, as well as the amount and type of support she experiences from significant caregivers, will affect her emotional reactions during this discovery period.

Each level is examined separately in terms of its prominent movements, its emotional themes arising from movement explorations, its spatial body orientations, and its qualitative movement-oriented awareness. While a child's exploration continues and expands, new levels of development and movement skills should come into focus.

Birth to 3–6 Months A baby's awareness of prominent movements at this age involves muscular tension fluctuations, head control, eye gaze, and breath flow. Because he has just arrived from the fluid-filled environment of the womb, he is experiencing the effects of gravity and body weight on his moving form. A baby's whole sensory system is stimulated as he encounters a wide variety of sounds, tastes, smells, feelings, and sights. As he senses his body in action, he is putting to use his proprioceptive and vestibular systems. The temperatures, textures, and types of surfaces he encounters all affect his moving experiences. The manner in which significant people in a baby's life move, touch, and interact with him is also important.

During this stage of a baby's life, the spatial theme is personal inner body space. It is essential for him to learn how to self-regulate to create homeostasis so that his body can function smoothly and enable him to focus on external surroundings. A baby's first movement-oriented awareness occurs when he gains some control over his internal body regulation with its neurological underpinnings. As he learns how to stabilize his senses, he becomes able to focus and to prolong his attention on the stimulation he is receiving from the outside world. As a baby works on this body regulation control, his most explored movement qualities are *tension flow fluctuations,* a term referring to the shift between free and bound flow that was developed by Judith Kestenberg, the creator of the nonverbal movement analysis tool, the Kestenberg Movement Profile (KMP) (Kestenberg-Amighi et al., 1999). These qualities are observed through the changes in a baby's breath; the muscular tension shifts from free to tense; and the sporadic actions of his limbs jutting out into space, created through joint flexion and extension. A baby's explorations and his growing ability to gain control of his internal multisensory system and moving body can be observed through the increasingly bright, alert state of attention in which he approaches people and other stimulating events in his environment. A baby draws people toward him because of his emotional and body states, exemplified by the ebullient, spontaneous smile that seems to suddenly burst from his face, accompanied by glittering focused eyes, and wiggling limbs. These experiences from birth to 3–6 months set the foundation for all subsequent experiences.

3–12 Months   At this broad age range, a baby begins to build on the foundation established during the previous stage. A baby continues to learn about the surrounding world through the sensations experienced by her moving body. She is accumulating experiences that enable her to make sense of this new life. Every time she uses her body to engage in the world, she has the opportunity to strengthen musculature and to increase overall body control. At this young age, engaging in the world is a complete physical workout! At 3 months, head control is mastered as a baby raises her head and peers over her mother's shoulder or, while lying on her stomach, uses her forearms to lift up her chest enough to raise and then turn her head from side to side.

A baby's natural spatial position is horizontal during these early months. Without the aid of a person or apparatus such as a car seat, swing, or baby chair, a baby physically experiences the world from a predominantly horizontal viewpoint, whether lying on her back or on her belly. A baby's body is most often in full contact with the world as she lies prone, supine, or on her side. These very corporeal encounters with a variety of surfaces, coupled with enticing activities offered by her surroundings, spur a baby's innate curiosity to find new ways of interacting with her world.

A baby begins to venture out into the world, first through eye gaze and focused attention, followed soon after by purposeful limb extension reaching out into space. His full body contact with surfaces provides immediate feedback as he pushes against surfaces and finds himself rolling into new positions. As he explores this pushing, he discovers variations that place him in a new physical and visual relationship with the world. A baby begins to explore crawling and may even begin walking. A baby's choice to explore her moving body and her surrounding world provides the emotional-body theme of this age. Through this exploration a baby will increase self-awareness and knowledge about spatial surroundings, objects, and other people. The most prominent movement qualities are spatial actions with either an indirect or direct focus. Indirect actions are all-encompassing, involving softer, more general sweeping actions toward a person or an object.

The pathway of the movement may take a few twists and turns before arriving at the final destination.

For example, a 4-month-old baby lying on her back may begin movement exploration by first enjoying the sensation of flexing and extending her legs out into space. She may follow this performance by grappling her toes toward her chest, which then leads to rolling over onto her side and ultimately onto her stomach. In contrast with the less specific focus of indirect movements, actions with direct focus create a sense of specific direction. Continuing with the image of the baby who has just rolled onto her stomach, an example of direct focus would be if she now develops rapt attention to the texture of the blanket on which she is lying. Her legs and torso quietly rest as she props herself on her elbows and studies the feel of the edge of her blanket with her fingers. As she stays absorbed in this exploration, time passes. Both indirect and direct movement qualities support all developmental levels of growth, and both are essential in establishing a movement repertoire. The indirect focus enables a baby to absorb her whole surroundings from all perspectives in an explorative and spontaneous manner, whereas the direct focus enables her to begin to feel control over her actions.

9–24 Months   This time period marks a baby's move into independent and purposeful mobilization—whether crawling, walking, or running. To accommodate the large variation between babies' navigational styles and abilities, this stage covers the very broad age range during which babies develop into toddlers. Around this time a baby begins to move through space in a very self-guided way. Through the earlier actions of rolling and pushing, the baby had created new physical and visual relationships with people and his surroundings. Now, through crawling, walking, and finally running, the toddler plays with balance and weight-shifting, discovering his own muscle strength and body weight as he mobilizes his entire body to pull himself up, fall down, start, and stop.

Weight is the prominent quality supporting movements of this period, involving the use of strength and lightness. The toddler creates a sense of limpness in his body weight or controls his use of weight in a more active manner to engage or resist the world. This passive use of weight is most obvious in the toddler's ability to make his body heavy as a way to avoid getting picked up. In contrast, the same toddler can suddenly engage his weight to prevent contact, quickly and actively mobilizing his body to move away from a parent!

Many complex body orientations are employed. The toddler learns how his upper body moves in relation to his lower body, how the left and right halves of his body support each other, and how he has the ability to perform more complex actions through contralateral coordination. Once he learns how to walk, he explores his body spatially by moving from a horizontal to a vertical relationship with his surroundings. As the toddler becomes able to stand and bear weight, he can create a solid base of support by spreading his legs. Through this wide stance that encompasses both vertical and horizontal spatial dimensions the toddler's body statement seems to be saying, "Here I AM!" Feeling the physical extension of his spine along with this wide lower body base, the toddler takes his place among his fellow bipeds. Aptly labeled, a young toddler of this stage progresses forward by balancing weight from one leg to the other, shifting from side to side, with a smaller emphasis given to the forward direction.

The emotional-body theme of this age range is the toddler's budding sense of self-will as he stretches up, feels the full length of his spine, and gains a new appreciation of his feet as weight bearing, balancing, and mobilizing tools that support his eager explorations. A growing physical sense of independence, coupled with his advancing cognitive understanding and social and communicative skills, encourage the toddler to utter such emphatic pronouncements as "No!" "Me do!" and "I do it!" as he attempts to accomplish more advanced tasks for the first time—including going up steps, climbing on chairs, and carrying his toys while walking alone.

18–36 Months   During this period, the older toddler begins to experience actions that move her forward and backward within what is called the *sagittal plane*. Movements in this plane allow a toddler the ability to mobilize her presence and enter more deeply into the environment. Once bipedal action is firmly established, a toddler moves from the statement "Here I am" to "Here I COME!" A toddler's body is really starting to work, taking her wherever she wants to go. Movement qualities covering the entire spectrums of time and speed become especially prominent. A toddler may be sitting quietly one moment and then suddenly take off running the next, stopping only when she encounters an obstacle such as a wall or the floor. Learning the gradations of time—acceleration and deceleration—will take practice. Holding, waiting, and resisting also involve a sense of time. It is no wonder that toilet training is a prominent issue for this age group.

By this point, the toddler has acquired many movement qualities that she can mix and match. In combining the qualities of space and time, for example, she can race forward directly into the living room filled with her parents' meandering party guests, and escape from her father's outstretched arms, creating a circuitous, helter-skelter pathway through the crowd. A toddler can explore rising up onto her toes, followed by falling down onto the floor, and then bursting back up and dashing off to a new place in the room to tumble and roll, perhaps culminating her experience with an upside-down pose! By the end of this stage, the growing toddler can balance on one foot, hop, and jump. She can differentiate movements that require rhythmic awareness such as clapping, stamping, marching, and galloping.

Toddlerhood is an exciting time filled with a sense of physical autonomy. The toddler is beginning to establish a basic proficiency on a bodily level, with a repertoire of movements at her disposal. Within a relatively short time, a toddler has gone from the stationary position that allowed her to become acquainted with her body parts; to a life of activity using these body parts first to lift and then to prop herself up; to rolling, reaching, crawling, climbing, and balancing; and finally to walking and ultimately running through her surroundings. Some toddlers welcome this increased mobilization with exuberance, confidence, and even reckless abandon. Others enter life more cautiously, hesitantly, or thoughtfully. The variations and sense of individuality of each toddler has become especially apparent (to this author) while teaching creative dance to this age group. The following is an excerpt taken from observations of children during a class when they were given time to create solo dances in response to a selection of music:

The strong reggae beat goes on, and immediately Josh jumps up, barely able to contain himself, so I ask him if he would like to go first. He responds by immediately running across the room, only stopping—and then just for a moment—as he bangs into the wall, gleefully slapping into it with his whole body. On impact, he instantaneously uses the wall to ricochet back through the room. His run is so free, leaning so far forward that it seems as if he might actually topple down. But giggling with glee, legs straggling out behind him, BANG! he is caught by the opposite wall and is off again. He has discovered something. The walls can act as springboards, containing and propelling his active energy, and boy is it fun! When I stop the music, he knows it is time to finish. I watch to see if he is able to suddenly freeze and hold his passionate exuberance. He tries to stop, but he succeeds only by drop-

ping to the floor in one continuous movement, sprawled out on his back. This again demonstrates his use of a surface to help him manage his body.

During Josh's dance, James watches, transfixed. So, I invite him to go next. As so often happens when a child is encouraged to express himself through his actions, the next child tries to imitate. But, if you observe the qualities of the actions carefully, his experience will be different. James runs to the wall with directness and purpose. He hold his body up straight and reaches his hands out to hit the wall—and then uses his hands as breakers to soften the impact when his full body comes into contact with the hard surface. His hands push him away as he makes a beeline for the opposite wall. When the music stops he freezes on his two feet without difficulty. But then, as if remembering that Josh landed on the floor, James suddenly drops down, lays on his side, and freezes again, causing his closing movements to have a two-part rhythmic quality rather than the continuous water-like splattering of Josh's culminating actions.

Adam's turn is next. He has watched Josh and James from his mom's lap. He smiles when I call his name but looks back at Mom, who gives him a smile and a nod before he enters the open dance space. As the now familiar music begins, he stands just 2 feet away from Mom with the front of his body slightly turned toward her. I quietly smile and nod when he gazes toward me, and I notice his head is slightly bobbing to the undulating reggae rhythm. "Oh! Look how Adam's head feels the beat!" I softly point out to the audience. Adam smiles and increases his nod. Mouth opened, he reveals his tongue, which is actually clicking to the beat as well! We all follow suit, clicking away. Adam beams and maintains this very articulate two-part body exploration until the music stops. ⌒

Toddlers have unique ways of delving into relationships with their surroundings. What they all share is the desire to be on the move, coming, going, exploring, engaging, and soaking up all there is to learn.

3–7 Years   From 3 to 7 years of age, a young child begins to work on integrating and more efficiently modulating all of the movement qualities and motor skills he explored in his earlier years. He can now perform actions requiring upper-lower body awareness, contralateral coordination, and balancing and weight-shifting his left and right body halves. A young child can perfect variations in his actions. He can also demonstrate a greater ability to perform these actions with subtle rather than extreme variations in his choice of movement qualities. For example, a young child is now able to walk slowly, then a bit faster, and finally, very fast in time to a changing melody, rather than being limited to a slow or fast response to the music. This is also the period of time when a young child makes extensive social, cognitive, and verbal communication leaps. A young child becomes more engaged in complex social interactions requiring a sophisticated understanding of nonverbal social cues. The experiential nature of a young child's repertoire of movement qualities assists him in interpreting these nonverbal cues. Young children of this age love to practice acting out a wide variety of feelings by creating imaginary play and dance scenes in which they embody characters from fairy tales, television shows, movies, songs, books, life events, and their own imaginations. By imbuing these characters with moods and events, young children explore how to express their own feelings. Through such explorations they learn about feelings and behaviors, as well as the nonverbal elements associated with them.

The emotional-body theme of this period involves mastery of basic motor skills, movement qualities, and emotional and communicative capabilities. Mastery builds confidence. A young child's increasing ability to create a wide communicative repertoire from which to express himself and be genuinely understood establishes a secure sense of self. This primary but essential degree of body mastery provides the foundation for the advanced skills required for his complex athletic and social interactions later in life. Through his investigation of the infinite variations and subtleties of movement qualities, a young child begins to develop his personal movement signature. A young child's preferred movement qualities become clearer as his more defined sense of self emerges—a sense of self that continues to grow into early adulthood.

Role of Parents and Primary Caregivers

Children's successes in moving through these emotional-body themes are dependent not only on their efforts but also on their experiences as they engage in their environment. Parents and other primary caregivers greatly contribute to how children perceive and interpret their experiences. During the early years, these significant caregivers guide and support the growing child's interactions with the world. Because of the co-constructed nature of attachment and interaction, nonverbal messages expressed through these early primary relationships act as powerful communications.

This can best be explained through simple examples. Visualize a mother holding her newborn firmly against her chest high up on her shoulder, with the infant's neck and head securely in the palm of one hand, while the other arm caresses the baby's bottom. Juxtapose this image with another picture of a mother holding her baby so loosely that the baby is continually sliding down her mother's chest with her legs dangling. What effects do these two contrasting holding styles have on a baby's physical and emotional experience? Wouldn't either of these holding styles (if developed into a predominant pattern) affect how the baby learns to hold her body or to develop a sense of trust about being held? Now visualize a toddler running after a ball down a slope in the park, with his father running after him. The toddler reaches the ball first, turns around and throws the ball at his father, hitting him on the leg. As the ball hits the father, he pretends to fall to the ground, saying with amusement in his voice, "You got me!" Contrast this scenario with that of another father with a similar-age child also playing ball in the park. This father stands within arm's length of the toddler, but when the father throws the ball, it rolls past the toddler down the slope. As the toddler turns toward the rolling ball, his father immediately yells, "Don't get that ball! Don't run down that hill! You might fall!" The toddler freezes a moment, startled, but being an impulsive 2-year-old, he ignores the order and instead runs after the ball. Reaching the ball, he picks it up and turns to throw it at his father, who is right behind him, glaring with a stern face. The toddler tenses his muscles as the father whisks the ball out of the toddler's hands, refuses to continue the game, and storms away, leaving the toddler standing alone.

How did each of these young children internalize their experience? If these styles of interaction are typical for each of these relationships, how might each child's developing level of physical comfort and confidence be affected? There are no definitive answers to these questions, of course, but these scenarios are offered to arouse the reader's attention to the experiential and nonverbal details of caregiver–child interactions. These questions direct the reader to look for typical nonverbal behaviors between and within each member of the dyadic relationship. Looking for patterns of *typical* behavioral interactions *over a period of time* and noting details can provide *potential* clues about the caregiver–child relationship and the infant or young child's developing nonverbal style. Typical, over a period of time, and potential are emphasized to avoid the tendency to make rash judgments or interpretations about styles of interaction. These nonverbal observations must be analyzed within the context of the uniqueness of each individual and each relationship. For example, the newborn whose legs dangle because of her mother's loose method of holding her may develop particular leg strength as an infant. This strength may encourage her to press her legs against her mother's waist, thereby developing a powerful lower body–pelvic–leg connection. This may eventually assist her growth into a sturdy, confident toddler, while in turn, her mother takes pride in her developing child's physical strength and self-confidence.

THE *WAYS OF SEEING* PROCESS

These motor, movement, and emotional-body themes are explored in the *Ways of Seeing* approach by using movement, dance, and body awareness activities through a four-part process:

- Dynamic Process I (*Establishing Rapport*)
- Dynamic Process II (*Expressing Feelings*)
- Dynamic Process III (*Building Skills*)
- Dynamic Process IV (*Healing Dance*)

The word *dynamic* is used to emphasize the nonlinear, interchanging progression of the four ways in which dance and movement can be used as well as to avoid any implication of hierarchical or stage level relationships between the processes.

Dynamic Process I
(*Establishing Rapport*)

The focus of Dynamic Process I is developing social-emotional and communicative relationships that establish meaningful rapport with a child and family. As described earlier, this involves analyzing nonverbal movements, exploring multisensory experiences, and educating parents to become aware of the impact of their nonverbal behaviors. A therapist who develops a positive social-emotional relationship inspires trust as well as the desire to relate and reach out into the environment—figuratively and literally. Trust is an essential component in motivating anyone who is having difficulties. Trust must be established to move children out of their worlds, which are often isolated and filled with highly charged emotional states. Trust is the key factor that will support them to attempt new ways of moving and being—especially when these new ways may feel very uncomfortable and even scary at first, due to their lack of familiarity.

This is especially true for children who have multiple sensory and communication difficulties. They usually have created extremely limited movement lives and know little about the pleasures of social *mobile* experiences. They do not yet have the necessary neuropsychological underpinnings, and only through connecting experiences can they learn about the rewards of relating to and exploring their surroundings. Using movement-oriented activities to build a relationship is especially helpful for infants and young children who do not have the ability to use words to clearly express themselves due to their age, developmental issues, or lack of emotional awareness. A therapist's development of a social-emotional relationship is the key to all other advancements. Once this is established, it becomes a primary motivator, even during skill building. Emotional and social rapport greatly enhances all other developmental areas. This was shown earlier in Lindsay's story, when the *Ways of Seeing* therapist successfully develops a relationship within the initial boundaries set by Lindsay, using her stationary position and her "wall" of animal figures. The story about their growing relationship continues in the following vignette:

Lindsay no longer starts each session building a wall of toy figures around her body. Now the animal figures do not even come out of the box. Instead, she enters each session placing her body in a position on the floor, gleefully exclaiming what animal she and I will be as we start on a crawling adventure that takes us up the "dangerous" mountain peaks created by a mound of pillows. At first Lindsay encourages me to follow her lead during these journeys, through gestures and verbalizations offering to help me by standing close by. Over time she voices her desire to attempt a "precarious climb" on her own, gesturing for me to go far away. From her perch atop the pillow pile she watches me as I (in animal character) crawl away backwards, keeping my eyes on her the whole time, verbalizing "I am going far away, but I am not too far if you need help!" As if testing this statement, high up on her mountain Lindsay begins to rock her body, causing the pillows to shake and slightly slip—all the while watching me intently. Immediately, my animal self prances to her shouting, "I'm coming!" as Lindsay reaches out toward me and exclaims, "Uh-oh!" On my arrival, she melts into my arms, relaxing her body as I gather her up. I hold her warmly and assure her that even when I am away, I am never too far away: She can come and go, and I will be waiting for her. When safely at the bottom of the mountain, Lindsay at once bounces back up the pillow pile to play the game again! This time, there is no need to test my connection to her. She climbs up the mountain and gleefully jumps off the side into a new pile of pillows, motioning for me to follow her lead and to try the jump too. Lindsay is able to use the whole room now to advance our interaction and no longer constructs a fortress to protect herself. ⌒

Developing this type of rapport requires a therapist to follow the child's lead rather than to direct the child. A therapist who follows the *Ways of Seeing* approach must translate information gleaned from keen nonverbal observations into playful interactions that physically match, complement, and support the development of a child's expressive communications. Chapters 8 and 9 provide more detailed descriptions of this method.

Dynamic Process II (*Expressing Feelings*)

In this aspect of the therapeutic process, a therapist encourages a child to express and explore feelings, emotions, traumas, and conscious and unconscious events (past and current) experientially through multi-sensory dance and play-based activities. During this process a therapist may take on multiple roles: joining in the dance-play story line, acting as a narrator by providing detailed descriptions of the events of the unfolding story, or verbally processing the content by providing insights and psychological interpretations of the story in a context and form appropriate to the child's level of understanding. Lindsay's ability to move into her deeper emotional concerns about separation and individuation from her mother portrays this second dynamic process.

⌒ *Lindsay begins our session by introducing a new dance-play. "You are Mommy horsey and I am baby horsey. Now go sleep over there," she directs, pointing to a pile of pillows. "I will sleep over here," she says as she curls herself up into a ball on the floor a few feet away. Settled into my cozy soft pillow pile, I gaze at Lindsay. I am struck by her choice of position, alone in the vast empty space of the room. I comment on our distant locations, being careful to add a caring but casual tone to my voice. "Oh, I see that you are all the way over there, alone in the rug without a pillow." "Yes," she says abruptly, "now close your eyes." Do I detect a bit of defensive pain in her voice, I wonder? I dutifully follow her directive and wait. It becomes quiet for almost a minute. Then quietly I hear Lindsay stir and sense her cautiously approaching me. Suddenly she pounces and is at my side burying herself into me. I welcome her closeness and offer a massage on her arms as I play the role of a mommy horsey by saying in a soothing voice, "Oh, here is my baby horsey. We were so far away in our beds. It feels nice to be close now." She gazes up at me and says "Neeiigh" as she bobs her head and her long, beautiful mane of hair up and down. Just as suddenly, she leaps up and proclaims in a baby voice, "Morning time! Mommy, need food!" "Oh, good morning, my baby horsey, let's gallop over here to the grass," I gleefully reply. We begin to gallop from side by side but soon Lindsay stops. "Up! Hurt! Can't do!" she whimpers. "Oh, I see, baby horsey needs some help?" I ask with concern as I approach her on all fours, curving my head toward her outstretched form. She nods and crawls eagerly onto my back. In tandem, we crawl to the "grassy" area. She partially slides her body over mine to nibble the grass. I respond to her gesture by noting, "Hmm, you are not coming down to feel the grass. You want to stay close to Mommy horsey even as we eat. You do not yet want to be far away from Mommy for too long." She gives me a warm squeeze, nestling her head into the crook of my neck.* ⁓

Lindsay and the therapist play this game over and over with little variations of the same narrations and interpretations. With each new episode, Lindsay's directive and defensive tones soften, becoming more playful and mischievous as she experiences her expressions met with understanding and mutual joy in sharing time together.

Dynamic Process III (*Building Skills*)

The primary focus of Dynamic Process III is skill building that incorporates physical and cognitive skill development into the social-emotional relationship. Specific tasks are added during this time, such as increasing body coordination and balance; accomplishing motor milestones; and acquiring language and cognitive skills, including cause-and-effect sequences. The main concentration is the development of specific skills to increase functioning. Activities include exercises and stretches, dance warm-ups, dancing steps, and the development of sequences with multiple steps and qualitative variations. Whereas the primary focuses of Dynamic Processes I and II are establishing rapport and expressing feelings, these same focuses are also important in Dynamic Process III, despite its emphasis on functional skill building.

The following vignette shows how skill development and emotional expression are explored together by the therapist's creation of dances, games, and drama play that requires the child to actively use her body.

⁓ *Lindsay's movement analysis profile reveals poor lower body strength and coordination, which is most noticeable in her inability to crawl with a smooth, rhythmic, contralateral relationship between her arms and legs.*

Instead, she hops with her legs together or drags them behind her. Emotionally, she struggles with separation issues with Mom. Her communicative issues keep her dependent, but her strong will and her need to protect herself from sensory overstimulation keep her fighting for independence.

Today Lindsay suggests we play "horsey" again, in which Lindsay is a baby horse who sleeps in a room all by herself, far away from me, her mommy horse. This time, when Lindsay hops and crawls over to give me a surprise wake-up call, we crawl together over to another part of the room to graze on grass for breakfast. In my role as a mommy horse, Lindsay allows me to teach her how to crawl like a "big girl horsey," through touch and demonstration. ⁓

Emotional independence, skill development, and adult support are explored simultaneously as Lindsay directs this dancing play. She succeeds in creating a storyline in which the baby shows her independence by choosing to sleep away from her mother and by controlling when her mother wakes up, yet she is able to show her dependence by allowing her mother to teach her how to crawl—because, naturally, one of the functions of a "mommy" animal is to guide and nurture her young!

Dynamic Process IV (*Healing Dance*)

The focus of Dynamic Process IV revolves around the power and joy of movement for movement's sake. This concept comes from the early pioneers of dance movement therapy (Boas, 1971; Levy, 1992) who acknowledged the healing properties that dance itself possesses. To simply move one's body for the pleasure of expression can be calming, energizing, releasing, and organizing, without a need to interpret meaning or function. As movement expression is allowed to take over, inner feelings, thoughts, and tensions often emerge. Many dance therapists feel dance is intrinsically therapeutic, enabling the expression of an individual's true spirit to be reflected (Boas, 1971; Levy, 1992). This use of dance to express joy and self-expression is shown in the following vignette:

⁓ *Several months later, as Lindsay enters the room, I compliment her on her pretty dress. She responds by twirling around. I suggest we add music as an accompaniment. Lindsay demonstrates her delight by fluttering her arms and cocking her head as she jumps up and down. I put on a lovely smooth waltz. Lindsay begins dancing around in circles, swaying her hips, and grace-fully curving her arms in a ballerina-like pose. She begins to create footsteps to the rhythm of the music. As she continues her free dance in time with the music, I am reminded of her first reactions to music and dancing 8 months ago. Then she would run around the room, sporadically spinning, picking up speed until she reached a fast-paced tension, and only stopped when she fell to the floor with her legs in a W-sit. She was unable to differentiate her arms from her torso or to sway her body to a musical rhythm for any sustained amount of time. It is wonderful to see her so joyously dancing. She now feels comfortable traversing the whole room!* ⌒

Clarification Through Awareness

A therapist will continuously assess which dynamic process (or which combination of the four processes) is being employed by a particular child throughout the intervention and educational program. In fact, clarification through awareness is the cornerstone of the *Ways of Seeing* approach. Throughout the program, therapists are continually asked to look more deeply into their own actions and into the actions of others. Clarity brings insight. Insight brings new awareness. New awareness bring new ways to see. New ways to see bring new ways to explore. Ultimately, new ways to explore will bring new ways to be.

4

The Language of Movement

From Dysfunction to Creative Expression

I think movement is liberating. I think that movement is good for you. The body is a reservoir of all sorts of tensions and dark forces. And it's also the potential source of amazing energy. This thing wants to live. It is a powerful engine—it connects it with the brain. A reservoir of images, dreams, fears, associations, language. And its potential we can't even begin to understand. Movement begins to negotiate the distance between the brain and the body and it can be surprising what we learn about each other.

B.T. Jones, *Still/Here* (film interview, 1996)

Bill T. Jones is an exquisite dancer who has spent his extensive career negotiating; listening to; and, most important, sensing this relationship between the brain and the body. As with most professional modern dancers, he has spent many hours in the studio delving into a single phrase of movement to discover its essence, to perfect its articulation, and to learn about its communicative power. Much can be learned about the moving body's beauty and its remarkable expressivity by studying such kinesthetically adept individuals. Dancers strive to learn about this brain–body–life force connection because to dance is to open one's self to this inner dialogue. Such exploration requires discipline, reaching the highest levels of fine art.

Watching a dancer perform enables us to formally study the power of movement as expression, but dancers are not the only source of this information. What is especially significant about Jones' study of movement and the body is that he has not restricted his exploration to trained dancers alone. He has taken his explorative journey through dance into the public arena, asking people to look inward, feel their feelings, and express them spontaneously through unspoken gestures.

99

The quotation that opened the chapter was taken from a documentary film *Still/Here* that Jones made about his work with people diagnosed with terminal illnesses. Using their gestures as his source, he choreographed a dance that he taught to his professional dancers.

Jones is not a dance therapist, but his project very much supports the dance therapy methodology. This type of investigation encourages a dance therapist to look for meaning in all movements. Viewing movement as emotional expression enables a dance therapist to look beyond immediate behavior to study its possible interior meanings. At times these deeper meanings are quite obvious—a child who is tired becomes cranky and flings her body down to the floor in complete exhaustion. But a therapist who pauses to look more deeply can often discover that the best clues to assisting people can be found in understanding the qualitative details of their nonverbal actions. Paying attention to details is especially effective in those cases in which the person's behaviors are most subtle, obscure, or difficult to read.

Many factors can influence the readability of an action, and the particular elements of the immediate internal and external environment all contribute to a person's behaviors. The internal environment includes a person's developmental level, sensory system regulation, current emotional state, medical conditions, and organic or acquired disabilities. The external environment includes other people (or the way in which the mover reacts to them) and the overall emotional and physical atmosphere of the surroundings. If approached under this frame of mind, behaviors that at first may appear to be quite dysfunctional can be often understood in a different light. This chapter's vignettes and discussions demonstrate how understanding each individual's unique movement style as an expressive language enables the observer to shift from perceiving dysfunction to recognizing creative expression.

SUBTLE, OBSCURE, AND DIFFICULT-TO-READ NONVERBAL CUES

~~ *Gentle music softly fills the room. Bruce stands alone in the center, opening and closing the videocassette box. I watch from the side. He seems to be mesmerized by the squeak and snap, repeatedly opening and closing the box with a monotone rhythmic beat. I pick up another video box and begin opening and closing it to match his beat. He looks up and smiles. We continue with this synchronous music making until he suddenly stops and walks over to the opposite side of the room. Once he settles into this new place, I follow suit and join him across the room. With Bruce as the leader and me as the follower, we spend the next few minutes creating a partner dance composed of traversing the room while stopping to open and close our videocassette boxes. At one point his travels take him over to his mother, who is sitting to the side watching intently. He gives her a hug and steps back. I hand Bruce another videocassette box, and he hands it to her. Mom smiles. A trio is created as we all become engaged in a dance of opening, closing, and exchanging videocassette boxes. At some point Bruce stops and sits down near his mother. I sit down behind him and straddle my legs so that our legs are touching, parallel to each other. I tuck my hands under his knees and cradle him as I gently lift his legs and rock back and then forward, dropping his legs to match the rhythmic pulse of our videocassette dance but add an accented emphasis. He turns to look at me, smiling. We repeat this and then he suddenly gets up, does a 360-degree run around me and climbs on to his mother's thighs, standing on them to give her a hug and warm smile. I get up and circle, too, giving him a firm hug. As I slide back, he leans away from his mother and falls into my arms, giving me a hug. He's off again, and after a moment, I follow. We now add this standing–hugging–running away sequence to our developing dance. It now has solo, duet, and trio components to it, an evolving improvisation as we spontaneously respond to each other. It feels especially magical because the whole interaction occurs without a single word spoken.* ~

The events of this vignette, which occurred over a period of 15 minutes, required the therapist to wait, watch, feel, and discover Bruce's behavior rather than to attempt to impose more conventional ways of creating an interactive exchange. At this point in his intervention, the therapist's goal was to improve and extend Bruce's social and emotional expressivity. Following his nonverbal actions and using them to create an interactive dialogue achieved this goal. As Bruce became able to experience his behaviors as communications, he became more emotionally available, as shown by how lovingly he incorporated his mother in the dance-play. This was especially gratifying to Bruce's mother because at that point, Bruce's nonverbal cues did not always reveal his affection and attachment to her. Most of his previous behaviors appeared to suggest his desire to be isolated from others, including his mother, but this session marked a turning point in their relationship. Bruce's mother began to understand that his behaviors were not rejections of her, but rather difficult-to-read nonverbal cues. This understanding enabled her to have more patience, as she learned to interpret his actions as ways to explore his environment. Over time, as she knew more of his interests, Bruce's mother has designed and implemented extensive programs to help him communicate with her and explore his environment. Her natural approach with her son is now more behavioral, and her programs provide Bruce with concrete prompts that he can manipulate. They return for additional *Ways of Seeing* sessions whenever she feels her own program is becoming too systematized and rote, or when she wants help in interpreting his behaviors. In fact, after Bruce acquires more strength in his movement repertoire much later in his intervention, he reveals a very different nonverbal style.

 Bruce suddenly grasps my hand, holding on to it with prolonged strength, twisting my fingers back as if he might break them off. At other times he grabs my arm, pinching the skin firmly without letting go. This pinch is performed with a similar strength and twisting as the hand grasp, but for a slightly shorter duration as he continues his pinching action all the way up my arm.

 Of course my first impression is that it feels aggressive. But if I look beyond this immediate instinct—what else can it mean? One interpretation could be that he is grasping for connection. What if he is unaware of, or unable to control, how strongly he grabs me? When I mirror Bruce's action by performing his pinching action on my own arm, I become acutely aware of my hand and wrist. As I pinch with that degree of strength, my hand and wrist seem separate and disjointed from the rest of my body, as if they are floating off alone in space. Extending this image, I begin to wonder what it feels like to be Bruce—is he caught in a maze of feelings and sensations that he cannot decipher or cannot share through typical verbal means?

 Working from this premise, I begin to respond by giving Bruce some tactile sensory feedback. I mirror the strength of his pinching action, matching its intensity, but without the twisting and prolonged holding that had made his pinch feel aggressive to me. Instead, my pinch actions are strong, direct, but very short in duration and create a pulsing rhythm as I firmly move up his arm. I move up his arm to give him the kinesthetic sense of how his hand is connected to his arm, and how we can use this physical sensation to stay emotionally and playfully connected in a more pleasant way. As I do this, I use words to describe my actions. Bruce stays engaged with me, and our play transforms into a full body integrated action as we mobilize. Matching our movements to this new pulsing rhythm, together we walk across the room, twice, in quick-pulsing beats.

Both of these vignettes depict nonverbal behaviors that require observers to look beyond their immediate impressions to search for alternative interpretations. Deciphering communicative expression from actions that at first glance appear dysfunctional requires observers to think about and experience such behaviors differently. There is no "dictionary of difficult behaviors" to provide already-established definitions of the meanings behind nonverbal actions. Attempting to use predetermined explanations of behaviors would be counterproductive anyway because this would discourage an observer from noticing the unique details that provide the most important clues to interpreting the communication underlying the action. Instead, observers must learn to notice not only what the action is, but also exactly how it is being executed. Noticing *how* an action is executed reveals its qualities, and it is the specific qualities of an action that determine the action's true meaning at a particular moment. This asks observers to be present, freshly engaged in the moment-to-moment exchange of nonverbal interactions. Engagement is a process that requires observers to abandon "knowing," and instead "ride" with the actions, noticing details of both the actions themselves and their own reactions. Observers must trust that there may be periods of not knowing during this process. Table 4.1 contains questions that can be used to maintain the desired level of "being in the moment" when observing subtle, obscure, and difficult to read behaviors. The questions invite observers to look for the subtle aspects of actions that can easily be missed or misinterpreted if insufficient time or attention is given.

The *Ways of Seeing* approach offers the information and questions concerning subtle, obscure, and difficult-to-read behaviors provided in Table 4.1 and the related Behavioral Descriptions Worksheet (see http://www. brookespublishing.com/dancing) to help guide a therapist's thoughts about the possible meanings behind a particular child's movements. Both the table and the worksheet are integral parts of the implementation of the *Ways of Seeing* intervention plan. The worksheet, described at the end of this chapter, helps a therapist to organize qualitative information that can then be used to create therapeutic explorations that enhance a child's functioning.

What Influences Communicative Difficulty in Nonverbal Behavior?

The *Ways of Seeing* approach's development of the questions concerning subtle, obscure, and difficult to read behaviors and the Behavioral

Table 4.1. Questions to be used when asking parents or caregivers about subtle, obscure, and difficult behaviors, or when observing child's behavior firsthand

Questions to obtain specific details about a child's behavior:

Does the child exhibit any subtle, obscure, or difficult behaviors?

- Hand flapping
- Head banging
- Biting self or others
- Licking self, others, or objects
- Unusual finger gesturing, such as picking, flicking, scratching, poking, pinching, fluttering, twisting, or tapping self or others
- Frequent manipulating of an object, such as a rubber band or piece of cloth
- Engaging in perseverative actions
- Rocking
- Jumping with intense self absorption
- Flinging or rubbing limbs
- Throwing body onto floor
- Acting unusually in approach and withdrawal within the environment
- Staring off into space with the whole body or individual parts of the body active or still
- Idiosyncratic gestures, postures, or sequence of movements

Questions to obtain details about specific movement factors in a child's actions:

- Is there a rhythm to the action? How would you describe the rhythm?
- How does the child start and stop the action? Does it seem related to anything in the external environment? To a personal directive?
- What is the intensity level of the action?
- Can the child modulate action (i.e., the speed, use of space, tension level, intensity, degree of strength) in appropriate response to the context of the environment?
- Does the child demonstrate ease or difficulty in maintaining the movement action to stay engaged in an activity or the environment?
- Does the child smoothly transition or add more complex movements to the current action sequence? In response to environmental input? In response to an internal personal directive?

Questions to obtain details about specific social factors in a child's actions:

- Does the movement enable the child to engage in, focus on, and participate with the surroundings?
- Does the movement distract or disengage the child from the surroundings?
- Does the action invite others to join in?
- Is the action a solitary experience that separates the child from the environment?
- Does the child use the nonverbal action to initiate, create, and extend relationships with others?
- Does the child use the nonverbal action with others to extend a personal, physical, or environmental exploration that does not really extend the social involvement of the person?
- What is the quality of eye contact during interactions with others while the child is performing this action?
- What is the child's emotion level of expressivity and engagement when performing the action?
- How is the child's emotional level of expressivity and engagement portrayed through the nonverbal movement action?
- How does the action support or hinder the child's ability to engage in verbal or nonverbal dialogue?

- Is the child able to respond to verbal or nonverbal dialogue within a natural time frame, maintaining a spontaneous banter, or is there a long pause or lack of response while the action is being performed?

Questions to obtain details about specific internal factors in a child's actions:
- Is the child receiving any sensorial feedback from this action? If so, what might that be, and how may it be serving the child?
- What may the purpose of this action be for the child? Focusing attention, discharging pent-up energy, tuning into internal sensations, tuning out external environment, "movement scripting," or traumatic reenacting of an image?
- Does this action provide self-regulation for the child?
- What degree of excitement is this action exuding?
- Does this action invite or elicit engagement from others and the environment?
- Does this action withdraw the child from others and the environment?

Questions to obtain details about specific external factors in a child's actions:
- To what elements of the environment may the child be responding?
- Is this a new environment?
- Are there elements in the environment—physical or emotional—that may be affecting the child's behaviors?
- How does the child respond (either overtly or subtly) when someone in the environment initiates contact?
  - Does the child's behavior become disorganized physically, emotionally, or socially?
  - Does the child tense or release body musculature?
  - Does the child pull away
    - in the torso by twisting, retreating, or making the body concave?
    - withdrawing a hand, arm, or leg; moving the whole body away; or turning the head away?
  - Does the child reach toward the person
    - in the torso—leaning into or expanding the body, creating a convex shape?
    - approaching by extending a limb, moving the whole body toward, or turning the head toward the person?
    - providing eye contact or looking away?
    - being emotionally expressive nonverbally?
  - Do the child's actions draw you toward or away from the child?

Descriptions Worksheet was influenced by recent works that drew on nonverbal and experientially based actions and interactions in studying the functioning and expressivity of several different populations. Research within the topics of nonverbal communication and sensory integration reinforced the point that *how* an action is performed should be highlighted when considering the effectiveness and efficiency of that action as communication. Donnellan and Leary pointed out that "all communication requires movement" (1995, p. 43) in their discussion about the movement differences characteristic of people who have conditions including ASD, mental retardation, Parkinson's disease, and Tourette syndrome. Through analyzing the mechanics of movement-making, they categorized each condition's movement differences as causing difficulties in "starting, stopping, executing speed, intensity, rhythm, timing, direction, duration, continuing, combining, and switching" movement activities and concluded that these movement difficulties "impede postures, actions, speech, thoughts, perceptions, emotions, and memories" (1995, p. 50). The *Ways of Seeing* approach employs these same categories in analyzing the qualitative aspects of observed movement actions that create the obscure and difficult-to-read elements of actions or cause a person's movements to appear bizarre, clumsy, or awkward. Although the difficult and bizarre nature of such actions often causes observers to ignore their value as communications, such observers are making a significant mistake.

The story of Bruce that opens this chapter exemplifies how movement differences, even those that are ostensibly meaningless, can be transformed into an effective social dialogue. At first glance, the monotonous rhythmic quality with which Bruce opens and closes the videocassette case could be dismissed as one of the repetitive mesmerizing actions often observed in children along the autistic spectrum who become fixated on an object and disengage in their social environment. The repetitive aspect of Bruce's action has an intense, focused quality that shuts out everything else. First observing and then mirroring the specific way that Bruce performs this action, the therapist wonders if it brings comfort to Bruce in some way, and uses it to socially engage him. She is successful when the same rhythm that initially isolates Bruce from interactions is transformed into an interactive dance. The therapist continues to support the rhythmic quality of this action by incorporating the rhythm into how she rocks Bruce on her lap as their interaction continues to grow. He experiences his action as a communicative tool. The therapist adds an accent and increases the spatial path of the movement by rocking backward and forward, keeping the same timing, but eliminating its monotone, mesmerizing effect. Without ever knowing with certainty what initially motivates Bruce to create this rhythm, the therapist employs several *Ways of Seeing* techniques, first to help her ponder what it is like to see the world through Bruce's eyes, and finally to create a dance of engagement.

Donnellan and Leary suggested that the idiosyncratic movements of people who have conditions such as ASD, mental retardation, Parkinson's disease, and Tourette syndrome may be the result of their conscious or unconscious responses to internal reactions, or be caused by deficiencies in their internal neuromolecular or neuromuscular systems as they attempt to interact with their external environments. These difficulties disrupt their abilities to develop efficient movement responses that are physically fluid and automatic. Refusing to merely dismiss these qualities as being clumsy or disordered, the *Ways of Seeing* approach instead uses the qualities of these difficult movements as clues to decode the communicative potential of an action. This approach analyzes behavior by taking into consideration potential contextual aspects of the person's internal, external, and social environment that may be influencing the situation. As shown by Bruce's story, the *Ways of Seeing* approach is able to use the information provided by idiosyncratic movements to develop improved social and emotional functioning.

Self-Regulatory Aspects of Repetitive Idiosyncratic Movements

Self-regulation is considered another significant internal force that may have an impact on, and even direct, the efficiency of a person's communications. The consistent, monotone, rhythmic quality in which Bruce opens and closes the videocassette case has a calming and focusing effect on him. It also greatly distracts him, enabling him to avoid socially engaging in his surroundings. By first observing this result and then mirroring his actions, the therapist's behavior communicates respect and acknowledgment of Bruce's self-regulatory needs. She enters Bruce's world on his terms, using his vocabulary. Bruce's acceptance is evident in his favorable reception that prolongs their interaction. These are their first steps toward building a relationship. Although his monotone rhythmic action is not efficient, Bruce's therapist is able to make an allowance for it and enable Bruce to experience this behavior—one that is well within his zone of comfort—as effective communication.

Research on nonverbal communication and social-emotional and communication development has examined the self-regulatory aspects of idiosyncratic or repetitive movements. Prizant et al. (2000), reviewed in Chapter 2, specifically addressed such movements in children with ASD. They described sensorimotor and presymbolic repetitive movements—including body rocking, spinning, averted eye gaze, and tactile and oral self-stimulation actions such as deep pressure massage and finger sucking—as the child's strategies to block off sensory input and to try to obtain emotional regulation. Emotional regulation requires an individual to modulate emotional arousal by staying calm and focused, in order to maintain communicative and social engagement. In their SCERTS™ Model intervention method, Prizant and colleagues (2000) acknowledged that these behaviors serve a function that must be considered during the early stages of forming a relationship with a child with ASD.

In an unrelated but similarly revealing study of nonverbal communication research, Davis, Walters, Vorus, and Connors (2000) studied the videotaped confessions of adult criminal suspects to analyze the idiosyncratic action patterns made by adults under stress. Their findings suggested that these idiosyncratic actions not only reflect the person's nervousness but also serve a discharge and a regulatory function. Davis and colleagues focused their attention on observable defensive behaviors and analyzed nonverbal and verbal details of the suspect's stress cues under the assumption that such cues provide information about the mechanisms of psychological defenses. They defined *stress cues* as those that reflect the person's coping style in dealing with struggles that present a deep personal threat or psychological conflict.

The researchers' discussion of an observed action pattern that continuously alternates between brief moments of self-focus and object-focus is of special interest. *Self-focus actions* involve self-touch and can initially serve a cognitive, self-organizing function. *Object-focus movements* involve simple hand gestures outward to the environment. Under severe stress, people often create this alternating action pattern, which "reflects a conflict between inner soothing or 'self-collecting' impulses and the effort to communicate and project one's thoughts to the other" (Davis et al., 2000, p. 112). These researchers argued that it is this patterning that represented the defensive adaptive function—not the discharge of nervousness. They emphasized the importance of looking at patterns of behavior as the true indicators of individual style, rather than looking only at their frequency and rates of occurrence.

Although this research may, at first glance, seem unrelated because of the radical difference in the studied population, it is presented because of its focus on people's reactions under severe stress. Indeed, careful analysis of the idiosyncratic movements of the child with ASD also reveals a pattern of actions that have both an inwardly and outwardly directed focus. One excellent example is the commonly observed gesture of hand flapping. A child with ASD can often be observed holding her hands up high symmetrically, about 6–8 inches to each side of her head—somewhere between her ears and peripheral vision—and seeming to be completely self-absorbed in shaking and flinging her hands in a rhythmic pattern with loose wrists. Observers who glance at this action devoid of its environmental context might think of it as a purely self-focused and self-organizing activity that serves no communicative purpose. More careful observers, however, will notice that the specific qualities of the hand-flapping action—such as the speed, intensity, tension level, and duration—can vary greatly depending on environmental input, including such simple variables as whether anyone physically approaches or speaks her name. In response, the child, although appearing lost in her stereotypic action, may suddenly increase the intensity of the flapping, causing her hands to pulse in a quicker and tighter rhythm, thus communicating the child's awareness of her changed surroundings. That is, a seemingly innocuous external stimulus—approaching or calling her name—can cause dramatic reactions in the child. Next, the child may accompany these gestures by body turning or jumping up and down. Each behavior communicates a different message to careful observers: They might interpret her body turning as evidence that she does not want to be disturbed; they might view her jumping up and down as an indication of her increased excitement. In other words the qualitative changes in how she executes her actions reveal that the child is quite aware of her surroundings.

Therapists must look for another interpretation of these seemingly self-focused actions. Might the child's behaviors have a defensive adaptive function, influenced by the perceived discomfort, sense of personal threat, or psychological conflict with environmental input? Davis and colleagues (2000) concluded that understanding such nonverbal cues may provide information about the mechanisms of psychological defense, whereas Prizant and colleagues (2000) suggested that such behaviors serve a self-regulatory function that must be used as the initial starting point for relationship building.

Both Davis and colleagues' (2000) and Prizant and colleagues' (2000) conclusions underlie the *Ways of Seeing* approach. Idiosyncratic actions are regarded as communicative elements that should be used to initially interact along a child's journey toward adaptive functioning and increased relating. The therapist who views nonverbal elements to be early communicative symbols brings a sense of understanding and acceptance of a child's efforts that reduces stress level and encourages improved relating.

THE *WAYS OF SEEING*
PERSPECTIVE REGARDING ASD AND PDD

Nonverbal expressive methods are an especially effective way to support both social and emotional relationships for children with ASD or PDD. So much of their behavior, which may initially appear to be idiosyncratic and dysfunctional, can transform into creative expression when viewed as a form of communication. Finding meaning and connection through movement and dance can be a very empowering experience that enables children to feel understood in a profound way. The following section specifically addresses how to understand and work with children with ASD or PDD. (See http://www.brookespublishing.com/dancing for a sample lesson plan that has been successful in engaging these children.) Readers who are not interested in this material may skip ahead to the section in this chapter called Sensory Sensitivities.

The difficulties with communication experienced by the child with ASD or PDD affect all aspects of development, including most significantly the child's ability to relate to others and to build strong effective social-emotional bonds. Bruce's vignettes show how children with ASD or PDD may appear to be listening to their own rhythmic beat, deeply lost in a personal solitary world as they run, jump, spin, leap, and roll through the room—often with unique details and precision. Nonetheless, the vignettes also demonstrate how the *Ways of Seeing* approach can effectively assist such children.

The key premise of the *Ways of Seeing* approach is that all nonverbal acts have the potential to be communicative. In light of this, therapists are encouraged to go beyond the behavioral aspect of an action and ask themselves what this child with ASD or PDD might be saying if this behavior or action is a communicative act.

Idiosyncratic Movements that Affect a Child's Sense of Emotional Self and Social Relating Skills

Certain actions affect how a child experiences and senses his physical, emotional and social selves. The movements that affect a child's sense of emotional self include

- Personal idiosyncratic actions

- Toe walking

- Movements that exhibit little torso differentiation

- Movements that convey the sense that his limbs are disconnected or unrelated to his torso
- Movements that lack fluid coordination or connectedness between body parts
- Movements that convey a difficulty in making fluid, sequential actions
- Movements that lack full extension of body parts; that exude stiffness, not reaching out into space, into environments, or even fully within own kinespheric space
- Movements with motor planning issues such as sequencing and following movement sequences of others

The movements that affect a child's ability to relate socially include

- Lack of eye contact
- Darting or turning away using a body part, such as the head, shoulder, limb, or hand
- Darting or turning away using whole body
- Running through a room
- Isolating himself in space

Therapists who work from the perspective that a person's physical, cognitive, and perceptual experiences are linked must ask themselves how these behaviors might affect a child's sense of self and social relating skills.

The *Ways of Seeing* Approach to Intervention

In designing an intervention, a therapist may find it helpful to observe the behaviors of a child with ASD or PDD within a dance-oriented frame of reference by asking two questions: First, what is the dance of interaction observable between the child and environment or between the child and his significant adults? This dance of interaction is the dialogue—the communication between self and other. Second, what isolated actions is the child doing and how can they be linked together like a dance? This last question is essential for a child with ASD or PPD because the answer can make the session's activities much more fun and imbued with heightened expressivity. When a child is able through his actions to experience extended relating, it helps extend his focusing and keeps him attending and relating for longer periods of time. By starting with the actions that a child brings to the interaction, a therapist can help the child make sense of his world. This approach also can be used to redirect undesirable behaviors by first matching the quality of the child's action and then modifying it (e.g., running transforms into leaping; then into fast marching; and finally into slower marching with a strong, direct, and focused beat).

In addition, a therapist may find that verbally narrating the actions during an interaction provides a child with symbolic verbal cues that label and follow his experience. Finally, when following a child's lead, a therapist may find it useful to watch for fragmentation, disorganization, or chaotic behaviors. If an activity does not become a mutual dancing dialogue involving sharing movements, affective reactions, and expressivity, then a therapist must look for new avenues in which to enter and connect with a child.

The *Ways of Seeing* Approach Movement Strategies for Children with ASD or PDD

A therapist may find it helpful to include the following elements in dance movement sessions for children with ASD or PDD to enhance their social skills:

- Having activities that shift between free individual movement explorations to structured group movement explorations and that include a wide range of variations from whole group, small group, and dyads to individual activities

- Identifying each child's "movement signature action for the day," remembering that this individual nonverbal expressive movement action may vary each session or may be similar for a period of time

- Having each child attempt to try the movements of peers

- Keeping the group moving and relating as a group, while allowing for the spontaneous breaks from relating that individual children may choose to take

- Attempting to keep children focused on specific movement activities or explorations while simultaneously being ready to change focus to keep the children engaged and interacting

The *Ways of Seeing* approach views the movements and behaviors of children with ASD or PDD from the following perspectives:

- Body and body sensations are the reference points from which a child with ASD or PDD decodes experiences.

- In the absence of typical communications skills, the language of a child's body becomes the main means of experiencing the world and communicating that experience.

- These experiences directly link a child's nonverbal expressions to communication.

- The discharge and regulatory function of a child's nonverbal stress behaviors supports their use as communicative elements.

- A therapist may use these behaviors to initially interact along a child's journey toward more adaptive functioning and increased relating.

- Responding to their physical actions assures children with ASD or PDD that their bodily reactions communicate information to which someone outside of themselves can respond.

- Relating to something outside of self by using music and/or props because this fosters individual expression while relating to others and builds group cohesion

- Using variations in music beat, style, rhythm, and volume to redirect and/or reconnect children

- Creating a theme around which to organize a dance (e.g., animals, jungle journey, beach, or feelings)

- Including group dance games (e.g., "Shoo Fly," "Old King Glory on the Mountain")

A therapist may find it helpful to include the following elements in dance movement sessions for children with ASD or PDD to increase their body awareness, sense of self, and control:

- Using a strong, clear rhythm with moderate tempo that organizes or creates full body or body-part coordination

- Including movements requiring increased body control

- Interspersing periods of relaxation, stretching, and breath awareness throughout the session as well as at the session's end. For example, the sessions might initially start with a relaxing circle activity, and progress to lying down over a period of weeks as the children become more adjusted and competent. Musical props such as a tone bar or other musical instrument can be used to maintain each child's focus.

SENSORY SENSITIVITIES: SENSORY INTEGRATION AND REGULATORY DYSFUNCTION PERSPECTIVES

As explained above, the *Ways of Seeing* method uses the communicative potential of nonverbal behaviors to help individuals develop relationships. In attempting to use these actions to communicate and form relationships, it is also important to consider the underlying physiological factors that may be influencing these behaviors. The early sensory integration work of Ayres (1980), which continues to be developed in the field of occupational therapy by such practitioners as Williamson and Anzalone (1997, 2001) and DeGangi (2000; DeGangi & Berk, 1983), is essential to understanding how a child's physiological functioning can affect experiences, styles of relating, and learning during all levels of development.

Sensory integration describes the ability to perceive and process sensory information from the body and the environment in an organized way. There are seven sensory systems that receive sensory input from the body and from the external environment. The first five are well known: taste, touch, sight, smell, and hearing. The last two sensory systems—the proprioceptive and vestibular systems—are less commonly known, possibly because these systems work in a more unconscious manner (Williamson & Anzalone, 2001).

The proprioceptive system is responsible for the muscular and joint sensations felt during active full body, body part, or limb movements. People sense movement and the positions of their bodies in space through their proprioceptive systems. It is through this system, for example, that a person registers such actions as standing (location and posture of the body) and reaching an arm overhead (movement and body part awareness) to get a book on the top shelf. This system plays an important role in motor development, for it is through proprioceptive awareness that initially explorative movements of the muscles and joints become instinctive learned-movement patterns. Motor control and motor planning are established through the proprioceptive system. That is, the proprioceptive system enables the body to acquire the movement memories that facilitate organized movement actions, which become automatic. It is through the proprioceptive sense, for example, that a baby establishes the proper leg and arm coordination to turn unstable and hesitant attempts at crawling into speedy, smooth sprints across the room.

The vestibular system supports the senses of balance and equilibrium; the regulation of muscle tone and coordination; the control of visual steadiness; the sustaining or shifting through different arousal and emotional states; and the ability to discriminate, select, and maintain attention during an action (Williamson & Anzalone, 2001). Located in the inner ear, the vestibular system registers speed, force, direction, and the continuation of a movement. It is engaged through head and body movements in response to gravity; such actions as swinging, spinning, and rocking rouse the vestibular system.

Sensory integration development occurs as the body learns to modulate each individual system in coordination with the other systems, creating organization and compatibility. The term *integration* emphasizes the dynamic processing that occurs as multiple sensory systems converge during the course of learning and mastery. This organization enables an individual to attend to and participate in surroundings both physically and emotionally. While swinging on a swing, for example, a toddler uses several systems as he coordinates the muscular pumping of his legs (proprioceptive and vestibular systems), maintains head alignment (vestibular system), engages visually as he smiles and waves to his mother (visual and proprioceptive systems), and senses and hears the breeze as the air rushes over his skin (tactile and auditory systems).

A sensory integration dysfunction is present when some or multiple aspects of an individual's sensory systems have difficulties in modulating internal and/or external input. Such difficulties have an impact on the overall organization of a child's whole sensory system and are especially observable in a child's nonverbal behaviors. Children with this diagnosis typically exhibit negative defensiveness reactions, displayed through a variety of physical or emotional behaviors, including distress, fear, anxiety, withdrawal, or increased activity. The degree to which a child displays sensory discomfort can vary from mild, to moderate, to severe. A mild reaction may cause a child to appear inflexible, finicky, resistant, controlling, or oversensitive. A moderate reaction is diagnosed when at least several aspects of a child's life are affected to a noticeable degree. A child may, for example, avoid social interactions or be too aggressive; have difficulties with eating, dressing, or other self-care skills; and have trouble paying attention at school. A severe reaction is diagnosed when a child has serious sensory issues and total functioning is compromised. At this level, multiple dysfunctions are often indicated, including ASD, developmental delays, and emotional disabilities.

For example, toddlers with auditory hypersensitivity sensory integration dysfunction may experience the underlying hum of a busy restaurant along a range from feeling mere discomfort to feeling the noise as an intolerable, piercing rumble. A toddler with only a mild discomfort may squirm in his chair, lose interest in eating, and remain very irritable even after leaving the restaurant. A toddler with a moderate sensitivity may forcibly resist entering a restaurant, refuse to eat her food, have difficulty concentrating and participating in conversations directed at her, and cover her ears at some point. A toddler with severe issues might place himself under the table and roll up into a ball, rocking and humming to himself.

Sensory integration intervention enhances the sensory integration process through specific physical techniques that are designed to improve this organization by controlling sensory input and activating more functional brain mechanisms. Williamson and Anzalone (1997, 2001) conceptualized this sensory integration process as having five interrelated parts:

1. Sensory registration—initially recognizing sensory input

2. Orientation and attention—identifying the location of this input

3. Interpretation—attributing meaning and integrating input across sensory modalities

4. Organization of response

5. Execution of response—the actual production of the cognitive, affective, or motor response that elicits new sensory input

This process occurs along a sensory threshold that measures a child's ability to modulate sensory input along a spectrum of hyperreactivity, mid-range reactivity, or hyporeactivity of the central nervous system. A child with sensory processing dysfunctions can have difficulty with one or more parts of this process. Hyperreactivity indicates a low threshold or tolerance for specific sensory input; in contrast, hyporeactivity is indicated in situations where a child needs a high level of sensory input to experience sensation.

Greenspan (1992, 1996, 1997) identified sensory integration dysfunctions as regulatory disorders, asserting that one of an infant's primary jobs in the early months is to obtain a sense of homeostasis—the ability to self-regulate internal sensations—balanced with an interest in the world through the senses. An infant's difficulty with self-regulation, sensory reactivity, or behavioral organizations should be observable by his behavior and his developing personal movement signatures. For example, an infant who cannot comfortably process auditory input may first display discomfort by shaking his head in a particular manner. As this infant gets older, if he has a severe reaction, this head shaking may be accompanied by a lack of eye contact, and evolve by his toddler years into the holding-the-head-and-rocking-under-the-table behavior previously described.

The term *sense of body* (discussed in Chapter 2) used in the *Ways of Seeing* approach, acknowledges that the bodily sensations, reactions, expressions, and experiences of all children—with or without special needs—come from their keen physical receptivity to sensations. These are their earliest experiences of self, for these body experiences define and continually inform them about who they are. Because of this understanding, the *Ways of Seeing* approach to intervention and learning focuses on helping individual children to become aware of

- How their individual sense of body affects their experience

- How these body sensations may overpower and distract their abilities to fully utilize and develop other aspects of self, emotionally, socially, intellectually, and communicatively

- How to transform and elaborate on their existing sense of body to develop their personal styles into more complex and functionally adaptive systems

In the *Ways of Seeing* approach, such awareness can be realized in the youngest population by the manner in which a therapist relates to and develops relationships with infants; the method that a therapist uses to touch, hold, and physically handle infants; and the types of experiences that a therapist provides for infants. A therapist observes infants' behaviors and attempts to find meaning in them. A therapist considers an infant's behavior within the context of her innate sensorial needs and her style of regulation. A therapist will also examine an infant's psychological responses to the environment, the communicative power of such responses, and their potential use in building relationships. The following vignette exemplifies how a therapist uses the *Ways of Seeing* method to help a young child, Nikki, respond to the repetitive, tension-producing actions related to Rett syndrome:

I place Nikki on her back between my straddled legs, her legs draped over mine. She has entered our session today in a very agitated mood, exhibited by her abrupt, spoke-like, arcing projections of her arms and legs into the space around her, followed by extreme tensing of her arms and shoulders as she struggles to draw her hands together at midline and up to her mouth. I am holding her hands, providing firm, direct input, and attempting to calm her down by circling her arms—first crossing them together down along the center of her torso, then widening them out to her side, continuing the circle by reaching them up over her head and then crossing them back down again. At first, we seem to be at odds. Nikki continually shifts her head from side to side, sometimes pulling her whole body into the action as well, creating undulations in her torso, bulging her chest forward, and extending her legs in a stiff manner. These actions are executed with great intensity, creating a sense of struggle and agitation as she holds her arms and shoulders in extreme tension and then abruptly tries to push against my hold and jut her limbs into space. At other times she seems to diminish the intensity of her bound tension while still maintaining it, which creates an appearance of stiffening. All of these actions initially exude a sense of resistance. Her abrupt attitude toward time, with its fluctuations in tension flow intensity, and the starting and stopping phrasing rhythm, create an agitated emotional state.

My experience is that she seems passionate in her approach but is not getting a clear message across beyond a sense of opposition. Having experienced the extreme tension her Rett syndrome condition can create in her body, I wonder if her agitation is more a physiological inability to relax than an outright refusal to be relieved of her agitation. As I move with her, I cannot believe that her physical or emotional state is a comfortable one and I become equally driven to help her calm down. At the start, the qualities of our actions seem opposing. I want to create sensations of soft, calm muscles, and she is fighting me with bound tension and avoiding eye contact. In the vigor of her actions, as she throws her head from side to side, her torso gets tossed about too! She is not able to apply true effortful strength because of her low muscle tone, so she must increase her muscular tension level in an attempt to achieve this.

*Through my actions and verbalizations, I attempt to respect her move-
ment efforts while keeping my goal of relaxation in mind. We begin an arm
dance of relating. As I hold her hands, I follow her initial arm projections
into the space around her and then gently, but with clear spatial intent, guide
them into arm circles. I support these actions with a long, low vocalization,
matching the fluid phrasing of our arms. She responds back, with shorter
vocalizations. Throughout, I am narrating our actions and my intention to
achieve a more relaxed state. "Open your fingers. . . . Let your legs relax. If
you want to dance, you must relax."*

*About halfway through this "dance," I direct her to focus on her breath,
and she momentarily looks at me and projects her chest forward—an action
she has used in the past to gesture breath awareness. I interpret this as a nonverbal cue of acknowledgment: She is with me. I begin to instruct her to relax
other body parts. "Let your teeth relax, now your hands. . . ." I support these
vocalizations by bringing my hands to my midline, and spreading them apart
in a gently explosive phrasing rhythm to emphasize the extending of my fingers. Nikki attempts to bring her own arm up and down her torso, with a
very indirect spatial action. The intent is subtle, but I don't miss it, and comment on her action. I feel as if she is now telling me that she wants to play.
She is eager to relax with me, but she does not have good neuromuscular control. We must do it together.*

*Nikki's resistance begins to soften. Her eye contact increases. At some
point I release my hold of her hand and begin to provide tactile input to her
torso. As she moves her torso, I adjust my touch to add awareness to these
areas. It is as if I am telling her through my touch, "I feel you moving that
leg, that arm, that belly, those hips. I'm with you. Connect to these places, too,
through my touch, so together, we can calm your body down." She suddenly
extends her right arm out toward me and then over her head in a sweeping
gesture. I am pleased and acknowledge it by mirroring the action with my
own arm and add the action of opening my fingers to demonstrate unlocking
them. She gently and indirectly reaches her right arm out and lets it rest on
my leg. She cooperates more and more as this sequence continues, enabling
me to place her arms up by her head against the floor to apply strong input.
At times she raises her arm and wiggles her fingers clearly in response to my
comments and actions, which indicates to me that we are in deep relationship.
She continues to release her tension and enables relaxation to take place. I am
reminded how much she learns through visual and physical input.* ～

The therapist catches Nikki's subtle nonverbal cues, providing her
with the feedback that they are communicative. By closely observing

the qualities of Nikki's nonverbal actions as communications, the therapist continually maintains, accommodates, and complements her own movements in response to the movement qualities Nikki presents. In essence, a "dancing duet" of relating is established. What is especially significant to consider with a child like Nikki—a young child who has specific movement issues that are not in her control due to the neurological factors Rett syndrome presents—is that these autonomic manifestations create behaviors that can be interpreted as psychologically defensive reactions or stress cues. Through the self-observation aspects of the *Ways of Seeing* approach, the therapist continually reflects on finding ways to introduce movement experiences that bring Nikki out of this defensive behavior and increase relatedness instead. These experiences lead to an increase in social-emotional expressivity. This is evident in Nikki's increasing ability to stay emotionally in touch through movement despite her initial aversion to eye contact; her successful efforts to redirect her tension-producing actions; and her ability to positively respond to the therapist's movement suggestions. Working together, the therapist creates an experience that assists Nikki to regulate her Rett symptoms, while encouraging social-emotional relatedness. Nikki's ability to maintain self-regulation enables her to more effectively interact with her surroundings. In the *Ways of Seeing* program this regulation takes on both a physical and social/emotional focus. As Nikki gains control over her Rett symptoms, as is illustrated in this vignette, she demonstrates an increase in focused attention, relating, and improved body coordination, along with a more qualitatively rich movement style.

ANALYZING DEVELOPMENTAL MOVEMENT PATTERNS

In the previous example, the therapist analyzes the specific qualities of Nikki's movements to support her improved functioning. Research has examined whether qualitative nonverbal analysis can assist the early detection of dysfunctions during infancy. Teitelbaum, Teitelbaum, Nye, Fryman, and Maurer (1998) used the Eshkol-Wachman Movement Notation system to determine if there were qualitative movement differences in how an infant who is later diagnosed along the autism spectrum has achieved particular movement milestones. These researchers reviewed early infancy videotapes of children diagnosed with ASD at 3 years or older and compared them with videotapes of infants whose development was more typical. The motor patterns studied included lying prone and supine, righting (rolling) from back to stomach, sitting, crawling, standing, and walking. After making their comparisons, the researchers detected disturbances in movement behaviors such as atypical shapes of the mouth and partial or complete deviations in specific motor-milestone acquisitions. These movement disturbances were present at birth and have an intrinsic role in the phenomenon of ASD. Teitelbaum and colleagues suggested that early detection of these movement disturbances may be effective in the early diagnosis and treatment of ASD, and they recommended employing early movement analysis to detect motor, emotional, and social development.

In a continuation of this analysis, Teitelbaum, Teitelbaum, Fryman and Maurer (2002) suggested that the disordered functioning of specific movement reflexes might be at the root of movement disturbances in children along the autism spectrum, including Asperger syndrome. Although a thorough description of the important role played by reflexes in a child's early neurological and motor development goes beyond the scope of this book, a brief explanation follows: *Reflexes* are early automatic movements controlled by the spine and brain stem that create the fundamental gross functional patterns that lie beneath all movements. Some reflexes are present at or soon after birth, and others appear later on in development. It is the development and integration of the primary reflexes that enable a more varied and complex action or series of actions to progress from needing volitional direction to providing autonomic control. During the course of typical development, certain reflexes appear to support development and then disappear or become inhibited at a later point to support more advanced development. Moreover, the absence, weakness, or incomplete development of a reflex may interfere with the underlying efficiency, coordination, and core structural support of a movement pattern. This can be observed in poor motor planning and may cause problems in other developmental areas. The atypical functioning of the reflexes found in the Teitelbaum and colleagues 2002 study included some reflexes that lingered too long in a child's neural development, and other reflexes that seemed to be either missing or quite delayed, sometimes years late. Both the lingering and the delaying of these reflexes seem to interfere with the development of more advanced movement developmental patterning.

The reflexes described by Teitelbaum and colleagues are the asymmetrical tonic neck reflex, the protective reflexes, and the head-verticalization reflex. The asymmetrical tonic neck reflex, typically present from birth to age 4 months, is characterized by one arm stretched out perpendicular to the body, with the head maintaining an orientation toward this outstretched arm. In typical development, an infant will roll over toward the direction of the head and the outstretched arm. In several infants in the study who were later diagnosed along the autism spectrum as having Asperger syndrome, however, this reflex remained present at 8 months and 11 months. The 8-month-olds maintained this head–arm positioning even while they rolled over onto the opposite side of their bodies. The presence of this reflex in the 11-month-olds interfered with their ability to balance while walking and standing, causing them to fall over in the direction of their outstretched arm.

The protective reflexes and the head-verticalization reflex fall under the category of righting reactions and equilibrium responses that emerge during the second half of the first year and remain engaged throughout life. The righting reflexes bring the head into a vertical spatial orientation in relation to gravity, and keep the head and torso in alignment with each other. The equilibrium responses enable a person to maintain balance when the center of gravity is off balance due to a personal movement action or the supporting surface elicits an imbalance. The Teitelbaum and colleagues' study found that the protective reflexes that create the extension of arms out and head up to block a fall were not present in three of the children with ASD at approximately 8 months, causing them to fall forward, backward, or to the side. Similarly, the neurological patterning that enabled an infant to maintain his head in absolute vertical spatial alignment when his body was tilted 45 degrees to the right or left, typically evident around 6–8 months, was absent in several of the children they studied. When these children were tilted slowly to one side, brought to center, and then to the other side, they kept their heads in alignment with the midline of their tilting bodies, rather than maintaining spatial verticality.

These studies showing the importance of careful assessment of sensory regulation, neurological reflexes, and motor developmental milestones, are presented to emphasize the importance of these factors in performing a *Ways of Seeing* assessment.

Relationally Based Nonverbal Cues

The studies just described used detailed observations of how infants and young children performed key developmental skills to glean information about possible discrepancies in their development. Nonverbal movement-based analysis can also be used as a significant tool to assess very young children's expressive functioning, specifically in regard to the social and emotional relating and interacting that provides the foundational focus of the *Ways of Seeing* intervention.

Greenspan and Shanker (2002) have used dynamic systems theory to study infant facial expressions in relation to dyadic interactions with significant adults. Especially interested in developing early interventions and understanding the early stages of ASD, Greenspan and Shanker have identified differences in facial expressions of infants at risk for developing ASD. Based on their own research and research done by others, Greenspan and Shanker found that these children exhibit atypical facial expressions that include less expressivity, asymmetries, and reduced eye and mouth movements. Moreover, these facial expressions occur for less time, are less intense, less complex, and more erratic, all characteristics that have been thought to impede social and emotional engagement.

The significance of this research for the *Ways of Seeing* approach is that these researchers have identified nonverbal, facial, body, and movement-oriented characteristics that influence a child's ability to organize and relate to surroundings. The Greenspan and Shanker (2002) research specifically stated that there seemed to be "an impairment in the rhythmicity of the child's movements and vocalizations in response to their caregiver's movements, vocalizations, facial expressions, and gestures" (p. 25). They developed the term *dyadic rhythmicity* to describe the presence of a steady and consistent beat of interaction between a caregiver and baby. This interactive rhythmicity can be intermodal but is not synchronous. The term describes the dyad's style of maintaining an extended tempo

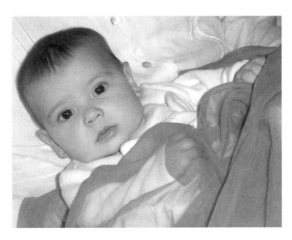

Nonverbal movement-based analysis can assess an infant's expressive functioning.

of interactive exchanges occurring through body movements, behaviors, and affective actions, including gestures; facial expressions; vocalizations/utterances; and eye, torso, and individual body-part movements. Using these criteria, the babies in their study demonstrated abrupt transitions from flat affect to pleasurable smiles that lacked intensity, complexity, and full facial muscular involvement; the transitions were also of short duration and often not accompanied by limb or torso actions. These behaviors were significant in that they all occurred while each child was in dyadic interaction with a caregiver who was quite energetic in attempting active engagement with the child. Despite the caregivers' animated efforts, these children lacked expressions of interest, curiosity, and surprise.

Greenspan and Shanker's research suggests the question of what neurobiological processes underlie these difficulties with "reciprocal affective gesturing" and "motor-mediated complexity and facial expressivity" (2002, p. 29). Their work stimulates practitioners using the *Ways of Seeing* approach to look closely at a child's affective expressivity, with the following questions in mind: How might such facial expressivity concerns play a role in other relationally based dysfunctions such as parent–infant attachment disorders, developmental delays, or posttraumatic stress disorder? Might these extended experiences of impaired social relating and communicating affect the child's neurobiological capacity to support healthy social-emotional development?

Neurobiological Development of the Infant and the Attachment Relationship

Research studies linking brain development with experience are especially relevant to the *Ways of Seeing* approach because it focuses on stimulating neurophysiological functioning by creating new experiences through body and movement-based interactions. Through extensive research, Hofer (1981, 1995, 2002, 2003; Tortora, 2004b) used the animal model to gain insight into the neurobiological development of an infant. Specifically, Hofer investigated the development of an infant–mother attachment bond by studying the infant–maternal separation experience. His research examined how separation from a mother in a variety of situations created stress management responses that affected the offspring's physiological, neurophysiological, and psychological functioning. Hofer's findings suggested that the mother's behaviors actually shaped and regulated multiple developing physiological and behavioral systems of her very young offspring.

These maternal behaviors were sensorimotor, thermal-metabolic, and nutrient-based, such as providing warmth and milk. The infant systems affected by these maternal behaviors included heart rates, activity levels, sleep–wake states, sucking patterns, and blood pressure. During mother–infant interactions, each of these systems worked independently from the others. This became evident when the infant experienced a complete separation from the mother that caused a deregulation and functioning in each subsystem. Under these circumstances, providing one of these maternal behaviors, such as warmth, did not have an effect on the change in heart rate. Hofer created the term *hidden regulators* to emphasize the fact that the regulatory effects of a mother's behavior are not readily evident in first observing a mother–infant interaction. The term regulatory is provided to describe how the level, rate, or rhythm of each system is controlled by specific components of the continuing maternal social engagement (Hofer, 1995). Hofer concluded,

> It is likely that during the early mother–infant relationship in humans, these hidden regulatory interactions come to be experienced by the infant as synchrony, reciprocity, and warmth, or as dissonance and frustration, depending on variations in their timing, contiguity, or patterning . . . .
>
> The discovery of these hidden regulatory processes provides new insights into the relationship of attachment to separation, the genesis of protest and despair patterns in response to loss, and the developmental processes whereby qualitative difference in early relationships may shape personality and future vulnerability to stress. They promise to afford a bridge between biology and psychology in the study of early development and social relationships later in life. (1995, p. 204)

In his continued discussion of the role of hidden regulators within the mother–infant relationship, Hofer stated that one implication of the regulatory aspects of the relationship is that these interactions— with variations in intensity and patterning—may actually shape the infant's developing brain, behavior, and physiology (2003).

Using Movement to Negotiate the Distance Between the Brain and the Body

In the beginning of this chapter, modern dancer Bill T. Jones describes his experience of the body as a powerful reservoir of feelings, images, and associations that connects to the brain through movement. Jones remarks about how movement begins to negotiate the distance

between the brain and the body, and he concludes that it can be surprising what we learn about one another. The *Ways of Seeing* approach
continually explores this distance, striving to find the relationship
between movement, the body, and the brain. The work of a diverse
group of professionals—a creative artist, a nonverbal-movement
researcher, a special educator, a speech–language therapist, a psy-
choneurobiology researcher, and several occupational therapists, child
developmental specialists, and researchers specializing in ASD—is presented in this chapter to highlight the connecting thread throughout
their work. Each uses some aspect of the body and its actions to drawn
conclusions about his or her subject's functioning. Matching and syn-
thesizing their discoveries together opens up a wide discussion about
the possibilities of using experiential, movement-based activities to
support children's development in all levels of functioning.

In considering Hofer's findings about the neurobiological and
psychological links of the mother–infant experience along with
Greenspan and Shanker's (2002) observations about the dysfunctional
expressive styles of infants at risk for ASD, for example, a therapist
might ponder how to use nonverbal, movement-based interactions
focusing on the parent–infant rhythmic exchange as a tool to improve
the development of both the infant's brain and attachment relationships. Moreover, a therapist might wonder what roles self-regulation,
early reflex pattern irregularities, and sensory dysfunctions play in
determining how an infant experiences surroundings and develops
relationships. Might a child's personal repetitive, idiosyncratic movements provide clues to evaluate how the child is experiencing and coping with the environment? How might a child's sensory and movement differences observable in his personal movement style affect the
ability of others to read the child's nonverbal cues? Might this also
influence the evolution of the child's early relationships with his significant caregivers? A therapist using the *Ways of Seeing* approach continually ponders such questions when working with children and their
families. The therapist also looks to see how a child's personal movement style—regardless of how difficult or dysfunctional it might initially appear—can be understood as a creative expression of the child's
experience. Finally, the therapist strives to see what can be learned
from this self-expressive movement to facilitate the child's healthy
development. The examples of successful interventions given at the
end of the chapter demonstrate how the *Ways of Seeing* approach proceeds from asking such questions to observing nonverbal behavior
before developing movement-based interventions.

Behavioral Descriptions Worksheet

The purpose of the Behavioral Descriptions Worksheet (see http://www.brookespublishing.com/dancing for a blank Worksheet) and Figures 4.1, 4.2, and 4.3 (examples of completed worksheets) is to help a therapist organize observations and questions by outlining specific behaviors, movements, events, experiences, and interactions. A therapist following the *Ways of Seeing* approach will find the information developed on this worksheet to be an invaluable resource.

The worksheet includes six sections: The first column, "Detailed general description," is provided to note the details of a child's general behavior that help the therapist clarify the specific behaviors being observed. Here the therapist jots down first impressions that are labeled "general descriptions" to distinguish them from the detailed body-movement descriptions that more appropriately fit in the fourth column to be described further. The second column, "Possible influences: internal/environmental," is provided to note details about possible internal or environmental influences. The third column, "What does it communicate to you?," asks for the therapist's self-reflections about the child's behavior so as to become more aware of how these personal responses may be influencing how the therapist is viewing, thinking about, and responding to the child. It is important to emphasize that it is the therapist's own feelings that should be listed here, and Chapter 7 presents a more comprehensive discussion of this self-observational aspect of the program. The fourth column, "Detailed description of body movements," is provided for the therapist to list details about a child's actions and body movements. This is the space where the therapist should note the specific qualitative nonverbal elements of a child's behavior, including the Laban-based elements described in Chapter 5 of this book. Such detailed descriptions should enable the therapist to complete the fifth column, "'Try on' action: Describe feelings/insights." Trying on a child's specific movements can provide the therapist with insights about the personal function or meaning of the action that may not have been evident from just observing it. The information learned from the experience of trying on certain actions, as well as the rest of the chart, should direct the therapist's decisions for the final column, "Movement-based interventions." This final column should be used to describe both interventions that spontaneously evolved during the specific session and to outline possible interventions the therapist wants to try during a future session. Each entry in this column should begin with the label "Tried" or "Future" to make this distinction clear.

The questions concerning subtle, obscure, and difficult to read behaviors provided in Table 4.1, discussed earlier in this chapter, can be used while filling out this worksheet to guide the therapist's thinking about specific idiosyncratic-movement characteristics. The *Ways of Seeing* approach has also developed six general categories to orient the viewer's observations. Described in detail in Chapter 6, these categories support the therapist's ability to sort the meaning and communicative potentials of nonverbal behaviors. They can also be used as a reference when filling out the Behavioral Descriptions Worksheet. The six categories are the child's

1. Ability to use gestures to communicate

2. Level of activity

3. Sense of continuousness in maintaining social-emotional engagement

4. Overall melody and rhythm of actions, especially when relating to others

5. Use of space and proximity to others

6. Reaction, response, and use of touch when engaged in interaction with others and objects in the environment

The reader will find elements from these categories and from the questions concerning subtle, obscure, and difficult-to-read behaviors embedded in the descriptions of successful interventions that follow. These vignettes provide examples of how the Behavioral Descriptions Worksheet can be used to describe and work with specific behaviors, encouraging their transformation from dysfunctional to creative expressions. In addition, the Behavioral Descriptions Worksheets completed by the therapist for Xenia, Perry, and Julius are provided as Figure 4.1, Figure 4.2, and Figure 4.3 in this chapter.

EXAMPLES OF SUCCESSFUL *WAYS OF SEEING* INTERVENTIONS

Evelyn and Xenia

~~~ *Evelyn, a first-time mother of 11-month-old Xenia, seeks a dance movement psychotherapy consultation because of her child's seeming avoidance of touch and lack of eye contact and facial expressions. During the ses-*

sion I notice that Xenia displays these avoidant behaviors especially when Evelyn or I are very close to her—within Xenia's arm's reach. I ask Evelyn to demonstrate how she plays with her. Sitting in front of Xenia, who is lying on her back, Evelyn lifts Xenia's legs, shakes them, and rocks them from side to side in a monotone, repetitive fashion, as she softly and kindly says her name. Evelyn looks at Xenia, but Xenia has a bland expression. Evelyn is sincere, but their play lacks joyful exuberance. Although Xenia is not resisting, her lack of enthusiastic response does not give Evelyn much encouragement; Evelyn's gentle style does not seem to reach Xenia either. Xenia's blank expression continues as she watches her mother and me interacting together. After she has watched us for a while, she does seem to become more engaged and demonstrates more emotional expressivity and interest—especially when there is substantial distance between us.

When we are several feet away, Xenia intermittently observes our activities with expressions of interest and pleasure and even crawls over to Evelyn or me, seeking increased engagement. I begin to wonder how a lack of physical space may contribute to her discomfort. In this comfort zone of being several feet away, I interact with Xenia by maintaining eye contact, smiling, calling her name, and describing my actions as I move around the room, dancing, running, and walking. I note that I am working especially hard to try to engage her and that it seems to take longer than with most babies her age. But at some point Xenia is completely engaged and stays engaged throughout an activity lasting several minutes. She watches my actions while maintaining eye contact, smiling, intermittently gesticulating with her arms and legs, and even rotating her body to look over her shoulder when I move behind her.

Encouraged by this, I want to see what triggers her loss of engagement. I begin to move directly toward her with quickness. Her attention wavers, evidenced by the change in her facial expression. As soon as I get close, she completely disengages. I step back, gain her attention again through my other actions, and this time I approach her slowly, talking to her about what I am doing and intermittently stopping my actions completely. We maintain eye contact as she stays with me with an expression of concentration. I stop again when I am very close to her. She is still watching me. I then begin to play with her physically like her mom demonstrated, but I use a firmer touch, add a more rhythmic pulsing phrase to the physical play, and greatly heighten the animation of my face and voice. Her social expressivity increases as her smile brightens and she giggles and vocalizes playfully. ⌇

Xenia's presenting behaviors (see Figure 4.1) makes the therapist wonder about her internal physical functioning as well as her

Behavioral Descriptions Worksheet

Name of child: Xenia   **Date of birth:** _____

Age: 11 months

Date: July 18, 2005

Observer: ST

Detailed general description	Possible influences: internal/ environmental	What does it communicate to you?	Detailed description of body movements	"Try on" action: Describe feelings/insights	Movement-based interventions
Difficult behaviors: • Avoids touch • Lack of eye contact • Often has a blank expression, even when Mom is very animated • Lack of spontaneous joyousness in their play • More emotionally expressive after she observes for a while or when contact is self-directed • Doesn't sustain physical contact • Social contact sporadic—doesn't sustain social engagement • Most often on her own in her own space • Not very physically active • Approach behavior compromised—more a sense of withdrawal from her environment	Possible sensory issues: • Tactile • Visual • Proprioceptive - hyposensitive Xenia may either be getting bombarded by the environment, so she is shutting down as a protective stance, or she needs a high level of input to register and respond to the environment. Xenia's behavior is not inviting/eliciting engagement from others, but rather pushing and keeping others away.	As I watch Xenia and Mom interact, I am taken by a deep sense of sadness. Mom clearly loves her child but seems to be at a loss about how to truly engage Xenia. I wonder how this makes Mom feel about herself as a new mother. Xenia's responses and nonverbal cues are often absent or are so subtle that they do not give Mom a lot to work with. In return, Mom seems to engage her in formulaic, rote manner. This is a harsh image. I must be careful about how to approach Mom about this, especially since I was able to increase Xenia's affective responses and extend her engagement with me by attending to her subtle nonverbal cues and by approaching her with slowness rather than quickness. Difficult relationship for both of them. Have concerns about attachment issues.	Phrasing: • More monotone and flat • Lack of melodic or rhythmic aspect to her nonverbal engagement • Momentary engagements seem to dissipate, seeming to drift off • Transitions between actions punctuated by stopping, with long pauses of stillness in between Effort: • Not much effortful affective, expressive engagement • Lack of direct, sustained eye contact, especially when in close contact with another person Space: • Mostly stays in own separate kinesphere • Some self-initiated exploration of surroundings • More avoidant behavior when someone approaches and enters near reach space	I experience a sense of separateness and avoidance of others and the environment. I feel a lack of interest in my environment, a fearfulness, and a sense of safety when I am alone. I feel that things are coming at me too fast! I don't want to be bothered—I don't have any urge or internal desire to engage.	Tried: I played with varying spatial pathways and tempos as I approached and withdrew social contact with Xenia, verbalizing her name as I moved. • When I moved slowly, I was able to sustain eye contact; she even followed visually as I moved around the room. • If I moved too fast, especially as I moved closer to her, she looked away. I used firm strong tactile input when I played with her physically. She responded to this rough and tumble play with heightened positive affect.

The Dancing Dialogue: Using the Communicative Power of Movement with Young Children, by Suzi Tortora, Ed.D., ADTR, CMA.
Copyright © 2006 by Paul H. Brookes Publishing Co., Inc. All rights reserved.

Figure 4.1. Xenia's Behavioral Descriptions Worksheet.

emotional experience. What is causing her behavior? Might she have some sensory integration and regulatory issues? Could her aversion to engage be a coping strategy to alleviate the stress? Is there an incompatibility between Xenia and Evelyn's personal styles that has not supported their experience of relating? How might the difficulties they are experiencing in their interactions influence their developing attachment relationship? Is this child at risk for developing an attachment disorder or dysfunction along the autistic spectrum? With such questions in mind, the therapist tests Xenia's reflexes, and reviews her motor developmental milestones. They are within the limits of typical development. Next she recommends that Evelyn modify her style of play with Xenia, taking into consideration the specific movement-based qualities she had found kept Xenia more engaged. This includes initially connecting to Xenia from a greater distance, using movement actions to initially gain her emotional attention. Once attention is obtained, changing the actions and varying the spatial distances between them can build on these movements.

The therapist advises Evelyn to use her own verbal and facial expressivity to encourage Xenia's responses. The mother is also instructed on how to use increased animation in her voice and facial expressions and a firmer touch to keep Xenia interested. Increasing Xenia's attention will facilitate extended social engagement. Evelyn is encouraged to notice when, how, and for how long Xenia loses engagement during their play and also to think about what might have provided the trigger. It is not unusual for a young child's attention to wax and wane, but considering the concerns about Xenia and their relationship, it was important to pay attention to such transitions. In addition, Evelyn is advised to more closely observe if Xenia demonstrates sensory sensitivities in her overall functioning. When sensitivities arise, Evelyn is given a series of sensory-based activities to explore ways to help Xenia learn to better modulate such input.

In the follow-up visit several weeks later, there is a marked improvement in Evelyn and her baby's interaction. Xenia is more engaged and animated, and affectively responds to her surroundings more quickly with more facial expressivity. Evelyn is also more animated during her interactions with Xenia and reports that Xenia seems to seek her out to play more frequently. She feels closer to her daughter, better about their relationship, and more effective as a mother.

Sara and Perry

The information provided by nonverbal-movement analysis is especially useful when trying to piece together a child's early history during times when parents have not been involved. Adoption presents
one such situation. Deciphering a baby's history can become an almost
detective-like task in adoptions in which an infant has been moved to
different child care settings such as a hospital, foster care, or institu-
tional setting within the first 6 months of his life. Often the child's
written records are sparse. In these situations, observing an infant's
nonverbal behaviors can help to create a picture of how his past may
be affecting his developing approach to the surrounding world (see
Figure 4.2).

Sara and Perry present an excellent example of a mother–infant
dyad in which a nonverbal analysis of the infant's behaviors helped
support their developing relationship. After several years of infertility
treatments, Sara and her husband Karl had decided to adopt a child
from Colombia. They were informed of Perry's birth, traveled to Colombia to pick him up when he was 3 months old, and stayed there
with him for 6 weeks while awaiting the final adoption filings. Perry
had been born in a hospital and then spent 4 weeks in an orphanage
and lived in a foster care setting with five or six other infants. By the
time Sara and Karl met him, he had been in three different child care
settings with multiple caregivers. One of Sara's most vivid early experiences of Perry was how much more vocal he seemed than the other
adoptive babies who were becoming acquainted with their new families. He made it very clear how he was responding to his surroundings.
Whether lying down, propped in an infant seat, or held in an adult's
arms, he was extremely aware of his environment and made his feelings known through his vocalizations, cries, and nonverbal behaviors.
Perry seemed inquisitive, and his gaze was alert as he visually perused
his surroundings. He readily gave Sara and Karl extended direct eye
contact. Perry was most content when his parents adhered to his
schedule, and Sara found that he functioned best when his environment was predictable.

When Perry was almost 5 months old, he and his parents came for
a *Ways of Seeing* evaluation. The therapist agreed with his parents that
Perry was visually inquisitive about his surroundings and very emotionally available. His smile was warm, and he had a lovely rapport
with both Sara and Karl. The therapist was particularly impressed with

Behavioral Descriptions Worksheet

Name of child: Perry

Age: 8 months   **Date of birth:** _____

Date: April 10, 2005

Observer: ST

Detailed general description	Possible influences: internal/ environmental	What does it communicate to you?	Detailed description of body movements	"Try on" action: Describe feelings/insights	Movement-based interventions
Is very visually and vocally engaged in people and surroundings Enjoys engagement with others Is very emotionally expressive via nonverbal affective and vocal cues: Lots of smiles, facial expressions, giggles, vocalizing, and great sustained eye contact Is not physically exploring environment—no attempt to roll or crawl to people/ objects—not transitioning from lying to sitting, sitting to belly, or into crawling position Has particular (obscure) behavior when he is especially seeking attention Obscure behavior: He sits tall, erect, and doesn't move his torso—extending his arms out horizontally, wiggling his fingers fast as he vocalizes	May not have physical strength to hold up, move stout body Has low muscle tone Obscure behavior: • Does communicate • Maintains, facilitates, and extends social engagement • Heightens emotional expressivity • Draws attention to self • Heightens excitement level • Maintains overall organization	Initially, I am drawn to idiosyncratic, yet cute image created by this tiny child performing this action. Soon I have the urge for him to move—for me to move him ("Come on, mobilize, reach for me or for the toys out of your reach!") He seems so set on NOT moving! Emotional themes arise: • How may early experiences related to adoption issues be expressed here? (i.e., he has been through so many transitions; literally handled by multiple caregivers.) • His posture exudes the statement, "I'm not going to budge!" • He attempts to use body weight to resist movement.	Body: • Erect, lengthened through torso • Movement distally—hands/ fingers, proximal/torso relatively still • Symmetrical use of arms and hands • Solid use of weight, centered in pelvis and legs • No weight shifting onto torso, legs, arms, or hands to enable rolling or crawling Space: • No motivation, movement, or level changes • Uses near and far reach kinespheres Efforts: • All are available, especially directness Phrasing: • Quick, rippling rhythmic quality to finger gesture Shape: • Directional: Reach from center out; torso is vertical and arms are horizontal	I feel a very balanced and determined sensation. My attention is focused. I feel solid, yet energized, and strong willed.	Future: I will support his visual strength by modeling for him different ways to mobilize: • Shift weight onto belly, hands, and knees • Demonstrate how to reach further beyond far reach kinesphere To physically mobilize his body, I will let him try weight shifting on physioball. I will use tactile support to stimulate transitions such as rolling and crawling. Emotional: I will empathize about early infancy experience.

The Dancing Dialogue: Using the Communicative Power of Movement with Young Children, by Suzi Tortora, Ed.D., ADTR, CMA.

Figure 4.2.   Perry's Behavioral Descriptions Worksheet.

Sara's keen ability to read Perry's cues. She knew just how much input he could tolerate: she understood when he should be approached or given a break and how much spatial distance and closeness made him most comfortable. Their dyadic rhythm of interactions had a very calm, reliable pace.

Karl also had developed a great rapport with Perry. As is often typical with dads, his interactions involved more rough-and-tumble play that Perry greatly enjoyed. Like Sara, Karl seemed to know just when play should stop so that Perry was never overexcited. The new family was off to a great start, and Sara and Perry came for a session every few weeks to support his development and their growing relationship.

At 8 months, Perry's interest in his world continued to grow. He appeared bright and eager to explore his surroundings. His visual sense was still his most dominant way of absorbing his environment. Now, sitting up very tall and erect, Perry would look all around him and watch everything that moved or talked. He giggled and smiled and drew attention to himself with delightful gurgles and grunts. When he especially wanted attention, he had a very specific gesture that accompanied his vocalizations and facial expressions: Stretching his arms out horizontally to his side and holding them there for an extended time, he would wiggle his fingers in a quick, rippling rhythm. What was especially remarkable was that despite all of his interest, visual attending, social engagement, and vocalizing, Perry never attempted to physically enter into his surroundings. When seated, he would keep his arms extending out instead of shifting his weight onto his hands and trying to crawl. When lying down, he never attempted to roll over or to push himself along the floor to grasp an object out of his reach. With his stout little body held erect and his arms outstretched to his side, his seated stance was reminiscent of a sumo wrestler and commanded tremendous attention. He seemed strong and determined—determined not to move but to still be in control of his surroundings.

The therapist considered Perry's stance from several perspectives and evaluated both the physical and the experientially based emotional aspects of the infant's early experiences. First the therapist wondered about Perry's muscular strength and tone: Might he not yet have enough muscular strength to hold up his body? Could the problem be related to low muscle tone? The therapist also pondered Perry's emotional state: How might his past experiences and his experiencing his surroundings from this stance hold expressive meaning? Reviewing his early history, the therapist wondered what it might feel like to be handled by so many different caregivers: Might his immobile stance be a coping strategy expressing his effort to stay put? Keeping all of these thoughts in mind, the therapist used several *Ways of Seeing* methods to encourage Perry to explore body movement. After first verbalizing what a stable and strong stance Perry's posturing had created, the therapist then supported Perry's visual learning style by getting down on her hands and knees to demonstrate exactly how to shift body weight to crawl. Next, the therapist supported Perry's hips and chest and assisted him to shift his own weight onto his hands and knees. This activity mobilized his body on the stable surface of the floor. The therapist also placed Perry on a physioball, both seated and on his belly, to help him experience weight shifting through his pelvis and torso. This taught him how to adjust his body on a moving surface. In addition, at the therapist's suggestion, Perry was given an early intervention evaluation that determined that he was several months delayed in his gross motor development. Within 2 months of physical therapy and continued *Ways of Seeing* sessions, Perry began to roll, crawl, and push up to sitting, thus catching up developmentally.

Perry's new ability to physically explore his world greatly facilitated his inquisitive nature. Now he was able to move and to go directly to those people and objects he had previously watched with such focused attention. Once he learned how to walk, he became especially engaged in trying to figure out how things worked, manipulating objects, and climbing. Often through nonverbal gestures and vocalizations, Perry would attempt to ask Sara for assistance. His determination was clear, and he often increased his communications and became frustrated if Sara's response was unsatisfactory.

Although this was an exciting stage for Perry, Sara's experience of these ever-growing explorations was very different. She found them to be both trying and provoking. The synchrony and reciprocity of their relationship was compromised as Sara and Perry began to get frustrated with each other. One example took place during a *Ways of Seeing* session when Perry was 18 months old, and he attempted to unscrew the cap of a water bottle to pour its contents into a sippy cup. After this unsuccessful attempt, he handed the bottle to Sara, who opened it and poured the water for him. Perry's immediate response was frustration, and he kicked his legs and vocalized angrily. Sara looked at the therapist and remarked that this was a typical example of their growing communicative conflicts. Sara and Perry had fallen out of sync with each other. The therapist suggested that perhaps Perry wanted assistance in learning how to open the bottle more than he wanted the water itself. After being shown how to open the water bottle, Perry's difficult behavior stopped.

The therapist and Sara began talking about how Perry's current behaviors might have originated in his early style of engagement with his surroundings. On reflection, Sara remembered how Perry had so outspokenly vocalized his needs when they first adopted him. Before he had command of his whole body, he had relied on his visual sense to absorb the world around him, and he wanted and needed to be actively involved in his surroundings. The adults discussed how Perry now used his mobility to continue this thirst for exploration. They realized that his requests, demands, and behaviors might be an extension of this process rather than defiant behavior. This reinterpretation of her son's nonverbal behaviors led to revolutionary changes in Sara's parenting style. Sara's description of her experience is revealing:

The most profound change in my parenting style happened when my health had broken down and my immune system was seriously compromised. After extensive testing, my doctor informed me that my chronic illnesses appeared to be stress related. I found this a bit ridiculous since I am a stay-at-home mother of an 18-month-old little boy. I did not equate what I did with stress—I thought that stress was reserved for career people, as I had been for nearly 20 years.

For me, mothering was hard, often unsatisfying work, with little inherent joy. I related to Dr. Tortora that my son was showing signs of being a discipline problem. I cited one example of his habit of throwing his full plate of food from his high chair and laughing as he saw my anger. I recounted how, as I knelt down at the foot of the highchair to clean up his mess, my son would spike his sippy-cup off the crown of my head.

I thought my child was exceptionally defiant and that my attempts to discipline him and teach him amounted to nothing. I felt defeated and frustrated at my new job as servant and policewoman. Dr. Tortora told me that my son was likely not hungry if he was throwing his food away as soon as he sat down. She suggested that when the food throwing happened again, I take my son down from his chair and go into his play area. She said that at my son's age, he is like a little scientist experimenting and learning constantly. Dr. Tortora explained that throwing was part of his learning process. Instead of forcing my son to learn "good table manners," I was to bring him soft toys and balls and we would have a throwing-fest together. When he was hungry he would eat. This turned out to be excellent advice. My son was not hungry and was learning about cause and effect, in this case by throwing. I have learned to apply this simple but profound change in perspective to many of the events of the day with my son. The result has been that I am having fun with him at last.

One aspect of this learning that fascinated me most was the effect it had on my well-being in general. When I was playing disciplinarian I felt like I had tapped into a part of myself that was rigid and perfectionistic. When I shifted my paradigm from school marm to learning-facilitator, I found that my whole attitude softened. It was as if this simple adjustment in my thinking had an unexpected chain reaction. I slowed down in general, felt happier, and my health improved.

I felt like Dr. Tortora imparted this simple information to me at a pivotal period in my son's development. What I saw as a discipline problem was actually the normal behavior of a bright inquisitive child exploring his environment. At this critical juncture my son was developing attitudes about learning. As the greatest influence in his life (I spend the most time with him) I could either enhance his experience of learning or I could shut him down by teaching him that learning and exploring make him a "bad boy." ⌇

Julius

Julius, diagnosed with PDD, began *Ways of Seeing* sessions when he was 7 years old (see Figure 4.3, Julius's Behavioral Descriptions Worksheet).

⌇ *Julius loves rock-and-roll musicians and dancing. He has a very unique personal rhythm and is very interested in mimicking the movement styles of his favorite rock-and-roll stars. On entering his Ways of Seeing session, he may break into a "moonwalk" or a rapidly spinning turn, involving stepping, gliding, and suddenly snapping his body around. He is fascinating to watch and appears to have a unique rhythmic sense and physical coordination of his body. Julius often holds a "tapper"—that is, any small, long object such as a rubber band or plastic twist tie—that he uses to tap out a rhythm when he is excited. While holding his whole body in check, he directs all of his energy into this tapper, rapidly flicking it with his hand and tapping in a tense, pulsing beat. Despite this affinity to rhythm, he has difficulty controlling his movements and his thoughts in social or academic settings in which he feels compelled to share his ideas. When he attempts to demonstrate some control, he often seems to be like a racehorse waiting for the signal to charge—often jumping the gun, unable to wait. He can talk in a stream-of-consciousness way about his personal themes of interest—often musicians—even if the conversation is not about music.* ⌇

Behavioral Descriptions Worksheet

Name of child: Julius   Date of birth: _____

Age: 7.5 years   Date: February 8, 2005

Observer: ST

Detailed general description	Possible influences: internal/environmental	What does it communicate to you?	Detailed description of body movements	"Try on" action: Describe feelings/insights	Movement-based interventions
Energetic personality Obscure behavior: He has his own distinct rhythmic pulse, often spontaneously and compulsively tapping out rhythm with a small object—sometimes accompanied by vocalizations. He has good expressive and receptive language skills, but he's functioning on his own time and rhythm. He doesn't respond in a timely manner or within context of conversation. He has intermittent engagement with people; he often seems to be in his own world and engages in "scripting," in which his actions and verbalizations mimic rock stars. He is easily distracted by inner thoughts and images (e.g., rock star postures, movements, music rhythms), and external stimulii (e.g., visually drawn to objects such as CD case or physioball).	Sensory concerns: • Sensory seeking: hyposensitive • Vestibular • Proprioceptive • Visual • Tactile Poor impulse control: He has difficulty internally modulating as if his nervous system can't turn off or is overfiring. Continual shifting of focus from internal to external Behavior doesn't seem related to immediate physical environment, but is instead more related to overall excitability and emotional tone of day. Regulation of systems—especially physical, emotional, social, and communicative—are key issues.	I am alert and energized; I need to stay constantly ready to move quickly to respond to unexpected actions, gestures, and verbalizations. I am intrigued by his sweet personality but also on my guard; my nervous system is really working when I engage with him. Movements: Dancing with him requires heightened strength to give him lots of proprioceptive feedback.	Body: • Has all levels of coordination, performed with unusual rhythmic timing • Differentiates body parts—legs, feet, hands most active rhythmically • Avoids eye contact • Is often in motion Space: • Fills all aspects of kinesphere • Creates linear and curving pathways all over room • Contains all levels of space Phrasing: • Stopping/starting rhythmic pulse, very personally directed—not maintaining rhythmic beat with others • No complementary or recuperative aspect to phrase, either moving or not moving • Sense of propulsion; explosive movement phrasing Efforts: • Bound flow • Quickness • Strength • Direct and indirect	I feel out of control, grasping onto ideas, objects, and rhythmic pulse in an attempt to gain some control. Perseverative actions hone my focus for a little while. Many things seem engaging, but I get stuck—my actions and ideas become scripted; I feel stuck, impulsively shifting to new ideas and actions to get out. I am lost in my own images; they keep out external focus because I can't maintain attention to external focus with any sense of organization or internal modulation.	I used strong rhythmic music and mirrored his actions, learning his dance steps: • He was able to respond in complementary way to rhythm and speed of music. • He increased the length of his social attention. • He enjoyed sharing his movement ideas. I attempted to have him follow my movement interpretations to the same music, but he was not ready to be a follower; he lost interest and started to do his own actions. I changed the music (slow, melodic) to follow his movements: • He was able to adjust his dancing actions to the slower tempo. • He spontaneously gradually decreased the tempo of his actions, made them smaller and then stopped—exactly following the ending of the music!

Figure 4.3. Julius's Behavioral Descriptions Worksheet.

Over the course of his several years in the *Ways of Seeing* approach, the therapist has used Julius's keen personal rhythmic awareness and musical affinity to help him gain more physical control, to improve his verbal self-expressions, to employ his rhythmic sense to engage more appropriately in social dialogue, and to explore psychologically his deep fascination with rock stars. During his early years of therapy, Julius and the therapist moved to ever-changing qualities of rock-and-roll music. First the therapist followed Julius's lead to feel how he interpreted musical shifts and changes. Soon Julius was able to take turns, following the therapist's inspirations. From there they progressed to moving together as synchronous partners, holding hands while following each other's movements as exactly as possible. Embodying musical changes developed in Julius an interest in learning how to write musical notes. Together, he and his therapist wrote the musical scores of the rock-and-roll music to which they were listening. Holding the sheet of music in front of them, they next created a dance of the written musical notes, emphasizing the difference between holds, whole notes, half notes, quarter notes, eighth notes, and sixteen notes. They correlated these differences in the music to movement time by stopping their actions during the holds, moving to a slower beat to match the quarter notes, and then speeding up as they progressed to the sixteenth notes. As their dances became more choreographed, they began to map out a floor pattern and perfect the actual dance moves. This required more body control from Julius as he concentrated on moving specific parts of his body in relation to others—such as learning where to hold his head, arms, and chest when making a full circle turn clockwise or counterclockwise.

Next, Julius's ability to gain this control enabled him to learn how to be a partner in ballroom dancing. These dances require each member to have specific steps that may be different or complementary to those of their partner. Julius practiced how to hold hands and help his partner move through the steps, supporting her without pulling or tugging, all the while keeping to the musical beat. During this partnering, they worked on extending eye contact and resuming eye contact while the partner spun around, turned, or twisted away from view. Through all of these actions, Julius began to increase his ability to maintain continuous social-emotional engagement for longer periods of time during the sessions. He is now (at age 9) able to maintain engagement for at least 90% of his session. Simultaneously, he is able to stay engaged in conversations, and he more easily stays connected to the conversational topic instead of going off on his own tangent.

As these gains have been established, further progress has been made using Julius's rhythmic sense as the key. Now Julius and the therapist take turns using a drum and mallet to tap out rhythms to which the other person dances. A spontaneous dialogue through rhythm and body movements ensues, and they try to keep a steady rhythm on the drum and match it with their bodies by maintaining a steady movement sequence. The action may be repetitive—such as continuously alternating between stamping the left foot then right, or moving the different parts of the body, such as the left arm then the right hand, the right foot then the head, in time with the beat. The goal is to maintain the beat with a steady pulse, whether it is fast, medium, or slow. As with his style of speaking, Julius has a tendency to speed up and start to blend all of his actions together, losing the distinct body-part awareness. Staying with the beat takes extended concentration. Other days they create a patterned rhythm—like quick, quick, pause, slow, slow, quick. This skill requires Julius to maintain engagement because he must really listen to detect the rhythm changes.

This is an especially useful activity that can draw Julius out of discussing the rock-and-roll stars he often likes to talk about. Connecting to the therapist rhythmically enables Julius to bring his attention to the here and now. The therapist's success in grounding Julius into his physical body through these activities has enabled her to verbally dialogue with Julius about what his deeper feelings are surrounding his fascination with these rock stars. He has been able to express concerns about their often violent and volatile behaviors, his identification with their Peter Pan-like desires to never grow up, and their heartfelt songs about feelings of love, sadness, and joy.

Movement, the Body, the Brain, and Creative Expression

This chapter guides the reader through various arts, sciences, and therapeutic interventions to reveal how such seemingly diverse fields have a common ground in their uses of the body and nonverbally and experientially based actions to assess a child's functioning. The *Ways of Seeing* approach weaves together the information from these fields to create a comprehensive intervention methodology using nonverbal action and experientially based activities to support a child's development. As these vignettes demonstrate, movement analysis can provide clues to the meaning behind behaviorally observable difficulties. These observations can be used to provide dynamic movement-based interventions. Interventions can repair difficult expressive and dyadic interactions to increase a child's ability to communicate. Acknowledging movement as a nonverbal language provides an opportunity to transform difficult or dysfunctional behaviors into creative self-expressions. The *Ways of Seeing* approach brings the brain and the body together through its understanding of movement expression.

II

Observation and Intervention

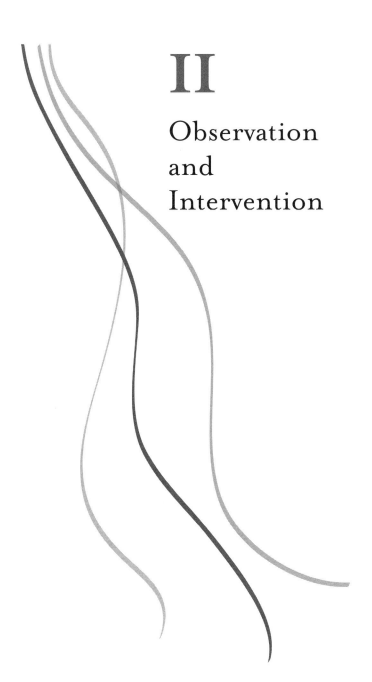

5

Elements of
Movement Observation

The deep association (conscious and unconscious) with body movement is reflected in the emotional content elicited by various rhythmic patterns. . . . Delineations of character and mood are evoked by their rhythmical associations with the body tensions they reflect. One's organism is organized into rhythmic patterns . . . shifting tensions in the body relate to space and Effort. . . . The characteristic rhythm of any given activity evolves out of the spatial/Effort sequencing and phrasing of its components. . . . The sensitivity to body, space and Effort rhythmic sequences is essential to the movement observer."

I. Bartenieff, *Body Movement: Coping with the Environment*
(1980, pp. 71–73)

All movement has rhythm and phrasing. These characteristics enable a person to relate, interact, and express himself or herself in the surrounding world. Rhythm creates the emphasis in a movement, whereas phrasing marks the unfolding flow of a movement sequence. Similar to a musical phrase, a person's *movement phrase* is created when the person performs a series of movements in a sequence that creates a complete action or expresses a feeling. There is an interwoven relationship between an individual and his or her body movements. An individual uses particular phrasings of his or her moving body parts to produce a unique rhythmic spatial organization that communicates feelings and information to the surroundings. Movement phrasing is created by the sequence shown in Figure 5.1.

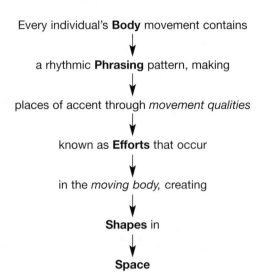

Every individual's **Body** movement contains

↓

a rhythmic **Phrasing** pattern, making

↓

places of accent through *movement qualities*

↓

known as **Efforts** that occur

↓

in the *moving body,* creating

↓

Shapes in

↓

Space

Figure 5.1. Movement phrasing is created by a sequence.

RHYTHM AND PHRASING

Each movement contains a rhythmic phrase because there must be a moment when an action begins, a duration as the action continues, and an ending to the action in order for it to exist in time. Time involves rhythm. The term *rhythm* is used here to mean the observable shift at some point in a movement phrase, which creates a demarcation or accent within the course of an action. The word *Effort* is not referring to its common use as an attitude involving exertion but is instead referring to its use in LMA (discussed in Chapter 6) to define the accents and specific characteristics of a movement. Such Efforts are observable because they are caused by qualitative differences in actions or exertions. Body actions not only take up time but also create shape forms that occur in space. A *Shape form* refers to the visible patterns a Body makes as it moves in Space that reflect each individual's unique style and manner. The physical space a body takes up is determined by the actual shape changes that occur as the person moves and adjusts his or her gestures and postures. These elements of movement—Body, Shape, Phrasing, Effort, and Space—are the key observational components of the *Ways of Seeing* approach's MSI Checklist.

MOVEMENT SIGNATURE
IMPRESSIONS CHECKLIST

The MSI Checklist (see Appendix A) was developed to guide a therapist's observations. The MSI Checklist, based on the LMA system described later in this chapter and in Chapter 6, enables a revisualization of nonverbal expression. An LMA profile provides very detailed information about a mover's nonverbal style. As suggested by its title, the MSI Checklist provides impressions of a mover's nonverbal style, taking into account the observer's subjective viewpoint. This distinction is important. A true LMA profile strives to be objective, and its goal is to create as exact and accurate a description of the movements as is possible. This notation system initially was developed by dancer Rudolf Laban to preserve the steps of a dance. He then began to use it to analyze and create efficient movement patterns for laborers in factories and other work settings. The best-trained movement analysis specialists often implement the LMA system, but it is not very accessible for those not specifically trained in movement analysis. Historically, this has been a problem for the LMA system that has limited its use outside of the dance world. The information obtained from it is invaluable, however, and so the MSI Checklist was developed to modify the LMA profile into a more general system that can be used by nonspecialists. The goal of creating the MSI Checklist was to make nonverbal information more accessible and to help professionals begin to understand how their own nonverbal style affects their interactions with people. As its name suggests, an MSI Checklist will provide an impression of the nonverbal style of the person being observed—through the eyes of the observer—by drawing awareness to, and taking into account, biases in observing. This differs from the LMA system's more objective account of the movements. This distinction is valid because the way an observer "sees," perceives, experiences, and interprets will greatly influence an interaction—regardless of whether the interpretation is accurate and valid. Moreover, an MSI Checklist is especially useful because it goes beyond the limitations of formal norm- and criterion-based assessments. An MSI Checklist does not focus on achievement or skill level but rather on the qualitative individuality of each person's style of existing, acting, and reacting to surroundings. The information it provides is used to develop intervention and educational programs applicable for each specialty, and thus an MSI

Checklist creates a universal language for the complete educational team conducting the intervention.

A full MSI Checklist includes observational and self-observational information, interactional analysis, movement metaphors, and closing comments. The five LMA-based components of an MSI Checklist and movement metaphors are discussed in this chapter. The self-observational elements are described in Chapter 7, and the interactional analysis elements are discussed in Chapter 10. The closing comments provide a synthesis of all of the information collected in each section of an MSI Checklist. As noted before, a full MSI Checklist outlining each section appears in Appendix A.

THE FIVE LABAN MOVEMENT ANALYSIS (LMA) ELEMENTS

The specific elements of an LMA add to a movement description by focusing on exactly how a movement is performed (e.g., with lightness or strength), instead of being satisfied with mere broad characterizations (e.g., describing a movement as *running*). Compare these two descriptions:

> *Jacob is running toward the barn. James is running faster, and he will get to the barn sooner.*

> *Jacob is swinging his arms with lightness and free flow, creating a floating sensation as he runs directly toward the barn. The strength and directness with which James is swinging his arms creates a pumping action that helps him run faster directly toward the barn.*

The added qualitative descriptions found in the second example provide information that enables a visual image to be formed.

The five LMA nonverbal observation elements used in an MSI Checklist to facilitate such descriptions are Body, Effort, Shape, Space, and Phrasing. *Body* describes how and what aspects of the body (e.g., how different body parts work together or separately) are used to execute an action creating a posture, gesture, or sequence of movements. *Effort* describes the qualitative intent that creates the feeling tone or inner attitude of a movement in four motion factors: space, weight, time, and flow. In early infancy, due to the underlying tension flow and lack of muscular strength, the qualitative intent of the actions— Effort—is not fully formed. The Kestenberg movement analysis system has created a category called pre-Effort to emphasize this stage

(Kestenberg, 1975; Kestenberg-Amighi et al., 1999). *Shape* describes the forms (such as shaping actions, shape-flow actions, or directional movements) the body and movements make in space. *Shaping actions* have clear body boundaries that mold around objects in space or create clear shapes in the surrounding space. *Shape-flow actions* are the movements that occur within the boundaries of the body such as breath movements. *Directional movements* are clear arcing and spoke-like actions that reach out from a person's center (torso) making clear lines in space. *Space* describes how a person moves the body to travel through the surroundings. *Phrasing*, similar to its musical counterpart, music phrasing, depicts how a person clusters actions together over a period of time, creating a flow, pulse, and rhythm as the actions start, continue, pause, and stop. Table 5.1 provides an outline of the qualities that define each of these five elements.

Space

This discussion begins with Space because space is the "container" in which all actions take place. Laban noted that space "is a hidden feature of movement and movement is a visible aspect of space" (1976, p. 4). He made a distinction between the space one's body occupies— known as the kinesphere or personal space—and the space that surrounds the body—the general space. How a person uses his body space and outside space influences and enables social interactions. For example, a person who holds his head down, gazing at the floor with shoulders slumped as he attempts to speak with his friend who is standing an arm's length away, delivers a very different message than a person who holds her body erect, with her head up, and looks straight into her friend's eye.

Movement in space involves a sense of self and the other. How someone actually moves across an area will affect people and objects occupying the same space. Visualize the following scene between two young children playing Hide-and-Seek while their mother is cooking in the kitchen. Juan enters, quietly tiptoeing as he crouches into the corner next to the refrigerator. His mother glances over her shoulder with a smile toward Juan as she continues with her cooking tasks. Suddenly, Nathan pushes the swing door—SLAM!—against the wall as he dashes into the kitchen, racing across the room just as his mother is taking the roast out of the oven. His mother tenses observably and tightens her grip on the pan as Nathan flies by. Without a word

Table 5.1. Overview of the five key elements of Laban Movement Analysis (LMA)

1. Effort		*related attitudes*
Space—direct	indirect	"where"—attention
Time—quick	slow	"when"—decision
Weight—strong	light	"what"—intention
Flow—bound	free	"how"—progression, precision

2. Structure of Body

Placement or movement of limbs in relation to torso
Proximal–distal initiation
Upper–lower body relationship
Left-to-right body relationship
Contralateral body relationship
Pattern of breath flow
Particular body parts or areas of which the individual seems aware
Particular body parts or areas that attract your attention
Most used parts of body during movement
Least used parts of body during movement
Use of body as a whole versus in parts
Symmetry or asymmetry
Place of initiation of movement
Weight shifting

Notice the overall sense of connection, fluidity versus disconnection, holding throughout body in stillness and in motion, sense of propulsion, locomotion, mobility, energy, intention, and motivation to move.

3. Space or spatial movement qualities

Use of space: Large or small; near, mid, or far reach of limbs (i.e., the kinesphere)
Enclosing or opening movements
Pathways in space
Level changes in space

4. Phrasing

How the movements are sequenced together to create rhythm and melody
Rhythm of movement phrase—exertion/recuperation, sequencing

5. Shape

Shaping
Shape flow
Directional movements (e.g., arcs, spokes)

---

spoken, the mother experiences each child's intent through the differences in the qualities of their nonverbal actions. Their actions influence her activities. Juan's quiet contained entrance enables the mother to keep attending to her tasks while Nathan's sudden burst catches her by surprise, adding an element of tension and concern due to the heavy, hot object she is in the middle of transferring onto the counter.

The *Ways of Seeing* approach looks at how children hold and move their bodies within their space (the kinesphere) in interaction with the outside space (the general space) to determine the children's orientation, comfort, and awareness of their environments. The *kinesphere* is the personal three-dimensional sphere around a body, whose periphery is reachable by extending one's limbs while staying placed in one spot. This limb extension is categorized as near-, mid-, or far-reach space—referring to the amount of distance between the body and the extended limb. Movements in the kinesphere involve level changes of low, middle, and high and also include front, side, and back actions. Rarely is an action performed by just one pure spatial dimension, and so several spatial placements are often combined to create a more complex action. Under these circumstances, an observer should note which direction is most prominent in determining the spatial dimensions of an action.

Because the kinesphere surrounds the body, one never leaves this movement sphere, but rather transports it, like an aura, when moving from place to place. The kinesphere can be thought of as a flexible bubble completely surrounding a person that creates the personal boundaries between self and another person. Each individual has his or her own level of comfort between self and others. The 2-year-old child who is testing his independence might situate himself beyond his arms' length from his mother in his far-reach kinespheric space as he examines a toy fire truck. Respecting his body placement, his mother might maintain her postural position at the outer edge of his kinesphere, smiling at him when he gazes at her, but not intruding on his body boundaries by leaning too deeply into his personal space or touching him with her hand. When he scoots next to her to show her how the ladder goes up and down, he draws his kinesphere in a bit closer around him, still maintaining his own body boundaries. His mother may extend her hand on his toy to try the ladder, too, entering into his kinesphere with her limb, while still holding her torso within her own kinespheric space. When he becomes tired and leans his body to rest on her lap, his mother embraces him with her arms and body, and their kinespheres merge.

The rest of space, known as the *general space,* lies outside of an individual's personal kinesphere (Laban, 1976). This is the public space in a given environment. *Interpersonal space* (Davis, 1975; Scheflen 1976; Moore & Yamamoto, 1989) refers to the interactive, changing spatial distances between people in a given environment. It involves the mingling, overlapping, or separateness of individual kinespheres. As people move their kinespheres through space, *spatial pathways* can be traced. They make straight, curved, direct, irregular, and/or circuitous floor patterns. Watching how an individual moves through the room, noting specific navigations of his or her body around, past, near, and next to other people and objects will reveal kinespheric preferences. The amount of kinespheric space required will vary depending on the activity or the interaction. This is exemplified in the following vignette:

Mom and her 14-month-old son by adoption, Darryl, come to treatment because of failure-to-thrive signs, manifested especially in attachment, calming down, and sleeping issues. Upon first observation I am struck by Darryl's long, straight spine as he sits with his left leg folded behind him and his right leg in front, with his knee up. The stillness of his arms and chest makes it appear as if his upper body is floating on top of his legs and pelvis. When he reaches out his limbs into mid-to-far reach space, the neutral/bound flow quality in his arms, mixed with extreme lightness, causes his arms to seem to glide gently through the air. His tendency to shift his weight to his left side creates the sense that his left side is pulling him away while his right side is reaching out into his far-reach kinesphere. Mom and Darryl sit directly across from each other, separated in space by the far edges of their kinespheres. One of them would have to move or lean far forward before their personal spaces could overlap.

In the room there is a cat. Darryl has positioned himself so close to the cat that her tail is swinging on his lap. Shifting to lean onto his left side, Darryl gently extends his right arm and torso—as if floating through the air—into his far-reach space to touch the cat's eyes. As he does this I match his movement quality, softly placing my hand around his wrist and briefly adding direct spatial Effort to redirect it toward the cat's body. Sensing the "No" in my action, with startled quickness, Darryl immediately recoils his hand back to his near-reach kinesphere, stills his whole body, and looks over to Mom, whimpering. He twists and extends his upper body so that he is leaning forward with his weight on both his hands intermingling with the outer edges of Mom's kinesphere, but he then stops a moment, frozen in this pose. Before he proceeds straight for her, he rocks toward and then away from her, shifting back on to his left side. Next, he lightly shifts forward into a crawl position and begins to move directly toward her. But just as he approaches, the far-reaches of their kinespheres completely overlapping, he stops abruptly again, looking toward her with tension in his face. His body is still. His approach is delayed once more. Mom reaches out and picks up his limp body.

Although Darryl looks at Mom and seems to want to head toward her, his actions create a sense that something is obstructing his pathway. It seems as if he is being pulled by some invisible force holding his left side. I am struck by this hesitation when he is so physically close to reaching his goal. I begin to notice this particular use of space in relation to his mother through-out the session in other situations when he moves toward her.

In this description, Darryl stays mostly within the close and comfortable range of his own personal kinesphere. On the occasions that he enters his surroundings by reaching into mid- to far-reach space, he anchors the opposite side of his body away from this forward reaching. He and his mom sit in their own separate kinespheres, requiring them to make a full body action through space in order to connect or overlap their personal spatial boundaries. During this session, Darryl does not travel significantly through the room to explore the space but instead barely mobilizes his body. His actions mostly take place within the confines of his personal reach space, sitting upright and only momentarily changing levels of space to crawl forward. Most significantly, when Darryl does attempt to crawl toward Mom, he stops himself at the outskirts of their overlapping kinesphere, requiring her to reach out to him, in order to make physical contact.

Three Developmental Space Orientations Spatial expressions are the varying uses of space within which relating occurs. Relating begins and develops within the context of both movement and motor development. Movement development, described below and in Chapter 3, is related and yet distinct from motor development. Both occur within a general spatial progression called developmental space. As discussed in Chapter 3, the concept of self, the experience of the moving body, and movement and gross motor development are influenced by various progressive spatial orientations. Such orientations can also be analyzed by three distinct spatial characteristics: horizontal, vertical, and sagittal.

The three spatial orientations used in the *Ways of Seeing* approach are adapted from the work of Bartenieff (1973, 1980); Bartenieff and Davis (1965); Kestenberg (1973); Laban (1976); Lamb and Watson (1979); and Cohen (1997). These orientations progress developmentally from horizontal to vertical to sagittal. They refer to the natural positions taken by an infant or young child in reference to the ground without assistance from others or supportive apparatus. Each spatial orientation is purported to have an affinity with specific movement qualities (Laban, 1976). These body positions orient a child perceptually, inform the child's visual perception of the world, and determine the child's experience of body in motion. Infants and young children continue to add orientations to their repertoire periodically during their development. Most children experience these spatial placements progressively in utero, during birth, and from birth onward, due to their own mobility and to their handling by their caregivers. The succession from horizontal to vertical to sagittal follows a young child's orientation during personal physical exploration through motor developmental advancement, first moving on the floor through rolling and crawling, next rising to sitting and standing, and culminating with walking and running.

Horizontal   The horizontal orientation is the initial position a baby is in when she is lying prone or supine. It entails all the space she can see in the front, to the left, and to the right. This position is known as the *communication plane* (Lamb & Watson, 1979). From this perspective a baby can both take in the people and elements of her surroundings as her visual field and physical actions sweep across the horizontal plane, or she can exclude her environment through actions that narrow, enclose, and contain her physical and visual fields. The movement qualities this plane facilitates are actions from side to side. Limb actions include gathering motions toward her body center and scattering motions away from her body center. Her torso or limbs experience the actions of enclosing, narrowing, spreading, and widening. Examples of actions in this orientation include looking around while a baby is lying on her stomach or back and log rolls.

Vertical   In the vertical, upright orientation, a baby or young child seems to be saying, "I am ME! Look at ME! I am HERE!". Whether sitting or standing, a young child who moves in the world from a vertical stance is able to expand her view of her surroundings. From this vertical position, she creates a sense of presence that can have the tone of simply being present or confrontational (Lamb & Watson, 1979). A young child's movements in the vertical position enable ascending and descending in space, both toward and away from others. A child uses her limbs to reach for others or to throw, pick up, or put down objects. A child experiences movements within her torso that lengthen or shorten her body. Examples of actions in this orientation include standing and jumping.

Sagittal   Movement in the sagittal orientation enables a young child to enter and advance or withdraw and retreat from the world. As a young child ventures out into or retreats away from others and objects in space, she seems to be saying, "Here I come" or "Away I go." Movements in the sagittal orientation initiate and terminate contact. A child's characteristic postures in this orientation include concave and convex shapes of her torso, and examples of full body actions from this orientation are walking and running.

Self-Achieved Spatial Orientation versus Assisted Spatial Placement During observations a therapist determines which spatial orientation—self-achieved or assisted—a child uses most to view the world. Although these spatial orientations were originally conceived in regard to the positions in which infants and young children could place themselves, with the advent of myriad types of apparatus that hold and carry babies, many very young children are spending tremendous amounts of time in positions they could not achieve by their own physical efforts. Babies placed in bouncy seats, car seats, jumpers, seated activity centers, and walkers are strapped in positions that they cannot hold for extended periods of time on their own. Moreover, these apparatus do not foster movement explorations that support self-initiated transitions through space. Under these conditions, spending extended time in such apparatus will affect a baby's free physical play.

When investigating the spatial aspect of a nonverbal assessment, it is necessary to differentiate between those spatial orientations a child can achieve self-assisted, and those that require a caregiver's assistance or supporting apparatus. It is particularly important to notice in which of the spatial orientations a child is most comfortable and able to maintain without assistance. For example, does an infant who often gazes at the world from the forward-tilted view of his car seat also enjoy the horizontal view when lying on his stomach—a position

A young child in a vertical stance seems to say, "I am ME! Look at ME! I am HERE!"

that requires him to push up with his arms to gain more perspective? The upright verticality of sitting and standing might enable another growing child to feel her presence and explore her surroundings from a broader visual outlook. Once she achieves this physical stance, however, how often and under what circumstances does she reorient back to the horizontal by crawling or lying down? Another question frequently appears once walking is achieved: Does a toddler predominantly use his forward movement to enter into the world and run around helter-skelter, or does he modulate his actions and carefully move through the room to investigate or stop and explore a new place, object, or person?

In other words, there are two general questions to ask when observing a child's spatial awareness:

1.   What spatial orientations predominate in the child's body and movement actions? For example, does the child prefer to sit upright and view the world from a vertical stance, or does the child prefer to explore through crawling (horizontal) or walking (sagittal)?

2.   What might motivate the child to maintain one spatial orientation over another? Factors to consider include the child's age, fine and gross motor skills, muscle tone, and general activity level, as well as internal, external, emotional, and previous experiential factors.

It is useful to determine which of the three Spatial categories—horizontal, vertical, or sagittal—is predominantly used by a particular child at a specific point in development. In making this determination of spatial preference, it is essential that an observer look beyond the child's physical skill level. For example, while it may be commonly expected that a 3-year-old who can walk will spend most of her time in the vertical and sagittal domains, close observation of a particular child may reveal that she avoids venturing out (sagittally) into her surroundings and chooses instead to engage in the world by standing or sitting in one spot.

This is the Spatial scenario presented by Darryl in the previous vignette. Darryl's most prominent spatial orientation is vertical. From this stance he observes his surroundings and reaches out cautiously, but he abruptly withdraws or freezes when engagement with others actually occurs. During his early dance movement psychotherapy work, he does not venture into the room freely, but instead chooses to

view the world from the confines of his kinesphere, where his movement involves shifting his weight from side to side or forward and back
rather than entering and reaching deeply into the opened general
space. The therapist wonders what factors motivate this cautionary
vertical stance, especially when close observation reveals that Darryl is
able to mobilize and coordinate his body through all three spatial orientations. The therapist asks about Darryl's early history and finds out
that during his first 3 months of life, Darryl resided in foster care with
a caregiver who did not believe in holding the children for fear they
would attach to her. This caregiver also did not believe in feeding the
foster babies more often than once every 4 hours because she didn't
want to spoil them. At 3 months, Darryl was placed with his adoptive
parents, who stayed with him in a hotel for several weeks before they
moved him from the warm South American climate to a cold North
American location in the middle of winter. As his parents and the therapist reflect on Darryl's history, they realize how many eating, sleeping, and relational issues he has encountered during his relatively
short life. Darryl's relative stillness takes on a new meaning, when
they consider his possible feelings of abandonment and safety. The
therapist knows that when a baby has so little regulation of his own
body during infancy, a primal way to assert control is by stillness. In
this manner the baby maintains control through vigilant withdrawal,
similar to the basic animal instinct of freezing in the face of danger.

Efforts

Efforts supply the feeling tone of a movement. Efforts are characterized by four motion factors—flow, space, weight, and time—that are
defined as the inner impulses from which movement originates
(Bartenieff, 1980; Laban, 1976; Maletic, 1987). These qualities create
the accent to the overall movement phrase. The particular combination of Efforts used in a series of actions is determined both by what
qualities are needed to perform the specific activity—considered the
physical aspect—and by the person's unique subjective movement
style—considered the mental aspect.

Each of the four motion factors—flow, space, weight, and time—
exists along its own spectrum and has its own distinctive correlating
attitude. According to Laban, it is these attitudinal qualities that provide information about a person's inner state of mind, although he
cautions that descriptive qualities of Effort elements are only indicators
rather than absolute defining descriptions. In other words, it is impor-

tant to regard interpretations as subjective guides and possible explanations rather than objective truths when trying to create a picture of how a particular child's movements depict her experiences. The true meaning of a person's style can emerge only when Efforts are studied within the context of the other elements of the complete movement event (Maletic, 1987). Continued observation and experience with children are required in order to provide a full perspective. While each of the Effort factors exist in all movements to some degree, everyone has a tendency to employ certain Efforts more often than others. It is these frequently used Efforts that contribute to a person's overall personal movement style that is known as the individual's movement signature, discussed in Chapter 3. Personal preferences, innate style, body type, and physical ability all contribute to a person's individual movement signature.

An example of individual differences in performing actions is often provided when an observer watches two children kicking a ball. One child may run toward the ball quickly with his legs and arms swinging helter-skelter. As the ball comes close, he makes an irregularly curved pathway in space as he kicks it; in contrast, another child may stand, lift her leg right under her, and swing it directly in line with the ball when it approaches. Both children are successful in kicking the ball, but they achieve this skill through very different techniques that tend to create differing images of each child as well.

A range exists within each Effort quality along the spectrum from diminished, to neutral, to clearly defined, to exaggerated. In an LMA-based analysis, a therapist notes not only how and what qualitative movement elements are predominately used but also whether a child has the ability to shift along the whole spectrum within each Effort. Moreover, a therapist should determine toward what range of qualities is a child's natural tendency. In analyzing the two children's different methods of kicking a ball, for example, the children each employ the Effort of space in different ways when swinging their legs. That the first child has not completely mastered spatial control of his limbs can be seen in his helter-skelter run. He uses diminished indirect spatial Effort to swing his leg from the side, but he successfully kicks the ball. In contrast, the second child uses clear directness, and she lifts her leg precisely to swing and kick.

No single Effort quality is superior to other Effort qualities. Certain Effort qualities, however, have affinities toward certain actions. For example, stroking a cat requires a child to use a light, sustained stroke because a strong quick action might cause the cat to startle and draw out his or her claws in defense. Similarly, a child on a swing will more likely be successful in flying high if she pumps her legs in a strong, direct manner rather than if she employs lightness and swings her legs haphazardly. Therefore, when observing the particular Efforts available in an individual child's repertoire, a therapist should look to see the range or lack of range of Efforts a child is able to employ in a given situation. In particular, a therapist should notice whether a child is able to adapt and adjust her Efforts to accommodate the needs of the situation, or whether her actions demonstrate a narrow, repetitive choice of qualities that are unlikely to succeed.

Physical ability, body structure, individual style, and personal comfort and preferences all contribute to how a person executes an action. Continuing with the cat scenario, the young child may not yet have acquired the right amount of lightness in her repertoire of Efforts to be able to gently stroke a cat. In contrast, the coordination and strength of the child in the swing, as well as her personal comfort level with assertive fast movements, all contribute to her success. In the therapeutic setting, a therapist should strive to help a child create a more balanced spectrum of Efforts to broaden her movement choices. Most often, a therapist should not take away a child's innate movement style but should instead supplement it by helping her learn better regulation and control over her movements. This develops a child's ability to relate and respond more appropriately to her environment. For example, finger-play songs that vary the strength and timing of how a child claps her hands and performs the gestures can become a therapeutic activity that improves her awareness and fine motor control skills. Similarly, a therapist can encourage a child's exploration of fast and strong movement qualities by creating a story dance that requires the child to move quickly with strong, stepping actions across a room.

Effort Attitude   In Laban movement analysis, Effort is also associated with specific feelings described as attitudes. These attitudes provide the emotional expressivity underlying the quality of an action and create psychosomatic sensations for both the person who moves and the observer (Maletic, 1987). Laban believed that all movement has an emotionally expressive element to it. The intent may be conscious or unconscious because the mover may not be aware and may not purposefully choose the attitudinal Effort quality within the movement. Moreover, the attitude is only one of many elements of nonverbal-movement analysis. A therapist must understand that the overall feeling tone of an action is reflected within the complex composition involving all the factors of the Laban-based analysis.

Flow Effort Flow is associated with a sense of *progression,* precision, and continuity. The term refers to *how* people maintain or interrupt the flux or normal continuation of their movements. Laban (1975) compares the flux of movement to a flowing stream that can move freely, be interrupted, or be stopped completely. The attitude associated with flow is characterized by movement along the spectrum of free to bound tension. All movements require a degree of muscular tension, and it is the quality of that tension that differentiates between free and bound flow. Movements performed with *free flow* have a care-free, alive, and fluid feeling. In contrast, *bound flow* actions create a sense of precision, resistance, restraint, control, and holding back, emanating the sense that the actions might stop at any moment. Again, neither a free nor bound quality is preferable to the other, and so a therapist must only look to see how a child's use of free or bound Effort supports the child's actions and emotions. For example, an observer would expect a 3-year-old to use extreme bound flow as he walks across a low balance beam for the first time. He may even request to hold his mother's hand as he goes across the beam. As he gains more skill and becomes more comfortable with crossing the beam, however, the extreme quality of his bound flow should diminish and be replaced by a moderate use of bound flow. Bound flow is necessary with this task to maintain control and exactness in body balance and foot placement. If the child continues to exhibit the extreme quality of bound flow, however, his body and movement attitude expresses a lack of comfort or adaptation to this task of crossing the balance beam. The picture of free flow is a child running down a hill with abandon; his movement effortlessly transforms into rolling should he fall. If that same child becomes fearful during that fall and tenses his muscles in an attempt to stop the roll, a sense of boundness will ensue. Mastery of both free and bound flow enables a controlled progression of attitudes from careful to carefree. On the other hand, a predominance of bound flow can portray caution, control, or severe tension at the extreme, while a predominance of free flow may exude the range from free abandon to excessive carelessness.

Space Effort The Effort attitude toward space is associated with the cognitive capacities of attention and thinking, orienting and organizing (Maletic, 1987). The mover's *attention* is revealed in how the qualities of space Effort are expressed. Space Effort determines the mover's intent about *where* the action takes her. The distinct movement qualities of space create a sense of the movement having either a *direct* spatial intent or a general *multifocused, indirect* quality. Space Effort is differentiated from the category of Space described at the beginning of the chapter. The LMA Space category describes how one's body and movements take up space and move through space. The three-dimensional properties of the physical body neccssitate that all bodies and movements must occur in space. Effortful space (space Effort) refers to the mover's exertion, attitude, attention or lack of attention t space. Spatial directness (direct space) creates an attitude that is single focused, specific, and pinpointing. The mover may get straight to her destination without distraction. A clearness and precision in the movement exists when directness supports the action. An indirect spatial focus (indirect space) references a more all-encompassing flexible attitude. Sweeping, scanning gestures and full body actions are created with an indirect spatial attitude. A person who moves with a flexible spatial demeanor appears to be gliding, circulating, and twisting throughout all levels of the surroundings (Laban & Lawrence, 1974). A child employs directness when attempting to get her father's attention by talking loudly, tugging on his pant's leg, looking straight up at him, and not stopping these actions despite being ignored. The child's actions make her intent clear that she wants his attention and is determined to bother her father until she gets it! On the other end of the space Effort spectrum, a child exhibits indirectness by sauntering across the playroom, observing everything but not focusing on any specific activity. The child may stop to examine a ball for a moment, but she may easily redirect her attention toward the sand table when she sees a red bucket and shovel out of the corner of her eye. Full development along the space Effort spectrum creates clarity in a child's alignment and execution of movements as she moves and relates to her environments. A natural tendency toward direct spatial Effort will emanate deep attention, focus, and concentration, whereas an exaggerated use of space will cause single-mindedness or inflexibility. Although a tendency toward indirectness encourages multitasking, an overemphasis of indirectness may create distraction, impeding a child's ability to pay attention.

Weight Effort The qualitative movement spectrum of weight includes strong, heavy movements on one end to light, limp movements on the other. The attitude of weight involves the assuming of a strong or light physical body *intention* when executing an action. The attitude of weight can be described as providing the *what* quality to a movement, for it reveals what level of body weight exertion is used to perform the action. The weight factor brings into awareness how a person is using body weight to affect the environment. The specific aspects of weight people employ during actions reflect how they sense themselves interacting with their surroundings. Mastery of this motion factor creates the feeling that people have clear body consciousness exhibited in their abilities to demonstrate responsive intent in the control of muscular engagement. The 3-year-old boy refusing to get dressed resorts to heavy weight Effort in his attempt to exert some control over his situation, whereas the 4-year-old girl who flits across the room deep in the fantasy of a dancing fairy demonstrates light weight Effort. As with all of the Efforts, the therapist should observe both a child's ability to shift along the whole spectrum and the child's natural tendencies. Some children exude an affinity toward a strong-weight Effort presence while others portray a light weight Effort. The therapist must determine whether children tread lightly or with strength in their approaches toward surroundings. A child with a balanced sense of weight Effort will demonstrate confidence with clear body boundaries, whereas a child who exerts great strength may fit along the spectrum anywhere from appearing imposing to appearing a bully. In contrast, a child with a tendency toward lightness may radiate a sensibility varying from gentleness to a total lack of presence.

Time Effort The movement qualities along a time spectrum range from sudden quickness to slow sustained movement. The attitude associated with time relates to *decision* making and *intuitive* readiness. The term *when* is associated with the Effort attitude of time, but it refers to a person's approach toward time rather than the actual duration, pace, or tempo it takes to execute the actions. A child performing along the quickness range proceeds with an urgent or driven attitude, whereas the actions of a child along the slow range may linger and lack a sense of urgency. Two people with opposing sensibilities toward time may share the same duration of time but create totally different atmospheres. For example, in the situation where a mother is rushing to put on her toddler's shoes and coat and get out the door while the toddler is resisting the end of playtime and is methodically trying to build his Lego car, the duration of time is the same, but mother and toddler's perceptions are very different. It is important to differentiate between slow motion, however, and the time Efforts of slowness and sustainment. When an action is performed in slow motion over an extended period, the focus is not on the time element but is instead on maintaining a smooth pace and even bound flow Efforts. In contrast, when an action is performed with the time Effort of sustainment, the attitude toward time is directed toward drawing it out while keeping an active awareness of it. Mastery of the time Effort creates a feeling of alertness, restlessness, and excitability along the quick-sudden end of the spectrum, or a feeling of calm, paused, and endless movement along the slow-sustained side of the continuum. A person who approaches with a predominance of quick and sudden Effort may appear efficient and decisive or rushed, harried, and careless if carried out to the extreme. A prevalence of slow to sustained Effort may create a sense of calm, thoroughness, and deliberate thoughtfulness, or if taken to excess, may create a sense of self-absorption and lack of connection or consideration of others.

Clustering Efforts The inner meaning of a person's intent is revealed by how Efforts are performed in combination; that is, by the specific ordering or sequencing of Efforts within the context of the entire movement event and the overall environment. Darryl's vignette is imbued with descriptions of Effort, and extracting these Efforts from the narrative crystallizes a better sense of the child.

Stillness – neutral to bound flow – floating – neutral/bound flow, mixed with extreme lightness – gently glide – shift his weight – shifting to lean – gently – floating – startled momentary quickness – still – leaning with his weight – stops a moment – frozen – lightly shifts – stops abruptly – tension – still – limply – hesitation.

Repeating these descriptive words over and over creates a picture of a child who treads lightly and cautiously in his surroundings. En route to engagement, Darryl appears to be held back by his own inner hesitations. He enters the world with trepidation, and the therapist wonders what is holding him back. Yet again, analysis of his Effort tendencies generates similar questions to those that appeared during the Spatial analysis. Might something in his early experiences have contributed to this extreme watchfulness, or is this caution genetically determined? Regardless of its origin, the therapist is determined to find a way that allows Darryl to experience more joyful and playful engagements in his life.

This image—created by the specific clustering of Efforts Darryl uses as he expresses himself through his body actions—adds the feeling tones to his movements and provides a more complex portrait of Darryl's experience. These words make Darryl's experience almost palpable, and they enable the reader to envision how it might feel to be Darryl. The words portray a child whose dominant Efforts use qualities within the spectrum of flow, weight, and time. Flow and weight are often combined during the active part of the movement phrase while the element of time punctuates the end of the sequence. Darryl uses time—mostly present through stillness—predominantly to stop the progression of his actions. This is an interesting way to use time because it arrests one of the salient characteristic qualities of flow in creating a sense of progression and aliveness. His prevalent use of bound flow assists his stillness, for bound flow exudes restraint and control and causes the actions to seem as if they could stop at any moment. Adding the weight Effort of lightness and limpness to flow makes his actions appear at times as if he is moving under a spell. The lack of clear spatial Effort awareness in Darryl's repertoire at this stage supports the dream-like quality of his actions. The therapist realizes that adding space Effort to his actions would produce a sense of precision and direction that is currently missing. Darryl seems unable to get where he is trying to go—it is as if he does not know how to express his emotional needs in a way that will enable him to receive the comforts necessary for growth.

The therapist's movement analysis considered his presenting symptoms of failure to thrive, including difficulties with sleeping, being soothed, and building a strong positive relationship with his adoptive parents. In the next section, Darryl's Effort actions are further illustrated as the therapist adds a body analysis to this unfolding image of Darryl's experience expressed in his nonverbal repertoire.

Body

The body is the vessel that generates all movement, feeling, and expression. These experiences are depicted in the specific ways that an individual chooses to move his or her body within the surroundings. *The Ways of Seeing* approach focuses on how a child moves, positions, and postures her body within the environment to communicate—this can be defined as the child's body attitudes regarding space. A therapist observes how a child's body attitude defines her personal space (kinesphere) within the general space. Such observations contribute to the developing pictures of a child by providing insight into how the movements of her body may be influencing her experience. Based on the LMA system, the *Ways of Seeing* approach has created four categories to organize body actions:

1. The limbs in relation to the torso

2. Specific body coordinations

3. Awareness of body actions

4. Overall sense of body actions

The Limbs in Relation to the Torso   Initially, a therapist observing a child should determine if her actions are performed using her body as a whole or if her movements are created with clear body-part differentiation. Is the child able to differentiate between her body parts? For example, when a baby rolls, does the action sequence separately through her shoulders, ribs, and hips, or does she roll over with her torso as one solid piece? The former description demonstrates successive movement sequencing through adjacent body parts while the latter uses the torso as one unit. Similarly, when a young child is sitting up during his first year, does he maintain stability by stretching his arms out wide and wiggling his fingers, or does he lean over, pushing his hands on the floor in front of him? These observations indicate whether the movement is initiated *distally*—at the end of the limbs, far away from center and torso as observed in the first description—or *proximally*—at the joints, close to the torso, or center, as in the second description.

Reviewing Darryl's vignette from this perspective, it appears that the initiation point of his actions do not seem to be as significant as how he moves his body as a whole. Darryl's movements often differentiate his body parts into large moving areas, with his limb and torso working as a unit. In sitting, there is an asymmetry in how he folds his left leg behind him and bends his right leg in front with his knee up. His erect spine and upper body stillness create a divide between his lower body and upper body. The bound flow of his upper body in comparison to the more active posturing of his lower body creates an image of disconnection between the two. This divide is further emphasized in the relationship of his left to right body side as he reaches with his right arm, leaning the right side of his body forward, while holding back with his left side and left arm. These descriptions of Darryl lead to the next category of body actions that analyzes body coordination.

Specific Body Coordinations Body coordination refers to the relationships that occur between different body parts as they work together to create an action. These coordinations relate to the movement developmental progressions described in Chapter 3 and were initially developed by Irmgard Bartenieff as the basis of a group of movement sequences known as the Bartenieff Fundamentals (Bartenieff, 1980). These coordinations are based on body structure and create inner support, integration, and balance during the execution of dynamic actions. The word *dynamic* is stressed to emphasize that this method is based on active movement rather than static positions and postures. Cohen (1997; Cohen & Mills, 1979; Eddy, 2005) placed these coordinations in developmental sequence to emphasize which body awarenesses are most explored at varying ages. All of these coordinations are explored at all times—this ordering only highlights their prevalence. The six coordinations are

- Breath flow
- Core–distal
- Head–tail
- Upper–lower
- Body-half
- Contralateral

Pattern of Breath Flow Breathing is the most primal rhythm of the body that supports all movement activities. Observing where and how the breath flows through the body provides information about body-part connectivity and movement fluidity. The intermittent stillness and overall bound flow of Darryl's torso, along with the stopping and starting quality of his actions, for example, create an image of shallow and constrained breath flow. Correct natural breathing involves a two-part sequence. When breath is inhaled, the body grows and expands; when breath is exhaled, the breath is emptied and the body releases, relaxes, and shrinks. This typically occurs as an ongoing flow: breathe in, breathe out, breathe in, breathe out. At times, however, the breath is held during some aspect of this sequence—it can be held between inhale and exhale or during inhale or exhale. Such breathholding in turn causes body parts to be held. Another common pattern of breath flow is where breath is shallow, seeming to barely exist at all or occurring only in the upper chest and collarbone area. These breathing patterns of behaviors are often exaggerated with heightened emotion. Movement flows best with fluid breath support. When a person's breath moves smoothly, it enables the person to experience subtle internal and external shape and relational changes as his or her head, limbs, and torso continually formulate new positions. This affects both how movement is produced and how it feels. Detecting breath-flow patterns when observing a child's body can provide a therapist with valuable information about areas of the body that may be contributing to the child's current state or lack of connectivity with the environment. In addition, adding breath-awareness activities to the movement interactions discussed in Chapter 8 can create a very simple yet profound way to relate to children and can greatly enhance their overall body and movement functioning.

Core–Distal Coordination   *Core* refers to the navel area, while *distal* refers to the six body parts: the head, the arms, the legs, and the tailbone (Cohen, 1997; Cohen & Mills 1979; Eddy, 2005). It is this coordination, which links the central core of a person's torso to his or her limbs, head, and tailbone, that enables a person to feel that his or her body is one connected whole made up of different parts. Such coordination provides differentiation and integration of the whole body as a dynamic moving system and kinesthetic awareness that body parts and limbs will not fly away or fall off! This sensibility develops early in utero and continues during an infant's wiggling, stretching, and contracting body explorations. These actions provide proprioceptive feedback that matures, stimulates, and teaches the neuromuscular system how to coordinate the body and its parts. It is this movement play occurring within a baby's kinesphere that enables her to develop a sense of her own body. The comfort and knowledge acquired through this play provides the psychophysical support needed for later mobilizations out into the larger world.

Core–distal connectivity is essential to efficiently and smoothly creating the more complex coordination that follows. The lack of effective core–distal relationships lies at the root of many of the issues encountered by children who are physically challenged. These "broken" connections may also correspond to places with breath-flow blockage. The therapist who creates movement experiences supported with breath awareness can help to awaken, energize, relax, or bring more relative connectivity to these areas, even in situations where the child's disability prohibits fully connected mobility. Regardless of needs, children who are comfortable with their core–distal coordination have a greater sense of inner movement fluidity and shaping within their bodies, creating the emotionally centered sensation of clearly feeling their bodies in their surroundings. Darryl's preference for asymmetry, noted especially in the use of his legs when sitting or crawling, stimulated the therapist to question how Darryl experienced his lower body in connection to his center.

Head–Tail Coordination   This coordination relates to the spine, with special emphasis placed on the two ends: the head and the tail-bone. A baby who develops a kinesthetic awareness of the length and flexibility of his spine within the relationship of his head to his tail-bone enjoys a dramatic advancement in mobility. This awareness greatly supports bending, rolling, spiraling, all three dimensional body shapes and actions, and the changes in levels of space necessary to mobilize from lying to sitting to standing. Cohen (1997; Eddy, 2005; Hackney, 2000) has suggested that a baby first becomes acquainted with this spinal awareness in utero as he yields and pushes his snug body against the uterine walls. Then, head–tail connectivity aids in the birthing process as the baby pushes and then reaches, leading with his head, to enter into the world. Once born, the baby continues this yielding, pushing, and reaching action as he squirms and presses to the top of his crib. Yielding enables the baby to feel his body weight as he connects and then releases the surface. This is followed by the push-ing against the surface that provides him with a feeling of his separate self against the surface. Through the push the baby learns to extend his head and neck, reaching out into the surrounding space. The baby then encounters weight bearing on the top of his spine as he learns how to lift up his head; he encounters weight bearing at the tailbone base of the spine as he kicks his legs and wriggles his pelvis. Slowly through such physical play the baby explores how the structure of his spine provides integrated support for his entire body. This discovery of the length of his spine provides the baby with a core sense of center from which he rolls, twists, and shifts his weight from left to right and from his upper to his lower body. This lengthening up along the spine, with the head perched on top and the tailbone providing weighted groundedness, creates a vertical presence and enables the baby to enjoy a new view of the world.

When observing this central-body coordination, a therapist should look to see how a child uses the spinal and head–tail rela-tionship for stability and flexibility. A therapist should also ask whether a child exudes a strong vertical presence complemented with a free bending and shaping of his environment or whether his vertical spinal stance acts as an anchor rooting the child to the ground. The latter description would fit if the child's pelvis-tailbone connection is prominent or seems to be floating him up to the sky—

a condition that is suggested where the child lacks a strong tailbone sense and instead demonstrates great fluidity through his head and upper spine. Darryl demonstrates a strong vertical presence, for example, but he lacks a sense of flexibility and free shaping (discussed in the next section) of his body with his environment. This preference for verticality without much bending and shaping makes him appear to be a perennial observer of his world rather than an eager and active participant.

Upper–Lower Coordination   Upper–lower coordination refers to how the head, arms, and chest of the upper body move as a unit in relation to the pelvis and legs of the lower body. Most often, movements in this body orientation work symmetrically. Drawing a baby up into a sitting position by pulling both of her outstretched arms is an example of a symmetrical upper-body activity. In this situation, the baby's lower body acts as the stable base that supports her upper body to bend forward. The child will later adapt and modify this activity when she rolls from her back to her side and uses both hands to push her upper body up to sitting, as her lower body weight shifts to complete the action. Alternatively, another example of a baby's upper-body stabilizing and her lower-body mobilizing occurs when she pushes or kicks her legs simultaneously while sliding along the floor on her back.

Another upper–lower coordination that is a precursor to crawling takes place when a baby on her stomach begins to rock her body forward and backward with her legs and arms up in the air in the "swimming" position. Upper–lower body coordination further develops during the yield, push, and reach patterns discussed in the head–tail connectivity above. This occurs when the baby, who is lying on her stomach, pushes up from the floor onto her forearms and lifts up her head. Cohen (Cohen, 1997; Eddy, 2005; Hackney, 2000) stated that these yielding and pushing patterns ground the baby's actions and enable her to begin to feel muscular power. In later development, as a baby experiments with movements such as crawling, frog jumping, and pulling up to standing, she will further mobilize her body out into the world when her reaching pattern is accompanied by pulling. Such reach-and-pull patterns enable a child to become goal oriented as she gains access out into her spatial surroundings, and the yield, push, reach, and pull patterns provide underlying support for all of the subsequent coordination patterns. In the vignette, for example, Darryl demonstrates upper to lower body coordination by his ability to dif-

ferentiate his two body halves, but this is not a prominent body posturing for him.

Body-Half Coordination This coordination involves the left
arm, leg, and side of the body moving together in relation to the
right arm, leg, and side of the body. A child's explorations in this
coordination enable the upper and lower parts of his body halves to
move in unison, thus stimulating kinesthetically and establishing
left-to-right sidedness. A child achieves balance when he shifts and
rolls all of his weight from his left side to his right side. This weight
shifting enables one side to act as the stable support so that the other
side can mobilize out into space. Movements that equally shift with
this left-to-right orientation balance the spine and integrate left and
right functionality.

Such body-half coordination is seen when a young baby pushes
his body as a unit to roll over, and then again during the early stages
of crawling. Lying on his stomach, the baby pushes with his forearm,
hand, flexed leg, and curled toes of one side onto a hard surface such
as the floor or wall and suddenly finds this side reaching, propelling
forward, and extending as the opposing side flexes. This same body-
half coordination underlies the wide stance of a newly upright toddler,
who progresses by waddling from side to side. Darryl appears particularly comfortable with his body-half coordination. He often seems to
enter his surroundings with the right side of his body while maintaining or withdrawing with his left side. This approach is also exemplified
when he sifts his body weight from left to right to extend his arms.

Contralateral Coordination This most complex coordination creates a diagonal relationship from one limb through the torso, in relation to the limb of the contrasting area of the body: left arm to right leg,
and right arm to left leg. True contralateral coordination develops a
sense of diagonal connectivity between the upper and lower quadrants
of the body, facilitated through an inner link passing through the central torso. This connection greatly facilitates the three-dimensionality
seen in the spirals, twists, diagonals, and the infinite number of other
shapes made by a body-in-motion. Three-dimensional movements
offer the most complexity and mobility and employ the whole range of
the kinesphere as a child shapes her body in space. In its simplest form,
a baby experiences contralateral coordination through her torso when
she is able to roll over by articulating through her torso rather than
rolling as one unit. In this diagonally connected action, for example,
the movement sequence begins as a baby lying on her back reaches her

left arm across her torso to her right side, pulls the left side of her ribs, then her left hip, and finally her left leg; a body-half connection occurs as the left side creates a diagonal in space and is supported by the contralateral connection made by the right leg that lengthens away to form a stable base.

Contralateral connectivity is most obviously seen in creeping—the anatomical term for crawling—as a baby reaches out with one arm, followed by her forward action of her opposing knee. The therapist can detect whether true contralateral connectivity exists by observing a baby engaged in this activity. Many variations of crawling observed in babies—including sliding one or both legs under the torso, hopping like a frog using both legs and arms together, moving the arms and legs in a body-half relationship, or almost sitting up dragging a leg under the torso and pulling and pushing with the arms—reveal the baby's lack of diagonal connectivity between limbs and torso. Fortunately, Darryl demonstrates some contralateral coordination when he twists at the waist to reach for the cat, and then again when he crawls toward his mother.

Awareness of Body Actions During this category of body analysis, a therapist begins to organize and think about the information gleaned from the first two categories. Once a therapist has determined a child's limb placement and movement in relation to the torso and has established the child's coordination, the next task is to analyze how this data can contribute to the whole picture of the child's experience. The therapist should question which of his body parts the child seems most aware, which of his body parts are the most used or active and which are the least used or inactive, which areas of his body are held with tension, and where on his body he initiates movement. The therapist should also consider whether the child's body parts are moved sequentially or simultaneously, whether they are individually articulated or moved as whole units, whether they are held and moved so as to create symmetry or asymmetry, and how weight is shifted through his body. By using such questions to guide the analysis, the therapist is able to develop a more complete image of a child's experience as reflected through his nonverbal style.

In analyzing Darryl's case, the therapist is most struck by the asymmetrical use of his limbs as he shifts his weight from side to side and forward and backward, thus entering and withdrawing from the therapist, his mother, and the cat. Darryl seems to move his body in units—arm and upper torso, leg and lower torso—creating a sense that an anchor holds him in his place in between his more active explorations. Lengthening up along his spine, Darryl seems stuck in his role as observer, and the therapist wonders if he consciously senses his strong verticality.

Overall Sense of Body Actions   This category describes the quality the actions create when viewed in their entirety. Questions arising from this category enable a therapist to summarize how a child uses her body because this category addresses the overall sense of body and movement integration. In assessing this category, a therapist looks to see whether the body movements create a sense of connectedness and fluidity or, in contrast, a sense of disconnection and restriction. A therapist questions whether or not there is a clear sense of energy and intention to the child's movements and whether the child's style induces a sense of mobility and propulsion or of stillness. This is the time for the therapist to wonder what it feels like to be this child and what might the child's actions reveal about her awareness and her relationships with others. Most important from a social perspective, the therapist should question whether the child's actions and body posturing support her to actively and emotionally participate with the people in her surroundings, or whether her body positioning and movement style separate her from social engagement and instead encourage her immersion into her own private world.

For many children, especially those with PDDs or communication disorders, these last questions are particularly significant. A therapist who pays attention to how and when children perform their signature movements receives clues to both emotional experience and sensitivities to the environment. In Darryl's case, for example, the therapist interprets his body actions as those of a child who has little body-part integration. His movements through space are sparse, and his actions are often interspersed with long stretches of stillness, punctuated by small, separate, body-part gestures. His asymmetrical use of his limbs produces an impression of a child simultaneously entering, holding back, and retreating from his surroundings. His most prominent body posturing is his verticality, which is especially noticeable when he sits and conveys the sense he is observing from afar. The therapist decides that this verticality, coupled with his propensity for stillness, indicates Darryl's reluctance to become engaged. The therapist thinks about how this physical lack of body-part integration may reflect or contribute to a similar emotional state.

Shape—Shape Flow, Shaping, and Directional Movements

The way people move and hold their bodies will create body shapes in space: spirals, arcing, or spoke-like action lines. People create a spiral through their spines when turning their heads to look at the back of their legs. People naturally arc their bodies to catch large beach balls. People who are pushing a child on a swing will make spoke-like actions in their upper bodies as they draw their arms from their chests, and then push their arms straight out to the child's back. These actions occur on a torso level when people create concave or convex shapes on their bodies or when they create a sense of flow by lengthening or shortening their torsos.

The Laban system has developed a specific category called *Shape* to represent the situations where a person's actions shape around and mold to objects or people, or a person gathers toward or pushes away objects or people in the surrounding space. This LMA category describes changing body shapes and forms in relation to oneself and the environment. A therapist should observe what body shapes a child makes and what internal or external factors may influence this shape as it is formed and changed throughout the movement experience. This category specifically addresses both how the child interacts within himself and how he interacts externally with the elements and people in his surrounding environment.

The three subcategories of Shape are shape flow, shaping, and directional movements. *Shape-flow actions* reflect body shape changes that are purely internally self-oriented because the external environment is not the focus of attention. A child is sensing his own internal changing body-part relationships with a conscious or unconscious focus on maintaining connection to his own body, even as it may be moving within the overall surroundings. Examples of shape-flow activity include the observable flow of breath within the torso or rippling actions through the body. A healthy use of shape flow exists in an infant who, while wrapped in his own movement exploration, twists and bends his arms and legs and sporadically sends them stretched out and away from center, followed by his recoiling them back toward the center. A shape-flow experience of more concern is a young child along the autistic spectrum whose movements around the room suddenly stop when he begins staring at his rippling fingers.

In *shaping actions*, the body movements shape, mold, or carve out space in relation to the environment. The body molds to the environment and changes shape to accommodate and interact with the surroundings. Shaping actions demonstrate a clear integration between oneself and one's surroundings, and they include such actions as the warm embrace. In another example, whereas a newborn tends to slide down his father's chest, as he grows and gains more body integrity, the older infant will be able to shape his body around his father's shoulder and stay perched high, with his head lifted so as to look around.

Directional actions create goal-oriented lines, cutting through space, that make clear connections between oneself and the environment. These movements link the internal intent of the action to something outside of self. One example of a *spoke-like* directional action is when a child pushes a heavy box by standing behind it, lifts his arms to chest height, and projects them forward against the box. An *arc-like* directional movement is created when a child extends his arm straight up above his head while holding a stick with colorful streamers at the end and then waves it by gliding his arms from side to side. A child's directional actions project clear lines of movement into space, thus defining his separate existence.

These terms were first defined by another Laban protégé, Warren Lamb (Lamb & Watson, 1979), and were adapted and elaborated on by Dr. Judith Kestenberg in her Kestenberg Movement profile (KMP), which she developed from watching young babies and mother–infant dyads (Eddy, 2005). The *Ways of Seeing* approach views these movement qualities as following a dynamic developmental progression. Although each individual quality is potentially present at each developmental age group, there seems to be an order of prevalence or more dominant acquisition during the early months, from shape flow, to shaping, to directional actions.

Shape Flow   Shape-flow actions seem to be the most prevalent quality dominating full body actions and body-part awareness during the earliest stages of infancy. These actions include the soft undulations and rippling actions of the full body and body parts and the mouthing actions commonly seen in a very young baby. Such actions seem to have several functions: First, they enable a baby to experience and exercise her newfound body, which no longer resides within the womb. This new body must adjust to a full array of sensory input, including gravity; a whole matrix of surfaces and textures, temperatures, sounds, smells and tastes; her own physical body and its complex functions; and the varying touching and holding styles of other people. Through shape-flow exploration, a baby begins to learn how to self-regulate this input in a very physical way, by moving and exploring and by focusing her attention for extending periods of time. Internally, this exploration includes learning about the inner workings of her body functions; externally, this exploration includes learning how to move. Babies are constantly reacting and responding to internal and external stimuli through shape-flow body awareness as they begin to process the world around them.

Embedded within shape-flow action is the human's most primal functional movement—breathing. The infinite variations in breath flow are an observable feature of self-regulation throughout the life cycle. Without conscious awareness, people hold, suppress, increase, or decrease their breath in response to environmental input. As infants breathe, they continually explore and adjust their breathing rhythms as they react to the interplay of internal and external input. An attentive therapist can contribute a great deal to assessment and treatment at all points of development. For example, a therapist should become aware of an infant's breath flow by noting her resting breath rhythm in comparison to how her breath adjusts during her state changes—whether she is excited, scared, tired, angry, alert, or focused. By holding a restless child and speaking to her in a soothing voice, the therapist can help the baby re-regulate to this stabilizing breath when she becomes agitated or difficult to soothe.

Through this process of shape-flow activity, an infant exercises her muscles and learns by experience how her muscles work. This includes experiencing the muscular strength it takes to work against gravity to create purposeful actions. The word *experience* emphasizes how a baby's way of knowing about her environment at this stage is through feeling, rather than conscious or cognitive knowing. As her muscles get exercised, an infant begins to function more effectively to build on her experience by relying on past experiences to support her new ones. This process relates both to the discussion in Chapter 2 about an infant's emerging sense of self (Stern, 1985) and to the discussion in Chapter 4 about the initial homeostasis stage of a child's development (Greenspan, 1992, 1996, 1997). An infant's playing with movement through shape-flow activities builds muscular integrity and contributes to the evolution of the self in a very literal sense.

Shape flow is a quality of movement that is accessible for all people at every age level. Shape-flow actions draw a person's focus inward, and often it feels as if these actions massage the body's connective tissues. Shape-flow actions can be very soothing and centering.

When people perform such actions for an extended period of time, they can enter into a deep inner space. Meditation techniques that focus on breath flow emphasize shape-flow awareness. For example, circling the head around the neck to get out a kink, shimmying the shoulder, or creating a rippling action down through the shoulders, rib cage and into the waist are all shape-flow actions. Shape-flow movements can be relaxing as well as sensual. Performing such actions alone can create a very personal space separate from others. This is the relaxing and centering function of shape-flow movements and can be extremely recuperative. Infants initially stay in this mode for extended lengths of time, while they focus both internally and externally. As they grow and extend their attention of the outside world, they often replace this movement quality with the others that are described below. Shifting into a shape-flow activity even momentarily can be recuperative, however, enabling infants and indeed people of all ages to reconnect to self, regroup, and then reengage with the world and activities outside of self.

If people limit themselves to shape-flow activities, they will not relate to others. Shape-flow movements can become self-stimulating actions and can develop into a way to self-regulate in order to avoid uncomfortable interactions. In contrast, if two people enter into shape-flow actions together, a condition without boundaries takes place, with each person experiencing a physical and emotional merging with the other. This is the root of sensual sensations. This phenomenon relates to Mahler, Pine, and Bergman's (1975) normal symbiotic attachment phase of development in which a baby experiences self and mother as sharing a common boundary. The mother–infant dyad's early nursing experiences are an excellent example of a merging shape-flow relationship: The baby's soft mouthing at the breast stimulates the mother to slow down and regulate her breathing pattern to match the sucking rhythm of the infant. In this satisfying interaction, the baby and mother are attuned to each other.

Shaping As the infant accumulates experiences through shape-flow actions, and begins strengthening his muscle tone, he develops a physical sense of integrity. He begins to develop shaping movements that enable him to mold himself to the environment. This is evident when the infant no longer immediately slides down when held on an adult's shoulder and instead uses a shaping movement that enables him to cuddle and snuggle. An infant needs a certain level of separate physical integrity to be able to mold and shape his body into another. This separation strengthens the infant's sense of differentiated self from other people although he is still able to relate to others. Once shaping actions are clearly established, the infant is able to adapt his body to his surroundings and to create body shapes that have muscular integrity. From early development onward, an infant experientially feels a clear sense of self as separate yet connected and relating to others through shaping actions.

Due to emotional and physical needs or differences, however, an infant may not develop clearly defined body-shaping actions. Physical and genetic disorders that affect muscular tone and strength may impede the infant's ability to move and hold his body with muscular integrity. Early emotional relationships that intrude upon, attempt to merge, or reject the infant's developing sense of a separate self can also interfere with his shaping explorations with the environment. A lack or loss of clear body boundaries can emerge from these environmental conditions, and the infant's resulting behaviors can be seen in his nonverbal body actions and postures that seem to melt into others and objects with which he comes into contact. As in the case of the young child who literally hangs or clings onto the arm or leg of another, such melting actions often involve a passive use of body weight. All of these actions are part of a normal movement repertoire; they should only be considered problematic if they are so prevalent that they dominate the child's movement style. When observing shaping actions, a therapist should also note the social, emotional, physical, and other environmental circumstances that might be influencing a child's actions and ponder how these might affect how the child is experiencing his surroundings at that moment.

Directional Movements   Directional actions are next along the dynamic progression that began with shape flow and shaping movements. Directional actions create a definite, defined sense of separateness between self and others. An infant's early sensations of autonomy and agency are literally and physically explored through these actions. Laban (1975, 1976) described actions with this quality as creating arcing and spoke-like lines in space. As soon as the musculatures become strong enough to make these actions, an infant sweeps and extends her limbs into the space around her. These actions enable the infant to reach purposefully out into the world, bringing things and people toward as well as pushing them away from herself. Although these actions most often encompass the limbs and torso, eye gaze can also possess directional qualities. Clear, focused eye contact is one way to create spoke-like directional movement. Moreover, it is arcing and circular eye actions that allow the eyes to gaze across the environment to gather visual information. When an infant does not have the physical capacity to move her body, eye gaze can provide another way to create connections between herself and others or surroundings.

It is important for the development of physical and emotional health that a child acquire each of these shape categories. Shape-flow actions enable a child's learning about the inner sensing self; shaping actions develop the child's ability to relate to self and other without losing personal integrity; finally, directional actions define the child's emotional and physical self as a clear presence, completely separate, but still an active participant in the surrounding environment.

In Darryl's situation, his movement repertoire most often displays directional actions that clearly separate him from his environment. These actions are prominent in the vignette, such as the times he becomes limp rather than shapes his body to his mother when she lifts and tries to hug him. The therapist considers how this movement propensity might be affecting or reflecting Darryl's difficulties in forming a secure attachment with his mother. The therapist also recognizes, however, that Darryl's prominent use of directional actions enables him to engage in his surroundings to a significant degree because he never becomes lost in inwardly directed shape-flow activities for extended periods of time. Deciding that Darryl's directional actions could be the starting point for developing his abilities to relate and connect with the significant people in his life, the therapist devises dance-play activities that transform movements beginning with directional actions into shaping actions that involve body-part touching. This enables Darryl to physically explore closer connections with others in a manner he finds nonthreatening.

Phrasing

As the body moves through space, its movements form sequences in time known as phrases. The manner in which the movements are sequenced reveals the root of the person's character—that is, his prevailing attitudes and his underlying drives. An individual's personal style of executing actions can be perceived in a general sense by noting his overall intensity and expansion of energy. Effort qualities provide the more specific descriptions of his movements.

The actual phases that define a complete phrase unit consist of the beginning action that serves as a preparation to the middle or main action, followed by the ending or recovery action. Mental and physical exertion and recuperation are inherent in both the preparatory and recovery aspects of the complete phrase, and this takes place by a person's selection of actions that complement or contrast with the main action. For example, a sprinter in a race will hold his body in sustainment with firm bound flow and direct Effortful attitude as he awaits the call to GO! These actions clearly shape his body in preparation for the activity to come. As he approaches the finish line, he will shift into acceleration and quickness by increasing his use of direct Effort as his limbs create clear arcing and spoke-like lines through space. Once crossing over the finish line, he will decelerate and eventually use shape-flow activity, shaking his arms and legs with free flow Effort, thus releasing the pent-up energy that mounted during the experience.

Recuperation is essential to enable a positive recharge of energy. This recharge is usually achieved by means of exertion rather than by an absence of movement altogether. There are different ways to achieve recovery, and short phrases of activity with repeated, frequent, resilient recoveries should function just as effectively as a long, single, continuous action phrase that includes a lengthy period of rest. The recovery phase of the former is achieved using the repetitive aspects of the recovery period, whereas recovery in the latter is provided by relaxation. Relaxation can be considered an active and necessary type of recovery because it enables a concentration in the neutral state of the Effort motion factors.

Actually, the beginning exertive and the ending recuperative qualities are the key factors designating the boundaries of the phrase unit. The length of a phrase does not always correlate with the number of phases in the sequence. A series of movements—such as a man's walking toward a counter, pausing to stabilize, followed by his reaching upward, then moving his arm back down and finally forward to place something on the counter in front of him—has four separate phases (that is, action – pause – action – action), but may be performed as one phrase. The simplest phrase contains two phases—exertion and recuperation—that may be symmetrical or asymmetrical, repetitive or unrepetitive. An even rocking action is an example of a symmetrical, repetitive action, whereas a slow, controlled body stretching followed by a quick body condensing and releasing is an example of an asymmetrical, un-repetitive, two-phasic phrase.

One phrase is composed of an infinite variety of patterns and ranges. An individual's movement style containing a diverse repertoire of movement phrases reflects vitality and freshness in his manner of responding and coping. In contrast, a person with only a limited range of movement phrase styles is revealed as having a more routine and predictable character. Notwithstanding, everyone has a few phrases that are more frequently used than others. These can be considered as the keynote phrases that best serve as the metaphors for their lives at the moment. For example, a person may often punctuate the end of his phrases with a strong push—in the air, on the table, or on the arm of the person to whom he is speaking. This push uses strength and direct Effort, with time Effort varying from quick to sustained. An observer might receive the sense that this person feels the need to constantly emphasize his point, leading the observer to wonder whether the person feels sufficiently "heard" in his life.

Children's preferred phrase timing may indicate their mode of mental and physical recovery. Consider a child with hyperactivity approaching the playroom with an abundance of quickness and tension. Her tendency to flit from one thing to another conveys the sense of her being rushed and her lack of true involvement with the toys or with the other children. Compare with her another child in the playroom who is displaying strong concentration skills by methodically building a Lego structure, using direct sustained Effort, intermittently pausing to search for just the right piece, and taking the time to chat with his neighboring playmates.

The types of transitions from one movement to the next within the phrase and between phrases also can indicate how an individual's movements fulfill his internal and external needs. The stop-and-start quality to Darryl's phrases, for example, reveals his hesitation to engage with his surroundings. Moreover, movement phrases that do not provide the individual with sufficient preparation and recovery will appear jerky and disconnected. Preparatory and recovery factors that overlap the action phrase might also shade the clarity and effectiveness of the movement. This often occurs when a child maintains one Effort factor throughout all of his phrases: An example of this would be a situation in which an exaggerated use of lightness produces a general vagueness to the phrases, while in another case, an overly emphasized use of strength could point to general inhibition (North, 1978, p. 27). In other words, the subtlest changes in Phrasing will affect the function and expressiveness of the movement phrase. The types of initiations, recuperations, transitions, timing, body or body-part use, and spatial and functional intent due to personal and environmental circumstances all play their roles in the Phrasing pattern being produced.

Based on North's (1978) and Maletic's (1987) descriptions of Phrasing types, the *Ways of Seeing* approach has delineated ten types of phrases, described next. The exertion of energy, observable by the Effort use that creates the accent and rhythm component of the phrase, is the most significant characteristic of each phrase type. Although an infinite number of combinations of actions and Efforts can make up a phrase, an example of a simple action and Effort description is provided to enable the reader to visualize each phrase type.

1. *Even:* The same level of energy is maintained steadily throughout the sequence, and no one area is accented or stressed more than another. The attitude created can range from calm, to detached control, to monotone uniformity (North, 1978). An example of even phrasing includes the action sequence of gliding (i.e., glide – glide – glide). Effort descriptions include: slow, light, indirect – slow, light, indirect – slow, light, indirect.

2. *Increasing:* The exertion of energy continually builds without a designated peak or accent. An example of increasing phrasing includes the action sequence: walk – walk a bit faster – still faster – fastest. Effort descriptions include: slow, direct, neutral flow – acceleration, direct, free – more acceleration, direct, slight bound – even more acceleration, direct, slight bound – quick, direct, slight bound – exaggerated quickness, direct, bound.

3. *Impactive:* The exertion of energy is maintained, or increases throughout, and ends with a distinct accent or peak. An example of impactive phrasing includes the action sequence: walk – walk – walk – jump! Effort descriptions include: direct – direct – direct – quick, strong!

4. *Decreasing:* The exertion of energy continually diminishes without a delineated area of accent. An example of decreasing phrasing includes the action sequence: run – run – a bit slower – even slower – slowest. Effort descriptions include: fast, direct, bound – decelerate, direct, bound – decelerate more, direct, decreased bound – slow, direct, neutral flow – exaggerated slowness, direct, neutral flow.

5. *Explosive:* The initial exertion of energy creates an accent followed by a maintenance or decrease in energy stress. An example of explosive phrasing includes the action sequence: jump! –

walk – walk – walk. Effort descriptions include: light, quick, direct! – decelerate, direct – slow, direct – slow, indirect.

6. *Increase–Decrease:* Energy builds and diminishes without peaks marking the transition. An example of increase–decrease phrasing includes the action sequence: walk – a bit faster – even faster – a bit slower – even slower. Effort descriptions include: slow – accelerate – increase acceleration – decelerate – slow.

7. *Swing:* The main exertion of energy is marked by a peak in the center of the sequence. An example of swing phrasing includes the action sequence: run – run – jump – run – run – run – jump – run – jump. Effort descriptions include: quick, indirect – quick, indirect – quick, direct, strong – quick, direct – quick, direct – quick, direct – quick, direct, strong – quick, direct – quick, direct, strong.

8. *Vibratory:* The exertion of energy creates an immediate pulsating series of repetitive similar actions that may decrease in emphasis as it continues. An example of vibratory phrasing includes the action sequence of a toddler's underarm ball throwing, followed by his arm bouncing against his leg, before his arm becomes still. Effort descriptions include: indirect, light, quick – free, light, decelerate – free, limp – free limp – stop.

9. *Resilient:* The initial exertion of energy is followed by a series of rebounding accents giving an effect of buoyancy and elasticity caused by the fluctuation between opposite effort dynamics with an emphasis toward one. An example of resilient phrasing includes the action sequence: jump! – bounce bounce – bounce. Effort descriptions include: direct, quick, strong – free, light – free, light.

10. *Accented:* The exertion of energy creates an intermittent series of stressed accents. (Effort combinations may fluctuate while maintaining one common Effort quality throughout.) An example of accented phrasing includes the action sequence: marching to the beat, hup – 2 – 3, hup – 2 – 3. Effort descriptions include: direct, strong – direct, diminished strength – direct, diminished strength – direct, strong – direct, diminished strength – direct, diminished strength.

Reviewing the vignette at the beginning of this chapter, visualize the lack of fluctuation of Effort as Darryl reaches his arm out into space with neutral/bound flow and extreme lightness (even phrase). Picture his arm dropping listlessly and landing with a slight pulsing before it comes to stop at his side (vibratory phrase). Envision his floating arm action and the lean of his body directed toward touching the cat, punctuated by his sudden recoiling away (impactive phrase). Sense the long pauses of absent activity. Darryl's Phrasing patterns, marked by Efforts of neutral to bound flow, gentle to light weight, stillness and sudden timing, create phrases that at times appear even, vibratory, and impactive. This particular arrangement of Efforts in these phrases creates a sense of detachment, for they lack the spontaneous dynamic variable adjustments that people usually make in reaction to environmental interactions. The repetitiveness of these Efforts and the scarcity of Effortful variation in his phrases do not create a sense of exertion and recuperation but instead add to his sense of detachment. The Effortful qualities that compose his sense of detachment add questions about Darryl's experience, leaving the therapist to wonder if his detachment actually belies a deeper sense of vigilance.

MOVEMENT METAPHOR

As these five LMA qualities (Space, Effort, Body, Shape, and Phrasing) unfold in a child, common themes will emerge. Personalized, stylized, nonverbal segments or sequences of movement that recur consistently within a child's movement repertoire are called *movement metaphors.* They often portray a specific attitude or expression, and so proper interpretation of these metaphors can reveal significant information about a child's experience. If a therapist successfully interprets these movement metaphors, they can become useful guides in planning interventions. But they are only guides—not absolutes. A therapist must be careful to avoid being so driven by a metaphoric interpretation that new information and insights about a child are being dismissed or ignored.

As previously mentioned, Darryl's most prominent movement metaphor is his strong vertical orientation, coupled with his tendency to physically engage his surroundings with his right side while holding back with his left side. This movement metaphor takes on increased significance as he suddenly stops, delays, and withdraws when confronted by the possibility of contact and increased engagement with others—including his mother. In the literature discussing attachment issues, this tendency to detach at the point of union has been identified as a sign of disorganized attachment (Main & Solomon, 1990).

The therapist's interpretation of Darryl's personal movement style is that he is a young child who is afraid of venturing into the world freely. The next task for the therapist is to create a playful environment that supports Darryl while also developing rapport with him, improving his relationship with his mother, and encouraging him to enter into his surroundings with less trepidation. Advice regarding how best to design a *Ways of Seeing* environment using the media of movement, nonverbal communication, dance, music, and body awareness techniques is provided in Chapters 8 and 9, but first Chapter 6 builds on the information just discussed to illuminate how to identify and find meaning in nonverbal expressions.

6

Nonverbal
Observation in Context

What you do speaks so loud that I cannot hear what you say.

R.W. Emerson (1803–1882)

Reading, responding, and reacting to nonverbal behaviors are part of everyday social interactions. Nonverbal behaviors are the underlying elements that act as the cuing system that provides the deeper meaning to words or actions. These behaviors are the information that people rely on when recognizing a friend or family member walking down the road in the midst of a crowd. One friend may cock his head in a particular way, whereas another friend lifts her right leg in comparison to her left in a way that catches the eye. Similarly, in the classroom, an observer can tell that it is naptime for 2-year-old Johnny because he is resistant to joining in with the boisterous play of his peers, preferring instead to lean his body passively against the bookshelf, with his head hanging over to the side.

These types of cues are so common that no one even thinks about their role in communication. People use nonverbal cues to determine their comfort levels with strangers and to evaluate another person's social savvy. Such cues include the distance separating two people who are standing across from each other during their conversation, the amount and length of eye contact, the absence or presence of touch and gesticulations used to support a person's words, and the rhythm and timing of words used to respond to or to interrupt another's conversation. These characteristics are the outline of nonverbal expression. They set up the structure of an individual's nonverbal behaviors and describe a person's nonverbal actions. The deeper interpretive meaning of these actions, however, is revealed in *how* they are performed. The answer to the "how" question provides the descriptive content to the actions, and it greatly contributes to both the feeling tone of the overall behavior and to the personal reactions of the observer. The primary focus of the nonverbal system used in the *Ways of Seeing* program is on this "how" aspect of nonverbal action.

FIVE CATEGORIES OF NONVERBAL DESCRIPTION

The *Ways of Seeing* approach divides nonverbal information into five categories:

1. General Nonverbal Descriptions
2. Nonverbal Intentional Acts
3. Physiologically Based Nonverbal Responses
4. LMA Descriptions
5. Potential Communicative Acts

These categories represent a hierarchy, beginning with the typical way of describing the quality of a nonverbal behavior and concluding with the more detailed way of describing a nonverbal behavior.

General Nonverbal Descriptions General nonverbal descriptions provide broad information about a person's actions without contributing very many qualitative details. These descriptions allow the observer to know only the most basic information about an action. An example of a general nonverbal description is the following:

~~~ *Nikki enters the room giggling and immediately lies on the floor. I ask her if she would like to crawl as she looks at me and claps her hands. I help Nikki roll from her back to her belly and support her hips as she pushes up to her hands and knees. She keeps pushing her hands until she is up on her knees.* ~~~

This description relates that Nikki, a child with Rett syndrome, lies down, looks at the therapist, rolls over, and is assisted onto her hands and knees. The outline of her movement actions are reported, but not much is told about Nikki's affect or attitude during the event, so it is difficult to visualize exactly how the actions are performed.

Nonverbal Intentional Acts The *Ways of Seeing* approach derives its concept of nonverbal intentional acts from the term *intentional* *communicative acts,* defined by Wetherby et al. (1988) as the gestural and vocal communications that are specifically performed with the goal of communicating. Gestures—the main nonverbal actions studied by Wetherby and colleagues—are regarded as the nonverbal means of communication in the service of, or taking the role of a precursor and support for, vocalizing and verbalizing. These nonverbal communications are most predominant in prelinguistic and one-word stages of communication. Most early childhood researchers in the fields of language acquisition and social-emotional development have limited their studies of nonverbal communications to actions and gestures that have known communicative implications. These actions and gestures include the presence or absence of eye contact, head nods, smiles, and finger pointing. A young child's ability to perform such acts indicates an important step in prelinguistic development, demonstrating the child's understanding that gestures have meaning and can be used to communicate. In the passage below, the nonverbal intentional acts that have been added to the previous description are indicated by bold font:

Nikki enters the room giggling and immediately lies on the floor. I ask her if she would like to crawl as she looks at me and claps her hands **with momentary eye contact, nodding her head as she looks away.** *I help Nikki roll from her back to her belly and support her hips as she pushes up to her hands and knees. She keeps pushing her hands until she is up on her knees,* **looking at me again fleetingly, and smiles.**

This addition of nonverbal gestural descriptions provides a few more clues to Nikki's state. It is now clear that Nikki is able to create a social connection through her eyes and smile. The words *momentary* and *fleetingly* imply that these gestures cannot be sustained, so the observer must be on the lookout for them. A bit more information has enhanced the possible visualization of this scenario, but there are still not enough details to completely comprehend the depth of the scene.

Physiologically Based Nonverbal Responses   Physiologically based nonverbal responses are also prominent in infancy research. Biobehavioral research has investigated how neural regulation of the autonomic nervous system may influence physical and psychiatric disorders (Porges, 1993, 2002, 2004). Based on the assumption that the regulation of the physiological system is embedded in early emotional relationships (Hofer, 1981, 1995), researchers have looked at physiological reactions to provide additional physically based nonverbal methods to determining an infant's experience. For example, Gunnar and her colleagues (Gunnar, 1980; Gunnar, Brodersen, Krueger, & Rigatuso, 1996) have studied the adrenocortical activity of infants and toddlers during stress-producing situations to determine how changes in this activity may relate to a young child's reactions and experiences. Lipsitt (1976) has studied physiologically based nonverbal responses in infants to track emotional responses—known as *psychophysiological responses*. His focus included heart-rate reactions, biological and culturally based differences and influences, a critical analysis of genetic determinants on development, the role of reflexes as precursors for such behaviors as the smile and sucking, and a discussion of the anger response observable by noting the intensity of autonomic and withdrawal responses to unpleasant stimulation.

Taking a position comparable to Lipsitt's regarding nonverbal communication, Brazelton and Cramer (1990) emphasized the neuromotor and psychophysiological characteristics necessary for nonverbal communication. They suggested that nonverbal communications require a level of internal regulation and homeostasis on the infant's part in order to develop the skills for effective nonverbal communication. These include the infant's ability to maintain an alert state by prolonging attention to affective and cognitive cues of others without getting overwhelmed by such stimuli. In the passage below, the physiologically based nonverbal responses are indicated by bold font:

⁓ *Nikki enters the room giggling and immediately lies on the floor. I ask her if she would like to crawl as she looks at me and claps her hands with momentary eye contact, nodding her head as she looks away.* **Her breathing becomes shallow as she begins to hyperventilate and then holds her breath as I approach. I place my hands on her chest to tactilely facilitate slowing and deepening her breath, and I feel her heart beating more rapidly. We breathe together, and gradually, her breath rhythm slows down.** *I help Nikki roll from her back to her belly and support her hips as she pushes up to her hands and knees. She keeps pushing her hands until she is up on her knees, looks at me again fleetingly, and smiles.* ⁓

This description reveals that the therapist can recognize how reactive Nikki's autonomic bodily responses are to her environment and can imagine how this experience might feel for her. This knowledge will be very useful to the therapist in thinking about ways to introduce new experiences to the young child. Because Nikki's physiological reactions can interfere with her ability to concentrate and interact with her environment, care must be taken to help her settle and calm her internal system before or during activities of engagement. A more detailed picture of Nikki's experience is now forming; however, there are still qualitative aspects of the event that cannot be ascertained.

LMA Descriptions   As has been discussed throughout this book, the LMA system provides an observer with detailed descriptions of nonverbal actions by supplying qualitative information. This information characterizes not only what the nonverbal actions are but also how they are performed. The "how" aspect of the action enables an observer to derive information about the feeling tones, emotions, and nature of the person who is acting and interacting. As Chapter 5 illustrates in depth, such qualities include the body parts performing the actions, the attributes of the movement exertion, the shape and spatial patterns of the actions, and the form the actions take as they are phrased together. Including this specific type of qualitative information in the descriptions reveals the specific elements that influence the nature of interpersonal interactions; such information is especially helpful when looking at a dyadic relationship.

A great deal of interest has been directed toward the factors that affect and demonstrate the early bonding relationship occurring in infancy, most notably between the mother–child dyad. As Brazelton (1974) noted, however, this literature has lacked qualitative descriptions. In regard to his own mother–infant research, Brazelton stated that the descriptive form and affective significance of the action—such as the quality and tempo of the behavior and spatial relationships within the dyad—cannot be revisualized by his detailed analysis (1974, p. 53). Such information about the therapist–child relationship can be provided by adding an LMA description to the previous vignette as indicated by bold font.

     Nikki enters the room giggling. **Both of her shoulders are lifted high, her arms are close to her sides and her elbows are bent as she claps her hands with a quick tense pulsing, creating a vibratory phrase. This pulsing clap increases as she sweepingly casts her gaze at me using indirectness. I clasp her hands, squeezing them with a strong sustained hold, and this time she looks me directly in the eye as she releases her body into passive weight and immediately sinks to the floor, lying on her back.** *I ask her if she would like to crawl as she* *looks at me with momentary* **direct** *eye contact and claps her hands* **again with that quick tense pulsing.** *She nods her head as she looks away* **with indirectness.** *Her breathing becomes shallow as she begins to hyperventilate and then holds her breath as I approach. I place my hands on her chest.* **I use strength, free flow, and sustainment in the quality of my touch** *to tactilely facilitate slowing and deepening her breath. I feel her heart beating more rapidly. We breathe together, and gradually her breathing rhythm slows down,* **creating a short, swinging phrase as she alternates between her inhale and exhale. By diagonally crossing her left shoulder and arm across her body holding her arm with strength and sustainment,** *I help Nikki roll from her back to her belly. I then support her hips* **with the same strong, sustained touch** *as she pushes up to her hands and knees. She keeps pushing her hands against the floor,* **adding more strength and sustainment, turning her vibratory phrasing into an accented phrasing rhythm. This added strength and the use of sustained timing enable her to** *push up on her knees.* **She lengthens her body vertically up along her spine** *as she looks at me again fleetingly and smiles.* ⌇

From this description, an image of the specific elements that foster this therapist–child relationship begin to emerge. Because of the detailed descriptions of Nikki's body posture, it is immediately evident that from the moment Nikki enters the room, the therapist is registering Nikki's emotional body state and is using this information to influence how she begins her interaction with Nikki. The therapist is particularly mindful to use the quality of her touch to attune to Nikki and to successfully draw her attention. Nikki's engagement with the therapist is shown by her direct eye contact and her release into passive weight. In this instance, creating passivity in her body implies trust, because without the support of the therapist's hand holding, Nikki would fall to the floor. Sharing touch and other similar and complementary movement qualities throughout this scene create an image of a therapist–child interaction imbued with reciprocity and dialogue. True relating is going on with barely a word spoken.

This description is filled with formal LMA terms: *direct, indirect, vibratory Phrasing, accented Phrasing, strength, free flow, sustainment,* and *passive weight.* This specific qualitative movement terminology is used to demonstrate the details provided by an LMA description. (The definitions for these terms are explained in Chapter 5 and many are also provided in the Glossary.) Learning to use these exact terms within an LMA orientation takes extensive training; but once correctly understood, these terms act as a shortcut, providing extensive descriptive information about the quality of a person's actions. They are included in this book in order to introduce a non-Laban-trained practitioner to new ways to observe and to a greater awareness of the nonverbal aspects of movement exchanges. Certainly, the LMA observational system greatly influences how this author perceives and engages with children during interactions and interventions.

Specific LMA terms do not have to be used, of course, to add an additional dimension of observational awareness to a therapist's understandings and descriptions of young children and dyadic relationships. Indeed, the vignettes sprinkled throughout this book are sufficient to provide readers with examples of ways to add more in-depth, qualitative descriptions to observations. In addition, the LMA terminology that is used has been modified in these descriptions to demonstrate how the qualitative perspective of LMA-oriented observation can enrich therapists' understandings and can facilitate their interactions with the children and families with whom they work.

Potential Communicative Acts   This category of actions, potential communicative acts, is broader than the common child-development concept that focuses on nonverbal intentional acts such as head nodding and pointing (Stern, 1985; Brazelton, 1974; Wetherby et al., 1988). These types of acts require a certain degree of self-regulation on the part of a child, who is thought to execute the actions with the expectation of response from the other participant. In contrast, the *Ways of Seeing* approach regards all actions as having the potential to be communicative and, therefore, pays attention to the qualitative aspects of nonverbal expression that provide valuable information about a child's intent. When emphasis is put on the qualitative aspects of the nonverbal actions, their communicative potential is heightened.

The qualitative LMA-based description allows an observer to attempt to interpret and understand Nikki's actions. In accordance with the LMA method, initial observations strive to provide clear pictorial descriptions of actions, separating potentially subjective interpretations from movement-oriented descriptions. Only after a perceptible image of the actions is defined can interpretation begin. The next step is to view the communicative potential hidden within these objective images to create a relationship.

Regarding all actions as having the potential to be communicative builds on the objective LMA-based observations. It enables a therapist to use the information gleaned from the detailed description to establish a place of connection with even the most uncommunicative child. Moreover, it enables the therapist–child dyad to create a common ground for initial contact, without the need for the level of cognitive processing required by verbalizations. In the story above, Nikki's upper body posturing, rapid hand clapping, and sweeping gaze as she enters the room communicate excitement and tension. She is perusing her surroundings but is not focused. The therapist takes these actions as a starting point for connecting. She meets these qualities with complementary ones— strength and sustainment—as she clasps Nikki's hands. Nikki's eagerness to respond is evident as their eyes engage. Through their touch, a sense of knowingness and familiarity transpires as Nikki gives herself to the therapist by releasing her weight and letting the therapist guide her to the floor. As Nikki and the therapist work together to calm the child's breathing, her compliance continues. Although hyperventilating is a common characteristic of Nikki's condition, Nikki's response to the therapist's firm fluid touch by slowing and softening her breath demonstrates both her ability to relate to the therapist and her own growing body awareness. This continues as she allows and supports the therapist by releasing the tension in her joints, enabling the therapist to roll her over to assume a crawling position.

Although Nikki usually communicates resistance by making her body very heavy or tense, preventing the free joint rotation necessary to support her to mobilize her body parts sequentially, during the vignette she communicates a desire to be helped through the quality of her body actions. The therapist's response in turn is to demonstrate her own support of Nikki's explorations as she provides time for the child to push up to her knees rather than insisting that she directly proceed into a crawling action. It is important to note that some of Nikki's physical restrictions and resistance are not solely caused by free will but rather by how her body and musculature work due to Rett syndrome. Nikki's ability to release her joint restrictions demonstrates the depth of "listening" and relating she and the therapist have created as they have worked together to discover how to facilitate a lessening of her tension.

Nonverbal Behaviors as Communication in the *Ways of Seeing* Approach

Nikki is able to maintain social engagement through the quality of her nonverbal actions. It is from such experiences that the *Ways of Seeing* concept that all actions have the potential to be communicative has evolved. This concept that nonverbal behaviors are a form of communication emphasizes the important role that the *Ways of Seeing* approach can play in communication development alongside the traditional social-emotional focus. A key aspect of the *Ways of Seeing* approach is communication: Nonverbally based communicative interchanges are considered self-expression, and they become the building blocks for the improvement and acquisition of communication and the development of social-emotional relationships.

This concept expands the more common, limited definition of nonverbal communicative actions. The essential criteria in a traditional definition consist of a relatively advanced degree of physical control and bodily regulation, as well as communicative and cognitive skills that require some degree of symbolic understanding. Broadening this traditional definition by accepting nonverbal actions as potential communications facilitates a child who has issues in communicating to begin to experience more successful relating.

Moreover, creating dialogue on this sensorimotor level supports the subsymbolic and presymbolic levels of communication described in Chapter 2. Learning how to read a young child's nonverbal cues, especially when the cues initially may be difficult to decipher, can greatly enhance the developing parent–child relationship. As the research cited in Chapter 2 discusses, the development of attachment is greatly influenced by both members' inputs and their abilities to accurately read the cues of the other. Creating repeated experiences in which a child is able to feel consistent patterns of response enables her to remember and generalize these experiences as meaningful interactions. Helping a child to feel that her actions communicate is the first step toward developing her sense of efficacy, which should support an eagerness to attempt further communication. This in turn supports the development of a strong, trusting relationship known as a *secure attachment* (Ainsworth, 1978) in the field of psychology, a concept that is discussed in more depth in Chapters 2 and 10. Patterns of interaction become established as they are put to practice during additional interactional experiences, continually expanding the child's social world.

The conversation below with Pepper, Nikki's caregiver and classroom teacher's aide, highlights the significance of nonverbal expression in the *Ways of Seeing* approach by discussing how Nikki has come to use nonverbal expressions in other aspects of her life.

Pepper: You can see as soon as she walks in that she's talking to you through her body. She's got that whole little head thing going. She shakes her head "no" and "yes" to show what she wants. She can give you the expression to let you know that she's excited when she lets her hands out, or she can let you know if she's scared. I mean it just brings it out. You can just see when she moves to the music that she lets you know what music she doesn't like; she lets you know. . . . And it works, you know the way she looks at people now, in the kindergarten class, she gives them that look . . . "I like your eyes!" That's what I feel like she's saying. "Hey, I like that shirt you have on!" I think she's saying stuff like that. . . . I see this different side [in dance movement therapy] in her and there are always little changes that happen throughout it, which is great. And you don't see that in ABA [applied behavioral analysis] and PT [physical therapy], and OT [occupational therapy]. You might see her do something now, but you just don't see the eye contact and the real expression of what she's feeling. You really don't. You get more of a vague kind of "I'm tuning out because I really don't want to do any more; I don't want to do what you're asking; this is too much" [in those other therapies].

Q: So are you saying because I work so much with her nonverbal cues that she's giving me a lot more nonverbal cues?

Pepper: Oh, yeah!

Q: Because I respond so much to those cues, she keeps using them more, and you're seeing that she's even using them in her school setting.

Pepper: Oh, yeah, definitely, definitely.

Q: But in the other therapies, because they are not looking for that, she may not try to be as expressive?

Pepper: Yes, definitely . . . . You know it's great to see another side of expression in her. That's what you wait for. You almost wish that she could speak, but then that's Nikki, that's who she is . . . that's how she expresses herself. . . . It's exciting when she does a new expression. It's like a regular 6-year-old learning a new word.

This dialogue with Pepper emphasizes that in dance movement psychotherapy sessions, Nikki's nonverbal expressions are regarded as effective a form of conversation as verbalizing. For a child with limited or no verbal skills, this is a lifeline that creates a link between her feelings and her relationships with others. This is also an effective technique for a young child who is first learning how to use verbal skills to support and express inner feelings. Nonverbal-movement exchanges can be supplemented with verbal dialogue to help this young child associate the relationship between internal experiences and personal movement expressions. When a therapist or any adult takes the time to read and respond to a child's nonverbal cues, it creates an emotional feeling of being known, being seen, and being understood by another.

The Benefits of Facilitating Nonverbal Expressions that Support Communication

Creating an environment that promotes a child's nonverbal expressions—especially if the child has issues with communicating and relating—necessitates a different initial structure to the therapeutic setting. Table 6.1 provides a list of strategies to create an environment that transforms nonverbal actions into communications. The main focus of each *Ways of Seeing* session is having a conversation through a movement dialogue—watching and listening to a child's nonverbal actions to glean information about the child—just as if the words were being used to converse. The moment-to-moment nonverbal expressions and

Table 6.1. Strategies to create an environment that transforms nonverbal actions into communications

1. Watch and "listen" to a child's nonverbal actions to obtain information about the child.
2. Be ready to adjust the environment to facilitate a child's optimal participation and interpersonal engagement.
3. Follow a child's lead.
4. Create conversation through movement dialogue.
5. Allow moment-to-moment nonverbal expressions and behaviors to guide how a session unfolds.
6. Act as a "container," receiving, holding, and trying on a child's behaviors.
7. Before redirecting or inhibiting a child's nonverbal action, consider what the action is communicating: What may it be saying? What feeling may the child be experiencing through this action? What can you do with your actions to enhance the communicative potential of the child's nonverbal behavior?
8. Be ready to abandon your goals for a session to assist a child in becoming more self-aware and self-controlled in the moment.

behaviors guide how each session unfolds. The therapist must rely on reading a child's nonverbal cues to create and adjust the environment to facilitate the child's optimum engagement with the surroundings.

The natural interactive nature emphasized in the *Ways of Seeing* environment plays a key role in a child's successful participation. The impromptu atmosphere, which is guided by following a child's lead, acts as a container that supports the child's current state as evidenced by movement expressions. In Nikki's example, the *Ways of Seeing* session unfolds as she experiences her nonverbal behaviors being carefully watched, commented on, and tried on by both the therapist and her mother. Their supporting of Nikki's nonverbal expressions through movement and verbal dialogue perks up the child's interest, often heightening her curiosity and enjoyment. This encourages further social-emotional relating and communication. Karen, Nikki's mom, emphasizes this in the following conversation:

Karen: She's happy! She loves coming here! She looks forward to it! She gets to be herself and tries to be a healthier self when she's here. She works herself to get rid of her quirky behaviors. She's so proud of herself that she can do it here.

She gets to come in and show you who she is at that moment. High energy—tired—she can be who she is—that stands out the most. . . . I always walk away learning something, either about her, or the way I should work with her. I really get to watch her here—she knows.

You don't have an obvious agenda. When we come in, you are working with whatever mood Nikki is in. When other therapists come into my house, it doesn't matter what mood Nikki is in—they have an agenda. They are going to work with what they are working on. . . . I used to go down there . . . to learn what they were doing to be able to integrate into my own work with Nikki . . . but I find I am watching them less and less.

Q: So you are saying that in our sessions you can be here with Nikki.

Karen: Yes, and I am enjoying what I see . . . even if Nikki, there are times when she comes in here and she is not performing or responding the way I would like her to, but it evolves. There is always something she has gotten out of it—where she found her place somehow, or she calmed down, or is in a happier state in her own self. You know, maybe one of the greater goals wasn't worked on that day, but something else was. I think that other therapies don't evolve as much as they do in this room.

The *Ways of Seeing* environment, which encourages Nikki's non-verbal self-expression, also appears to positively influence Karen's ability to connect emotionally to her daughter. Experiencing her daughter's enjoyment is contagious! Using Nikki's nonverbal expressions to guide the session enables these behaviors to evolve into meaningful interactions, rather than actions that must be inhibited or redirected into more purposeful actions. Nikki's caregiver also emphasizes her appreciation of the discoveries that occur during each dance movement psychotherapy session.

Pepper: With dance therapy, [you are] focusing on what she's all about . . . she's going in to see you, and you see what kind of balance, what kind of mood she's in, what you can work from at that point. What you can salvage from her day. You get different things out of her every day. That's fascinating.

Both Karen and Pepper's comments reveal how much they have learned from the *Ways of Seeing* approach that focuses on seeing nonverbal behaviors as potential expressions. They have come to rely on Nikki's nonverbal expressions to understand her. Her nonverbal cues play a significant role in how they communicate with her. Obtaining this level of communicative understanding from nonverbal actions requires an observer to develop a new way to look at behavior. The five points below outline the preliminary steps a therapist must take down this road.

Key Points to Keep in Mind
When Reading Nonverbal Cues

Therapists must keep several factors in mind in order to adjust their focus to see nonverbal actions as potential communications.

Point 1: A dictionary type of fixed interpretation
should not be used to understand nonverbal actions.

Although universal actions and gestures do exist within a culture—such as a wave to say hi or goodbye—the *Ways of Seeing* approach does *not* advocate a dictionary approach that provides a fixed interpretive definition for every nonverbal behavior. Never look at an action and assume meaning without looking at how a child's personal style of performing the action may be contributing to the action's overall sensation and intention. The word *seeing* in *Ways of Seeing* is derived from an observer's keen awareness of a child's unique idiosyncratic way of performing even the most common nonverbal action. This is the point in which the quality of the action comes into play in providing the personal meaning of every movement. For example, a baby may have a smile on her face as an adult approaches her, although her head may be leaning back away from the adult and her hands may be clenched tightly. Assuming that the baby's smile indicates pleasure may cause an observer to ignore the subtle retreat revealed by the position of the head and the clutching of the fists. Look at the meaning of the movement for a particular child. Avoid making assumptions.

Point 2: No nonverbal action or quality is good or bad in and of itself.

No nonverbal action or quality of movement is, in and of itself, either good or bad. All movement behaviors must be analyzed with consideration of the context in which they occur. Reserving judgment greatly contributes to the understanding of the deeper meaning of an action. Deciphering the specific characteristics and reasons why a child is using a certain movement quality and action in the immediate setting reveals the child's experience and provides insights that can help a therapist's continued interactions. An example of this is a toddler who does not make good eye contact, has a very active movement style, and seems unable to quiet or still his body. These characteristics may cause a therapist to believe that the child is not paying attention. Close analysis of the child's movement path may reveal, however, that despite these behavioral characteristics, the child continually circles near the therapist whenever the latter is speaking. This reveals that the child is demonstrating some degree of attention that can provide a "way in" for the therapist. When the child comes close, the therapist can bend down to the child's level, catch his eye for a moment, and give firm sensory input by squeezing the child's hands and saying "Oh! I see you're listening!" If the child can stay attentive, the therapist might add, "It's just hard for you to slow your body down. I'll help you with that." This can become a game of making contact and letting go, progressively increasing the moments of contact as the movement game develops. The therapist's actions and words convey an understanding of the young child's experience while simultaneously offering an additional experience that models and teaches the child a new way to gain control over and find stillness in his body.

Point 3: Determine if the nonverbal
behaviors are motivated by a need to satisfy a sensory-
related reaction, a social or emotional drive, or all of the above.

Think about other internal factors that may be influencing a child's behaviors. Are a child's nonverbal behaviors motivated by a need to satisfy a sensory-related reaction, a social or emotional drive, or both? In the previous example, the toddler may be unable to make eye contact due to a visual sensitivity. His predominantly mobile body actions may be caused by an innate inability to modulate motor activity. This could be creating a fearful, fright-and-flight type of emotional reaction. Thus, the behaviors have a sensory-based cause that is affecting his emotional experience.

An alternate explanation could be emotionally based. In this scenario, the toddler's avoidant and distracted actions could be due to unpleasant or traumatic past experiences in which a significant adult has demonstrated volatile behavior toward or in the presence of the child. The child's movements may be depicting an inner emotional vigilance. Determining which interpretation is accurate is paramount because it will dramatically affect how the movement game continues to unfold: If the sensory-related interpretation is accurate, the therapist may focus on providing more sensory input, extending the length of physical contact and guiding the child toward increased physical calmness. In contrast, if the cause of the toddler's behavior is emotionally based, the therapist will need to pay close attention to his or her own personal presence when the child is near to present a peaceful, safe container for the child. Under these circumstances, the emphasis of the intervention may be to support the child's ability to move away from an adult when uncomfortable and to stay close when he is feeling safe. When close, the therapist can help the child relax his body. Holding the child's hands may not be wise, and the therapist instead should use verbalizations, imagery, simultaneous breathing, or quiet play with toys to best facilitate obtaining the child's internal body tranquility.

Point 4: Determine if body actions, vocalizations, verbalizations, or a
combination of all of these elements are influencing perceptions of the behavior.

When observing a child's behaviors, determine which of the child's communication systems is being used to glean information. Body actions, vocalizations, and verbalizations are all sources of communication that may be unconsciously influencing one's sense of a child. It is often useful to videotape a child and then view the tape both with and without the volume. This exercise should help determine which aspects of behavior are contributing to one's understanding and impressions of a child.

> *Point 5: Notice if a prominent nonverbal body action occurs facially, gesturally, posturally, or as a combination of all of these expressive modes.*

Notice which feature of a child's moving body attracts special attention. Is this feature occurring facially, gesturally, posturally, or is it a combination of all of these expressive modes? The distinction is important because each of these nonverbal forms articulates feelings in very different ways. Although facial movement may be the form of expression most often cited to decipher feelings, an observer is also influenced by full body actions and gestures. A *gesture* is defined as an action that is contained within a specific body part—such as a fling of a hand, the nod of a head, or the shrug of a shoulder. In a *postural* action, the whole body is used in the expression. Postural expressions include stepping backward, shifting the torso to the side, or leaning forward. Once again, an observer who notices how these actions are performed will obtain valuable information about a child's inner experiences. Such actions reveal which areas of the body a child employs—consciously or unconsciously—to get her message across. These different expressive modes will also display the level and amount of muscular control a child has in each mode to assist effective communication.

Regardless of which body form a child displays, notice whether the action appears strained, contained, free and easy, or out of control. It is a child's ability to effectively use these forms of nonverbal expression that most influences her success in using nonverbal cues to get her needs met and her feelings understood. Determining to which modes of body expression a child has access will guide in deciding how to support both nonverbal and verbal dialogue with the child. It will also offer insight into which aspects of a child's behavior are influencing how information is being acquired and ideas are being developed about the child. In fact, learning about which modes of body expression one is drawn to may highlight one's own preferred style of nonverbal expression. Some people rely a great deal on facial expressions to determine a child's feelings, and interact accordingly. Conversely, others may have a more reserved facial affect, relying mostly on gestures to accent communication. If people's expressive modes are more postural, how and where they place and move their whole bodies during conversations will punctuate their interactions. Most people, of course, will use a combination of these body-focused modes. Still, understanding these categories can be helpful in organizing nonverbal observations and can help to bring understanding to one's own reactions and responses during interactions. An in-depth discussion about how to observe personal reactions is provided in Chapter 7.

The vignette below will demonstrate how these five points direct the therapist's interaction with Eric, a 3½-year-old diagnosed with PDD:

Eric loves jumping on the mini-trampoline. He seems to go deeply into his own private world, propelling his long, firm body up and down in a mesmerizing, rhythmic pulse. His face is frozen in a gaping smile and his eyes are glazed. He bounces for several minutes as Mom and I watch from afar. Where is Eric right now, I wonder? What is he thinking about—is he aware of us? There is nothing in his current actions that say he is registering our presence at all. In an effort to engage him socially, I stand on the floor in front of his bouncing body and bend and lengthen mine as I say, "Where is Eric?" Without missing a beat or gazing toward me, Eric adds a turn to his jump and immediately has his back toward me! At once, I run around to face him, and again, without a sound, he adds a turn away from me! Yes! Despite the lack of eye contact, his actions say he is definitely aware of my presence. Next I place my hands at his waist and support him to jump even higher. I help his jump get so high that I hold him above me suspended in the air and say, "Where is Eric? Let me see those eyes." I hold him like this until he looks directly at me. I then let him resume his jumping with my assistance. After a few more jumps I repeat these interactive actions, requesting social engagement through eye contact. He enjoys the added bounce my assistance provides, and in turn is willing to give me the facial emotional feedback I'm requesting. A social relationship begins to bud.

The five points to keep in mind when observing from a nonverbal perspective are depicted in Eric's *Ways of Seeing* session. The first point is clearly made: Eric likes to jump. Jumping is often associated with excitement. But seen in the whole context of this session, Eric's jumps do not reflect excitement but instead seem to be self-stimulatory. The second point is also implicit: Despite the fact that this jumping activity seems to keep Eric in his own world, disengaged from others, the therapist does not immediately judge or inhibit the jumping but instead observes it carefully and then finds a way to work with it. The therapist uses the jumping as a point of entry to create a movement dialogue. The third point is brought out when the therapist notices that the mesmerizing rhythmic pulsing quality of Eric's jump points to a self-stimulatory, sensory motivation: By performing the jump in this way, Eric is receiving very deep proprioceptive input in his joints. In addition to this sensory aspect, Eric's behavior has an emotional result in that it shuts out more effective social engagement. The fourth point is carried out when the therapist recognizes that it is Eric's overall full-body actions that most influence her own perceptions of the boy. Finally, the fifth point is also apparent: Both Eric's lack of active, animated facial affective expression and his full body actions greatly influence the therapist's response and the intervention. The therapist uses Eric's full body jumping and turning away to initially stimulate a way to relate. Eric's physical compliance—noticeably his lack of struggle to turn or get away—motivates the therapist to "up the ante" so to speak, by requesting and receiving his eye contact. The deep bodily nature of the interaction seems to support Eric's ability to make a social connection; likewise, the nonverbal activities communicate understanding and a desire to relate.

OBSERVING AND DECIPHERING NONVERBAL CUES

Therapists developing the observational skills to decipher nonverbal cues may find it helpful to keep these five points in mind. Such awareness will greatly enhance how they can use nonverbal observations in further interactions and interventions. Nonverbal cues include both actions that are intentional communications and actions that may be unintentional, but still have the potential to be communicative.

Intentional Nonverbal Communications

Intentional nonverbal acts are culturally acknowledged actions and gestures that possess symbolic meaning. These gestures can be deictic or representational (Iverson & Thal, 1998). *Deictic gestures* establish reference by drawing attention to an activity, event, or object through pointing, reaching toward, holding up, or showing an object. In contrast, *representational gestures* create reference and have associated semantic meanings. These gestures can be object-related or culturally established and include such actions as stretching arms out to depict an airplane or bending one's head to rest on clasped hands to indicate sleep. As has been noted in child development literature, a certain degree of physical control and regulation over the body is required to successfully perform such actions. These intentional nonverbal communications develop a young child's rudimentary cognitive understanding that an action can portray meaning, and they are often cited as the primary precursors to language acquisition. (There is an extensive body of literature and research that discusses the acquisition and role of gestures in the development of communication and language. For further information beyond the scope of this book, see Bruner, 1981; Iverson & Thal, 1998; Prizant et al., 2000).

The *Ways of Seeing* approach highlights the following actions and gestures because they are considered the most basic ingredients of intentional nonverbal communication. These movements create the foundation for building emotionally rewarding relationships.

Eye Gaze   The earliest such action is eye gaze. Eye gaze and other facial expressions are included because of their strong communicative capacity. At the beginning of life, a newborn infant does not have the ability to focus her gaze to far distances, but instead limits eye contact to short moments at relatively close distances. One of the initial activities that begin to develop an infant's ability to sustain eye contact are feeding interactions in which the baby is held at chest height. The image of a nursing baby at the mother's breast has often been depicted in art, capturing the tender, nurturing relationship just budding between mother and child. During these early experiences a baby begins to learn how to read the subtle and complex nonverbal cues provided by facial expressions as she and her mother create a facially expressive dialogue. It is at this early stage that prob-

The earliest example of a child's intentional nonverbal communication is eye gaze.

lems with eye contact can interfere with the baby's learning how to read those cues.

Smiling   Smiling is the next nonverbal action that gives an infant communicative power. Despite the controversy over whether those early smiles during the first few months of life are truly imbued with emotional content, everyone responds with such joy as a baby begins to discover the pleasures a smile brings! Of course, smiles and other affective facial reactions such as frowns and expressions of surprise or fear are not initially intentional on a baby's part. They are included in this discussion, nonetheless, for they are classified as culturally acknowledged nonverbal cues that people use to understand the feelings of another person. Over time a young child learns how to use these expressions to communicate his feelings and needs as well as how to interpret the feelings and needs of others. Indeed, a child's learning to communicate and understand these facial actions is the foundational skill needed to develop his successful relating skills. In fact, for a child with PDD or other disorders that have problematic social and relational components, his inability to accurately read and respond to such cues is at the core of his struggles.

Body-Part Articulations   These actions address the circumstances in which specific parts of the body are used to communicate meaning. Some variation of these actions can be found in all cultures. Head nodding, pointing, shoulder shrugging, hugging, pulling, pushing, and throwing objects or people toward or away from self are other examples of intentional nonverbal actions that a young child uses to communicate.

Unintentional Nonverbal Communications

Unintentional nonverbal communications contrast with intentional nonverbal communications in that the former are unconscious; nonetheless, unintentional can be just as significant as intentional nonverbal communications. All nonverbal behaviors have the potential to communicate meaningful knowledge; therefore, it is important to pay attention to the specific qualitative information of a person's movements. (More specific interventions for nonverbal behaviors are discussed in Chapter 4, and although the information is outside the framework of this book, further discussion and research about the use of sign language to enhance communication and support early language development with infants who are preverbal can be found in Acredolo and Goodwyn [1988, 2002].)

Elements to Consider in
Potential Nonverbal Communications

The following issues to consider when observing potential nonverbal communications apply to both intentional and unintentional actions, but can be especially useful in analyzing unintentional behaviors that have the potential to communicate meaningful knowledge (see worksheet at http://www.brookespublishing.com/dancing).

Ability to Use Actions or Gestures to Communicate   As a therapist enters into the realm of qualitative nonverbal analysis, it is useful to determine if a child has developed any full body actions or individual gestures—either original or those commonly understood—to communicate. Is a child able to point to the object of her desire (a gestural action) or does she grab adults by the hand and drag them to the desired object (a full body action)? Does a child who wants his blanket use self-created distinctive gestures such as lying on the floor, or instead use more commonly acknowledged nonverbal gestures such as sweeping his arms across and then hugging his body while lifting his shoulders and rocking from side to side? Does a child use vocalizations, such as high-pitched screams to indicate displeasure and melodic vocal tones to express enjoyment, or does the child make desires known using language, such as expressly stating, "I want blanket"?

Whether a child uses a standard or a distinctive gestural action to communicate, noticing the qualitative way in which the child performs these actions can provide helpful information. Becoming aware of these distinct modes of nonverbal cuing enables a therapist to learn more about how specific aspects of nonverbal communicating influence a child's interactions and can guide in modifying the overall intervention. Reading nonverbal cues is a significant aspect of many of the activities in the *Ways of Seeing* approach.

Level of Activity   Children's physical activity levels may influence the communicative aspects of their nonverbal actions and gestures and may assist or impede their ability to attend to their surroundings. Accordingly, it is important to assess children's levels of physical activity and how much their bodies are used to attend. For some children, physical activity (full body or gesture) supports their ability to focus, whereas for others, it is distracting. Children's physical activity levels can influence how communicative are their nonverbal actions and gestures.

A therapist should begin by asking how active or inactive is the child being observed. Whether a child is an infant without the muscle strength to push up unassisted or a toddler already walking, the child's activity level will be detectable. Does a child seem to want to be on the go, continually taking in her surroundings in a very active manner through her eye gaze, head turning, or full body mobilizations? Conversely, is a child more stationary, quiet, and inwardly focused; sitting and/or otherwise displaying a more contained and controlled visual or physical exploration of the room? Is a child's activity level somewhere in between these two extremes? What environmental stimuli or situations may be influencing a child's interest and ability to attend to the surroundings? How may a child's level of activity reflect or support other aspects of behavior and influence the feelings of others about the child?

Sense of Continuousness A child's sense of continuousness reflects the ability to stay continually engaged through social-emotional relatedness while attending cognitively and/or physically to a session's activities. This sense, which includes a child's awareness and ability to engage with those in the room, will influence a child's nonverbal communications. Noting the link between a child's social-emotional abilities with her cognitive and physical focus is essential. A therapist should determine whether a child experiences a continuity of social and emotional engagement or if the nonverbal behaviors create some degree of intermittent or total lack of engagement. A child, for example, can maintain continuous physical activity, such as running all around the room, without demonstrating any awareness of others. Similarly, a child can become very engaged in a seemingly cognitive task, such as counting the number of cars in a row, without acknowledging or allowing social input from a peer or the therapist. Alternatively, another child may move from activity to activity while still engaging with those around him by maintaining intermittent eye contact from afar or by staying near other people.

A therapist should also look for the more obscure ways a child may be maintaining engagement. To view a child from this perspective, a therapist should notice in what manner and how frequently the child moves through the room and transitions from activity to activity. A therapist should also observe a child's awareness and ability to engage with others. Does a child have a fluid, logical, and naturally progressive way of exploring and transitioning through activities? Does a child reference, notice, or include others in any way during these activities? Or, is there a stop-and-start quality to a child's engagement, with periods of time in which the therapist may wonder "where the child is" due to a lost or empty expression, extended lack of eye contact, and physical interruptions of engagement in the child's movements, play, or attention? Such "lost" behaviors often require a therapist to constantly refocus and redirect to keep the child relating and on task. Finally, a therapist might find it helpful to imagine how a child's experience on a body-movement level might influence how the child feels because this sense of continuousness is reflected in the ability to (cognitively) attend, physically engage, and stay emotionally connected.

Overall Melody and Rhythm of the Child's Actions   Relating in a general way to the LMA element Phrasing discussed in Chapter 5, the phrasing of movements performed in a sequence depicts the overall feeling tone or story a child is telling through nonverbal actions. By pondering the overall nonverbal components linking together to create the phrase, a therapist can determine its melody and rhythm. Similar to its use in music, a *movement melody* is a harmonic composition of actions sequenced together that often exude a lyrical quality. The melody provides contour, tone, texture, and color, creating a recognizable shape and theme to the movement phrase. To find the melody, a therapist searches through the nonverbal details that contribute to his or her overall impression of a child.

When moving with a melodic sensibility, a child may seem to glide through the room, with actions moving smoothly from one to the next. The child may maintain focus and develop a theme during play, or instead may seem to be engaged in one activity and then somehow just gravitate toward something else without the therapist even having noticed how or when the change occurred. Melody can create continuity or discontinuity in the action and the child's focus. Melodic continuity can be seen in a child who is acting out a story of gliding through the air on a space rocket, and then, by suddenly accelerating, is transformed into a laser beam blast. Both the actions and the imaginary theme follow a natural progression. In contrast, melodic discontinuity occurs when that same child loses the storyline focus and changes from being a laser beam blast into a baby bear rolling on the floor. The actions flow into each other, in that rolling is a natural action to do on the floor, but the content does not relate.

Rhythmic accents may occur within the melodic tone, adding structure and emphasis to the quality of the movement phrase. When a child's actions portray a more rhythmic quality, there will be more of a patterned sense of immediacy and timing to the actions. To continue with the space rocket story, the child may replay the gliding space rocket acceleration into the blast, running across the room, jumping and then falling on the floor over and over again with the same timing and movement dynamics. The places of accent and emphasis in the phrase create the rhythmic aspects of the phrase. Rhythmic movements are organized by time and create a sense of pulse or beat to the action. The rhythm can be regular, formed by a regulated or patterned set of actions repeated in a sequence over a period of time; alternatively, the rhythm pattern can be irregular, as occurs when the movement pattern is not organized in a regularly recurring beat but, nonetheless, has a sense of pulse and accent to it. The placement of the emphasis or accents within the phrase will determine which of these rhythmic types the movement phrase portrays. A therapist can check if a child's actions are rhythmic by trying to clap out (literally or mentally) a regular, sustained beat that corresponds to the child's actions: If a regular sustained beat is possible, the actions are rhythmic; if there is a beat, but it does not have a steady or repeatable pattern, it is arrhythmic.

A child who has a rhythmic quality to his actions often seems guided by an inner pulse or drive. For example, he may have a bounce to his walk; may approach and move in a room with sweeping, accented or rhythmic dance-like actions; may have a patterned or systematic way of doing something, such as lining up his toy cars; or he may enjoy the sense of order and regularity that counting or numbering objects creates. The repetitive rhythmic quality can add formal structure to the child's experience. It can also be perseverative if there are no variations to the rhythm or no social or emotional pulse underlying the actions. This is often the case in which a child with ASD systematically lines up objects in a rote manner.

When observing a child from this perspective, a therapist should ask the following questions: Does the child tend to move through the room in a melodic way or with more rhythmic accent? When and how is the child interacting in her surroundings in a melodic way? How and when does she use rhythm to explore the environment and express her feelings? Does the child have access to both melodic and rhythmic movement, or does she favor one style over the other?

As with all movement qualities, neither action is good or bad in and of itself. In a balanced movement profile, each of these qualities should be available; problems only arise in cases in which a child overutilizes a particular quality and is not able to adapt his style to the situations at hand. A child with an overly melodic style may not be able to sustain rhythmic actions or to stay engaged for an extended period of time. This may also be reflected in his difficulty in attending to his classwork.

One example of this situation is Jake, a very bright 5-year-old child with a seizure disorder, who is not able to sustain the rhythmic action of stamping his feet in a dancing sequence beyond two counts. After two counts, he melts into fluid, undulating, full-body actions that send his focus either all over the room or silently into himself. The overall melody of his movements portrays a languid sensibility, filled with soft yet weighted actions that continually ooze and then dissipate into short-and-then-long pauses of stillness and emptiness.

Billy, a precocious 5-year-old child, is equally unable to sustain focus, but for different reasons: His movement style exemplifies more of a rhythmic Phrasing quality, and his actions are driven and punctuated with sporadic quick starts and stops of continually varying durations; however, his rhythm is so unique that he is unable to sustain a rhythmic dialogue to an external beat. He is unable, for example, to clap his hands or move his body to follow the beat of a song. When he initially came for intervention, this intelligent child presented himself as very creative and inquisitive, completely filled with ideas involving complex physical constructions based on the many scientific and natural facts he had mastered. Early in his intervention, he explained that he liked to work on projects because they keep his mind focused, and he described his inner mind as very busy and easily distracted. Although these descriptions demonstrate his keen awareness of his inner experience, Billy's difficulties with attention and hyperactivity manifest nonverbally in how he executes and carries out activities. He often begins with a jump-start, maintains his engagement with a strong pressured or tense pulse, and then he has such difficulty ceasing his actions that he seems to have a live electric wire inside. Indeed, in an effort to explain what it feels like to be him, Billy once gave the following description of his difficulties in stopping his actions and his inner pulsings: "You know when you try to turn off an electric current, but it keeps going for a little while longer, on its own? It just keeps vibrating and won't turn off right away." The story of Billy shows how thinking about a child's actions as melodies and rhythms can provide further insight into how that child may be experiencing connection.

Use of Space and Proximity to Others   Also relating in a general way to the Laban Spatial category, this element is included to remind observers to notice how comfortable a child is moving throughout her space and how aware she is of her surroundings. How and where a child physically places herself in relation to objects, other people, and activities going on in the room reveal her sense of personal boundaries and body awareness, as well as her social comfort level. A child's sense of her own body boundaries will be reflected in how she uses her body in space in relation to other people and objects.

The *sense of body boundaries* can be defined as an awareness that one's body is contained, integrated, and physically separate from others. It is this sense that enables a mover to judge how close to place her body next to someone else during interactions. A child without firm body boundaries often bumps into people and objects. To this child, the ability to judge the correct proximity to people and objects may be elusive. Often such a child seems to have a heaviness to her movement quality as well, for example, when the child seems to throw or drop her body or particular body parts when walking, running, or transitioning during a movement action, such as shifting from standing to sitting, or from being mobile to becoming still. From a sensory standpoint, such a child may be seeking deep physical sensory input due to an imbalance of her proprioceptive and/or vestibular systems.

Although these systems are discussed in more detail in Chapter 4, to review, the proprioceptive system is the internal feedback system that provides information to the joints and muscles about where the body is in space, whereas the vestibular system manages the body's sense of balance and muscle tone. The quality of muscle tone (hypo- or hypertonic) will affect a child's abilities to contract or stabilize her muscles. When these systems are functioning properly, clear sensorial knowledge about her body's spatial placement enables a child to attend to other stimuli in the environment. Conversely, seeking or avoiding proprioceptive and vestibular stimulation may interfere with a child's ability to fully attend and maintain her focus.

Relevant questions involve determining how close a child places herself in relation to other people when engaged in a joint activity. For example, does the child often want to sit on a grownup's lap during storytime? Is the young toddler often engaged in rough-and-tumble play with a peer? Is the baby's body comfortably molded into the caregiver's shoulder when held or is it tensed and arched away? A therapist should observe if the child in these situations holds her body firmly or strongly while engaged with the other person— reflecting a clear, separate sense of body boundaries; or, conversely, if the child seems to melt or lean her body into the other person—

reflecting a softer or lack of separate sense of body boundaries. It is essential for a therapist to notice if the child tends to place herself clearly separate from other people or activities because this may indicate whether a certain amount of distance is required in order for the child to feel comfortable.

Touch   Touch plays an integral role in a person's sense of body boundaries, for it involves being able to feel where one's body begins and ends in relation to someone or something outside of oneself. Questions regarding touch involve both how a child touches and how a child reacts to touch. The answers should influence how much a therapist or caregiver uses touch to interact with the child as an extension or a replacement of verbal communication.

Touch may be a personal interactional style, increasing enjoyment (such as giving a hug), or it may add accent or emphasis to the dialogue to facilitate or support self-expression. For an adult interacting with a child, touch may be used to keep the child directed or to redirect him, especially if he is not able to understand verbal cues. In the therapeutic setting, touch may be used as a tool to help calm and settle a child or to provide sensory input. For a child, touch may support or replace verbal dialogue, as in grabbing an adult's hand and walking over to the refrigerator for a drink. Perhaps the most important question to ask is whether a child avoids or seeks touch. Children who avoid touch may tense their bodies, pull away, scream, or if mobile, move their bodies completely away from an uncomfortable touch. Children who seek touch place their bodies close to others and objects, often leaning, pushing, climbing onto, or stroking these surfaces. At the extreme, the type of child who overrelies on touch may not possess a sense of personal body boundaries.

Interactional, Social, or Emotional Nonverbal Analysis

The next set of nonverbal cues looks at a child's movements specifically in relationship to her interactions with others. These nonverbal qualities relate to the interactional analysis section of the MSI Checklist and include observational categories and questions that address general nonverbal concepts and concepts related to the LMA system. This category of observations identifies the nature of a child's interactional style by specifically asking the observer to notice when the child's nonverbal interactions have a social or emotional focus.

General Social Activity Level This category refers to a child's overall social ability during a session. Does a child seek and maintain social interactions for most of the session or are social interactions avoided? How are these social exchanges nonverbally expressed through a child's actions? For example, one infant may use eye contact and shared visual attention during an interactive activity while keeping her body relatively still to display a connection. Conversely, another infant may be very energetic, increasing his arm movement in a rapid swinging fashion equally displaying attention. In particular, observers should notice when and how social engagement changes a child's emotional state. This is often observable on a body or movement level. For example, an observer should determine a child's level of social comfort by noticing if the child's behaviors display an increased or decreased sense of calm or focus, or convey a reduction in muscular tension during social interactions. An observer should also ask what types of activities and social exchanges specifically contribute to these nonverbal behaviors.

Nonverbal Social or Emotional Relating Style A salient question for an observer to answer when assessing interactions is how does a child sequence from a place of calmness and self-soothing through other stages ranging from attending, active participation, excitement, and overstimulation, then back to self-soothing and calmness (Tortora, 1995). Again, the focus here is on how these behaviors are exhibited through nonverbal actions and behaviors. While cycling through this sequence, does a child elicit, invite, or reject interactions with others? How does a child portray this nonverbally through Body and facial expressions, Body Shapes, use of Space, Phrasing, and choice of available Efforts?

The observer should also question whether a child's partner demonstrates attunement to the child's interactional style through nonverbal actions, giving room for the child's self-expression before responding. Does the nature and nonverbal quality of the dyadic interaction change depending on whether the child's partner is a parent, a professional practitioner, a sibling, or a peer? How does a child nonverbally demonstrate support of social and emotional interactions initiated by others?

Movement Synchrony When Interacting Movement synchrony specifically refers to how an individual mover's actions relate to each other. *Synchrony* occurs when the participants of the movement activity are moving in relationship to each other without needing to copy the actions exactly. This differs from the concepts of attunement and mirroring in that the actual movements do not match but instead relate to each other. An example of this is when a child's arms reach up at the same time a therapist is sitting down. The actions are not the same, but there is a relationship between their movements. This relationship creates a complementary or even opposing quality to the interaction that depicts a conscious or unconscious sense of response and awareness between the two participants. Movement synchrony creates an atmosphere of potential connection to a sensitive and observant observer. This is often the first detectable sign of interaction observable during early relating experiences with children in the PDD and autism spectrums.

For example, Sally, a 3-year-old child with ASD, despite looking away, repeatedly flaps her hands at shoulder height in a quick, pulsing beat in response to the therapist's stamping of feet to the moderate, even, rhythmic beat of a nursery rhyme. Although the action does not replicate the music or the therapist's actions, it does demonstrate an awareness of a change in the environment. It can become an avenue for the therapist to expand their interaction—through verbal and movement acknowledgment and further exploration. A therapist can build on nonverbal engagements such as these by identifying how each moving member is contributing to the interaction.

Child-Led versus Adult-Led Interactions   An observer should notice when and how often a child initiates the social exchange and how often an adult initiates such engagement. Again, the focus here is about how a child uses his body actions to support interactions even if vocalizations and verbalizations are available.

Turn-Taking Sequences   An observer should ascertain whether there is room for turn taking once social engagement is established, or whether the exchange is mostly child or adult led. This relates to Greenspan's (1992) description of "closing circles of communication," in which the goal is to keep the dialogic interaction going. Turn taking in the *Ways of Seeing* approach is established when a reciprocal interactive sequence involves each participant taking at least one turn. Observing from a body-movement perspective will reveal a child's ability to keep her body, actions, and cognitive, social, and emotion focus in interactive control.

Initiation, Withdrawal, Maintenance, or Resumption of Contact   This category of questions takes an observer deeper into nonverbal analysis. How do a child's actions reveal the child's ability to initiate, withdraw, maintain, or resume social-emotional contact? During any analysis of social interactions, it is important for an observer to note who keeps the engagement going and how this is accomplished through actions in addition to words. These four aspects of relating are integral parts of typical social engagement as discussed in the mismatch-and-repair work defined and described by Tronick (Tronick, 1989; Tronick & Gianino, 1986). It is natural and expected, especially during early infancy—when a baby does not have the cognitive or physical capacity to stay attending for long periods of time— that the baby may need to disengage her attention during social exchanges and may not always be able to communicate her needs and wants in an understandable way on the first attempt. It is a baby's experiences of striving and eventually succeeding in initiating and reengaging in dyadic relating that provide her with an emotional sense of agency, thus developing and expanding her capacity to relate in a social context.

Nonverbal Ways of Maintaining Social Engagement An observer must be open to the sometimes obscure ways a child may be attempting to maintain social engagement, because such observations are a key tool in creating, supporting, and extending potential relatedness even in the seemingly distant or noncommunicative child. Careful observation can reveal how and when a child has nonverbally stayed connected to an interaction in ways that traditionally would not be regarded as maintaining connection. The LMA-based elements— Body, Efforts, Phrasing, Shape, and Space—provide the necessary tools to detect specifically how a child uses his body movements to nonverbally maintain a social connection. Described more fully in Chapter 5, these LMA elements provide important descriptive details about what specific body and movement characteristics each person is using to contribute to the social-emotional dialogue. Once an understanding of these five LMA elements is obtained, an observer should look to see how they are used to continue social engagement.

Body How are participants in a social engagement using their full body and individual body parts to initiate, maintain, and close interactions?

Efforts Are the Efforts used by each participant the same, complimentary, or opposing?

Phrasing Styles Do each mover's phrases synchronize or complement, or do their individual Phrasing styles not relate at all? Within this dyadic context, general nonverbal qualities to notice are the length of each mover's phrase—whether short, medium, or long—and the quality and activity level of the phrase—whether agitated, lively, calm, or relaxed. Do the members of the interaction enable each other to prepare and recuperate during movement interactions or is one mover continually intruding, interrupting, or ignoring the other mover? What types of movement transitions occur during interactions? What is the duration of the interactions and the general activity level and tempo of the interactions?

Shape   How the movers use their bodies and the level of their body boundary awareness in relation to each other and their surroundings will become apparent in the types of body shapes—whether shape flow, shaping, and directional actions—they create as they move through the room together. From an image standpoint, do they seem to be creating an interactive sculpture as they move together, or two separate sculptures that do not relate?

Space   What is each mover's level of active engagement and awareness in space—constant contact, some contact, minimal contact, or no contact at all? What levels of space are used most often? What is the level—ranging from constant to none—of active engagement and awareness of others in the surrounding environment? An observer should notice each mover's spatial pathways to determine whether they intersect, follow, or do not relate at all to the pathways of others. As discussed earlier, spatial proximity often comes into play in relationships between the self and others.

These questions focus on how and which elements of an individual's movement style affect and contribute to the interactional dialogue. This is exemplified when observing Nikki's interactional style.

Nikki enters the room seeming very excited to start with dancing today. This becomes evident when I ask her what she wants to do. At first her gaze is all over the room, seeming to take in the opened space and the scarves on the wall. When I say "dancing," she nods her head as she looks me directly in the eyes with bright eyes and a broad smile. I guide her over to her computer communication board and, on her own, she chooses and pushes the dance button using directness and bound flow. As I turn around to put on music, Nikki wanders away from me with a slow yet determined gait into the opened dance space, clapping her hands as she then circles back, passing near me and the CD player. Watching her self-initiated energetic yet characteristically slow-paced tempo, I decide to put on an Etta James CD. James' sultry and jazzy voice will support Nikki's slow qualities yet provide a stronger syncopated rhythm to ground and direct our dancing.

Without looking at me Nikki takes my hands as we assume partner-dancing positions—me walking backwards so I can face her—and we circle around the room together. She relaxes the tension in her arms, enabling me to lift her arms up high above her head, guiding her to turn under our clasped hands, followed by me bending down to also turn under our raised arms. As we resume our positions facing each other, Nikki glances up at me and gives me a bright smile and delightful giggle. Our dancing dialogue continues as we drop one hand while raising the remaining hand. Nikki spontaneously steps and turns under this raised arm to do a single arm turn. At the completion of this pivot, Nikki disengages our clasp, and turns her head to glance at Mom, who verbally acknowledges how much she is enjoying Nikki's partner-dancing sequence. Nikki wanders through the room, first toward Mom, clapping her hands to the beat of Etta James. I follow her actions and again she finds a way to circle her pathway near to me. When she passes without looking at me, she flings her arm off to the side in my direction. I take this as an invitation, grasp her hand as we resume our partnering positions, and begin another series of arm and full body turns and pivots throughout the dance space. Nikki's eye contact with Mom and me most often occurs after the completion of one of these dancing sequences. We continue in this way for the duration of the song. ⌁

This vignette exemplifies Nikki's interactional style. Through careful, detailed analysis of Nikki's movements, it is evident that even when she is not providing eye contact (a common nonverbal gesture of communication), she is maintaining the relationship through her movement choices. In general, Nikki's qualitative preferences reveal that she uses her body parts to continue following the movement dialogue (LMA-Body); she participates and creates movement phrases that enable the interaction to continue (LMA-Phrasing); and she keeps her body in continued and close proximity to the dance movement psychotherapist (LMA-Space). Nikki invites interaction: Her movement phrases are often complementary, her movement pathways follow or intersect the dance movement psychotherapist's pathways, and she demonstrates continual awareness of her surroundings. Nikki often resumes eye contact after these movement and body-oriented ways of staying connected are acknowledged. In this specific vignette, Nikki sustains a social-emotional dialogue by keeping her body fluid, enabling the psychotherapist to hold her and guide them through an extended sequential-movement experience (in a sequence that involves moving around the room in a partnering "swing" dance containing underarm turns, pivots, and complicated large-arm movements). They move to a rhythmic beat to the music and Nikki is in sync with the psychotherapist's actions, reaching one of her limbs toward the psychotherapist and maintaining touch. In response to Nikki, the *Ways of Seeing* practitioner keeps the dialogue going with her own movements, which match, attune, or complement the child's actions.

Specific Interactional Questions   The MSI Checklist of the *Ways of Seeing* approach (Appendix A) addresses these nonverbally focused interactional considerations in relation to early childhood social-emotional development. Based on the child development concepts discussed in depth in Chapter 2, the MSI Checklist asks the following key questions, focusing on nonverbal interaction styles (Tortora, 1995):

1. How do the movements of the adult establish a holding environment through her use of Space—whether kinespheric, general, interactional, or pathways—Body levels, Phrasing, Shaping, and Efforts?

2. How are the turn-taking sequences opened and closed through each participant's movements, focusing specifically on initiation, withdrawal, and resumption of contact via the use of Space, Body, Shape, Efforts, and Phrasing?

3. How do mirroring, attuning, and mismatch-and-repair cycles occur through body-movement dialogue, as observed by their qualitative use of Space, Body, Shape, Efforts, and Phrasing?

4. How does the adult attune to the child's style as reflected in the child's cues: Does the adult give room for the child's expression before intervening, or does the adult instead respond without attending to the child's style first? How is this expressed through the movement qualities of Space, Body, Shape, Efforts, and Phrasing?

5. How does the adult establish a "base of support" from which the child receives pleasure, understanding, and comfort when exploring the surroundings and when returning to the adult in times of perceived danger or discomfort? Describe how the adult and child's behaviors are portrayed through their movement qualities of Space, Body, Shape, Efforts, and Phrasing.

In summary, attending to a child's nonverbal expressions is a key element of the *Ways of Seeing* approach that facilitates the interactions and the development of an emotional relationship with the child and supports the child's growth in other developmental areas. Nonverbal analysis is a component used by many early childhood theorists (Beebe, 2004; Brazelton, 1974; Stern, 1985). The feature that uniquely identifies the *Ways of Seeing* program is its attention to the qualitative aspects of the nonverbal exchange, both through observational analysis and through spontaneous, improvisational interactions. This chapter provides questions to assist a therapist or other observer in becoming aware of how a child uses body and movement behaviors when an interaction is initiated and as it continues to unfold. Laban-based categories are especially useful in providing clues regarding a child's nonverbal actions. Careful and detailed observation of the quality of a child's movements often reveals that the child may actually be attending to surroundings in ways that typically go unnoticed when qualitative aspects of the child's nonverbal behaviors are not considered.

7

Witnessing,
Kinesthetic Seeing,
and Kinesthetic
Empathy

As I witness you move, I cannot know your experience. I can only
know my own experience in your presence. I commit to tracking my
experience as best I can. It is my intention, my practice, to notice all
that occurs within me as I witness.

J. Adler, *Offering from the Conscious Body* (2002, p. 10)

This quote describes the role of the external observer, known as the
witness, in the discipline of Authentic Movement. In this discipline participants discover their own inner experiences through a profoundly simple process of movement and stillness. It is a type of meditation through
movement that occurs by listening to one's own body. Originated by a
dance movement therapy pioneer, Mary Starks Whitehouse, and further
developed by Janet Adler, Authentic Movement has greatly influenced
the role of the therapist in the *Ways of Seeing* approach. As shown in Table
7.1, the principles that guide Authentic Movement are deeply embedded
in the *Ways of Seeing* approach, especially in the attitude of the therapist
in the self-observation process. Typically, Authentic Movement is employed exclusively with adults. In the *Ways of Seeing* approach, however,
Authentic Movement principles are modified to adapt this practice to the
state of mind and abilities of a younger population. A brief description of
the adult discipline is provided below because understanding Authentic
Movement's history and development should both elucidate the "seeing"
in *Ways of Seeing* and provide a structure to organize the therapist's experiences when observing and moving with young children and their family members.

Table 7.1. Principles of the Authentic Movement discipline adapted and applied to the *Ways of Seeing* approach

Witnessing involves a mover and a witness.

The *mover* is the person actively moving and being observed.

The *witness* is the person observing the active mover.

Movement actions include all degrees of activity from stillness to very active.

Both the mover and the witness step into a place of not knowing in order to enter into a place of listening moment to moment.

The mover suspends deliberate will, listening to his or her body, enabling body sensations and feelings to direct the actions rather than be directed by mental thoughts.

The witness observes by listening with focused attentiveness, relinquishing preconceived ideas and images while simultaneously tracking his or her own internal experiences.

The process allows the mover and the witness to have an active experience in which the witness is *seeing* for the mover, who is *being seen.*

The witness creates a safe holding environment for the mover to feel free to reveal himself or herself.

The result is the emergence of a new awareness of self and self and other.

The process develops the internal witnesses within both the witness and the mover.

The mover–witness relationship is a co-constructed experience for both participants.

MOVER–WITNESS RELATIONSHIP

The form in the discipline of Authentic Movement is basic—it involves a mover and a witness. The practice commences as the mover closes his eyes and directs his focus inward, beginning to move only when sensing an impulse to do so. Dropping into this quiet place, the mover suspends deliberate will and surrenders, allowing his body to direct actions rather than choosing actions with thoughts and mind. All the while, the witness sits to the side, looking on with clear intent, creating a sense of presence. The witness is not simply watching but rather listening with focused attention, *seeing* the mover, who is *being seen.* Through this seeing, the witness maps each action element of the mover while tracking her own internal experience that transpires during the observation. Witnessing becomes an active experience that may inspire images, sensations, feelings, ideas, personal memories, and sensorial reactions. By "holding" the experience for the mover in this way, the external witness creates a safe environment in which the mover can bring emerging unconsciousness material into consciousness. Afterward the witness and mover exchange their experiences using such mediums as the spoken word, prose, poetry, drawing, clay work, and other expressive arts techniques. The witness models the development of the mover's own inner witness through the process of providing detailed descriptions of all that was seen—within the witness's own self and the mover.

The mover increases conscious awareness of his inner experience as reflected by the external witness. The external witness actively processes both her own internal activity and the pure movement seen in the mover. Through personal mapping, the witness develops an internal witness tracking of herself as well. In this way the discipline of Authentic Movement is an active, indivisibly coupled experience for both the mover and the witness. The witness develops mover consciousness and the mover develops inner witness consciousness. As the mover and witness advance though the Authentic Movement practice, the mover internalizes the witness, learning to consciously observe himself, finding form for the unconscious through personal body actions. As stated by Adler (2002, p. 6), "The inner witness learns to accompany the body into the shapes of the moving self, discovering one's truth. The inner witness learns to honor that which the body directly knows." Both Adler and Whitehouse acknowledged the body as a preternatural vessel that holds each person's deepest perceptions of self. Simply put, "The body is the physical aspect of the personality, and movement is the personality made visible" (Whitehouse, 1987, p. 17).

It is only out of being seen extensively by an external witness that the inner witness is developed in Authentic Movement discipline. After studying this process at length, Adler concluded that from the experience of being seen arises the instinctive ability to witness internally, which then prepares one to witness another (1987). The *Ways of Seeing* approach has built on these ideas the recognition that we each have an innate longing to be seen by another and a desire to be acknowledged for our uniqueness and truth. These longings typically first occur at birth when we are seen by our parents. It is the experience of being seen, or not seen, in our earliest relationships that greatly contributes to our sense of being understood and cherished. Aspects of this need to be seen are also revealed in early childhood development literature discussions about the necessary elements needed to create healthy primary relationships. The ability of a parent and baby to successfully read the nonverbal cues of each other, and a parent's capacity to accurately and sensitively perceive and reflect on a baby's behaviors, known as reflective functioning (discussed at length in Chapter 10), greatly influence how the baby learns the skills of relating. It is a parent's role as a baby's first witness that creates a safe environment for the baby to navigate his surroundings through embodied and sensory-felt exploration. As a young infant uses his budding body-directed awareness to freely explore his surroundings, the ways in which his primary caregivers reflect and respond back to him create reliable dyadic interactions. These familiar interactions in which a parent both echoes and responds to a baby's expressions and experiences are a central process in the baby's getting to know himself as a social emotional being.

Indeed both Adler (1987) and Whitehouse (1999) related the adult mover–witness experience to a baby's earliest explorations and discoveries within primary relationships. Adler compared the development of the mover's inner witness with a baby's sense of self, which grows through interactive experiences with his mother acting as a reflector of, and in response to, the baby's actions and expressions. As emphasized in the mover–witness relationship, and discussed in Chapter 2, infancy theory also highlights this process as an active experience for both parent and baby. Each experience is co-constructed by the qualities, actions, and reactions each member of the partnership brings to the interaction. The baby's bright, alert smile encourages his mother to sweetly chant her baby's name, physically responding with a swaying tilt to her head. The baby's response is evident as his arms and legs start to wiggle with increasing speed, intensity, and excitement. The mother's reaction supports and helps to define the baby's experience of his behavior. This response tells the mother that the baby enjoys her presence and is eager for deeper engagement. If, instead, the mother responds to the baby's smile with little emotional and physical expressivity, the baby will have a very different experience. The baby will not experience the power of smiling as an emotionally positive communication. Similarly, if the mother receives a blank look from her baby every time she coos his name, she will feel very ineffective in her ability to emotionally engage her child. This can potentially compromise her feelings about her ability to be an effective mother. This co-construction acts as the building blocks that shape how both the infant and the parent come to know their developing relationship.

Whitehouse (1999) pointed toward the free-forming unmediated movement explorations of the infant—including the first movement of the first moment of life, which occurs through the very physical act of the lungs' expanding to breathe—as the infant's first language. She believed this initial movement language is self-guided but becomes altered, losing its authentic, internally inspired voice as a young child is taught to model the expectations and values of guiding adults, which demand particular behaviors to meet personal, cultural, and social beliefs. Whitehouse believed that the authentic voice gets lost in the acquisition of this learned behavior; it was her pursuit to reveal this lost authenticity that inspired her to develop the Authentic Movement discipline.

It is obvious that the adult discipline of Authentic Movement is not a feasible method to use with young children. A child cannot be expected to move with his eyes closed for any length of time or be able to reflect on his personal experience to the same extent as an adult. Both Whitehouse and Adler discussed the young child's lack of conscious awareness of actions. Therefore, when using the *Ways of Seeing* approach, which focuses on the young population, changes must be made to adapt this practice. The extensive discussion of Authentic Movement is included here, however, for the analogies that can be made between this practice and work with young children and their families. In addition, the depth of self-awareness resulting from the principles and development of this discipline provides an excellent structure from which a therapist can work with very young children and their families. Understanding the evolution of Authentic Movement, adapted from the writings of Adler (1987, 2002, 2003), Pallaro (1999), and Whitehouse (1987, 1999), should clarify its application to the early childhood population focused on in the *Ways of Seeing* approach.

Mover–Witness Development: The Early History

As a professional modern dancer, Whitehouse was deeply aware of the powerful emotional exchange that occurs between the dancer and the audience during a performance. There is mutuality in this exchange: A performer is moved to use her body to communicate, whereas an audience is moved by the experience of watching the performer's actions. Especially in a live performance, this exchange is palpable! A trained dancer has an evolved kinesthetic sense imbued with a deep understanding of how the body can communicate emotion. Her movements are a learned and codified language acquired from extensive training that the dancer expresses through her body.

As Whitehouse's interests in dance developed, she shifted her focus from the learned movement vocabulary of dance to exploring the process of dance as a medium for inner life self-expression. In a talk Whitehouse gave to the Analytical Psychology Club of Los Angeles in 1965, she stated that she was most interested in "the psychophysical connections in movement" (Whitehouse, 1987, p. 16). As a student of the early modern dance leaders Martha Graham and Mary Wigman, Whitehouse learned about improvisation and was especially drawn to the unique material that arises in each dancer during the improvisational experience. Wanting to find the authentic voice in her dancers, she attempted to replicate in her studio the experience of a dancer being observed on stage by an audience. Taking on the role of the audience, Whitehouse became the single witness for many dancers' self-directed movement explorations. Through this process, Whitehouse began to detect when individual dancers were moving from a prepared movement language executed with purpose, versus when they allowed themselves "to be moved," which occurred when their bodies rather than their conscious minds directed their actions. Whitehouse concluded that it was this experience of "being moved" that drew out a dancer's authentic voice. At these moments Whitehouse felt that the dancer's purposeful action was suspended; instead, the dancer appeared to be guided by movements that arose from within, taking a form of their own, which revealed the dancer's deeper aspects of self. Whitehouse took this work with dancers in her studio to an inpatient adult psychiatric ward, prior to the time that medication was extensively used as a modality for intervention. Bringing along her own music, Whitehouse invited each patient to join her in the dance. By supporting and following the unique moves of each patient, she successfully enabled these adults with psychosis, many of whom exhibited isolating and avoidant behaviors, to move and dance, forming relationships with others.

Adler, another dancer and early student of Whitehouse, dedicated her life's work to exploring and defining in detail the discipline of Authentic Movement, extensively focusing on what specifically happens within the relationship of the mover and witness. She believed that relationship is at the core of the discipline of Authentic Movement. Early work with children with autism first drew Adler to the study of relationships, and her work with children with autism—the focus of her classic 1970 film *Looking For Me*—has greatly influenced many dance movement therapists working with children today. Adler's views that this early work with children with autism established the roots of her development in the adult discipline of Authentic Movement were expressed at a National Dance Movement Therapy conference:

> Forty years ago, autistic children were described as those beings who never had an experience of relationship with another human being. In such a child there is no hint of an internalized other, a mother, an inner witness. There is no internalized presence. For a decade I worked in big and empty rooms where autistic children, one by one,

filled the space with their absence, until, because of a momentary presence, we experienced a connection. Such moments of grace created resonance within our relationship, revealing a glimpse of light. Autistic children represented the unknown to me. Now so many years later, my desire to experience the unknown persists. . . . With the children and within the discipline of Authentic Movement, there is so much learning about distinguishing when we are here and when we are not here. (2003, pp. 8–9)

Through her work with Whitehouse, Adler learned firsthand the experience of being witnessed as a mover in a way that supported her finding her own true spirit embodied in her movements. She began her work with Whitehouse because of her own self-searching, driven by her desire to step into the unknown and untouched parts of herself. She acknowledged this work with Whitehouse as deeply influential in how she approached her work with children with autism. As an embodied witness (i.e., one who moves with the mover, as opposed to one who observes without moving), Adler (2003, p. 12) carefully followed the "precious detail" of the gestures that a child often repeated, thereby creating a personal distinctive movement pattern. Moving with a child, Adler experienced the child "in a merged state" with these action patterns (p. 12). She believed that was occurring due to the child's lack of an internalized witness. Taking on the role of an external "moving, open-eyed witness," Adler was able to create a dialogue with the child with autism (p. 12). Adler felt that during these moments of relationship, the child was able to experience the early beginnings of the development of an inner witness in which one comes to know and develop one's own true sense of self. Adler was convinced that this relationship with others strengthened the child's sense of self and supported growth in all other aspects of development.

The Place of Not Knowing

To step into a dialogue with another that creates a mover–witness relationship requires each member of the dyad to relinquish preconceived perceptions and be willing, instead, to enter into a space of not knowing. Through this process of abandoning knowing, directed instead by moving and feeling through listening, a sense of immediate presence—a consciousness of the movement—becomes possible. This conscious presence helps to develop an individual's deeper knowledge and awareness of his or her authentic feelings, which may reveal different information than was previously assumed.

In the *Ways of Seeing* approach, this aspect of the discipline of Authentic Movement is applied and adapted in specific ways to work with young children and their families. Significantly, infants and young children also begin their explorations of their surrounding world from a place of not knowing: Their experience is about discovering and making sense of their explorations. They are coming from a place of bringing organization to the unknown rather than relinquishing knowing; they are just beginning the process of developing both intersubjectivity (i.e., the reciprocal sharing of emotions and felt-sense that enables two individuals to each have a sense of self that is separate yet in relationship with the other) and objectivity as perceptions about their experiences are forming. It is from this experiential learning that they will slowly become conscious of their presence in the moment and the effect of their presence on others. They may be able to experience their behaviors and their effects on others from the beginning, but their having conscious understanding and objective awareness of their feelings about personal behaviors—and the effect of these behaviors on others— are perceptions that take time to develop. Acting as the observing and embodied witness, a therapist holds the conscious awareness of the interactional experience both for himself or herself and for a child. It is through this embodiment that the child will be able to learn about actions, such as how they feel, how they communicate, and how they affect the environment. Through these experiences, the child develops a sense of presence and an internalized inner witness.

In taking on this role, the therapist must simultaneously be mindful of how the experience feels personally and also the possible interpretations of how the experience might feel for the child, without ever assuming that this can be known for certain. Maintaining this lack of certainty is essential because it keeps the therapist open to being present from moment to moment and enables the relationship to feel spontaneous and alive. Such improvisational spontaneity is the element that encourages a relationship to grow, thereby creating a reliable and trusting attachment.

It may seem contradictory that abandoning a sense of knowing can foster the development of a secure relationship. After all, it is the familiarity of experiences as they occur repeatedly that enables an infant to create the sense of knowing and constancy that builds secure attachments. In the *Ways of Seeing* approach, however, a therapist's lack of certainty regarding a child's feelings does not preclude the development of consistent patterns of interactions that become the foundation of a developing relationship. Instead, it asks the therapist merely to always stay open to the moment, fostering active, spontaneous involvement and creating a sense of discovery in interactions. This discovery comes from being receptive to the child's cues rather than having preconceived notions based on the therapist's knowledge.

To be willing to enter into a dialogue with self and other, to surrender knowledge, and to be open to discovery are especially difficult tasks for a therapist, who is trained and skilled in highly developed teaching and treatment techniques. This process asks a therapist to not only set aside important training in order to really listen to a child but also to turn the focus inward and listen to personal responses. This assumes that this act of looking inward might reveal important perspectives about the role of the therapist's personal responses in relation to the child. The range of such responses may be quite vast, varying from something as simple as being reminded of another child, to experiencing an intensely unsettling feeling of despair related to a time when the therapist felt personally misunderstood. It requires the therapist to see the child as the teacher, in a place in which they both enter the unknown space together in relationship, watching, listening, and feeling. It asks the therapist to trust that through this process the appropriate course of intervention will unfold. Ultimately, of course, the therapist's training and knowledge will deeply influence and sustain the experience by guiding rather than dictating the interactions. The fuel for these interactions must come from the therapist's attitude of being present with the child, and open to any spontaneous explorations that might shed light on growing possibilities and potentials.

Adding Trained Knowledge to the Self-Observation Process

The *Ways of Seeing* approach adapts this method of working, rooted especially in Adler's early work with children with autism and in her thorough investigation of the witnessing experience, by incorporating knowledge from the fields of education, neurobiology, and all aspects of child development. In practice, a therapist is asked to suspend the sense of knowing—not to forget about it completely! The therapist suspends his or her wealth of knowledge in order to see the child more authentically. It is a way to gather more information about the child, the therapist, and their developing relationship. In addition, instead of attempting to alleviate the observer-therapist bias, the therapist is asked to become more consciously aware of personal responses and reactions to a child. All this information adds to the therapist's studied understandings and enriches the experience for both the therapist and the child. This is illustrated in the following vignette about Brianna, who was first introduced in Chapter 1 to readers. Here, Brianna is 2 months into treatment. The first part of the entry provides an objective description of the interaction, interspersed with the internal dialogue the therapist has with herself. (The terms *objective, kinesthetic seeing, kinesthetic empathy,* and *witnessing* used in this internal dialogue will be discussed following this vignette.)

Objective: Brianna lies on her back on the floor with her body totally extended, arms out horizontally, rocking and rolling her head from side to side. When she stops, she draws her fingers close to her eyes, watching them intently as she ripples them delicately in a continuous fluid Phrasing rhythm. I lie down, mirroring her actions, rippling my fingers close to my eyes.

Kinesthetic seeing: As I lie here on my back I feel mesmerized by my fingers. Held so close I lose track of them as my fingers. Instead, I am drawn to the light and space behind them creating twinkling images like a strobe light.

Kinesthetic empathy: As I continue to stare, I am no longer aware of anyone else around me. I am content and alone, enjoying this visual sensation.

Witnessing: As I try on her "dancing finger" and head-rocking actions I begin to wonder what these movement metaphors might be expressing for Brianna. Caught in this entrancing visual and kinesthetic world and given Brianna's substantial physical, communicative, and social developmental delays, how can Brianna know the pleasures of the world of interpersonal interaction? How can I approach her in a way that can interest her in social engagement?

Over the next few weeks the therapist begins to use these movement metaphors as a means of social dialogue. Her internal dialogue continues:

Witnessing: So I have begun to do the head rock and roll with her, drawing her attention to me through words and touch and then repeating her actions, playing with varying the timing and the duration. She totally enjoys this and immediately stops her rocking to watch me. She also begins it on cue after I have stopped. Might this relate to Stage 3 of Greenspan's Functional Emotional Developmental Levels—interactive intentionality and reciprocity—for ages 6–12 months? Great! She is beginning to learn about being able to engage in cause-and-effect social interaction, using and demonstrating purposeful signaling!

During this internal dialogue the therapist continues to monitor her own reactions, evidenced in her session notes a few weeks later:

Witnessing: I am very aware of my consciousness in trying to read and encourage Brianna to communicate and express herself—following Greenspan's stages, we have established Stage 1—mutual attention and engagement. Now I want to encourage Stage 2—intentional 2-way communication— and Stage 3. I am still working on skills such as crawling, upper-body awareness, and exploring sounds through vocalizing and stimulating her diaphragm. But I really want to encourage her to try to use nonverbal movement and vocalizing cues to get into a (dancing) dialogue and exchange. I have been noticing that her family is focusing on her mastering physical skills. I recognize that this keeps their hopes up. I have seen this with many families. Seeing the child accomplish a new task keeps the parents going. But I want to make sure we don't forget there is a child with feelings and a personality behind all the effort to keep her skills' building. I am ascribing such an attitude to Brianna—but who knows? Maybe she is this cognizant!! Why not work from the premise that she is cognizant of the feelings and moods around her? Even if it isn't a mature awareness, I think she does respond and react to the "essences in the air."

WITNESSING, KINESTHETIC SEEING, AND KINESTHETIC EMPATHY

The *Ways of Seeing* program has defined three categories of self-observation to organize a therapist's observations and embodied experience: witnessing, kinesthetic seeing, and kinesthetic empathy (see Table 7.2). The author's experience with the discipline of Authentic Movement has greatly influenced how personal observations, reactions, and responses in her work with children and families have been ordered. She has developed the content of these three categories out of her own explorations in adapting the principles of Authentic Movement to this younger population. These categories encourage a therapist to review and ponder each of these aspects while working with a child and family. The therapist's awareness uncovers how subjective bias may be influencing actions, which in turn influences the child's experience. Through this inner

Table 7.2. The *Ways of Seeing* approach's three categories of self-observation to organize a therapist's observations and embodied experiences

Witnessing: Includes 1) a therapist's objective mapping of actions and 2) self-reflective comments that describe the therapist's awareness of general thoughts, personal reactions, and sensations that may come up when moving with or observing a child.

Kinesthetic seeing: Knowledge gained about a child through a therapist's own sensory experience reveals the possible ways the child may be experiencing his or her surroundings; knowledge obtained from trying on the child's movements is then used to inform subsequent therapeutic interventions.

Kinesthetic empathy: Includes a therapist's emotional reactions due to experiencing and trying on a child's movements while moving with the child; through this experience, the therapist can reflect on how the child might be emotionally experiencing his or her surroundings.

dialogue, the therapist reveals how the goals of the intervention are continually revised as she listens to both personal reactions and to the child's responses. This differs from other nonverbal observational approaches that strive to alleviate the observer's bias (e.g., Scheflen's Context Analysis (Davis, 1977)).

Witnessing

The *Ways of Seeing* approach intentionally uses this term to maintain its connection to the discipline of Authentic Movement. Witnessing emphasizes the importance of a therapist's acknowledging perceptions to include all observations and embodied experiences. For clarity, the *Ways of Seeing* approach has delineated two aspects of witnessing:

- A detailed descriptive tracking of a child's actual actions

- Self-reflective comments of this experience, discussing thoughts, personal reactions, and sensations in response to moving with or observing the child

During this second aspect of witnessing, a therapist makes connections between personal experiences and trained knowledge. The first aspect of witnessing has been depicted throughout this book by objective descriptions of experience. In this first aspect, a therapist provides a detailed descriptive tracking of actions and attempts to map them as objectively as possible so they can be clearly visualized. These descriptions can take the form of an LMA profile as discussed in the previous chapter, or well-defined characterizations of specific behaviors. This objective aspect of witnessing should always precede the specifically self-reflective aspects of the second aspect of witnessing. The *Ways of Seeing* method asks a therapist to first clarify what he or she is seeing, and through this mapping of the actions, differentiate this objective viewing from personal reactive reflections. This initial tracking, void of reaction, is then followed by emotional, felt-sensed, and knowledge-based interpretations to help the therapist become aware of how each aspect of personal experience might be influencing his or her interactions with a child. To clarify these two separate aspects of witnessing, the reactive aspects of self-reflection are labeled as witnessing, and the mapping aspects are left unlabeled or are labeled as objective. Below is an excerpt from the first 25 minutes of a session with Nikki.

Objective: Nikki enters today with increased hand wringing. I decide to attempt to start with relaxation, but she is not able to settle her tense pulsing. I see this tension all over her body. Instead, she indicates that she wants to use the drum. She does this by looking over at it very intently using directness and sustainment and then nods her head very eagerly when I ask her if she wants to play it. So I take out the drum.

Witnessing: I am very happy that Nikki is trying to communicate and I want to support it—whatever form it takes. I feel excited that she is really seeming to register the activities we do here, and perhaps even getting a sense of what activities might help her. The choice of the drum seems like an excellent way to re-channel her bound flow hand wringing.

Objective: Nikki now adds arm movements, reaching out in space as she hits the drum. She reaches her arms in arcing directional actions from her side, next reaching down low, then diagonally forward hitting the drum. She accompanies these movements by bobbing her head up and down. These actions get us into a continuous drumming dialogue, improvising with our own beats like a spontaneous conversation.

Witnessing: I am very drawn to extending this experience with Nikki. She seems intent on communicating through the drum, and I find myself so ready to follow and add to her rhythms.

Kinesthetic seeing: By now, though, we have been drumming for about 25 minutes. I am aware that through my excited state my body is very riled-up. My actions are quick and a bit tense. I'm concerned that for Nikki this could cause her to increase her bound state. So I decide to transition us into relaxation at this point. Perhaps now she will be ready to settle down, since the drumming seemed to match and redirect the tension she entered with today.

The therapist relies on reading Nikki's nonverbal cues to create and adjust the environment as a way to facilitate Nikki's participation. Throughout this process she continually monitors her own nonverbal, sensorial, and emotional reactions in an attempt to pay attention to how they may be contributing to the experience. The kinesthetic description that is added here details how the therapist is specifically attending to how her own excited state may be affecting Nikki.

Kinesthetic Seeing

This aspect of self-reflection draws attention to a therapist's own sensorial experience. A therapist is asked to notice shifts in his or her own sensory awareness including increased or decreased physical reactions. Becoming aware of bodily reactions provides information about how a therapist is physically experiencing a child through observations and shared actions. For example, 1) "There is a rapid change in the rhythm of my breath as I playfully try to run after Jane"; 2) "I feel a surge of warmth throughout my body as Janice kicks and coos in response to my smiling at her"; or, 3) "The muscles in my arms and chest begin to tighten as I watch Carol carry her new baby without supporting his head." These sensations may affect how the therapist interacts with the child or family and also may lead him or her to reflect on possible ways the child may be experiencing the surroundings. This knowledge informs subsequent interventions and interactions. Continuing with the situations outlined above, the therapist may conclude in noticing the rapid change in breath described in the first example that "I must stop, but she is not ready to do so." The second example may create a response from the therapist such as "I am encouraged and respond back with heightened enthusiasm." The third example may produce yet a different response in the therapist: "I find myself approaching Carol with an air of disapproval that I try to cover up with a smile, but as I begin to greet her my words are sharp and irritated."

How might these varied reactions by the therapist affect continuing interactions? These interactions might evolve in an infinite number of ways. In the first example, the child might be empathic and slow down or get upset and run farther away; in the second example, the baby might also respond more robustly or get upset, tuning the therapist out if the approach is too strong; or in the third example, Carol might pick up on the therapist's curtness and respond with a cool defensiveness, or she may not be sensitive to it at all.

These examples are very simple, everyday occurrences that happen so frequently that the specific details contemplating how one behavior may affect another often goes unstudied. The point of emphasizing such examination is to urge the therapist to become acutely aware of how personal reactions may color responses. Every action and reaction has the opportunity to communicate, thereby influencing the resulting interactional exchange. This supports the concept, discussed in Chapter 2, that relationships are co-constructed. The *Ways of Seeing* approach demands that a therapist go beyond the usual associations such as "I am tired today so I have less patience with the children," to define instead exactly what physical and sensory-based sensations may be fueling personal behaviors. Developing the ability to read personal nonverbal cues develops a therapist's capacity as an inner witness, which, in turn, enables the therapist to be more receptive in reading the nonverbal cues of others. This process strengthens a therapist's ability to witness another person, and such understandings reveal patterns of behaviors specific to individual relationships. The following scenario shows how such awareness may unfold:

    I watch Amy playing gleefully and wildly at the water table. She hits the water hard repeatedly as she scoops a cup deeply into the water. She then raises the cup of water high into the air and turns it upside down, letting the water pour into the basin. As I observe this, I realize I'm holding my breath. Suddenly she makes an extra-large splash as she scoops the cup into the water. Spontaneously I run to her shouting, "STOP!" The toddler responds with a startle and begins to cry. Now she can't stop crying!

After watching this reaction and recalling that Amy's regulatory issues can show up as poor impulse control, the therapist now considers the situation.

    As I call to mind holding my breath, I now realize I was anxiously awaiting a disaster. This in turn causes a reaction in Amy. My spontaneous reaction demonstrates a sudden change in behavior that supports Amy's sensitive reactivity, rather than modeling a more controlled reaction response. Perhaps next time, when I first feel myself holding my breath, I can use that as a signal warning me of Amy's escalating behaviors. I can take a deep, relaxing breath and assess whether her actions are truly depicting an escalation. If so, I can then approach her at the water table and help her modulate her actions, fostering regulation before her behaviors get out of hand.

Kinesthetic Empathy

Often such self-reflection on the part of a therapist elicits an emotional response, as well. The kinesthetic empathy category includes a therapist's emotional reactions derived both from observing and from experiencing a child's movements by trying them on. Using personal awareness of emotional bodily reactions, the therapist can contemplate how the child might be experiencing the surroundings emotionally. For example, continuing with the water table scenario, the therapist's inner dialogue might reveal the following:

As I think about it, I often hold my breath as I watch Amy engage in physical play. Her actions make me feel like the room is not safe. What might Amy's actions reveal about her sense of safety? What can I do with my nonverbal actions to address safety issues? Could I have gotten the message across without moving so quickly and shouting? I can use my breathholding as a signal to myself of my discomfort. Then I can observe Amy's behaviors to see what the intentions of her actions might be communicating. She might be signaling me to help her gain control of her actions. Children who do not have good impulse control often need limits set to help them learn how far they can go. Conversely, can I give her another minute before I intervene, to see if her actions are simply expressing her playfulness?

This realization enables the therapist to reflect on ways she might adapt her behavior as well as explore potential themes with the child. By being aware of how personal emotional reactions may be influencing bodily and physical responses, the therapist strives to maintain a nonjudgmental attitude toward the child's actions and the interactive exchange.

Kinesthetic empathy occurs by first being present in the moment, observing and embodying a child's actions through experiencing, mirroring, and attunement. This enables a therapist to be available—both empathically and physically—to perceive even the smallest hints of communicative exchanges. Several elements happen simultaneously during this process. By approaching a child from a place of compassionate understanding, the therapist stays open to first sensing and feeling the child's actions rather than immediately interpreting them. The therapist assumes an initial position of "not knowing" that enables a primary emotional connection to occur on a body experiential level. Mutuality can develop as emotions are shared; staying empathically opened during each interaction enables the therapist to continually check and adjust perceptions and to modify them based on the child's responses. The therapist cannot truly know, of course, exactly how this experience feels for the child—the therapist can only know how it feels as a participating member of the experience. Still, it is through shared emotional experience that one gets to know another and a relationship grows. From such knowing, trust and a sense of self emerge—both within the self and as reflected in the other.

Objective: Brianna sits between my straddled legs on the floor with her back against the front of my torso. I take each of her hands in mine and attempt to circle her arms forward, up, back down, and around. She leans her body forward, stiffening her arms, and slides her hands out of mine using quick, indirect, pulsing actions. This is accompanied by a high shrieking sound. She is resisting my contact. I narrate her reaction, "Oh you do not want to move like this? Okay, let's try one hand at a time." I place her left hand in mine and begin again. But this time I lean forward as she does, following her lead as she bends her elbow, making smaller and more free-form gestures in the air with her arm. As Brianna continues to direct this arm dance, her arm becomes more flexible, swooping in front and to her side. Our bodies sway forward and back in unison. Suddenly she comes to a stop and turns her head to look at me with a smile. "Yes, what a lovely arm dance," I say as I slide my legs out, situating myself across from her. Now facing her, I take her arms to continue our arm dance, but she suddenly stiffens again. Dad comes up behind Brianna and supports her just as I had done. With Dad behind and me in front, the three of us begin to sway and swoop, still following Brianna's lead. With this support, we assist her to stretch a little further each time we feel that she is receptive to it. She lets us know by keeping her arms loose and flexible. She giggles and smiles.

Witnessing: I feel like we are really working as a team—the three of us (Dad, Brianna, myself). I kept us connected to Brianna's ebbs and flows of attention and strength—always stopping to converse with her—narrating what we are doing and looking and getting eye contact as Dad follows right beside me. We are both led by Brianna's guidance.

Kinesthetic seeing: I stay connected to Brianna by reading her body cues and vocal cues with my own body. I feel resistance as our limbs and bodies stiffen, which stops the movement. Her high-pitched vocalizing feels like a tightening in my throat. This sound greatly differs from the more mid-level tone she produces when straining during actions that require physical exertion.

Kinesthetic empathy: I feel my excitement growing as our trio dance ensues. It feels to me like a true improvisational dancing dialogue as we follow Brianna's lead, mirroring and attuning to her swaying body and swooping arm actions. Her vocalizations, giggles, and smiles add to her socializing ability. I feel uplifted—might she, too? Her eyes look bright and she sustains eye contact with both Dad and me. Dad smiles back broadly and gives her a warm embrace when we bring this session to a close. As we say goodbye, the whole room feels bright and light!

Through these processes of witnessing, kinesthetic seeing, and kinesthetic empathy, Brianna is "seen," supporting her ability to join in a delightful communicative social exchange. By seeing Brianna, the therapist and her father do their best to truly experience her. Behavior is what is seen; experience is what is felt. By witnessing Brianna, the therapist and father create a sense of presence, empowered through kinesthetic seeing. By observing Brianna's actions from a place of kinesthetic seeing, they begin to experience what it might be like to move like Brianna. Through kinesthetic empathy they begin to gain an emotional understanding of how Brianna might be experiencing her surroundings. Of course, it is their own interpretation of her experience; they cannot know for sure what her experience is. Watching and trying on her movements, however, provides a window into the possibilities of what Brianna might be encountering and enables a mutual emotional exchange. It enables them to become more understanding of Brianna's idiosyncratic actions, and in turn, to use them to develop their rapport with her. Through the moment-to-moment movement exchange, each of their actions contributes to the interaction. This excerpt illustrates the power of attending to nonverbal cues to support relating and communicating. For this young child who does not have the ability to engage in verbal dialogue,

When an adult observes a child by witnessing, kinesthetic seeing, and kinesthetic empathy, the child is truly "seen."

nonverbal clues become invaluable in enabling Brianna to develop her relationships.

Working in this manner, a therapist follows a similar path as that of the ethnographic researcher doing field research. A researcher enters into a new culture, perhaps with some information, but mostly staying open to what might be found by experiencing this unknown world. Similarly, a therapist begins a journey of discovery with a child and family, always looking for what may be revealed by sitting, watching, and interacting. Thus engaged, the therapist may go down a previously unnoticed new passageway, always staying careful to keep all senses alive in experiencing this new "culture."

The following vignette of Nikki demonstrates how the self-observational process affects the *Ways of Seeing* therapist's awareness over time through the knowledge gleaned from mirroring Nikki's actions (with modifications).

(November 24) Objective: Pepper gives Nikki two dolls. I take two and dance with them into the center of the room, verbally encouraging Nikki to join me. She watches glowingly without moving for a few minutes. Then she begins her own dance of stepping, rocking, turning, and moving across the room, dropping the dolls. She continues to direct our dance, with me following her for 20 minutes. I follow, mirroring her with modification. Basically, I follow the form of her dancing actions, but I allow my own qualitative differences in performing these actions to come out. She is able to keep the movements continuous rather than her usual stop-and-go rhythm!! Her dance is accompanied by lots of joyous vocalizing.

Witnessing: I choose not to match Nikki's movements exactly to enable her to experience this as a true social dialogue rather than me just following her. I want her to feel the unique contribution of each of our actions without changing the action too drastically—I'm concerned how that might cause her to lose her ability to continue to follow the exchange. What I do seems to work, for she is able to keep the movement dialogue going. It is as if she is saying through her movement, "Okay, if you vary the movement that way, I'll vary it this way."

(February 25) Objective: At the end of our dance improvisation sequence, Nikki walks us over to the dolls and looks up at them with a steady gaze. I ask her if she wants to dance with them and she eagerly nods her head yes. I slowly hold them up one by one, saying their names, asking her if this is the one she wants. She shakes her head no until I show her the

sixth one. I hand it to her and take one myself and direct her to the open floor and hold the doll out, dancing with it—mirroring, with slight modification, the dancing movements I just did with her as my partner. Nikki watches with a broad smile and holds her doll close to her body. Intermittently, in a time delay, she looks at the doll, stretching it out to mid-reach space and shakes it or lifts it in an approximation of what I have just done. When I see her action, I then attune to her action, copying it, but add more effortful emphasis and increase my actions as they extend out into space. She seems encouraged by this and gleefully expands her movements to include more full body actions, such as head nodding and lifting the doll higher up along the vertical dimension.

Kinesthetic seeing: I realize that I constantly mirror her actions but that I modify them, often by adding larger actions that use more flow and space. Actually, trying to do her movements exactly like her—mirroring—is very difficult. It makes me feel too confined! I wonder if it feels like that for her. She seems so visibly relieved and joyous when we get into these movement flows, and her movements become larger and more relaxed. Perhaps Nikki does not know how to find these more expanded actions on her own, but she can embody them when she is helped to find them as we play with these kinds of movement progressions.

Initially, the therapist describes her motivation to modify Nikki's actions as a way to support more natural dialogue with Nikki. Although this is true, she also discovers over the course of time that she finds it difficult and uncomfortable to maintain Nikki's movement style. She uses this information to expand Nikki's movement repertoire, which in turn expands Nikki's ability to express herself through their dancing dialogue. Nikki is able to feel successful in her ability to have an interactive exchange through these nonverbal means. The therapist's ability to be aware of, and then to respond to, Nikki's altered forms of communication is the essential component that enables the child's actions to become a dancing dialogue. Mirroring Nikki's actions gives the therapist ideas about how the movements may feel for her. But it is the modification of these actions, and the ways that the therapist varies them through attunement and the addition of other movement qualities that enables the experience to convey the give and take of a true communicative dialogue.

This *Ways of Seeing* approach encourages Nikki's self-expression, interaction, and communication. It also reflects dance movement therapy's roots as an artistic form. The *Ways of Seeing* approach strives to create an environment similar to that of an artist, encouraging, seeking, and honoring a child's unique view and experience. In Nikki's story, it is through the dance movement therapist's artistic understanding of her own body as a tool for self-expression and communication that she is able to demonstrate and teach Nikki how to nurture this type of expression and communication within herself. It is from this perspective of artistic self-expression that the therapist closely observes the qualities of Nikki's nonverbal actions as communications—continually maintaining, accommodating, and complementing her own movements in response to the movement qualities presented by Nikki. In essence, the therapist and child establish a dancing duet of relating, and the experience leads to an increase in the child's social-emotional expression.

EXERCISES TO DEVELOP SELF-OBSERVATIONAL SKILLS

The first step in developing self-observational skills that have a kinesthetic focus is to gain awareness of one's personal nonverbal style. This involves learning about how to use one's body and movement actions to communicate, react, and respond to surroundings. It is not necessary to be a trained dancer to explore personal nonverbal expressive modes. However, a dance movement therapist who has extensively explored the use of dance and movement as an expressive medium and as healing art can provide helpful guidance. Developing self-observational skills is a very thorough and intensive process that includes studying a variety of classic, modern, folk, and ethnic dance techniques and methods of choreography to understand the roots of this expressive medium as a pure art form and to develop a broad movement-based vocabulary. Deeply intrinsic to dance study is the exploration of improvisational dance techniques that enable a student to uncover personal dance vocabularies. In this process a student discovers movement-quality preferences and learns about the personal meanings hidden within these actions. This is an invaluable and unique experience in a dance movement therapist's training. The depth and breadth of this training prepares a dance movement therapist to assist others in finding their own unique nonverbally based expressive vocabulary. Such experiences bring insightful information about themselves to the dancer and nondancer alike and support their development in becoming strong inner witnesses.

The activities in this section start from developing a general awareness of a person's nonverbal style to gaining very specific knowledge about a person's nonverbal signature. Each exercise contains information about how nonverbal styles reflect and express a person's emotional self. A personal profile of nonverbal tendencies and preferences can be created from these exercises.

Such profiles should enable people to develop greater wisdom about their bodies and actions as they reflect on their feelings and how they relate to their environment. These exercises have people step into the unknown by asking them to not assume that they know how they feel, but, instead, to obtain information about their bodies and feelings by listening to how they feel moment by moment. Gaining such a sense of personal knowing is especially helpful for therapists in learning how to use their bodies and their nonverbal understandings more effectively to support the development of a child's nonverbal awareness in the context of building communication and relationships with self and others. These exercises should each be repeated over a period of time.

While doing these exercises, it is very helpful for a person to keep a journal of his or her experiences, recording insights and looking for patterns to emerge. These patterns will describe the individual's nonverbal style. Once the exercises have been completed, individuals may want to find someone that they feel comfortable with to create a mover–witness experience. Ideas for sharing these experiences with another mover are provided at the end of these exercises.

General Nonverbal Awareness

These exercises (see Figure 7.1) consider what internal and external elements of the environment contribute to a person's sense of well-being each day. The goal of these exercises is to reveal how personal reactions interweave with environmental influences. Individuals should answer these questions by thinking descriptively, using their imagination and any images or metaphors that can help describe how they feel. The best advice is for individuals to be spontaneous and not to edit their responses because the aim is to get first impressions without censorship! Again, it is helpful to keep a journal of personal responses as these exercises are to be completed over a period of time.

Personal Specific Nonverbal Signatures

These exercises enable individuals to discover what happens on a body and feeling level in relation to their mood shifts. The exercises are based

General Nonverbal Awareness Exercises

Exercise 1

Think about your tolerance level for

1. Order
2. Disorder
3. Noise
4. Personal space
5. Energy level of others
6. Conflict
7. Maintaining a single focus
8. Maintaining multiple focuses

As you ponder each alternative, notice any specific associations you may have with that word or term. These can include people or events in your current or past life. If so, notice if these associations bring pleasant or unpleasant feelings. Notice as well whether you experience any of these feelings internally on a body level.

Exercise 2

Listen to a variety of music with different tempos and moods. Select a song to match each of these attributes: relaxed, calm, happy, focused/concentrated, excited, tense, angry, fearful, or tired. Notice what thoughts each style of music elicits from you. Notice which songs you favor. As you play each selection, notice if the song reminds you of anyone. Visualize that person interacting with you, and then notice your reactions.

Exercise 3

Describe yourself in general terms. Next, describe yourself using three movement-oriented words and pretend you are playing Charades. Visualize how you would demonstrate each movement-oriented word to someone else who has to guess its meaning. Think about what movement terms you might use to describe yourself when you are busy, tired, angry, happy, excited, or calm.

Exercise 4

Turn your focus on your present situation. What is the "essence in the air"? How would you describe the physical feeling or mood of your current environment? How does it relate or compare with how you are currently feeling? What movement-oriented word might you use to describe this feeling? Ask yourself these questions when you are alone, then again in a group setting, and yet again with a particular person.

Figure 7.1. Exercises that develop general nonverbal awareness.

on the concept that a continuum exists between mind, body, and feelings. In essence, there are always physical reactions to emotional responses that register consciously or unconsciously in the mind. Sometimes this connection is obvious; other times, it is very subtle. These exercises draw awareness to how individuals' minds, bodies, and feelings react to different internal and external stimuli. Perhaps that is why the word *action* is in the word *reaction*. The goal of these exercises is to map out a person's tendencies along this continuum.

To become aware of personal nonverbal styles, a person should focus on breath flow; muscular tension level; and posture, including body alignment and balance. Becoming aware of these elements can help a person to discover neutral or normal comfortable activity levels, as well as to reveal the body areas in which one holds stress. In doing these exercises, a person should pay particular attention to how one's body reacts to stress and how stress affects one's body. This will draw attention to how physical stress reactions relate to stamina, tolerance, and behavioral tendencies toward children and others. It is important for therapists in particular to learn to detect stressful and uncomfortable reactions, especially when working with children and families, for these reactions can greatly interfere with creating an optimum environment for growth. At the end of this section, a simple movement sequence is provided that is designed to increase full body awareness and help lower stress levels. This sequence will teach how to find and move from an individual's "center." Moving from center creates a sense of stability, inner core strength, and balance—both on a physical and an emotional level.

Breath-Flow Awareness   At the core of all action is the flow of breath. Gaining awareness of personal breath flow underlies all other body awareness because learning about breath-pattern tendencies and breath regulation supports all other actions and interactions. Figure 7.2 describes several exercises that will develop breath-flow awareness.

Muscular-Tension Level   The goal of the exercises described on Figure 7.3 is to draw awareness to those places in a person's body that may be held more excessively than necessary, and then discover if this tension is associated with specific emotions. *Muscular-tension level* refers to the amount of extra exertion or holding of the muscles beyond the normal effort necessary to maintain muscular integrity. Muscular tension should not be confused with muscle strength. *Muscle strength,* or power, comes from the natural increased exertion during the active stage of muscle engagement. This is followed by a recuperative phase following the completion of an action. It is during this second phase of muscular functioning that muscular tension often arises. Although the muscle's job is complete, the mover may neglect to entirely release the muscle. Frequently, this is not within the mover's conscious awareness but rather has become a habitual behavior.

Posture: Body Alignment and Balance   Posture is one of the most popular nonverbal actions described by both trained movement analysts and people without formal movement training. It is the sub-

Breath-Flow Awareness Exercises

Exercise 1

Draw your awareness to the flow of your breath during different times of your day. Breath flow involves three actions—inhaling, exhaling, and pausing. Notice the following things:

1. How deeply your breath enters your body
2. If you pause between the inhale and exhale, the exhale and the inhale, or both
3. How much air you take in comfortably and how much air you let out
4. If and when you hold your breath
5. If your body pulls in or expands when inhaling
6. If your body releases or contracts when exhaling
7. If the breath flows freely in and out of your body or, in contrast, if you pull it in or push it out

Exercise 2

Explore your specific feelings in relation to this breath awareness. Pause during your day and register how you are feeling, then notice your breath pattern. Do this periodically as your mood shifts. Determine what your breath-flow pattern is when you are relaxed, calm, happy, focused/concentrated, excited, tense, angry, fearful, or tired. Notice which emotions share the same breath pattern. Notice what is your preferred breath pattern, and then notice if this pattern is also your most prominent pattern.

Figure 7.2. Exercises that develop breath-flow awareness.

ject of fashion magazines, healthful living tips, psychological studies, and old wives' tales. Within each of these contexts, a person's posture is regarded as providing clues to the person's feeling state. The goal of the exercises described in Figure 7.4 is to explore how posture is used to support nonverbal expression. *Posture* includes body alignment and balance: *Body alignment* refers to the way in which a person places different parts of the body in relation to other parts; *balance* refers to how a person creates a sense of stability in this placement by shifting weight from one area of the body to another during both stationary and mobile actions.

Sequence: Moving from Center The movement sequence described in Figure 7.5 was developed to provide an individual with both an organized series of movements in which to explore particular movement tendencies and with a structured movement activity to improve body coordination. The movement principles of this sequence are based on the natural ways that a human body is designed to move. Through this sequence a person can experience the innate coordination and alignment that is based on proper anatomical structure and

Muscular-Tension Awareness Exercises

Exercise 1

Start in a stationary position, sitting, standing, or lying down. List the places in your body where you know you typically hold tension. Some of the most commonly held places of tension in the body are the muscles of the abdomen, rib cage, back, shoulders, neck, and face. Now notice if you can release any of these places a bit more during a breath cycle. Do this by actively breathing into the area and then consciously letting your breath go as you exhale. Find an image that evokes a sense of relaxation for you, such as melting or softening the area. Also notice your fingers, arms, legs, and feet. Are they at rest or unconsciously being held, clutched, fisted, or entwined in some way? Try breathing into these areas as well.

Exercise 2

Walk around the room, paying attention to both the commonly held places of tension in the body and the other places that you specifically tend to hold tension. In particular, notice how freely your limbs swing from your torso during this active state of walking. How much can you release in these areas while still feeling strong and steady as you walk? (Releasing can occur by breathing into a specific area of your body as described in Exercise 1; shaking out the body part to make your muscles loose; or stretching the area and extending it out into the space, making arcing and circular actions.)

Exercise 3

Draw your awareness to your level of muscular tension during the active times of your daily life. In contrast with Exercises 1 and 2, which help you establish your muscular tendencies while in a contemplative, investigative state, Exercise 3 asks you to correlate this information to real-life events. This can occur by focusing first on your body experience and second on your emotional feeling state.

For the body-focus perspective, randomly turn your awareness inward, sensing your level of tension at different points of your day. Specifically notice which areas of your body are drawing your attention.

Notice what your emotional feeling state is at that moment. Try to discern over time if there exists a pattern between where you are holding body tension and what you are feeling emotionally. Starting from a feeling state focus, take a moment to register your emotional state, and then notice if you are holding tension anywhere in your body. Notice if any of these places are key areas of your body that you have previously identified as the places where you typically hold tension. As you map out your muscular tension style, make sure that you review all of your emotional states because tension can arise out of positive as well as negative emotions.

Once you've identified an area of your body that holds tension, notice if any metaphors come to mind in regard to that area. For example, you may notice an upper body posture in which you hold your left arm close to your torso as you pull your left shoulder inward as if you are protecting your heart from pain. Perhaps you may notice an image of exhaustion coming over you as you focus on the tension of your lower back holding your whole body up. You may notice a sense of fluidity as if a stream is flowing throughout your body when you have accomplished a task on which you have worked hard. Or, you may feel your chest is light as a feather when you feel triumphant. Notice how these images relate to your current and past life experiences.

Figure 7.3. Exercises that develop muscular-tension awareness.

Posture as a Means of Nonverbal Expression Exercises

Exercise 1

Stop! Without moving, notice the position of your body right now. Observe what areas of your body you are leaning into to hold your body up and what areas are bearing little weight. Are you leaning over more to one side than the other, or do you distribute your weight symmetrically? Pay particular attention to how your large body parts are aligned with each other. Where is your head in relation to your neck, shoulders, arms, ribs, abdomen, hips, buttocks, legs, and feet? Notice this in different positions—lying, sitting, and standing. How does your breath flow play into this posturing? Emotionally, what is your mood right now? What is on your mind?

Exercise 2

During a time when you are actively engaged in some activity, notice the relationships between the same areas of your body that you noticed in the previous exercise. Draw your focus inward while you are involved in an activity or interaction with someone. How does moving affect your alignment? What body-part positions keep you most balanced and which create more instability? How comfortable are you moving all areas of your body? Do you find yourself mobilizing some areas more so than others?

Exercise 3

Notice your posture during moments when you have specifically registered your emotional state. What links can you make between your body postures and your feelings? Does your posture reveal information that you wish to relay? Might your posture be expressing aspects of yourself of which you are unaware?

Figure 7.4. Exercises that develop an awareness of posture as a means of nonverbal expression.

principles of kinesiology. This sequence, which can be done with or without music, can be used both to energize and to reduce stress in the body. Whether its effect is to energize or reduce stress will depend on the focus that a person takes while performing it: Performing the sequence in a smooth, slow tempo following one's breath flow will relax one's body; conversely, performing the sequence to a lively, rhythmic beat will be energizing. Once the sequence is learned, a person should feel free to embellish and improvise any aspect by listening and attuning to one's body and mood. After all, listening and responding to one's own body and emotional cues are the preliminary steps to learning how to listen to these cues in someone else.

A few points should be kept in mind throughout the movement sequence: It is important to notice one's breath from time to time, especially during the exertion and recuperation cycles; a person's body should expand on the inhale but should release and come back to a more neutral state on the exhale. Whenever possible, an individual should lengthen through the spine before bending it in any direction.

Exploring Movement Tendencies and Improving Body Coordination

Movement 1 *(Walking)*

Walk around the room, drawing your awareness to your joints starting from the base of your body. Feel how each ankle flexes with each step as you place your heel on the floor, roll through your arch to the ball of your foot, and then to the toes, finally pushing off with the toes to lift up your next foot to take another step. Notice how your knee bends and you swing your leg in your hip socket. As you lift your feet, alternate rolling through your feet with pausing momentarily, to balance and circle them around at the ankle joint. Once your gait feels stable, add circling the hands at the wrist joints and rippling the fingers individually. You can also transition the circling actions to small, quick, and free shaking actions of these extremities. Now add bending and circling of the elbows to correspond to your lifting of the knees. Next, enlarge your arm actions to include rotating at the shoulder joints and take larger steps, lifting the legs deeply from the hip sockets in relationship to the shoulder rotations of the arms.

Movement 2 *(Body-Part Awareness)*

As you do the actions in Movement 1, pay attention to how each body part is moving in relation to one another: the hands to the feet, the wrists to the ankles, the elbows to the knees, the shoulders to the hip sockets, and the chest to the pelvis. Also pay attention to what your specific preferences are today, depending on your mood: For example, are you in the mood to make the actions large or small? Do you want to move quickly or slowly?

Movement 3 *(Body Coordination)*

When you feel ready, find a place in the room to pause and stand tall. Notice where in the room you gravitate: Are you drawn to the open space, the natural sunlight, or to the only available place in which to stand in your house? From this stance, place one hand at the base of your torso in the front and one at the back. Slowly glide your hands up your body as you visualize zipping up your body as you lengthen through your spine.

Next, bring your arms down to your side. Starting from your side, swing your arms forward symmetrically, then up as high as you are comfortable, and then swing them down, creating a gentle curve of your spine, bringing your head with you as you bend at the waist and soften your knees slightly. Then, reverse the action, swinging back up. Keep these actions going freely, like a pendulum, allowing your momentum to guide them. Notice how high and low you can go while still maintaining a comfortable balance. After a while, have this action slowly come to a close, getting smaller and smaller, until you stop when you are standing tall.

Now widen your legs evenly into a small V (slightly wider than your shoulders) and lengthen along the left side of your body by scooping your left hand in front of and to the left side of your body as you extend your left arm all the way up vertically. Reach your left hand and arm up toward the ceiling and your left foot and leg down toward the ground. Now, feel this whole left side as one long line, and imagine it is one half of a hinge. Shift your weight to your right side. Lift the left leg and simultaneously swing it with your left arm, in front of your body, crossing your midline, then swing it back, planting your foot back on the floor. Repeat this action a few times, keeping your right side still and stable as you swing your appendages on your left side. All of your weight will shift to this right side to enable the free-flowing action of the left side. It is as if the left side is folding over the right side of your body. Then repeat this action on the right side.

Finally, lengthen your left arm high up to the upper left corner of the room and then scoop it down across and close to your torso toward your right leg and foot, swooping it down to the opposite corner of the room, and then back up away from your body, back to the high left corner. You are making an undulating arc with your left arm. Repeat this on the right side.

Movement 4 *(Weight Shifting)*

Lunge the right leg forward as you arc your left arm down toward it as in Movement 3, creating a contralateral relationship. Take your time to feel the weight shift onto this leg and lengthen through your spine. As your arm begins to arc back to the upper left side, push the weight off of the lunging leg. Find the right amount of push to enable you to bring your body back to your standing place while balancing on the left leg with your left arm extended high. Feel this full extension through your torso, creating a vertical axis in space. Notice how long you can comfortably hold this position. Repeat this action on the opposite side.

Movement 5 *(Centering Breath Flow)*

Bring your arms to your sides, and breathe deeply and freely. Feel your rib cage expand while you inhale and release when you exhale. Try to quiet down your actions in order to feel your ribs slightly expand in all three directions. Focus on each direction, one at a time: forward and backward, side to side, and up and down. Then, slightly shift your weight on your feet (while keeping toes down at all times) to match these directions, swaying your whole body and passing through center as you move in each direction. Keep your legs and lower body stable as you sway your upper torso freely. Imagine you are a willow tree, with your lower torso and legs as the trunk and your upper torso and arms acting as the branches and leaves. To complete this weight shifting movement, circle around your center, shifting forward, then to the side, to the back, and then to the other side, starting forward in both the left and right directions.

Movement 6 *(Rolling Down and Up Spine)*

Shift your weight to center. Leading with your head, slowly roll down your spine, feeling each body part fold over one at a time and bending at the waist and the knees to go down as far as you can. Follow this body part progression down: head, neck, shoulders, arms, chest, abdomen; then bend at the waist and knees and scoop your tailbone under. Reverse, leading with your tailbone and making sure your head is the last thing to come up. Repeat this whole sequence as much as you like, sensing how your body parts are aligning themselves along your center. At some point complete the roll all the way down to the floor, scooping your legs and arms under your body to make a small ball. Resting on your shins, you will be enclosed, with your lower legs, forearms, and the top of your head resting on the floor. Gently breathe in this position.

Movement 7 *(Up on Hands and Knees)*

Leading with the top of your head and moving down your spine, push up onto your hands and knees as if you are a table. Alternately arch and round your back, lifting your head on the arch and dropping it when you round your back. It may be helpful to envision yourself as a cat stretching as you do this action. Do this as many times as desired.

Movement 8 *(Knee Spirals)*

Starting on your hands and knees and leading with your tailbone and buttocks, shift the weight of your lower body to the right side, sitting on the floor, letting your knees shift to the left, and keeping your hands centered to your body on the floor. Feel the diagonal connection between your hands and upper body and your hips and legs. Now roll onto your buttocks with your hands behind you through a gentle spiraling action.

(continued on next page)

Figure 7.5. *(continued)*

Begin the spiral by lifting your left arm up and stretch it diagonally behind you as you take a breath in. Let your chest naturally follow and then lift your knees to face the ceiling, rolling from the sides of your feet to place your feet flat on the floor. Now both of your hands are behind you, and your feet and chest are facing forward. Let your breath out, and take another breath in, feeling the whole front of your body expand. Next, you will continue the spiral action, crossing over the front of your body to end up on your hands and knees to your left side.

On your next exhale, initiating the action from your tailbone, drop your knees to your left. Feel the action create a diagonal twist through your hips and into your chest. Now lift your right hand diagonally up and across the space in front of your chest, placing your right hand parallel to your left hand shoulder-width apart. Starting the action with your tailbone, swing your buttocks up until your weight is evenly distributed between your hands and knees. At this point you are back in the table/cat position. You can repeat this spiral motion a few times varying the tempo.

Movement 9 *(Closure)*

At this point notice how you feel and how your body feels. Decide if you want to end this sequence with relaxation or if you want to stay active and repeat the whole sequence.

To end this sequence with relaxation, you should repeat the first half of the knee spiral, pausing when your hands are behind you, your knees are up, and your feet are flat on the floor. Now lie completely down on the floor on your back. To do this, straighten your legs out by slowly sliding your knees down, then slide your arms out to your sides onto the floor. Find a comfortable resting position and breathe comfortably, paying attention to your body expanding on the inhale and settling back to a neutral place during the exhale. Keep this focus, sensing how your body feels now compared with when you first began the sequence. Notice if you are holding in any parts of your body. If so, visualize sending your breath flow to this area, releasing, relaxing, and melting the tension.

To repeat the whole sequence, you should lift your tailbone as you begin to straighten your legs by tucking your toes under. Now step or jump your legs to land between your hands. Slowly, leading with your tailbone, roll up your spine as you did in Movement 6 of this sequence. When you are standing, you can begin the whole sequence over again from the beginning.

Figure 7.5. Movement sequence to explore particular movement tendencies and to improve body coordination.

Moreover, an individual should think about adding space between the rib cage and the hips, thus lengthening the torso from the center. In fact, adding space and breath within the torso is the key to developing inner strength and finding and moving from one's center.

Final Advice and Considerations Those who participate in these exercises and movement sequences may find it helpful to review their journals of their experiences. Have patterns emerged as these exercises were repeated over a period of time? Do these patterns reveal and describe their personal nonverbal styles? After reviewing their journals, therapists, in particular, may want to find someone that they feel comfortable with to create a mover–witness experience; again write in their journals; and finally share portions of their accounts with each other, with the mover always speaking first. (Please note that specific exercises such as those described here are not typical in the discipline of Authentic Movement. In that discipline, the mover simply begins by closing his or her eyes and listening inward. These exercises are provided to introduce the concept of listening to one's body within the context of learning to apply this knowledge to support work with children and families.)

Self-Observation While Working with Children and Families

The final step of this self-observational process is to relate this way of observing one's self within the context of one's work with children and families. Keeping a journal of interactions and observations of the children with whom one is working for at least a week is one excellent approach. Track each child's specific actions in detail, and then take a moment before, during, and after interactions to notice one's own immediate thoughts, specifically sensing how one is feeling physically and emotionally.

The Interactional Behavior Log was created to facilitate this process. It was developed to help professionals—or parents—chart their experiences and self-observations with a specific child, both when thinking about the child and when interacting with the child. The six categories of the log include Date, Visualize, Observe, Self-Observation, Think, and Interaction. The "Date" charts the calendar date of each interaction, enabling the adult to keep track of how the experience progresses. The "Visualize: Detailed description" column asks the adult to describe the child's behavior in as much detail as possible from memories of experiences with the child. The "Observe: Detailed description" column asks the adult to track the child's behaviors as they are actually occurring or by watching a videotape; this particular column relates to the objective aspect of witnessing described earlier in this chapter. The adult will start with either the Visualize or Observe column, depending on whether he or she is actually with the child (or watching a videotape) or reflecting on the child. In the "Self-Observation" column, the adult is asked to describe the effect that the child's behaviors have on how the adult feels. This is the space for the adult to include self-reflective witnessing comments, kinesthetic seeing responses, and kinesthetic empathy reactions. In the "Think" column, the adult is encouraged to use the information gleaned from the previous two columns to substantiate perceptions about how the child's behaviors affect the child; that is, how the child may be experiencing his own behaviors. Finally, in the last column, "Interaction: New approaches," the adult is asked to record both ideas of possible approaches to future interactions with the child (perhaps gleaned from doing this analysis), as well as new approaches that have already evolved during recent interactions with the child. These new interactions reflect how the adult's understanding of the adult–child relationship is dynamic, involving the qualities, experiences, and perceptions that each person brings to the interaction. To demonstrate how this chart should be used, two completed Interactional Behavioral Logs using the vignettes of Brianna in this chapter are provided as Figure 7.6 and Figure 7.7, and a blank Interactional Behavioral Log can be found at http://www.brookespublishing.com/dancing.

Interactional Behavioral Log

Name of child: Brianna

Age: 23 months   **Date of birth:** _____

Date: January 16, 2005

Observer: ST

Visualize: Detailed description	Observe: Detailed description	Self-observation: Its effect on you	Think: How does it affect the child?	Interaction: New approaches
	Analysis obtained from review of video: She lies on her back on the floor with her body totally extended, arms out horizontally, rocking and rolling her head from side to side. When she stops, she draws her fingers close to her eyes, watching them intently as she ripples them delicately in a continuous, fluid Phrasing rhythm. I lie down, mirroring her actions, rippling my fingers close to my eyes.	*Witnessing:* Trying on her "dancing finger" and head rocking actions, I wonder how to approach her in a way that will interest her in social engagement? What movement metaphors might these actions be expressing for Brianna? *Kinesthetic seeing:* Lying on my back, I feel mesmerized by my fingers. Held so close to my eyes, I lose track of them as *my* fingers. I am drawn to the light and space behind them that creates twinkling images like a strobe light. *Kinesthetic empathy:* Continuing to stare, I'm no longer aware of anyone else around me. I feel content and alone, and I enjoy this visual sensation.	Caught in this entrancing visual and kinesthetic world, and given Brianna's substantial physical, communicative, and social developmental delays, how can Brianna know the pleasures of the world of interpersonal interaction? She may be quiet and content in her own world. She may not even notice I am following her hand movements. She may not even feel my presence next to her. Perhaps her sense of body boundaries is not developed. Maybe her proprioceptive sense is hyposensitive.	I want to try to get her to perceive her own body in movement and to sense the presence and movement of others nearby as they try to relate to her. I'll try making my touch very firm and exact. I'll create clear pathways in space as I move her body and individual body parts. I'll try to get some type of cue from her such as eye contact, body part movement, breath flow change/adjustment, change in speed, or cessation of her finger actions when I first approach her and/or touch her. Maybe I'll add vocalizing and verbalizing, such as her name and greetings, as I first approach and figure out what tone, length of verbal phrase, and quality of vocalization works best to get her attention. I'll continue this as I move with her, if she seems to respond well to it.

Figure 7.6.   Brianna's Interactional Behavioral Log at age 23 months.

Interactional Behavioral Log

Name of child: __Brianna__   Date: __February 18, 2005__

Age: __24 months__   Date of birth: _____   Observer: __ST__

Visualize: Detailed description	Observe: Detailed description	Self-observation: Its effect on you	Think: How does it affect the child?	Interaction: New approaches
She's on her back on the floor rocking her head side to side. I lie nearby, placing my face within 12 inches of her and gently say her name in a singsong manner, matching the rock of her head, "Briaaa" as she rolls it toward the floor; "naa" as she returns it. She stops her head actions, pausing, though she does not immediately look at me. I rock my head like her, saying her name again in the same way; then I stop. When I stop, she begins to rock her head again. We do this sequence several times. I move—she stops; I stop—she moves; she stops—I move, etc. I place my hands firmly embracing her ribs and gently roll her onto her side so she can look at me. Her eyes focus and slightly brighten. We continue this game—I vary the length and speed of my head rocking and pausing. So does she, without matching my timing.		*Witnessing:* I draw her attention to me through words and touch, repeating her actions. I play with varying the timing and the duration of my actions. She totally enjoys this and immediately stops her rocking to watch me. She seems to begin it on cue after I have stopped. Might this relate to Stage 3 of Greenspan's Functional Emotional Developmental Levels—interactive intentionality and reciprocity—for ages 6–12 months? Great! Maybe she is beginning to learn about being able to engage in cause-and-effect social interaction by using and demonstrating purposeful signaling! *Kinesthetic empathy:* My own excitement mounts as I see her look toward me, her eyes brightening. I hear myself say her name with a sudden burst the next time! *Kinesthetic seeing:* I must remember to keep my breath free and consistent as I move with her and say her name. In my excitement at her following me, I notice I start to hold my breath.	She sees me! She may feel my presence. Maybe she is enjoying the contact, the interaction. Perhaps her sense of body boundaries is developing. Maybe she feels her cues are being understood. At the very least she is enjoying the rhythmic exchange.	I want to extend this reciprocal dancing dialogue, to make it last as long as possible, while trying to keep her affective response fresh and engaged the whole time. This seems to be possible by changing the length of time of my rocking and vocalizing as well as playing with the speed within each movement phrase. I'll continue to play with changing these dynamics and see if this keeps her attending. I want to create a true rhythmic pulse, and I may try doing it to music with a simple, strong beat to see if this keeps her engaged. I watch her cues. Is she signaling in other ways? Is she moving other parts of her body such as her legs or fluttering her fingers? I will teach Mom how to read these subtle cues and play with her like this, and then I will watch to see if Brianna responds differently with Mom—perhaps she will show an even more heightened affective response. If so, I'll be sure to help Mom see/recognize this. This will support their growing relationship.

The Dancing Dialogue: Using the Communicative Power of Movement with Young Children, by Suzi Tortora, Ed.D., ADTR, CMA. Copyright © 2006 by Paul H. Brookes Publishing Co., Inc. All rights reserved.

Figure 7.7. Brianna's Interactional Behavioral Log at age 24 months.

252

8

The *Ways of Seeing* Technique

Rather than suppressing the fantasy of a psychotic individual, we should fly with him for a while, then descend with him for a soft landing on this earth. In giving shape to his visions, he will create a work that fuses fantasy with reality.

T. Schoop, Won't You Join the Dance? (1974, p. 150)

Maria, age 2½, is sitting on the floor with her legs spread wide and her back hollowed forward, head lifted, looking out into the room but avoiding eye contact. Her breath is shallow, her torso is relatively still, but her fingers and hands are tense, intermittently twitching and touching different parts of her body with quick dabbing taps. During the first phase of our work, the stimulation phase, I mirror Maria's posture and hand movements to draw attention to them. Maria glances toward me momentarily as her actions become more intensified. The activating phase now follows as Maria spontaneously begins to increase the twitching, adding more frequency and turning the movements into sharper flicking actions that reach out into the space in front of her. This sequence becomes a more purposeful action, as she begins to say, "Go away!" looking toward me but still avoiding eye contact. Verbalizing and enlarging the movement phase causes Maria to deepen her breath flow and expand her rib cage, increasing her kinesthetic body awareness. I follow her actions, exaggerating the flicking motion, and I introduce an increased use of the surroundings by moving my body toward and away from Maria. The mobilization phase has begun. This movement through space attracts Maria's attention, noted by how Maria leans her body slightly toward me, adjusting her head to enable a better sideways view of me. When I come closer to Maria, our hands meet,

push against each other, and turn into a backward arm circle. Physical con-
tact has been made.

As these actions are repeated, Maria begins to watch me more openly,
directing the placement of her hands to meet mine. A rhythmic arm circling
begins as our movements take on a dance-like form. The rhythmic structure
organizes our connection. Our dance of relating expands as, together, Maria
and I begin to move around the room. The actions become more fluid and
sweeping. I hand Maria a scarf to support this arching flow as we move in
synchrony throughout the room. Maria's breath becomes very calm as she
playfully moves around, toward, and away from me. Her actions are now
more free and full-bodied. She smiles and giggles as this gentle chasing dance-
play evolves. To create closure I tell Maria I will follow her, encouraging her to
find her own way to finish the dance. Maria responds by running around me,
wrapping us together in the scarf. ⌒

In this vignette Maria experiences how it feels when someone
responds to her actions and then transforms them. Through the movement dialogue, Maria learns that her physical expressions can create
connections with other people. Left unacknowledged, her initial
actions and postures potentially could become behaviors that isolate
her and interfere with communication. Instead, this positive experience
teaches her that with help, she can redirect her behavior in a very physical way, gain control over her feelings, and alter the outcome.

This chapter describes in detail the principles and activities that
comprise a typical *Ways of Seeing* session. It begins with a short summary of the concepts underlying the *Ways of Seeing* approach discussed
more fully in Chapter 3 of this book. The general principles, strategies,
and specific techniques that guide each session follow, providing the
reader with a toolbox full of ways to understand how the use of movement, dance, and nonverbal expressions can facilitate a child's growth
and development. The techniques described are those traditionally
used to create dance movement-oriented therapeutic sessions. Adding
any of these specific activities to other forms of therapeutic and educational services will provide a practitioner with added tools for understanding a child as well as enhancing the child's experience. This does
not replace a dance movement therapist's role as a contributing member of a child's treatment team; instead, it enables other practitioners
to work more fully with the whole child, creating a deeper common
ground among each of the professionals involved with the child.

SUMMARY OF *WAYS OF SEEING* CONCEPTS

The *Ways of Seeing* approach follows many of the elements of Authentic Movement (see Chapter 7) and general dance movement therapy practices. What singles out the *Ways of Seeing* from these other approaches is how its material is organized into a full program that can be used as a bridge from observation and assessment to intervention and educational programming. The theoretical aspects of the *Ways of Seeing* approach encompass early childhood development concepts, as explained in Chapter 2 of this book. The program also places a strong emphasis on LMA-based observations detailed in Chapter 6. The LMA aspect of the program is emphasized because, although all dance movement therapists have some training in LMA, not all dance movement therapists integrate it as deeply into their work as was done in this program.

The influence of the LMA system is most evident in the MSI Checklist, a nonverbal assessment/observational tool (see Appendix A) that is described in more detail in Chapter 5. A dynamic interactional relationship exists between the MSI Checklist and the activities of a therapeutic session, and often they occur simultaneously: MSI Checklist observations continually inform the intervention, and the intervention translates the MSI Checklist information into action—which leads to more MSI Checklist observations and further intervention and educational programming as a child's best learning style is discovered. This process is further developed when a dance movement therapist interacts with an educator and uses these discoveries to develop educational guidelines that optimize a child's learning potential.

The *Ways of Seeing* approach is especially helpful for children with developmental delays for two reasons: First, its belief that nonverbal expression underlies how a young child experiences motor development and learns about self in relation to other; second, its emphasis on how early preverbal experiences influence communication and cognition. The *Ways of Seeing* approach provides:

1. An avenue into seeing how a child is functioning and experiencing the surroundings—cognitively, socially, emotionally, physically, and communicatively, especially if that child is not able to communicate effectively

2. A support into communicative interactions at all levels of language acquisition

3. An insight into prelinguistic stages when verbalizations are not available

4. A technique of intervention that increases the communicative functions of children with delays and other symptoms of developmental disorders, while simultaneously developing their physical skills

The dance movement therapy technique that most clearly facilitates this progress is becoming aware of and focusing on the qualitative aspects of nonverbal actions. As the opening vignette portrays, bringing awareness to nonverbal expression creates an atmosphere of encouragement and connection to a child. This both supports the child's eagerness to succeed and provides needed support for parents in building their relationship with their child, in their trusting of the therapeutic process, and in increasing their sense of hope and acceptance of their child's disabilities.

A unique element that the *Ways of Seeing* approach brings to intervention is the concept of a dancing dialogue. A *dancing dialogue* involves an exchange between a child and a therapist (or other adult) through movements based on spontaneous improvisations. Such dialogue focuses on social engagement by the therapist's following the child's nonverbal cues. This creation of a social relationship through a dialogue of movement facilitates both the intervention and the child's development.

The *Ways of Seeing* approach strongly emphasizes an awareness and conscious use of affect and nonverbal qualities of movement to first establish a social interaction before continuing on with explorations in other areas of development. As described in the previous vignette about Maria's session, the qualitative aspects of her nonverbal style were used to heighten her sociability. The information obtained through this process led the therapist to further exploration. The *Ways of Seeing* approach unfolds in such a way that themes emerge, become a focus, and then evolve. The *Ways of Seeing* approach thrives on staying open to changes that occur through movement interactions that play a key role in the evolution of the therapeutic experience. Uncovering who a child is, and how a child's ability to express her emerging personality affects those working with her, becomes part of the discovery.

The term *Ways of Seeing* was chosen to emphasize the many ways there are to look, assess, and receive information about self and other. The *Ways of Seeing* approach encourages practitioners to strive to become more conscious about how they look, see, assess, think, and read the cues of the children with whom they work—and about themselves. This is based on the belief that every individual creates a nonverbal movement style composed of a unique combination of select movement qualities known as a movement signature that is used to interact with the surroundings. These qualities make up an individual's expressive communicative style regardless of how conventional or atypical that style might be. From a nonverbal analysis perspective, skill and developmental levels are considered within the context of the quality of an individual's nonverbal behaviors. Even severe movement limitations have a qualitative element to them: It may be in the level of tension in a person's musculature, the position the body habitually takes, or the frequency or infrequency of eye contact. How a person expresses these qualities creates in that person a sensation, an attitude, and a response to those observers in the environment. In return, observers of these behaviors have a reaction based on their own personal experiences. It is this action-reaction that influences the developing social-emotional relationship and affects therapeutic and educational interventions.

KEY PRINCIPLES AND STRATEGIES THAT GUIDE EACH SESSION

All activities in a session should give a child the opportunity to show a therapist who that child is. All nonverbal actions have the potential to be communicative. Nonverbal behaviors are expressions of self and as such have the potential to be used for meaningful communication. Therefore, a therapist must always look through, behind, under, and over these nonverbal behaviors to think, "What might this child be trying to tell me through these actions?"

Three questions are discussed more fully in Chapter 3 that a therapist must continually ask during each session, creating an internal running dialogue. These questions are:

1. How does relating and moving in a unique way color this child's experience?

2. What does it feel like to experience the world through this child's particular expressive movement repertoire?

3. How can a therapeutic environment be structured to enable this child to experience a way of relating and functioning as a com-

municative tool, while simultaneously enabling the child to use the experience to explore new ways of interacting?

The answers to these questions can best be found by experiencing a child's movement style by actually trying on the child's movements. This intervention strategy focuses on how individual children are using their own unique internal structures to cope, adapt, and respond to the environment. In the therapeutic setting, a child's personal non-verbal movement style directs the movement interactional dialogue among the child, the therapist, and any other significant members of the child's life who are participating in the session. The "dance" in the dance therapy process begins as these movement elements unfold during the child's spontaneous choreography. These may involve actual dance actions as well as creative play and storytelling activities. The *Ways of Seeing* approach has coined the term *dance-play* to incorporate all of these aspects of movement-oriented activities that may occur during a session. The salient dance-play elements of each session become reconstructed in the new dance-play that takes place during the next session. Thus, initially spontaneous sequences of movement often become choreographed elements for use in subsequent sessions. Keen attention is paid to how a child's subsequent actions may provide windows of opportunity for expanded interaction and developmental progression.

As described in depth in Chapter 3, movement and dance-based activities are conceptually structured within a four-part dynamic framework. The goal of Dynamic Process I (*Establishing Rapport*) is to enhance social-emotional and communicative development and at-tachment. In Dynamic Process II (*Expressing Feelings*), children are en-couraged to express and explore feelings, emotions, traumas, and con-scious and unconscious past and current events experientially through multisensory dance and play-based activities. In Dynamic Process III (*Building Skills*), children with developmental difficulties are helped to acquire physical and cognitive skills in tandem with social-emotional development. Although physical skill building is not always a part of the typical dance movement therapy program, the *Ways of Seeing* ap-proach includes skill building as an additional interactional activity that can build or strengthen a child–adult relationship. Dynamic Pro-cess IV (*Healing Dance*) acknowledges the intrinsically healing aspects of dance and movement. Dancing and moving feel good, enable a re-lease of bodily tension, and provide an avenue of playful interaction with others.

The Therapeutic Process

The therapeutic process occurs through a four-part procedure:

1. Match: Feel the quality of the nonverbal cues through attunement and mirroring

2. Dialogue: Create a dialogue through the use of these movements

3. Explore and expand: Explore, expand, and develop these movements

4. Nonverbal to verbal: Move communication from nonverbal to verbal excfhange

Match   Trying on a child's movements can occur in two ways: attunement and mirroring. *Attunement* is a term taken from dance movement therapy and defined in detail by Kestenberg (1975; Kestenberg et al., 1999) that is used by the *Ways of Seeing* approach to describe a person's matching of a particular quality of another person's movement, but not completely depicting the entire shape, form, or rhythmic aspects simultaneously, as in mirroring. In attunement, a characteristic of the action will be portrayed but may not occur with the same body part, spatial attention, or intensity. For example, a therapist may clap hands and nod his or her head to the rhythm of a child's jump, rather than actually jump with the child. The distinct essence of the action that the therapist is drawn to is portrayed through the handclapping and head nodding.

Mirroring, in contrast, involves literally embodying the exact shape, form, movement qualities, and feeling tone of a person's actions, as if a therapist is creating an emotional and physical mirror image. It is important, however, to distinguish mirroring from mimicking an action. In mimicking, the actions may be copied without matching the emotional attitude; in mirroring, there is a qualitative emotional connection between the therapist and the person whose actions are being mirrored. The *Ways of Seeing* approach has defined three additional variations of mirroring: In *mirroring modified,* the overall style and quality of the movement is left intact, but some aspect is changed. In the jumping scenario described previously, the therapist may match the depth of the bend of the jump but may vary the rhythmic pulse by alternating the speed of the jump in order to encourage the child to break out of the monotonous, trance-like quality that an unvaried rhythm might create. In *mirroring exaggerated,* the embodied movement qualities are enlarged, but the overall sense and style of the movement is retained. Continuing with the jumping scenario, for example, the therapist may decide to increase the depth of the bend downward and exaggerate the knee bend to help the child connect more deeply through the whole body before pushing up off the floor. In *mirroring diminished,* some aspect of the movement quality is reduced, but the overall sense and style of the movement is left intact. This would be the case if the therapist in the above scenario decides to soften the landing of the jump to demonstrate how to create a more gentle, buoyant body sensation.

The initial goal of both attunement and mirroring is to create an emotional connection with a child. Through these actions, a therapist reaches out to a child, using personal body actions to assure the child that his actions communicate. Attunement and mirroring both signify a therapist's desire to meet a child on the child's own terms by demonstrating an interest in learning what the child may be experiencing. Whether a therapist chooses to use attunement or mirroring depends on the moment-to-moment dynamics of the therapist–child relationship. Choosing effectively requires both a therapist's skill in knowing how each of these methods affects the interaction and a therapist's experience with a particular child. This knowledge is obtained over time as a therapist becomes familiar with these techniques and develops a growing relationship with a child.

Therapists often prefer the technique of mirroring as precisely as possible when first meeting a child. It creates a direct connection that is most completely child-centered. Mirroring makes a tacit statement that the child is the sole leader and the therapist is the follower. It requires a therapist to resist providing personal input and requires the least amount of modification on a child's part to enable relating to occur. In this way, mirroring can create a primary sense of safety for a child who is unable or unwilling to enter into a social-emotional dialogue. It is often a good way to start in situations in which a child is presented as being completely self-absorbed in his or her own personal world. It is impossible, of course, to mirror exactly. Even when mirroring a child's actions, a therapist creates a sense of presence of other. Inevitably, the child takes note of this presence and creates reactions that range from curiosity to enjoyment—or even anger. A child's reaction may be subtle, such as a fleeting gaze toward the therapist; slightly exaggerating or quieting an action; pulling or turning away; turning toward the therapist; or extending the action, creating a longer interactive movement sequence. All of these responses become avenues into relating and provide valuable information about a child's feelings and comfort level during an interaction.

In responding to a child with one of the three variations of mirroring or attunement, a therapist is beginning to add personal input. A therapist is clearly defining himself or herself as a separate other in relation to the child. This is an important and inevitable step in forming relationships. It moves the relationship from the more symbiotic stage in which there is little separateness between self and other into a more differentiated experience of self and other. A therapist's decision to respond to a child through attunement or through one of the three variations of mirroring should be specific to the situation, the relationship, the goals, and the child's ability. Attunement is a more subtle way to connect to a child and still establish this differentiation. By only responding to an aspect of a child's movements, a therapist gives the child a great deal of room, literally and figuratively, to take up space. It allows the child to feel distinctly separate while still relating. A therapist's chosen movement response creates an independent voice that immediately opens a dialogue of interpretation. It can be less intrusive to a child who may be sensitive to being overpowered or who already has a sense of autonomy.

The three variations of mirroring maintain a more united experience but allow the budding of differentiation. A therapist's decision to alter a quality of a child's action, for example, invites shared dialogue. A child's attempt to modify, exaggerate, or diminish some aspect of the action reveals a level of skill, perception, and awareness of the social exchange and the environment that should not go unnoticed by a therapist. This is where keen qualitative observation is essential. A therapist must have the ability to detect a child's strivings, which may at first be quite subtle. A therapist can then acknowledge the child's efforts, verbally or nonverbally, through smiles, head nods, and an extension of the movement dialogue. From this joint shared experience between therapist and child, a relationship grows and develops into spontaneous dialogue.

Dialogue   Once the movements are matched and a social-emotional connection has occurred, the next step is to use a child's movements as the primary vocabulary that can develop the relationship further. The therapist draws from this movement vocabulary to create new spontaneous dialogues. Novel interactional exchanges occur as the therapist combines movements to make fresh reciprocal sequences that both support and challenge a child: The child's comfort level is supported because the movements used for dialogue are familiar, yet the child is challenged because her familiar movement vocabulary is now being used in a new way.

⌒ *Nikki, age 17 months, never leaves Mom's lap. She does not travel through space to explore her surroundings but instead looks out at the world perched on Mom. At our first session we all sit on the floor and I roll a small plush ball to Nikki. She watches it approach, but only attempts to reach toward it if it rolls right within arm's reach. She gently squeezes it but does not throw it. We begin a "reciprocal" game of ball rolling, in which I do all the rolling—making sure the ball rolls right to her so she can touch it. Repeatedly I lean forward, squeezing the ball like she does, but add a bit more strength to the squeeze to accent and highlight her action. Through my actions I tell Nikki that I'll play within her expressive movement range. Using more strength and repeating the rolling game beyond her one squeeze response adds challenge by inviting Nikki to enhance the quality and level of her active engagement.* ⌒

Explore and Expand   This movement vocabulary is further extended as the therapist provides new movements that act as a bridge to expand experiences into the environment. This movement-based vocabulary is a natural outgrowth from a child's core movement signature, expanding the child's repertoire of movements by introducing novel elements that encourage the child's potential. This step relates to Vygotsky's notion of scaffolding tasks to support learning (1978). A child is introduced to tasks that cannot be done alone, but can be accomplished with the guidance of a teacher.

⌒ *While respecting Nikki's sedentary posture, I want her to get a taste of what it might feel like to mobilize, so I place Nikki in my lap facing her mom and provide deep sensory input to her body through firm touch. I begin to rock her side to side, supporting and shifting her hips. Because my body acts as a container, I enable her to experience moving without feeling off balance. Nikki cries. As Mom reaches for her, Nikki pulls her arms back, seemingly threatened by someone coming toward her. Mom places Nikki on her lap and Nikki observes me demonstrating how to rock her hips. Safe in Mom's aura, Nikki experiences the rock. During the next 2 weeks in session and at home, Nikki plays with these new movements. By the fourth session, Mom*

puts Nikki on the floor and sits one body length away from her. Looking at
Mom and vocalizing, Nikki continuously rocks her whole body, inching her
way toward Mom. Mom and I cheer her on. Feeling triumphant, Nikki
reaches Mom and is scooped up into her lap. ⌒

Many things can be learned by watching Nikki's nonverbal cues
during these early sessions. First, Nikki relies on visual cues to get
information. Demonstrations become a key teaching tool. Nikki's
resistant reaction to even her mother's reaching toward her implies
that she may be overly sensitive to input when it comes too abruptly
and seems too close to her physical boundaries; the therapist wonders
about tactile defensiveness and visual motor processing. Nikki's ability
to mobilize on the floor so quickly suggests that she was ready to
move, but she didn't have a clue about how to start. The therapist's act
of setting up an experience that enabled Nikki to feel her body in
motion—yet respecting her sensitivities and allowing her to stay within
the comfort zone of her mother—encouraged Nikki to reach beyond
her current style of existing.

Stimulate, Activate, and Mobilize   The vignette in the beginning of the chapter demonstrates a specific *Ways of Seeing* method
known as "Stimulate, Activate, and Mobilize" that is especially useful during this stage to help a child explore the environment in new
ways. Stimulating, activating, and mobilizing a child through movement-oriented activities supports Thelen and Smith's (1994) idea
that children learn best when given the opportunity to explore and
discover development. That is, through spontaneous explorations
children can discover their own developmental progressions; when
children are given the chance to use their bodies to explore their
environment, stages of development naturally unfold. This is especially important now that children spend so much of their time in
containers (e.g., car seats) and in stationary positions watching
screened media instead of physically exploring their own environments. These concepts can also be used to help children discover
how movement can be expressive.

Stimulation is the initial step in the process of supporting a child to
explore the environment through self-discovery. The primary task of
stimulation is to bring a child to an awareness of some aspect of the
child's behavior. This awareness can be directed toward all developmental areas simultaneously, or with an emphasis on a particular area.
Stimulation involves arousal. The purpose of stimulating a child is to

create an initial engagement between self and other. It is important that a therapist be clear about the intent of this initial engagement because it can have a primarily emotional, social, physical, cognitive, or communicative focus. Even if the primary focus of the engagement is to reach a physical or cognitive goal, however, a therapist should always approach the contact with social and emotional intent because this attitude will automatically add a communicative focus. Although this may seem self-evident, it cannot be overly emphasized. It is very easy for a therapist to get so caught up in trying to get a child to achieve a physical milestone, for example, that the actions unintentionally overshadow the relating aspects of the interaction. An example of this would be the situation in which a therapist is working with a child to meet the goal of catching a rolling ball. This task can get very methodical if the ball is routinely rolled back and forth. Instead, to maintain social rapport, the therapist can modify the interaction so that each attempt to catch the ball is met with new enthusiasm and an effort to create eye contact. This can be elaborated further if the therapist develops a storyline by personifying the ball and pretending it is a visiting friend. If an activity becomes rote and dry, it is time to change the dynamics of the activity or change the activity altogether.

The task of the stimulation phase is to bring a child to a basic awareness of some aspect of her body, actions, or self. The phase first starts by watching a child, carefully ascertaining to which components of the child's presence is the therapist especially being drawn. This might be, on a physical level, her shallowness of breath flow, or how her body parts move independently in relation to other body parts or as full body movement. In the case of a child's shallowness of breath, the therapist can stimulate the child by adjusting his or her personal breath flow to model a new breathing rhythm. In another example, if observation reveals a lack of mobility of a child's left arm in comparison with her right arm, the therapist can draw attention to this asymmetry by simply putting a hand on either of the child's arms, stroking the arm, applying pressure or mirroring its movement or lack of movement, while providing verbal descriptions. The use of touch focuses the child's attention kinesthetically even if she is initially unable or unaware of her own body; on a social and emotional level, such actions initiate contact.

If a therapist starts by first following a child's moves and limb placement, rather than immediately attempting to adjust the child's body into better alignment, this acknowledges the child's presence and nonverbally tells the child that the therapist is open to dialogue. It states that the therapist is interested in what the child can say and do. Adding verbal dialogue can support these intentions. A therapist who takes the time to talk with a child at the beginning of each session or during transitions to new activities within the session keeps the rapport, first and foremost, with the child. For a child who is severely challenged and very closed off to external contact, the intervention may stay at this point for quite a while. The primary focus is to get the child to sense, respond, and attune to the therapist's outward stimulation.

Activating is the next step in this process. The choice of this term was influenced by the sensory integration work done by occupational therapists Williamson and Anzalone (1997). Activation in the *Ways of Seeing* approach involves a child taking an active part in the engagement to facilitate and develop the focused elements of the stimulations into something new. During the activating step, instead of merely accepting a child's simple reaction to a stimulus, the therapist pays close attention to her response and encourages her to take a leadership role in the expanded interaction. This occurs by reading the child's body and vocal cues and facilitating her movement-oriented engagements to stimulations.

Specifically, this follows the principles that a dancer employs when studying a particular phrase of movements before "setting" the choreography. First, the steps are marked out. Next, the initial qualitative style in which the steps have been performed are defined. Then, one by one, each core qualitative element of the sequence is explored until the exact effect for which the dancer is striving is reached. During this process, elements are exaggerated, emphasized, or diminished, or are changed in terms of direction, level of strength, or fluidity. These are the Effort qualities discussed in Chapter 6. Continuing with the example discussed in the stimulation phase of the child who reveals a lack of left arm mobility, during this activating phase an exploration may now add shaking the child's right arm with more vigor, while putting more emphasis on the stillness of the left arm. The therapist is an active participant, for it is the dancing dialogue that creates the change. At this point, as the therapist witnesses the child performing this modified action, the emotional meaning to the actions may begin to emerge.

In the *mobilizing* phase that follows, actions are developed into deeper expression. Mobilizing a response enables a child to explore her body's moving further into her surrounding environment. Mobilizing can involve actually moving through the room, or moving a feeling as in emoting. As the child moves her body around the room, her actions take on the qualities of a dance in that they are regarded as expressive aspects of the child's inner experience. Movements transform into dance when they are viewed as the child's own expression. The term *mobilizing* that is used here to highlight this dance and movement perspective refers to the *Ways of Seeing* concept that encourages therapists to continually think about linking isolated actions together into movement and dance-like phrases to convey deeper expressions. On a physical, literal level, this promotes a sense of fluidity and connectedness in the moving body. As isolated actions are joined together, focus and attention are lengthened. On a more symbolic level, the child experiences how abstract relationships work. The child explores the complex and varied ways individual elements can be put together to create meaningful expressions. Extending the example given above into the mobilizing phase, the child with a lack of left arm mobility may move her whole body around the room but keep the left side still and the right side shaking and wiggling. The therapist observing this dichotomy may mirror her actions and ask the verbal child what these actions feel like. As the child puts meaning to her actions, a story might evolve that can be danced out with narration adding voice to the actions. Dancing out the story enables the release and expression of the child's feelings, and offers an opportunity for her growth and change.

For a child who is able to verbally participate in the narrative, this dialogue provides a creative avenue that links physical feelings with the emotional self. The child will develop a sense of empowerment as she literally experiences her body supporting her feelings. For a nonverbal or very young child, a therapist can decide whether to include verbal interpretations from personal observations and witnessing experiences along with information provided by the child's parents and caregivers. For some children just experiencing the mirroring and extension of the actions, creating emotional and social dialogue can be the complete support they need. For other children, a therapist's verbalizing provides the words they cannot produce but are searching for, even when their understandings are extremely basic due to their age or challenge. A therapist can tell that the feeling tones and the essences of his or her interpretations—verbal and nonverbal—are accurate by observing a child's nonverbal responses. Often a child's response is expressed through calmed breath; steady, extended, or excited eye contact; an increased sense of activation or integrity in the musculature or movement sequence; or further elaboration of the child's movement interactions. Even without words, these actions seem to be saying to the therapist, "You've got it! You understand me!"

Nonverbal to Verbal   The fourth and final process in the *Ways of Seeing* therapeutic procedure—*verbalization*—is best demonstrated by continuing the vignette to show how verbalizations were used to support Nikki and her growth. It is important to note that these episodes all take place during Nikki's first 2 weeks of *Ways of Seeing* sessions. In other words, all aspects of this four-part therapeutic procedure can occur right from the beginning of an intervention. A therapist should continually navigate fluidly through each of these strategies, moving freely through the four-part sequence, assessing and securing the relationship along the way. This fluidity enables the emotional relationship to grow. Throughout the sessions, a therapist can reestablish a sense of trust by returning to the first level—mirroring and attuning to a child's action—as a way of saying that the child's needs, concerns, and expressiveness are always of the utmost consideration. It is by moving without encumbrance through each level of this four-part process that a deeper relationship is built over the course of time.

⌒   *As Nikki rocks and rolls her body and reaches toward Mom, Mom and I exclaim, "Go Nikki! Yes, you can crawl to Mom! You can do it!" When she reaches Mom, Nikki's whimpers turn into a smile, her eyes lock with ours, and she holds her body tall and alert as if to say, "Yes, I did it!" We verbalize, "You did it! You can reach your mom!" During this session and those that follow, Nikki continues to attempt to mobilize her body on the floor after watching me demonstrate how to move from sitting to lying to moving forward. With each demonstration, I narrate my actions. "Rock, rock, and reach, rock, rock, and reach. Nikki is watching me, rock, rock, and reach. . . . Look, Nikki is trying it. Rock, rock, and reach."*   ⌒

During this part of the intervention, the therapist uses her words to support the child's experience. These words may simply narrate what is going on by describing the child's actions or by describing the scene in which they are involved. In the previous vignette, Nikki is provided with the verbal vocabulary to match her actions. During later sessions, simple pictures and photographs of these actions will be used to make the link to symbolic representations of language. *Narrating* provides an objective description of the events of the interaction as they are occurring. For example, narration is used to enable Nikki to become part of a pretend story.

⌒ *At 3 years old, Nikki is able to take her actions into symbolic play. We begin to add dolls to our dances, holding them as we turn and spin. As we put them down to "rest," a story evolves. I tell her, "These dolls want to rest. They are tired from dancing. (As Nikki lays one on a pillow) We are putting them to sleep. Let's get a scarf and pretend it is a blanket for them. Nikki, where are the blankets?" Nikki walks over to the wall of scarves, yet she is unable to actually lift a scarf on her own. She stops next to them, and gazes fleetingly at them. I read this as a cue that she is following my suggestion and reply, "Yes, here are the blankets. Let's take one and cover the doll." Together, we hold a scarf as we walk, and drape it over the doll as we approach her bed.* ⌒

Narration serves to label actions for a child, designating their placement in the sequence. It provides a child with a sense of acknowledgment and accomplishment. This can be very helpful for a nonverbal child. In Nikki's case, it put literal meaning into her actions.

Verbal processing is the other form of verbalization used in the *Ways of Seeing* approach. In *verbal processing*, a therapist defines the nonverbal experience to explain or interpret its meaning as it is occurring. In this form of verbalization, a child is provided with words that give possible understandings to feelings and reactions. This process is akin to the use of interpretation in traditional psychotherapeutic practice.

⌒ *As Nikki, now age 4, enters today, she is squeezing and ringing her hands in a start-and-stop pulse and holding her breath. Her gait has a jumpy start-and-stop pulse to it as well. I know these are characteristics of her condition (Rett syndrome), but I also know these behaviors can increase under stress. I first narrate Nikki's actions, "Your movements are very jumpy today. You are squeezing your hands very tightly." I then add an interpretation, "These actions can happen when you get very excited and cannot calm yourself down. I will help you calm yourself down." I take her hands, gently squeezing and releasing to match her pulsing rhythm, as we begin to run around the room to music with a lively rhythm that also matches her state. As Nikki connects to our actions, the tension in her arms and hands releases. We slow down our run and change the music to a more lyrical, softer melody. Nikki looks me in the eye with a steady gaze. "Nikki, you have calmed your body down. Do you feel that feeling inside?" I inquire. Nikki nods her head. Her eyes sparkle. Her experience is understood.* ⌒

When a therapist imbues interpretive meaning to a child's movements, it is important to keep in mind that these comments reflect the therapist's perceptions and may or may not match the child's intentions. It can be helpful to preface such comments with a statement to clarify this. For example, a therapist might say to a verbal child, "When you fall to the ground so slowly, it feels like sadness to me. What does it feel like to you as you do that motion?" Taking ownership for the interpretation gives a verbal child the chance to respond back, confirming the interpretation or modifying it to match the child's intention. Providing interpretations to actions introduces to both verbal and nonverbal children the important idea that movements possess meaning.

Children do not automatically attach meaning to their movements. At first their movements just *are*—that is, children view them as simply part of themselves. Providing children with an interpretation, even in situations in which it may not be a completely accurate description of their intentions, demonstrates to children that movements possess meaning. This understanding enables children to compare their intentions with the adult's interpretation.

Processing

Interpreting and describing nonverbal actions during a session is a basic element of dance movement psychotherapy. Traditionally, in the dance movement therapy practice designed specifically for adults (discussed in Chapter 7) known as Authentic Movement—sometimes depicted as a meditation through movement—movement improvisations bring specific characteristics of a person's nonverbal actions into conscious awareness. After these experiences, a discussion known as *processing* occurs, during which time the salient aspects of the experience are defined to heighten understanding of inner aspects of the self. Processing provides a way to highlight and reinforce concepts learned through the session. This processing can take several different forms: verbal dialogue or nonverbal communications; movement; or art materials, such as clay or drawing paper and crayons.

The use of the verbalization stage in the *Ways of Seeing* approach can be analogized to the processing procedure contained in these adult dance therapy approaches. With a very young child, processing often occurs simultaneously during activities. The key goal during all interactions should be to help increase each child's self-awareness and communication skills. Putting words to a child's movements gives the child an opportunity to connect meaning to experiences. For a very young child, it introduces concepts through words. A therapist can introduce connections between words and actions by making simple comments such as "Let's go forward and back" while rocking a child, and then repeating those words when the child is later rocked in the swing. Many practitioners make such comments intermittently and automatically, without giving it much thought. It is emphasized here to draw attention to the therapeutic value of saying these words with awareness. It begins to build a child's repertoire of communication.

A more symbolic use of words to express feeling can also be introduced to a child unable to verbally communicate due to age or developmental challenge. A therapist's providing the same words to describe a reaction each time a child performs a particular movement or sequence of movements puts communicative meaning to emotional actions. This happens by first describing the action and the meaning it seems to create. Over time the therapist can use just the key words to make these links. The initial comments may be, "You are breathing very fast again. Sometimes this happens when people feel nervous or excited. What are you feeling? I can help you slow down your breath." This comment can be condensed if the therapist, looking straight into the child's eyes and looking for nonverbal acknowledgment, says, "Oh, there goes that fast breathing again. Can I help you slow it down?"

For a nonverbal child, processing often occurs through eye contact and body posturing. Her eyes may look at a person with more direction and intensity, or may have a sense of relief and a softening of expression. Her actions may momentarily become more still, or suddenly increase, in recognition or excitement that the therapist has acknowledged her attempt to express his feelings. If this gesture is in her repertoire, head nodding, either gently or more overtly, may occur as a form of confirmation. Each child has her own individual ways of expressing herself with her body. The careful observer can heighten a child's attempts to communicate nonverbally, however, by providing words of interpretation.

For a more verbally cognizant child, putting words to his actions gives him the chance to see if his experiences match the adult's understandings. Adding words to gestures and actions also increases their communicative value. Of course, a word of caution must be made again: Whenever observers attempt to interpret a child, they must always acknowledge that it is their own interpretation; they cannot assume that they know for sure what the child is thinking until he signals some type of verification.

Art materials such as clay or markers, crayons, and paper are very effective tools to enable the processing experiences for both verbal and nonverbal children of all age ranges. These items allow nonverbal and younger children to use a tangible medium to depict their experiences. For verbal or older children, these materials can serve as a transitional expressive activity between the experience and verbalization. There is no right way to draw—children convey their feelings in both abstract and realistic designs. Rather, it is important to pay close attention to the colors and the physical qualities that children use to form their images. For example, notice whether artwork is created fast or slow, or with strength or gentleness. Observe whether it covers the whole page or uses a great deal of clay, and if it is organized or chaotic. Verbal children can be asked to describe their artwork so that they begin to develop their associations with their experiences.

BEGINNING A SESSION

To begin this dance of relating, always keep several elements in mind. Each session should begin with the basic assumption that a child's non-verbal behaviors are a form of communication portraying her experiences and her sense of self. The communicative message may not initially be clear. Nonetheless, the therapist must believe that a child's actions have the potential to become communicative. The *Ways of Seeing* therapist's specific initial intention should be to observe and respond to a child's particular movement expressions as the child interacts within her surrounding spatial environment. It is this interaction between self and environment, observable in the child's personal characteristic movement patterns, which will reveal how the child is relating, adapting, and responding to her surroundings. In this way, the child becomes the primary catalyst of her own therapeutic interventions.

From such observations and interactions, the therapist can derive an understanding of the whole child. This includes being open to all aspects of the child's development and experience—whether motor, sensorial, verbal–communicative, emotional, or cognitive—that may influence how she perceives and responds to the world.

Starting Where the Child Is

This phrase describes the focus a therapist should take when beginning a session. The concept of beginning a session at a child's level is a prominent procedure in most intervention and educational programs, implying that activities should be appropriately structured to the child's level of functioning. When putting this concept into practice in the techniques of the *Ways of Seeing* dance movement therapy, however, its meaning should be expanded further. In these sessions, tasks are not only directed to a child's functional level but are also often created by the child. This includes the specific dance activities as well as the particular format and sequence of events. The dance-play activities and overall structure of the sessions unfold as the child explores and engages in self-expression in a therapeutic setting. The child's moods and actions guide each session. This focus on a child's style, level of functioning, and needs arises from the concept that everyone has a need to be seen, held, and listened to.

Being Seen, Held, and Listened To

These words, rich in sensorial imagery, are used here to symbolize every person's innate need to be acknowledged for his or her uniqueness. They are used both literally and figuratively. In its literal sense, the word *seen* is used to describe how a *Ways of Seeing* therapist should carefully observe a child's nonverbal expressions. A therapist's use of eye contact, trying on movements, and verbal narration of a child's actions are techniques that make it clear that the therapist is eager to learn about the child and the child's experiences. In the figurative sense, mirroring, attuning, and watching a child move expressively reflects the therapist's acknowledgment and support of the child's uniqueness. Pawl (1995, p. 5) addressed this same notion by stating that we each have a need to be "held in another's mind." This statement implies that we all have a need to be special within another's thoughts, and having this need met from birth onward is necessary to enable healthy growth in all areas of development. Literally and symbolically, touching, holding, and embracing a child are among the most significant *Ways of Seeing* techniques that support this concept.

Being *listened to* completes this sensorially rich metaphor. Listening connotes thoughtful attending. Its image is one of a listener stopping other activities to provide full attention. It is differentiated from the term hearing, which is also about sound recognition but can be qualitatively very different. A person can hear a noise while maintaining a different focus, but one cannot truly listen to another while otherwise engaged. Figuratively, all these terms recognize the imperative need for children (and for all individuals) to feel honored for their distinctiveness. When therapists or other adults give attention to all of their forms of communication, children are provided with a clear sense that others have a deep interest in them personally. It enables children to feel recognized, cared for, and loved unconditionally.

Sense of Presence

One of the most important goals in beginning a *Ways of Seeing* session is for a therapist to create a sense of presence by providing uncondi- tional, nonjudgmental attention toward a child. This involves watch- ing the child from an open place, being ready to receive whatever information is revealed by the child's actions, gestures, and vocal communications—seeing, holding, and listening to the child. In dance movement therapy, a therapist is viewed as an open vessel, receiving information about the individual being worked with by experiencing that person's verbal and nonverbal expressions. As an open vessel, the therapist is ready to receive and hold whatever materials a child brings into session. In this way the therapist creates an environment similar to the holding environment described by Winnicott (1965).

In this next description of the experience of another child, Lindsay, the therapist acts as a nurturing container, creating an over- all sense of safety to explore all depths of experience. In the *Ways of Seeing* approach, this sense of safety and containment sometimes occurs quite literally.

As Lindsay, age 4, enters the session today, her sitter informs me in quite an exasperated voice that Lindsay has had a tough weekend. Lots of acting out, not following the household rules, and talking like a baby. Lindsay walks into the room with her head down and her feet dragging. We sit down to take off her shoes (part of our opening ritual) and Lindsay softly crawls into my lap in a fetal position. I ask her if she needs to play the baby game for a few minutes. She silently nods yes. I gently stroke her back for a few minutes. Using words of comfort to acknowledge that she had a tough week, I talk about how this happens to all of us sometimes. Sometimes going back to being a baby seems easier. I ask her if it was difficult for her to use words to explain what she needed. She nods and whispers, "Yes." We share just a few words describing what those needs were that had been so difficult during the week. Suddenly she sits up gleefully and says, "Suzi! Let's play now!" as she bounces out of my lap. This introduction to our session takes no more than 3 minutes, but it supports her activities throughout the rest of the session, which focuses on her defining herself as a "big girl."

Included in this sense of presence that therapists must create is their obligation to become aware of how their personal responses may influence children's experiences during the sessions. To reach such understanding, therapists must stay aware of what aspects of their own sensory systems and emotional selves are stimulated while watching and working with the children or the parent–child dyads. This is accomplished best by the therapists' participating in the self-observation experiences of witnessing, kinesthetic seeing, and kinesthetic empathy described in the previous chapter. Awareness occurs through observations and through actually trying on a child's movements. Watching personal responses within the context of the whole environment acts as a third objective eye. How these elements—watching, receiving, and self-awareness—interweave will influence how a therapist facilitates each session.

AS SESSIONS CONTINUE

An interesting thing occurs when a therapist begins and conducts sessions with the perspective inspired by the *Ways of Seeing* approach. Regardless of a child's age or ability, after several sessions a repetition of actions and a sequence of their occurrence will unfold. As this occurs, the therapist detects patterns as minirituals evolve that provide a structured beginning, middle, and ending to each session's sequence of activities. The specific needs and abilities of a child dictate how structured each session need be. For many children, structure helps lend a feeling of safety during the session. It enables them to focus and know what is expected of them. This is especially helpful with children with difficulties maintaining attention, such as ADHD, ASD, or attention difficulties caused by seizure disorders. For Jake, age 7, diagnosed with severe seizure disorders, a four-step procedure has evolved in his weekly 1-hour sessions that follows the Stimulate, Activate, and Mobilize structure described earlier in this chapter. Steps 1–3 take up the first half hour; Step 4 takes the second half hour of each session. The elements of each activity are outlined below.

1. *Stimulate*: Increase Jake's full body awareness and body part relationships. We do this through tactile support using deep joint press—applied directly to joints—as well as having Jake use his arms/hands and legs/feet to push against me.

2. *Activate*: Add relaxation/breath awareness to this joint pressure and pushing work to prevent Jake from holding his breath, and help him find an even, steady breath-flow rhythm.

3. *Mobilize*: Take this body awareness out into space by creating a sequence of four movements that we do as a warm-up exercise.

We each create movements for this sequence. Each action is performed 10 times. Jake, a true math whiz, very much enjoys coming up with very creative mathematical ways to think and count out these actions.

4. *Expression*: This section of the session is creative dance-play. Jake creates a scene for us to move in. It may reflect his emotional needs or a personal interest. We often use music and/or drawing materials to support these ideas. Most often we create a story involving a journey. We outline the journey by drawing a map of the events in a floor pattern and then we dance or act it out. Working on sequencing using fine motor skills and then translating it into gross motor activity is a very important part of the session. These activities keep Jake focused and attending and help him move back and forth more smoothly from his visual to motor capacities.

Creating routine and structure can be very important. It is equally important, however, for a therapist to know when to relinquish the structure to allow a child's immediate needs to unfold more spontaneously. Learning when to hold on to a structure and when to let it go takes time, practice, and a reliance on intuition in regard to one's relationship with a child. Room must always be left open for variations on any themes that may emerge. Letting the child lead the session provides an additional window into his moods and his functioning each session. Noting how and when the child chooses to hold onto or change minirituals encourages a deeper understanding of the child as well as a more concentrated focus on his nonverbal cues. More thorough information about what factors are affecting the child or his environment may become revealed. By carefully watching over time when and how a child varies his activities, a therapist can thoughtfully use this information to choose when it is necessary to assist the child in adhering to a structure, and when it would be better to relinquish it. The decision to hold onto a structure is often indicated when a child's veering off is due to his distractibility or avoidance.

Maintaining a structure helps the child learn how to refocus and regulate. A therapist should not, however, immediately and automatically assume this is what is needed each time a child seems distracted. Instead the therapist should always take a moment to assess what else might be going on emotionally for a child, making it a conscious decision each time the therapist decides to reign the child back into a routine. Often the most valuable information about a child's feelings and current experiences can evolve very unexpectedly from these ventures away from the routine, as the following example shows:

〰 *For the whole summer, Nikki's sessions have had a routine. We use the picture board to outline the structure. Relaxation activities such as breath awareness, massage, and yoga stretches begin each session followed by dialoguing through rhythms with the drums. Then come doll dance-play and improvised dancing. Sessions end with a rhythmic song that seems to help her feel socially connected and strong, keeping her hand wringing and hyperventilating in check. But from mid-September into October, Nikki has been entering each session tense, with an increase in hand wringing and hyperventilating. She is too agitated to lie down for any of the relaxation activities. As soon as she walks in the door, she begins to vocalize and gesture toward the wide, open floor space of the Ways of Seeing studio. Each time, I respond to these cues as indications that she wants to go right into improvised dancing. Sometimes she chooses to include the dolls, sometimes she dances alone and I follow her lead. I put on music with a lively yet melodic beat. She takes us all through the room, bending and stretching, then rocking and shaking. As I move with her, I feel my body stretch and release. It feels good to just plain move! That's it, I realize. Perhaps, Nikki is saying, "I need to MOVE!!" I verbalize this to Nikki, and she looks me straight in the eyes and starts to giggle, slightly nodding her head, and adds a jump to her step. "You've got it!" she seems to say. She seems so appreciative. I notice that all during our dance she has been effectively keeping her hands down at her sides, avoiding wringing them—a state we usually only reach after our opening relaxation, massage input. She is really working hard to connect with me and knows what is expected of her. After about 5 minutes of this free dance, she slows down her steps. I switch the music to a soft calm melody and we lie down for relaxation. Together, with Mom present, we begin to discuss what's been happening in her life lately. What's different? What's new? Mom explains that Nikki just started a new school with children with a variety of special needs. The setting, the classroom routine, and many of the children's behaviors are very unfamiliar to Nikki. As we speak, Nikki listens attentively, calming her muscles and slowing her breath. She begins to relax.* 〰

This vignette dramatically portrays the value of giving up an established routine and instead taking cues from the child. This particular episode required the therapist to really question her own logic. She knew Nikki had started a new school and it was natural that the transition would take some time. The opening relaxation activities had been specifically structured to help Nikki regulate her agitation. So why not be a bit more insistent and guide Nikki to use these tools, continuing the work of helping her gain control over her regulatory issues? The best answer is that in taking that approach, the therapist would have been following her own directives rather than focusing on the child's needs. Allowing Nikki to dance first enabled her to express her feelings in the only way she could. It sent Nikki the message that her mother and the therapist were willing to listen to her—to share, complain, and express herself purely—something that everyone does, or wishes they could do, when they are agitated about something. Nikki's dance was free yet contained. It provided her with a safe and fun way to get her feelings out when she did not have, or perhaps did not even know, the words to verbalize these feelings. The therapist's recognition of Nikki's need to vary her routines conveys the essence of the *Ways of Seeing* approach.

Finding Novelty within Routines

Even a choreographed dance or sequence of activities can never be regarded as a codified exercise or routine. There is always room for change. Each time a dance-play is executed, a *Ways of Seeing* therapist keeps an eye open for variation. The movement piece always has the potential to continue to grow and change—to become a new improvisation on a more current theme. Sometimes the changes are very subtle and a therapist may not be able to pinpoint when the actual changes occurred. But on reflection, a child's movement journey may perhaps have shifted focus from where it was several weeks or even months ago. These types of observations and openness to improvisations are essential to avoid having movement activities become rote or mechanized. A therapist's goal must be to keep the movement activities alive with the sensibility that every time an activity is executed, even if its form has been established in the past, it can be performed with a fresh and unique awareness of the moment.

The previous vignette discusses a time when the shift in the improvisation was quite large, varying from one session to the next. In contrast, the following vignette, which starts from a simple ball-rolling activity, demonstrates how a sequencing ball dance of many steps may evolve over time. This occurs because the therapist allows Brianna's body cues exhibiting discomfort to change the session's focus from skill building into a whole new series of movement explorations.

~ *At age 2½, Brianna is still uncomfortable lying on her belly. In the winter, I place her on her stomach on the ball to provide an experience of being prone on a softer surface. After being on the ball a few moments, she begins to arch her body, rotating her spine as if attempting to twist onto her back. Responding to her cue, I assist her onto her back, appeasing her desire to be in her preferred position, supine. I rock her on the ball vigorously to stimulate her proprioceptive system and get her emotionally engaged. She looks up at me smiling and cooing. She loves large strong movement. She is a true sensory seeker, staying more engaged if the activities are more active. Back on the floor, I notice two distinct qualities in regard to how she uses her body: 1) Her upper body lacks strength, causing her to move with little upper body awareness or active intentional movement connection with the rest of her torso; and 2) Her strong preference for supine posturing causes her to move her torso as one solid body part, with little differentiation or articulation within the spine, hip, and shoulder joints.* ~

These body and movement-based observations provide clues to Brianna's problem with crawling. Besides her obvious lack of physical strength, her posturing prevents her from experiencing the more enclosed positioning necessary to be on her hands and knees to crawl. The therapist decides to use the activity of rolling her on the ball to create more upper body awareness and full body enclosing. The ball dance sequence expands.

~ *I put on lively music with a strong, invigorating beat and place her on her belly on the ball. I roll her vigorously forward and backward, stroking her upper back. Her dad assists her in extending her arms and flexing her wrists when the ball rolling lets her touch the floor. At this moment Dad stops Brianna, giving her a big hello and smile, and provides quick tactile joint compression to help her push her way back up the ball. When Brianna wiggles as if she wants to get off, Dad and I help her roll forward off the ball, in a tucked position. She is able to feel her body in a compact rather than lengthened position. Once lying on her back on the floor (the ball beyond her head), I use verbal and physical cues to encourage her to reach her arms to the ball. When she does, I lift her legs up over her head, placing her back over the ball onto her tummy.*

When she attempts to roll onto her back, I support this action and repeat this rolling game lying supine. In this position I firmly stroke her chest as she extends her arms overhead, rolling forward and backward down to the floor. As I support her hip sockets and then help her to scoop her knees into her chest, Brianna does a backward roll onto the floor. At first she resists this position, lengthening her whole body and legs out flat in a plane as she rolls off the ball. But slowly, over time, she begins to keep her body enclosed and even stays there a few moments before she pushes her whole body down to lie prone with her full body surface flat against the floor.

By spring, she is able to keep her legs enclosed smoothly as she rolls over. During a session when Mom and Dad are both present, for the first time Brianna actually pushes up to sitting on her knees from a crouched position and holds it for a moment.

By summer we have begun to add more elements to this ball dance. Now following her own initiative, she rolls along her vertical axis, too, while on top of the ball—log rolling from prone to supine and then back again. After a few of these rolls, she decides when to reach back with her arms rolling onto the floor to her knees, and then uses the ball to push up to kneeling. We realize this supports the leg strengthening work she has been doing in physical therapy. She has been working on high kneeling. Next she uses the ball to push into high kneeling, extending our choreography.

Brianna continues to find ways to creatively and spontaneously incorporate her physical therapy exercises into our dance-play. In the fall, she is practicing standing. Now, as she rolls backward on the ball while prone, she stretches her legs all the way down to the floor and stands, using her feet to push off the floor to continue the roll forward on the ball. On her back, after she rolls over with her legs completely tucked into her chest, she uses her arms and hands to push up to tall kneeling and then lifts her leg to push up to standing with the support of the ball. I give her small tactile support along her tailbone and spine to help her initiate the action from her pelvis and feel the sensation of lengthening along her torso.

One day, while Brianna is lying on her belly on the floor, she begins to roll onto her back as she is looking at a piece of paper her dad is crumpling above her head. She doesn't stop! Maintaining her focus on her dad and the paper, she begins to log roll all over the room. I only provide gentle touch to her torso and verbal encouragement intermittently along the way. ⁓

Following the Child's Lead

As demonstrated in Brianna's story, following the child's lead describes how a therapist enables a child's level of functioning and unique style to extend into the content of a session. Allowing a child's actions to direct how the session unfolds is a prominent technique in dance movement therapy in which a therapist pays particular attention not only to what a child chooses to do but also to how the child specifically performs an action. This includes noticing what parts of the child's body are used to execute the action, where in the room the child chooses to go, and the sequence in which the activities occur.

A therapist's letting a child direct the interactions relates to Greenspan's Floor Time techniques (Greenspan, 1992; Greenspan & Lewis, 2002). In Greenspan's Floor Time model, a therapist enters into a child's activity and attempts to attract attention by following, intervening, challenging, and adding new elements to the child's focus. The therapist lets her presence be known to the child and seeks to draw the child into a more interactive, socially engaging relationship by manipulating the environment in some way. For a child engaged in lining up a row of cars, such activities may include the therapist's sitting with the child, handing the child a car unexpectedly, taking a car away from the lineup, or building a similar row of cars across from the child.

Although such activities may occur in a *Ways of Seeing* dance movement therapy session, there is a distinct difference in the approach and attitude. In the *Ways of Seeing* approach, a therapist follows with kinesthetic empathy (defined in Chapter 7) and physical dialogue, which may include both verbal and play activities. This distinction underlies a philosophical variance from Greenspan's Floor Time model. In the *Ways of Seeing* approach, a therapist initially follows a child's lead to gain a better sense of the child's experience, to literally try to feel what it might be like to experience the world in the same way as the child. Of course, the therapist, not being the child, cannot know exactly what it feels like. But trying on a child's movement style by mirroring and attuning to the qualities of the actions does provide the therapist with personal insights. This insight is what the term *kinesthetic empathy* implies. By trying on movement qualities, a therapist becomes physically open to the possible feelings and meanings that a child's movements create. Approaching a child from this empathetic reference reflects an attempt to first and foremost understand and appreciate the child's unique experience rather than highlight the child's dysfunction, difficulty, or abnormality.

Role of the *Ways of Seeing* Therapist

Starting where the child is and following the child's lead should not, however, mean that the child takes over. Allowing a child to take a leadership role during the sessions takes skill and practice and requires a therapist to create a delicate balance between freedom and control. Freedom entails the therapist's encouraging the child to take the time to explore the environment. This may mean holding back directions, exercises, and a lesson plan in order to give the child the space to develop her own ideas. Control within self means holding back from jumping in too quickly, while still creating a sense of authority. This lets the child know that even though she is given room to explore freely, the therapist is overseeing, always interested and connected to her explorations, as well as monitoring the overall level of safety. Control also lies in knowing when to interject more structure. A therapist must determine when and if a child's behaviors are so fragmented that they are not leading to interaction and active engagement. If this is the case, a therapist must interject and transform the activity to support an interactive dialogue.

Although the *Ways of Seeing* approach emphasizes improvisational exploration, it also supports the organization that directions, exercises, and lesson plans create. The *Ways of Seeing* approach acknowledges the usefulness of these more structured aspects alongside the continuous discovery that the child's improvisational explorations inspires. Herein lies the sense of balance that the program strives to create. The *Ways of Seeing* approach aims to produce an atmosphere that enables discovery and spontaneity within a structured safe environment. The primary focus is on honoring a child's explorations with the ultimate goal of bringing order to what

The therapist should always follow the child's lead.

may at first appear to be chaotic or nonsensical. The attitude of the *Ways of Seeing* practitioner is to continually look for the potential form from the formless, order from disorder, and structure from lack of structure. It is from this perspective that therapists can begin to enter into the children's experiences, joining them on their journeys of self-expression and discovery. Ultimately it is through this process that therapists can begin to put meaning into children's movements as they strive to increase the communicative potential of these actions.

Establishing such a presence involves a mix of respect, openness, patience, clarity, and authority. A therapist must exude a sense of respect for a child's initiations, waiting, watching, and listening to the child rather than immediately jumping in with an idea or suggestion that seems obvious to the therapist but less so to the child. From this observing attitude, a therapist tries to stay open to where a child's actions may lead and to what they may relate. Patience lies in giving a child's actions time to develop. This may mean waiting, observing a child a few moments longer before joining in, or supporting the child to continue further when at first an action seems to be repetitive. It may also mean allowing a child to continue an action for several sessions and staying open to seeing how it might evolve.

It is essential for a therapist to maintain clarity of focus and belief in the process to pull off this balancing act. A therapist must exude a sense of presence that is calm and clear, and at the same time maintain a sense of authority that creates a safe environment for all participants. Children will ultimately feel the freedom to truly explore only if they sense that their actions are being observed from a place of genuine interest. Details about how therapists can create such a *Ways of Seeing* therapeutic milieu and design specific *Ways of Seeing* activities are illustrated throughout this chapter—and throughout the entire book.

Closure

Creating a specific way to bring a session to an end is as important as planning an effective way to begin a session. This relates to a basic principle in dance choreography—each piece must have a beginning, middle, and ending. The dance begins as the dancers get the viewers engaged. Often the dance starts when the dancers actively draw attention to themselves. This may involve large movements or even stillness. The key feature is that the movers and viewers are engaged through a mutual focus. During the middle of the dance, both the movers and the audience become involved in the elements of the unfolding storyline, whether it is abstract or quite literal. Although the immediacy of live movement causes each action to disappear as soon as it is performed, the participants—both the dancers and the viewers—are left with the memory of the movements and the feelings they evoke. As the piece continues, these memories begin to relate to one another, creating a theme. The end of the piece comes at some point after the movers have shared their nonverbal information with the viewers. In a successful performance, both the movers and viewers feel a deep sense of satisfaction. The movers feel the physical high of having strongly connected to self and other in a physical way. They have united their whole selves by using their bodies to communicate a feeling or message. The audience also feels a connection between self and other by being intensely touched by the movers' actions. Through the act of witnessing the movements of another, the viewer feels moved. An awareness of self occurs when the movement message has a personal reference for the viewer. Both parties feel fed by the experience.

Applying this experience to each *Ways of Seeing* session reinforces the underlying focus of the program and creates a social connection between a therapist and a child. Each session should end with an activity that highlights the relationship. A clear sense of closure acknowledges and celebrates the time shared together. A closing ritual should be soothing and centering to help the child make the transition to the next activity. It often includes a verbal or movement-based summary of the activities, thoughts, and feelings that might have come up during the session. The specific activities that support this will differ with each child. They may involve touch—literally or figuratively—either through an embrace, an activity that involves eye contact or breath work, or jointly engaging in an activity that places the therapist in close proximity with the child.

With very young children, this may include listening to a selection of music or singing one of the children's favorite songs. Some therapists find it very calming to hold infants in their arms and dance and sway to the gentle three-beat rhythm of a waltz. Toddlers and older children can clearly define the end of a session by creating an improvisational good-bye dance. Sitting together to share a good book or making a drawing can help some children to focus. Relaxation activities involving breath awareness, touch, or yoga stretches direct other children's physical energies. Singing good-bye songs that include children's names while maintaining eye contact encourages language awareness. Cleaning up the room and helping children put on shoes and outer clothing creates structure and order in the environment. Having the room organized and familiar each session supports the children's knowing that the room will be found the next time just as it was left during the last session. For older children, closure may also involve discussing and writing plans of activities and themes for the next session.

The key emphasis during these closure activities should be creating social connection and exchange. A therapist commonly assigns "homework" to older children and parent–child dyads, asking a child or family to apply some of the insightful themes and body/movement awareness that came up during the session to their lives during the week. Often, a closing ritual will naturally develop, but even then there is always room for subtle or more overt changes to the closing activities if a child expresses a desire to elaborate on a particular aspect of the ritual. As always, watching how and what a child chooses to do or change continually provides the therapist with additional information about the child.

Daily Notes Form

The *Ways of Seeing* approach has created a Daily Notes Form (see http:// www.brookespublishing.com/dancing) to provide a thorough and efficient way for a therapist to document how each session unfolds, with attention paid to categorizing the particular movement or dance-based activities that evolve during each session. This form logs the order of the specific activities and the therapist's immediate reactions during the session.

The Daily Notes Form has four sections:

- Key Impressions of the Session and Techniques Used

- Key Themes Addressed During the Session

- Movement Metaphors

- Impression of Key Psychological Themes

Key Impressions of the Session and Techniques Used This section provides space for a therapist to write a chronological narrative of the events of a session, described both objectively and subjectively. The *objective* description maps out the sequence of events. The subjective description section includes the terms *witnessing, kinesthetic seeing,* and *kinesthetic empathy* described in Chapter 7. These terms outline the self-observation process in the *Ways of Seeing* approach in which a therapist is asked to pay attention to personal thoughts, memories, and bodily reactions while observing and interacting with a particular child and family. There is also a list on the right for the therapist to check off which techniques were used (i.e., body awareness, developmental space, breath flow, Authentic Movement, improvisation, developmental movement, dance, choreography, play, verbal processing, narrating) for the specific activities that were described in the narrative portion.

Key Themes Addressed During the Session   This section is a checklist for a therapist to note which categories were most focused on during a particular session (i.e., body, emotional, stress reduction, rehabilitation, Efforts, Space/kinesphere, Phrasing). The therapist can check off as many categories as applicable.

Movement Metaphors   This section is provided so that a therapist can describe any specific, personally stylized nonverbal qualitative element, posture, or sequence of movements that recurred within a child or parent's repertoire during the session, including a description of the actions and possible metaphoric meanings.

Impression of Key Psychological Themes   This section provides space for a therapist to define which psychological themes were worked on during a session.

9
Movement and Dance-Based Tools

On with the dance! let joy be unconfined!

Lord Byron, *Childe Harold's Pilgrimage*
(Canto III, stanza 22, 1816)

Many modes of nonverbal communication can be used in the therapeutic environment. The *Ways of Seeing* approach emphasizes the use of movement and dance as the key tools for intervention. Movement and dance are regarded as similar but different aspects of nonverbal expression. The term *movement* refers to the everyday actions a person uses consciously and unconsciously to mobilize or perform a task. As discussed in Chapter 6, the actual action chosen and how a movement is performed can reveal a great deal of information about a person's mood, feelings, attitudes, and abilities. The term *dance* is used to emphasize the emotionally expressive phenomenon that occurs when movements are put together in a lyrical way. Dance transforms movement by imbuing the movement with self-expression. Because dance is not task-oriented, its ultimate purpose is to enable the dancer to fully engage in experiencing himself or herself moving. Looking at movement and interaction as a dance can shift one's vision into seeing how movements link together. Linking movements together lengthens focus by helping individuals, especially children, attend and relate for longer periods of time. Through these actions, individuals can experience extended relating, which helps them make sense of and interact more fully in the social world. The *Ways of Seeing* approach strives to always use dance and movement as media for emotional and social exchange.

THE DANCE DUET

The elements that two dancers must consider when performing a duet best explain this perspective. In a dance, the essence of each dancer's actions combines to create the overall feeling tone of the duet. A successful dancing partnership ensues when both members trust and are acutely aware of each other. This awareness is communicated primarily from a bodily, felt-sense level. An expressive interaction transpires that is palpable to the audience. Throughout the dance, each dancer is sensitive to the quality of how they touch and hold each other. Each dancer adjusts his or her body and limbs to provide a stable or mobile container for the partner. Full body shifts and weight placement are assessed moment by moment to create a fluid balance. A particular muscular tone and tension ensues to support the dancing theme. Each dancer must modulate his or her use of strength and lightness to create a continuity of form. Mutual gaze and focus occur, not only through eye contact but also through physical sensing of the location of each other's moving body on the dance floor. All of these elements combine to support how the dancers approach, initiate contact, and withdraw contact as they come toward and then move away from each other. The energy level and tempo of each dancer adds to the overall qualitative feeling of the dance. A mutual dialogue occurs as each dancer finely tunes his or her mobile rapport, keenly attuning to the individual style of the other.

A true dancing dialogue only "clicks" when these elements create a synergy of feeling, energy, and expressivity, developed through deep kinesthetic listening, that creates rapport between the dancers. Regardless of how choreographed a sequence may be, it only truly becomes alive when each movement is executed freshly and anew in the spontaneity of the moment. The duet becomes its own expressive form that transcends the confines of the dancers' individual styles. The magic of the dance for the dancer is experiencing this sharing and connection with another. The thrill of the dance for the audience is to be able to witness, understand, and find a place from within that relates to the dance's expressiveness. The dance becomes a message that is verbalized through this nonverbal medium.

It is this frame of reference provided by the *Ways of Seeing* approach that a therapist should use to observe and interact with a child. To become acutely aware of the nonverbal elements that comprise an interaction, a therapist should ask two questions with this dance-like frame of reference when approaching a child:

- What is the dance of interaction observable between the child and the significant adult in the child's life?

- What isolated actions is the child doing—and how can the therapist link them together like a dance?

The term *dance* is representative of two elements. It is the dialogue, the communication between the self and the other. It also suggests that this dialogue can become a true dance when the elements of the interaction are understood along a continuum of nonverbal expression. These elements can then be used to create playful interactions with children. This makes the activity much more fun for children by imbuing their actions with heightened expressivity.

TURNING NONVERBAL DIALOGUE INTO DANCE-PLAY

The *Ways of Seeing* approach uses the term *dance-play* to describe the varied ways that dance and movement are used in a session. The term *dance* emphasizes the nonverbal expressive aspect of the activities. The term *play* emphasizes the playful and play-like aspects of the interactions.

Turning a nonverbal dialogue into a dance-play requires an understanding of the following concepts: how the body can be used as a therapeutic tool; how the awareness of physical space and spatial placement of the body can be used for intervention; how movement and dance can be transformed into dance-play activities; and how rhythm, music, relaxation, visualizations, and storytelling can be used as additional intervention tools. In the *Ways of Seeing* approach, these elements are combined with a sensorially rich environment to create an atmosphere that supports a child's deepest self-expression.

The Body as a Therapeutic Tool

The body is the most significant therapeutic tool of intervention for the *Ways of Seeing* therapist. This cannot be underscored enough. No other tool is as important or necessary as the body. Thinking about the body as a tool provides therapists with endless possibilities for assessment, intervention, and relating. It is the starting point for all other tools and methods. Therapists receive information about the children and families with whom they are working through their clients' bodies. It is through bodily interactions that people relate to others. Viewing the body as a tool expands the therapist's perspective, providing a broader information base from which to work with children and families.

When therapists regard the body as a tool and information source, they put the emphasis on the individuals involved in the interactions rather than on the props and toys that may be used to stimulate the interactions. The focusing of attention on the body does not diminish the value of other tools, however, but instead keeps the primary awareness on the individuals involved even when other tools are being used. This focus keeps social interactions and relationships between the self and the other paramount and prevents an interaction from becoming too object-focused.

When therapists become more conscious of how to use their own bodies, they can model additional ways for parents to create meaningful social interactions with their child, especially if their child has difficulties communicating. Helping a family adapt to an attitude of seeing the body as a tool and communicator can often alleviate the frustrated perceptions felt by many parents that their role with their child is purely custodial—feeding, bathing, changing diapers, putting the child in front of the TV, or giving the child a toy. If parents always use toys to relate to their child, they may come to feel that it is to the toy rather than to them that the child is relating. Parents may feel unable to connect to their child unless they have an object as a mediator to attract the child's attention.

The perception acquired from seeing one's body as a tool creates additional avenues into understanding children. Therapists and parents can use their bodies to mirror and attune to children. The body provides a spontaneous interactive structure with endless possibilities to stimulate qualitative variations through changes in affect, muscle tone, physical shape, touch, breath, and movement. The body can even become an apparatus for children to use in rolling, crawling, and pulling up. Using the body as a tool continually provides children with social and tactile feedback as they physically feel an adult's body respond through touch, movement, breath flow, warmth, coolness, sound, and muscular input. Bodies are alive! They respond and react, and this response naturally causes bodily reactions from others.

Such body awareness can become a principal tool in encouraging and enabling a child's self-expression. Acknowledging a child's physical reactions associates meaning and connects emotions to actions and reactions. Traditionally, this acknowledgment primarily occurs through verbal dialogue. For example, an adult may respond to an infant who has a broad smile and is shaking his hands exuberantly by saying something like, "Oh, what a happy look you have today!" Often the adult is supporting these comments with increased emotional and physical affect, concurring with the child's actions. This physical response on the part of the adult occurs naturally. Regarding the body as a tool capitalizes on this bodily interaction by reminding and instructing the adult to highlight and expand this bodily reaction and use it as a starting point for expanded ways of relating.

Extending the Dancing Dialogue Through the Body

Attunement and mirroring have already been discussed as two methods that use the body as a tool. These techniques use the whole body or some aspect of the body to follow a child's actions. Attunement and mirroring are the initial techniques that enable a therapist to learn about a child's personal nonverbal language. This provides insight into how a child experiences surroundings. Once a therapist has entered into a child's worldview, the dancing dialogue begins. Now the perception of the body as a tool of intervention takes on a deeper meaning and becomes an important facilitator of communication and reciprocal relating. The body becomes a primary tool to encourage and enable the child's self-expression. The therapist and parent use their bodies to mirror and attune to the child. The specific body tools the therapist emphasizes in the *Ways of Seeing* approach are eye contact and responses to music through the body, rhythm, sound, breath, touch, and muscle tone.

Eye Contact   Eye contact is one of the earliest elements of connection that provides emotional feedback between two people; however, it is not always a comfortable modality for a child with sensory sensitivity. It is easy to fall into a pattern of not providing eye contact when a child with whom a therapist is working avoids it. Therapists must become aware of how they use eye contact to relate, especially paying attention to how they use the expressivity in their eyes to engage a child. It is important for therapists to learn the most effective ways of softening their gaze or exaggerating excitement or surprise with each child. Therapists should know when to look away to provide a child with visual rest and when to maintain eye contact so that she can find the therapist available when she is ready to visually return her attention. Most important, therapists should never miss an opportunity to read the visual expressivity especially apparent in a nonverbal child.

—— *Nikki cannot stop the sporadic pulsing of her taxed nervous system today, but I cannot miss her eagerness to dance with me. It is her eyes that sparkle so brightly every time I look at them to acknowledge that I've noticed how she is using some part of her body to respond to our dance music. These responses are quite subtle. They are in competition with the continuous side to side rocking of her whole body that she cannot control. Despite this, she holds my gaze with steadfast visual contact as she strives to respond to the qualitative changes in the music—shaking her head to the beat, quickening her movements as the music accelerates, and even trying to contain her rocking when the music pauses.* ⌇

Responding to Music   Using her body to respond to the qualities of music enables a child to begin to gain a sense of control over her body while supporting interactions with others. Interpreting a piece of music through bodily self-expression enables a child to share her experiences without the need for words. Asking a child to hear music through her body requires her to match her movements to an outside rhythm rather than to listen only to her own innate rhythm. The dance-play activity section later in this chapter will provide more extensive ways to use the body, movement, and music.

Rhythm, Sound, and the Body   The body is an instrument of rhythm and sound. Vocalizing, singing, hand clapping, and foot stomping are the most common associations made when thinking about the body as an instrument. Rhythms can also be made by tapping different body parts. Of course, there are the "head, shoulders, knees, and toes" (to quote the classic children's song), but there are also the chest, belly, arms, legs, ankles, fingers, facial details, and even the bottom! From the most basic single two-beat rhythms to vastly complicated multipart syncopated patterns, human bodies are a wealth of rhythm, sound, and structure. The voice should also be included in this discussion for its use in producing sounds and accents, in addition to its most common use—language. As with body movement, it is important for therapists to become cognizant of how the levels and tones of their voices can be used to facilitate interactions. Using the voice to exchange sounds, tunes, or rhythms is a wonderful way to support a dialogue, especially if words are not available.

Breath and Muscular Tension   Breath, the essential life force, also exhibits rhythm. The depth of breath and the flow of inhaling and exhaling form this rhythm, and can indicate the level of body tension. *Breath awareness* involves noticing the length of inhale in relation to exhale and the amount of pausing between these two points. Breath awareness reveals an individual's resting breath pattern and how this may change under different situations and stressors. Muscular tension occurs when the muscles of an area of the body are being held tight even when they are not being used. To help a young child learn about his breath, a therapist must become aware of his or her own breath patterns and body tension. A therapist must detect how his or her breath changes depending on different emotions and what circumstances alter breath and muscular tension levels. This understanding becomes very significant when therapists are in physical contact with children, for their muscular tensions and breathing patterns are felt through tactile input.

Breath activities help deepen a child's breath, support physical activity, and promote relaxation. These activities involve vocalizing during different stages of the breath pattern and adjusting the breath flow to music or instrumental tones. A child can be assisted to experience new breath patterns by breathing in unison with the therapist. During breath activities the therapist creates a breathing rhythm to which the child can adapt. This may require the therapist to slow down, shorten, or even slightly speed up the breath to accommodate the child's breath capacity. The therapist's vocalizing or audibly blowing air in and out provides additional kinesthetic and auditory input.

Synchronous breath flow is also an effective way to create an emotional connection with a child. Sitting back to back or back to front with a child while providing full torso contact during breathing can support tactile awareness between the self and the other. Placing one's hands on a very young child's rib cage, gently widening one's holds during the inhale and enclosing one's holds on the exhale can provide tactile instruction and support the child's breathing mechanisms. When taking breath into account during actions, inhaling generally occurs during the preparation or the opening/enlarging/extending aspect of an action, while exhaling is performed during the action's exertion or enclosing aspects. This breath-flow pattern facilitates ease in motion by expanding the body as it fills with air and using the release of air to provide power for the action.

Touch and the Body   Touch, whether through the hands or other body contact, is another way to communicate. The quality, tension, and pressure of touch become another language from which both participants receive information. Touch is an additional way to see and listen to another person. Touch can be used therapeutically to support a child's movement initiations, continuations, or completions. Massaging touch can stimulate or relax a child's body. Clear, careful placement of a therapist's hands through touch communicates and maintains a sense of connection between the self and the other. When a therapist uses touch to help guide a child's body through a series of actions, the child can experience fluid consecutive movement phrases that build on each other. This enables the child to encounter, in a very primary, physical way, a sense of continuity that can be especially helpful with motor-planning issues. Thoughtfully planned, a therapist's consecutive touch can act as a tactile guide to teach a child the correct motor or muscular rhythm necessary to execute a series of actions.

Paying attention to how a child uses, welcomes, or avoids touch may also reveal valuable information. Some sensory-seeking children crave touch. These children have poor body boundaries, and do not have a clear kinesthetic sense of where their bodies end and others' begin. Using her whole body, a sensory-seeking child may bump into objects or may lay, rub, or "pour" her body over other people during conversations or activities. She might not be able to properly judge what a comfortable spatial distance might be between herself and another person. Often she does not have an accurate awareness of her own body weight. When she takes others by the hand, she frequently puts her whole body weight into the action, tugging and pulling people to lead them across the room. In contrast, a child who is sensorially sensitive to touch may keep his distance from other people. As people approach, he may retreat, pulling back the nearest part of his body or even his whole body. Such a child may often place himself apart from others and avoid group activities. Both sensory-seeking and avoiding reactions affect how children experience interactions with others, and such responses, repeated over time, will influence how children form relationships.

Both behavioral descriptions reveal issues related to body weight, timing, and spatial placement. Dance-play activities that emphasize these qualities support increased awareness and facilitate interpersonal engagement. One excellent activity that develops body and spatial awareness is to ask children to create imaginary bubbles that surround and enclose their bodies. A group of children can be instructed to find their own personal spaces in the room and then mark these spaces by extending their arms all around them as far as they can reach—up, down, and to the sides—thereby delineating their far-reach kine-spheres. They can decorate the inside of their imaginary bubbles with rainbows or spaceships or whatever else they envision. Then each child can test his bubble with that of his neighbor by approaching her but stopping before they physically touch. Once this distance in which their bubbles nearly touch is defined, the children can pretend that the edges

Dance-play activities can support awareness of a child's body and spatial placements.

of their bubbles bounce them away from each other; or, they can stay at the edge of their bubbles' points of contact and take turns mirroring their partners' actions without touching. The group can experiment with moving throughout the room to different tempos of music, creating pathways around each other without touching.

Adding rhythm to a game of tag—which uses time and weight— is another way to explore these issues. This activity is introduced when the children have established a clear sense of their body boundaries by means of the bubble imagery. In this activity, the children allow their bubbles to become so close (near-reach kinesphere) that they can actually touch other children's bodies. Playing music with a strong medium beat, the therapist may suggest to the children that they approach and tag each other with actions that move to the rhythm. The quality of the touch on the body can be varied—from light to firm or quick to prolonged. The location of the touch may also be changed—from arms to hips, and so forth. These parameters provide variations of weight, time, and space.

Space as a Therapeutic Tool

Space can become a prominent intervention tool when a therapist pays attention to both the placement of each mover's body in relation to another and how the whole room and floor space are used in the navigations that take place throughout a session. The spatial concepts of the LMA system provide the underlying structure from which the awareness of the physical space and spatial placement of the body are used in the *Ways of Seeing* approach. As discussed in depth in Chapters 5 and 6, the key Laban concepts applicable for intervention are kinesphere, general space, interpersonal space, shape flow, molding/shaping, directional movements, and spatial pathways.

The *kinesphere* is the personal space around each individual that is reachable while staying in one spot. It includes level changes—low, middle, to high space; spatial distance from the body—near, middle, to far-reach space; and spatial placement in reference to the body—any variation of movement in relation to the front, side, or back of the body. The *general space* is all of the public space outside of an individual's kinesphere. *Interpersonal space* refers to the area of space shared when two individuals are engaged. It represents the interactive changing distances between people in a given environment and involves the mingling and overlapping of each individual's kinespheres.

Shape flow, molding/shaping, and directional movements refer to spatial actions the body makes as a person moves through the room. *Shape-flow* actions occur within one's internal body space and create internal movement fluidity. The motion of the breath through the body is a shape-flow action. *Molding/shaping* actions describe when a mover forms his or her body around an object or another person. Sitting in a chair requires a mover to mold his or her body to fit the chair's dimensions. Hugging also requires a mover to adapt his or her body to form comfortably around someone else. Adapting one's body around people, objects, and the surroundings while maintaining clear physical boundaries facilitates relating; in contrast, holding one's body too firmly while attempting to mold, as in a hug, can create a feeling of distance and rejection. When one's style of molding creates boundaries that are unclear by being too loose, soft, or passive, enmeshment occurs. *Directional movements* are the spoke-like and arcing actions that happen when a mover's limbs are projected into space. These actions create clear lines in space, delineating boundaries and conveying a sense of separateness between the self and the other. *Spatial pathways* are the floor patterns that the body makes as a mover traverses a room.

In the *Ways of Seeing* program, a therapist must keep all of these spatial considerations in mind as he or she moves with and watches a child or parent–child dyad during a session. How individual movers navigate through their spatial environments provides valuable information about how comfortable they are within their surroundings. In turn, activities that use the space around them can support social-emotional exploration and growth.

⁓ *Jake saunters into the center of the room (the general space), creating a wiggly floor pattern that matches his arms swaying this way and that, only settling down as he plops himself on the pile of pillows in the corner. His soft body takes on the contours of the pillows by molding into the grooves made where the pillows meet. When I remind him that we always begin sessions by taking shoes off, he is still for a few moments, and then log rolls off the pillows toward the door. This "log" is a very crooked, bumpy one, formed as his legs splinter open and his arms flop and push along the floor. Jake's roll enters into my personal kinespheric space, intermingling our interpersonal space as he lifts up his feet and drops them onto my lap in a gesture that seems to ask me to take off his shoes. Jake's sensory-seeking movements clearly portray a lack of solid body boundaries between self, objects, and others. Without this clear sense of physical self, Jake has a difficult time focusing and staying on task, especially in group settings. We begin our session with the stimulation and activation activities (described in Chapter 8).*

Today, during our mobilizing activities, Jake creates a story about being lost in space. I am instructed to save him as he waits for me on a faraway planet. I am to get to this planet by leaping across a wandering pillow path that he has designed and ordered by numbering each pillow from 1 to 13. It feels like a mobile dot-to-dot.

The irregular format of this path matches the way Jake enters his space. The numbering supports how his mind works and serves to organize his movements in space. The rescuing theme allows Jake to acknowledge his need for help during this difficult emotional time, when his cognitive focus has been interrupted by seizures that have been occurring more intensely. The image of being "lost in space" seems to be an accurate emotional analogy.

Transforming Movement and Dance into Dance-Play Activities

Jake's outer-space story fits perfectly within the dance-play category of *Ways of Seeing* activities. Dance-play activities utilize movement and dance-based explorations to foster body awareness, social-emotional expression and growth, as well as physical, motor, cognitive, and communicative skill development. These activities support Thelen's (1996) emphasis on the importance of spontaneous movement for all levels of development. Dance-play activities encourage a child to experience movement in a fun way. Individual creativity is tapped as the child begins to learn how to spontaneously play with movement. There are six categories of dance-play in the *Ways of Seeing* approach:

1. Improvisation
2. Individually composed dances
3. Drawing and dancing

4. Choreographed dance
5. Drama and storytelling dance-play
6. Developmental movements using exercises, warm-ups, and yoga

Improvisation In improvisation activities, therapists set up an environment to encourage children to create their own spontaneous movement sequences. This technique is used for two reasons: From an emotional-social perspective, it enables children to use their own movements to express their needs, concerns, joys, and past and present experiences. Children especially enjoy this technique because it provides them with the freedom for self-expression. It is a time for children presenting with issues along an emotional or social spectrum to share their feelings in self-directed ways without feeling pressured, forced, or guided. For children with physical or communicative special needs, it is often the only time in their therapeutic schedules that they are not asked to perform codified exercise sequences. Instead they are given full reign to use their bodies freely in whatever ways they are able to move. Their actions can be constructed completely within the range of movements that feel comfortable, totally accommodating any limitations. For some children, this dance may involve simply rocking their bodies from side to side, or gliding their arms along the floor. Others may move all around the room rolling, running, jumping, sliding, or being silly, serious, cautious, or boisterous. All the while, the therapist observes with the sole intention of getting to know the children better as unique individuals; this attitude enables the children to feel a sense of agency and safety with the environment.

From these spontaneous explorations, children often discover new movements. This is the second aspect of this technique that is especially useful when children have been working on specific movement skills. When children are given the opportunity to freely explore movements, often their improvisations incorporate elements of the movements they have been learning in their occupational or physical therapy sessions. Suddenly, during their spontaneous dance-play, they find the movement sequence on which they have been working. Discovering a movement skill on their own lifts their self-esteem, as they enthusiastically try it over and over again, thereby owning the action.

Improvisation fosters spontaneous interactions. These interactions can then be turned into dances, which can then be varied and transformed into choreographed dance sequences to foster neuromuscular learning. A therapist can take three different approaches toward a child's dance during improvisational activities:

- Follow
- Watch
- Watch, narrate, and interpret

Follow the Child's Dance In this approach, a therapist follows a child's actions by dancing alongside the child and creating an immediately social experience. For the child with social awareness, the dance-play may become an affable exchange of movements incorporating the therapist into the dance. For the child not yet able to relate socially, the therapist becomes a shadow. As the therapist reflects the child's actions back to the child, the therapist stays open to any opportunity for the actions to facilitate verbal or nonverbal social dialogue.

Over time, the child may begin to respond to the therapist's presence. At first, she might stop the action to look at the therapist, or she might push the therapist away. She might change some qualitative aspect of her movement, such as speeding up the action, altering the timing of the movement. Another child might change his position in space by turning his body away from the therapist. He might add more strength or lightness to his movements, altering the weight of the overall action. Sometimes a child will expand her movement or contain it, affecting the use and orientation of space occupied by the movement. Her body may tense or become more fluid, causing a change in the flow of her actions. Changes in the movement quality—time, weight, space, and flow—or in the body's orientation in space may occur subtly or overtly during a movement sequence that may go unnoticed to the untrained eye; but for a movement-oriented therapist, these qualitative aspects of movement provide occasions to enhance interactions by expanding, elaborating, and responding to these qualities.

Watch the Child's Dance Sometimes a child seeks to move purely for the sake of moving, neither wanting nor needing direct feedback from a therapist. Under these circumstances, the therapist's role is to just watch. Such dance-play improvisation functions as a release, or a personal exploration in a form that neither desires nor requires explanation. Those who have attended a modern dance performance may recall an abstract piece that could not be ascribed direct meaning but was enjoyed nonetheless. A classical ballet viewer might relate this experience to a solo or duet section of a performance that showcased skills and virtuosity more than it moved the storyline forward. For both the modern and classical dancers themselves, these moments epitomize the power and wonder of the body in motion similar to the sense of a peak experience known to any athlete. It is satisfying to feel the body move! Young children seem to know this, too, for so many of them are on the move for so much of the time.

Watch, Narrate, and Interpret the Child's Dance   At some point while watching a child's dance-play improvisation, a therapist may begin to narrate or interpret some aspect of the movement sequence as a way of using verbalizations to process the experience and facilitate an understanding of the child's movement expression. This method is discussed in depth in Chapter 8.

Individually Composed Dances   Individually composed dances are the next step along the continuum of dances that begin with improvisation and end with choreographed sequences. Although they may originally be considered an extension of improvisation dance-play, improvisational dances that are repeated over time become individually composed dances. In these dances, an established pattern of actions is created that usually includes repeated actions and rhythms. There is still room for free exploration, but individually composed dances differ from improvisation dance-play in that there are more composed, repeated movement aspects or themes to a dance that is worked on over a series of sessions. The ability to consciously reconstruct the loose patterns and themes each week supports and requires a degree of cognitive processing; however, these dances are not classified as a choreographed dance because they do not require a set number of steps or repetitions of actions.

Individually composed dances create a sense of ownership and accomplishment for a child. These dances say, in essence, "Here I am. Look at me. This is what I have to say. And I can say it again and again!" These dances can be used to help the child link emotions to actions by describing and titling his dance—"This is how I feel when I am excited. This dance is called, My Excitement Dance!" The use of movement and dance actions in these dances correlates to the use of play in play therapy. In play therapy, the therapist pays particular attention to the content of a child's play to discern the emotional themes that underlie the storyline of the child's play each week. During *Ways of Seeing* sessions, the child will playfully create dances with repeated themes depicting his most prevalent concerns and perceptions.

Sometimes individually composed dances first arise by exploring choreographed sequences from dances the child has learned through play with other children or through popular songs, folk dances, and movement and finger-play games. Often such movement-based games act as a safe, nonthreatening, or even self-revealing way to introduce nonverbally based explorations. This occurs when a therapist pays close attention to the specific style in which a child performs a dance, and through observation and discussion with the child, ascertains specific movement difficulties and preferences that arise from these choreographed dances that can later become themes for child-composed dances. That is, the therapist encourages a child to develop some specific aspect of the dance to make it her own composition. A child's unique personality is highlighted when she has the opportunity to pick the specific music and movements she wants to include in her dance.

In other instances, the therapist may assist a child to add particular challenges to his personal dance. This may involve purely physical skills, such as using body parts that need strengthening or balancing on one foot; alternatively, the focus may be placed on social interactions, such as exploring how to stay engaged through appropriate eye contact or touch, or examining how to transfer weight so that neither dancer is pulling nor leaning on the other. A child can also explore body regulation and control by creating a dancing sequence that involves slow and calm movements continuously supported by breath-flow awareness.

Drawing and Dancing   Art materials have already been discussed in previous chapters as excellent tools for processing emotional themes. Artwork can also be utilized as a movement catalyst. A toddler's involved scribbles when danced out can become an elaborate story about a superhero fighting a bad guy, complete with an action in which he jumps off the castle wall to safety. The crayon markings of the young child, described next, become a visual and socially supported floor-patterned road map.

Juan, age 4, has sensory integration issues, particularly noticeable in his inability to maintain eye contact and his jumpy actions that keep him sporadically moving. He uses a red crayon to drawn a series of overlapping, irregularly shaped circles and squiggles all over the page. Following his lead, I first mirror these marks on the corresponding page. When he enters onto my page, I begin to trail after him, tracing his marks. Eventually we bump, cross, and meet each other on the page, in a game of drawing chase and dodge. Contact seems less threatening on the drawing sheet.

Eventually we move this game to the dance floor, running, bumping, and crossing paths. Each time we cross paths or meet, I encourage eye contact and firm hugs. Juan responds with glee and increased social connection.

The more realistic drawings of an older child can become scenes and characters capable of embodiment through improvisational and individually composed dances. Detailed drawings can be made into obstacle courses that support perceptual motor development as the child moves throughout the room. These drawings and maps can be imbued with a storyline pertinent to the child's emotional focus. Jake's outer-space journey, discussed in a previous vignette, which had originated several weeks before as a mapped-out obstacle course, provides an excellent example.

Other art medias, such as clay and found objects, can be added to the artwork to form sculptures. The actual process of making the clay sculpture is very physical. A therapist may find it useful to pay attention to the quality, such as the strength or lightness, in which a child manipulates the clay; how much clay is used, and whether the clay is pulled, ripped, thrown, roll, squeezed, or separated into different shapes or colors; and how much or how little of the body is involved as the child works the clay. These details reveal information about a child's physical abilities and emotional moods as well. For the older child, clay structures and found objects often become characters that can be acted out. Here again, a therapist should pay great attention to the different movement characteristics each character possesses as potential insight into a child's expressive experience.

Choreographed Dance Choreographed dances are action and rhythmic sequences that are created and repeated exactly. They have a set pattern of movements that require cognitive processing to support the attention given to the qualitative and repetitive details of the sequence. These dances include established dances that a child is taught, such as folk dances, large motor singing movement games such as the Hokey-pokey, and self-developed finger-play songs or dances. In self-created choreography, a child makes a signature movement sequence that focuses on a particular theme. The theme can be functional—such as body-part coordination or skill development—or social-emotional—such as a dance about feeling sad.

Choreographed dance provides form and structured movement experiences for a child, and often organizes her actions. These dance activities foster increased social opportunities, as they are often performed with a group of participants. A therapist has several roles during choreographed sequences. When presenting a folk dance or singing movement game, the therapist acts as a teacher, encouraging a child to learn the steps of the dance. During a child's own choreographed creations, the therapist acts as a notetaker and interpreter, helping the child identify and keep track of the exact actions of the sequence. The therapist can record and discuss symbols, drawings, and key words to support the child's expressions and her ability to put meaning to her intentions. Once the sequence is established, the therapist becomes the student, asking the child to teach the sequence as a way to better understand its meaning and feelings. In a group setting, each child can also share and teach the choreography to other participants.

Folk Dance and Singing Movement Games   Folk dances and other structured group dances such as contra dances and large motor singing movement games offer extensive opportunity for both individual growth and socialization for mobile children. The organized, structured actions of such dances provide a nonthreatening way for children to explore their bodies in motion, especially if they are not comfortable with self-expressive movement. It can be a wonderful lead into self-awareness as each child's unique ways of performing the actions can be highlighted and praised. Dance movement therapist pioneer, Marion Chase (Chaiklin, 1975), extensively developed the use of folk dances and other forms of group dancing; she distinguished the use of folk dances for recreational as opposed to social-emotional therapeutic purposes in her classic work. In their recreational use, folk dances are enjoyable community building activities that develop body skills in the execution of the actions. The movement actions of folk dances often portray specific tones of a culture and frequently represent common lifestyle activities of that culture, such as the farming and pearl-gathering actions of Japanese folk dances. They may include quite lively and complicated rhythmic foot-stepping actions as in classic Israeli and Russian folk dances. In their social-emotional therapeutic use, the emphasis is not on the technical execution of the movements but rather on their function to both build community and enable self-awareness. Used in this way, the participants are encouraged to create their own styles within the structure of the dance. This simultaneously supports group cohesion and self-expression.

The *Ways of Seeing* approach supports the use of these dances for both physical skill development and social-emotional therapeutic use, but therapists must be clear regarding their intentions before introducing these activities. When using these dances to promote social-emotional engagement, the proficient execution of the actions must be abandoned; however, once a sense of group cohesion and enjoyment is experienced by all the participants, carefully introducing increased attention to the specific details in the performance of the actions can add to both the individual and the group's senses of pride and accomplishment. Ultimately, as has been expounded on throughout this book, supporting social-emotional growth must underlie all activities in a *Ways of Seeing* session.

The intrinsic actions of each dance provide opportunities for growth on many levels. Feder and Feder (1981) emphasized that the wide variety of rhythms, movement patterns, and postural stances available in international folk dances enables the knowledgeable therapist to choose particular folk dances to address specific physical and social-emotional objectives. They distinguished seven specific objectives supported by folk dances: the promotion of socialization, the exploration of nonverbal communication, the experimentation with leading and following, the exploration of timing and rhythm, the relief of tensions and aggressions, the explorations of variations in the flow of qualitative Effortful action and Body Shapes, and the encouragement of humor and enjoyment. Feder and Feder cited various examples to demonstrate how different cultures' dances aid these objectives, ranging from the vigorous foot stamping actions of Rumanian dances that promote a healthy organized expression of tension and aggression, to the continual line leading changes of Greek dances that support leading and following skills.

Through these dances, children increase their movement vocabulary and range of motion as they learn about moving and being with others. They take turns in leading and following, while developing patience in waiting their turn. Social development is increased as the dances provide a reason to engage with others. Children acquire skills in observing others and sharing movements with one another. They learn about the similarities and differences between themselves and others as they see and feel the movement steps on one another's bodies. Learning about others can be extended into cultural exchanges by studying the origins of the folk dances from other countries. The actions, rhythms, and music of the dances often reveal extensive information about a culture's attitudes and lifestyle.

The circle, line, and multiple partnering formations intrinsic to many of these dances enable children to experience interaction and physical closeness to others in appropriate ways. This provides opportunities to experience relating through suitable forms of touch. Most of all, group dances are fun. They stimulate laughter, conversations, and expressions of joy. All of these aspects of dance encourage communication and a sense of belonging.

The specific actions of a group dance provide an excellent diagnostic tool for a perceptive therapist to observe each child's style of executing the movements. Individual differences in social engagement and comfort; abilities to maintain coordination, focus, and composure; or difficulties with regulating excitement will quickly be revealed. Coordination, balance, and increased range-of-motion activities can be embedded in the dance as new versions are performed within the context of trying to create unique variations of the dance theme. Regulation of excitement can be addressed by adding sequences of breath awareness and centering actions that will be elaborated on later in this chapter under the relaxation subheading.

Whether they are used for socialization or skill improvement, folk dances and singing movement games support multiple levels of cognitive and physical development by fostering the simultaneous integration of listening, observing, and doing. Children are asked to follow directions, imitate actions, listen and produce rhythms, and move their bodies in a wide variety of ways. The group forms include large circles, lines, stars, squares, and curves as well as smaller clusters as children break into dyads and other mixed partnering. The specific actions of the dance often require children to put their own bodies in a variety of shapes, reaching, bending, and curving their bodies in time to the rhythm. Within any one dance, children will explore variations in timing, direction, fluidity, use of strength, and spatial placement of their bodies in reference to self and others. Physical and emotional tension can be released in a structured way as the children vigorously stamp, clap, and use large actions to move their bodies throughout the room.

Finger-Play Songs Finger-play songs provide the same advantages as folk dances, singing movement games, and individually composed dances. Because these songs predominately involve finger manipulations as the category's name suggests, smaller actions and fine motor skills are emphasized. These dance-play games are often used with younger children and are a great introduction to the world of group dancing. Many of the songs can be performed sitting down in a circle. Often they provide an added opportunity for tactile stimulation and closeness between an adult and a child as they perform the songs together. For sensory-seeking children (and any child who enjoys cuddling), being held on someone's lap while singing and acting out the words to a song brings great pleasure and stimulation. Varying the tempo of the music, the Phrasing emphasis of the actions, the strength of the movements, and how much space is taken up by the dance encourages social awareness while invigorating the proprioceptive and vestibular systems. When large full-body actions are included in these songs, children explore the containment of their bodies within their surroundings. Body boundaries of self and other are experienced as a child is instructed to stay in place, jump, bend, and balance from one side to the other. These actions can be developed further to mobilize through contained space, if the children move around a circle. Encouraging individual children to add their own large body action interpretations to the gestures adds self-expression and provides a sense of agency.

As with the folk dances, singing movement games, and individually composed dances, these finger-play songs and games can be modified to accommodate individual children's needs. Children's specific challenges can be incorporated and tried on by each participant by being introduced as "Mary's way of doing the song."

⌒ *Nikki's excited vocalizations and increased whole body activity every time I put on the singing dance game "Jump Jim Joe" tells us that she loves the song. But the fast-paced words on the CD describing the actions to perform do not give her enough time to try an action before the next movement is required. So we play the song through to get in the mood and then play it again pausing during each instruction to give her the time to try out the action. Pepper, her teacher/sitter, watches the session and comes back the next time with a new modification. She has been helping Nikki create nonverbal signals to assist in communication. So Pepper and Nikki have adapted a recorded line so that they nod their heads yes and shake them no instead of shaking and nodding their heads as the song requests, which both describes the actions more clearly and supports Nikki's communication goals.* ⌒

Drama and Storytelling Dance-Play This form of dance-play occurs when symbolic representation exists or is about to emerge and fits along the continuum of the interpretive improvisational dance-play. Dramatic and storytelling dance-play encompasses pure dance actions as well as acting out dramatic expressions. Movement and pantomime become the main media rather than dance. During these activities, the storyline unfolds with an emphasis on acting out instead of, or in addition to, dancing the information. Aspects of existing stories from fairy tales or favorite children's books may also be incorporated into a child's original drama dance-play. A child may choose to have the therapist participate by joining in, watching, or narrating the story. Narrating, writing, or drawing the storyline during each session records the story and enables it to be extended during subsequent sessions. Each week the story can be reviewed and added to, providing a chronological history of the story's evolution. This was an especially helpful tool for Darryl, the adopted child discussed in Chapter 5, who attended the *Ways of Seeing* sessions for one month at age 14 months and then again from ages 22–25 months due to signs of failure to thrive, manifested especially in issues of attachment, calming down, and sleeping.

In our first session I am struck by how long and straight Darryl holds his back when sitting and crawling. He seems to exude a sense of separateness between him and those in his environment. This strong vertical stance creates a distinct difference in how he uses the left and right sides of his body. He seems to most often use his right side to mobilize, initiate, and explore his environment, while the left side acts as stabilizer and follower. This is especially seen in his crawl, which occurs as a three "and" beat. He initiates the action with a push from his right leg, transferring his weight into his upper body as his right arms reach forward, followed by his left leg scooping forward and his left arm reaching forward on the "and" beat. This vertical also does not support Darryl molding into his mom during hugs or when he is carried. Helping Darryl mold and soften his body during playful interactions becomes our first goal. Symbolically, molding supports emotional closeness. Over the next three sessions, we begin to create a story about Darryl being born from his adoptive mother by crawling and rolling over her body. When he rolls over her back onto the floor, I use his outstretched legs to push him toward Mom as she lifts him up and says "OH! Here is my boy! I am so happy you are here." They embrace in a warm, firm hug. Mom and Darryl spend the next few months on their own, playing this story game at Darryl's request whenever he is feeling anxious.

Mom calls 7 months later to say that she thinks Darryl wants to elaborate on this story. Darryl demonstrates much better left-to-right and full-body integration, molding more to his mom and his environment. His love of the vertical is still present but is now just a part of his more expanded movement vocabulary. Mom reports that he is much more attached to her, accepting her comfort during times of distress, and is easier to calm. He begins the session by running through the room and then jumping, jumping, jumping, and falling on the floor and bumping his head. I follow, verbally describing his actions as I go. The falling and bumping feel purposeful. I exaggerate the action and say "Oh! I bumped my head." Darryl loves this and keeps repeating the action, requesting my narration. This story develops further during the next session. He again begins with this running and falling sequence, requesting that I describe it. This time I ask him if someone can help him when he falls. He points to Mom. Of course! He is now starting to realize and accept Mom's care and attention over these months. Each time he falls, Mom runs over, places his head in her hands, and gives him a kiss. Over the next few sessions, Darryl creates all kinds of dancing games in which he falls or bumps his head and points to Mom to come and "rescue" him. Sometimes he just bends down so his head taps the floor and then stands up requesting Mom's kiss. Darryl and Mom begin to create a beautiful dance demonstrating their newly developed sense of attachment to each other. ⌒

Exercises, Warm-Ups, and Yoga Organized movement forms can be used in a session to complement the other dance-play activities. Exercises and yoga poses are activities that add structured movement exploration to the improvisational aspects of a session. They do not replace the improvisational dance-plays, but rather can augment the more child-directed movement explorations. They can be used as warm-up actions at the start of a session to get a child's body prepared for physical activity, interspersed during the session to help regulate or calm the child's actions, or inserted at the end of the session as part of a relaxing closure ritual. Sequencing actions that support the developmental movement progressions discussed in Chapter 3 and based on the Laban (1975, 1976), Bartenieff (Bartenieff & Lewis, 1980), and Cohen (1997) movement experiential work will foster improved movement coordination. This progression moves through actions using breath, spinal movement, upper to lower body awareness, left-to-right body half awareness, and contralateral body actions.

Teaching a child existing exercises has strong merits such as building strength, coordination, balance, overall body awareness, and instruction-following skills. These are essential elements of any therapeutic program for a child with motor difficulties; however, even when teaching a standard exercise, emphasis should be placed on the specific way that a child is performing the actions. Noting a child's speed or particular placement of limbs while executing the movement, for example, can help the child make a personal connection to each element of the actions. Even when teaching the technical aspects of a movement skill, the emphasis is best placed on how the child is producing the action. This adds a self-expressive personal element and orients the exercise around the child. During these explorations, a child can increase body awareness by discovering how specific body parts move, both alone and in sequence with larger body-part actions. Exercises, warm-ups, and specific yoga poses can also be used to introduce creative dance-play stories that portray emotional and social themes. For example, after learning how to execute the cat, dog, and cobra poses, one 4-year-old spontaneously sequenced these yoga poses together to tell a story about three friends who were arguing. Each wanted to show off as "the best performer," but in the end they all took turns and became better friends.

In a group setting, such yoga activities can be used to support and improve social relatedness. Children can assist one another to form yoga poses. They can also create group stories interspersed with poses as they work on such themes as conflict, aggression, cooperation, individuality, and self-expression.

Teaching Skills

Skills can be introduced as forms of dance-play, although several points should first be considered. A therapist can link together specific steps of a skill to make a minichoreographed sequence, giving special attention to the rhythm and timing of particular elements. A skill can be treated as a movement phrase, and a therapist can note places to emphasize; for example, by adding strength or slowing down the action. Typically, a therapist will teach a skill by stressing the specific body parts used in an action. When dissecting the body parts needed to create a skill, a therapist may think about how the parts move in relation to one another: Which body parts move together simultaneously? Which body parts move in sequential order? Asking these questions when teaching a skill can make even the simplest action feel like a dance by helping the movement segments flow together more smoothly. A therapist may pay attention to the placement of the body in space—using high, middle, or low levels of the spatial surroundings. A therapist can also add rhythmic emphasis by including qualitative aspects to movement skills. (See Chapter 6 for further discussion of these qualitative aspects of movement.) Skills that can be taught include both motor skills, such as crawling or walking, and more complicated dance steps for more advanced movers.

Rhythm and Music

Research has begun to look at the critical role that rhythm and timing play in communication, motor planning, perception, and affective interactions.

Research on newly developed auditory programs that use sounds to guide the listener by combining a musical metronome and computer technology has demonstrated improvements in children's motor planning sequencing and timing, attention, language processing, reading, and regulation of aggression (Shaffer et al., 2001). Nelson (2001, p. 10), a speech and language therapist, has commented:

> Rhythm and timing are involved in a number of skills critical to communication: attention, eye contact (knowing when to look and how long to look, where to look), two-way purposeful interactions, gestural communication, imitation skills, creating ideas (imaginative play, realistic play, symbolic play sequences, responding to others, prediction of how others will feel or act in given situations), articulation, syntax, auditory processing, problem-solving skills, graphomotor skills.

Rhythm is an intrinsic part of dancing and music and is used extensively in *Ways of Seeing* sessions, both with and without musical accompaniment. Rhythms are used to create mutual attention; develop social engagement, communication, and self-expression; and support motor skill development. For example, placing a rhythmic accent during a particular aspect of a motor skill facilitates its execution. Touch is often used to articulate this type of rhythm. This is shown in the earlier vignette in which the therapist repeatedly uses a light touch on Brianna's upper torso to support her as she log rolls throughout the room. Adding music with a strong rhythmic beat creates external auditory support for action execution. When movers respond to a beat, their actions become more organized. Rhythm can also be added to actions to emphasize feelings.

⌒ *Jasper, age 4, enters the room angry, flinging and flailing his limbs around the room. Suddenly he slashes at the large physioball. When asked, he says he is angry because everything is stupid, and the ball is bad. Aiming to support this emotional outburst while preventing it from getting out of control, I clap my hands to the beat of his ball slashing. He adds vocals, "Ahhhyaaa." He slashes the ball all the way across the room accompanied by my claps. I tell him he can continue the actions, but I add more rhythmic parameters to provide even more organization to his body actions: When moving across the room from the wall to the windows, his actions with the ball must include punches, but when returning, he can repeat his slashing actions. I ask him if he would now like music to support our claps and vocalizations.*

"Yes!" he responds. I choose a fast-paced rhythmic instrumental piece. The strong beat of the violins, accordions, and piano "Old Time" American dance music fills the air as Jasper moves to the beat. Exerting so much strength is very tiring. After a few minutes Jasper is able to stop and rest as we begin to talk about his feelings of anger and frustration. 〜

Rhythms are contagious! It is almost impossible to put on a rhythmic piece of music, such as a march by John Philip Sousa, without foot tapping or finger snapping. Even the youngest and least-mobile children respond with alert attention when a rhythmic piece of music is played. For all ages, the use of music and rhythm adds mood and emotion. Music is used in the *Ways of Seeing* session to match a child's mood as expressed through movements. The careful selection of music can support specific qualitative aspects of a child's actions that are particularly representative of themes or issues the child needs to express. Music can create vast emotional landscapes such as mystery, fear, gaiety, freedom, or comfort. A wide variety of music must be on hand for each individual's response, and every child's connotations to a specific piece of music will be unique. Music can calm, relax, mobilize, energize, and regulate a person's body.

Relaxation and Visualizations

Creating experiences in which a child can feel her body calm down has become an invaluable tool for even the most organized and healthy child living in this fast-paced and overstimulating world. Relaxation activities involve both stationary and mobile movements. Stationary relaxation occurs while the child sits or lies down. The focus of these activities is to systematically relax each part of the child's body through awareness of her breath flow using guided verbal descriptions and visualizations with or without touch. The therapist's verbalization can be technical or can involve storytelling. The therapist may instruct the child to breathe in and expand her torso while inhaling and to release her body while exhaling. Alternatively, a storytelling example might involve a beach scenario in which the child imagines lying on the sand, with a soft summer breeze entering into her body on the inhale, and the warmth of the sun softening her body on the exhale. Through the visualization that is developed by both the therapist and the child, the latter's images of concern and comfort will unfold as they create a story together.

Using soothing music, lowering the lighting, and resting and being wrapped in soft, textured objects such as pillows and scarves can also facilitate relaxation. Touch may be added to provide tactile guidance to these descriptions. Jake's vignette, described earlier in the chapter, displays one example of how a firm joint compression touch can provide tactile body-part feedback that serves to calm and integrate body awareness. Touch in the form of massage during breathing can also help to physically relax muscles. The therapist's thoughtful touch can be used to guide a child's breathing by placing the hands on either side of the child's rib cage, lightening and expanding the distance between the hands and the child's body on the inhale, followed by holding the hands more firmly and drawing them slightly together on the child's ribs during the exhale. Gentle, small rocking rhythms through touch can also be very soothing. A therapist who uses touch to facilitate actions must be especially aware of personal breathing and tension levels. It is essential for a therapist to relax muscular tension and create a comfortable regular breathing rhythm in order to act as a child's physical role model.

Active relaxation includes whole body dances and weight-shifting activities, often using music and musical instruments. Although choosing music that supports relaxation is very personal, it can be generally assumed that music with an easy, fluid, or undulating rhythm exudes a feeling of calm, softness, and gentle wonder. The violin, harp, cello, flute, and piano are just a few of the instruments that can create such a mood, and the waltz is a good example of a type of music that can be very successful in soothing children of all ages and needs. The three-part rhythm of the waltz step is especially helpful in calming busy children because it enables them to add structure to their need to move. While keeping to the languid but mobile rhythm of the waltz, children can glide through the entire room, varying their steps down—up—up in a repeated, fluid manner. Any variation of this pattern is fine, such as going up on toes and bending down at the waist, stamping on the down and lightly stepping on the up, or turning on the down and moving straight ahead on the up beats. A dance in which children move with their partners to mirror the actions of a leader supports socialization and emphasizes an awareness of self and other in space. Lullabies and lilting vocal songs are very effective as well.

In contrast to this more rhythmic music activity, children can also explore moving to a selection of music with a slow, even tempo that creates a sense of continuity. A child can lead by moving his whole body or by moving only one body part. Another variation might be alternating leadership, with the goal being to sustain calm actions as children explore increased and more organized body coordination through space.

Another activity to calm a child's busy body is to ask her to dance when the music is played and to hold a pose when the music is paused. Once a child shows some control during the pauses, the therapist can establish a certain number of seconds for the child to hold her pose. During these pauses the child can count how long she is still. If she moves during the designated holding time, the counting must begin again from the number one. Initially the child may burst back into movement when the music begins again. Over time the child and therapist can work on reinitiating her actions in a gradual manner, perhaps one limb at a time. As the child progresses in this movement game, the length of holding time can increase. The therapist's tracking and verbal acknowledgement of this achievement will create a sense of pride in the child and provide her with very tangible positive feedback.

Following this activity, a child can stand tall and straight, lengthening her body up along her spine. Placing one hand at the base of the front of the torso (by the pubic bones) while placing the other hand at the tailbone in the back, the image of zipping up her front and back can be used to help the child grow tall, aligning her body up along the vertical stance. The therapist or another child may assist a classmate with this image, providing added tactile support by placing his or her own hand at the base of the classmate's spine and then moving up the spine. Once established, the child can shift her body weight front – center – back; side – center – side; then circling around front – side – back – side – front.

Children often enjoy the image of circling on the top of a doughnut with the center being the doughnut hole. Shifting weight while maintaining a long torso enables a child to create a calm centeredness through action. Once a child has accomplished this, the therapist can add balancing poses to further develop body control. Starting with aligning each child's body as described above and then shifting the body weight over onto one side, still maintaining that length over the standing leg, the therapist should instruct the child to lift her free leg, balancing on her standing leg to a count of three. After a child is able to hold this position, she can create her own balancing poses by changing the levels of space or which body parts bear the weight. A child's imagination will soar as she twists and turns her body into different shapes.

Both mobile and stationary relaxation activities develop body regulation and support motor planning and sequencing. In the *Ways of Seeing* sessions, the physical experiences that teach body regulation and organization are then extended to helping a child gain better control over his emotional states. Throughout the sessions, a therapist pays close attention to a child's range of emotion, especially noting the qualities of more difficult emotions such as angry outbursts, temper tantrums, and overexcitement. A child may be directed toward one of these relaxation activities during such times, or these activities may be interspersed throughout the session as a way to help the child learn when he needs to draw his focus back to himself to connect and center his behavior. For example, if a child is beginning to escalate with excitement, the therapist might verbally label his behavior, helping the child to become aware of his rising excitement. Often when a child escalates to such states, he may not be able to immediately stop and gain control over his actions. If this is the case, the therapist might turn on music with a strong rhythmic quality to both match the emotional state and to give it some directional purpose. A therapist can use words to describe this, or demonstrate through his or her own body by emphasizing the beat and joining the child's actions. The actions can be taken into the larger space through such movements as runs, leaps, rolls, and jumps. But then the music can be paused and the child instructed, through words and/or demonstration, to take long, deep breaths, stretching his body into a big shape on the inhale. This is followed by collapsing and folding his body on an exhale and lengthening his whole body up along his spine on the next inhale. Varying the speed from quick to slow motion as the child opens and encloses his body provides added breath and body control.

When the music is turned back on, a more structured movement may be required, such as counting the running steps or making a sequence of running – running – running – jump – jump – jump – stop. The breathing sequence can be repeated again. Often at this point the therapist may decide to change the music and movements to a slower and calmer selection. This series of activities is recommended when a child's movements demonstrate excitement, but he seems able to regain some degree of control quickly as the therapist takes the first directive steps. At other times in which a child's behavior is too out of control, as evidenced by excessive falling, bumping, or true aggressive actions, he may need more assertive guidance from the therapist to learn how to regain control. The vignette at the end of this chapter provides an example of this more instructive approach.

Through the therapist's words, actions, and experiences of relaxation during the session, a child will gain new experiences that help him develop control over his behaviors. These experiences accumulate over time, especially if through these activities the child is able to sustain better regulation of his body, behavior, and feelings throughout a whole session. At first such control may only occur during a session. The therapist can help the child and the attending parent begin to read the nonverbal cues that precede the child's more difficult behaviors, however, and help them adapt these deep body awareness and focusing activities when at home and school.

Adding Instruments to Relaxation

Instruments that have resonance, such as bells, chimes, buffalo drums, tone bars, and Tibetan singing bowls, are also very useful for relaxation, whether used in recorded music or actually played during a session. By keeping the room quiet and drawing the children's attention into their bodies, the tone of these instruments can be felt inside. Children can be instructed to move their bodies to match the fading resonance of the tones, moving into stillness when they no longer can hear the tone. The quiet that comes over the room is magical. At this point the children are then asked to become aware of their breath flow, in and out. When they become restless, the instrument can be played again, repeating the sequence.

As their concentration and skill increases, children will be able to maintain their still postures for longer periods of time. Counting the seconds of quiet rest provides an external focus for restless children. Describing the different poses the individual children make during the calm, silent period increases their body spatial awareness. Listening to their poses being described also helps children extend their abilities to maintain this sense of stillness and inner balance as they eagerly wait for their poses to be noted. The tone bar instrument—a hollow metallic tube with a small hole on the top surface—is an especially fun instrument for children to hold and play while they are focusing on their breaths. Once this chiming instrument is struck with a mallet, the musician covers the small hole on the top surface with a thumb, changing the tone of the sound, and then releases the thumb. This creates a pulsing sound that is regulated by the speed in which the hole is covered and uncovered. The children breathe in and out in time with this pulsing tone. Initially, the therapist who is guiding the children to respond to the different qualities and sounds plays these instruments. As the children become more attuned to the sounds, however, they can each be given a chance to be the musician, directing their peers to dance to the changing tones and tempos. Allowing them to lead each other in an activity that fosters increased control and concentration empowers children, builds their self-esteem, and heightens their social awareness.

The Sensorially Rich Environment

The dance-play activities described in this section can be combined with a sensorially rich environment to create an atmosphere that supports a child's deepest self-expression. The therapeutic environment is sensorially rich because all the props are open-ended, fostering a child's own imagination and use. Although some typical play-therapy toys may be included, such as stuffed animals, dolls, tea sets, and a sand box, the focus of props used in sessions is discovering which ones support a child's full body play. Rather than use objects to manipulate and play out an emotional theme, a child and therapist in essence embody the theme by becoming the characters of the experience.

Objects that support more physical play include musical instruments; scarves; balls of all sizes; flashlights; fabrics of varying textures and shapes, including tubed fabric; large spandex bags that children can wrap themselves inside and close; simple costumes such as capes and hats; streamers; pillows; mats; blankets; tunnels; squares of carpet; and even chairs. A mini-trampoline, large physioballs, and suspended apparatus such as a hammock, a trapeze bar, and a large fabric bag made of stretch fabric create added thematic drama. They can be used to depict birth and womb experiences that also provide vestibular, tactile, and proprioceptive input. Tape, string, and art supplies such as drawing materials, clay, stamps, stamp pads, stickers, and scissors are also essential. Children use these materials to construct and build their environment and then place themselves inside it. There must also be enough open floor space so that children can freely move around without worrying about bumping into or breaking objects.

Children can also use art materials to create maps and books that act as a kind of journal that they can narrate to a therapist to record their experiences. Video filming and photographing children's stories and watching them as a way to process the experience together can be a useful approach, especially for older children. The following vignette of Savannah portrays this approach. Savannah had been exposed to domestic violence and was diagnosed as an infant with sensory integration dysfunction and overall developmental delays—manifested especially with attention and language processing issues. Because of very successful early intervention treatment, however, Savannah was doing well and had entered a typical kindergarten program with some special education assistance to address the remaining attention issues and learning differences. At age 6, she began dance movement psychotherapy.

⁓ Savannah enters the session, week after week, constructing two very specific stories. In the first scene she stacks two mats up high, placing them on either side of the trapeze bar. Under the trapeze bar, between the mats, she scatters all the scarves in varying sizes and colors. These are the deadly alligators she must try to avoid as she swings on the trapeze bar from mat to mat. Inevitably her actions get out of control and she falls into the sea of alligators. When this happens she lies down on the mat as I assist her to calm and gain control of her body. She places her hand on her heart to feel its fast beat. I place my hand on top of hers and guide her to breathe in and out slowly, matching my breath with my words. As her pulse slows, I suggest she directs her breaths one by one, to the areas of her body that are still tense—her fingers, her legs, and her arms. It takes awhile for her to calm her itches and jerky actions. When she does, she stands up to begin the story again, but this time she is more composed.

A year later Savannah begins her second story. She scatters all the props throughout the room. She swings on the trapeze, crawls through the tunnel, throws the scarves, and jumps on the trampoline in a haphazard manner, acting out "Crazyman." As I narrate and ask questions about Crazyman's behaviors, Savannah explains that Crazyman just likes to be crazy because he just does. That feeling is simply inside him. Other times she instructs me to be completely silent, watching Crazyman's antics without questioning or describing them.

At her request we videotape this story every week. Each week she numbers the episode, just like the TV series she watches at home. Every time, the ending is the same. Savannah curls herself into a ball, hiding, completely still—under the trampoline, behind the mats, or under the scarves—poking her head out just a bit, with eyes wide. We view only short excerpts of the tape together. Savannah gets very excited, actively moving her body as she watches, but she soon loses interest. We end these sessions with calming breath work, using gently undulating music to create a change in the atmosphere of the room.

The number of taped episodes accumulates until one week in which Savannah states that we are soon approaching the final episode. The final episode session occurs. The scene unfolds as usual. Again there is not much verbal processing during the closure of the session. But she notes with satisfaction that we have taped all of the episodes. Her actions and simple words seem to imply that she takes comfort in knowing that her experience has been recorded and witnessed. The new dance-play activities that follow the final episode develop organization and control. Once in a while Savannah brings up the idea of Crazyman's visiting again, but ultimately she concludes that he is away and isn't available right now. ⌒

The therapist has her own responses to the story of Crazyman.

Kinesthetic empathy: As I watch, narrate, and videotape these episodes, I feel as if I am an onlooker watching a chaotic, and at times violent scene. I am instructed often to keep silent. I wonder why? I am struck by the ending—I feel as if I am looking out at this event from a hiding place. I feel alone and scared. This image stays with me. I sit with it a little while, and suddenly I recall a session with Savannah's mother in which she tells me that her daughter was often silently present during some violent events with her husband. She also reveals that Savannah had hidden under tables and chairs throughout her early childhood.

Witnessing: As we move on into dance-plays that encourage organization, I feel as if Savannah has found a way to gain control of and process her early experiences. She is now working hard to move forward.

Summary of Dance-Play Activities

Each of these techniques is considered a dance-play because of the implicit orientation of the session. During each activity a therapist must continually pay attention to the nonverbal expressive quality of a child's involvement. The focus should not only be on *what* a child is saying or doing, but also on *how* she is saying or doing it. Interventions should address how a child's actions reveal deeper aspects of self. This draws awareness to the meanings beyond a child's verbalizations and actions to address her experiences. These techniques look for a child's own unique contributions and create an environment that enables her to take the therapist along on personal journeys, sharing the child's experience of the world. Through this process a therapist's role is to uncover and integrate a child's felt-sense memories, fantasies, and action-based representations of experiences and translate them into multilevel expressible understandings. This therapeutic environment acts as a secure container for a child's expressions—a holding framework from which she can experience a response to her movement language. A child can feel a sense of wholeness and completion as her symbolic expressions are heard.

As a child receives recognition for her efforts and expressions, she becomes receptive to engaging in expanded movement exchanges. This mutual sharing of experiences provides a safe environment to explore alternative communicative methods while simultaneously encouraging growth in physical, emotional, social, communicative, and cognitive development. Through this unique movement dialogue, a therapist first meets a child primarily on a nonverbal level, entering into her symbolic movement world. Once engaged, the therapist assists the child by creating pathways from nonverbal to verbal communication. Through her exposure to the *Ways of Seeing* approach, a child can develop self-awareness, social and emotional expressivity, and more effective ways to cope with specific personal challenges as she interplays with the demands of her environment.

III

Movement as an Interdisciplinary Tool

10
Working with Parents

Once there was a little bunny who wanted to run away. So he said to his mother, "I am running away."

"If you run away," said his mother, "I will run after you. For you are my little bunny."

M.W. Brown, *The Runaway Bunny* (1942/1991)

In the classic story for young children *The Runaway Bunny*, a little bunny discusses with his mother an imaginary journey he wants to take to run away from her. During these adventures he proposes that he will become quite a variety of different personas—a fish, a rock, a bird, and even a circus trapeze artist, to name a few. But with each image he presents, the mother bunny responds with a companion image that continues to nurture, support, and find her child. As a fisherman she will fish him from the waters; if necessary, she will become a mountain climber to retrieve him from whatever mountaintop he may climb. But the final image sums up her devotion to her child best. When he proposes to become a little boy running into a home, she proclaims that she will be there as his mother, to catch and caress him. The little bunny concludes that he might as well stay put as her little bunny!

This lovely story poignantly describes the commitment each parent makes along the voyage of parenthood. Like the mother in this story, at times parents may feel like they must persevere through a child's explorations and self-discovery, acting as an ever-patient presence, allowing the child to freely explore while being always available at arm's length. It is an especially striking metaphor for parents of children with special needs. Parenting a very young child who cannot easily express needs, or is not following a typical developmental progression, often requires the parents to transform and place themselves into the most unimaginable states in their desire to support their child's optimal growth and development. But despite their efforts, it is not always easy to decipher a child's needs or to know the right course of action. The parents of a child with special needs, especially if the child's condition includes severe communication difficulties that impede social engagement, may feel as if it is their job to convince the child to join the social world. Situations are often filled with disappointment, rejection, and projection for these parents, as they attempt to imbue meaning to their child's behaviors without any clear or concrete way of knowing if their interpretations are accurate.

EARLY PARENTAL THERAPEUTIC EXPERIENCE

This state of disbelief and unrest is the position in which parents often find themselves when their children are first entering the *Ways of Seeing* approach. The beginning of intervention is a sensitive and fragile time for families of children with special needs. The discovery that their truly precious young child may not be developing in a typical manner is wrought with many mixed emotions. They may experience disbelief that anything could really be wrong, especially if the pediatrician has been taking the "wait and see—you are just being an anxious parent" attitude. Often one or both of the parents have felt a sinking feeling in the pit of their stomachs for quite awhile, in that something about their interactions with their baby just hasn't felt right. A parent's initial attitude may be directed toward herself or himself: "Is there something I did during the pregnancy that caused this trouble?" "What is it that I am doing wrong now that is not supporting my baby's healthy development?" Despair and a feeling of being overwhelmed often follow and will resurface throughout any intervention. Initially, there is much angst and strife in not knowing what step to take to begin the process of finding out what might be wrong. Finding the right practitioners (especially if a diagnosis is not easily discernable), navigating smoothly through early intervention and school-based reports and service programs, and finding the monetary resources to cover expenses can be extremely arduous. Once intervention is begun, there begins the unceasing need to monitor the level of progress and to determine the next steps.

Interwoven with these difficult emotions are feelings of hope and faith. Initially parents may hope that all will go well and the intervention will succeed. In some cases this will become true. But if their child's condition has lifelong implications, the hope must be adjusted over time, with realistic goals supporting the child's progress. The hope that, despite the struggles, this experience will ultimately enrich and strengthen a family becomes an important goal in the *Ways of Seeing* approach, which supports the family's development and acceptance of the changes that will occur. The parents must develop faith in themselves as parents who will do what they can to support their child's needs; they must put faith in those practitioners with whom they choose to work, and, ultimately, they must possess some sense of an inner faith in the goodness of the world in general. Each of these feelings is continually acknowledged and addressed throughout the *Ways of Seeing* experience.

PARENTAL INVOLVEMENT IN THE *WAYS OF SEEING* APPROACH

Although most often the initially designated patient in need of treatment is the young child in a family, the *Ways of Seeing* approach considers the whole family's needs within its intervention paradigm. The parents are always welcomed and are encouraged to participate as much as possible throughout the program. Their needs, views, and knowledge about their child are respected and form the foundation of the intervention. A *Ways of Seeing* therapist views the parents as partners and co-explorers along the journey of discovery about how to best support their child's growth. Parents attend sessions with their child as well as meet with the therapist in separate sessions to discuss the child's progress, the family members' needs and concerns, and any other relevant experiences occurring in a child's life that may be influencing the child at that particular time. Team meetings with parents, other practitioners, and teachers provide additional avenues to maintaining a continually open dialogue.

The most important first step in an intervention is to establish a supportive and respectful relationship with the parents. Their views and concerns always must be received and treated with great care—even if their perceptions of their child are different from the therapist's own experience when interacting with the child. The self-observation roles of witnessing, kinesthetic seeing, and kinesthetic empathy, as described in Chapter 7, become especially important when there is a discrepancy between the therapist's experience and the parents' experience of a child. As witness, the therapist must review these different descriptions from a clear place, being open to the interpretations and factors that might be influencing each person's viewpoint. This is exemplified in the vignette below.

Parents are partners and co-explorers along the journey of discovery about how to best support their child's growth.

⌒ *Tanya and Everett brought their son Eric (diagnosed with PDD at age 3) to dance movement psychotherapy. Despite a full intervention program for the last 1½ years—including sensory integration, applied behavioral analysis (ABA), and speech and language therapy—they felt he was not progressing enough. Eric was not relating socially in a typical manner at all. He avoided play with other children, wandering away from them and isolating himself; had very limited verbal language skills; and was very reactive to transitions, including refusing to change from pajamas to clothes. He became fixated on musical videos and their companion CDs, acting out whole sections of these musicals in a mesmerized manner and becoming very upset when they were turned off. Eric would resist severely during everyday transitions that required him to change his personal focus, such as needing to get in the car, get dressed, go to the store, leave a room, enter a new situation, or stop an activity. His resistance often turned into full-blown tantrums in which he would scream and fling his body down to the ground, rolling and kicking on the floor.*

Tanya became quite adept at understanding her son's behaviors and adapting to his wishes. With her beautiful voice and professional acting skills, she would continue the musical numbers he was entranced by in an effort to cajole him to the next task at hand. She avoided things and activities he did not like. When he was really upset, he would nurse. Mom became Eric's sole mediator between himself and the world. Eric often became inconsolable when she left his side. Understandably, Tanya and Everett felt Eric was controlling their lives. And he was. ⌒

The behavior described by Eric's parents was very evident during the first month of sessions. Eric would not freely enter the dance movement psychotherapy room, but instead would cling to his mother, making his body limp as he refused to walk down the three steps at the doorway. Tanya would very attentively watch her son and try to ease his tension and support his difficulties in several ways. She would always start by verbally reassuring him, saying in a very kind, soothing tone, "It's okay, Eric, I know it is hard for you, but it's okay, Eric. You can have fun here, Eric. It's okay, everything will be okay, Eric." She might suggest that she sing one of his favorites songs, and then break into song, attempting to ease his discomfort by distracting him with something that she knew he enjoyed. Or, she would sit with him against the wall, gently holding him on her lap. At first, if he tried to lift her hands and wrap her arms around him to assume the nursing position, she tried to avoid his attempts to nurse by making her arms limp or redirecting them. Inevitably, the nursing won out. Taking on the role of witness, the dance movement therapist paid close attention to her own personal reactions to these parent–child interactions, as is evidenced in session notes.

Witness: As I watch Tanya and Eric, I am torn. Tanya is a very attentive mother who seems to know and understand what elements in the environment make Eric uncomfortable and how to ease his discomfort. She creates an atmosphere of great support for Eric, especially when it comes to expanding and developing his truly precocious interest in music. Eric clearly responds to his mother. I want to support these strengths in her parenting style. However, despite this attunement, I feel great unrest as I experience their interactions here in my studio office. They seem to be caught in an isolating dyadic loop—they are stuck with these particular coping techniques that don't actually enable their relationship to develop into a spontaneous, interactive dialogue. There is an odd scripted feeling that creates a sense of emotional dependence on Mom and that does not easily translate to supportive emotional interactions with others. But I want to commend her abilities to find such creative ways to connect with her child.

Kinesthetic empathy: What must it feel like to have to continually expend so much concentrated effort to assist Eric as he transitions through even the most everyday activities? As I experience this mother and child, I feel both awe and sadness. Awe for her undying efforts and true love, but sadness in her having to work so hard. A sense of tiredness sweeps over me in my empathy for Mom.

This family situation must be treated delicately. The family clearly acknowledges their need for help, for they have sought out assistance, but nonetheless, they must be approached with care. Tanya has developed a parenting style that demonstrates a depth of caring and attunement to her child's unique style. Mother and child clearly have a strong emotional connection to each other, but these strengths create an exclusivity that will not make it easy for Eric to socialize in the world around him. The therapist needs to address Tanya and Everett's parenting strengths while providing them with alternative ways to support their child's growth. The therapist empathizes with the difficulties this family must encounter in their attempts to parent Eric, and looks for alternative approaches to expand Eric's repertoire of relating skills.

To support this focus, the therapist wants more information about Eric's experiences in other environments, and she plans a home visit to overlap with his ABA teacher's home-based session. The home visit provides more valuable information about Eric's life and the family dynamics. Their home is set up to support Eric's interests. In every room there are activities and objects of interest to engage Eric's attention. In the kitchen is a dress-up corner and mirror hung at Eric's height, ABA-related toys are provided in the living room, a television and stereo are in the study next door, and a cozy futon bed is placed low to the ground so that he can easily climb into it in his bedroom upstairs.

As Eric sits diligently with his ABA teacher, the therapist and Eric's mother watch, unnoticed, in the adjoining kitchen. The therapist is very impressed with Eric's ability to stay focused during his ABA session. The talented ABA teacher supports Eric to point to objects and say their proper names, praising him with verbal and concrete food reinforcements, and keeps him going just when he is about to get distracted by letting him manipulate and study a toy car. The therapist sees the ABA teacher as an astute adult, who is very attuned into Eric's style and who is able to maintain a good rapport with him by reacting and responding to his fluctuations and redirections of attention. The extremely structured and continually repeated ABA activities create organization and familiarity in Eric's environment in a similar way to the set of interactional strategies Eric's mother has developed with her son. They each have found a particular repertoire of activities that Eric is able to engage in to develop their rapport with him. Tanya says she has learned much from observing the ABA sessions, in which she does not participate, and has incorporated these ideas in her parenting style.

The therapist again notes Tanya's receptivity and openness to learning how to best support her son's growth.

Once the ABA teacher leaves, Eric begins to wander around the house, momentarily stopping in each room to manipulate an object of his interest, to listen to a piece of music, or to put on a musical video for a moment or two. Tanya watches, follows, and responds to Eric's activities—talking to him and trying to get him to stay engaged with her and the object, but he quickly wanders off to another location. Within a few moments we have traveled the whole house, and Eric heads for the front door. Despite Tanya's objections about going outside, Eric, taking his clothes off on the way, gets the door open, and steps outside. With the whole outdoors as his playground, Eric's boundaries for exploration expand dramatically. Before long, as we follow Eric's path, we have traversed up and down the stairs numerous times, balanced along the porch railing, and run in circles around the driveway. We are headed up the hill and over to the faraway neighbor's trampoline when Tanya is finally able to stop him—kicking and screaming in protest—and she has to physically hold him as we go back inside.

Witnessing: As Mom and Dad have described, Eric does seem to run the household. In our effort to follow and support Eric's engagements, we have started but not completed or become emotionally engaged in a single activity! I feel scattered, bombarded, and have to work hard to stay focused and connected to Eric as I follow his lead.

Kinesthetic seeing: As I follow Eric's wanderings through his house and then into the greater outdoors, I feel as if I am in a world without walls. Nothing is stopping me. It is as if I am on a continual search—I'm not sure for what—but I am compelled to move forward. I am struck by the lack of contact with others and my deep experience with the physical world of objects and the natural environment. I feel the activeness of my body as we run up and down the stairs, and the exertion of my legs as we climb the hill. I feel the prickly early spring grass on my feet and the April wind on my cheeks. I have a heightened focus on myself and a diminished awareness of anyone else around me.

This home visit helps the *Ways of Seeing* therapist understand the difficulties Tanya and Everett are having in parenting Eric. They have set up a very supportive environment, filling it with things and activities that interest their son. By participating and following Eric's interests, they are able to engage and hold his attention for periods of time. In this way they have been able to build a relationship with their son. Their motives become crystal clear. Due to Eric's limited ability to stay emotionally connected, they have accommodated as much as possible to his desires, learning to read and respond to his most obscure cues, in order to feel connected to their son. It is a case of overattunement (too much adaptation), driven by their deep love and desire to relate to their child. The therapeutic path becomes very lucid. The *Ways of Seeing* approach will build on their deep understanding and ability to read their son's nonverbal cues by creating experiences that expand their repertoire while developing interactions that require true, more in-depth, spontaneous, and ongoing emotional connection.

Sessions become organized to help each member of the family become an active participant in the intervention. Twice-weekly sessions are set up and Tanya attends and participates actively. Everett joins them when he can take off from work. The weekly sessions are videotaped on a regular basis and shared with both parents at periodically scheduled parent sessions. These sessions enable each parent to discuss their feelings and concerns about their son and issues that have come up about their parenting differences. Reviewing the videotapes together is an invaluable additional teaching tool that helps to keep Everett informed about Eric's sessions and enables a concrete review of the events and themes evolving through the *Ways of Seeing* approach.

Relational and Personal Movement Metaphors

As has been discussed, in order to support parents, a therapist must recognize what has influenced the parents' understanding of their child's nonverbal behaviors. The story of Eric and his family exemplifies the process, which can be summarized by focusing a therapist's initial observations about a child on the following seven questions:

1. What feeling am I receiving through the child's movements and behaviors?

2. What do I think the child's needs are, based on these movements and behaviors?

3. How specifically does the child express his needs through these movements and behaviors?

4. What are the parents' concerns about their child?

5. What are the parents' attitudes about their child?

6. How are the parents' concerns and attitudes (from questions 4 and 5) being expressed through their nonverbal interactions with their child?

7. What is the child's embodied experience of this interaction? How might it feel for the child to be touched, held, moved, and manipulated in the way that the parent or parents physically handle him? (adapted from Tortora, 1994).

In addition, Table 10.1 outlines a series of principles of nonverbal interactions and related questions that a therapist can discuss with parents to help them increase their awareness of their nonverbal interactional behaviors with their child. It is a general guide to stimulate discussion. As these questions are answered and principles are discussed, the patterns, elements, and qualities of each member's nonverbal movements should become apparent as they influence and play out

Table 10.1. Key principles and related questions to improve parent–child interactions

Principles

- Parents may find it helpful to learn their children's movement styles (rhythms) and their own.
- It is best to look for similarities and differences and compatibility rather than exact matches.
- Finding compatibility takes the blame away from the individuals and helps both parents and children learn why they are reacting in the ways they do regarding each other's actions.
- Parents and children can use this knowledge to figure out which aspects of each other they must accept and which aspects they might want to work on.
- An understanding of compatibility encourages parents to respect their children's behaviors as a form of communication and to not perceive these behaviors automatically as deviant actions.
- It is most helpful for parents to understand that most often, a child's behavior is communication—even if it is inappropriate.

Questions for Parents

1. What meaning do you "read" in your child's body expressions, and what message is your child "reading" in your nonverbal behaviors?

2. Spend some time watching your child. How does your child show his or her emotions—whether happy, sad, angry, tired, or frustrated? What body signals are used?

3. What are your physical and emotional reactions to these body expressions and signals?

4. What might a child be saying by how he or she is moving? Mirror the movement by trying it on. What does it feel like to you? What is your reaction?

5. Most crucially, do you attune to your child's style as reflected in the child's cues, giving room for his or her expression before intervening? Or, do you respond from an internal impulse to help without attending to your child's style first?

within dyadic and family group relationships. A therapist should specifically look for unique stylistic patterns that occur and recur beyond the immediate context of these actions to see how they might be expressing deeper feelings. Quite often, seemingly random actions, when observed more closely, reveal core themes, feelings, and emotionally based coping systems. These recurring, stylized, emotionally expressive patterns are called *movement metaphors* (described in Chapter 5). Movement metaphors often are the key nonverbal elements that act as the foundational systems depicting individual and family dynamics. The *Ways of Seeing* approach calls the recurring nonverbal patterns of relating that are detectable in an established dyadic interaction *relational movement metaphors,* and observable individual nonverbal patterns are called *personal movement metaphors.*

As discussed in Chapter 2, infancy research supports the concept that the dynamic quality of the dyadic relationship is co-constructed (Beebe et al., 2000; Beebe & Lachmann, 2002; Fogel, 1992). This co-construction involves the interplay of both self-regulation and interactional-regulation. Each member must sustain a certain level of control of his or her internal system to be able to maintain external engagement (Brazelton & Cramer, 1990; Greenspan, 1996; Greenspan & Wieder, 1993; Sander, 1977). From quite early on, parents begin to respond both consciously and unconsciously to their young infant's self-regulating behaviors. These self-regulating behaviors are expressed largely through the baby's nonverbal body actions. Of course, vocalizations—especially coos and cries—are also operative. But even vocalizations have a body component, for they are performed through the use of a body system.

Nonverbal actions are emphasized to draw attention to the physically experiential aspect of these behaviors that communicate fundamental information to the new parent. For example, right from the start, a mother will begin to determine when her baby is alert and receptive to play—even if this ability lasts only for moments during the first few weeks. She will make this determination by the particular way the baby holds her head, focuses her eyes, and moves her arms when alert as opposed to the way the baby changes the quality of these actions when she is tired or almost asleep. A baby's particular way of using her body to display attention is perhaps among the earliest personal movement metaphors. This simple, consistent movement pattern says, "I see you. I am here. I am paying attention to you and the new world around me." Indeed, these early unique stylistic expressions are among the very first elements that contribute to the parents "falling in love" with their new precious child. Parents look on with wonder and joy at these initial facial expressions, gestures, and gazes. The distinctive qualities an infant employs to perform these nonverbal actions are the most basic and earliest statements from the baby, which she will build on as she develops her own signature way of being. The specific qualities of these early traits—initially governed largely by the baby's regulatory needs—are what the family begins to recognize as their baby's budding personality. As the baby matures she will gain more control over her internal needs, establishing regulatory stability. With self-regulation in place, the baby's movement expressions will expand and become more elaborate. These expressions will be less tied to internal needs and are therefore more receptive, influenced, and responsive to external stimuli.

It is important to highlight that internal regulation occurs in both the adult and the young child. How the members of the dyad regulate their personal internal systems to support their individual needs will affect what each contributes to the interactional experience. The interactional experience develops out of, and is continuously influenced by, the moment-to-moment reactions of each dyadic participant. This is why the relationship is co-constructed rather than directed by one member of the dyad. The unique patterns of interaction that the dyad establishes become their relational movement metaphors. Self and interactional regulation is especially significant in early infancy, when a baby is only able to maintain internal homeostatic stability for a short time. A parent's own reactions and ability to accept and navigate through a baby's waxing and waning of attentiveness will greatly affect how each of them experiences the relationship (Brazelton, 1974; Stern, 1985). Over time, the dyad will create a system of relating that becomes familiar and expected. As discussed in Chapter 2, many child developmental specialists have described this process of growing expectancy. These established and expected ways of relating are the observable relational movement metaphors. The ways that a parent and a baby are speaking to, getting to know, and establishing a relationship with each other become the foundation of their developing attachment.

These repeated interactional exchanges have a strong nonverbal component that can be seen easily when observing a young baby's responses to playing with his mother as opposed to his responses toward a stranger. By this age the dyad already has established an assortment of interactional games—relational movement metaphors—involving both vocal and movement elements. It is not just the sound of the mother's cooing that causes the infant to squeal with joy, smiling as his arms wiggle wildly in the air and his legs kick robustly. The baby has already come to know the feeling of his mother's presence. This feeling of presence is imbued with the specific qualities of his mother's nonverbal style. The repeated nonverbal aspect of the exchange is observable as the relational movement metaphors that define that particular dyad's style of relating. Watching the nonverbal exchange reveals the dynamic qualities of the attachment, and can be viewed as the relational movement metaphors unique to that dyad. It is important for a therapist to observe these relational movement metaphors because the *Ways of Seeing* approach recognizes that these nonverbal components of the interactional experience depict and can greatly affect the qualitative aspects of the developing relationship.

Witnessing: I watch Mina and her 6½-month-old baby Crystal play on the floor with such pleasure. I experience them having such delight with each other. What exactly is it about Mina playing with Crystal that is drawing my attention? As I observe the details of their nonverbal actions, it becomes clear. Crystal is not yet able to pull herself up to sit, or to lift her hips up to crawl supported on her hands and knees. At this point she is moving around by reaching with her arms, pushing with her toes, and sliding her belly on the floor. As Crystal slides on her belly first toward Mom and then swivels away, Mina moves with her in an arcing pathway, placing her body arm-distance away, first to Crystal's side, then in front of her, intermittently catching Crystal's visual attention. In this lovely dance, their kinespheres overlap in varying degrees as Mina and Crystal extend their heads toward and away from each other, giggling and gurgling. As she sees Crystal's gaze shift away from her toward the big ball a few feet away, Mina clears Crystal's path by slightly moving her own head and body back. "That's a big ball!" she coos to Crystal as Crystal reaches, pushes, and slides toward it with determination.

This relational movement metaphor is observable throughout their interaction. Mina's careful reading of Crystal's nonverbal cues tells Crystal she is nearby, attentively following Crystal's cues to support Crystal's interests in her or something in the room. Mina expresses this nonverbally by placing her body within varying arms-reach distance of Crystal, leaning toward her at a gentle speed and with a broad smile when Crystal shifts her gaze toward Mina. When Crystal shifts her gaze away, Mina follows Crystal's gaze, giving her room to explore physically and verbally by slightly moving away and commenting on Crystal's new interest. Mina's actions create a sense of waiting and attentiveness, with a calm-paced rhythm that exudes a confidence in her baby's interest in exploring.

When the Cues Are Difficult to Read

Nonverbal information plays an especially important role in early childhood. During the preverbal period, this is the main conduit through which information is expressed and received. For a child whose development is compromised with language, communication delays, or mental health concerns, it continues to be a significant way to receive information beyond the typical preverbal time period. Even though such a child may be relying a great deal on nonverbal experiences to understand her environment, her expressive nonverbal cues may be very limited and/or not easy to decipher depending on her particular difficulties. This is a crucial point that can greatly affect her developing relationships with significant family members.

When a young child's personal movement metaphors are difficult to read or are very limited, the relational movement metaphors often display tremendous emotional discord. Efforts to relate become compromised, for the misreading of nonverbal cues creates a deep internal sense of discomfort, upset, disappointment, and agitation, heightening the need to self-regulate. How each member of the dyad self-regulates is quite individual because there are an infinite number of ways self-regulation can be displayed on a body-movement level. It may cause an increase in either person's activity levels, observable in intensified muscular tension and a rocking or shaking of limbs. Gaze may be averted or the whole body may recoil into itself, pulling away quite noticeably by turning or arching away, or moving by walking or running away, leaving the other person alone. Or, the movement may be quite subtle by a tightening or freezing of the gaze or the body, creating a blank stare and vacant coldness. These self-regulations can also go in quite the opposite direction, decreasing the muscular tension to the point that the body becomes limp or heavy. This form of disengagement creates a sense of apathy and deadness. When a young child takes on such a stance, it often causes the frustrated parent to think about responding to the contrary by shaking or pulling the child. Yet another response may include self-touch of personal body parts or clothing.

Each member of the dyad often feels these exchanges, but their emotional effect is not necessarily consciously interpreted. Instead, a standard set of reactions and actions become established, without a deeper understanding of the implications of these reactions/actions on the developing relationship. The emotional potency of these reactions/actions is observable to a therapist trained to look at the qualitative nonverbal aspects of both individuals and their dyadic exchange. Helping parents become aware of the nonverbal qualities of their own and their child's reactions within the context of their emerging relationship enables them to begin to reflect on the emotional implications of these behaviors. This can be the first step of the powerful process of using nonverbal understanding to revise and heal their growing relationship.

This is exemplified in the story of Sharon and her daughter Casey, who began attending *Ways of Seeing* sessions when Casey was about 10–14 months old. During her first 10 months, Casey was not easily comforted, often crying and averting her gaze when held by her mother. She slept a great deal and tended to prefer to be alone. Sharon was not sure how to engage her daughter and had concerns about how their relationship was developing. She did not feel that she and Casey were really connecting.

The therapist concluded that the relational movement metaphor of their nonverbal interaction revealed arrhythmic disharmony. Sharon actually read her daughter's cues very well but was not aware that she was successful in responding to Casey's behaviors and therefore failed to follow through when Casey attempted to regain her mother's attention. Casey's discomfort in being held was due to tactile and proprioceptive sensitivities. When Casey averted her eye gaze, arched her back, or darted her arms and legs in jerking actions as Sharon held her in an attempt to play, Sharon would immediately put her down, but did not give Casey eye contact. Sharon displayed little affective facial expressiveness and was mostly silent as she attempted to hold and play with Casey. When she said Casey's name, she spoke in a quiet, monotone manner. Once Casey was put down, she would quickly settle by looking out into space for a few moments. She then would look toward her mother, but Sharon did not see her daughter looking toward her. When Casey quieted her body, Sharon would again attempt to engage her in physical play, but she did not provide eye contact or verbal support. Casey did not look at Sharon, and the arrhythmic dance of relating would begin again.

When the *Ways of Seeing* therapist played with Casey, she noticed that the infant seemed to initially prefer to provide and respond to eye contact from afar. She welcomed the therapist's physical contact only when the therapist came closer in a slow, even pace and touched her with firm contact. The therapist was able to sustain eye contact by holding Casey firmly as she moved the baby's limbs in playful, rhythmic dance actions and spoke to her in a melodic voice, adding tonal and timing variations. The therapist's interactional style was qualitatively different from Sharon's. The therapist changed the timing, physical force, directness of her gaze, Phrasing, and use of Space. Through observation, modeling, videotape analysis, and instruction, Sharon learned how to adjust her nonverbal movement style, changing the quality of her voice, touch, eye contact, and the surrounding space to approach and extend her play with Casey. By 14 months, Casey's ability to tolerate touch increased and she sought her mother's contact by crawling onto her lap, vocalizing more, and staying engaged for longer periods of time.

In the *Ways of Seeing* approach, a therapist's job is to observe, decode, and explore individual and family system-based relational movement metaphors. This initially occurs through observations and experientially based interactions, but as understandings become clear, verbal dialogue also becomes important for both parent and child. This brings tangible, cognitive awareness to each family member's nonverbal expressions and supports the young child's acquisition of language as a principal communicative tool. The verbal communications integrate verbal and nonverbal expressions and support higher order thinking. For a child, matching language with physically felt and sensorially based events creates concrete experiences that stimulate and support receptive processing.

Using Nonverbal Awareness to Support Reflective Functioning

Bringing conscious awareness to the nonverbal aspects of a parent–child relationship requires parents to be sensitive to, reflect about, and act on their experiences with their child. To have such insightful awareness, parents must be able to "keep the baby in mind," a phrase coined by Slade and her colleagues in their discussion about reflective functioning

(Slade, 2002a, 2002b). Reflective functioning illustrates the necessary internal traits a person must have to support sensitive emotional attentiveness with others. It involves one's ability to perceive that each individual's observable behaviors are actually a result of underlying dynamic internal mental intentions and emotional states that may not be immediately obviously visible (Fonagy, Gergely, Jurist, & Target, 2001; Slade, 2002a, 2002b; Slade, Belsky, Aber, & Phelps, 1999).

The capacity to reflect on another's intentions greatly influences one's ability to anticipate another's actions. Reflective functioning has been described as an essential element in supporting the development of a healthy parent–child relationship. Reflective functioning has two vital aspects: Parents must have the ability to recognize that their young child has his own internal mental states involving feelings, intentions, desires, and thoughts that are separate from the parents' internal states. Parents must also have the capacity to then connect this understanding of each person's individual states to their own personal behaviors. These behaviors include both external actions and other internal mental states that affect these behaviors and the resulting experiences of the interaction and developing relationships.

The *Ways of Seeing* approach highlights the role nonverbal understanding can play in supporting reflective thinking. It emphasizes that helping parents notice their own and their child's nonverbal cues can greatly contribute to their ability to be reflective about their child. The *Ways of Seeing* program includes a series of worksheets—Assessing Your Child's Nonverbal Cues and Your Responses to Them—to help parents become more aware of their nonverbal readings/reactions to their child (see http://www.brookespublishing.com/dancing). These worksheets teach parents how to understand their nonverbal interactions with their child. Although these worksheets can be used with children of any age, they were originally created to foster increased parental observation during the first 2 years of the child's life to support and build the evolving attachment relationship. Worksheet 1 focuses on helping the parents to become aware of both their child's personal style of communication, interaction, and self-expression through body postures and actions and their own responses to them. In Worksheet 2, the goal is for parents to explore ways to expand the nonverbal dialogue between themselves and their child in the context of play, and to become aware of the unique expressivity portrayed by each of their movement styles. New experiences are encouraged through playful movement exchanges. These experiences facilitate greater awareness of body and self and at the same time develop expressive skills for both children and parents. As parents and children find new ways to play within their own relationship, their senses of self-resourcefulness will be fostered. Each element of the worksheet series is described next.

ASSESSING YOUR CHILD'S NONVERBAL CUES AND YOUR RESPONSES TO THEM

These worksheets, which can be done during sessions or as home assignments, are designed to help parents begin to see the relationship between physical states, mental (emotional) states, and nonverbal expression. Because many people are not familiar with nonverbal elements, it is best for therapists to go over the concepts and begin these worksheets together during a session. In addition, a *Ways of Seeing* therapist may need to do some body awareness experientials with parents before they can answer some of these questions; in other words, this series may not be a home assignment for all parents.

Worksheet 1: Awareness

In Worksheet 1, parents are encouraged to focus on their child's unique personal styles of communicating, interacting, and self-expressing through body postures and actions as they answer these questions (see Figure 10.1 for a copy of the worksheet describing 5-month-old Julian, completed by his mother; see http://www.brookespublishing.com/dancing for a blank worksheet). Exercises 1 and 2 of this worksheet ask parents to first think about their child's behaviors without the child being present. Parents are asked to create pictures of their child in their minds, clearly visualizing their child's responses. It is designed in this way to immediately engage parents in reflective modes about their child. The quality of the parents' responses to these questions directly reveals the parents' current levels of nonverbal representation of their child and awareness of their own bodily reactions. Initially, parents are asked to write down their first impressions to maintain the true spontaneity that live interactions require. The questions that follow progressively lead parents to contemplate their responses more thoroughly, learning more about nonverbal understanding.

Exercises 3 and 4 ask parents to observe their child as they answer the questions. In this section of the worksheet, parents compare their images of their child with what they actually see their child doing. This provides a concrete way to see how their preconceived thoughts about

Assessing Your Child's Nonverbal Cues
and Your Responses to Them
Worksheet 1: Awareness

Name of child: Julian   Date: 7/22/03

Age: 5 months   Date of birth: 2/18/03   Observer: Julian's mother

Goal: To become aware of both your child's personal style of communication, inter-action, and self-expression through body postures and actions and your own responses to them.

Exercise 1:
Take a few minutes to think about these questions at a time when you are *not* with your child. As you read each question, create a mental picture of your child, visualizing his or her response.

A. Write a few words or phrases to describe your first impressions about how your child expresses the following emotional and physical states on a body or body movement level.

Emotional States:

Calm
—Soft body, with arms and legs resting at sides or crossed over body
—Facial expression is neutral, and breath flow is even

Content
—Same as calm, but his arms and legs may intermittently flutter
—More varied facial expressions, along the range of calm to focused attention

Happy
—Very active arms and legs, extending, bending, and circling in bursts that create a rhythmic pulse
—Gleeful facial expression, eyes sparkling, as he looks at me in an extended gaze, then looks away for a moment, and then back at me with that sparkle and a bursting flutter of his arms and legs

Alert
—Has bright eyes and holds his mouth a little tight, with his lips parted a bit when he focuses on something
—Seems to want to take in his surroundings and doesn't get overwhelmed
—Will hold his body still and then suddenly burst into his happy behavior when he's been surprised and "tickled" by what he has been focusing on

Excited
—Similar to "happy" description, but without the rhythmic pulse to his actions
—Seems to be more of a transition stage (if his actions become rhythmic, he shifts into "happy," but if his actions stay sporadic and arrhythmic, he can shift into becoming upset)

Inquisitive
—Similar to alert state, in that he first becomes still, focused, and then a bit tight in his musculature, but finally he begins to move his arms and torso, attempting to reach out and explore in a slow, investigative way
—Has great concentration already and can stick with his focus

Sad
—Soft body, drooping head, and really pouting lips!

Angry
—Whole body becomes tight
—Arms and head are thrown from side to side

Figure 10.1.   Worksheet 1: Awareness for Julian at age 5 months.

Bored
—Body held still
—Eyes unfocused
—Seems to be in a dream state, and doesn't respond immediately when I try to get his attention

Unfocused
—Similar to his bored state, except that his body becomes intermittently active, and he immediately responds with eye gaze and arm and leg activity when I try to get his attention

Physical states:

Hurt
—Suddenly stops all of his activity, waits a moment, and then suddenly bursts out into tears and holds his body very tight (even when I pick him up to cuddle and comfort him)

Hungry
—Very cranky, not able to settle his focus on anything
—Can't find a comfortable body position, constantly adjusting himself, but never calming down
—Becomes physically agitated, only settling down when he is fed and held with a firm, embracing hold

Tired
—Similar to hungry in his cranky attitude, but instead of agitated, he can barely hold up his arms
—Drops his head, arms, and body to his side limply as if they are too heavy

B. Now visualize the specific body gestures your child uses to express the following emotional states and reactions and write a few words or phrases that come into your mind.

Quiet
—Stillness
—Body relaxed, yet contained, with arms resting on chest and his legs relaxing
—Eyes have a soft, relaxed gaze

Smiling
—Bright, energetic   —Sparkling eye contact
—Limbs swinging freely

Focused
—Steady eye contact   —Firm, muscular body

Laughing
—Joyous all over
—Moves his arms toward and away from his torso with a bouncy, quick action
—Shining eyes as he looks at me, looks away, and looks at me again in quick succession

Questioning, uncertain
—Head tilting to side   —Shoulders lifted
—Muscles of face held tight

Frowning
—Lower lip protrudes   —Head pulled down and in
—Shoulders lifted, with arms sporadically lifting and dropping in erratic rhythm

Crying
—Face, arms, and legs held tight   —Whole body shaking in one, tight, rhythmic pulse

Pain
—Delayed reaction (a pause, then sudden tightness throughout his body, followed by the crying behaviors described above)

Uninterested, uninvolved
—Staring off into space   —Body very unengaged, making very few actions
—When body is moved, actions seem to have no purpose or effect

continued

Figure 10.1. *(continued)*

Distracted, vague
—Jumpy attitude, with arms and legs that seem to sputter into action, but aren't directed anywhere
—Difficult to get or maintain eye contact with him

Sleepy
—Very intermittent eye contact   —Almost in a daze
—Arms and legs almost limp
—Becomes agitated if he is picked up quickly or if he sees or hears a sudden, loud action

C. Select one of the states described above and focus on the specific movement qualities.
Alert State

1. Does your child use his or her whole body to express this state, reaction, or feeling, or just an area or a specific limb?
His whole body is involved.

2. What body parts/areas accompany the expression (e.g., arms shaking while excited)?
His eyes and arms are most active as he becomes more engaged and interested.

3. What is the feeling tone quality of the action in regard to the flow/tension level, strength/gentleness, singular/multifocus, and quickness /slowness?
He becomes more single focused. He increases his muscular tension at first, and then he bursts into a free-flowing swinging of his limbs, especially of his arms, as if he suddenly understands something.

4. Is there a specific rhythm or tempo to the action?
First he pauses, and then he swings his arms rhythmically.

5. Within what area are your child's actions focused and contained: The child's own body, the immediate surrounding area within easy reach, or directed outside of self toward others or the general surroundings?
His focus is outside of himself toward others.

Exercise 2:
Review the images from Exercise 1, and notice your internal bodily responses when you visualize one of the emotional and physical states of your child. Which of your emotional states best describes this physical feeling? Are these physical and emotional reactions familiar to you? What other times in your day or your life do you have these feelings?
I am visualizing Julian's "alert state," which is a lot like mine. When I am feeling alert and involved, I feel very jumpy inside in a happy and excited way. I notice that I hold each breath an extra moment in my excitement.
I love seeing my son being so engaged. I want to keep him going like this as long as possible. I often feel this way when I'm excited about starting a project or learning something new.

Exercise 3:
Take a few minutes to answer these questions during a time when you are actually in the presence of your child. Observe his or her particular way of expressing each of the emotional and physical states as they are happening.

A. How does the image you had of your child match this presentation of the expressed emotion?
His alert state matches my image well, but I hadn't noticed the role that his body plays in conveying his feelings.

B.   What is similar? What is different?

I had not noticed before that his body seems to become fluid and more coordinated in his alert state.

C.   At this very moment, what is your internal bodily response to your child's expression?

I am very motivated to attract his attention and engage with him. I feel very alive inside, as if I'm bursting, and I want to talk to him. I want to catch these moments when he is most attentive and interested.

D.   What happens next? How does this expression influence the continuation of your interaction with your child?

I approach him excitedly, with a wide smile, and I bob my head up and down. He looks at me immediately with an equally broad smile. Then his eyes shift to a lock of my hair that has fallen in front of my eyes and is glistening in the sunlight, and he stops moving for a few moments, intently watching. His lips tighten as he concentrates. I stop, too, as he looks at my hair. Suddenly, his face brightens into a smile and reaches for my hair, flinging both of his arms toward it.

Exercise 4:

At this point, you and your child may want to introduce different modes of acting and reacting to influence the outcome of your interactions. Are there any actions you would like to accent, emphasize, diminish, or change?

As soon as he becomes active again, I, too, become active and bring my head closer, shaking my hair so that it crosses over his hands. He squeals with glee, and his legs and torso become engaged, rocking to the rhythm of my shaking. I'm encouraged, and I shake my hair across his belly, matching his beat, and then I add an extra "oomph" by cooing "whoo, whoo," which makes him giggle even more.

their child and their child's ways of nonverbally expressing himself fit with the child's actual nonverbal cues as they are occurring. The questions in these exercises ask parents to be self-reflective, turning their awareness inward toward their own nonverbal responses. It is similar to a therapist's own self-observational process described as witnessing in Chapter 7. It introduces the idea that their personal reactions may contribute to their experiences of their baby. This question is built on the "ghost in the nursery" notion first put forth by Fraiberg (1980) and now a well-supported concept in early childhood practice. In Fraiberg's understanding, the parents' own early childhood experiences may affect how they perceive their child's current experience. Not all parents may be able to make a link between past and present experience. For some it may be enough to simply reflect on current interactional experiences. Thus, these questions direct parents to first pay attention to their own subtle physical, sensorial reactions, and then asks them to link their physical states to their mental reactions about an immediate event ("what other times in your day") or an historic event ("your life").

Each of these awarenesses occurs within the context of the parents' reactions to their child's emotional states. Answering these questions may not be easy for every parent. They require parents to be able to identify their child's reactions and then, separately, to reflect on their own reactions. Parents are directed to define both their nonverbal and emotional reactions. The research on reflective functioning suggests that a parent's ability to recognize and emotionally reflect on a baby's mental state is a strong indicator of the parent's ability to "hold [his or her] child in mind" as a separate feeling person. The level to which parents will be able to answer such questions may reveal the parents' abilities to use reflective thinking to link their mental states and their baby's mental states to behaviors. Such ability fosters the development of healthy parent–child relatedness (Slade 2002a, Slade 2002b).

The *Ways of Seeing* approach adds a nonverbal component to this understanding to help parents understand how physical reactions relate to emotions, and how they may also influence the nature of their interactions with their children. This relationship between physical reactions, emotional reactions, and interaction works in all directions, as the nature of the interaction can be influenced by the child's or the parent's current mental and physical states. In addition, the experience of the interaction can also have an effect on each member's mental and physical states. An understanding of this continuous relationship supports self-regulation and co-regulation of the dyad.

Adding nonverbal awareness to this understanding will most likely be a new way of thinking for many parents. How they respond to this part of the exercise will reveal their self-awareness of their own nonverbal experiences. The parents' personal awareness may indicate their abilities to be reflective and considerate about their baby's physical and mental states. Their responses should guide the *Ways of Seeing* therapist in selecting a starting point from which parents can begin to learn how to read their child's cues. Parents with high physical and mental awareness may readily accept the concept that their child's nonverbal gestures may have expressive meaning. In contrast, other parents may have difficulty recognizing the relationship between their own physical states and their emotional states; they may need to be guided through some experiential exercises to help them first feel these relationships on their own, before they can relate these ideas to their child's nonverbal cues.

In Exercise 3, parents are asked to observe their child during the different emotional and physical states outlined in Exercise 1, paying particular attention to how their images of their child match what they are actually seeing. By this point in the worksheet, parents have been contemplating their child's nonverbal expressions from a variety of perspectives. They have formulated general images of their child's nonverbal cues and have been provided with specific nonverbal qualities to look for to expand their thinking about their unspoken dialogues with their child. Now parents are asked to compare in a non-threatening way just how their images of their child fit with what they experience during live interactions. This is where a therapist must be especially supportive of the parents. A therapist should acknowledge the parents' strengths in their keen perceptions and knowledge of their child, and should be encouraging about the new information that the parents are learning about their child through this worksheet series.

Parents' abilities to accurately see their children and read their cues may vary. Again, it is essential to keep in mind that the child's ability to express his needs may not be clear as well. In addition, it is best if therapists start this process with a great sense of respect for the parents' interpretations. A therapist might apply the self-witnessing tools discussed in Chapter 7, comparing their thoughts and their knowledge about early childhood development, in situations in which they have a different interpretation of the child's cues than that of the parents.

Exercise 4 asks parents to think about their interactions with their child. It actually leads into Worksheet 2, which will focus on actively developing the nonverbal interaction between parents and child. Here parents can contemplate what nonverbal elements they enjoy or would like to modify as they interact with their child. Parents arc invited to employ the same tools used by the *Ways of Seeing* therapist, accenting, emphasizing, diminishing, or changing their wordless interactive dialogue with their child, thus finding new ways of nonverbal play. This question provides yet another way for parents and the therapist to bring to light the parents' feelings about how they nonverbally have perceived their experiences with their child. The therapist's providing potential opportunities to vary the interaction through these nonverbal means may stimulate a discussion about what parents expect and want their interactions with their child to be like.

Worksheet 2: Interactions

In Worksheet 2, parents are asked to observe and then try on their child's actions as a way to feel what it is like to experience the world from their child's physical perspective (see Figure 10.2 for a worksheet completed by Casey's mother Sharon; see http://www.brookespublishing. com/dancing for a blank worksheet). During these exercises, the *Ways of Seeing* therapist emphasizes that the parents' experiences may not be the same as their child's. The goal of trying on these different physical modes of being is to enable parents to actually embody how different postures and ways of physically exploring the surroundings can affect experience. A basic construct of the *Ways of Seeing* program is that physical experience has an effect on one's emotional state. These embodiment experiences make very tangible the concept that even babies *can have* and *do have* their own experiences. These exercises enable parents to postulate such thoughts and then explore them. It is the beginning of an awareness of self and other having two different but related experiences.

These experiential exercises should instill in parents this sense of differentiation in a very concrete way. Exercise 1 guides parents to observe their child for a few minutes, keeping different qualitative movement focuses in mind. In Exercise 2, parents try on their child's particular current movement state. Exercise 3 directs parents to mirror their child's movement states, following their child's nonverbal actions. Exercise 4 provides parents with qualitative movement suggestions about how to dialogue with their child. Exercise 5 asks parents

Name of child: _Casey_   **Date:** _8/08/04_

Age: _10 months_ **Date of birth:** _10/06/03_   **Observer:** _Sharon (Casey's mother)_

Goal: To explore ways to expand the nonverbal dialogue between you and your child in the context of play, and to become aware of the unique expressivity portrayed by each of your movement styles.

General directions: Begin each exercise by observing your child's current state. Repeat these exercises over a period of time until you have observed your child in several of the movement states and focuses listed below. As you repeat these exercises, you will notice which states and focuses are most predominant in your child's style.

Exercise 1:

A. Write a few words or phrases that describe the activity level of your child's current movement states while still, stationary, active, mobile, stable, or unstable.

Still

Casey is often in this state when she is left alone. She doesn't seem to move much. She looks around but doesn't seek my eyes or try to make contact with me, or anyone else, really. She doesn't try to move her body out of whatever position she is in—she is not very curious to explore the world with her body. Now she is sitting, her arms are very still at her sides, and her back is pretty straight. She is looking out into space but not at anything in particular.

Stationary

Active

Mobile

Stable

Unstable

B. Think about your child's current movement state as a musical sequence and write a few words or phrases that describe its Phrasing quality.

Continuous

Sporadic

continued

Figure 10.2. Worksheet 2: Interaction for Casey at age 10 months.

Figure 10.2. *(continued)*

Rhythmic

Arrhythmic

Breath flow

I guess the movement state that I would describe as a musical sequence would be her breath flow. There is no regular rhythm to her actions since she is not really moving besides breathing. I see her chest slightly rising and falling as she breathes gently and calmly.

C. Describe the direction of your child's current focus. Is the focus directed toward

Self

She seems to be in her own world, just looking out but not focusing on anything going on around her or inside of herself either. Actually, I am not sure where her focus is!

Child's surroundings

People in the surroundings

Objects in the surroundings

D. Describe your child's position and use of:

Torso

She is holding her back up pretty tall and straight for a 10-month-old.

Head

Her head is looking straight ahead.

Arms

Her arms are still at her sides.

Hands

Her hands aren't moving.

Legs

Her legs are stretched out in front of her and still.

Feet

Her feet aren't moving.

E.   What parts of the body are active in your child's current movement state?

Nothing really.

F.   What parts of your child's body are supporting his or her weight to enable the maintenance of this movement state?

She is sitting with her weight evenly balanced on her bottom.

Exercise 2:

Try out this movement state on your own body and describe how it feels to explore and view your surroundings with this movement expression.

I feel very quiet, as if I am meditating. I'm not tuning into anything around me. Actually, it feels very peaceful. I don't want to be bothered.

Exercise 3:

Watch your child and mirror his or her movement states, following your child's cues as the qualities of his or her movement varies.

A. What is the overall mood of this interactive dance?

When I sit across from her, not moving, just sitting with her, everything seems very quiet. Nothing is disturbed.

B.   What specific feelings do you believe you are expressing? Your child is expressing?

I feel anxious. I feel as if I should do something to get Casey to look at me. She makes me feel as if she is ignoring me—maybe she doesn't even like me. Still, as I sit here and watch her, she seems quiet and serene and not very emotional at all.

Exercise 4:

Vary some element of your movement state, encouraging your child to follow you: Accent/emphasize/diminish/change some aspect of your nonverbal dancing dialogue. For example: Increase/decrease the force; change the rhythm or tempo; accent a point in the Phrasing sequence of your child's actions; enlarge/condense the shape of your body in space; add/subtract other body parts to those already involved in the movement; or use your whole body or just one body part to continue the action.

A.   How do these variations change the overall mood and specific feeling of the interaction?

First, I do what I normally do. I move closer to her, speak to her very softly, and lift her gently in a slow, even pace. She doesn't look at me at all, but she arches her back away from me, suspending herself in the air away from my body. I immediately put her down, away from me, and she quiets herself down. I don't feel we connect at all.

The second time, I call out her name in a louder, singsong voice before I approach. Once we make eye contact, I begin to slowly move toward her, holding her gaze. I firmly place my hands on her rib cage and give her a playful squeeze. She looks at me and then she smiles. I scoop her up and place her on my lap, bouncing her. Her face brightens, and she begins to wiggle her arms. We are having fun.

B.   Name the qualitative movement variations your child responds to the most. Which do you respond to the most? Why?

She likes firm touch and more energetic actions. I am so surprised! My natural tendency is to be very gentle and soft. I don't like abrupt actions, and I thought I would startle her if I was firm.

Exercise 5:

After playing with your child several times in this way, notice what nonverbal interactive patterns seem to emerge repeatedly.

continued

Figure 10.2. *(continued)*

A. What patterns are initiated by you? By your child?

It is clear that she prefers to look at me for a moment before I approach her. If I initiate the contact and get her attention first, she seems receptive to play. She will actually show increased excitement, swinging her arms and legs as if telling me to bounce her more!

B. What is the overall mood of each of these patterns?

If I approach her without her first seeing me coming, she becomes agitated. If she watches me come over, she is more prepared and seems to gradually shift into a playful mood. Sometimes, she even seems to try to continue our play by enlarging and repeating her actions.

C. What specific feelings arise in you with this pattern?

I feel rejected when she gets agitated, but I am relieved and excited when she seems to want to play more with me.

D. What feelings do you think your child is experiencing?

Maybe it wasn't me that she was rejecting but just that she couldn't handle how I was approaching her. Maybe she didn't know how else to communicate this except to get agitated. Maybe she is relieved and is eager to play with me, too!

E. Do you think you and your child have the same feelings, or are they different?

It is hard to know exactly how she feels, but she certainly seems to be more expressive when we play together now compared to how she acts when she is sitting alone. I think she is now as happy to play with me as I am to play with her.

F. How do you know? How can you tell? Are there specific aspects of your child's nonverbal style that support these ideas about his or her expressions and experience?

She lets me hold her more, and she looks at me longer. When she is sitting alone, I can see that she is looking for me. If I catch her gaze, she stares at me. Then, when I say her name, she brightens. If I hold her firmly (instead of my usual gentle, cautious style), she becomes more excited, moves her arms and legs more freely, and even starts to giggle.

to continue to play this qualitative movement game with their child and notice if any patterns of engagement develop. They are then given a series of questions to contemplate the nature of this new nonverbal dancing dialogue.

Section A of Exercise 1 uses descriptive words to define the child's physical state. At this point the qualities of the child's overall movement and posture are emphasized to avoid having a parent immediately trying to interpret a child's emotional state. This focus on the physical state heightens the parent's ability to pay attention to a child's nonverbal body actions (cues). A child may be exhibiting several of these qualities at the same time. These choices are just suggestions to guide the parent's perceptions. There is space left after each choice to enable parents to use their own words to describe their child. Parents' word choices can be very insightful in depicting their experience of their child.

Still movement should be chosen when a child is not moving at all regardless of focus. She may be staring off without a focus or intently focusing on a toy or her parent's face. *Stationary* action means a child's activities are confined to her current placement—lying down, sitting, or standing—without moving away from her center or changing her full body spatial orientation either up and down, rolling, or moving around the room. *Active* is the appropriate label when a child's movements are lively; the level of activity (active, very active, or extremely active) should also be described, and the parent's own description of the activity level is encouraged. Such actions can occur whether the child is stationary or moving or whether the child's focus is internal or external. The key element that defines this choice is the sense of active engagement of a child's movements, regardless of how much space she takes up, whether she travels through space, or the manner in which she focuses. *Mobile* describes the spatial orientation of a child's actions. This is chosen when a child's movements actually traverse through the space. Rolling, crawling, walking, running, jumping, sliding, and hopping are just a few of the many ways a young child may mobilize her body. *Stable* and *Unstable* describe the sense of security a child's movements create. A child moving around the room in a very active style, falling, bumping, tumbling, and losing her balance as she goes has an unstable quality; while another equally active child who exudes a stable quality may navigate the room with agility and litheness, never losing her balance. Children do not have to be actively moving for these qualities to define their actions, though. These qualities are present even when a child is stationary. A child may be sitting quite still but have so much tension that it may seem as if she might fall over if someone brushed against her, creating an unstable sense; or, she may have such a solid presence that it may seem as if nothing could topple her over.

Section B of Exercise 1 begins to introduce some movement analysis concepts more directly by asking parents to think about their child's movements as a sequence, similar to a musical phrase. As with Section A, a child can display a variety of these Phrasing qualities in his movement repertoire. It is helpful to describe the particular series of actions and the context in which they are occurring when choosing these Phrasing descriptions. In a *continuous* phrase, the movements flow from one action to the next without a noticeable stopping or starting. The speed and tempo of the actions may vary, but the overall sense is that the sequence is flowing and ongoing. A *sporadic* phrase has clear stops and starts to it. A child may run to a place in the room and suddenly stop and linger; then slowly begin to play with a toy, increasing his activity level; and finally become disengaged and still, just looking around the room for a while. A younger baby who is not yet mobilizing may shake his arms a moment; pause; shake his arms and kick his legs; then stop shaking his arms but keep his legs kicking. *Rhythmic* Phrasing occurs when the movement action has a pulsing definite accent. In this Phrasing there is a regular beat that organizes the actions. Babies at all ages are capable of rocking, shaking, and kicking their limbs and bodies in a rhythmic Phrasing style. Even the youngest infants' actions can have rhythm, albeit very short, and they may have a vibratory rebounding quality. In an LMA profile, a strong accented rhythm and a vibratory rhythm would be distinguishable, but at this level of analysis it is enough if the parents can just notice the existence of a rhythm. As babies get a little bit older, putting on music with a detectable beat can often elicit a rhythmic rock, shake, or sway from a young child. *Nonrhythmic* Phrasing occurs when a clear rhythmic sense is not observable. Many actions fit into this category. A child may begin his movement phrase with a burst of energy and then keep moving but maintain a neutral, even tempo to his actions. His actions might steadily increase or decrease in intensity, strength, or size. Although in a full movement analysis there would be several additional categories of Phrases to classify nonrhythmic Phrases; at this level, however, the only goal is to provide parents with new ways to observe and think about their child's actions, so this more general category is sufficient. *Breath flow* is the final type of Phrasing pattern. As the name suggests, this Phrase resembles and is often directed by the rise and release of the breath. There is a soft, undulating quality to these actions. This Phrase is frequently observable in very young babies as they lie quietly gazing around a room. It is also observable in the older toddler caught in a reverie as he wanders around the room. This Phrasing style has an inwardly focused quality to it.

Becoming aware of Phrasing styles prepares parents for Section C, which requires them to describe their child's focus. Self-focus is an internal focus. A very young baby will spend lots of time self-focused as a way to regulate the stimulus of her external world. This ability plays a very important role in how a young child learns to organize and coordinate her whole physical and emotional body systems to navigate through all the new experiences she will encounter. As she learns how to maintain inward regulation, she will become more and more engaged in her surroundings for longer periods of time. She will begin to direct her attention outward toward her surroundings. This external focus on her surroundings may be directed to the outer world in general, or she may have a specific focus toward people or an object such as a toy or a ray of sunshine pouring through the window. In healthy development a child will demonstrate all of these focuses. This exercise teaches parents to become aware of their child's natural shifts of attention. This knowledge is essential to support a child to develop her own ability to physically modulate internal and external stimuli as well as navigate social interactions. Successful relating requires a child to maintain enough internal stability to be able to stay outwardly focused. New parents who are sensitive to a child's ebb and flow of attention create positive interactive experiences for their child, rather than impose interactions when the child is not able to stay attentive. As these positive experiences accumulate, the child develops a repertoire of experience supporting continued interactions and strengthening turn-taking abilities.

Section D asks parents to notice how their child uses his body to engage in his surroundings. This preliminary question increases the parents' general awareness of their child's use of his body. Parents who learn how to look at the way their child specifically uses his body are prepared for the next step—paying attention to their child's movements as nonverbal expressions. Sections E and F provide parents with more specific movement analysis concepts to guide their observations. These questions increase the parents' nonverbal observational skills, helping them to begin to develop a nonverbal language to describe their child's actions. This provides parents with a nonverbally focused context to view their child's actions, without asking them to interpret the meaning of their child's actions. It is vital that parents learn to first observe their child's nonverbal actions from a descriptive and objective perspective to ensure that they see their child as his own person—separate and apart from themselves—with his own style of feeling and being.

In Exercises 2 and 3, parents are asked to embody their child's movements to experience what they feel like. They are cautioned not to assume that their own reactions are what a child is feeling. Rather, they are asked to try on these actions as a way to gain perspective about how different the world might feel for the child. Such knowledge will facilitate dialogue about what possible experiences the child might be having. Unspoken messages will be revealed as parents have the opportunity to watch, experience, contemplate, and talk about the child's nonverbal cues over time. Exercise 3 instructs parents to explore their child's actions and then contemplate the experience. By asking the questions in this order, parents are taken through a progression of steps; they will become increasingly more aware of the potential meaning of their child's actions by first differentiating their own responses.

In Exercise 4 parents are asked to play with their child by changing some qualitative aspect of their actions in the same way that a *Ways of Seeing* therapist would engage a baby. Parents are then asked to reflect on the interactive experience in Sections A and B. Arranging the exercise in this order supports the developmental and phenomenological concept that experience influences how one thinks about and comes to understand that experience. As parents move through this worksheet, they are continually asked to first experience and then reflect on their experience. This process will help them become more sensitive and conscious of watching, feeling, and thinking about all their interactions with their young child.

In Exercise 5, parents are asked to identify the ongoing nonverbal relational movement metaphors that are becoming established and expressed. They are asked a series of questions to help guide their thinking about these developing patterns. Discussing these questions and exploring these new ways to play enable parents and children to increase and develop their understandings of each other. They learn about the power of their interactions as they experience their reactions and responses to each other. When both a parent and a young child successfully and repeatedly read each other's nonverbal cues, each member of the dyad experiences the rewards of this wordless communication. A trusting and secure attachment relationship can develop as successful and experientially based interactions accumulate, are remembered on a very sensorial level, and are built on, creating a sense of competence in both parent and child.

Reading and responding to nonverbal cues is a natural process. Detecting the qualitative aspects of these nonverbal cues is a mostly unconscious process that underlies all social interactions. The qualitative elements of these cues are the subtleties of nonverbal communication that create the overall feeling tone of an interaction. These worksheets are designed to teach parents to become alert to these more subtle cues.

Parameters of General Interactive Nonverbal Cues

Observing nonverbal interaction between parent and infant as a way to discern the quality of the attachment relationship is a prominent practice in early childhood development literature (Beebe et al., 2000; Brazelton & Cramer, 1990; Stern, 1985; Isabella & Belsky, 1991; Tronick, 1989; Tronick & Gianino, 1986). Table 10.2 outlines the basic interactional cues most commonly observed. The more subtle qualitative cues described above should be viewed within the context of these more general nonverbal parameters.

Variables Affecting Parent–Child Interactions

This chapter stresses the joint creation of the parent–child relationship based on the qualities of each dyadic member's reactions and responses. Influenced by early childhood development and attachment relationship theories, the *Ways of Seeing* approach includes seven variables for a therapist to consider while studying a parent–child dyad. These interdependent variables, which build on and influence the others in a dynamic and ever-evolving manner, are the following:

1. Sensitivities to cues
2. Reciprocity of interaction
3. Regulation—sensory sensitivities—arousal
4. Affect
5. Flexibility
6. Proximity and distance
7. Cultural influences

Sensitivities to Cues   These interactions include a parent's ability to discern, be attentive to, interpret, and be aware of a child's sig-

Table 10.2. Parent–child interaction nonverbal observational points

---

1. Notice the clarity of the child's cues.
   - Does the child employ clear use of eye contact, vocalizations/verbalizations, smiling, gestures/nonverbal expressivity (e.g., increased movement of limbs to show excitement), pointing, or focused attention when he or she wants or refuses something?
   - Does the child demonstrate differential qualities (e.g., demonstrate a range of different vocal qualities) when crying and vocalizing to communicate needs and wants in response to vocalizations or interactions with others?
2. Notice any child-initiated actions.
   - Does the child attempt to engage adults through eye contact, vocalizations, smiling, gestures/nonverbal expressivity, pointing, or focused attention when he or she wants or refuses something?
   - Does the child attempt to engage environment through body movement, gestures, vocalizations, or focused attention?
   - Does the child use noncrying vocal signals and/or eye contact to gain attention (e.g., smiling, pointing, focused attention)?
   - Does the child increase or decrease motor activity along with eye contact and vocalizations to demonstrate attentiveness?
   - Does the child increase vocalizations and language use to imitate and sustain contact?
3. Notice the responsiveness of the parent(s).
   - *Contingent responses*
     - Does the parent accompany the child's behavior with language that parallels action?
     - Is the parent's response contingent on the child's cue in a way that demonstrates that the parent has an understanding of the child's communication (e.g., engagement, play, hunger, discomfort, boredom, fatigue)?
     - When the child is expressing feelings that are understood by the parent, does the parent verbalize or enunciate for the child—as a reexpression of the child's expression to label the child's emotions?
   - *Noncontingent responses*
     - Does the parent offer no response (acknowledges with no reaction) or ignore (does not acknowledge) the child?
     - Does the parent's response show a lack of awareness or insensitively to the child's behavior?
     - Does the parent's response overstimulate the child, or is it intrusive, passive, or remote?
     - Is the parent's affect too intense, flat, labile, or rigid?
     - Does the parent's affect not match or comply with the affect of the child?
4. Notice how the parent facilitates interaction with the child.
   - Does the parent help the child to focus by drawing attention to the task at hand, reducing stimuli in the environment?
   - Does the parent position the child to maximize interaction with the environment?
   - Does the parent notice and share the child's success through gesture, eye contact, and/or vocalizations and encouragement?
   - Does the parent maintain eye contact, allowing room for the child's attention to wax and wane?
   - Does the parent imitate or mirror the child's vocalizations and expressions with playfulness?
   - Does the parent facilitate the child to do things on his or her own when he or she is able to?

---

nals. Signals may include postural and gestural nonverbal cues, vocal and verbal cues, and eye contact. A parent's ability to sensitively read a child's cues represents the parent's awareness of the child as a human object separate from her- or himself. Such recognition enables the parent to nurture and meet the child's needs, assuring the child's survival. Discerning a child's signal of discomfort as different from the child's signal of fatigue is an example of this skill portrayed in the story of Sharon and Casey earlier in this chapter. Even before formally learning about her child's tactile and proprioceptive sensitivities, Sharon accurately read her daughter's cues, provided her with time and space to settle herself down when she displayed discomfort, and attempted to reengage her as soon as she saw her daughter quiet her body down.

Reciprocity of Interaction   By using their abilities to read their child's cues, parents can formulate responses that accurately meet their child's communications and needs. From this, a growing and turn-taking cycle of communication and interaction can develop. The evolving and enlarging cycle of turn taking includes initiation of interaction and balanced participation by both parent and child. Inevitably, misinterpretations will occur in these exchanges. Through effort and practice, however, the individuals in the dyad can mend such mismatches in communication, leading to an expansion of their communicative repertoire and growing intimacy. For example, a lack of consistent positive reciprocal interactions initially caused Sharon to seek therapeutic help. Because Sharon did not realize that her daughter was seeking her mother's attention once Casey's sensory sensitivities quieted down, the two were prevented from successfully developing a playful reciprocal nonverbal exchange. As Sharon learned to read Casey's cues better and changed her approach—adjusting Space, Time, Phrasing, and physical touch (which involves the weight Effort)—their ability to relate improved.

Regulation—Sensory Sensitivities—Arousal   Through an accurate reading of cues and reciprocal interactions, a parent can help an infant sustain homeostasis. Through growth and experience, a child will develop a range of situation-appropriate states (e.g., arousal, responsiveness, attention, intensity, intention) that become increasingly under the control of the growing child. In Casey's example, she became able to attend for longer periods of time as her sensory needs were met by her mother.

Affect   The quality of the dyadic relationship will elicit, regulate, and influence the expression of each member's mood and emotional state. Innate qualities can be shaped, modified, or entrenched during their interactions. For example, Sharon's subdued facial expressivity and quiet, monotone vocal quality did not successfully engage Casey.

Flexibility As a relationship develops, both parties introduce and experiment with an ever-expanding range of communicative and interactional qualities that have the potential to deepen and broaden their attachment. As stated in Chapter 2, flexibility in a relationship supports healthy attachment. Once Sharon learned how to vary her nonverbal style, she was able to provide more interactional variations. Casey immediately responded, and as their repertoire of playful physical and vocal exchanges continued to expand, their relationship began to grow.

Proximity and Distance This includes how the members of the dyad position themselves in relationship to each other and to objects within the room to promote attuned interaction. Here a therapist first looks at how close or distant each mover places him- or herself in relation to the other. Specific observations include noticing if their kinespheres are completely separate, touch at the far-reach edges, overlap, or merge. Observations might also include noticing how each mover orients his or her body within the personal kinesphere to support attending to the other member of the dyad. In addition, a therapist may note if, how, and how often the kinespheric and body orientation of each mover varies throughout an interaction. The use of touch, voice, eye contact, and body placement dynamically contributes to this experience. Once Sharon changed her approach regarding body space, touch, and eye contact, her interactions with Casey became far more successful.

Cultural Influences The use of the word *culture* refers to the family's ethnicity as well as the family's personal systems, customs, and rituals. Considering cultural differences can become especially significant when a therapist is working with a family with a different ethnicity. All observations must be done with an understanding of the family background and customs. It is especially important to consider a family's personal value system, specifically in regard to child-rearing practices and beliefs. What child-rearing principles have family members embraced and rejected from their cultural background? What aspects have they adapted or discarded from their own experience of being raised by their own families? What child-rearing practices are they creating on their own, and what current elements in their immediate environment may be influencing these decisions? Due to her own personal early childhood experiences of neglect, for example, Sharon's initial parenting style was to immediately respond to her child's signals of discomfort rather than waiting to see if Casey would settle down before making any changes. The therapist respected this attitude by helping Sharon to develop more ways to interact with Casey once the child's immediate discomfort stopped.

WORKING WITH DYADS WHEN THE PARENT HAS A MENTAL ILLNESS OR INTELLECTUAL DISABILITY

These variables become especially significant when working with parents who have a mental disability. Such parents may not demonstrate sensitivity to their child's cues or support reciprocity during their interactions. They may not be able to regulate their own, never mind their child's, sensory sensitivities or arousal level. Their affect may be flat, or at the other extreme, quite bizarre. Flexibility and innovative interaction may be replaced by rigid and limited patterns of engagement. Physical spatial awareness, body boundaries, and a sense of self and other as separate feeling people may not exist.

When a parent has a mental disability, an important question arises: How can a therapist support healthy infant development when a parent's skills and judgment are compromised? These parents may not be able to respond initially to parent worksheets, which require a certain degree of self-reflection. In such instances, parents should be first provided with movement-based experiences to help them become aware of how they use their own bodies and personal movement styles for self-expression.

The next section describes an intervention that took place in a program in an outpatient psychiatric hospital facility that served mothers of young children (from birth to age 5) who had been hospitalized for mental illness after they returned home. Mothers and their children attended a variety of outpatient services at the hospital on a daily basis. Dance movement therapy was provided twice a week. Mothers could attend group dance therapy sessions with other mothers and dance therapy dyadic family sessions with their children. The dance movement therapist also saw each child individually. In addition, the dance movement therapist videotaped sessions periodically and used these tapes to do an in-depth movement signature analysis of mother–baby interactions. She showed portions of the tapes to the mothers as another tool to help them reflect on their interactions with their children.

This program is described first by presenting in a narrative form the author's movement analysis of a mother, Rosa; her 18-month-old son, Tito; and their nonverbal dyadic interactions to enable readers to visualize how family members can express themselves through their movements. The specific dance movement therapy-based activities that the therapist created to work with them both individually and in dyadic sessions are also provided to put their movement signature profiles in context. This story is presented to demonstrate how information obtained through nonverbal observation can be translated into effective therapeutic intervention. (See Chapter 5 for definitions of the LMA qualities used in this description.)

Movement Analysis of Rosa and Tito

Rosa   The most outstanding feature of Rosa's movement style is her continual effort to avoid interactions and encounters with the environment by maintaining an inward focus. This is especially apparent in the rhythm of her Phrases, the Body Shapes she makes, and her use of Space during group dance therapy sessions. Rosa's physical participation is minimal. She spends much of the time on the periphery, sitting along the edge of the designated movement area. Periodically she takes herself outside of the whole situation by leaving the room. By physically excluding herself from the group she attracts attention, for it becomes obvious that she is not participating. When confronted with an unavoidable encounter from the environment—such as when the dance movement therapist sits with her on the outskirts—Rosa's responses are polite but sparse and controlled, maintaining this inward focus.

Phrasing   The swing-type Phrases that dominate Rosa's movement style enable her to conduct herself in this manner in which she avoids engagement with others and stays in her own inner world. These Phrases are characterized by an initial period of movement involving little dynamic Effort exertion, appearing almost monotone in rhythm. By beginning the Phrase without an Effortful energy commitment, Rosa enters an interaction with little engagement. The more accented middle portion of her Phrase is marked by actions that often appear as slips or body readjustments. Examples include weight shifts, in which she momentarily changes the course of her gait, or redirects the placement of her body during mid-action in space. These actions enable her to have a response to the environment while still maintaining her focus on herself. Although she creates an action in space, it enforces personal attention. These actions are followed by a return to her previous state—employing a minimal exertion of Effort energy to complete the sequence. Monotone Phrases, which are also evident in her phrasing style, are marked by her use of bound Effort.

Efforts Bound energy flow is the salient feature of the entire Phrase that produces this barrier between self and the environment. During the first and last portions of the swing Phrase it presides over any other use of Efforts, creating the monotone effect. This boundness is accompanied by a slight acceleration in pace during the spatial readjustments just described, creating the peak to the swing phrase. Though this focus is inwardly directed, it momentarily adds direct spatial and time Effort to her movement repertoire.

During early observation of Rosa's movement style, the time Effort seemed to be a salient characteristic. However, on repeated analysis of the tape it became apparent that the quickness seen during actions in which she actually maintains engagement with her environment, like patting Tito's back, lacks dynamic energy and has a mechanical quality. Moving without a fluctuation in energy stress, her Phrasing rhythm is often monotone, occurring at varying times in a slow or quicker tempo. Actually Rosa seems to perseverate on a single Effort such as boundness, creating a monotone Phrase, especially when she is asked to participate in her environment—observable when interacting with Tito. By maintaining such a Phrasing rhythm, Rosa is able to physically participate while emotionally detaching herself from the situation. This isolating use of one or two Efforts limits Rosa's ability to participate with full emotional expressivity. Her predominant use of bound flow does not support her to experience a sense of recuperation in her body, causing jerky transitions between her movement Phrases and creating a feeling of tension and discomfort.

Shape This discomfort is also apparent by observing the Shapes her actions make in the Space directly surrounding her body (kinesphere). Her initial actions, both gestural and postural, always come back to herself. Her movements never travel far from her body, only extending into mid-reach space. Her physical self actually seems to become the pivot point from which her actions go and return. A movement in the surrounding space, such as a walk, appears to rebound back to her own self as the central focus, when she momentarily makes some type of bodily adjustment by shifting her weight back and then forward. Repeating dimensional pathways in space along the sagittal, horizontal, and diagonal axes are formed by these actions.

Space   Due to Rosa's weight shifts and inward actions, she inscribes linear and zigzag pathways when she moves through the room. This inward, bodily focus actually is counterproductive for her because it draws attention to her, making her the focal point of action for Tito.

Tito   Similar to his mother, Tito does not involve himself in any of the activities going on around him, and he rarely acknowledges the presence of other people in the room throughout the dance therapy session. His involvement in his surroundings focuses on one specific object—his mother. His attitude appears ambivalent, however, for he alternately shuns and demands his mother's attention. His Effort choices, Phrasing, and manner of moving his Body in Space reflect this controversy.

Phrasing   His movements often do not appear as complete phrase segments involving clear, Effortful action sequences with preparation, main impetus, and recovery. Rather, they occur as isolated accented, vibratory, or monotone Phrasing movements, followed by long periods of no movement. What precedes the dynamic action of the phrase can vary. A pulsing, even-tempo rhythm using strength and quickness, performed by jumping up and down, often interjects the long periods of relative stillness. At times this accented Phrase seems to begin on the upbeat via a body-part shift or postural readjustment, caused by first leaning over before the action occurs. Thus a spatial rather than an Effortful action acts as a preparation for the main action. It is cut short with bound flow, however, which is the prevailing Effort in Tito's repertoire (the same prevailing Effort favored by his mother).

Effort   Using bound flow enables Tito to remain with his inner self as he directs his focus outward. When bound flow occurs as a response to an interaction that he does not want to be a part of, at times it creates a vibratory rhythm following his initial bound Effort exertion. In a vibratory Phrase, one exertion of Effortful energy creates a pulsing series of immediate actions that decrease in emphasis as it continues. The utilization of boundness enables Tito to withdraw emotional investment, for this bodily response—creating a blank attitude—is observable as an action with no outward spatial intent. By disengaging his inner self from the environment, he is able to choose exactly when to get involved. When Tito wants a response from the environment, especially from his mother, his actions accelerate, dominated by the time Effort of quickness. Thus, an unaccented walk initially appearing monotone in Phrase takes on an increasing Phrase quality as the tempo hastens. However, the relatively sparse amount of active actions (both when stationary and moving through the room) in relation to the large amount of stillness and stopped actions characteristic of Tito's repertoire reveal a cautious attitude toward his surroundings. The stillness seems to enable him to observe his environment before he gets involved. Directing his focus almost solely toward Rosa and getting involved only in response to his mother's actions exemplifies his attachment to his mother.

Body The varying ways he uses his body to respond to his mother, however, display his discomfort with his surroundings and his mother in that space. Tito does not move himself freely when placed on the floor. His arms are held close to his body or reach out to Rosa. He often uses his legs to jump up and down within his own vertical space, or he swings his body into the farthest reaches of his personal space, making his whole body stiff when he wants to disengage with his environment.

Space Tito does not explore spatial level changes on his own. He most often demands to be lifted off the floor to be held by reaching his arms out, but he does not soften his body to mold into his mother's body once held. His preference to view the world from this high place suggests that he chooses to be out of his own naturally reachable kinesphere by entering into this higher surrounding space. This enables him to share his personal space with his mother rather than be alone. The floor pattern of his spatial path reveals that most of his actions occur when in this shared occupation of space with Rosa.

Rosa and Tito Interacting At 18 months of age, as balance and bipedal stability are becoming established, Tito is developmentally at a stage in his life that is ordinarily characterized by experimentation with independence and self discovery. As their physical skills become more secure, this is a time that most children commonly fill with great exploration of the environment, within the comfort of knowing that their mothers are within reach when needed. This is not the image, however, portrayed on examining Rosa and Tito's nonverbal interactive style. Tito's marked disinterest in his surroundings and vigilant focus on his mother interfere with such free exploration. Separation anxiety coupled with ambivalent attachment permeates his actions. Detailed qualitative movement analysis makes this especially evident. Tito's strong desire to be held; his avoidance of independent exploration by not physically mobilizing himself through crawling, walking, or running when on the ground; and his sparse engagement with others are indicative of these tendencies. It is his bound Effort flow when held, however, that truly reveals his ambivalence. By holding himself rigidly and grasping his mother tightly rather than molding into his mother's body, Tito is floating alone high up in space.

In turn, Rosa's prevailing bound flow and swing Phrases, involving little dynamic Effort exertion, do not provide Tito with the types of responsive cues that are essential to develop an interactive dialogue that supports a secure primary relationship. By not providing Tito with positive expressive responses, Rosa fails to give Tito the necessary encouragement to venture confidently away from her into the world. Observing Rosa's manner of holding Tito reinforces this pattern. Rosa maintains her boundness, seeming to guard herself from letting Tito get too close, whereas Tito fights this barrier by jumping up and down with the same boundness his mother displays, insisting on being held. The dancing dialogue created by this dyad is one of increasing tension, with Tito vigilantly seeking his mother's presence and striving to be in physical contact with her.

Tito's use of bound flow is the key element that constructs his personal movement metaphor, expressing his struggle between separation anxiety and his drive for individuation. This bound flow both holds him to his mother and acts as a distancing tool that separates him from his mother. Tito's use of bound flow physically separates him from others and abruptly cuts his actions short, resulting in complete stillness or responses that create a vibratory Phrase. Boundness has also taken on an adaptive developmental purpose, enabling Tito to gain information about his world through observation while not dynamically participating. This boundness in his Phrasing best displays both his adaptability and ambivalence to adapt. While Tito seemingly detaches himself from his mother with stillness and bound flow, this Effort quality and the overall Phrasing of his actions very much relate to Rosa's Effortful Phrasing tendencies. The rhythm of Tito's accented Phrases fit proportionately in between the slower tempo of Rosa's swing Phrase. Tito's stillness occurs in response to his mother's actions, and Tito's actions occur during his mother's stillness or Effortless, undynamic portions of her Phrase. One movement sequence between mother and child occurred as follows: Rosa shakes a rattle at Tito with pulsating boundness for 2–3 seconds. Tito watches, holding his body in bound flow. His mother stops, and Tito jumps up and down with strength and quickness, matching the beat of the rattle. Tito's actions stop as Rosa slightly lifts Tito and places him on the floor as Rosa stands up and walks away. Being left alone in the space, Tito picks himself up and walks over to his mother with an unaccented rhythm to his gait.

This nonverbal dyadic interaction between Tito and Rosa has become their relational movement metaphor, shaping the overall way in which Tito engages in his surroundings. Tito expresses himself by using dynamic Efforts within the boundaries of his mother's Phrasing pattern. His use of Space coincides with this tendency. The majority of his expressive actions occur when he shares the (kinespheric) Space with his mother. In general, Tito is most engaging with others when he is lifted up and held, placing him in the surrounding space far above him. This suggests a fearful, untrusting attitude toward the surrounding space reachable within his kinesphere by his own locomotive actions. When his mother is not nearby, Tito does not demonstrate a dynamic use of his available Efforts or explore the surrounding Space. Tito's response to his mother's constant striving to make little impact on her environment is to exert the majority of his energy toward his mother.

The *Ways of Seeing* Intervention

The dance movement therapist initially begins meeting with Tito in private sessions. The therapist believes it particularly important to develop a relationship first with the child because the mother's emotional stability is compromised. The therapist hopes to be able to act as a stable and safe figure to support Tito in developing his own sense of self. Then, when his mother begins to attend sessions, Tito will have an established relationship with the therapist, who will become a positive role model for Rosa to support the growth of her relationship with her son. The therapist's first goal in developing a relationship with Tito is to help him overcome his fear of actions in his immediately surrounding space. During the beginning weeks of the intervention, Tito displays his discomfort with a stranger's presence (the dance movement therapist) by crying, insisting on being held by a familiar adult (the caregiver), or being put in his crib. This occurs even when the therapist is not directing her attention toward Tito. The therapist eventually achieves this goal by accepting Tito's initial need to keep his distance and remain off the floor. Their initial interactions involve a minute or two of greeting and gentle talking while Tito is held in his caregiver's arms. After a few weeks, Tito is able to come into the therapist's arms, while his teacher stays close. During the next month, all of their interactions occur in this holding position high off the floor. Activities include the therapist's encouraging Tito to release his body tension by molding into the therapist's body rather than holding on by grabbing the therapist's body with increased bound flow. The therapist achieves this by helping Tito feel his own body through rocking him up and down in the vertical dimension with a pulsating rhythm, attuning to the accented Phrasing of his breathing, thus enabling Tito to sense his body weight.

Slowly, in the next month, the actions are brought down to the floor, maintaining the same rhythm while getting Tito involved in stationary activities. In a game in which Tito and the therapist exchange sticks back and forth, the sticks take on a symbolic meaning as they become the active movers traveling through the space to create a bridge of connection between the therapist and Tito. When a ball replaces the sticks, the space opens up, and Tito himself becomes the active explorer, with the ball as his focus. The therapist begins to employ narrative to support their dance-play, constantly questioning the whereabouts of the ball and Tito. The therapist supplements this narrative by exclaiming exuberantly when Tito picks up the ball, providing encouraging feedback to Tito's actions. Tito also becomes more expressive, running toward the ball with quickness and directness, laughing joyfully as he shows the ball to the therapist. Tito begins to move more freely through the space, actively engaging himself with Effortful and emotional affect, and he even changes body level by crawling under objects to retrieve the ball. His floor pathways inscribe large arcing and circular forms around the therapist. His tendency to relate his actions to another person are still apparent, but he is now much more confident in mobilizing through his surroundings, away from a central figure.

The *Ways of Seeing* sessions with Tito and Rosa together focus on continuing this positive exploration. Tito becomes the focal point from which all actions are initiated. With Tito as conductor, Rosa is encouraged to become aware of the rhythm of Tito's exertions of energy as Tito directs the activities in the space. Tito uses the ball as the object for relating to both his mother and the therapist. Placing himself between them and running back and forth, he passes the ball to Rosa and the therapist. At times he engages himself solely with one of them and throws the ball back and forth a few times before proceeding to the other person. The rhythm of the activity is set by Tito's back-and-forth pace. Placing the adults between him and the space enables Tito to receive positive feedback from both areas. In this way, Tito is able to obtain a response at the beginning and ending of his action sequence—an experience his mother's swing Phrasing pattern has not previously provided. By creating this situation, Tito is able to have a figure to relate to while he explores a larger use of space. As his drive to find his own identity is growing, allowing Tito to direct this specific activity has enabled him to expand his proximities and take personal initiative, although still staying within the protective bounds of familiar people.

Closing Comments

Whether a family is compromised by difficulties in reading their child's cues or by a parent's own emotional capacities, *The Runaway Bunny* analogy that opens this chapter prevails. When therapists begin to work with these children, they are alone in their isolated world—detached. It is the therapist's job, just like the little bunny's mother, to never allow them to truly go away, but instead to follow them, going deeply into their world, wherever it may lead—together—then, when trust, relating, and communication have been established, bringing the children back home where they belong, engaged in the world of relationships.

II

Focusing on the Child

From Nonverbal Assessment to Intervention to Educational Programming

"Will you, won't you, will you, won't you, will you join the dance?
Will you, won't you, will you, won't you, won't you join the dance?
You can really have no notion how delightful it will be
When they take us up and throw us, with the lobsters, out to sea!"
But the snail replied "Too far, too far!" and gave a look askance—
". . . What matters it how far we go?" his scaly friend replied.
"There is another shore, you know, upon the other side.
The further off from England the nearer is to France—
Then turn not pale, beloved snail, but come and join the dance."

   Lewis Carroll, *Alice's Adventures in Wonderland* (1865/1992, p. 122)

The individual's perception of the world is itself affected by the status of his motor activities; information concerning the position and status of the body itself regulates the way in which subsequent perception of the world takes place.

Howard Gardner, *Frames of Mind:
The Theory of Multiple Intelligences* (1993, p. 211)

In the lyrics of the Lobster Quadrille dance, the whiting invites his friend the snail to join in a dance of play and fun. Is the snail game? The whiting seems to be coaxing his dear friend, hoping he can convince him to perceive this as amusement. As Gardner points out, however, how a person perceives his or her world is dependent on how the person physically engages in it. How the person physically engages in the world will influence the person's experience. How the person experiences the world will influence how that experience is internally processed. How the person internally processes that experience will affect how that experience is stored in memory. How the person remembers an experience will affect how subsequent similar experiences will be perceived. How the person perceives an experience will be reflected in how that person engages with the environment. How the person engages with the environment will become apparent in how that person's behaviors communicate engagement. And so, just as the whiting suggests when trying to lure the snail into joining him, partaking in the world is like a dance—a partner dance between the individual and the surrounding world, filled with opportunities in which one can choose to participate.

The *Ways of Seeing* approach views this dance, with strong emphasis on its very physical nature, as a most necessary element at the very core of a young child's engagement with the world. In its broadest interpretation, dance implies interaction and relationship between the self and the other. In its most specific interpretation, actual dance activities inform the *Ways of Seeing* program. How a young child uses his bodily system to experience the world affects the quality of this engagement. If there is no dance—no mutually playful and enjoyable communicative interchange—between an infant and his surroundings, the quality of engagement can be impaired. This, in turn, influences the infant's ability to develop relationships within his surroundings. As this chapter links nonverbal assessment to intervention and educational programming, the focus must remain on the child—on how a child engages in his surroundings and how this engagement is depicted through the child's behaviors.

The *Ways of Seeing* nonverbal assessment looks at this dance of engagement in a variety of surroundings—the home, the clinical intervention setting, and the school. In looking at engagement as a communicative dance, the *Ways of Seeing* nonverbal assessment continually questions the nature of a child's participation in the dancing exchange between the child and his environment. At its most basic, a *Ways of Seeing* therapist simply asks, just as the whiting asks his friend, *Will you, won't* you join the dance? In asking this question, an assessment process takes into account which aspects of a child's internal and external experience may be influencing how and if he is participating in the dance of interaction. This dance is communicated through his nonverbal behaviors. It is through the creation of enjoyable interactions—often including creative expressive dancing elements that a young child can grow in the *Ways of Seeing* approach and engage more fully in the dance. The two case studies at the end of the chapter exemplify how the *Ways of Seeing* approach uses the elements of nonverbal observation, dance, and movement to integrate home, intervention, and school. In addition, Table 11.1 provides a list of the five levels of development (motor, communication/ language, emotional, social, and cognitive) that need to be evaluated in assessing a child's improvement in relation to age-appropriate or

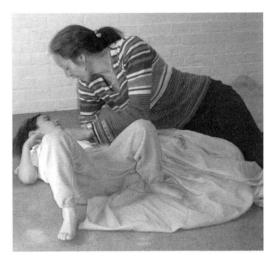

The focus of all nonverbal assessment and intervention must always remain on the child.

disability-appropriate levels. The information in this table can be used as a quick reference to determine progress. It supplements the MSI Checklist (see Appendix A) that assists an observer to describe the nonverbal elements of a child's behavior.

CONTINUUM BETWEEN NONVERBAL ASSESSMENT, INTERVENTION, AND EDUCATION

In order to create this dancing engagement and use dance as an element to support engagement, it is necessary to determine how a child's nonverbal expressions communicate his experiences, how new experiences continue to influence and affect his cumulative experiences, and how these new experiences become depicted in his nonverbal expressions. This is an ongoing process. As a young child learns about his surrounding world, he is continually registering new experiences within the context of his preexisting experiences. In this way he is building a repertoire of experiences that, over time, develop into his core expressive style. As new experiences accumulate, they have the potential to influence and modify a child's developing perceptions of his environment, which in turn will be apparent in how he interacts with his surroundings. This change will be perceivable in his nonverbal expressions. It is this ongoing process that has influenced the *Ways of Seeing* concept that assessment, intervention, and educational programming

Table 11.1. Evaluating a child's improvement in home, school, or therapeutic program

This evaluation follows the five levels of development (i.e., motor, communication/ language, emotional, social, cognitive) and assesses improvement in relation to age- or disability-appropriate levels.

Motor

- Is there improvement in the child's fine and gross motor abilities?
- Is there improved coordination in the child's general movement style?
- Is there an increased movement vocabulary? Is there a broader range of some or all five Laban Movement Analysis (LMA) movement qualities observable? Describe:
  - Body
  - Effort
  - Space
  - Phrasing
  - Shape

Communication/Language

- Does the child's personal nonverbal action take on expressive, communicative meaning understood by observer?
- Does the child intentionally use his or her own nonverbal cues as communication?
- Does the child understand the observer's nonverbal cues as communication?
- Does the child use conventional nonverbal cues to communicate (e.g., pointing, head nodding, increased use of eye contact)?
- Does the child use single words to communicate and support nonverbal cues?
- Does the child create two- to three-word sentences?
- Does the child create complex sentences?
- Does the child use the words *I, you, me*, and *mine*?
- Does the child understand the questions *which, what, where, who,* and *why*?

Emotional

- Does the child use full-body nonverbal actions to express personal emotions?
- Does the child use facial expressions to express affective expression?
- Does the child participate in dance-play activities that describe a variety of emotional states?
- Does the child create dance-play activities that describe a variety of emotional states?

Social

- Can the child maintain eye contact?
- Can the child extend the length of time he or she is able to stay jointly engaged with others?
- Can the child engage in mutual attention using a variety of nonverbal cues?
- Can the child engage in turn taking—this includes waiting for turn without interrupting partner—through nonverbal expressions and actions?
- Can the child lead a partner in a movement sequence (matching some aspects of the five LMA movement qualities)?
- Can the child follow a partner in a movement sequence (matching some aspects of the five LMA movement qualities)?
- Can the child lead a partner in a movement sequence correctly mirroring the movement qualities?
- Can the child follow a partner in a movement sequence mirroring the movement qualities?
- Can the child lead and follow a partner in a dramatic story dance-play?

Cognitive

- Can the child stay on task without getting distracted by personal idiosyncratic actions?
- Can the child follow a sequence of several movements together, maintaining engagement with a teacher, a therapist, or another student?
- Can the child follow a one-part verbal direction with body actions supporting/ complementing the completion of the task rather than distracting from the task?
- Can the child follow a two-part verbal direction with body actions supporting/ complementing the completion of the task rather than distracting from the task?
- Can the child follow multistep verbal directions with body actions supporting/ complementing the completion of the task rather than distracting from the task?

---

should be considered along a continuum, freely flowing from one aspect of this continuum to the other. As has been discussed throughout this book, the *Ways of Seeing* approach has developed a specific tool, the MSI Checklist (see Appendix A), to guide a therapist's nonverbal observations. The MSI Checklist provides a way to add qualitative information to assessment. This tool is not used solely as a formal assessment to be performed at a predetermined, structured time as an isolated event. Rather, it is constructed as a set of nonverbal observational guidelines that can be employed as a way to see how a child is nonverbally expressing his experiences at any time in any setting. Viewing assessment in this way supports current best practices, which focus on creating an environment that aims to determine a child's strengths and potential healthy growth (Meisels & Fenichel, 1996).

The qualities of the particular assessment designs that influenced the development of the MSI Checklist will be discussed below. An *assessment* is defined as an information-gathering process for the purpose of making evaluative decisions. The word *gathering* is included to create the image of the physical gesture of taking in and embracing the information. The word *process* is included to emphasize the ongoing aspect of this procedure. Assessments take many forms and are executed in a variety of ways. Styles of performing assessments have evolved from more traditional standardized evaluations, performed in isolated settings by specifically trained evaluators, to informal assessments occurring in natural settings familiar to a child, such as the home and the school, that include information obtained from family members and other significant people in the child's life. (An excellent discussion of issues and principles of appropriate assessment practice that goes beyond the scope of this book can be found in Meisels & Fenichel, 1996. See also Losardo & Notari-Syverson, 2001; Bagnato, Neisworth, & Munson, 1997.)

Overall Tone of Movement Signature Impressions Checklist and *Ways of Seeing* Approach

Authentic – engaged – active – responsive – interpret – explore – analyze – discover – embedded – apply – contextual – personal interests – ability – process oriented – dynamic – descriptive – cumulative – shape learning styles – develop competencies – collaborative – guide development – broad range – qualitative – interactive – multisubject domains.

These are examples of the terms commonly found in educational assessments that take the child's perspective into account (Darling-Hammond, Ancess, & Falk, 1995; Gardner, 1991, 1993b). In the realm of education, students are being asked to become actively engaged in the assessment process, responding to curriculum subjects through analysis, exploration, and discovery, enabling them to reveal their personal strengths, talents, and abilities through the process. Assessments are built from a broad range of sources that include descriptive statements taking consideration of each child's learning style and personal interests. The information in the assessment is accumulated over time and across subject domains. Students are encouraged to work collaboratively in interaction with other children who are often their friends. In this way assessments support the power of relationships to stimulate and encourage curiosity, creativity, and optimum performance. Assessments aim to ascertain and encourage competencies rather than only to define deficits. They inform and guide continued development and shape additional learning. These assessments act as a dynamic support for reflections and actions that inform and become part of the learning process (Darling-Hammond et al., 1995). A blurring of the line between assessment and learning occurs as the assessment enables students to accumulate and explore information across subject domains and develop competencies along the way.

Meisels and Fenichel (1996) apply similar terms in their discussions about early intervention assessments: *multiple sources – encourage – support – optimum performance – integrative – multiple components – direct observation – spontaneous natural settings – interactions with significant others – developmental – honor differences – elicit – coaching – building alliances – continuous growth model – identify competencies – attention to child's level and pattern – complexity – contextualized.*

In a performance-based assessment, a child is observed in natural settings to provide an environment that encourages and supports her optimum performance. Data are accumulated from a wide variety of sources, encouraging input and interaction from family members and significant people in a child's life. The goal of these assessments is to elicit a child's best responses by building an alliance with the child and the significant people in her life. This includes coaching and supporting the child and adults during the assessment process and encouraging her best efforts, with the goal of identifying competencies. The assessment process occurs over time, paying attention to a child's personal level and patterns of interacting that affect her performance. This process supports a model of continuous growth, acknowledging the complexity and plasticity of a child's development. Thus, the intervention assessment is not viewed as a static measure, but rather is regarded as dynamic, causing and creating changes even as it is executed.

The concepts of intervention-based assessments and education-based assessments are parallel and complementary. Meisels (1996) advocates a continuum of assessment and intervention. In this model, the assessment and intervention relationship is bidirectional. Information gleaned from assessments influence intervention strategies and intervention experiences are utilized in the assessment process. An additional continuum exists between intervention and education. This is not to say that a therapist should become an educator or that an educator should also act as a therapist. Rather, practitioners in each field can benefit from the general knowledge base of these complementary practices. It can be very useful for an educator to have an understanding of how specific emotional, social, cognitive, physical, and communicative developmental factors may affect a child's learning. Similarly, an intervention specialist with knowledge of both learning theories and a specific child's learning style can provide additional tools to support the child's total functioning. Broadening the practitioner's knowledge base has implications for the training of all practitioners, regardless of their field of specialization.

In her work to build higher standards for the profession of teaching, educational reformer Linda Darling-Hammond advocated, among other criteria, the necessity that teachers have an understanding of development: how children think and behave; what is of interest to them, and with what concepts they may have difficulty; awareness of differences that shape a child's experiences such as family, language, culture, gender, and community; differences in preferred learning approaches; and specific difficulties in learning that may arise. This last point emphasizes the need for teachers to be sensitive to how children's experiences may shape their learning so that teachers can design curriculum that connects to each student's knowledge base and supports optimum learning (Darling-Hammond, 1997).

Social-Emotional, Embodied Experience, and Cognitive Focus

On a similar note, to create a continuum between assessment, intervention, and education with an eye toward nonverbal experience, the *Ways of Seeing* program proposes that—in addition to their specialty— all practitioners working with children should be knowledgeable in the following three areas of study (with special attention paid on their nonverbal implications): social-emotional, embodied experience, and cognitive focus. Therapists can use these three categories to more easily and methodically organize the information they obtain from their observations of nonverbal behavior. These three components are at the core of the *Ways of Seeing* assessment process, whether the assessment is occurring in the home, during intervention, or in the classroom environment. A child's intervention and/or educational program should be based on these three categories, described in more detail next.

Social-Emotional Focus   The *social-emotional focus* emphasizes the role that nonverbal expression plays in a child's developing sense of self and encourages therapists to be aware of how nonverbal movement qualities express an individual's sense of self. This focus asks therapists to keep in mind how early nonverbal relationships, especially with primary caregivers, may affect overall development, and more specifically, the developmental process of social relatedness.

Embodied Experience Focus   The *embodied experience focus* explores the interrelationship between physical development and a sense of self. It emphasizes how a child's actual physical makeup, sensory processing, and corporeal experiences influence his behavior and total functioning in all developmental levels. This focus, discussed extensively in Chapters 2, 3, 4, and 5, greatly enhances an understanding of how a child's physical functioning affects his experiences. It will influence the planning of strategies for optimal performance in intervention and learning settings. (Sensory processing has been extensively explored in the field of occupational therapy. See Chapter 4 and the pioneering work of Ayres, 1974, and the recent work of DeGangi, 2000, and Williamson & Anzalone, 2001, for more information.)

Cognitive Focus   The *cognitive focus* relates to a child's perceptions of her surroundings: what a child understands and how this understanding affects her actions, behaviors, and ability to learn. This focus underscores how the qualitative elements of a child's embodied experience can influence how the experience is perceived. The cognitive focus provides a framework for therapists to learn how to reach all children by supporting their specific learning styles.

It is important to note that communication is a salient component within each of these three areas of development. Communication takes different forms depending on the study area. In the social-emotional focus, communication occurs through qualitative nonverbal expression. In the embodied experience, it is observed in the effect that a child's physical abilities have on self-expression and exploration. In the cognitive focus, communication occurs within nonverbal and language acquisition and cognitive processing. These three focuses are shown in the story of Lily, an 11-month-old baby who is not crawling.

⌒ *Observant and quiet, Lily spends most of her day in the arms of adults or in a baby seat. On occasion she sits on the floor playing with a toy. When she attempts to move, she does so by reaching forward, bearing weight on her arms, but she has not figured out how to unfold her legs into the crawling position. After attempting to crawl for a few moments, Lily shifts her weight back onto her bottom and resumes looking around or begins to play with a nearby toy. When she wants to move, she bounces her body up and down as she reaches her arms toward one of her parents and vocalizes. Once lifted into her parent's arms or placed in a child seat she settles immediately and engages in her surroundings by watching the room. Lily allows other adults to hold her as well. If the adult holding Lily looks at her, Lily responds with pleasant affect and a steady gaze. She appears quiet and content, gently smiling when someone approaches her in a friendly way. Most often, from this high perch, she intently observes her surroundings or keeps busy playing by herself.* ⌒

What do these behaviors communicate about Lily's present state? Although only a small description has been provided, a preliminary picture can be formed. From a social-emotional focus, Lily's nonverbal actions portray that she is aware of people and her surroundings. She has the ability to form pleasing interactions and is also content to engage herself. She shows interest in people but is a bit reserved, often not engaging or drawing attention to herself unless she needs something.

Do these observations provide any information about her experience of, and relationship with, her parents? Clearly, Lily has confidence in her parent's presence, expecting and receiving a response to her gestures and vocalizations. Her immediate settling in their arms, and the arms of other adults, as well as her ability to quietly engage emotionally with adults, demonstrates that she enjoys the close contact created by being held. Yet, for the therapist, her nonverbal behaviors spur questions. Her quiet affect, watchful style, and lack of initiation of playful emotional engagement cause the therapist to wonder if this is a temperamental style or a learned response. Have her accumulated experiences with significant adults taught her not to ask for much? Have her experiences taught her, in essence, to be seen but not heard? These questions are especially significant because Lily's mother is experiencing postpartum depression. Although Lily's physical needs are being met, the therapist questions how emotionally available is Lily's mother and wonders what Lily is processing from a cognitive standpoint.

Lily's cognitive focus is communicated in her ability to use gestures and vocalizations to make her needs known. Her ability to respond, request, and make choices about how she would like to engage in the environment with such control and interest suggests that Lily has created a level of understanding and organization about her surroundings.

The therapist's look through the lens of Lily's embodied experience ties the social-emotional and cognitive focus together. Careful analysis of her attempts to shift into a crawling position reveal that Lily cannot lift her pelvis up high enough to hold her legs under her hip sockets to create a perpendicular relationship to the floor. Her knees slide out to her sides and her belly slides to the floor. This physical component of her experience contributes to her tendency to stay in more stable still positions rather than freely exploring. Analysis of her motor ability and movement style communicates that Lily is more easily able to engage when upright; she is not physically reaching out into the world, nor does she emotionally initiate engagement.

New questions arise for the therapist. Why is Lily unable to support herself in a crawling position? Is there a lack of strength or coordination in her lower body or instability in her hip joint? Is this why she has tolerated being held so much? The therapist wonders whether Lily's predominant daily experiences of being held in her parents' arms or in a baby seat contribute to her lack of movement exploration. If not, why has she tolerated being held so much? Recognizing that Lily clearly finds comfort in being held, the therapist ponders whether the child has learned to rely on this physical closeness to receive emotional attention. This description and related questions are stimulated from a

Ways of Seeing therapist's single observation that attends to the nonverbal aspects of a child's actions. Although these questions cannot be answered from one observation, they give the therapist a starting point that provides an array of directions—from a social-emotional, physically embodied, and cognitive perspective—to pursue in the intervention of this child and her family.

Influence of Learning Styles

The salient point in adding a *Ways of Seeing* perception to the continuum of assessment, intervention, and education is first to become aware of how children reveal their experience through their nonverbal movement repertoire, and second to then think of how to use the elements of nonverbal expression to enhance, stimulate, activate, and develop interactions in a way that facilitates growth and communication. Numerous examples of how the *Ways of Seeing* approach works in an intervention setting have been discussed throughout this book. In this chapter the link between intervention and education is emphasized within the context of the understanding that many children have individual and particular learning styles. Acknowledgment of differences in how children learn is now a widely recognized factor in the intervention-education continuum. Identifying that not all children learn in the same way has led to the development of more diverse teaching strategies. Curricula are more individualized, to work with and build on each child's strengths, which in turn also supports children's growth in areas of less strength. Understanding how children learn provides a framework in which to think about how they process experience. (Although discussion of particular learning style differences and educational programs goes beyond the scope of this book, please see Gardner 1991, 1993a, 1993b; Levine, 2002 for more information.)

The *Ways of Seeing* approach includes an awareness of how nonverbal and sensory information interacts with a child's particular learning style. Supporting the principle of learning differences, the program draws on and honors each child's uniqueness. The educational piece of the program builds on a child's differences to create an adaptive learning program for him. (Examples of two complete *Ways of Seeing* approaches are provided in the case studies at the end of this chapter.) A child is supported to reach his potential in both the intervention and education aspects of the program by the concept of zones of proximal development (Vygotsky, 1978). Zones of proximal development refer to the expanded range of a child's ability to problem solve and respond to input at a higher developmental level. This is achieved through guidance and collaboration with adults and more able peers. The zone indicates the level of a child's potential. What a child is able to achieve with assistance indicates what he may be able to do independently in the future. In the *Ways of Seeing* approach, an adult acting as a support uses information obtained through nonverbal observation to engage a child in movement explorations in the therapeutic environment and to encourage behavioral explorations that facilitate improved learning and behavior in the classroom. As a student becomes more comfortable in the classroom setting, peers can take on the role of the adult to help a child integrate with the other children.

This is exemplified in the case of 3-year-old Xavier, discussed in Chapter 1. Xavier first encountered the *Ways of Seeing* approach in his integrative preschool. Diagnosed with failure to thrive, he had difficulty maintaining attention, participating in group activities, and forming relationships with his peers. He was very physically active, walked on his toes, and avoided activities that required him to sit and focus. The therapist worked with him in private sessions as well as in the classroom. Movement games were developed in private sessions that extended his attention while still respecting his need for action. These games included running in a large circle with the therapist, while each took turns changing some aspect of the run, such as speed, stopping and starting, hopping on two feet like a bunny rabbit, or side stepping. When group movement activities initially were conducted during circle time in the classroom, Xavier would not join the group. He would stand in a different part of the room, watching from afar, intermittently following the activities of the group. Observant of his presence, the therapist would add his movement contribution to the group without requiring him to actually join their circle. Once the group was over, the therapist, acting as the catalyst and trusting the relationship they had developed through individual sessions, created a small movement game for him and a peer who was interested in continuing a dance-play activity. Over time, their relationship grew, and with the support of his new friend and the therapist, Xavier began to join the group in a variety of circle-time activities.

Use of the Movement Signature Impressions Checklist as an Assessment Tool

The example above demonstrates how Xavier's nonverbal behaviors were analyzed, worked with individually, and then used to support his participation in the classroom. The continuum between assessment, intervention, and educational programming proposed in the *Ways of Seeing* approach does not eliminate the need for systematic nonverbal assessment of a child's abilities at any one point in an intervention. Even while advocating the need to support a child's potential growth during all interaction, there are times when a therapist needs to look clearly at a child's level of functioning. To accommodate this need, the MSI Checklist (see Appendix A) can be used as a designated assessment tool whenever a formal evaluation is necessary.

The general theoretical perspective used to determine the MSI Checklist guidelines was developed by creating a composite of select features of assessment techniques in the fields of early intervention and general education. The assessment criteria that most closely parallel the approach of the MSI Checklist are Zero To Three Performance Assessments (Meisels & Fenichel, 1996) and authentic assessments described by Darling-Hammond and colleagues (1995) and other professionals in the field of education (e.g., Gardner, 1991, 1993b).

Guidelines Underlying the Movement Signature Impressions Checklist

Ten guidelines create the overall tone of the MSI Checklist:

1. The assessments are to be based on an integrated dynamic developmental model, taking into account the context of a child's family and the child's emerging abilities and potential communicative acts apparent during supportive interactions.

2. The information about a child is always collected from multiple sources, with emphasis placed on the influential role of family members and significant others.

3. The focus is maintained on assessing a child's optimum core level of functioning, with the goal of discovering the child's capacities, potential, and challenges. This focus contrasts with the assessment practice of ascertaining a child's deficits in an isolated room with an unknown assessor, comparing results either to norm-referenced measurements that rank children numerically in comparison to a set of external standards, to criterion-referenced measurements that base scores on a specific performance level or degree of mastery in a particular domain or subject area with an independent set of standards, or to curriculum-based instruments that emphasize achievement of specific curriculum related criteria.

4. A child's own abilities should become the reference for continued achievement rather than comparison with other children in the class or predetermined norms. Qualitative criteria is valued more than quantitative criteria, taking into account a child's personality, general knowledge base, and unique skills.

5. A child is observed in spontaneous interactions even when "formal" MSI Checklist assessments are performed. Formal assessments and reassessments may occur as frequently as needed— a reassessment can occur impromptu when a specific aspect of a child's behavior (e.g., an advancement or question) suggests a more thorough investigation in addition to the scheduled reassessments that are arranged monthly; quarterly; or at the beginning, middle, and end of the year.

6. A planned assessment will use the people who are both familiar with and actively involved with a child.

7. A child is observed demonstrating what he can do. The elements of performance are based on activities that allow a child to act on the environment, solve problems, show higher order thinking, and encourage interactions with others; moreover, assessments rely on broad samplings of such behaviors rather than one scheduled performance.

8. The skills and abilities that are acknowledged and fostered have contextual relevance in a child's life and help prepare him for ways of interacting in the social world.

9. The opportunities for a child to engage in interactions and collaborative learning are encouraged.

10. A continuum is recognized to exist between assessment and intervention, and assessment and educational curriculum. The assessment becomes a means of informing, altering, and influencing continued development of specific elements and strategies of intervention and education, enabling these programs to be created with an emphasis on a child's specific needs and styles.

The Movement Signature Impressions Checklist as a Formal Assessment Tool

Using the MSI Checklist as a formal assessment tool is best done through analysis of a videotaped session with the participants. This enables therapists to repeatedly review in detail the specific qualities of each mover's style. Videotape can be viewed in fast motion or slow motion to further study a mover's nonverbal expressions. Multiple viewings of the videotape are essential to enable the qualitative elements to become lucid. Due to the level of detail and attention needed to do a formal nonverbal analysis, it is best to pick only one section of videotape to view and be analyzed at a time. This section should be between 5–20 minutes long and should include details of the events that precede and follow the behavior of particular interest. (Keeping the time code visible on the videotape facilitates accurate continuous review.) More specific details regarding the recommended procedure are described in Table 11.2.

QUALITATIVE NONVERBAL ASSESSMENT IN VARIED SETTINGS

A continuum between assessment, intervention, and educational programming occurs by using the nonverbal assessment process fluidly,

Table 11.2. Suggested procedure for analyzing videotaped sessions

1. Clear your mind of all movement information and interpretative material in order to view each mover objectively.
2. View the entire session once with the sound turned on, noting the sections from which you would like to make a detailed nonverbal analysis.
3. Select a section of tape you would like to analyze in more detail, noting the time code for each behavior to be analyzed.
4. View each tape section a minimum of three times following this three-part procedure:
   a. View the section with the volume turned off to enable complete concentration on the nonverbal qualitative elements, noting general nonverbal elements and the sequence of events.
   b. View the section with the volume turned off to analyze specific qualitative details using the MSI Checklist guidelines.
   c. View the section with the volume turned on to see how the verbal and vocal content may relate to the nonverbal observations.
5. When analyzing a parent–child or significant adult–child dyad, several additional steps are appropriate:
   a. Choose a section of tape in which the adult and child can be seen together and separately.
   b. Focusing on just one mover, view the tape following the steps in Step 4 to determine the individual's movement signature.
   c. Repeat this with the other mover.
   d. View the segment again, this time focusing on the dyad moving together to observe the interactional style of the adult and child. Use the interactional section of the MSI Checklist to guide your observations.

as both a formal tool and an informal way of looking at and interacting with a child and family. The *Ways of Seeing* therapist always looks to see how a child's nonverbal behaviors are communications or have the potential to communicate. As stated in the beginning of this chapter, nonverbal assessment through the *Ways of Seeing* method focuses on how a child's behaviors reveal the nature of the child's engagement and exchange with the surroundings—including the home, clinical, and educational settings. The *Ways of Seeing* approach has been developed so that both home and educational aspects of the program are used to inform clinical work, and a therapist can use clinical information to make recommendations for home and educational settings.

Assessments Should Include Information Regarding a Child's Home Setting

When possible, home visits are the preferred method of assessment for this setting because they enable a therapist to actually experience the home on a firsthand basis. Assessment in the home involves learning about the home environment in several ways. Through the process of self-observation described in Chapter 7, a therapist should be able to describe the experiences and stay attuned to his or her personal reactions while observing a child in the child's primary surroundings. It is also very useful to view how a child has mastered early developmental milestones and overall past history in the home by reviewing family videotapes, if they are available. Using the qualitative nonverbal movement analysis provided by the MSI Checklist when viewing family tapes can reveal the development of a family's unique dynamics. Looking at the qualitative way in which an infant accomplished movement milestones—lifting the head, rolling over, sitting up, crawling, pulling up to standing and walking—can provide insight into later developmental concerns. (See Chapter 4 for a discussion of the research of Teitelbaum et al., 1998, which studied the particular motor patterns of infants with ASD).

Finally, to obtain important information in regard to a child's home experience, a therapist should conduct interviews with the child's parents and other significant people through both verbal discussions and questionnaires of the prenatal and perinatal history. (See http://www.brookespublishing.com/dancing for an example of a birth history questionnaire.)

Assessment within the Clinical Setting

After a child has been recommended for intervention by parents, an allied practitioner, or a teacher, the assessment process typically begins in the clinical setting. Assessment initially occurs with a minimal amount of information about a child's background in order for a therapist to obtain a fresh view of the child and family.

The *Ways of Seeing* protocol consists of three sessions. The first two sessions are videotaped to enable a therapist to have the opportunity to review experiences with a child and family using the MSI Checklist without being biased by the reports and the observations of others. During the first and second sessions, the therapist follows the methods described in Chapter 8, following a child's lead. During these sessions the therapist is looking at how behavior may indicate a child's functional developmental level. While following a child's lead, a therapist will also attempt to create and initiate interactions that present information about the child's social, emotional, physical, cognitive, and communication developmental levels. Medical and school reports that the parents feel are important are provided at the end of the second session so that the therapist can review them before the third session. The third session is held with the parents alone to discuss the therapist's findings, to interview and answer questions from parents, and to set up a *Ways of Seeing* approach for intervention.

Assessments Can Also Include
Information from a Child's Educational Setting

It is helpful for an assessment to include specific nonverbal movement criteria (see Table 11.3) that are features of an educational environment if such information is available. A child's nonverbal performance during classroom observations is divided into three categories:

1. The child's use of space during specific activities
2. The child's body level awareness
3. The child's changes in nonverbal style during different classroom activities

Use of Space   Observations about a child's use of space note which parts of the room are most used by the child as well as how the child uses space during specific activities. The therapist might notice whether a child conducts her body differently in a group or circle time

Table 11.3. Nonverbal movement cues to look for in an educational setting

Space

How is space used during group activities or circle time?

How is space used during individual activities or deskwork?

Is the whole room used?

Is only part of a room used? Which part?

Are some areas used more than others? Why?

Body awareness

Describe eye contact and eye gaze.

What is the body boundary awareness of individual children?

- Between self and other
- Between self and objects
- When standing, sitting, and walking, describe the
  - Breath flow
  - Body-part coordination/gestures
  - Body-part mobility
  - Whole body movements and postures

Nonverbal style

How does child's nonverbal style change during

- Large whole-group activities
- Class lectures by the teacher
- Small-group activities
- Individual work (whether individual is active, alone at desk, or with others at a group table)
- Quiet time or study time
- Test taking
- Snack
- Free play

compared with individual tasks or deskwork tasks that demarcate private space. An example of this is the $3\frac{1}{2}$-year-old preschool child who is able to move independently through an obstacle course with great body control but loses her physical, mental, and social attention, and leaves the group when her class joins in a circle dance.

Body Level Awareness Here the body criteria of the MSI Checklist are applied to view how a child conducts himself when engaged in classroom activities that require him to be aware of other students and nearby objects. Is the child able to maintain his personal body boundaries and avoid bumping into other students? Can the child navigate through the classroom without bumping into desks, tables, or shelves? Does the child's body awareness and level of body activity change when standing, sitting, or walking? How are these behaviors observable in his breath flow, body-part coordination and gestures, and mobility of body parts and full body movements/postures? Does the child's eye contact, eye gaze, and visual focus change during different classroom activities?

Changes in Nonverbal Style   A therapist might also find it helpful to ascertain whether and how a child's nonverbal style changes during different classroom activities, including

- Large whole-group situations
- Teacher-led lectures
- Small-group tasks
- Active individual work that allows a child to move around freely
- Individual work at a separate desk or group table
- Quiet time/study time when a child is required to rest or look at books quietly
- Structured test-taking activities
- Snack time
- Free play

Each of these situations requires different attentional and body-awareness skills. Closely observing a child's nonverbal styles in each of these situations reveals which settings are most difficult and which best support the child. Moreover, an analysis of the particular elements that influence each setting may help a child's teacher determine how to match the child's strengths with the best possible learning environment.

In summary, the preferred way to develop a child's total *Ways of Seeing* approach is to use the child's behaviors as revealed through home-based, clinical, and educational observations and assessments. Two case studies provided at the end of this chapter demonstrate how this continuum from assessment to clinical intervention to educational programming occurs in the *Ways of Seeing* approach. The roles that home, clinical, and educational settings play in this continuum will be described next to clarify their use in the case studies that follow.

The Role of Each Setting

An overlapping relationship exists in the home, clinical, and educational settings. The foundational base of this relationship is the home. The home is the primary setting that initially forms and informs a young infant's life. Once a child is identified with special needs, the next step often becomes the clinical setting that defines the difficulties and treats the child within the context of the family. When a child is ready for an educational experience, the clinical setting can become the bridge between home and school, be it a self-contained special educational or an inclusive educational environment. The educational setting consists of a structured community that organizes a child's growing experiences outside of the home and expands them into the larger social world.

The key goals of an educational setting are academic and involve the shaping, expanding, and building of a child's cognitive abilities; however, learning actually occurs on many levels, crossing all areas of development. Due to the advent of programs such as infant and toddler child care, Early Head Start, and preschool, many young children are exposed to larger social group settings at very young ages. It is in these settings that a young child's special needs may first be identified due to the child's difficulties in adapting to the structures and routines of the center in comparison with the behaviors of the other children. Some programs, especially Early Head Start, can be seen as preeducational settings that focus on developing school-readiness skills. For many children, these settings are the first step toward socializing and education. The *Ways of Seeing* approach considers any program that aims to support children by strengthening their cognitive understandings of their surrounding world while providing a healthy social environment to be an educational setting.

All three milieus—home, clinical, and educational—should be compatible and continually involved in and informing a child's total program. This represents both an interdisciplinary and a transdisciplinary approach. It is interdisciplinary in that the intervention team, who work collaboratively, is made up of distinct individuals from each aspect of a child's total program. It becomes transdisciplinary as members of the team become educated about and apply what they learn from other members to their own specific experiences and roles with a child and family.

Home Environment   The role the home environment plays in the lives of infants and children is foundational to all other aspects of development. It is at home that children develop primary attachments with their families (both nuclear and extended) and with other significant people in their lives. The home is where social-emotional relationships originate. The quality of children's early and primary attachments to their caregivers and each family's overall dynamics will influence how children relate to others and how they fit into larger group dynamics later on, in school and other social settings. From the earliest moments of an infant's life, specific home-based environmental experiences begin to shape how the infant processes and comes to understand the surrounding world. These experiences can both provide opportunities for growth and expose a young child to environmental experiences that may interfere with or limit healthy development.

Clinical Setting   The role of the clinical setting in the *Ways of Seeing* approach is to explore a child's primary experiences and relationships to repair and enhance the child's ability to function in the home and other environments. It is only through learning about a child's home environment and relationships that the *Ways of Seeing* therapist can focus on the child's social-emotional development. Many therapists find it helpful to identify how the home influences a child's experience of outside environments. This knowledge can enable a therapist to create a relationship with the child and family that allows both to feel safe in a clinical setting. Once a child and a therapist are in such a relationship, the child can be supported in the clinical setting to express and explore past experiences, concerns, and developmental or organic challenges through child-centered activities. A therapist uses the clinical setting to create new experiences for a child to process and synthesize in ways that enhance emotional relating, develop new relationships, and support healthy functioning. In the *Ways of Seeing* model, the clinical setting also acts as a link between the home and the educational environments.

Educational Environment   The educational setting provides children with structure and teaches them organization while supporting their group socialization. It requires children to experience adaptation, modulation, and regulation of their entire physical, mental, and emotional systems. Children must adapt their internal structures to work within the external structures of school environments. Teachers provide them with external organization and structure through rules, routines, and group activities that necessitate social skill and cooperation. Ideally, children will adjust their internal structures, modifying and compromising their personal needs, desires, and focuses to stimulate and challenge their cognitive functioning. This requires them to have inner body regulation, impulse control, the ability to have extended attention, and emotional and physical modulation.

Two *Ways of Seeing* Case Studies

Eric

Recall the story of Eric, a $3\frac{1}{2}$-year-old child diagnosed with PDD, who was first discussed in Chapters 6 and 10.

Impressions Regarding Eric's Home Setting   The therapist gathered information about Eric's home through home visits, parent sessions, and live and videotaped analyses of the parent–child interactions during initial *Ways of Seeing* sessions. Chapter 10 describes how hard Eric's parents have worked to understand and accommodate Eric's behaviors. They have learned to read his nonverbal cues and adapted and adjusted the environment to create a world that feels comfortable to him. In the process they often feel controlled by him, creating an atmosphere that enables Eric to stay confined to his very narrow social existence and avoid interactions that involve mutual affective exchanges, eye contact, emotional understanding, and expressivity. Although his natural style is sweet, Eric becomes easily agitated and has full-blown tantrums when he is not understood due to his very limited vocabulary and processing difficulties. The *Ways of Seeing* therapist wants to support the deep commitment and understanding that Eric's parents have about their child, while helping them to develop ways to interact with him that will encourage increased social relatedness.

Eric's Experiences in a Clinical Setting   Chapter 6 offers a look at an early *Ways of Seeing* clinical session, outlining one of the first extended exchanges the therapist has with Eric while he is jumping on a small, individual trampoline. At home, Eric enjoys the rhythmic and deep sensory input he experiences while jumping. As he jumps with even-tempo Phrasing, he can become mesmerized by the perseverative quality that the repeated jumping action creates. In the movement play during the session, the therapist interrupts this monotonous rhythm and solitary play. While standing on the floor in front of Eric, holding him at the waist, she bends her knees in a bouncing rhythm that matches his jumping rhythm. Periodically she assists Eric to jump higher, breaking the monotonous rhythm by holding him far above her head and requesting his eye contact to continue this play. He thoroughly enjoys this added height and readily looks at her each time to communicate his desire to sustain their play together. It is a simple but profound gesture for Eric. In this moment, he learns that connecting to others through sustained eye contact has value. It opens an avenue in which to have his needs and wishes understood. Eric's mother is witness to this play, and through these demonstrations she learns how to encourage eye contact with Eric during her interactions with him at home.

Many other dance-play games are developed during Eric's *Ways of Seeing* sessions to support his need for full-body active input while requesting that he intermittently engage in playful exchanges with his mother and the therapist. Eric's seemingly random running through the room becomes a "high-five" hand-slapping game each time he and the therapist run past each other to meet in the middle. Soon Eric begins to anticipate this social exchange by slowing down and seeking the therapist's contact by extending his arm and hand and looking at her as she approaches. Both at home and in session, Eric demonstrates keen musicality. He listens with deep interest to the instruments, lyrics, tempo, rhythm, and feeling tone of the musicals he watches, intently reenacting the dancing steps he has learned by studying classic musical videos. This is initially a solitary activity he performs by himself. Thinking of him as a "musical learner," the therapist employs the music of these musicals as a key teaching tool to expand Eric's ability to relate. She uses his acute awareness of the rhythmic and qualitative changes in a musical score to help Eric engage with more affect and emotional connection.

About 2 months into sessions, Eric makes a major breakthrough in his ability to stay related. During this session, the therapist follows Eric's lead, mirroring his Irish step-dance stomping as he jumps on the trampoline to the strong rhythmic pulse of *Riverdance* music. When this beat changes to a languid, soft, yet heartfelt melody, Eric slows his actions down, and with the therapist's assistance, slowly melts onto the bed of the trampoline, lying on his back. The therapist holds his legs, gently swinging and rotating his body around as they gaze into each other's eyes. She then lifts Eric off of the trampoline, all the while maintaining eye contact with him. They continue their gaze as she scoops him into her arms, slowly swaying him closer and farther away from her face while moving him through the air—first high above her head, then at shoulder height, then slowly bending at her knees to hold him upside down. She varies the distance and position of his body to hers, while keeping him mobile (to help him stay attuned) in order to explore what particular spatial positions enable him to most comfortably keep his eyes focused.

This constant motion supports Eric's enjoyment and desire for mobility so that he stays engaged for an extended amount of time. Immediately, as the music again changes to a faster, more rhythmic pulse, Eric begins to take their dancing dialogue across the floor, repeating his step-dancing stomp and smiling broadly as the therapist follows suit. When the slow section of the song returns—the therapist had programmed the CD to repeat the song as the best means of supporting, without interrupting, Eric's potential to connect—Eric and the therapist find themselves in a small alcove in the room. The therapist takes Eric into her lap and begins to slowly rock and sway with him to the melody. Eric softens in her arms and gazes into her eyes. The therapist senses the moment acutely.

Witnessing: As I rock Eric, warmly embraced in my arms, I am immediately transported to those early days of holding my own infant son close, as we gazed into each other's eyes, soaking up the details of our faces. These moments felt timeless and all-encompassing; precious moments when the outer world seemed far away, for we were deep in our own safe world getting to know each other intimately just through our loving gaze.

Kinesthetic empathy: Seeing Eric, now 3½ years old, I wonder about the types of exchanges he had with his mother as an infant. Where have they gone inside of him? Such early affective exchanges seem not to have accumulated in the typical way, building on each other to develop a reservoir of emotional bonds with others. Rather, up until now he has avoided such engagement. But at this moment, through our dance-play he seems to have found the pleasure such connectedness can bring.

Objective: As the music begins to shift into a more active beat, I place Eric next to me on the floor. Still gazing into my eyes, he reaches his hand to touch my face. I follow suit and touch the same places on his face, softly labeling them. Together we clap our hands to the music. Eric seems to be relearning—or learning for the first time—the pure joy of sharing oneself with another. As the music swells, Eric gives me an excited look and stands up. Taking a Riverdance-*like pose, he begins to prance with distinct rhythm, across the room, looking over his shoulder to check that I am with him. Now our private little world opens up as our partner dance takes up the whole room. We are everywhere; traversing the space; gliding past each other; and making big, arcing pathways as we come together and separate. Though our dance takes in the whole space, this time we remain dancing partners, for our movements are in sync and our emotional connection is clear.*

Eric stays engaged with the therapist and his mother for more than 85% of this session. As the session continues, his mother joins in, taking the therapist's place during the slow sections of the music, engaging Eric in a waltz. It is a beautiful and memorable moment. Eric and his mother leave the session quite peacefully. His mother reports that during that whole afternoon, Eric was calm, composed, and very loving toward her.

Soon after, Eric is able to initiate such partner dancing by imitating parts of the musicals he so enjoys watching on video. Humming the tune "Shall We Dance" from *The King and I,* he approaches the therapist, placing his arms in the male partner waltzing position as if asking her to join in his dance. His facile melodic and visual memories of these musicals become the starting point for relating. They are used to initiate engagement and are then transformed to become spontaneous mutual exchanges by varying the movements to fit the moment-to-moment interactions.

This point is important to note: A child, especially along the PDD and autism spectrums, can get very caught up in repetitive actions by repeating them in a robotic manner, losing affective connection to his surroundings. In the *Ways of Seeing* method, a therapist uses these actions as a way to enter into a child's world but changes some qualitative aspect of the action to stimulate focus, attracting the child's attention to the here and now, drawing him out of his private self, and asking him to connect and respond to the immediate action at hand.

Eric's Experiences in an Educational Setting The next step in intervention is to help Eric's family find a preschool placement for him. Here the parents face a dilemma: His PCSE (Preschool Committee on Special Education) yearly conference strongly suggests that Eric be placed in a self-contained, special education setting that can provide many of the services he is currently receiving at home (ABA and speech) and in a clinical setting (OT). Although this is a wise economic solution, it does not meet Eric's specific needs. Eric's budding ability to relate only occurs in one-to-one settings that are not overstimulating or overcrowded. Equally significant, every special education program Eric's mother visits says either that there is no room for him in that program or that Eric is not ready for that program because of his lack of social awareness. His current level of relating cannot support a group setting that does not have a one-to-one aide. The *Ways of Seeing* therapist recommends providing a trained one-to-one aide in a small general preschool setting. The small class size will create a supportive and less busy setting with children who are typically developing who can provide strong role models for appropriate social engagement. Once Eric creates a relationship with his aide, she can act as a bridge between these children and Eric.

The parents find such a placement, and together with the therapist, they immediately begin training Nila the aide to learn how to read Eric's cues to support her developing relationship with him. Once Nila establishes a relationship with Eric, she can act as a liaison between Eric and his peers.

Early in the school year, the *Ways of Seeing* therapist visits the preschool and makes a videotape of the experience, which she later reviews with Eric's parents, Tanya and Everett, as well as with Nila. While at the preschool, the therapist demonstrates through activities and discussion how to encourage more social engagement with Eric and his peers. This school visit enables Eric and the therapist to put their work into immediate action.

I enter school with Eric and watch as he takes off his coat and is greeted by Nila. She immediately engages Eric in a lovely exchange using a stuffed bunny to sing to him. The bunny hops on different parts of his body as she labels them. Eric provides her with good eye contact and warm smiles, clearly delighted in this play. A classmate, Josh, looks on, gleefully commenting on the bunny play. A little while afterward, Josh leaves the room and begins to paint at the art table in a different room. Eric enters the painting area, lingering and looking around but not getting engaged in the art activities. Josh verbally acknowledges Eric's presence and asks if he is going to paint. Eric, seeming not to notice, begins to wander around the three rooms. Josh asks, "Where's Eric?" I jump in and say, "I don't know? Where do you think he is?" Josh responds, "Maybe he is playing Hide-and-Seek!" What a great idea! Leave it to the creative mind of a child to direct the intervention. Not wanting to miss this opportunity, I chime in: "Yes! He must be playing Hide-and-Seek. Let's go find him!" Josh is game immediately and begins to search for Eric, stopping for a moment to cover his eyes and say, " One, two, three. Ready or not, here I come!" as he runs off to look for Eric. With me close behind, Josh finds Eric standing in the center of the room alone with his back to Josh. Josh steps nearby, gleefully pointing and saying, "Here he is!" Eric barely looks at him and begins to wander away into yet another room. I take this as acknowledgment and enthusiastically say, "Oh! Yes! Josh found you! You found him, Josh! Oh! Where is he going now? Can you find him again?" Josh is deeply invested in our game. He covers his eyes right away and starts to count "One, two, ready or not, here I come." This time when he finds Eric, I ask him to look into Eric's eyes so that Eric can notice and acknowledge that Josh is there. Josh says, "I found you," as he looks directly at Eric. He then comes over to me and begins to talk about how he notices that Eric speaks differently.

Encouraged by the intervention the *Ways of Seeing* therapist makes at the school, Eric's teachers ask for more contact with her. Nila begins to attend *Ways of Seeing* sessions several times a month to continue to learn how to encourage Eric's social-emotional expressivity and to create a continual link between the school and the clinical setting. Nila is a great addition to the sessions. With Eric's mother Nila and the therapist together on his team, Eric now has his home, school, and clinical settings well represented. He learns about social turn taking as he dances and plays with each of them during each session. Throughout the sessions the therapist explains and demonstrates how she is encouraging Eric to maintain and extend social engagement. Nila brings these insights into the classroom on a daily basis.

The therapist's key point is to never miss an opportunity to turn Eric's solitary behaviors into a social interaction. This occurs by following Eric's lead and by joining in the activity he presents but turning it into a social contact. In one session, for example, Eric pulls out a brightly colored sheer flowing scarf hanging on the wall of the studio. He turns his back to the therapist and Nila and begins to run with it across the floor. Immediately, the therapist and Nila follow him, grasping a section of it as well. The three of them begin to float through the room together. The scarf extends their ability to connect as they work together to billow it up and down, forward and backward, and swaying side to side. Eric experiences the emotional satisfaction of teamwork and the physical sensation of modulating his actions as they work together to create the smooth flowing qualities of the scarf. Whenever Eric lets go of the scarf, Nila and the therapist float after him, draping the scarf over him as they scoop him up inside of it. With this simple prop, a gleeful game of running and capturing ensues, further extending Eric's ability to maintain social engagement. After the session, Nila takes this scarf with her to school and it becomes the highlight of a group activity, creating a bridge for Eric to interact with all of his classmates. Eight months into his *Ways of Seeing* intervention, Eric has made significant strides in his ability to relate to others.

Jerome

Jerome, 4½ years old, is recommended for a *Ways of Seeing* intervention by his OT Joan. Diagnosed with sensory integration dysfunction, and questions about ADHD, Jerome's issues include difficulties with impulse control, movement and motor planning, and social settings, along with problems with concentrating, maintaining attention to tasks, feeling calm, and modulating emotions including excitement and aggression. Most significantly, the OT is concerned about the emotional content of Jerome's behaviors during her sessions with him. As Jerome engages in typical sensory integration activities such as rolling in the ball pit and using his whole body to climb up the apparatus, his play images are extremely violent. When Jerome gets caught up in these images, his anger increases and he loses the ability to restrain himself. This undertone of aggression is displayed both physically and verbally, such as swinging his arms defensively when people get too close to him and punching the physioball while exclaiming, "Kill, asshole, idiot." At other times, when frustrated at a physical task such as one that requires fine motor skill, he directs this aggression toward himself, saying things like "I'm dumb," "I can't hold things," and "I'm stupid." The OT's objective in recommending dance movement psychotherapy is to provide Jerome with a safe environment that supports his physical expression and exploration of the emotional content of these behaviors, enabling the OT's sessions to focus on the more physical aspects of his sensory issues. The initial *Ways of Seeing* assessment occurs through discussions with the OT, Jerome's parents, a pre- and perinatal birth history report, a review of past medical and school reports, and the dance movement therapist's own observations and nonverbal movement analysis of Jerome during his early *Ways of Seeing* sessions.

Early Clinical Sessions   The OT's concerns are immediately apparent in Jerome's first two *Ways of Seeing* sessions. During his first session, Jerome presents himself both as a sensory seeking and sensory avoidant child. He enters the room as if his body is floating in space, moving from place to place on his toes, without stopping in any one place for very long. As the dance movement therapist approaches, Jerome suddenly dives under a pile of pillows. With the therapist providing deep pressure by rolling him under the pillows, Jerome becomes calm. As suggested by Joan, Jerome needs an enormous amount of proprioceptive feedback to feel his body in space. Jerome begins to respond back by attempting to push the pillows with his feet, but he is not able to direct them very well and misses. This frustrates Jerome, and his anger rises as he pulls his body out from under the pillow and runs around the room high up on his toes. When it is time to end the session, he has a difficult time slowing his body down to put on his shoes and socks. When his mother holds him to accomplish this task, he struggles to get free, flinging his body to and fro and yelling at her that she is "stupid."

Jerome enters the second session and begins to attack the large physioball with obvious aggression. After observing this for a minute, the dance movement therapist creates a structure for his actions by incorporating Jerome's movements into a game. First, she asks Jerome what he is doing to the balls. He replies that he is a knight fighting the bad guys. "Great!" she thinks, "He has a theme." She tells Jerome that this is a terrific story and now they must organize how the knight fights these guys with his trusty sword. While moving in one direction across the room, he must turn before he hits the ball, using slashing actions. When he returns, he must stab these "bad guys" using poking actions. In LMA, the slashing actions are performed using indirect, quick, and strong movement qualities, while the poking action requires direct, light, and quick actions. The therapist's intent is to see if Jerome has the capacity to modulate his feelings both physically and emotionally. Jerome incorporates these ideas immediately. Although he is not yet able to execute each individual action smoothly by using good rhythmic body control, the therapist's setting up of such a structure organizes the overall rhythmic flow of the game. Jerome's turns and slashes occur at regular intervals, creating a recurring accented beat that provides a pattern and focus to his play. It supports Jerome's enjoyment of the experience, and he does not get frustrated. Seeing this increased organization, the therapist introduces a new level of control. Now Jerome must hold his body still for the count of five, providing eye contact with the therapist as they count in unison. Jerome holds it together again! These pauses clearly juxtapose his slashing and poking movements so much that even Jerome takes note. He begins to exaggerate these mobile actions by adding more strength and quickness as he vocalizes his anger with gusto, "Take this!" "Take that!" "Aughhh! I got you, you bad guys!" and "You stupid idiot!"

His added verbalizations are encouraging. He is using language to support his play actions. Might these verbalizations provide another avenue into Jerome's internal experience? The therapist keeps up with Jerome, running side by side, both narrating and verbally processing his actions enthusiastically. "Yes! You got those bad guys! Oh! You are strong! You are angry!" The next time Jerome pauses for the count of five, the therapist, pausing beside him, asks him what makes him angry. During each pause, he begins to share his feelings. Through the continuation of this dance-play, Jerome speaks about his anger at his mother, himself, and his body for not doing what he wants and feels he needs to do. For a 4-year-old, Jerome demonstrates keen intrapersonal awareness and strong verbal processing skills, using language to express his inner thoughts quite clearly. Jerome's intrapersonal awareness is marked by an inwardly directed focus. This ability will enable Jerome to have conscious access to the range of his feelings, affect, and emotions, and these skills will become key tools during the intervention process. Through these abilities the therapist will help Jerome discriminate between his feelings both physically and emotionally, using language to label and reference them, leading to personal understandings that guide his behavior.

The last 15 minutes of the session following this dance-play are devoted to relaxation. Using three large pillows, Jerome constructs a "house" in a corner of the room. He settles in, making his body small, and the therapist covers him with a soft, sheer scarf. He sits quietly, hugging his body close. At some point, he begins to press on the scarf as if pushing out. The therapist wonders about his birth experience and his need for deep proprioceptive input. She provides strong tactile input, pressing on his torso as he triumphantly pushes out and into her arms. Bringing closure to the session, she lifts him up and brings him over to his mother. She receives him with joy, and everyone helps him to put his shoes and socks on.

Jerome's Parents' Perspectives   In a private separate session, Kelly, Jerome's mother, shares her concerns about Jerome. At home Jerome frequently becomes out of control using aggressive and bad language as he talks back to her. He has been a difficult child since his birth. Kelly's answers to the pre- and perinatal birth history report administered by the therapist reveal that Jerome's birth experience was difficult. Due to fetal distress and a 27-hour labor with medication intervention, a caesarian section was performed. Jerome spent 2 days under the bright yellow lights used to treat jaundice before coming home. Although he was alert and had good eye contact, Kelly reports that he was "difficult to comfort and screamed for hours." As a breast-feeding mother, Kelly had to eliminate many foods from her diet because it was clear they were troubling Jerome's digestion. Jerome was difficult to put to sleep, and he did not like car rides or the stroller. As he grew, he became very affectionate and social, but he did seem to get overstimulated in group situations, especially those with too much sensory experience. Kelly recalls a music class she attended with Jerome when he was 2 years old, in which he went from holding her hands and dancing to suddenly becoming very scared as his excitement increased.

By this age Jerome seemed sensitive to sunlight and his clothing. He had difficulty transitioning out of the tub and getting his fingernails cut. When he got excited, he flapped his hands and toe walked. When in one-to-one or small-group settings with fewer than three children, Jerome was very talkative. But when in a larger group, such as in his preschool setting, Jerome's difficulties became most apparent. He would shut down and withdraw, not participate, and get defensive, lifting his arms up in protest if anyone came close. He was placed in a special education preschool. The preschool's supportive environment helped him to a degree, but his basic difficulties remained. As he became older, he began to express his concerns verbally through both fears and anger. He spoke about being bad, bad guys, and wanting to kill. He was afraid of the dark, doing things wrong, and his mother and father's dying.

As Kelly shares this information, she speaks about how difficult it has been to parent Jerome. There are many times when she does not know what to do or how to support his needs. Although she wants to be understanding, some of his behaviors are so difficult that she also finds herself reprimanding him. This causes problems with David, Jerome's father, who has a very different parenting style. In a separate session, David speaks about how he believes that Jerome is very much like him. He can relate to Jerome's behaviors and takes a less directive approach than his wife when engaged with his son. Due to his identification with Jerome, David feels that when Kelly is reprimanding Jerome, she is also criticizing him. These discussions demonstrate a family dynamic that must be considered when working with Jerome.

Clinical Goals for Jerome   The goals of intervention are clear yet complex. Jerome's difficult emotional reactions have to become separated from his physical actions so that he can engage in his surroundings with less defensiveness. Jerome's more physically based issues—sensory integration dysfunction and lack of body control (along the spectrum of hyperactivity)—directly feed his aggression, fears, and low self-esteem, and must be addressed. These emotional feelings so evident in the quality of his current movement style need to be explored within the context of the therapeutic environment, enabling his feelings to be listened and responded to. The goal is to expand his experiential movement vocabulary, helping to increase body awareness and control, while simultaneously providing a safe place to explore the depth of his embodied emotional experiences. Jerome's strong verbal skills and intrapersonal intelligence style will support this approach. The first task to accomplish this is to guide Jerome to express his feelings verbally through activities that are physically organizing and modulating. As has been described, such activities include sequencing movements together and matching these actions to specific emotions. The therapist includes experiences that physically calm and center Jerome's body, imbedded in and between these sequencing and matching activities. The therapist also provides Jerome with literal experiences of emotional and physical control when she creates dance-play games that cause Jerome to spontaneously pause and contemplate his feelings within the midst of these more active and aggressive actions. Such accumulating experiences build a new repertoire that he can draw on to support his developing emotional and bodily sense of control.

Home Goals for Jerome   The therapist recognizes that it is essential to pay attention to Jerome's parents as well. David's integrity must be preserved while Kelly's concerns are acknowledged. David needs to be educated about his son's struggles in a way that does not criticize David or his parenting style. Kelly needs support for her feelings of frustration, acknowledgement for her devotion in helping her son, and assistance in finding additional ways to work with him. She and Jerome also need to explore the tension in their relationship.

The Plan of Intervention   The intervention plan devised by the therapist is designed with several layers. Initially, Jerome participates alone in individual sessions once a week to enable him to freely express his aggressive feelings without being concerned about his mother's feelings. Both parents are also seen separately on an as-needed basis to enable their needs and parenting styles to be addressed individually. After a few months, Jerome's mother is brought into her son's sessions, during which time they reconstruct Jerome's early infancy period, discussing and creating new ways to experience and repair the discord that occurred at that time. Later, Jerome and his mother participate in the first half of the session together to discuss current events, and Jerome attends the second half of the session alone to work on physical skill building.

Jerome's Clinical Sessions   The combative dance-play between Jerome and the "bad guys" ball juxtaposed with his hiding in a contained space continues to grow during his early private sessions with the therapist. Over the first 2 months of intervention, Jerome appears to relish expressing his aggressive feelings, embellishing his angry language with profanity and impaling images that are quite gruesome. It is through these very images that he has a breakthrough in one particular session.

Objective: Jerome enters today and immediately runs over to the balls, holding his body stiff as he jumps up and down on his toes. "I'm going to kill you, stupid bad guys, real bad! Just you see!" "Oh! You have some fighting feelings today," I say. Jerome quickly begins to slash and poke at the ball, in an accented Phrasing rhythm. Soon he is in quite a groove, moving back and forth across the room as if he is on a runway. At the end of the room is an arched floor-to-ceiling window. This window intrigues Jerome. Looking out from this second floor window, he sees a quiet street with a few cars and occasional neighborhood children and adults walking by. Across the narrow street is a small brick building with a flower garden. Beyond this quaint setting through the treetops are the majestic Storm King Mountain and the Hudson River. The sun is setting, and the sky is filled with the jewel-toned colors that were made popular years ago by the famous Hudson River painters. Curiously, this tranquil setting provokes further thoughts of violence for Jerome. "Oh! I'm going to push you bad guys out this window, and it will be so funny when you crash on those people outside and kill them!" he announces with a stilted laugh, slowing down his body as he looks at me from the corner of his eye.

Witnessing: This statement is chilling. Up until now his images of destruction were directed at imaginary figures. Does he really think it would be funny to hurt innocent people just happening to be passing by? How developed is his interpersonal social consciousness? His body actions and peripheral eye gaze tell me he might be questioning my reaction to this statement. I must ask him to think about what he just said.

Objective: "Jerome?" He pauses, as he encloses his body, making himself smaller as he looks at me. "Do you really think it would be funny to kill those people outside?" He pauses, replying slowly, "No." "How would you feel if you did kill them?" I ask. "Bad," he says softly, holding his body tensely, yet with his chest passively concave. "I am bad already," he says looking away and suddenly jerking his arm free from his hold as if to swing at something. "Oh, you feel like you are bad," I say quietly. "Yeah! I can't do anything. My body is stupid," he spits out. I respond, "I understand. Sometimes it feels bad in your body. It doesn't always do what you want it to do. And that makes you feel bad and this makes you have angry feelings too." He looks up at me with a softened expression and murmurs, "Yeah."

This session seems to have opened a door for Jerome. This dance-play game becomes a forum for him to not only discuss his overall feeling of inadequacy but also to report his current out-of-control thoughts and feelings as well.

Three months into intervention, amidst Jerome's hitting, slashing, and poking at the bad guy ball with a streamer, the therapist adds another body controlling instruction to his play: He has to stamp his feet rather than toe walk as he advances on his opponent. This is difficult for Jerome. Again he describes how his body doesn't work for him. He sits on the floor with the therapist and practices using his feet to push against her hands with strength and direct action. He clearly does not like this, but he does it anyway. He begins to tell the therapist that today he got so angry at a little girl in his class that he got very close to hitting her. He demonstrates the hit. He speaks about the feeling of hating and wanting to kill because he is bad. Having a body that does not seem to work properly makes him bad, causing him to feel inadequate. Suddenly he crawls over to the corner of the room and hides. Might he be hiding from his aggressive thoughts? The therapist constructs a way for Jerome to physically feel his body behaving with control. Using a bell, drum, and rain stick, she instructs Jerome to maintain stillness when he hears the bell tone; to come out quickly when he hears the drum; and to use slow, quiet actions to emerge during the rain stick sounds. Each action represents a different body state. He embodies each quality quite successfully. These different movement qualities evoke different emotional states in Jerome: calm, aggressive, and active yet controlled. He crawls over to the therapist and curls up on her lap. He says he wants to be a baby again. He pretends to drink milk while in her arms. The therapist pats him on his back, matching his oral sucking rhythm. Jerome is leading them into his deepest earliest memories of his troubled infancy. It is time now to bring his mother into Jerome's sessions.

Jerome's Mother Joins the Sessions   Jerome's mother's presence in the *Ways of Seeing* sessions brings their home life into the therapeutic environment. It enables Jerome to explore his youngest experiences with his primary attachment figure—his mother. This is important for both Kelly and Jerome. The retelling through embodied experience provides an opportunity for Jerome and his mother to reenact those early events, creating new alternative outcomes. Jerome's acquired developmental skills include his increased ability to attend, to control his body, and to use language to describe his experience. The depth of his intrapersonal awareness and his growing interpersonal social thinking inform these new experiences with his mother. These revisions serve to repair the misunderstandings and miscommunications of his early life events. The reexperiencing of these early events through reenactment will enable a retelling with revisions, repairing and healing the primary attachment wounds. As Jerome's mother cradles her boy in her arms like an infant, she shares with true emotion her feelings of despair in not knowing how to comfort her much-loved child. Jerome, in turn, describes through words and actions how difficult it was to be so sensorially disorganized and sensitive. He demonstrates his experiences: his jerky and uncoordinated actions, his aversion to molding into his mother and providing eye contact, and his inability to crawl with fluid, rhythmic coordination. Together during their dance-play, they experiment with new ways to hold Jerome. Their physical and verbal negotiations help to further desensitize Jerome's defensive aversions to contact, both emotionally and bodily. Jerome and Kelly take this "baby-game" dance-play home. It is defined and organized very specifically, relating to the therapeutic session as a way to help Jerome with his feelings. It is structured like this to keep it from becoming a regressive behavior that Jerome slips into when he is having difficulty or is seeking attention. Their home experience becomes a very significant part of intervention, creating a link between home and the clinical setting. In both settings the mother and son begin to rewrite history. This time Jerome practices tolerating tactile stimulation and learns through the help of the *Ways of Seeing* therapist to move with smoother, more fluid, limb–torso coordination. As he feels more comfortable in his body and more acceptable to his mother, Jerome begins to desire other social interactions. His behaviors become more appropriate, and his dance-plays begin to include imaginary friends.

Educational Goals for Jerome   In September, Jerome enters a typical public school kindergarten. The *Ways of Seeing* therapist arranges to do a school visit within the first few weeks, followed by a team meeting with all the teachers involved in Jerome's program. There are 10 adults at the meeting, including Jerome's mother, the main teacher, school psychologist, school-based OT, gym teacher, and special education chairperson. This school is very committed to integrating children of all abilities. Jerome is given a full-time aide to support him in the highly organized classroom setting. Based on her own observations, along with reports and discussions with Jerome's teachers, the *Ways of Seeing* therapist writes a plan to support Jerome's class-room learning experience. See the School Intervention Plan for Jerome at http://www.brookespublishing.com/dancing.

Home–School–Clinical Continuum The school adapts these suggestions and in addition Jerome's parents, under the guidance of Joan the OT, create a sensory motor room in their home. Jerome does a minimum of 30 minutes of deep pressure physical activity before school each morning. The baby game continues to be a theme both at home and during private sessions throughout the next year. In session, the baby game and the combative dance-play ball game provide a safe structure that Jerome uses to express his aggression, fears, and concerns. In conversations stimulated by these games, Jerome de-scribes how his sensitivities to touch, light, and too much activity cause him to excessively cry and want to hide. These activities and discussions now take up approximately 20–30 minutes of the hour-long sessions.

Jerome's *Ways of Seeing* sessions now also begin to help the boy develop his strengths. He begins to focus more on activities that increase his sense of body control. His very creative mind supports elaborate drawings of swords, monsters, and intricate bug creatures that develop his fine motor skills. Jerome enjoys recorded singing movement games that require him to listen to the words and tune, moving different parts of his body in rhythmic coordination to the music. As he begins to feel more in control physically, he begins to speak more about his aggressive feelings.

Aggression as an Embodiment of Feelings At age 6, a year and a half into intervention, Jerome talks about wanting be a "baby in dis-guise as an adult to buy weapons to hurt everything." He discusses how he wants to scare people because he used to be so scared as a baby. The therapist speaks about his need to feel powerful and strong. Together they create more dance-play games to help him feel physi-cally competent. Such activities include dodge ball and obstacle courses that require him to jump with precision using varying heights and dis-tances, as well as to crawl, swing, and climb using a variety of tempos. These activities improve articulation and coordination; use his muscles actively to weight shift, balance, and align his body; and explore full body direction and level changes. The obstacle courses, designed each week by Jerome and the therapist, are especially effective in helping Jerome learn how to physically modulate his extreme risk-taking behavior.

As they create a new course each week, the therapist and Jerome discuss proper ways to execute specific actions, adding safety elements such as places to pause while counting to six, to make sure that Jerome's body is poised and ready for the next move. This is especially helpful for moves that have a high jump or a big swing and require a strong, solid, "sticking" landing—as opposed to falling on the ground limply. Each session ends with a relaxation exercise.

In June, at the end of kindergarten, Jerome enters the session stating that he just wants to talk. He has had an especially difficult week culminating with hitting his mother during a school outing when it was time to go. The conversation begins with him noting his feelings of being stupid and bad, quickly moving to his feelings of guilt about his behaviors with his mother. Guilt is defined and linked to hitting himself after he hit his mother. Jerome, his mother, and the therapist discuss the importance and appropriateness of his guilty reaction, separating it from the more destructive reactions that followed—anger, pain, and aggressive negative thoughts about self, resulting in his physically attacking and punishing himself. The theme of sharing difficult feelings rather than acting them out is revisited. With his mother and the therapist, Jerome is able to list his strengths, including his empathic sense, evidenced early in the intervention during the bad guy combative game when Jerome wanted to crash the ball onto the people outside. The therapist shares that Jerome's ability to acknowledge, in the midst of his angry play, the pain of hurting someone demonstrates a boy who is very caring inside and just needs help to learn how to work through his angry, frustrated feelings. Jerome participates fully in this discussion and seems markedly relieved. Jerome's intra- and interpersonal skills continue to develop, with language being a strong tool.

The Home–School–Clinical Continuum Continues   Conversations between home, school, and therapist continue during Jerome's next year in first grade, through school visits and phone and written contact. With his school-based OT, he designs a My Input Book, describing in detail the activities he has created with his dance movement psychotherapist and his OT that help him stay focused and regain his focus during classroom activities. Improving Jerome's physical strength and control and developing his emotional understandings dominate individual *Ways of Seeing* sessions. His sessions are now structured so that he and his mother use the first half hour of the session to discuss events of the week; Jerome uses the second half hour to work on organized physical skill-building activities based on gymnastics tricks. The following session notes written in the early winter exemplify these sessions:

Great day today! During our initial talk time, Jerome is able to sit with his body relatively still, only adjusting his legs from cross-legged to straight rather than needing to play with the ball, squirm, move, jump around the room using lots of space, or get deep pressure input from me and Mom. He reports that he has had 2 good weeks in school. Mom later tells me that his student aide hasn't even been there this week due to illness. Jerome tells me he is now like the other kids, saying, "Now I am human." When I ask him to explain this further he says, "Well, it's not that I wasn't human . . . it's hard to explain . . . . " I ask if he meant that his behavior was more like the other children now that he was able to be in better control of his body and sit with them without drawing attention to himself. "Yes! That's it!" he exclaims. Jerome is able to maintain this good behavior throughout our session, staying completely in control of his body movements, and is able to demonstrate fine listening skills and good conduct. He shows me some new moves he has been playing with on his bar at home including skin-the-cat, and moose shadow, which he performs by inverting his body and putting his legs through his arms. I marvel at how strong and in control of his muscles he is becoming. Next he wants to create an obstacle course with the pillows, scarves, and streamers. He makes a very complicated pattern that requires him to jump, stretch, crawl, slide, and balance through different levels of space. He demonstrates terrific motor planning skills, and I marvel at them in reference to the trouble he used to have when he was a "little kid." He keeps making the course more and more challenging, adding barriers he has to move around and "alligators" (streamers) he cannot touch. If he does touch them, he has to stay still for 29 counts, which equals 29 days. He does this with great eye contact and body control. If he moves during our counting, he starts again.

A key element we include to facilitate his success is to let him adjust and get into a comfortable position before I start the counting. He often chooses a cross-legged or enclosed position to help himself. This is terrific, and resembles the relaxation/calming down poses he has been working on here and in school with his OT to help when he needs input in class. (He now has 23 pages in his My Input Book.) I also note the calm rhythm of the whole session with no accelerated movement. Even during the ending transition, when we have to abruptly move more quickly because we have waited for Mom to come to see his obstacle course, he does not need as much direction to keep on task.

He did accelerate a bit, running around the room with quick darting actions and attempts to bounce and throw the ball, but he is able to let us guide him back on task with minimal resistance. ⌒

Conclusion of Jerome's *Ways of Seeing* Intervention

As Jerome's physical abilities improve along with his deep emotional insights and cognitive understandings, he becomes ready to join an athletic class. He successfully attends a local gymnastics school. The physical nature of his combined therapeutic and home programs has truly built up his muscular strength. Over time, Jerome adds soccer, baseball, and hip hop lessons to his growing athletic activities. After 3½ years of *Ways of Seeing* sessions, Jerome has learned to discriminate his feelings both physically and emotionally. He also uses language to label and reference his feelings, leading to personal understandings that guide his behavior. Having successfully completed the goals of intervention, Jerome is ready to move on. To support Jerome's continued emotional growth and school participation, the *Ways of Seeing* therapist helps Jerome through his transition and adjustment to a verbal therapist specializing in working with children with sensory integration issues.

Summary

An individual's perception of the world is dependent on how that person physically engages in the surroundings. By watching how a child physically engages in the world through his behaviors, much can be learned about how he perceives his surroundings. This is the communication that the *Ways of Seeing* approach describes as the dance of engagement, the dancing dialogue. The *Ways of Seeing* approach strives to discover the nature of a child's participation in the communicative exchange between self and the environment by paying close attention to the details of the child's nonverbal behaviors.

This chapter links nonverbal assessment to intervention and educational programming through the use of the information found in Table 11.1 that supplements the MSI Checklist to enable an observer to describe the nonverbal elements of a child's behavior. The information obtained can be used in an intervention to support a child's growth in home, clinical, and educational settings. The nonverbal information gathered from the assessment is organized within three categories: social-emotional, embodied experience, and cognitive. The *Ways of Seeing* strategy uses the information gleaned from a therapist's observations of a child's nonverbal behavior to create an environment and experience of comfort and understanding for the child. The case studies in this chapter demonstrate how this nonverbal approach can support children's growth. Chapter 12 will detail how a nonverbal focus can support children in the classroom.

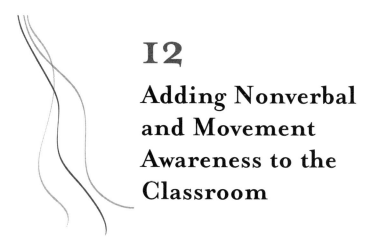

12

Adding Nonverbal and Movement Awareness to the Classroom

Everyday I count wasted in which there has been no dancing.

F. Nietzsche (1844–1900)

Chapter 11 discussed how to use observations of nonverbal behavior to gather information about individual children and apply this information in an intervention or classroom setting. This chapter will take this discussion deeper into the classroom setting to provide ways to incorporate nonverbal understanding into group dance activities and everyday classroom environments. Why and how movement explorations facilitate all developmental domains will be highlighted. The final section of this chapter will discuss how to analyze the elements of an overall curriculum to create a rhythm and flow that supports each child's learning style.

BENEFITS FOR THE CLASSROOM ENVIRONMENT

An awareness of the nonverbal elements of expression and interaction is useful in a classroom environment, both for individual children and the whole group. Having an understanding of nonverbal behavior in mind while teaching is helpful in several ways. Including group dance activities within the curriculum supports children's total development, enables a release of their accumulated restless energy, and facilitates their transitions through the daily classroom program.

Early childhood classroom curricula in many American preschools and elementary schools are becoming increasingly structured. With the recent strong emphasis on academic achievement and national and statewide testing at the elementary level, teachers at the early childhood level are being asked to strengthen their academic curriculum. This has created a shift away from the focus on the developmentally appropriate curriculum of the 1970s, 1980s, and even 1990s, which was based on Piaget's understandings of cognitive development. During this time children were encouraged to explore a great variety of materials, linking the arts and sciences to support learning through physical engagement with their surroundings. Academically oriented activities might have included prereading and writing—such as letter recognition and inventive writing—and math skills with nominal (using a number by its name) and ordinal (ordering things based on their quantitative differences) numbering. In recent years this emphasis has changed away from exploratory activities so that more stress is now directed toward academically focused activities that require higher levels of thinking and more focused attention spans. Piaget (1970) calls this the *concrete operations stage*, which generally occurs when children are 6 or 7 years old, and they begin to construct and work with concepts and more complex symbolic representations. It is this type of understanding that facilitates reading and writing acquisition.

The ability to read and write is a complex skill that has many components (Levine, 2002). The mechanisms of reading include the cognitive ability to decipher sounds auditorially, translate these sounds into symbolic representations, and then identify the sounds visually with abstract letter clusters that form words. The requirements of writing include three dimensions: the technical aspects of translating language into the written word, vocabulary, and creative ability. The technical aspects of translating language into the written word include two elements. The first is graphomotor skills, encompassing the physical aspects of forming letters and the production of writing: spelling, punctuation, capitalization, spatial organization of words on a page and letters into words, and the linguistic organization of sentences and paragraphs. The second element is the ability to organize words into sentences, ideas into paragraphs, and paragraphs into a complete concept or story. The vocabulary aspect of writing entails the quantity and quality of word usage available to a child. How a child is able to formulate, express, and develop her ideas reflects her creative abilities. Although having creative ideas is the first step, being able to write these ideas down requires a complex interplay of three elements: vocabulary, technical skills, and creative thought. In the early elementary school years, children typically do not have all of these faculties functioning at the same levels.

Despite this, an increasing number of schools (and parents) have begun to focus on early reading and writing abilities as the key elements of early childhood curriculum. Free play and recess times are being cut short or eliminated in the struggle to include more academically oriented activities in the daily schedule. This places children in more sedentary activities. Children are being asked to sit at tables and desks or to look at computer screens for extended periods of time, demands that require them to have great physical control over their bodies. This can present quite a problem for a young child who is new to a school environment and not yet ready to be in such control. As noted by Dr. David Elkind in his now classic book *The Hurried Child,* the process of learning about the world of things, including their various properties, is a "time-consuming and intense process that cannot be hurried." Elkind comments further that anxious parents, driven by an increasingly competitive economy, fuel the increased pressure toward early academic training.

Introducing creative movement activities into an early childhood classroom curriculum can simultaneously provide avenues to strengthen children's cognitive learning while still maintaining developmentally appropriate practices. It is a way to bring academic pressures and realistic abilities of young children back into balance. Creative dance facilitates active engagement with the environment through activities that enable children to explore their bodies moving in space. Dance also assists children to gain increased body awareness and control; auditory and visual organization; and social, emotional, communicative, and physical development. Through movement and dance, children play with sequencing, focusing and attending; following instructions; maintaining perceptual, auditory, and motor organization; and creating a sense of balance and internal regulation. All of these skills support cognitive understanding. The self-expressive aspects specific to creative dance allow children to stimulate their own creative instincts, thus honoring and encouraging their personal input.

Although the ideal solution would be to add a specific creative dance time into the curriculum, it is not always feasible in all school districts. By understanding the elements involved in a creative dance program, however, teachers can learn how to include nonverbal movement-oriented elements within everyday school activities. Teachers can also apply such understanding to organizing the overall classroom schedule.

Dance Enrichment

It is important to make a distinction between movement and dance activities designed to enrich the classroom experience and those designed from a psychotherapeutic perspective, such as the *Ways of Seeing* approach. Dance enrichment supports the use of dance for the pleasure and joy of moving, exercising, learning dance skills, increasing body awareness, and improving coordination and overall physical development. It is a natural assumption that the active use of the body will support physical development. An added benefit to a creative approach to a dance and movement-oriented program is a child's ability to review and relearn in a playful manner important physical developmental stages that may have been missed or rushed through at an earlier age.

A recent phenomenon (discussed in Chapter 3) is that many babies are skipping the crawling stage. Some speculate that the cause may be related to infants' spending less time on their bellies a result of the medical recommendation that infants sleep on their backs to avoid sudden infant death syndrome; another factor may be the increased time infants spend in supportive apparatus such as car seats, rockers, swings, walkers, and stationary entertainment centers during the stage of physical development when they need to experience their world by physically acting on it. This decrease in physical exploration through crawling has been associated with numerous weaknesses in development, including poor upper body to lower body coordination; poor hand, wrist, and shoulder stability; and poor visual-motor perception. It has been further speculated that such weaknesses may contribute to graphomotor problems and issues in executive functioning.

Graphomotor difficulties become apparent in the conceptual and physical organization of thoughts into the written word. This encompasses many aspects of writing, including the physical task of forming letters correctly; placement and spacing of letters into words and words onto the page; spelling; the ability to accurately apply punctuation; and the linguistic organization of sentences and paragraphs. Executive functions are the levels of cognitive functioning corresponding to graphomotor abilities, such as organization, mental manipulation, planning, sense of time, sequencing, capacity to anticipate, and the ability to maintain sustained attention.

Dance Enrichment in the Classroom: One Example

The sequences, patterns, and rhythms of dance naturally support cognitive development and visual motor perception. Group dance experiences also encourage socialization and self-expression. The creative dance approach enables these skills to be developed playfully through each child's imagination. A teacher can structure a dance activity by giving children certain parameters that they must move within while encouraging them to use their imaginations.

For example, children can be sea creatures who are on a journey into the depths of the ocean. With the accompaniment of appropriate music, they must first "swim," in whatever means possible, through the designated dance area, never allowing their stomachs to leave the ground. This will require them to use their stomachs, arms, shoulders, and legs in coordination as they navigate through the "sea" of other children. This type of activity can help children to acquire awareness of their bodies moving through space while maintaining clear body boundaries in relation to other children. When the children get to the center of the ocean, the teacher can elaborate the story even further by telling them that they have discovered a shipwreck with openings into which they can climb. Children can describe the type of opening they found and the distinctive way they created to gain entry. Once the experience is tried with the whole group, volunteers can demonstrate personal stories through solo dances that portray how they remember and sequence the whole story.

This aspect of the class can be very informative to an observant teacher. The level of detail, the order in which each movement is sequenced, how each action is executed, and what personal imaginings each child adds will provide pertinent information about the child's physical skills, emotional expressivity, and cognitive processing. This information—which portrays how a child perceives and interacts with the social world—can assist a teacher's ability to ascertain each student's unique learning style and to design appropriate activities for specific students. The *Ways of Seeing* approach emphasizes this aspect of the creative experience.

The *Ways of Seeing* Therapeutic Focus

The *Ways of Seeing* approach continually links physical and cognitive skill development with emotional, social, and communicative functioning. Movement activities have an additional function that not only supports physical skill development but also assists communication, social-emotional, and cognitive development as well. This process starts at the beginning of life. Right away, an infant's movements function as communication and provide interactional exchange and regulation between the infant and significant caregivers. As discussed in Chapter 2, an infant's movements are cues to how he is experiencing his surroundings and how he is using his internal system to regulate his external environment. In return, his attuned significant caregivers respond to these cues by both adapting and contributing their own unique behavioral styles to the infant's actions. Much of this non-verbal exchange takes place without conscious awareness. Infancy researchers looking at the role of communication and language acquisition are finding links with sensorimotor development. It is now thought that a continuum exists between the nonverbal movement-oriented experiences and the formation of a symbolic understanding that is necessary for both the development of language and the ability to form strong emotional and social relationships (known as *attachment* in the field of psychology) to others (Appelman, 2000; Bucci, 1994).

An infant's early sensorimotor experiences provide information about self and other, influencing how the child will organize and understand the social-emotional world of relating. Physically experienced interactions are received, processed, and stored first on a visceral, sensory level. As stated by Appelman (2000), this level of understanding is presymbolic and acts as a building block to later symbolic formations that use language as the symbolic medium. The nonverbal movement-oriented experiences and exchanges that initially occur before the acquisition of language mark the beginning of symbolic ideation. This concept is significant for learning because the ability to use symbols requires a higher level of cognitive functioning for all levels of academic understanding. Furthermore, a child's emotional and social states and abilities also can greatly affect the child's capacity to learn.

The *Ways of Seeing* perspective appreciates the integral role movement experiences play in overall development. A *Ways of Seeing* dance movement class encompasses the same dance principles carried out in a dance enrichment program, but puts specific emphasis on supporting each child's own self-expression. In the *Ways of Seeing* approach, breath and body awareness, movement, dance, and rhythmic activities are regarded as the tools of practice that support social, emotional, and communicative development. All movements are regarded as potential expressions and communications and should be responded to as such by teachers during the classroom group experience. As has been stated throughout this book, people have their own individual nonverbal movement signatures that are composed of unique combinations of movement qualities. During group *Ways of Seeing* dance activities, children are encouraged to use their unique movement vocabulary to express their feelings and to learn how to observe and understand their classmates' movement expressions. Specific activities are designed to have the children try on the movements of their classmates in order to increase their own movement vocabulary as well as to become aware of the expressive power of movement and dance.

Working on dance skills that promote physical development and drawing out movement qualities for self-expression are two different focuses. Each is important in a child's overall development, and they can be worked on separately or simultaneously. However, it is helpful to make a distinction between teaching the skills of dance and supporting self-expression because this distinction influences how a teacher might comment and encourage a child's movement responses and contributions to dance activities. This can best be explained through an example.

During a particular dance class, a teacher might announce to students that the theme is exploring movements that travel across the room. To explore this concept and build physical skills, the teacher might describe and demonstrate different locomotion actions such as galloping, prancing, skipping, hopping, and leaping. The teacher might also select musical selections that support these actions and explore the stepping pattern and rhythmic quality of each of these movements. First, the teacher asks that the children clap out the rhythm of the music. Next, the teacher invites the children to attempt to make these steps with the musical accompaniment, both as a group and individually. The teacher especially compliments those children who execute the movement with skill and precision and assists those who were unable to perform the action correctly. The teacher's compliments might include comments such as "Look how Kirin is keeping the same foot in front, the whole time she gallops across the room. Her front foot is landing right on the beat. Let's all clap on the beat and watch Kirin's—front—foot—step—forward—with—each—clap." The teacher might assist a child having difficulty keeping the same foot in front by holding hands and galloping with the child: emphasizing the step forward with the leading leg by taking a larger and stronger step, and then quickly gliding the back leg forward with a smaller, lighter step. This will create a very specific rhythmic pattern of "1 and 2 and 3 and 4 and," with the step occurring on the 1 and the quick glide on the "and."

To contrast this skill development approach with one that emphasizes self-expression, using this same galloping exploration, the teacher might initially ask the children to demonstrate their own ideas about how to move across the room. Leaving the directive very open-ended allows the less experienced or able movers to perform an action that follows the instruction without the pressure or concern about doing it correctly. This approach alleviates fears of criticism that can often impede the less adept child's early attempts. During this initial stage, the teacher might comment on how each child moves across the room: "Look how John gets very low to the ground, crawling on his hands and knees. Amy goes high up on her toes, holding her arms in a circle over her head." These comments acknowledge each child's own ideas. Each child then becomes the leader, demonstrating and instructing the group to try his or her movement. The children are asked to comment on how it feels to do an action like their classmates in order to develop their abilities to use language—symbolic representations—to explain their concrete, physical experience. Attempting to move like their classmates opens their awareness of others and supports their social engagement; watching and discussing individual differences stimulates the children's abilities to discern and accept diversity.

If a teacher decides to move a creative dance class to the next level of experience by introducing the actual skill of galloping, the teacher might ask students what they think a gallop looks like. As the children demonstrate their ideas, the teacher's comments again initially focus on how each child attempts to execute the gallop, even if it is not done perfectly. The teacher might say, "Look how quickly Mary's legs move her across the room," "Watch how Vladimir's feet seem to bounce off the floor when he gallops," and "Look how high Lucia's gallop goes into the air." Commenting qualitatively on how the gallop is executed enables the teacher to acknowledge and regard each child's action as an appropriate response to the movement task, rather than critiquing whether it is done correctly to evaluate its successful achievement. Such supportive comments encourage a child to continue to try to accomplish the skill over time. Once each child's gallop is commented on, one by one, children take their turns acting as leader by demonstrating and teaching their individual ways of galloping. As children try on the different galloping styles, the teacher can encourage them to share how it feels and notice what makes each child's gallop different. Trying on different gallops supports children's sensorimotor learning. Commenting on the children's movements encourages the use of words to explain their kinesthetic experience. Attempting to move like their classmates opens their awareness of others and supports social engagement. Exploring the gallop in this way maintains the focus on each child's specific self-expressive interpretation of a gallop rather than on the proper execution of an actual skill.

Once all of the gallops have been explored, the teacher may want to shift the focus toward learning the actual skill of galloping. The teacher can discuss and demonstrate how a gallop is performed by stepping with the front foot, followed by quickly gliding the back foot to tap the heel of the front foot, which sends both feet momentarily into the air as the front foot steps forward again. Each child can then attempt the movement, trying to keep a rhythmic foot pattern. As in the first part of this experience, having the teacher add comments that focus on how each child's action is unique will enable the self-expressive aspect of the skill to be maintained even as the skill is being practiced.

In the final part of the class, the children can create their own dance sequence made up of several different "moving across the room" actions they have tried during the class. These spontaneous "choreographies" can be demonstrated as solos during which the teacher and other children are encouraged to comment on the specific qualities of the soloist's actions, differentiating galloping steps from other movements across the room. The teacher might say, "Look how fast Jacque's gallop gets him across the room. Watch how he changes it to a small slow step just the way Karin did her gallop," or "Notice how Jacque finishes his solo by sliding his body down to the ground. It reminds me of a leaf blown by a strong wind! What does it remind you of? Jacque, what were you thinking about while you were dancing?"

During the next creative dance class, the teacher can expand on this lesson by asking the children to think of new ways to move across the room. Galloping can be included and practiced again as new locomotion steps are introduced. Teaching a structured locomotion step while leaving room for children to invent their very own movements, which do not resemble a formal dance action places the children's self-created movements on the same level as the teacher-initiated actions. Skill development and self-expression are integrated into the same lesson. This builds a sense of respect for each child's ideas and supports continued focus, concentration, and commitment to the group activity. The children develop the attention, symbolic thinking, and interactional skills that can be useful in all subject domains.

Using Comments to Support Self-Expression   The teacher's comments above have a very specific style. First, the teacher uses qualitative words to describe the actions, making sure that the comments are descriptive of the actions and provide children with movement vocabulary rather than evaluation. Simply complimenting a child's efforts through remarks such as "That was very good. I like the way you used your feet to jump so high," can create a complex situation. A dynamic may be established in which children become motivated to please the teacher rather than to explore their own movement ideas. Other children are often acutely attuned to the child who is being complimented and may attempt to copy that child's actions or ask if the teacher likes their actions too. The focus becomes pleasing the teacher rather than self-expression. It is fine for teachers to express pleasure and enthusiasm for children's ideas, but they must be careful to balance such comments with more descriptive ones that focus the attention back on the students. See Table 12.1 for examples of remarks that a teacher might use in making comments to students about their dancing.

Teachers may also use images to elaborate on descriptions. For example, they might preface a statement with the phrase "It reminds me of. . . ," "It makes me think of. . . ," or "When I watch you move like that, it makes me feel like. . . ." Such observations allow teachers to share their own images and reactions but leave room for other interpretations by the children. Comments such as these help children learn how movement is expressive and provokes feelings. They emphasize the nonverbal communicative aspects of movement and encourage an understanding of how children's actions portray their feelings. These expressive behaviors can be translated into words, helping children to experience a sense of being respected, seen, and heard. When children realize that their actions have an impact on others, their own creative expressions are often sparked.

Teachers should also make sure that children who are exploring or watching another child's actions have time to share their own experiences of the mover's actions. This teaches children that their perceptions and thoughts are valid and worthy of discussion. Teachers should always give the moving child time to share the ideas that motivated the movement. With such teacher encouragement, a rich expressive dialogue can begin between the teacher and children. Guided by the teacher, children will learn how to verbalize their thoughts, behaviors, and sensorimotor experiences.

Panthea, age 4, chooses the solemn music of Bach/Busoni's "Chorale Prelude Adagio," for her dance. She begins on the floor crawling, then slowly gets up, with her head down. Slightly accelerating, she adds a twirl that takes

Table 12.1.   Sample movement-based words for making comments to students about their dancing and encouraging classmates to add their comments

Make note of a child's movements by describing the action's qualities using Effort words or by commenting about Body, Shape, Space, or Phrasing. Add your image ideas after the students make their suggestions.

Effort qualities

Speed (i.e., time)
- "Wan is moving soooo fast. What animal does he remind you of? I think he is as fast as a cheetah."
- "Jolie is soooo slow. Watch how slowly and gently she lifts her feet. It is as if she is stepping on a floating cloud."

Strength (i.e., weight)
- "Kelley is stamping her feet so hard that I can hear the beat."
- "Shhhh, listen. Wanda's dance is so light that I can't hear her footsteps. Can you?"

Focus (i.e., space)
- "Watch how clear and determined Nastasha's dance is. She wants to get across the room, and nothing will stop her!"
- "Look how Oscar's dance takes him everywhere!"

Muscle tension (i.e., flow)
- "Kyle's body is so long, stretchy, and bouncy as he dances that he looks like a rubber band to me."
- "Carl's body is so loose that it makes me think of a flowing stream gushing over the rocks. What does it remind you of?"

Body
- "Look how Anna is only wiggling her _____ (e.g., toes, eyes, fingers, tongue, nose)."
- "See how James is holding up his head so high."
- "Keisha is sliding her belly on the floor when she crawls."

Shape
- "Look! Ahred's legs make a triangle!"
- "Sorin's curvy back pose makes an arc."
- "Amy is holding her arms and legs so strong and stiff that her body is making lines in the air."
- "Oh! I see the letter *L* in the way Keith bends his body over his legs."

Space
- "Jacob is making big circles around the whole room. Oooh, look where his dance has taken him now—he is making smaller circles inside the big circle!"
- "Watch the path Cameron's dance is making on the floor. What letter do you see? I see an *S*."
- "Cara's dance is making such straight lines in and out of the center like the rays of the sun."
- "What does Justin's arcing curve across the room remind you of? I see a rainbow! What color might his dance be about?"

Phrasing
- "Listen to the rhythm of James's feet. Let's try to clap it out as he dances."
- "Paco's arm is flowing to the music. Can you tell which instrument he is listening to as he dances?"
- "I see the beat of the drum in the way that Karla is moving her arms."

her once around, landing back on the floor with a quick, almost stumbling drop. Her head and gaze stay down for the remainder of her dance. Now on the floor, Panthea extends her leg out with pointed toe, as she stre-e-e-tches her arm across her body to resume her crawl position, rocking her body side to side on hands and knees. Her dance becomes a series of standing twirls that drop to the floor in abandonment, made more dramatic by accelerations and decelerations in her tempo. This is followed by a variety of crawling actions, which include moments in which she pauses, extending her arm, reaching up toward the ceiling, or lengthening her leg over the other leg, before resuming her crawl position. The children watch in quiet reverie. When Panthea is finished, they join her on the floor, following her every move as Panthea repeats her dance to teach it to them.

The teacher and children sit down to discuss what it felt like to dance like Panthea.

Teacher: *Who can guess what that felt like?*

Tyrese: *Hmmm, like mixed with happy, tired, and sad all mixed together (as she vigorously circles her hands around and around), because the twirls looked like happy, and the crawls looked like sad (matching her statement with a sad expression).*

Shawn: *Happy!*

Teacher: *Happy? What part of the dance seemed happy to you?*

Shawn: *Down on the ground (in a shy whisper).*

Ana: *It was like she was crawling on the ground and she didn't have no family.*

Teacher: *So she was crawling on the ground with no one; she didn't have any family. . . .*

Ana: *Well, she had friends, but no family (stated with aplomb, holding the teacher's gaze for an extended moment).*

Teacher: *Okay, Panthea, can you tell us a little about what you were thinking about in that dance?*

Panthea: *Sad and mad and not feeling well, all mixed together (appearing satisfied that the children have gotten her message, she lifts her knees up to her chest and down, softening her spine and chest into a relaxed posture).* ⁓

The themes and events that arise from creative dance sessions can be incorporated into other aspects of the classroom curriculum. Stories can be written, musical rhythms and artwork can be made, and play activities can be explored to extend the children's creative thoughts. For older children, these themes can be brought into math class by analyzing the rhythmic structures, floor patterns, and shape designs of the dance sequences. The social sciences can also be explored by choosing movement themes that have a cultural focus. The products of the academic activities can then be examined through the medium of dance and movement, creating a continual link between subject domains.

Adding a Group Creative Dance Program to the Classroom Curriculum

Planning a group dance time within the classroom curriculum enables a teacher to address many topics within a single lesson. The prominent focus of any dance movement class is to enhance group socialization, emotional self-expression, cognitive functioning, and physical coordination. In dance class, each child gets to learn about group processes, follow rules, take turns, and let off steam by getting a chance to share personal styles and current feelings with all those involved. (To read more about the kind of classroom planning and assistance that can result when a *Ways of Seeing* dance movement therapist works directly with an educator, see the School Intervention Plan at http://www. brookespublishing.com/dancing.)

The next section will describe the general format of a group dance class. This will be followed by a discussion of the elements to consider when designing a class, how to sequence these elements, considerations for specific age ranges, and how to embed movement activities within the everyday classroom curriculum. The section will also detail how to draw out each child's unique expressive dance and how to use movement and music to help children increase their attention and their ability to move through classroom transitions. Specific activities appropriate for different age groups and abilities will be interspersed throughout this section. See a *Ways of Seeing* Dance Therapy Session lesson plan and different activities using dance, movement, and music progressing with different age groups at http://www. brookespublishing.com/dancing.

General Format

Before beginning a class, it is important for teachers to be clear about their goals and expectations. Is the main focus on group socialization and all of its supporting elements, such as relating to others, turn taking, listening, and sharing ideas and movements? Or, is the focus instead the acquisition of motor skills through a creative process? Is self-expression through increased body awareness a goal for the children? Does the teacher want to use movement and dance exploration to tie into a current class curriculum theme? Alternatively, is dance being used as an inviting way to support the children to release their restless energy, calm down, and focus on a guided relaxation? Adding dance and movement curriculum into the school schedule provides ample opportunity to address each of these concerns.

Regardless of the teacher's focus, the overall structure of the class remains the same. The most important factor to keep in mind when planning a creative dance class is finding balance: balance between whole group actions and individual expression; between teacher-guided activities and student-led actions; between more lively, energizing movements and more centering, relaxing activities; between movements that are large and take up a great deal of space and more contained movements that occur within the boundaries around each child's own body space; and between structured movements and pure dance-play. Moving back and forth between these contrasting qualities creates balance. Keeping in mind this idea of balance will enable a teacher to guide and respond more spontaneously to the class as a group as well as the individuals within the group. Individual expression and group cohesion can dance side by side if the teacher pays attention to the qualitative elements of the movements and the specific activities.

Elements of a Creative Dance Class

A movement-based lesson plan incorporating the *Ways of Seeing* principles should strive to facilitate individualization and socialization through a group experience. The primary tools of a *Ways of Seeing* curriculum approach are the use of music, body awareness, movement, dance, and relaxation techniques (see http://www.brookes publishing.com/dancing for some suggestions about how to apply Laban Movement Analysis, Bartenieff Fundamentals, and Creative Dance principles to a dance class). Each lesson should include the following elements:

> *Element 1: Activities that offer each child*
> *opportunities for individual self-expression*

Throughout the class, continually look for opportunities to comment on each child's unique movement responses. These comments can be very simple, such as "This music makes John feel like jumping," or more explicit, such as "Look how deeply John bends his knees as he begins his jump. Let's all try jumping this way." Such comments tell children that the teacher is paying attention to them as individuals. It fosters a sense that their contributions are welcomed. These comments also help direct the other children to pay attention to the ideas of their classmates. Describing the actions of each child conveys the concept that all actions are acceptable and supports diversity and tolerance for different styles and ability levels. This builds a sense of community and group cohesion.

Give children opportunities throughout the class to individually demonstrate their movements and to lead the class as other students try on their movements; children should also be provided with time to perform a solo in response to the music or movement theme chosen for that session.

Element 2: Movement sequences, both with spontaneous, free movement explorations and with more structured movement patterns

Free movement explorations are activities that enable children to interpret the music or respond to a broad directive such as, "Make your dance as big as you can." This enables children to be as creative as they want, tapping into their own personal reservoir of ideas that may or may not actually correspond to the directive or the music. For example, the music may be very slow and languid, but Kirin may choose to run quickly across the room for her dance. Although this may not be the most likely response one would expect, during free improvisations it is very important that a child be given permission to make their own interpretation of the music. This is not a time for corrections or directives, but rather a time for children to feel that they are being seen, acknowledged, and supported for their imagination and contributions. This can be a difficult role for teachers to play because it requires them to refrain from their natural instinct to teach children how to listen to the directive or musical selection. Instead, the teaching that takes place helps the children to learn about themselves.

After individual children perform, a teacher can encourage them to think about their interpretations by asking them to describe what they were thinking and feeling during the dance. Other classmates can be asked to describe how they saw and experienced their classmate's movements. This will enable the children to become more aware of how their

424 · The Dancing Dialogue

actions do or do not support their feelings and ideas. Moreover, as they listen and watch the children interpret and respond, the teacher can learn salient information about individual children. When Kirin was asked to speak about her running dance to the slow music, she explained that she experienced the soft music as sleepy music. She was pretending that she was playing a chasing game with her mom to avoid going to bed! How individual children think, organize, and process their personal worlds will be revealed during these improvisations.

Including structured movement patterns during the same class is also essential. Structured movement sequences have an organizing effect. They involve motor planning and perceptual motor integration. Movement sequences increase a child's attention space, improve focus and memory, require turn taking, and support whole group processing. There are many ways to work with structured movement patterns. A movement sequence with these patterns can be taught by the teacher; created by the students; or learned by following an organized dance, such as a folk dance or a dance song that includes dance-step instructions.

A teacher might include a structured movement activity by creating a three-step dancing pattern such as step—jump—turn, repeated several times as the children move across the floor. This can be taught in several ways. A teacher could describe these movement terms verbally—asking each child to try the sequence; ask one child to demonstrate each action; or demonstrate it to the class herself. The children can move across the room individually or as dyads, repeating the actions in sequence. Maintaining individual focus and creating group cohesion should be instilled as the observing children identify and call out the movements as their classmates perform them.

The children's own movements can also be used to create a repeated movement sequence. A teacher might start out with two children contributing one movement each. More children can add dance elements as their ability to follow and remember increases. Additional movements can be included until each member of the class has contributed to the choreography. This type of sequencing activity becomes imbued with each child's individual personality. The qualitative elements of the sequence—the speed, the space, the directional pathway, and the body parts used, for example, will reveal each child's personality.

Children can be helped to become aware of how each person's contribution changes the feeling of the sequence. Over time they will come to know and expect certain children to contribute a certain quality to the dancing game. For example, Isabella loves to float lightly on her toes. This action very much depicts the delicate, quiet personality of this child who enjoys fantasy stories about being a princess. Katie, on the other hand, loves to take risks. She is boisterous and energetic. Her movement contributions inevitably take her running as fast as she can go, and end with a sudden fall to the ground! Eden, a complex, deep thinker, creates actions that turn and twist his body into the most unusual shapes. They require skill in balancing. When the children combine these movements by performing each action to the count of four, they all have the opportunity to feel what it is like to move like their classmates. It is a very different experience for Isabella—whose preferred actions are light and floating—to run full force across the room and to drop to the floor. However, in the context of this dance-play, she will try these new actions and experience what a free-flowing movement might feel like. In contrast, Katie will learn about control as she strives to contain her actions to mirror the gentle quality of Isabella's movements. Both Isabella and Katie will gain a sense of controlled strength as they attempt to form and balance their bodies into the twisting shapes that Eden has added. Placing each of these individual actions sequentially together enables children to develop motor planning, increase attention span, adapt to variability, and experience feeling tone changes. This sequence starts them off in a gentle and calm manner, quickly becomes energetic and free, and finishes with a sense of strength and focus. The children experience a sense of mastery as their ability to perform these qualitatively diverse actions improves.

Element 3: Activities that sequence through group and individual experiences: whole group, small group, dyads, and individual

Varying how the children are clustered together throughout the dance class will contribute to both their sense of individuality and the creation of group cohesion. Interspersing the focus on individual attention and different clusters requires children to continually stay aware of themselves within the context of each other. Children naturally break off into dyads and small groups based on their friendships. By organizing activities from the perspective of individuals to dyads, to small group, and finally to the whole class, all within the span of a 45-minute to 1-hour class period, children can interact with their favorite friends as well as get to know and learn about children to whom they may not ordinarily gravitate. Because varying groupings of children will occur throughout the experience, children recognize that they will have turns with their good friends and turns to shine on their own. Therefore, they should be more compliant and less resistant to dancing with a child or group of children they may not know as well. This is an especially helpful format for the shy or more reserved child who tends not to initiate contact or readily contribute personal ideas. Pairing off this type of child with a more outgoing child places both children on equal ground. This sets up a situation that provides them with an opportunity to encounter, relate, and share themselves with each other through a playful yet structured activity. This practice supports diversity and understanding amongst all types of children.

Element 4: Movement sequences that keep the group moving and relating as a group

Sequencing the elements of a dance class so the children shift from individual to dyadic to small-group to whole-group activities develops a sense of group membership. As children learn and have the chance to experience each other through movement-based sharing, a deep sense of knowing one another is instilled. Helping and instructing the children to pay attention to the individualized qualitative aspects of each child's unique movement interpretations supports the group relationship.

Element 5: Experiences that help children relate to something outside of self, through music and rhythm

A sense of group cohesion develops over a period of time through shared group experiences. Providing a medium that all the children can simultaneously focus on outside of their own ideas provides both a structure and a thread that joins them together as a group. Music is a good stabilizing force. Starting out with focusing on the rhythm of a piece of music organizes everyone to attend to the same element. Within this attention there is room for each child's individual interpretation. At first the children can be asked to find the beat of the music by clapping it out. A group consensus can be taken to determine if the rhythm is slow, medium, or fast. Once the group has determined the music's tempo, all can be asked to clap out the rhythm, following the acknowledged speed. Invariably there will be differences in how each child performs this task. One girl may clap her hands high above her head, another boy may wiggle his hips as he claps, and still another boy may tap his feet along with the clap. One by one, each child should be given the opportunity to express a personal response to the musical rhythm through demonstrations that other children can try to emulate. The children can move across the room as a group trying on these different rhythmic responses.

Following steady rhythmic structures supplies predictability and provides an organized moment in each movement to emphasize. This is useful when first forming a group. Children learn how to move through the room maintaining their own personal space by making sure their actions react to the music specifically during the beat of the music. Once the sense of group interactions feels firm, the focus can switch to the melody of the music, which may have a less predictable and regulating beat to it. Children can swoop and sway and swirl around to music that floats and meanders. Elements to look for in music to encourage self-expression will be discussed later on in this chapter under the music heading.

Element 6: Periods of relaxation, breath
awareness, and movements requiring increased body control

These activities improve body awareness and focus a child's attention. Relaxation provides a break from focusing and enables the body to recuperate. Relaxation also requires both control and a relinquishing of control in order to support the body to release. Relinquishing control is obvious—one must release action on the body in order to allow muscular and mental activity to relax. Control is needed to allow the body to let go without becoming silly or wild. This can be quite difficult for young children to do. Children often respond to relaxation instructions about letting go or freeing their bodies by either throwing or collapsing their whole bodies or some part of their bodies down to the ground, running around the room, or using great effort to forcefully hold their bodies stiff. Relaxation activities require body stillness, but it is a calm, quiet stillness. Children must learn that stillness can be a comfortable state of being rather than an inhibiting action. This is not a typical body attitude for an active child, but acquiring this body attitude fosters the focused attention necessary for learning. Calm stillness is complementary to the alert, quiet state that is best for receptive learning.

Movement experiences that help foster this type of body awareness include creating visual images to provide a mental focus and using external props such as lighting, music, musical instruments, and touch to stimulate kinesthetic and sensorial awareness. Suggesting to children that they pretend to be melting snow or ice cream, a train slowing down, a flower wilting, a leaf blowing in the gradually softening wind, or ripples of water responding to a gentle breeze are good images with which to start. Choosing calm, soft music that gradually gets quieter in tempo supports these images as well. Violins, pianos, flutes, and bells are instruments often used in pieces made especially for relaxation. Classical orchestral renditions of lullabies can also be useful; in contrast, using popular lullabies sung with words might be too distracting for those children who feel compelled to sing along.

Breath awareness is an important element of true deep relaxation. Children can be instructed to take a deep breath and slowly let it out as if they are letting the air out of a balloon. Each breath gets softer and slower as the balloon slowly becomes more and more soft, until the children breathe so very quietly and gently that their bodies have become smooth, like deflated balloons. A light with a dimmer switch can be used in the same way. The children can be directed through the same gradual process, attempting to blow the lights out, one breath at a time. Slowly turning down the volume of a piece of music is a similar strategy. Whichever prop is used, the culminating experience is the same: By the end of the sequence, the children are asked to become aware of the quietness and gentle stillness of their bodies and their surroundings.

At first, this awareness time may last barely a minute. This period of time should be extended, however, as the children become more able to sustain a relaxed state. The important elements to stress during breath-flow relaxation activities are becoming aware of one's body expanding during the inhale and softening and settling during the exhale. Although most children readily respond to the strong, deep inhale, it is ultimately the softening quality of the exhale that will most facilitate the relaxation effect. Drawing attention to both inhale and exhale supports the reciprocal process of a complete breath sequence and creates a balance between exertion—the inhale—and recuperation—the exhale.

Adding a safe, positive touch to the classroom environment can be a useful tool. As children experience being touched, they can be instructed to work as partners helping each other relax through this organized touch technique. A teacher's moving around the room and placing a hand directly and firmly on each child's stomach or back to feel the quiet breath flow, for example, can provide tactile support as children attempt to regulate their breath. It is important to note that touching can cause very powerful reactions, however. It is best to discuss the topic of touching with school officials and, if allowed, with the whole class before adding this element into a structured relaxation. It is essential that the proper steps be taken to make sure each child is comfortable being touched. A child's individual preferences regarding being touched are important to respect. This type of touch must be very purposeful. If it is too light it will tickle, but if it is too firm it will feel intrusive. Paying attention to each child's reaction to the quality of the touch should help the teacher determine how and if a child is comfortable being touched.

A similar gradual process must be followed to take children out of a relaxation period and back into a more active alert state. How children come out of relaxation is as important and as much a part of the process as how they get into it! This whole sequence—into relaxation, staying in relaxation, and coming out of relaxation—experientially teaches children how to regulate their bodies and increases their abilities to attend and focus. To come out of relaxation, children can be asked to slowly start to move just one part of their bodies by making small circles or flexing and extending at the joints. They can then increase the size of the movement and add new body parts in a gradual and progressive way until their whole bodies are involved in the movement. A teacher can instruct students to keep the whole action on the floor, or to find a way through their movements to gradually come up to a standing position. Using images of seeds growing into flowers or fairies coming out of a deep sleep and floating around the room can facilitate this process. Music that gets progressively fuller or is slowly increased in volume also supports children's awakening back into a more active state. Dyads can be formed, having the children mirror each other's process. Children really enjoy being each other's teacher as they help their classmates "come back to life."

Sometimes creating a whole relaxation activity is not possible. The room may not have enough space for children to stretch out on the floor, or there may not be enough time to devote to the complete sequence described above. If the children are too active or energetic, such a relaxation sequence may be overly demanding. It may require too extreme a shift in energy level for the children. In these situations, the sequence above can be modified to accommodate such issues. For example, the children can use their tables or desks to rest their upper bodies. A good transitional activity under such circumstances is to create a movement-based activity that requires body control. These movements can include holding poses and balancing, such as when a teacher instructs the children to stop or freeze when a piece of music is paused. While the children hold their positions, the teacher can move around the room and describe some quality of each child's pose. For example, the teacher can pick a theme for the children's poses such as their shape: "Look at the long shape Sara's body makes. Nathaniel is making a round shape. I see a triangle shape in Maria's arms." Or, the teacher can identify how the children are using space: "Carly is making a large shape. Yael is as small as a mouse. Elfie's body is making a line, while Peter is making a squiggle!" The children's eagerness to be described motivates them to hold onto their still forms.

As children become more able to hold these shapes, they can be directed to gain more control over their bodies by developing the shapes into balancing positions. Learning how to balance requires increased body control and visual focus. It builds central body awareness and coordination of the limbs in relation to the torso. Balancing can be taught by having the children stand erect and first shifting their weight from foot to foot while keeping their feet on the floor. The focus is on weight shifting from side to side rather than weight bearing on one foot. Next, children can be instructed to shift all of their weight onto one side of their bodies, extending their arms on that side high up into the air above their heads. The teacher can bring to their attention the long line they have created, starting from their ankles, going up to their hip bones, their rib cages, shoulders, ears, and extended arms. Each body part is in line or resting on the body part below it. When this line-up is felt, the children have created a firm, stable support for that side of their bodies. Next, children can be instructed to slowly lift the opposite foot off the ground. The lifting side is known as the mobile side. As their skill improves, their whole leg can be extended forward, to the side, and back while their stable side maintains a solid center of support. Each side of the body must have a chance to be the stable and mobile side to build strength coordination and balance between the limbs and torso. It is very common, however, for children to be able to balance more easily on one side than the other. The challenge is in learning how to make it feel stable and balanced on both sides. After working on this structured balancing activity, the children can be asked to create their own balancing poses. All of the children can attempt to try on each of their classmates' balancing poses. While holding the poses, the children can then be asked to change places with a classmate or move to another part of the room. Through these balancing games, children learn how to gain control over their bodies. This improves their body awareness and supports them to be able to transition into the relaxation activities described above.

Element 7: Movement themes to explore

Structuring each dance session around a theme can help to organize the dance experience, keep the children focused, establish a routine, develop an understanding of dance class as another avenue of classroom learning, and support all levels of developmental growth. Movement and dance activities can be very stimulating for children. Encouraging a child to freely move can be a very powerful experience. Without a clear focus and structure, however, the class can quickly spin out of control. The challenge in directing a creative dance class is to create a balance between maintaining organization while allowing for each child's individuality and self-expression. Too much organization will stifle individual input from the children. Too little organization will create chaos! Focusing the class around a theme can help achieve a balance. Creating rituals by beginning and ending the class in the same way should also support the overall structure of the lesson. Other elements to ritualize include hello and goodbye songs that enable children to create personal movements that describe how they are feeling that particular day toward the beginning of class, and then again toward the end of class, noting if their feeling dances have changed as the class progressed. Maintaining the same songs but encouraging the children to respond to their current feelings supports the comfort of a routine but makes it fresh each class. Having children take out props and put them away during a specific time in the class sequence creates ritual and helps children refrain from continually asking to use props when the teacher is encouraging them to first focus on body movement awareness. Repeating a dance activity they especially enjoy for a few classes in a row can become a miniritual that enables them to work more deeply on a particular theme. Through this concentration, a new ritual often develops.

An infinite number of themes can be explored through movement activities. The seven elements described above are good thematic structures to use when first starting a dance movement curriculum in the classroom setting. These include sequential movement explorations that are choreographed by using established folk and children's song-and-dance activities or creating spontaneous choreographies from the children's movement suggestions. This theme can be contrasted with free improvisations that reflect the children's moods at the moment.

Along these lines, stories and poems can be read to spark new images for dance interpretation. Interpretative dance supports transmodal learning. Auditory perceptual motor development can be stimulated when children are asked to create movements in response to different tempos and rhythms of music. Body regulation is increased as children learn how to adjust their bodies and actions to different tempos, rhythms, and themes of music. Relaxation, breath awareness, and large-body stretches are additional themes that support enhanced body regulation. Social and emotional development along with body awareness is enhanced as children use their bodies to tell stories about themselves and their lives. Feeling dances expressing moods such as sadness, anger, and happiness can support emotional regulation. Images of animals are a popular and safe way for children to address emotional themes such as strength, power, control, aggression, and nurturance that are so dominant in a young developmental age.

Laban/Bartenieff System   The Laban/Bartenieff system provides a limitless structure to develop themes for creative dance class. (For additional reading, see Gilbert, 1992; Guest, 1990; and Laban, 1968.) The five basic categories discussed in Chapter 5, Effort, Body, Space, Shape, and Phrasing, can be focused on as organizing themes in and of themselves, or they can be incorporated into any of the themes discussed in the preceding paragraphs.

Effort   The four elements within the Effort category—space, time, weight, and flow—define the qualitative feeling tone of an action. Each of these elements features two opposing aspects described along a spectrum encompassing the specific quality. Each Effort quality is also associated with an attitude that can be used to add a deeper understanding of the feelings. The feeling tone, opposing elements, and attitudes of each quality provide the emotional expressiveness to a movement.

Every individual's personal movement style is made up of a unique cluster of these qualities. Children's personal Effort tendencies tend to become defined as they describe their spontaneous movement improvisations. Children can be encouraged to experience the other qualities when they try on their classmates' movements. Specific music can be explored that the teacher and children feel best exemplifies each of the Effort qualities. Teachers can help children make distinctions between which qualities create the melody and which create the rhythm in the chosen music.

Body   The body category relates to coordination and a sense of connectedness between different body parts. Children's abilities to move with a sense of bodily integrity and connection vary greatly. Closely observing the children's styles will reveal which parts of their bodies they favor and which parts they are less able to connect. Bodily strengths and weaknesses should become obvious.

Bartenieff characterizes the body elements of movement into six themes

- Breath flow
- Core–distal
- Head–tail
- Upper–lower
- Body-half
- Contralateral

Breath flow involves sensing the fluid movement of the breath through and within the whole body. Children can be instructed to send their breath to a specific body part, from one specific body part to another, or to follow their own natural breath path. They can use their whole bodies to physically express this pathway, draw it on a piece of paper, and then dance it out. Full body actions that create a feeling of expansion followed by a contraction can also provide breath flow experiences. (Think of a floating balloon, and then think of letting a little air out of it quickly.)

Core–distal awareness, including *core*—relating to the navel and central body—and *distal*—relating to the six extremities (head, arms, legs, and tailbone), describes the early sensations experienced by young infants. Through the process of expanding and contracting their bodies as they inhale and exhale, babies begin to sense their physical inner sensations and their outward expressions of these sensations. Core–distal awareness activities can be subtle—related to breath flow— or active—involving large-body actions that connect the center of the body to the extremities. One example of an active full body core–distal action is asking children to lie on their backs in a fetal position, with their head, legs, and arms curled close in, and then suddenly expand by shooting out and extending their extremities.

A quiet breath flow activity that supports full body awareness through relaxation is to support the children to send their breath start-ing centrally from their stomachs (navels) to their six extremity points: up their spines to their heads; diagonally up through their left shoul-ders and left arms; diagonally down through their left hips and left legs; down the spines to their tailbones; diagonally down through their right hips and legs; and diagonally up through their right shoulders and arms. Asking children to create a dance that emphasizes these connections can expand on this internal awareness sequence. Combinations of these body coordination patterns—such as a movement sequence that accents the stomach and head and stomach and upper left body—can be explored. Continual focus on each of these connections can greatly increase the children's kinesthetic perceptions of their bodies in space.

Head–tail movements draw kinesthetic attention to the role of the spine and central torso muscles, which obviously play a very essential part physically in alignment and stability. Less obviously, movements and postures involving the spine and torso musculature also affect and reflect a child's attentional abilities and emotional expressivity. Those movements associated with squirming in a seat, hunching over a desk, or holding head in hands greatly involve spinal muscular activity. People who hold their heads up high on strong, vertical backs portray an image of alert attention. Eyes held in steady visual attention are most often associated with people who are holding their heads erectly. Exploring movements that emphasize awareness from the head through the spine to the tailbone lengthens and stretches the torso and creates a deep-felt sense experience of core strength. Asking children to pretend that they are fiddlehead ferns curling and uncurling is one activity that works well with toddlers and school-age children. Other images include pretending to be a marionette doll being pulled up by a string on the top of one's head; evenly stacking blocks or stringing beads to represent each vertebrae and balancing a ball or large bead on the top of the stack for the head; and placing one hand in front of the pubic bone and tailbone, gliding one's hands up to "zip up" one's body with an imaginary zipper. These actions feel good on the body, are a relief from the collapsed postures that people often sink into unknowingly when standing and sitting, and stimulate alert focused attention. Head–tail movements are valuable activities to spontaneously interject in the midst of a lesson, especially if it seems that the children are losing their focus, enthusiasm, or attention.

Upper–lower, body-half movements draw awareness to the upper limbs and torso—chest, neck, head, shoulders, arms, hands—and to the lower limbs and torso—pelvis, hips, legs, and feet. This body-awareness is associated with actions that reach, push, and pull. A frog jump is one example of an action that exemplifies upper to lower body-half coordination. It involves crouching down on feet or lower legs, reaching arms and upper body forward as the feet and legs propel the whole body forward onto outstretched arms, and completing the action by landing on the feet or lower legs. Try having the children also reverse this action by starting with the legs first, jumping backward! Movement qualities that stimulate this awareness include folding and unfolding the body halves toward and away from each other, holding one half of the body stable as the other half moves, and forward or backward rolls.

Left–right body-half actions accentuate the spine as the central connection of the body. These movements differentiate the left side of the body from the right. Movements include opening and closing each body half, pretending to be the front and back covers of a book, with the spine of the book represented by the book's spine. Balance and alignment are greatly enhanced through this left–right awareness. Children can imagine they are rocking on a boat as they shift their weight from their left to their right while maintaining a clear vertical stance. Keeping their body parts aligned on one side of the body and then shifting the whole alignment to the other side accomplishes this.

For example, ask the children to place their feet parallel and about one hand width apart, and then with legs straight to bend all the way over and let their bodies hang. (This starting posture stimulates upper–lower, body-half awareness.) Next ask the children to slowly, starting from their tailbones, roll up their spines—the image of pretending to be a zipper discussed above works well. When upright, ask the children to check to feel that their heads are resting evenly above their shoulders, that the shoulders are placed on top of their rib cages, that their rib cages are aligned with their hips, and that their hips are squarely above their ankles. Once this body placement awareness is established, the children can rock their weight to the left side while still maintaining this vertical alignment. Lifting their left arm straight up holding onto the sky can enhance this sense of verticality. In this posture, the left side becomes the stable side and the right the mobile side. The children can lift first their heels, then the balls of their feet and then their toes off the ground. They can progress to full leg extensions to the front side and back, holding each position or swinging the legs forward, back, and to the side. The children can count how long they can stand on one leg and can try to catch themselves in a pose before they fall to the ground. This activity develops increased body control and focused attention. From this structured exploration, the children can be encouraged to create their own movements and balancing poses using this left-to-right body awareness.

Contralateral awareness is the next level of coordination. It develops torso strength and underlies actions that cross the midline. A mobile baby's explorations involving sequential rolls from back to tummy and pushing up to sitting introduce this kinesthetic awareness; these are the preliminary actions that support later contralateral actions such as crawling and creeping. Many children navigate through this stage differently. Having children emulate animal actions provides many opportunities to revisit this stage of development while strengthening greater contralateral integration. Contralateral integrity also plays a role in balancing. It is the coordination between opposing limbs that secures movement actions that require balance. The windup and throwing action of a pitcher is a great example. Viewed in slow motion, pitchers are continually placing their limbs in diagonal opposition as they reach back and then step forward to release the ball.

Space   This category of movement includes both personal space around the body and how the body moves in space. Explorations involving the body moving in space teach body boundary awareness. The body can take up a large, medium, or small amount of space. The term *kinesphere* is used to describe the personal space surrounding an individual that is reachable from a stationary position. The image of a flexible bubbles made of unbreakable plastic can be used to help children explore moving their limbs within their own personal space without moving from their center. *General space* is all the space outside of one's personal kinesphere. Moving through the room in their bubbles and stepping or jumping away when they sense the presence of another person in their bubbles increases children's physical awareness of their moving bodies in relationship to others. How children move through the room can be explored through different spatial pathways—zigzag, straight, curved, circular, or diagonal, for example. In this way geometric forms can be explored physically. A sense of direction can be taught as children respond to directives that ask them to move their bodies, up/down, forward/backward, left/right, or diagonally. Level of space—low, middle, and high—is an additional spatial concept that develops children's kinesthetic senses of their moving bodies.

Shape   Shape refers to the forms the body can take. Mathematical relationships can be explored as children move by making their bodies very wide or by pulling them in and squeezing through the room in narrow body shapes. Children experience angles as they bend their limbs into sharp shapes. Children can explore placing their bodies in a straight shape and contrast this position with curving and twisting their body shapes. Symmetry, asymmetry, and balance can come into play as the children work with body shapes. Linking shapes made by more than one person supports group process and further develops kinesthetic, visual, and spatial concepts.

Phrasing The phrasing of a series of movements creates sequence and rhythm. Clapping, stamping, and jumping to the beat of a song is the simplest way to introduce Phrasing and rhythmic awareness. A drum or tambourine can be used to create spontaneous phrases that encourage children to move and stop. Making stepping floor patterns with rugs squares is another way to introduce phrases. Phrasing patterns can be explored by placing each square a certain distance away from the previous one. For example, a teacher or child can create a pattern by placing the first and second rugs 2 inches apart, and the third rug 5 inches away from the second, and having the children repeat the sequence several times. A 4-year-old can create something similar by making a step – step – jummmp, step – step – jummmp Phrasing pattern. The teacher claps, counts, or labels the step-and-jump actions as a child performs the movements. By being presented with a variety of musical styles such as a waltz, march, or polka during their interpretive dancing, the children will spontaneously begin to feel their way through new Phrasing possibilities.

Other Elements in Designing a Creative Dance Class

When starting a dance curriculum, it is useful to have a clear lesson plan. The structure of a lesson plan helps a teacher to learn how to think about and organize the ways different movement activities relate to one another. A teacher should have a general lesson plan in mind that reflects how he or she would like the class to flow, while being continually open to the spontaneous opportunities that may arise as the children respond to the dance and music. A teacher should try to balance each class, taking in the children's responses while maintaining some of the teacher's planned direction. If a teacher only responds to the children's responses, a class can lose its focus, but if a teacher only directs a class based on preplanned ideas, he or she can miss the richness of each child's self expression. The goal is to support the children's expressions while still maintaining guidance to create an overall sense of safety. How to create this balance is shown in the descriptions that follow. A detailed explanation about how to read the feeling tone and energy level of the group to determine in which direction to take the class will be provided after a discussion of specific age-related considerations.

Parental Participation   If parents are to be included in the class, it is important for a teacher to make sure that they are comfortable with dancing and moving. It is great to have parental participation, but not all parents enjoy moving. A teacher must make sure that parents are prepared to move around and are clear about when they are being asked to participate and when they can just watch and rest. Parents also tire more easily, so it is best for a teacher to balance the class with parent–child and solo children activities.

Preparing Materials and Props   The most useful props to include in dance class are music and a CD player (or electronic music devise such as an iPod). Choosing the right music involves several considerations that will be discussed in a later section of this chapter. At this point it is sufficient to note that CDs or electronic music devices work best because they can be programmed to start, stop, and repeat at a particular song, and can be used to link a sequence of assorted songs together. With the use of a remote control, a teacher can control the music while dancing among the children, rather than being stuck near a music player.

Additional useful props include musical instruments, scarves, streamers, gym mats, large physioballs, rug squares, fabric tunnels, and assorted-size pillows. These props can be used to respond to the music, to support the imaginative stories and characters children create in their dances, and to create obstacle courses. Such props are fun, but they can also be very distracting, depending on the age range. For the youngest children (birth through 2 years old), they are an integral part of the experience stimulating sensory awareness. In the 2–3-year-age group, however, they can also be very distracting, and can take the children's attention away from using their bodies to explore the music and movement-based themes. If props are used incorrectly, a beautifully articulated full body dance full of runs and jumps in response to a strong rhythmic beat can turn into a child standing still and simply shaking a streamer. To prevent this, it is best for a teacher to start out without props, and add them intermittently and slowly into the class over a few weeks.

Additional Important Factors   Several factors should be kept in mind when planning the sequence of activities for a specific dance class, including the class size in relation to the space; available props; and the age, attention level, and ability level of the children. These factors may greatly influence how specific elements of creative dance unfold. It is always best to have a clear, open floor space where children can move freely without worry about bumping into other children or objects. Although open space is desirable, totally wide-open space such as a full-size gym can be too cavernous. An overly large space seems to suggest to children that they must race through it, running, sliding, and falling to the floor. If it is necessary to use such a space, it is best to mark off a section of it into a square or rectangular area to provide a designated domain for dance class. This will help focus and contain the children. A carpeted reading corner or quiet area of the classroom often works well. Creating open space by pushing desks and tables away can also be effective. The process of clearing the space can become a preparation ritual signaling the beginning of dance. If the space is too small to accommodate the whole class, running several dance sessions with smaller groups of children can also be effective. These groups can dance on alternate days or during different activity periods on the same day. The composition and exact size of the group should vary depending on the children's ability and attention span. The key factor to keep in mind is to create a group that will be able to attend for a long-enough time that each child can participate in solo movement sequences. This means that children will be able to both observe the dances of others and dance their own dances. This criterion is best determined by each teacher's knowledge of the students.

The children's age, attention, and ability level will determine the length of the dancing session, the types of movement activities that can be explored, and how these elements unfold during the session. Nonetheless, there is a basic sequence of activities that is effective with all age levels.

The Sequence to a Dance Class

Beginning the Class   When possible, it is best to have all children dancing without shoes or socks. This is suggested for some period of time even for children who may have splints in their shoes for orthopedic reasons. Feeling the floor against their feet stimulates sensory awareness of the foot and exercises the muscles. Activities that accentuate rolling through the feet from heel to toe as the child steps on each foot to bear weight, adds increased awareness of the whole foot and articulation through the toes. This contributes to creating a core sense of balance in the whole body. Taking off shoes and socks can become part of the ritual that signals the beginning of dance class. Create a specific place where shoes and socks can be stored out of the way and designate another specific place in the room where the children can gather to begin the dancing activities.

The initial focus at the beginning of class is to create a sense of group cohesion while acknowledging each participant. This can be accomplished by starting off with a movement activity that encourages the group to respond as a whole, and group members to share their own interpretations of the activity. This will warm them up to feeling like a group while simultaneously offering the opportunity for them to voice their own individual presence and feelings on that particular day. This also can provide a gentle way to join in for children who are hesitant, shy, or uncomfortable in large groups. For the boisterous children who are raring to go, this type of activity can enable them to direct their excess energy into movement while making their presence felt in socially accepted ways. In essence, it is best to begin a class with an energetic activity rather than one that is sedentary such as everyone sitting down for circle time. Sedentary activities require children to immediately gain control of their actions and to attend both emotionally and socially. Starting with an energetic activity warms the children up, preparing them to become a cohesive group once they have had an opportunity to express themselves.

Body Warm-Up and Movement Awareness   Once the class members have had time to express themselves and get a sense of the group, a more structured group activity should be introduced that acts as a body warm-up and an introduction to basic dance and movement actions. This usually occurs 10–20 minutes into a 45-minute to a 1-hour class. Relaxation activities can be included to help the group calm down and be ready to focus on the more structured activities to follow. By this time, children should have a good sense of each other, so a circle time using a greeting song that acknowledges each child can be included.

Introduction of Theme   A theme for the class should be introduced at this point. This theme can be explored with any arrangement of children from whole group to individual interactions. Although the theme may be predetermined, it is best for teachers to take a moment to review how the class has been going. Has a theme developed through the children's participation that might support their learning in an interesting or valuable way? For instance, through their warm-up play the children might have begun to imitate animals such as a bird taking off into flight or a snake gliding across the grass.

Now is the time for a teacher to determine the natural progression of the class. A teacher may decide to explore a theme that developed spontaneously or may introduce a predetermined theme. As discussed above, the list of potential themes is virtually endless. Everyday activities such as waking up, going to bed, or playing outside are often popular in parent–baby and toddler groups. Transportation vehicles, seasons, fairies, dragons, and combat characters can also be fun. Themes around social experiences are a wonderful way for children to dance out their budding awareness of self and others. These include searching, finding, playing, and parting from a parent or favorite friend. Feelings associated with being lost and found, happiness, excitement, confusion, anger, sadness, and fear can be safely explored through the drama of dance. (Toddlers love to bring in their favorite teddy bear or doll to participate as partners in such dances.) Themes can also focus on movement concepts such as awareness of Body, Efforts, Shape, Space, and Phrasing elements; and dance concepts such as partnering, trios, group dance sculptures, and choreographies involving visual interest and sequenced movements that make patterns across the floor. A teacher can introduce these dance concepts in a simplified form to children by the time they are 4 years old, and can introduce more complex concepts as children become school age.

Solos   Children can be asked to create a dance sequence to share with class members. Students can learn about being good observers and audience members as they watch and discuss what they think the dance is about when it is finished. During the solo, the teacher can describe elements of the spontaneous choreography that may help children learn about the child or the theme. This helps the children stay focused and be active participants even when they are not dancing. Over time, children can also be encouraged to describe what they see as it is happening.

Closure   The purpose of a closure activity is to support group cohesion and prepare children for the transition into their next scheduled activity. This can take many forms and be of varying duration, depending on the group's energy level and the nature of their next event. Regardless of the age, closure should always include gathering the whole group together and acknowledging each member. This can occur through a good-bye song sung to each child or a final good-bye signature movement contributed by each child. Closure can start with breath awareness, relaxation, visualization, or a group dance to a song with a slower tempo to gather the children and calm their bodies. Singing a few finger-play songs together before the final good-bye song can help focus younger children to begin the closure process.

Choosing the same last one or two songs each time and using these songs along several age ranges creates a sense of ritual, connecting and supporting all age groups. This is especially significant as children grow into other class ranges or when a special event may combine different age ranges for a joint activity or performance. A teacher should create a systematic way to assist children with putting their shoes back on to bring the whole experience back full circle to the beginning, thus completing the closure ritual.

Specific Age-Related Considerations

See http://www.brookespublishing.com/dancing for a chart offering specific advice and questions to keep in mind in encouraging early childhood creative movement explorations in various age groups. In addition, the following age-related suggestions and observations may be helpful to those who work with young children.

Birth–2 Years Movement explorations with children from birth to 2 years old are very free flowing. Activities and peer interactions with this age group are intermittent. It is best to keep these sessions small and short. If the parent–infant or caregiver–infant ratio is equal, a reasonable length for a session containing six dyads is 20 to 30 minutes for babies under 6–8 months; this time can be extended to up to 45 minutes for older babies. However, if a teacher is the only adult, no more than three to four children should be included at one time, and beginning sessions should only last 10 minutes, progressing to 20 minutes over time. During this period the teacher will be moving from baby to baby as the babies' abilities to attend fluctuate. There should be lots of flexibility, with babies coming and going throughout the activities. Be prepared for the baby's attention to wax and wane. It is okay if not all of the babies participate at all times. Often a teacher may find it best to dance one-to-one with a baby as other babies watch and try some interpretation of the action off on their own at a later point. A teacher can include or acknowledge babies from afar through eye contact, smiles, and vocal encouragement if they are trying the actions on the side, or if they are being good observers.

At this young age, the focus is to provide an environment that piques a baby's interests. Including parents or other significant caregivers in the class provides the opportunity to enhance the attachment relationship and communication within the dyad. It is a reciprocal process between the baby and the parent. Adults are guided to become skilled in reading their baby's budding nonverbal cues and personal movement style, while the babies use their moving bodies to explore and express themselves as they develop knowledge and expectations about their parent's nonverbal style of relating to them. See http://www.brookes publishing.com/dancing for a description of activities that support this developing parent–infant relationship.

The movement and dance should stimulate the senses, encourage exploration on all developmental levels, and enhance communication. Babies will learn about sensory integration and regulation as they are introduced to a wide variety of activities. This age group benefits from lots of gross motor play using tunnels, large balls, pillows, and safe objects for them to climb and explore in between group activities. These children respond to strong rhythms and simple movements such as rocking, rolling, crawling, clapping, bouncing, swinging, stamping, and running. Participating parents and caregivers learn about their baby's unique style of relating by providing times in class to specifically watch and follow their baby's movement actions, no matter how small or subtle they may be. Adults are instructed to pay close attention to how their baby is using his body actions to react and respond to different stimuli: such as the rhythm or melody of different music selections; the baby's ability to sustain eye contact; the introduction of different tactile sensations like the quality of the adult's touch, a silk scarf or the texture of a soft ball rolled on the baby's limbs; experiencing different movements in space such as bouncing, swaying, and rolling; as well as how and if the baby attunes to the adult as they engage in songs and singing finger games. Throughout the class, pertinent child developmental information can be shared with the adult participants as they play with the children. As the adults and caregivers participate in these classes they will learn about new ways to play with their babies at home.

A typical session may start with the children exploring gross motor activities. At some point the teacher can play a musical selection that elicits a group movement experience. This may be a piece that has a distinct rhythm that encourages bouncing movements, or a waltz that invites the adults and children to sway, swoop, and step. Simple recorded dancing singing games, like "Shoo Fly, Don't Bother Me" are very enjoyable for this age group. The adults can hold the babies in their arms, swinging, swaying, and turning with them as they respond to the words of the songs. As the weeks progress and participants become familiar with the activities and form a sense of group, this section of the class may extend in time and become very active. A teacher should be flexible, however, about the manner in which and how long each individual baby or dyad participates as a group because this will vary greatly.

This gross motor activity may be followed by a circle time activity. Infant massage, gentle stretches, Peekaboo, and other finger-play games that involve touch will encourage body awareness and support social engagement as the child and adult playfully interact. Listening to and playing a wide variety of musical instruments and exploring textures by dancing and rolling in scarves and different textured fabrics can be explored. These activities will stimulate the babies' sensory systems. At this point the teacher might select a piece of music to encourage the babies, or the babies and the adults, to freely respond through dance.

For this activity, the teacher can form a circle, leaving enough open space in the middle in which all the children can crawl, stand, step, or dance safely. The teacher looks to see how the babies respond to the new music. This response may be subtle or overt. One baby may start to open and close her fingers to the beat very gently while another might bounce his body up and down exuberantly. A child newly upright may simply stand motionless! Sometimes this dancing involves clapping hands to the beat or rocking side to side. Each of these actions is considered a dancing movement and should be acknowledged and tried by the other participants.

After these activities, a final group activity should be conducted to create a sense of personal centering and group closure. A slow, soft waltz ending with everyone in a circle swaying and gently stroking his or her children creates a calming closure. Children can also sit or lie on their caregivers as they massage or rock and sway, gradually slowing down their actions into quiet stillness.

Preschool Age   An obstacle course is a useful first activity for a preschooler or for any classroom in which there is great variation in the children's attention spans. The elements of the course should require children to go in, under, over, swing, crawl, squeeze through, jump, balance, and roll. Such actions stimulate early basic motor and movement development skills. Physically, the actions enable children to gain an awareness of their moving bodies in space in relation to objects and other bodies. The observant teacher can learn much about individual children's perceptual motor planning abilities as they navigate through the course. Their emotional states—affects, levels of tiredness, abilities to attend, and the attention and nonverbal quality in which they initiate engagement with the obstacles—can be assessed by watching the amount of energy and focus they are able to expend on the specific elements of the course. Children have the opportunity both to be on their own and to get the teacher's individual attention as they move through each element. Children may choose to do each element of the course alone, with the teacher's assistance, or with a peer. Children watch other children as they move through each element and wait their turn. Each child's own way of performing each action can be verbally acknowledged as the children pass through the elements of the obstacle course.

The innate nature of an obstacle course itself supports cognitive skills by teaching concepts such as sequencing movements together, maintaining a sense of continuity, extending concentration, and following pathways. Perceptual motor and gross motor skills involving body coordination, rhythm, and motor planning are also explored. Socially, obstacle courses provide an active way for children to begin to learn about rules and turn taking. Paying attention to how each child navigates through the elements of the course will reveal information about each child's mood for the day, individual pace, and overall affect and emotional style.

One example of an obstacle course might begin with the teacher placing colored rug squares on the floor in some type of pattern. This immediately creates a mobile focus for the children to direct their moving bodies. A pattern is formed by varying how close or far away each square is aligned to another rug square. For example, four squares can be placed equidistant from each other followed by a larger space and then four more squares of the same distance. A simple walking rhythm is created following the beat 1 – 2 – 3 – 4 jump, 1 – 2 – 3 – 4. After a few days of this pattern, it can be revised by placing three squares in a vertical line close enough that a child can easily step from square to square, with the fourth square placed far enough away that the child must jump or leap to land on it. This pattern can then be repeated with additional rugs to make a pathway. A stepping and jumping rhythm of 1 – 2 – 3 – jump – 4 is created with this pattern. The rug squares might lead to a foam block over which the children must crawl, followed by their crawling through a tunnel. At the end of the tunnel, the teacher might lay out more rug squares in the same stepping–jumping pattern. This could lead the children into stepping onto folded mats on which each child is asked to tap out the rug pattern on a tambourine. This activity extends the rhythmic stepping pattern into an auditory musical sequence, crossing sensory modalities. Next, each child waits and then takes turns to climb over and slide down the "mountain"—created by placing a three-folded mat on its side and diagonally opening one of the folded sides, supporting it with pillows. Pillows can be placed in a jumping pattern, creating a larger gross motor rendition of the rug pattern. These actions could lead each child to rock on or roll over a large physioball. The child might finish the obstacle course by doing a full turn inside a hula-hoop. These later actions stimulate the vestibular and proprioceptive systems. Watching how each child navigates through each of these elements enables a teacher to learn about each child's ability to attend, follow directions, work on motor planning, and get along with others.

Kindergarten–Second Grade   For this age range of children with a greater attention span and increased body awareness and control, the creative movement class can begin by interpreting qualities of varying music selections through body movements that take the children moving across the room. For example, children can be asked to create a movement in response to the rhythm, tempo, or melodic quality of the music. The children can move across the floor as a group or individually, demonstrating their reactions. In the group experience, the children can be instructed to spread out in the room, taking time to individually feel the music in their bodies as the teacher watches all of them. One by one the teacher describes and demonstrates a particular quality of each child's action. The teacher can ask the whole group to try on the children's individual actions as they move across the room together. Children's ideas can be highlighted in an even more individual way by having individual children demonstrate their ideas as a solo. At first the teacher can use descriptive words to help the children learn how to look at the qualities of the actions such as, "Look how Amy's feet take quick, tiny steps as she goes across the room!" After the child first demonstrates her action, she leads her classmates through instruction and demonstration across the room as they try on her action too. These activities simultaneously build group cohesion while fostering individual expression.

Children with increased body awareness, physical control and coordination, and attentional abilities can begin their creative movement classes with movement actions that create a challenge, such as following a movement sequence involving balancing. This will immediately draw the group together as individual children each concentrate their visual and physical focus.

The next activity might involve more concentrated group cohesion, such as asking all of the children to create movements in response to the rhythm of a song. Again, there is room for individual expression as each child has the opportunity to shake a body part in a unique way, with the group following. Common, structured, age-appropriate movements such as running, jumping, gliding, and turning can be introduced at this time. These are also the elements of dance that the children can be reminded to use later when they make up their own dances. At this point, the teacher should determine the group's feeling tone, energy level, and attention span. Based on the teacher's reading of the group's needs, the next activity can either draw the children into a more focused activity such as sitting in a circle and rolling a ball to one another or doing a formal hello dance and song, or it can allow the children to move into more individualized expressions following the movement theme of the day.

How to Read the Feeling Tone and Energy Level of the Class

Determining which direction to take requires a teacher to read the feeling tone and energy level of the group, as well as that of individual children. The *feeling tone* refers to the mood of the group or child, while the *energy level* depicts the actual body and movement behaviors the children are exhibiting. The feeling tone relates to emotions while the energy level refers to the physical feelings created by the children's actions.

For example, the mood of the group may be excited, exhibited in facial expressions such as smiles and giggles and quick, large motor actions such as running, jumping, and darting around the room. The overall energy level of the group in which they are performing these body movements may be portrayed with strong, direct, focused, and organized execution. This can be a fun mood to support by putting on lively music with a strong beat to help the children express this feeling in a group dance of excitement. Then the group can form a circle and each child can demonstrate a dance action for the group to try. A dance can be choreographed as each child's actions are performed to make a sequence. This activity supports the flow of the group while acknowledging each child's unique contribution.

If the whole group or individual members present these excited actions with an energy level that is unfocused or too multifocused, however, this will create an atmosphere that is on the verge of getting out of control. Evidence of this might include floppy movements, agitated tension, too much variability in the choice of actions, or an excessive amount of bumping or falling behaviors. The way to prevent this from happening is to create organization within the context of the actions that the children are exhibiting. To do this, a teacher must first mentally define the specific qualities of the movements that individual children are doing. These qualities should influence what the appropriate next step will be.

There are several directions a teacher might take. The energy level of the children's actions can be shifted to compliment their excited feeling tone. For example, a teacher might shake a tambourine and ask children to suddenly freeze into an interesting pose at the sound of a drumbeat. When the children have all frozen into positions, the teacher stands next to each child and describes his or her shape. Next, the children shake their body shapes as the teacher shakes the tambourine, asking them to form new shapes at the next drumbeat. The anticipation of having their shapes described and forming new shapes creates excitement and focuses the children's attention, for each child welcomes the individual acknowledgment. Another variation on this freezing/posing dance-play is to instruct the children to move as a drum is lightly tapped or a tambourine is shaken, and to freeze when the music stops by catching themselves right before they fall, making a pose. Each child can demonstrate his or her falling pose and have the other students try it. Posing just before falling is an exciting challenge that brings focus while developing attention and body strength and organization.

Adding recorded music is a quick way to change the atmosphere of a whole room. A strong yet medium tempo beat can provide children with an external structure to use in setting their actions. A melodic musical score can soften their actions and stimulate imagery. A teacher can instruct the children to experiment with movements that get bigger and smaller or higher and lower as the volume of the music is adjusted. An alternative choice is to juxtapose the presenting energy level and feeling tone. A teacher might play a recording of very full, solemn music that suggests large, slow, serious movements such as lunges and actions low to the ground. The fullness of the music will compliment yet redirect the children's excited feeling tone while channeling their unfocused energy level into large-body experiences.

A teacher's ability to work with and decipher the subtle differences in these two distinct qualities—feeling tone and energy level—greatly affects the overall flow and success of the group experience.

This skill will take time to acquire and requires the teacher to watch each child's actions and the overall group feeling closely. The teacher must look to see if and how the emotional feelings of the group and individual children support, compliment, or are dissonant with the actions they are performing. It is of paramount importance for a teacher to determine the qualities of the actions in order to use these qualities to make a bridge to the activities that follow. The bridging movements, activity, or theme suggestions should match or compliment the qualities of the children's actions, creating organization and direction, without escalating their behaviors. This is how to achieve a sense of flow in the whole class that signifies that the magic of creativity, cooperative sharing, and a sense of group connection is at its peak. A teacher might also notice his or her own reactions prompted by the group and individual behaviors, for this will influence the paths the teacher is most comfortable in taking in order to continue the experience. The best approach is when a teacher's attitude exudes a sense of curiosity, support, and guidance. A teacher taking this approach will be open to the children's suggestions and movement expressions while still maintaining just enough direction that the experience feels monitored and safe for each child.

There are numerous directions to be considered when reading movement cues to guide the group experience. These include picking up on emerging themes inspired by the children's actions of the moment, creating activities that enhance class cohesion, transitioning the group to a new focus, and redirecting difficult behaviors. There is more than one way to conduct a class correctly. The key is for the teacher to closely observe the children's responses. If the children are enthusiastic, engaged, and expressive, if they contribute to and solidify the group experience as well as find opportunities to share their uniqueness, the chosen direction is a success.

Drawing out Each Child's Unique Expressive Dance

The goal of the *Ways of Seeing* approach to creative dance is to support each child's self-expression. Numerous examples of how to draw out the specific qualities of each child's personal style have been provided in this chapter and throughout this book. Supporting each child's self-expression enables a child to participate in a variety of different ways according to abilities and inclinations. Children vary greatly in their interest and eagerness to express themselves physically. Some children cannot stop moving while others tend to recoil in shyness when asked to join a group. The creative dance experience has room for these types of children and for all of the variations in between.

Very Active Children These children are always on the go. They often have a difficult time sitting still for too long. Their movements can be large, full body actions that take them racing through the room. They are comfortable throwing their bodies on the floor or bumping into objects to stop their projections. Alternately, if asked to stay still, they can become very fidgety, shaking and rocking their bodies or different body parts like fingers or limbs in an effort to contain their energy. Their ability to regulate their bodies and feel in control is not well established. This may become one of the creative dance class's goals. Asking them to stop and start as the music is turned off and on is a good full-bodied activity for these children. The duration of the pauses can be extended as they gain more control. The next step is to have the teacher or a classmate shout out a particular type of movement to perform while the music is on—such as a hop or a skip—and a particular type of shape to hold when the music is paused—such as a large shape or a twisting shape. Stepping, stamping, or clapping to a strong, regular beat of music supports auditory processing as the children work on regulating their bodies.

Very active children often do not differentiate between varying tempos of rhythm. Having them step or clap right to the beat or asking them to clap out a simple rhythm designed by the teacher focuses their attention. Having the children leap onto evenly spaced rug squares or tap their feet to the beat of the rhythm extends this activity. Working on balance is also extremely useful for these children. The whole class can count aloud as different balancing poses are found. To come out of their poses, the children can be asked to fall and then catch themselves in another pose before they drop to the floor. Obstacle courses are also useful because they require children to spontaneously change the mode of their movements to be able to follow the course. Any of these suggestions can be used as a warm-up before playing music with varying tempos and asking the children to create their own movement responses. All of these suggestions teach children how to organize their bodies while still being able to move.

Shy Children Children along this spectrum appear hesitant to freely express themselves. They may try to avoid creative dance class altogether or sit on the sidelines observing from afar. When they do join in, their actions appear tentative or may reflect an attempt to copy those of a classmate. When asked to contribute their own movement, they may stand still or reply that they don't know what to do. Despite these initial reactions, these children can be successfully integrated into the creative dance class experience. Initially, such children can be allowed to observe the class. During this time the teacher should notice if a child is inadvertently responding to the movement activities despite her resistance. For example, a child may sway to the rhythm of the music or giggle in response to a classmate's playful action. At first the teacher can acknowledge this nonverbally by smiling or nodding to the child. This is a private contact between the child and teacher supporting the child's responses without drawing too much attention. From time to time the child can be given a gentle invitation to join. Whether or not the child actually joins in, she should be acknowledged during the hello and good-bye song rituals. Often parents report that children recreate many elements of the dance class in the safety of their homes. This may happen for weeks before they are willing to participate during class.

Once a child does participate, even if it is only to copy the action of a classmate, the teacher must look for some subtle uniqueness in the quality of the child's actions and verbally describe it. It can be in the softness of the child's step, how the child's head is held, or how well the child is able to mirror another child's actions. The goal is to help shy children feel seen and honored for their contributions without feeling that too much attention is drawn toward them. Also, a teacher should keep in mind that all actions are considered dancing responses in creative dance class. Therefore, when a shy child's reaction during a solo is to "freeze" in place, the teacher can address the power of stillness and the strength it takes to hold a pose. The teacher might also ask the other children to watch closely to observe if they can see any part of the performer's body moving. This helps the shy dancer to feel empowered by the command she exerted over the group. Often this will inspire the child to move some small body part ever so slightly to see who is watching. The observing children become delighted in their detective work, as they attentively attempt to find the mover's action.

Children with Special Needs and Challenges

Adding children with special needs to a class can be an enhancing experience for everyone. When successful, every child gains an understanding and appreciation of each person's uniqueness. How to integrate children with special concerns depends on each child's unique strengths and challenges. If a teacher has not met the child before, a private session or interview is recommended before the child joins the group. This will give the teacher an opportunity to learn about the child's style. It can be helpful to hold several private sessions during which the teacher introduces the dance and movement concepts so that the child may become familiar with aspects of the class and begin to develop a personal relationship with the teacher. It is essential that the child feels comfortable with and trusts the teacher. Children who are physically independent, are able to maintain joint attention and focus with the group, and are socially comfortable can be in a dance class without a one-to-one aide. If needed, the other children can take turns being the partner of the child with special needs. However, if a child needs physical assistance to move, has difficulty maintaining attention, or is socially disconnected in a way that is disruptive to the whole class, a one-to-one aide will be necessary to shadow the child.

A creative dance class that includes children with special challenges is an ideal way to develop social awareness and friendship because each child's unique movement expression contributes to the group experience. As children try on the movement suggestions of other children, they begin to reflect about how it feels to move in ways they have not previously experienced. Dance activities can be structured so that no movement is too large, too small, too fast, or too slow. Any action a child creates can become part of the group dance. As children become more comfortable, even if they cannot follow as completely as the other children in the class, their actions can be incorporated to contribute to the overall dance.

The Use of Music

Music is instrumental in evoking each child's qualitative style. As has been illustrated throughout this chapter, music is an invaluable tool that can greatly assist students in developing their unique styles and expressivity. Music for creative dance is used in four different ways:

1. To provide a background

2. To create a feeling or mood, such as calming children or stimulating a more lively response

3. To evoke an emotional or self-expressive experience through a specific piece

4. To emphasize a particular rhythm to support a movement or motor skill

Using music purely as background should be limited. Background music sets a tone and influences the environment, both consciously and unconsciously. It is important to be careful and clear about the particular goal of the piece of music selected. When it doesn't serve a function other than filling in an empty space with sound, music can desensitize children's auditory awareness and their responsiveness to a particular musical selection. This especially occurs in what is often known as elevator music, which does not have a distinct quality or enough variation in tempo and style to evoke a dynamic response. If the music does not stimulate the children's senses and emotions, this will be reflected in their movement reactions. Inevitably children will begin to tune out the music or to respond to it in rote ways. They will get bored and easily distractible. This is when children will begin to act out in ways that disrupt the sense of class cohesion. Varying the musical selections often and drawing from a wide variety of musical styles and cultures can prevent this response. Such variations include changes in tempo, rhythms, melodies, and types of instruments, as well as using multiple layers of musical themes and energy levels.

Tempo refers to the speed of the music. The tempo of a piece of music can be constant or varied. Classical music often has several changes of tempo within the same piece. Different tempos can evoke different themes and feelings. Each person has a unique response to these variations. Careful listening to music will reveal that often there is an obvious theme (the melody), and also other supporting themes that seem to be behind or underneath the melody. This is what adds richness to the total sound. Having children tune into these multiple layers of music greatly enhances their enjoyment and understanding of the music. Cognitively, it strengthens their listening and attentional skills.

The rhythm of the music influences its overall organization. In its most general definition, *rhythm* marks the passage of time, emphasized through marked pulses. It is created by a sequential flow between sound and silence in a distinctive temporal patterning. Rhythms can be regular or arrhythmic. *Regular rhythms* create a predictable steady beat, whereas in *arrhythmic rhythms* the timing between the sounds' emphasis does not follow a consistent beat. Encouraging children to find the beat and respond to it through their bodies helps them gain a sense of organization, regulation, and control over impulsive actions.

The tempos, melodic themes, and rhythms create the overall energy level of music. The energy level can be high and stimulating; neutral or calm; or lethargic, requiring very low energy. A teacher can select music to reflect the children's current mood or can set a new tone in the classroom. Both the children's current energy level and what the focus of the creative dance experience is will determine what music is chosen. It is important for a teacher to take the time to get a sense of the overall mood of the group. Does the teacher want to support the children's energetic enthusiasm or have them calm down? There are many ways to use music to approach both situations. Surprisingly, selecting a lively piece of music with a strong beat can be the first step for either focus! The lively melody will match the children's energy levels and draw their attention to relate to something outside of themselves, while the strong rhythm will begin to organize their movements on personal body levels. Matching the children's mood first attracts their attention and provides a focus for their energy without escalating it.

How a teacher works with this music and uses the subsequent piece of music determines what direction the class will next take. Playing with music by instructing children to make their movements larger and smaller as they hear the volume increase or decrease will add further control over their actions. Intermittently pausing the music and requiring them to freeze and then move again will improve their body awareness as well. Once children have gained more control, the new music selection can either maintain this lively rhythmic focus—as they respond with their own dance combinations based on the movement themes explored—or calm their energy level if the teacher chooses a musical piece that is slower and softer. Such slow, soft songs can naturally lead into a relaxation experience. This whole music sequence explored through body movement expression enables children to feel their bodies gradually becoming more organized and quiet. Children learn, through physical experiencing, how to bring their busy bodies down to a calmer state.

ADDING MOVEMENT ACTIVITIES TO EVERYDAY ACTIVITIES

Adding a full creative movement curriculum is not always practical in a classroom setting. Even if that is the case, there are still ways to add movement explorations in a classroom to enhance each child's experience. First, a teacher can provide organized physical group activities using the principles discussed in this chapter, both during lessons and as a transition between lessons. A teacher should always watch how individual children add their own styles to the actions. This will ensure that movement activities are self-expressive rather than just an exercise.

For example, a teacher might have the children stand up and follow a game of Simon Says. As the game progresses, the teacher looks around the room and comments about how individual children touch the named body part. The teacher can focus on body awareness in space by having the children move in front, behind, or next to

There are always ways to add movement explorations in a classroom to enhance each child's experience.

their desks and chairs or by having other students making shapes as they stand in those spaces. Several children can be asked to create zigzag pathways over to their cubbyholes to get their coats and then the next group of children can be challenged to see if they can follow one of those paths to reach their own coats. The teacher can watch how each child performs the action differently and then describe it. This will encourage the children to add their own signatures to their actions. They may change the level of space of the action by walking on their toes, or by taking long strides. A teacher might add a rhythm through hand clapping or might play music to see how movements are transformed. The different times in a day when children are asked to line up provides an excellent opportunity to work on rhythmic stepping patterns, simple dance steps, marching, and increased body boundary awareness.

Storytime is an excellent opportunity to include movement activities. The story can be used as the basis for a whole dance experience. This activity provides prereading skill. A teacher can start by having children identify the movement words in a story. Movement words are words that provoke images that can be expressed easily through actions. Often they are the descriptive or action words of the story. For example, in the sentence "The dog ran through the barn," the verb "ran" is the action word. Individual children can be asked to demonstrate how they think the dog ran—some will crouch over as they run, while others may shake their heads and pant with their tongues out.

Feelings and interpersonal relationships can also be portrayed and explored in the dancing out of a story. Children will learn about the important role of nonverbal behaviors during interactions. After listening to the sentence "Jessica was walking all alone through the park and suddenly saw her best friend Inez playing by the swings," the children can be asked to demonstrate how Jessica felt when she was walking alone and how she felt when she saw her best friend. Interpreting books through movement will stimulate the children to create their own stories for their dances. (See Appendix B for a list of recommended books.) Adding movement explorations to any part of the curriculum supports multisensory learning.

Analysis of Overall Classroom Curriculum

Applying an understanding of nonverbal communication to the overall classroom curriculum can create a rhythm and flow that supports each child's learning style. There are seven qualitative elements to consider in curriculum planning:

• Tempo
• Rhythm
• Energy levels
• Tension levels
• Body awareness
• Use of space
• Sequencing

Designing a classroom curriculum with the first six elements in mind, and becoming aware of how these six elements sequence together over the course of the day, will create a balance among activities that has an active and a recuperative relationship.

Tempo Tempo relates to speed. Although the two opposing tempos, fast and slow, most readily come to mind, it is important to remember all the tempos in between—medium, medium slow, medium fast, and gradual tempo increases and decreases. Tempo-related questions include asking how a person moves into a fast or slow tempo, how that tempo is maintained, and for what duration the tempo is kept once it is attained. When thinking about tempos in the classroom, teachers should consider children's individual tendencies as well as the required tempo of a particular learning activity. Both factors have their own natural style. Some children speed through an assignment, whereas others linger and need continual direction. Learning new material may require a slow, steady pace, whereas familiar tasks may be approached more quickly and easily. Thinking about the pace an activity requires in relation to the time of day, the activities that precede and follow it, and the overall classroom tempo created by the students contribute to the effectiveness of the planned activity. Interspersing activities that vary in duration and require different levels of attention provides variation in the pace of the day. Such structures create an active and recuperative relationship between lessons.

Rhythm   Rhythm involves the organization of the passage of time through accented pulses. A sequential flow develops over time as these accents are interspersed with elements that have less emphasis. This flow can create a pattern as it is repeated. Applying the concept of rhythm to classroom curriculum refers to the level of emphasis the actual academic activity has within the overall sequence of activities throughout the day. The rhythm of a specific curriculum activity is defined by the qualitative elements that are required in order for children to participate. These requirements relate both to skills on the children's parts as well as tools needed to teach the lesson. The children's skills include the level and type of attention needed. Does the task require the whole group's attention such as in a lecture? Does the task require a dyadic or small-group sharing such as in a joint project? Is individual attention needed to complete a test? Each child's cognitive ability should also affect the rhythm of the lesson. How well the children know the material of the lesson will affect the rhythmic flow in which the lesson is taught. New material may require a stop and start arrhythmic pace filled with pauses as questions are asked and answered. The speed in which different children obtain an understanding of the material will also affect the whole classroom rhythm. Once the material is well known, a regular rhythmic beat may evolve.

The tools the task itself requires will also affect the rhythm of the activity. Some activities require a certain amount of preparation, such as getting out the materials to prepare for painting or handing out worksheets for a desk assignment. Other activities have a natural flow, such as when the teacher reads a book to the class. How long the class stays with a particular lesson affects the rhythm of the whole day. Interspersing lessons of varying lengths will create a recuperative rhythm involving more active or intense attention followed by activities that are freer flowing, having a restorative and replenishing effect.

Energy Levels   Classroom activities also can be classified in regard to the level of energy they require or create. *Energy level* in this sense refers to the amount of concentration a task demands in relation to the resulting mental and physical activity exuded from the group—

as a whole or as individuals. This relationship between individuals, the group, and the task will greatly affect the success of a lesson plan. Energy levels are categorized as high, neutral or calm, low, or lethargic. High-energy activities work best when students are in a state of alertness both mentally and physically. Students in this state emit a sense of aliveness. In its most extreme, there is a sense of electricity felt in the children's bubbly eagerness. Neutral or calm energy activities require children to be alert and well regulated in order to be able to absorb information. In this state their bodies can focus on the lesson without needing to mitigate between their inner sensations and external stimuli. In this state children are good listeners. It is useful for children to be in this state during reading time when they are being asked to listen and relax. Activities with a neutral energy help to calm the classroom down and take off the pressure of performance. It can be a time of relaxation and centering. Low energy activities require even less participation from children. Relaxation lessons fit into this category, as well as activities that require little skill and are easy and familiar. Simple coloring tasks in which children do not have to follow many directives also support this level of energy. This state is most useful to create deep recuperation for children before engaging in a lesson that requires more active participation. Lessons that create a sense of lethargy should be avoided. This occurs most when children feel overloaded due to their personal circumstances or they have been presented with too much material for too long a time.

When executing a lesson, it is helpful to consider the amount of energy a task requires in relation to the students' current energy levels. Many factors influence a child's energy, including sleep, hunger, mental state, and developmental ability. The time of day, season, overall classroom environment, current events, and the teacher's energy level are also very influential. In addition, different lessons will stimulate a shift in energy level. The active and recuperative flow of the breath rhythm is again a useful analogy to keep in mind when creating a lesson plan. This does not mean, however, that a slow activity must follow an active one. Instead, the emphasis is in creating balance and variety rather than simple activities that have opposite qualities. The intense yet contained high energy required for a new writing task can focus the whole group into an alert state. Nonetheless, once the task is completed, this intense high energy will need to be released. A large motor activity such as stomping to a rhythmic beat redirects this high energy through another activity that allows children to use their whole bodies in a vigorous yet directed manner. It enables a release of energy that will prepare children for the next task that may require them to sit again and listen.

This example can also be analyzed from the standpoint of the children entering the classroom in a state of high energy—a common occurrence after recess. The focused concentrated requirements of a writing task for the young kindergarten child may be too demanding to be the first task. The fluid actions involved in painting lines, circles, and curves with markers, finger paints, or a brush, however, are wonderful transitional activities that might start to focus them mentally and physically and act as a precursor to letter writing.

Tension Levels   Tension levels work hand in hand with energy levels. *Tension level* refers to the overall feeling tone and sense of intensity in the classroom. Tension levels move along a spectrum from free, to fluid, to neutral, to directed, and finally, to bound. *Free tension* creates a sense of carefree freedom and abandon. Outdoor play, such as running and swinging, or the joyous imaginary play that goes on in the pretend play corner, fits into this category. A *fluid tension* level is similar to free tension with a bit more direction. This is exemplified when the children have learned the routines of the classroom, easily moving from activity to activity. It is that content feeling the teacher has when the children have had no problems deciding on activities during choice time. *Neutral tension* is that feeling in the classroom when nothing in particular is standing out. It is needed every day, but if it is the only or most prominent state of the class, it can feel boring or uninspiring at times. *Directed tension* is also a necessary state in the classroom. It reflects that the class is hard at work, and often is felt when students are concentrating on a new skill or one that requires all of their attention. *Bound tension* occurs when the directed tension goes awry, or when there is discord among the children or between the teacher and the children. For example, bound tension may result when a task has required too much effort and has taken on a very strained, unnatural level of focus or when an event compromises the children's social interactions. It is not a comfortable state and should be avoided whenever possible. When children are new learners experiencing more complex social relations in a group setting, it is important to evaluate activities to see if they may have inadvertently set up a sense of competition rather than of cooperation and tolerance for differences. If a sense of bound tension is felt in the classroom, these factors may be contributing.

Body Awareness Body awareness relates to the personal, physical, cognitive, communicative, social, and emotional sensibility of each classroom participant. This includes the teacher as well as the students. In its broadest sense, body awareness extends the tension level category previously discussed and applies it on a personal level. The individual's tension level may affect how the student or teacher processes input cognitively and emotionally. How comfortable people feel about their physical, social, emotional, communicative, and cognitive selves can influence how they receive and interact with information in their environment. When thinking about body awareness in relation to classroom curriculum, a teacher must ask how the lesson may affect each student's sense of self in all developmental domains.

Many body awareness factors can influence the learning experience. On a purely physical level, these include tense or sluggish musculature, tightness or holding of breath, and poor body alignment, most noted when children sit with their torsos in deep, concave shapes exuding a sense of passive weight. Taking a moment to breathe deeply, release or wake up the muscles, and realign the posture can do a lot to help refocus attention. Children's body awareness will be revealed socially in how they use their bodies and where they place their bodies when interacting with others. Are they able to have clear body boundaries observable by maintaining a comfortable distance between themselves and others? Or do they stand too close or need to touch other children when they interact? How children regulate their emotional reactions and how their emotions are displayed physically can be expressed in how they hold and move their bodies. Are they very physically expressive when they are happy, agitated, or sad?

How children combine nonverbal and verbal actions to express needs and understandings will demonstrate their communicative styles. Children greatly vary in their abilities to use verbal language. The skills of using nonverbal gestures and reading nonverbal cues can play a significant part in communication. On a cognitive level, individual children's abilities to attend and maintain focus will affect their abilities to advance intellectually.

Use of Space This category has both a personal and an environmental focus. On a personal level it relates to the individual's awareness of his or her body in the surroundings. Does a child take up a great deal of space, figuratively or physically? Is a child able to organize himself and his classwork neatly within his reach? Does another child seem to create a trail of her personal items extending beyond her immediate surroundings into the shared space of her classmates? How aware is a child of others and objects in the room?

This category also analyzes how the room and activities in the room are organized. The pathways created by the placement of objects in a room can greatly influence how children interact and participate in a classroom. Is there a mix of contained and open areas? Can the children pass by each other without needing to squeeze their bodies? Does the placement of the furniture and other classmates present clear lines of vision enabling students to focus toward the direction of the lesson? Is the classroom visually pleasing and inviting? Conversely, are there so many objects piled and stacked that it is difficult to know where to focus attention?

How the objects are placed can greatly influence how the room feels. This can influence how children move around the room and how they interact with one another. For example, the continuous curve of circles tends to create a sense of community and equality. Evenly spaced desks in rows create individual private spaces. Diagonals cut across a space and stimulate a sense of traveling. When organizing the objects in the classroom, teachers should consider how it feels to move through the pathways created. This can be extended to include where lessons and activities are executed throughout the day. Can they be organized in ways that children have an opportunity to systematically move through the room?

Sequencing Analyzing curriculum activities with these elements will reveal the sequence of events throughout the day. This sequence is called the *pattern of flow*. This pattern is analogous to the melody of a song. It represents the major qualitative themes of the classroom environment. Charting this flow pattern each day for several days will reveal the themes, rhythms, and energy levels that predominant in a classroom. Flow patterns that develop over time become routines of interaction between individuals and within groups, affecting the whole group's cohesiveness. From time to time during the day, teachers might want to consider the flow pattern by thinking about how they are sequencing their activities together. Teachers can take a reading of the classroom environment by asking, "What is the essence in the air?" and "How does it relate or compare to how I am feeling?" Key points in the day that significantly influence the overall themes, rhythms, and energies are preparation for activities, activities, transitions, and times of day—morning, afternoon, end of day, and night.

Creating Flow in the Classroom

Teachers may find it useful to classify activities in terms of the seven listed elements when planning their lessons. They might also find it helpful to be mindful of how they sequence lessons together to create patterns of flow for each day. It is best to sequence activities so that they follow the breath flow marked by exertions and recuperations of energy. Teachers might also consider activities in regard to how they use space, and vary the activities so that the children can experience the space in diverse ways that will refresh their energy and focus. Teachers may decide to hold some activities in the center of the room and have others use the periphery. Teachers might also organize activities so that the children can experience a variety of spatial relationships with one another—working in dyads, triads, and different group clusters. Teachers can try taking a "temperature" reading of the students' moods, tempos, and energy levels at key points of the day to notice how their states are influencing the overall pattern of flow. Children can be introduced to this awareness as well, if teachers help them to become aware of their own patterns of flow. Children can learn to study how their movements and energy levels reflect their feelings and productivity. This will teach them to pay attention to their own body signals. Teachers may also pay attention to the room design and lighting because changing these can redirect energy and focus.

When interacting with children, teachers may find it useful to tune into their body alignment, breath flow, and muscular tension level. If teachers remember to add more room between hip and chest, stretch through the whole left or right sides of their bodies as they pass out papers, lengthen through their diagonals, and shift their weight equally on both feet as they are standing, they will take pressure off their bodies and ease their physical stresses during their active days.

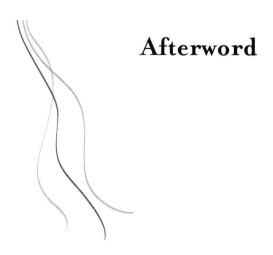

Afterword

> Dance is an absolute. It is not knowledge about
> something but is knowledge itself. . . . I am certain
> that movement never lies.
>
> Martha Graham,
> *The Notebooks of Martha Graham* (1973)

The Dancing Dialogue ends with some final reflections and a discussion about a spiral image that in many ways encapsulates the entire *Ways of Seeing* approach. These last points, which highlight the centrality of dance in all of its forms, are provided to enable readers to reflect on the new ideas and experiences they have developed from reading this book. The opening image of this book describes how many professionals in the field of early childhood are reaching beyond the boundaries of their individual disciplines to create a collaborative dancing dialogue. It is now time for readers to begin to contribute to this image, creating their own journeys by using the power of movement to better communicate with young children.

Readers may find that this journey of designing a nonverbal assessment-based program requires some narrowing of focus to prevent it from becoming unwieldy. It is true that there must be a tapering process—but not in the usual sense of the word. It is not a tapering to create a gradual lessening, to diminish, or to reduce the derived information. It is not a tapering to produce the typical kind of assessment scale that tries to compile a list of characteristics of a child to be used to compare and contrast that child with standardized means and variables. Instead, this tapering is in the service of unwinding—but not unraveling—each element that is brought out and looked at, so that its connection to all other elements can be discovered or revealed.

As mentioned before, the *Ways of Seeing* approach is best visualized as a spiral ever turning and ever expanding. The spiral image emphasizes the embracing, dynamic continuum between each element of the *Ways of Seeing* approach along the path of a child's development. Every element is considered equal, rather than ordered within some hierarchical spectrum. Key to this spiral image is the concept of movement—a therapist/observer can start at any point along the continuum and move to a new place with fluidity, in his or her nonverbal dancing journey of discovery with a child.

Movement plays a significant role in all aspects of the *Ways of Seeing* approach. It is a therapeutic and educational tool, an essential part of a body's activities, and a means of nonverbal communication. Movement is the thread that holds all of this together.

This spiral is not a line with a single thickness, equally spaced as it spins outward. Instead, its width may expand and contract, taking up more and less space as it travels. The width and space between each coil can vary, depending on each individual's experiences. That the spiral wraps around a center point is implicit in this image; it is only through ongoing investigation, spiraling deeper in and out, that the central understanding of our deepest selves can be made visible.

Active and dynamic movement exploration is essential to this discovery. The term *movement* is used both figuratively and literally. Movement is used figuratively in the sense that a person must be open to taking action, moving from one point, position, or opinion to another, and must also be open to accepting whatever help the information gleaned from an observational assessment can provide. Movement is used literally in observing how a person's physical movements create a dance; that is, the repertoire of movements unique to that person, that in essence provides the means of understanding that person and that person's experience. The spiral image shown on page 465 illustrates the factors that affect each individual's ways of being in the world. The factors can be depicted by eight major themes, beginning with the innermost curve, spiraling outward. At the center of the spiral is an unborn child embraced by a pregnant mother, followed by a sense of body, sensorial experiences, movement and motor development, parent–child interaction, experience, creative ways of living, and nonverbal observation.

Moving inward depicts the more specific elements of ways of being in the world, whereas moving outward incorporates the more general external elements that influence a child's experience of the world. The outermost curve, nonverbal observation, encompasses all of the elements by making them observable through nonverbal action.

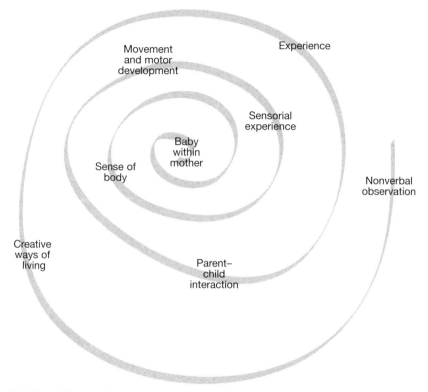

The *Ways of Seeing* spiral.

Specific Elements of the *Ways of Seeing* Spiral

Baby within Mother At the very center of the spiral is the unborn child within the mother. This is included to suggest how the in utero experience may influence both the mother's and the child's perceptions. During pregnancy a woman begins to create images of her baby based on the sensations that she experiences of her baby moving within, along with the events in her outer life that may be affecting her impressions. The advent of sonograms has enabled the viewing of an unborn child's private life before birth. Although a discussion of how this time period affects a child goes beyond the scope of this book, the *Ways of Seeing* spiral includes this element to acknowledge the potential influence of this time and to highlight the unspoken dance that begins between a mother and her child from the conception of life.

Sense of Body In the *Ways of Seeing* approach, the body is the key experiential focus. The body of an infant functions as the core organizing principle that determines how she processes her experi-

466 · The Dancing Dialogue

ences within her surroundings. The development of this concept was drawn initially from my experiences observing and working with infants using movement, dance, and other nonverbal modes of communicating. While moving with children with diverse needs, I began to ask, "What is a child's first sense of self?" Continually, the answer seemed to be a physical, sensorial self. Regardless of the child's level of functioning, whether emotionally, socially, physically, communicatively, or cognitively, she was constantly reacting and responding to sensations from and toward her body. I realized that the body must be the initial focus! Before the brain can conceptualize the idea of self, before an emotional self and other is discerned, before a verbally communicative self is available, a young infant experiences her body. This leads to the next curve of the spiral.

Sensorial Experiences   Sensory experiences, which are body related by nature, play a key role in providing a reference point for an infant's sense of his body. It seems to follow that an infant must first begin by sensing sensations through his body. Internally, a young child must try to regulate these sensations to create homeostasis. Externally, physical responses simultaneously interplay with social and emotional interactions. A child's physical orientation to the world interrelates with his sensory responses. Thus, movement and motor development become the next embracing curve.

Movement and Motor Development   Movement development is differentiated from motor development in the *Ways of Seeing* approach. Movement development depicts a child's process of acquiring the qualities of movement involving muscular tension, strength, timing, and spatial organization that make up the feeling tones or essences of nonverbal behaviors. They are the descriptive elements of movement. A child's experiences in the environment are influenced by the combination of movement development in association with the child's level of physical mastery (i.e., motor development). These experiences inform the child's ever-evolving sense of body. A dynamic flow exists as the child moves through the spiral from center out and back in again, accumulating new experiences.

Parent–Child Interaction   The parent–child relationship becomes the next embracing element of the spiral, for it has the most initial impact on a baby during experiential navigations of herself in relationship to others. It is this primary dance between a parent and a child that will set the tone and continue to influence how the baby first experiences, explores, and comes to understand her surroundings.

The nonverbal messages and cues expressed as each member of this pair relates will influence how the baby learns to communicate, as well as develop a sense of herself emotionally, physically, and socially. Fascinating new research points out the role that a mother–child relationship plays in the development of an infant's brain.

Experience   Experience becomes the next element of the spiral. In the *Ways of Seeing* approach, experience is viewed from the phenomenological principle that our experience of existence informs our sense of existing. A young child's accumulated explorations between himself and others will inform how the child processes, becomes acquainted with, and forms ideas about his surroundings. How a child experiences the world, and how these experiences influence and inform preexisting and ever-evolving constructs of existence within his surroundings, will influence his unique ways of being in the world. These experiences first and foremost occur as his sensorial moving body explores the world. Each child's unique ways of being affect all levels of his development, specifically influencing how he feels about himself, expresses himself, relates to others, and learns. These are all necessary components of actively being in the world. The structure and form of the *Ways of Seeing* approach is designed specifically to highlight each child's creative individuality in constructing his ways of being in the world.

Creative Ways of Living   Developing creative ways to process experience is the next element on the outer curve of the spiral. The term *creativity* is used here to denote the unique process in which each child creates her own sense of self from her experiences and perceptions, as well as to emphasize the importance of creative activities such as the arts and play in helping a child perceive and process her experiences. The natural, spontaneous creative impulse that exists within each child directs her continuously changing, distinctive sense of being and how her sense of self is represented on a cognitive level. It is through original, real, imaginative, and self-generated exploration that a child explores ways to understand and integrate experiences, and to create new images that support new ways of developing her sense of self. Creativity fosters inner expression. The creative movement explorations that are a signature of dance movement therapy and the *Ways of Seeing* intervention provide direct contact with the creative process. This method encourages a young child's own discoveries within the context of a supportive relationship. A child's movement qualities are matched to form a relationship and then their expansion is fostered through movement dialogues.

This process encourages the child's own creative explorations and perhaps a "rewiring" of her neuromuscular pathways.

Nonverbal Observation Nonverbal observation becomes the last, totally encompassing curve of the spiral because it is through such analysis that all of the other curves of awareness can be revealed. It is the finely detained observation of the qualitative aspects of a child's actions that enables the therapist/observer to begin to understand how the child is experiencing the world and expressing that experience through his body. It also includes the therapist/observer's own personal awareness gained through careful self-observation of his or her own nonverbal, sensorial, and movement style of expression and being in the world.

I hope that the information, images, and stories in this book have stirred readers in thought, feeling, sensation, and, perhaps most of all, into action. It is my hope that as the readers are gliding along processing and envisioning the ideas presented, that a sense of exploration emerges provoking them to actually embody, experience, and play with the concepts, entering deeply into their own spiraling path of self-discovery—finding at the "the still point" the unique dance that informs their personal and professional ways of seeing themselves and others. As new ways of seeing emerge, new ways of thinking and being with others will also evolve, setting the stage for new collaborations and dialogues—dancing dialogues—that, at the center point, bring to light how movement and nonverbal understanding can be used as a powerful tool of communication with young children.

Dance is about community, connection, and life. It stimulates expression, understanding, unity, and harmony. I envision a time when the term *dance* is used more universally, beyond its metaphoric implications, in the classroom, home, and therapeutically. If this book has inspired you, the reader, to put on your favorite music even just once and dance freely across the room to feel yourself in motion or to connect with a friend or loved one, then I feel my goal has been achieved. If this book has transformed and informed the way you have looked at someone's unspoken actions, then my deepest aspirations have come to fruition.

May you embrace the dance in all of its forms—to evoke the words of a beautiful song sung by Lee Ann Womack, "I Hope You Dance" (Sanders & Sillers, 2000).

Suzi Tortora, Ed.D., ADTR, CMA

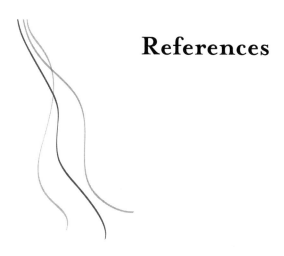

References

Acredolo, L., & Goodwyn, S. (1988). Symbolic gesturing in normal infants. *Child Development, 59,* 450–466.

Acredolo, L., & Goodwyn, S. (2002). *Baby signs: How to talk with your baby before your baby can talk.* New York: McGraw-Hill.

Adler, J. (Producer). (1970). *Looking for me* [Documentary Film]. (Available from Berkeley Media LLC, Saul Zaentz Film Center, 2600 Tenth Street, Suite 626, Berkeley, CA 94710)

Adler, J. (1987). Who is witness? *Contact Quarterly Dance Journal, XII*(1), 20–29.

Adler, J. (2002). *Offering from the conscious body: The discipline of authentic movement.* Rochester, VT: Inner Traditions.

Adler, J. (2003). American Dance Therapy Association 37th Annual Conference Keynote Address: From Autism to the Discipline of Authentic Movement. *American Journal of Dance Therapy 25*(1), 5–16.

Ainsworth, M.D.S. (1978). *Patterns of attachment: A psychological study of the strange situation.* Mahwah, NJ: Lawrence Erlbaum Associates.

Allport, G., & Vernon, P. (1933). *Studies in expressive movement.* New York: Macmillan.

Appelman, E. (2000). Attachment experiences transformed into language. *American Journal of Orthopsychiatry, 70*(2), 192–202.

Ayres, A.J. (1980). *Sensory integration and learning disorders.* Los Angeles: Western Psychological Services.

Bagnato, S.J., Neisworth, J.T., & Munson, S.M. (1997). *LINKing assessment and early intervention: An authentic curriculum-based approach.* Baltimore: Paul H. Brookes Publishing Co.

Bartenieff, I. (1989). How is the dancing teacher equipped to do dance therapy? *A collection of early writings: Toward a body of knowledge, Vol. I,* American Dance Therapy Association, 145–150.

Bartenieff, I. (1973). The roots of Laban theory: Aesthetics and beyond. In I. Bartenieff, M. Davis, & F. Paulay, *Four adaptations of effort theory in research and teaching* (pp. 1–27). New York: Dance Notation Bureau Press.

Bartenieff, I. (with Lewis, D.). (1980). *Body movement: Coping with the environment.* New York: Routledge.

Bartenieff, I., & Davis, M. (1965). Effort/shape analysis of movement: The unity of expression and function [Unpublished monograph]. Bronx, NY: Albert Einstein College of Medicine.

Beebe, B. (2004). Co-constructing mother-infant distress in face-to-face interactions: Contributions of microanalysis. *Zero to Three, 24*(5), 40–48.

Beebe, B., Jaffe, J., Feldstein, S., Mays, K., & Alson, D. (1985). Interpersonal timing: The application of an adult dialogic model to mother–infant vocal and kinesic interaction. In T. Field & N. Fox (Eds.), *Social perception in infants.* Norwood, NJ: Ablex.

Beebe, B., Jaffe, J., Lachmann, F., Feldstein, S., Crown, C., & Jasnow, M. (2000). Systems models in development and psychoanalysis: The case of vocal rhythm coordination and attachment. *Infant Mental Health Journal, 21*(1–2), 99–122.

Beebe, B., & Lachmann, F. (2002). *Infant research and adult treatment: Co-constructing interactions.* Hillsdale, NJ: The Analytic Press.

Beebe, B., Lachmann, F., & Jaffe, J. (1997). Mother–infant interaction structures and presymbolic self- and object representations. *Psychoanalytic Dialogues, 7*(2), 133–182.

Beebe, B., & Stern, D. (1977). Engagement-disengagement and early object experiences. In M. Freeman & S. Grand (Eds.), *Communicative structures and psychic structures* (pp. 35–55). New York: Plenum Press.

Berger, J. (1977). *Ways of seeing.* New York: Viking Press.

Blau, B., & Reicher, D. (1995). Early intervention with children at risk for attachment disorders. In F.J. Levy (Ed.), *Dance and other expressive art therapies: When words are not enough* (pp. 181–189). New York: Routledge.

Boas, F. (1971, October). Origins of dance. *Proceedings of the sixth annual conference of the American Dance Therapy Association,* 75–78.

Bowlby, J. (1969). *Attachment and loss: Vol.1. Attachment.* New York: Basic Books.

Brantlinger, E. (1996). Influence of preservice teachers' beliefs about pupil achievement: On attitudes toward inclusion. *Teacher Education and Special Education, 19*(1), 17–33.

Brazelton, T.B. (1974). The origins of reciprocity. In M. Lewis & L. Rosenblum (Eds.), *The effects of the infant on its caregiver.* New York: John Wiley & Sons.

Brazelton, T.B., & Cramer, B.T. (1990). *The earliest relationship: Parents, infants and the drama of early attachment.* Reading, MA: Addison-Wesley.

Brown, M.W. (1991). *The runaway bunny.* New York: HarperCollins. (Original work published 1942)

Bruner, J. (1981). The social context of language acquisition. *Language & Communication, I,* 155–178.

Bucci, W. (1994). The multiple code theory and the psychoanalytic process: A framework for research. In J.A. Winer (Ed.), *The Annual of Psychoanalysis, 22* (pp. 239–259). Hillsdale, NJ: The Analytic Press.

Caf, B., Kroflic, B., & Tancig, S. (1997). Activation of hypoactive children with creative movement and dance in primary school. *The Arts in Psychotherapy, 24*(4), 355–365.

Carroll, L. (1992). *Alice's adventures in wonderland and through the looking glass.* New York: Alfred A. Knopf. (Original work published 1865)

Chaiklin, H. (Ed.). (1975). *Marion Chase: Her papers.* Columbia, MD: American Dance Therapy Association.

Cohen, B.B. (1997). *Sensing, feeling, and action: The experiential anatomy of body–mind centering.* Northampton, MA: Contact Editions.

Cohen, B.B., & Mills, M. (1979). *Developmental movement therapy.* Amherst, MA: The School for Body/Mind Centering.

Darling-Hammond, L. (1997). *The right to learn.* San Francisco: Jossey-Bass.

Darling-Hammond, L., Ancess, J., & Falk, B. (1995). *Authentic assessment in action: Studies of schools and students at work.* New York: Teachers College Press.

Darwin, C. (2002). *The expression of the emotions in man and animals.* New York: Oxford University Press. (Original work published 1872)

Davis, M. (1975). *Towards understanding the intrinsic in body movement.* New York: Arno Press.

Davis, M. (1977). *Methods of perceiving patterns of small group behavior.* New York: Dance Notation Bureau Press.

Davis, M., Walters, S., Vorus, N., & Connors, B. (2000). Defensive demeanor profiles. *American Journal of Dance Therapy, 22*(2), 103–121.

Davis, P., Monda-Amaya, L., & Hammitte, D. (1996). Where have we been and where are we going? Views from the presidents. *Teacher Education and Special Education, 19*(3), 235–247.

DeGangi, G. (2000). *Pediatric disorders of regulation in affect and behavior: A therapist's guide to assessment and treatment.* San Diego: Academic Press.

DeGangi, G., & Berk, R. (1983). Assessment of sensory integrative dysfunction in the preschool years. *Learning Disabilities, II,* 1.

Delsarte System of Oratory (4th ed.). (1892). New York: Werner.

Donnellan, A.M., & Leary, M.R. (1995). *Movement differences and diversity in autism/mental retardation: Appreciating and accommodating people with communication and behavior challenges.* Madison, WI: DRI Press.

Eddy, M.H. (2005). *Perceptual-motor development: Movement disciplines* (3rd ed.). State University of NY Empire State College: Xanedu Proquest Press.

Ekman, P. (1984). Expression and the nature of emotion. In K.R. Scherer & P. Ekman (Eds.), *Approaches to emotion* (pp. 319–343). Mahwah, NJ: Lawrence Erlbaum Associates.

Ekman, P. (2003). *Emotions revealed: Recognizing faces and feelings to improve communication and emotional life.* New York: Henry Holt & Co.

Ekman, P., & Friesen, W. (1976). Measuring facial movement. *Environmental Psychology and Nonverbal Behavior, 1,* 56–75.

Elkind, D. (2001). *The hurried child: Growing up too fast too soon* (3rd ed.). Cambridge, MA: Perseus Publishing.

Feder, E., & Feder, B. (1981). *The expressive arts therapies: Art, music & dance as psychotherapy.* Upper Saddle River, NJ: Prentice-Hall.

Fogel, A. (1992). Co-regulation, perception and action. *Human Movement Science, 11,* 505–523.

Fonagy, P., Gergely, G., Jurist, E., & Target, M. (2001). *Affect regulation, mentalization, and the development of the self.* New York: Other Press.

Fraiberg, S. (1980). *Clinical studies in infant mental health: The first year of life.* New York: Basic Books.

Gaensbauer, T.J. (2002). Representations of trauma in infancy: Clinical and theoretical implications for the understanding of early memory. *Infant Mental Health Journal, 23*(3), 259–277.

Gaensbauer, T.J. (2004). Telling their stories: Representation and reenactment of traumatic experiences occurring in the first year of life. *Zero to Three, 24*(5), 25–31.

Gardner, H. (1991). *The unschooled mind: How children think and how schools should teach.* New York: Basic Books.

Gardner, H. (1993a). *Frames of mind: The theory of multiple intelligences.* New York: Basic Books.

Gardner, H. (1993b). *Multiple intelligences: The theory in practice.* New York: Basic Books.

Gilbert, A. (1992). *Creative dance for all ages.* Reston, VA: National Dance Association, American Alliance for Health, Physical Education, Recreation and Dance (AAHPERD).

Graham, Martha (1973). *The notebooks of Martha Graham.* New York: Harcourt Brace Jovanovich.

Greenspan, S. (1992). *Infancy and early childhood: The practice of clinical assessment and intervention with emotional and developmental challenges.* Madison, CT: International Universities Press.

Greenspan, S. (1996). Assessing the emotional and social functioning of infants and young children. In S. Meisels & E. Fenichel (Eds.), *New visions for the developmental assessment of infants and young children* (pp. 231–266). Washington, DC: ZERO TO THREE.

Greenspan, S. (1997). *The growth of the mind and the endangered origins of intelligence.* Reading, MA: Addison-Wesley.

Greenspan, S., & Lewis, D. (2002). *The affect-based language curriculum (ABLC): An intensive program for families, therapists, and teachers.* Bethesda, MD: Interdisciplinary Council on Developmental and Learning Disorders.

Greenspan, S., & Shanker, S. (2002). Differences in affect cuing: A window for the identification of risk patterns for autistic spectrum disorders in the first year of life. *The Journal of Developmental and Learning Disorders, 6,* 23–30.

Greenspan, S., & Wieder, S. (1993). Regulatory disorders. In C.H. Zeanah (Ed.), *Handbook of infant mental health.* New York: The Guilford Press.

Guest, A.H. (1990). *Your move: A new approach to the study of movement and dance.* New York: Gordon & Breach.

Gunnar, M. (1980). Control, warning signals, and distress in infancy. *Developmental Psychology, 16*(4), 281–289.

Gunnar, M. (1998). Quality of early care and buffering of neuroendocrine reactions: Potential effects on the developing human brain. *Prevention Medicine, 27,* 208–211.

Gunnar, M., Brodersen, L., Krueger, K., & Rigatuso, J. (1996). Dampening of adrenocortical responses during infancy: Normative changes and individual differences. *Child Development, 67,* 877–889.

Gunnar, M., & Cheatham, C.L. (2003). Brain and behavior interface: Stress and the developing brain. *Infant Mental Health Journal, 24*(3), 195–211.

Hackney, P. (2000). *Making connections: Total body integration through Bartenieff fundamentals.* New York: Routledge.

Hagberg, B. (Ed.). (1993). *Rett syndrome: Clinical & biological aspects*. London: MacKeith Press.

Hamberg, J., & Hammond, A. (1991, July/August). Laban-based dance activities to improve coordination and sensorimotor function in children. In S. Stinson (Ed.), *Proceedings of the 1991 Conference of Dance and the Child*, 173–182.

Hofer, M.A. (1981). *The roots of human behavior: An introduction to the psychobiology of early development*. San Francisco: W.H. Freeman.

Hofer, M.A. (1995). Hidden regulators: Implications for a new understanding of attachment, separation, and loss. In S. Goldberg, R. Muir, & J. Kerr (Eds.), *Attachment theory: Social, developmental, and clinical perspectives* (pp. 203–230). Hillsdale, NJ: The Analytic Press.

Hofer, M.A. (2002). The riddle of development. In D.J. Lewkowicz & R. Lickliter (Eds.), *Conceptions of development: Lessons from the laboratory* (pp. 5–29). New York: Psychology Press.

Hofer, M.A. (2003). The emerging neurobiology of attachment and separation: How parents shape their infant's brain and behavior. In S.W. Coates, J.L. Rosenthal, & D.S. Schecter (Eds.), *September 11: Trauma and human bonds* (pp. 191–209). Hillsdale, NJ: The Analytic Press.

Isabella, R.A., & Belsky, J. (1991). Interactional synchrony and the origins of infant-attachment: A replication study. *Child Development, 62*(2), 373–384.

Iverson, J.M., & Thal, D.J. (1998). Communicative transitions: There's more to the hand than meets the eye. In S.F. Warren & J. Reichle (Series Eds.) & A.M. Wetherby, S.F. Warren, & J. Reichle (Vol. Eds.), *Communication and language intervention series: Vol. 7. Transitions in prelinguistic communication* (pp. 59–86). Baltimore: Paul H. Brookes Publishing Co.

Jaques-Dalcroze, E. (1918). *The eurhythmics of Jaques-Dalcroze*. Boston: Small, Maynard, & Co.

Jaques-Dalcroze, E. (1976). *Rhythm, Music, and Education*. New York: Arno Press.

Jaques-Dalcroze, E. (2003). *Thirty Melodic Lessons in Solfege*. Ellicott City, MD: Musikinesis.

Jones, B.T. (1996). *Still/Here* [Documentary film]. (Available from WNET, Post Office Box 2284, South Burlington, VT 05407)

Kestenberg, J. (1975). *Children and parents: Psychoanalytic studies in development*. New York: Jason Aronson.

Kestenberg Amighi, J., Loman, S., Lewis, P., & Sossin, K.M. (1999). *The meaning of movement: Developmental and clinical perspectives of the Kestenberg Movement Profile*. New York: Bruner-Routledge.

Laban, R. (1968). *Modern educational dance* (2nd rev. ed.). London: MacDonald & Evans.

Laban, R. (1975). *The mastery of movement*. Boston: Plays.

Laban, R. (1976). *The language of movement*. Boston: Plays.

Laban, R., & Lawrence, F.C. (1974). *Effort*. Boston: Plays.

Lamb, W., & Watson, E. (1979). *Body code: The meaning in movement*. London: Routledge & Kegan Paul.

Levine, M. (2002). *A mind at a time*. New York: Simon & Schuster.

Levy, F.J. (1992). *Dance movement therapy: A healing art*. Reston, VA: American Alliance for Health, Physical Education, Recreation and Dance.

Lifter, K., & Bloom, L. (1986). *Object play and the emergence of language.* Unpublished manuscript.

Lipsitt, L. (Ed.). (1976). *Developmental psychobiology.* Mahwah, NJ: Lawrence Erlbaum Associates.

Loman, S. (1995). The case of Warren: A KMP approach to autism. In F.J. Levy (Ed.), *Dance and other expressive art therapies: When words are not enough* (pp. 213–223). New York: Routledge.

Loman, S. (1998). Employing a developmental model of movement pattern in dance/movement therapy with young children and their families. *American Journal of Dance Therapy, 20*(2), 101–115.

Loman, S., & Tortora, S. (Eds). (1999). *ADTA: American Dance Therapy Association* [Brochure]. Columbia, MD: American Dance Therapy Association.

Losardo A., & Notari-Syverson, A. (2001). *Alternative approaches to assessing young children.* Baltimore: Paul H. Brookes Publishing Co.

Mahler, M., Pine, P., & Bergman, A. (1975). *The psychological birth of the human infant.* New York: Basic Books.

Main, M. (1996). Introduction to the special section on attachment and psychopathology: Overview of the field of attachment. *Journal of Consulting and Clinical Psychology, 64*(2), 237–243.

Main, M., & Hesse, E. (1990). Parents' unresolved traumatic experiences are related to infant disorganized attachment status: Is frightened and/or frightening parental behavior the linking mechanism? In M.T. Greenberg, D.C. Cicchetti, & E.M. Cummings (Eds.), *Attachment in the preschool years: Theory, research and intervention* (pp. 161–182). Chicago: University of Chicago Press.

Main, M., & Solomon, J. (1990). Procedures for identifying infants as disorganized/disoriented during the Ainsworth strange situation. In M.T. Greenberg, D.C. Cicchetti, & E.M. Cummings (Eds.), *Attachment in the preschool years: Theory, research and intervention* (pp. 121–160). Chicago: University of Chicago Press.

Maletic, V. (1987). *Body, space, expression: The development of Rudolf Laban's movement and dance concepts.* Hawthorne, NY: Walter de Gruyter.

Meisels, S. (1996). Charting the continuum of assessment and intervention. In S. Meisels & E. Fenichel (Eds.), *New visions for the developmental assessment of infants and young children* (pp. 27–52). Washington, DC: ZERO TO THREE.

Meisels, S., & Fenichel, E. (Eds.). (1996). *New visions for the developmental assessment of infants and young children.* Washington, DC: ZERO TO THREE.

Merleau-Ponty, M. (1964). *The primacy of perception.* Chicago: Northwestern University Press.

Merleau-Ponty, M. (2002). *Phenomenology of perception* (2nd ed.). New York: Routledge. (Original work published 1945)

Moore, C., & Yamamoto, K. (1989). *Beyond words: Movement, observation, and analysis* (2nd ed.). New York: Routledge.

Moyers, W., & Grubin, D. (Producers) (1997). *Bill T. Jones: Still/here* [Documentary film]. (Available from WNET, Post Office Box 2284, South Burlington, VT 05407)

Nelson, L. (2001). *Motoric & rhythmic bases of communication.* Speech-language pathology white paper for American Speech-Language-Hearing Association. Weston, FL: Interactive Metronome.

Nelson, C., & Bosquet, M. (2000). Neurobiology of fetal and infant development: Implications for infant mental health. In C. Zeanah (Ed.), *Handbook of infant mental health.* New York: The Guilford Press.

North, M. (1978). *Personality assessment through movement.* Boston: Plays.

Pallaro, P. (Ed.). (1999). *Authentic Movement: Essays by Mark Starks Whitehouse, Jane Adler, and Joan Chodorow.* Philadelphia: Jessica Kingsley Publishers.

Panksepp, J. (2001). The long-term psychobiological consequences of infant emotions: Prescriptions for the twenty-first century. *Infant Mental Health Journal, 22,* 132–173.

Pawl, J. (1995). The therapeutic relationship as human connectedness: Being held in another's mind. *Zero to Three, 15*(4), 1–5.

Piaget, J. (1962). *Play, dreams and imitation in childhood.* New York: W.W. Norton.

Piaget, J. (1970). *Science of education and the psychology of the child.* New York: Penguin.

Piaget, J., & Inhelder, B. (1969). *The psychology of the child.* New York: Basic Books.

Porges, S. (1993). The infant's sixth sense: Awareness and regulation of bodily processes. *Zero to Three, 14*(2), 12–16.

Porges, S. (2002, April). Biosocial rhythms in development. In S. Porges (Discussant), *Biosocial rhythms in development.* Symposium conducted at the meeting of the International Conference on Infant Studies, Toronto.

Porges, S. (2004). Neuroception: A subconscious system for detecting threats and safety. *Zero to Three, 24*(5), 19–24.

Prizant, B.M., Wetherby, A.M., Rubin, E., Laurent, A.C., & Rydell, P.J. (2006a). *The SCERTS™ Model: A comprehensive educational approach for children with autism spectrum disorders. Vol. I: Assessment.* Baltimore: Paul H. Brookes Publishing Co.

Prizant, B.M., Wetherby, A.M., Rubin, E., Laurent, A.C., and Rydell, P.J. (2006b). *The SCERTS™ Model: A comprehensive educational approach for children with autism spectrum disorders. Vol. II: Program planning and intervention.* Baltimore: Paul H. Brookes Publishing Co.

Prizant, B.M, Wetherby, A.M, & Rydell, P. (2000). Communication intervention issues for children with autism spectrum disorders. In S.F. Warren & J. Reichle (Series Eds.), & A.M. Wetherby, & B.M. Prizant (Vol. Eds.), *Communication and language intervention series: Vol. 9. Autism spectrum disorders: A transactional developmental perspective* (pp. 193–224). Baltimore: Paul H. Brookes Publishing Co.

Reinhiller, N.(1996, Winter). Coteaching: New variations on a not-so-new practice. *Teacher Education and Special Education, 19*(1), 34–48.

Rilke, R.M. (1992). *Duino elegies* (D. Young, Trans.). New York: W.W. Norton.

Sander, L. (1962). Issues in early mother child interaction. *Journal of American Academy of Child Psychiatry, 1,* 141–166.

Sander, L. (1977). The regulation of exchange in the infant-caregiver system. In M. Lewis & L. Rosenblum (Eds.), *Interaction, conversation and the development of language* (pp. 133–156). New York: John Wiley & Sons.

Sander, L. (1980). Investigation of the infant and its caregiving environment as a biological system. In S. Greenspan & G. Pollack (Eds.), *The course of life: Vol. I. Infancy & early childhood.* Bethesda, MD: National Institute of Mental Health.

Sander, L. (2000). Where are we going in the field of infant mental health? *Infant Mental Health Journal, 21*(1–2), 5–20.

Sanders, M., & Sillers, T. (2000). *I hope you dance.* Nashville: Rutledge Hill Press.

Sapolsky, R.M. (1992). *Stress, the aging brain, and the mechanisms of neuron death.* Cambridge, MA: MIT Press.

Scheflen, A.F. (1965). *Stream and structure of communicational behavior* (Behavioral Studies Monograph No. 1). Philadelphia: Eastern Pennsylvania Psychiatric Institute.

Scheflen, A.E. (1972). *Body language and social order: Communication as behavioral control.* Upper Saddle River, NJ: Prentice-Hall.

Scheflen, A.E. (1973). *Communication structure: Analysis of a psychotherapy transaction.* Bloomington: Indiana University Press.

Scheflen, A.E. (with Ashcraft, N.). (1976). *Human territories: How we behave in space-time.* Upper Saddle River, NJ: Prentice-Hall.

Schilder, P. (1978). *The image and appearance of the human body.* New York: International Universities Press. (Original work published 1935)

Schoop, T. (1974). *Won't you join the dance?* Palo Alto, CA: Mayfield Publishing.

Schore, A. (2001a). Contributions from the decade of the brain to infant mental health: An overview. *Infant Mental Health Journal, 22,* 1–6.

Schore, A. (2001b). Effects of a secure attachment relationship on right brain development, affect regulation, and infant mental health. *Infant Mental Health Journal, 22,* 7–66.

Shaffer, R., Jacokes, L., Cassily, J., Greenspan, S., Tuchman, R., & Stemmer, P., Jr. (2001). Effect of interactive metronome training on children with ADHD. *American Journal of Occupational Therapy, 55*(2), 155–161.

Slade, A. (2002a). Keeping the baby in mind: A critical factor in perinatal mental health. *Zero to Three, 22*(6), 10–16.

Slade, A. (2002b, December). *It takes relationship to build relationship: Insights from modern infant–parent psychotherapy.* Plenary session presented at the ZERO TO THREE National Training Institute, Washington, DC.

Slade, A., Belsky, L., Aber, J.L., & Phelps, J. (1999). Maternal representations of their relationship with their toddlers: Links to adult attachment and observed mothering. *Developmental Psychology, 35*(3), 611–619.

Smith, L., & Thelen, E. (1993). *A dynamic systems approach to development: Applications.* Cambridge, MA: The MIT Press.

Stern, D. (1977). *The first relationship: Infant and mother.* Cambridge, MA: Harvard University Press.

Stern, D. (1985). *The interpersonal world of the infant.* New York: Basic Books.

Stern, D. (1995). *The motherhood constellation: A unified view of parent–infant psychotherapy.* New York: Basic Books.

Sweigard, L. (1974). *Human movement potential: Its ideokinetic facilitation.* New York: Harper & Row.

Teitelbaum, P., Teitelbaum, O., Fryman, J., & Maurer, R. (2002). Reflexes gone astray in autism in infancy. *Journal of Developmental and Learning Disorders, 6,* 15–22.

Teitelbaum, P., Teitelbaum, O., Nye, J., Fryman, J., & Maurer, R. (1998). Movement analysis in infancy may be useful for early diagnosis of autism.

Proceedings of the National Academy of Sciences of the United States of America, 95, 13982–13987.

Thelen, E. (1996). The improvising infant: Learning about learning to move. In M. Merrens and G. Brannigan (Eds.), *The developmental psychologists: Research adventures across the life span.* New York: McGraw-Hill Co., Inc.

Thelen, E., & Smith, L. (1994). *A dynamic systems approach to the development of cognition and action.* Cambridge, MA: The MIT Press.

Tortora, S. (1994). Join my dance: The unique movement style of each infant and toddler can invite communication, expression and intervention. *Zero to Three, 15*(1), 1–12.

Tortora, S. (1995). Seeing ourselves as a way to see young children. *Insights From the Center for Infants and Parents, 2*(1), 4–7.

Tortora, S. (2004a). Our moving bodies tell stories, which speak of our experiences. *Zero to Three, 24*(5), 4–12.

Tortora, S. (2004b). Studying the infant's multisensory environment: A bridge between biology and psychology: An interview with Myron Hofer. *Zero to Three, 24*(5), 13–18.

Tronick. E. (1989). Emotions and emotional communication in infants. *American Psychologist, 44*(2), 112–119.

Tronick, E., & Gianino, A. (1986). Interactive mismatch and repair: Challenges to the coping infant. *Zero to Three, 6*(3), 1–6.

Vygotsky, L. (1978). *Mind in society.* Cambridge, MA: Harvard University Press.

Wetherby, A., Cain, D., Yonclas, D., & Walker, V. (1988). Analysis of intentional communication of normal children from the prelinguistic to the multiword stage. *Journal of Speech and Hearing Research, 31,* 240–252.

Whitehouse, M. (1987). Physical movement and personality. *Contact Quarterly Dance Journal, XII*(1), 16–19.

Whitehouse, M. (1999). Creative expression in physical movement is language without words. In P. Pallaro (Ed.), *Authentic Movement: Essays by Mark Starks Whitehouse, Janet Adler, and Joan Chodorow* (pp. 33–40). Philadelphia: Jessica Kingsley Publishers.

Williamson, G.G., & Anzalone, M. (1997, May). *Sensory integration in infants and toddlers.* Paper presented at the New York ZERO TO THREE Network, New York.

Williamson, G.G., & Anzalone, M. (2001). *Sensory integration and self-regulation in infants and toddlers: Helping very young children interact with their environment.* Washington, D.C.: ZERO TO THREE.

Winnicott, D.W. (1965). *The maturational processes and the facilitating environment.* New York: International Universities Press.

Winnicott, D.W. (1982). *Playing and reality.* New York: Tavistock Publications.

Winnicott, D.W. (1987). *Babies and their mothers.* Reading, MA: Addison-Wesley Publishing.

Appendix A
Movement Signature
Impressions Checklist

Note to Reader:

    All the blank forms mentioned in this book, including the Movement Signature Impressions Checklist, can be downloaded by going to http://www.brookespublishing.com/dancing. Please see p. vi for information on the conditions under which these forms may be used.

Movement Signature Impressions Checklist

Name of child: _____ Date: _____

Age: _____ Date of birth: _____ Observer: _____

I. Observational information

Parent(s) name and address: _____

_____

Date(s) of observation/interaction: _____

Note the setting (visual, auditory, and physical elements of the surroundings): ____

_____

_____

Note the other sources of information used: _____

_____

_____

Note the overall developmental level of the child (include sources):

Motor:
    Gross motor:

    Fine motor:

Communication:
    Nonverbal:

    Verbal:
        Expressive:

        Receptive:

Social/emotional:

Cognitive:

II. Self-observational information (the qualitative aspects of the observer's verbal and nonverbal responses as expressions of personal feelings and reactions to the child)

1. Which of my senses are responding to the child?

2. How does the child's developmental level, way of moving, and interacting in the environment make me feel?

3. What feelings, thoughts, or impressions is the child stirring in me and what parts of me are drawn out when watching the child?

4. What is the tension or relaxation level of my body, limbs, and facial expressions while watching the child?

III. Movement signature impressions (the range of movement qualities and elements observed during this assessment that the child uses to express himself or herself)

A. **Space analysis** [Focus on the child's sense of self and other—how the child uses his or her body space and the outside space to enable social interaction.]

1. Note the general impression of the child's relationship to outside influences and others and the child's awareness and active engagement with his or her surroundings.

2. Check the terms that describe the child's relationship to developmental space (i.e., gross motor development involving a progression through various spatial orientations).

Horizontal "communication":

_____ Inclusion	_____ Exclusion
_____ Gathering	_____ Scattering

Torso action

_____ Narrowing	_____ Widening

Vertical "I am ME":

_____ Presence	_____ Confrontation
_____ Ascending	_____ Descending
_____ Throwing down	_____ Reaching up

Torso action

_____ Lengthening	_____ Shortening

Sagittal "entering and withdrawing from world":

_____ Forward	_____ Backward
_____ Venturing out/advancing	_____ Retreating
_____ Initiating	_____ Terminating contact

Torso action

_____ Concave	_____ Convex

3. Check the terms that describe the child's relationship with his or her kinesphere (i.e., the personal space around each individual).

Level changes: __ Low __ Middle __ High
Reach space: __ Near __ Mid __ Far
Direction: __ Front __ Side __ Back __ Diagonal

4. Check the terms that describe the child's relationship with the general space (i.e., public space outside of self). Then fill in the blanks as indicated.

Level changes: __ Low __ Middle __ High
Use of space: __ All __ Some __ Small area
Direction: __ Forward __ Side __ Backward
Describe the location (Where?): _____

5. Check the terms that describe the child's relationship with the interpersonal space (i.e., interactive, changing distances between people in environment).

__ Touching __ Overlapping __ Separate individual kinespheres

6. Check the terms that describe the child's relationship with spatial pathways (i.e., floor patterns).

__ Winding __ Linear __ Arcing __ Spoke-like
__ Circular

7. Describe at least one movement sequence exhibited by the child that portrays the qualities detailed in this section.

B. **Body and Shape analysis** [Focus on the child's body attitude toward space—his or her attitude toward defining personal space within the general space as well as the child's body shape relationships to self and the surroundings.]

1. Check the term that best describes the placement/movement of the child's limbs in relation to torso.
__ Proximal __ Distal initiation

2. Check the term that best describes the child's Body part relationships.
__ Upper–lower __ Left to right __ Contralateral

3. Check the term that best describes the child's Body axis orientation in space.
__ Horizontal __ Vertical __ Sagittal __ Diagonal

4. Check the term that best describes the child's spatial pulls.
__ One-Dimensional __ Planar __ Three-Dimensional __ Combination

5. Note the child's
Pattern of breath flow:

Particular body parts of which the child seems to be most aware:

Particular body parts that most attract your attention:

Most used parts of the body during movement:

Least used parts of the body during movement:

Body parts held:

Place of initiation of movement:

Simultaneous or sequential movement through parts:

Use of body as a whole or in parts:

Sense of symmetry or asymmetry:

Manner of shifting body weight:

6. Check the terms that best describe the shapes that the child's body makes.
   __ Spiraling   __ Arcing   __ Spoke-like
   __ Concave torso   __ Convex torso   __ Flow within torso
   __ Lengthening torso __ Shortening torso
   __ Shaping to objects/people
   __ Gathering space toward self
   __ Pushing away from self

7. Check the term that best describes the child's most prominent Body-Shape relationships.
   __ Shaping (external)   __ Shape-flow actions (internal)
   __ Both

8. Note the child's overall sense of connection, fluidity versus disconnection, and holding throughout the body in stillness and in motion.

9. Note the child's sense of propulsion, locomotion, mobility, stillness, energy intention, and motivation to move.

10. Describe at least one movement sequence exhibited by the child that portrays the qualities detailed in this section.

C. **Phrase analysis** [Focus on how the child clusters his or her actions together over a period of time, creating a sequence that has a flow, pulse, and rhythm as the actions start, continue, pause, and stop.]

1. Note some general impressions of the child, including expressivity, liveliness, fluctuations, sequencing, structure, dominant elements, and tempo.

2. Note the rhythm of the child's movement phrase: Is there exertion/recuperation sequencing? Does a complete phrase exist (i.e., initiation/preparation–main action–recuperation/recovery)? Describe.

3. Check the term that best describes the child's breath type rhythm.
   __ Rhythmic   __ Arrhythmic   __ Free breath type rhythm

   Check the terms that best describe the appearance of the child's rhythm of whole movement in relation to body.
   __ Harmonious   __ Unharmonious
   __ Within whole body   __ Within body parts

4. Check the type(s) of the child's rhythmic phrase.
   __ Even (monotone)   __ Increasing
   __ Impactive   __ Decreasing
   __ Explosive   __ Increase–decrease
   __ Swing   __ Vibratory
   __ Resilient   __ Accented

5. Check the characteristics that affect how the child's phrase boundaries are determined.
   __ Level/direction changes   __ Body parts
   __ Postural shifts   __ Weight shifts
   __ Effort   __ Dynamic shifts
   __ Pauses   __ Stops
   __ Intent of child's actions (e.g., was task completed?)

6. Check the term that best describes the duration of the child's phrase.
   __ Long   __ Short
   __ Simple phases   __ Multiple phases
   __ Pauses between phrases   __ Pauses during phrase

7. Check the term that best describes the transitions *between* phrases.
   __ Smooth   __ Jerky
   __ Even   __ Uneven
   __ Enables recovery   __ Merges with recovery

8. Check the term that best describes the child's flow of movements *in* the phrase.
   __ Smooth   __ Jerky
   __ Connected   __ Unconnected

9. Describe at least one movement sequence exhibited by the child that portrays the phrasing qualities detailed in this section.

D. Efforts used [Focus on the variable qualitative aspects of movement exertion that create a feeling tone to movement within the four motion factors below.]

1. Check the terms that best describe the child's Effort qualities regarding

   Time (*when* decision):   __ Quick   __ Slow

   Weight (*what* intention):   __ Strong   __ Light

   Flow (*how* progression, precision):   __ Bound   __ Free

   Space (*where* attention):   __ Direct   __ Indirect

2. Check if the child's movements involve single Efforts or a combination of Efforts.
   __ Single   __ Combination

3. Note which Effort(s) predominate throughout the sequence.

4. Note the range of Efforts that are available in the child's movement repertoire (even if the Efforts do not predominate throughout the sequence).

5. Note how Efforts are used to create the phrase.

6. Describe at least one movement sequence exhibited by the child that portrays the Effort qualities detailed in this section.

E. Movement metaphors [Focus on the salient repeated movement sequences within a movement signature impression.]
Describe a repeated movement sequence, designating qualitative description separately from interpretation or subjective inference.

IV. Interactional analysis (i.e., which elements of the child's movement style affect and contribute to the interactional dialogue and how)

  A. List the participants of the interaction being observed and their relationship to the child. Note if the person filling out the Movement Signature Impressions Checklist is also a participant in the interaction or is only observing the interaction of the child with other participant(s).

  B. Answer the following questions while observing an interaction with the child:

  1. What is the child stirring in me and which parts of me are drawn out when observing an interaction/interacting with the child?

  2. What is the tension or relaxation level of my body, limbs, and facial expressions while observing an interaction/interacting with the child?

  3. How do the elements of the immediate surroundings feel as I embody the child's nonverbal style? Does the presence of others feel inviting or does it feel too noisy and distracting?

  C. Answer the following questions detailing general impressions of the participants' interactive styles:

  1. Initial the terms that describe the participant's movements.
     Time: ____ Quick ____ Sudden ____ Racing ____ Careful
           ____ Slow

     Weight: ____ Strong ____ Light ____ Gentle ____ Careful
             ____ Heavy ____ Limp

     Flow: ____ Tense ____ Excited ____ Relaxed ____ Neutral

     Space: ____ Large ____ Small ____ Contained
            ____ Opened ____ Direct ____ Crisp ____ Unfocused
            ____ Meandering

  2. Note the participants'
     Energy level—tempo—Phrasing:

     Use and quality of touch and holding style:

     Body balance to provide a stable or mobile container for the child:

Use of Body Shape (i.e., directional, shaping, shape-flow) actions in relation to the child:

Voice tone:

Use of Effort:

Approach, initiating, and withdrawal of contact during interaction:

3. Note the amount of space between child and participant (e.g., at what point in the general space, kinespheric space, or interpersonal space, does the observer begin and end an interaction?).

D. Answer the following questions detailing general impressions of the child's interactive style:

1. Note how the child sequences from a place of self-soothing and calmness to attentive, active participation, excitement, and/or over-stimulation, and then back to self-soothing and calmness.

2. As the child cycles through this sequence, does he or she elicit, invite, or reject an interaction by other(s)?

3. How does the child portray this nonverbally?
   Body/facial expressions:

   Use of Space:

   Phrasing:

   Shape (e.g., directional, shaping, shape-flow actions in relation to participant):

   Effort:

E. Answer the following questions to describe the general interactional experience:

1. Phrasing
   Check the terms that best describe the child's styles of Phrasing.
   __ Synchronous   __ Compliant   __ Do not relate

Check the terms that best describe the participants' styles of Phrasing.
__ Synchronous   __ Compliant   __ Do not relate

Do the Phrasing styles enable the participants to prepare and recuperate during the movement interactions? If so, how?

Note the types of transitions during interactions.

Note the duration of the interactions.

Note the general activity level and the tempo.

List the Efforts used.

Are these Efforts (check one)
__ Same   __ Complementary   __ Opposing

2. Use of Space
Check the term that best describes the participants' level of active engagement/awareness of each other in space.
__ Constant   __ Some   __ Very little   __ No contact

List the levels of Space used.

Check the term that best describes the child's level of active engagement/awareness of the surrounding environment.
__ Constant   __ Some   __ Very little   __ None

Check the term that best describes the child's pathways.
__ Intersect   __ Follow   __ Do not relate

List the pathways.

F. Key questions

1. How is the waxing and waning of attention to establish a holding environment created in the participants' movements through the use of Space, Body, Phrasing, Shape, and Effort?

Use of Space (e.g., kinesphere, general, interactional, pathways):

Body:

Phrasing:

Shape (e.g., directional, shaping, shape-flow actions in relation to the other participant):

Effort:

2. How are turn-taking interactions (i.e., circles of communication) opened and closed through the participants' movements, specifically looking at how they each initiate, withdraw, and resume contact via the use of Space, Body, Phrasing, Shape, and Effort?

Initiation of contact
Use of Space (e.g., kinesphere, general, interactional, pathways):

Body:

Phrasing:

Shape (e.g., directional, shaping, shape-flow actions in relation to the other participant):

Effort:

Withdrawal of contact
Use of Space (e.g., kinesphere, general, interactional, pathways):

Body:

Phrasing:

Shape (e.g., directional, shaping, shape-flow actions in relation to other participant):

Effort:

Resumption of contact:
Use of Space (e.g., kinesphere, general, interactional, pathways):

Body:

Phrasing:

Shape (e.g., directional, shaping, shape-flow actions in relation to other participant):

Effort:

3. How do mirroring, attuning, and mismatch-and-repair cycles occur through body-movement dialogue observable in the qualitative use of Space, Body, Phrasing, Shape, and Effort?

Use of Space (e.g., kinesphere, general, interactional, pathways):

Body:

Phrasing:

Shape (e.g., directional, shaping, shape-flow actions in relation to other participant):

Effort:

4. Does the adult attune to the child's style as reflected in the child's cues, giving room for the child's expression before intervening, or does the adult respond without attending to the child's style first? How is this expressed through the movement qualities of Space, Body, Phrasing, Shape, and Effort?

Use of Space (e.g., kinesphere, general, interactional, pathways):

Body:

Phrasing:

Shape (e.g., directional, shaping, shape-flow actions in relation to other participant):

Effort:

5. Describe the type of "base of support" established between the adult and the child from which the child receives pleasure, understanding, and comfort when exploring the surroundings and when returning to the adult in times of perceived danger or discomfort. Note how these behaviors are portrayed in both the adult and the child through the movement qualities of Space, Body, Phrasing, Shape, and Effort.

Use of Space (e.g., kinesphere, general, interactional, pathways):

Body:

Phrasing:

Shape (e.g., directional, shaping, shape-flow actions in relation to other participant):

Effort:

V. **Final comments** (e.g., salient impressions, interpretations of data, emerging themes, learning styles/multiple intelligences, and implications for intervention and education)

Appendix B
Recommended Resources

CHILDREN'S BOOKS THAT CAN BE USED TO ENCOURAGE DANCE

Because a broad range of young children enjoy the stories, rhythms, and imagery of these books, they are categorized according to content rather than age group. Although reading just a part of a story can get a child's body moving, if you add a little music, you will have a dance! The books are divided into three categories: simple imagery, rhythm play, and imagination builders. Simple imagery books provide concrete images (e.g., animals) to explore and general body awareness activities. Rhythm play books provide rhythmic language that translates into fun, organized body movement patterns. Imagination builders inspire a young child's imaginary world and emotional expressivity.

Simple Imagery Books

Boynton, S. (1985). *Good night, good night.* New York: Random House.
Ets, M.H. (1989). *In the forest.* New York: Scholastic.
Fleming, D. (1991). *In the tall, tall grass.* New York: Henry Holt.
Haus, F. (1986). *Beep-beep I'm a jeep!* New York: Random House.
Hindley, J. (1999). *Eyes, nose, fingers, and toes.* New York: Walker Books.
Jorgensen, G., & Mullins, P. (1989). *Crocodile beat.* New York: Bradbury Press.
Kaplan, R. (2003). *Jump, frog, jump!* HarperCollins.
Oxenbury, H. (1986). *I can.* New York: Random House.
Walsh, E.S. (1993). *Hop jump.* Orlando, FL: Harcourt Brace, Voyager Books.
Wood, A. (1982). *I'm as quick as a cricket.* Swindon, UK: Child's Play International.
Ziefert, H., & Lobel, A. (1987). *Where's the cat?* New York: HarperCollins.

Rhythm Play

Baer, G. (1989). *Thump, thump, rat-a-tat-tat.* New York: HarperTrophy.

Boynton, S. (1993). *Barnyard dance!* New York: Workman.

Martin, B. (1994). *The wizard.* New York: Harcourt Brace & Co.

Raffi. (1987). *Shake my sillies out.* New York: Crown Publishers.

Imagination Builders

Berger, B. (1984). *Grandfather Twilight.* New York: Philomel Books.

Bornstein, R. (1978). *The dancing man.* New York: Houghton Mifflin.

Butterfield, M. (2000). *Who am I?* North Mankato, MN: Thameside Press.

Frasier, D. (1991). *On the day you were born.* New York: Harcourt Brace & Co.

Plourde, L. (2001). *Snow day.* New York: Simon & Schuster.

Rosen, M. (1997). *We're going on a bear hunt.* New York: Simon & Schuster.

Seuss, Dr. (1998). *My many colored days.* New York: Random House.

Shulevitz, U. (1969). *Rain rain rivers.* New York: Farrar, Straus & Giroux.

Shulevitz, U. (1998). *Snow.* New York: Farrar, Straus & Giroux.

Skofield, J. (1981). *Nightdances.* New York: Harper & Row.

Titherington, J. (1990). *Pumpkin pumpkin.* New York: HarperTrophy.

Williams, L. (1986). *The little old lady who was not afraid of anything.* New York: HarperCollins.

Yaccarino, D. (1997). *Zoom! Zoom! Zoom! I'm off to the moon!* New York: Scholastic.

Zolotow, C. (1952). *The storm book.* New York: HarperCollins.

Zolotow, C. (1981). *Flocks of birds.* New York: Thomas Y. Crowell.

Zolotow, C. (1992). *The seashore book.* New York: HarperCollins.

BOOKS THAT TEACH
CREATIVE DANCE TECHNIQUES

Barlin, A.L., & Kalev, N. (1993). *Goodnight toes! Bedtime stories, lullabies and movement games.* Pennington, NJ: Princeton Book Co.

Gilbert, A.G. (1992). *Creative dance for all ages.* Reston, VA: National Dance Association, American Alliance for Health, Physical Education, Recreation and Dance (AAHPERD).

Joyce, M. (1994). *First steps in teaching creative dance to children* (3rd ed.). Mountain View, CA: Mayfield Publishing Co.

Stinson, S. (1993). *Dance for young children finding the magic in movement.* Reston, VA: National Dance Association, American Alliance for Health, Physical Education, Recreation and Dance (AAHPERD).

FURTHER READINGS ON RELATED TOPICS

Bernstein, P. (1979). *Eight theoretical approaches in dance-movement therapy.* Dubuque, IA: Kendall/Hunt Publishing Co.

Bernstein, P. (1981). *Theory and methods in dance-movement therapy.* Dubuque, IA: Kendall/Hunt Publishing Co.

Berrol, C. (2000). The spectrum of research options in dance/movement therapy. *American Journal of Dance Therapy, 22*(1), 29–46.

Bertenthal, B., & Campos, J. (1990). A systems approach to the organizing effects of self-produced locomotion during infancy. In C. Rovee-Collier & L.P. Lipsitt (Eds.), *Advances in Infancy Research, 6* (pp. 1–60). Norwood, NJ: Ablex.

Bertenthal, B., Campos, J., & Barrett, K. (1984). Self-produced locomotion: An organizer of emotional cognitive, and social development in infancy. In R. Emde & R. Harmon (Eds.), *Continuities and discontinuities* (pp. 175–210). New York: Plenum Books.

Blakeslee, S. (1999, January 26). Movement may offer early clue to autism. *The New York Times*, p. F4.

Blau, B., & Reicher, D. (1995). Early intervention with children at risk for attachment disorders. In F.J. Levy (Ed.), *Dance and other expressive art therapies: When words are not enough* (pp. 181–189). New York: Routledge.

Bloom, L. (1993). *The transition from infancy to language: Acquiring the power of expression*. New York: Cambridge University Press.

Boas, F. (1941–1942). Psychological aspects in the practice of teaching dancing. *Journal of Aesthetics and Art Criticism, 2*, 3–20.

Boas, F. (1978). Creative dance. In M.N. Costonis (Ed.), *Therapy in motion*. Chicago: University of Illinois Press.

Boas, F. (1989). Origins of dance. In *A collection of early writings: Toward a body of knowledge*. (Vol. I, pp. 23–29). Columbia, MD: American Dance Therapy Association.

Bowlby, J. (1969). *Attachment and loss: Vol. 1. Attachment*. New York: Basic Books.

Cohen, D., Stern, V., & Balaban, N. (1997). *Observing and recording the behavior of young children* (4th ed.). New York: Teachers College Press.

Davis, M. (1972). *Understanding body movement: An annotated bibliography*. Bloomington: Indiana University Press.

Davis, M. (1973). Effort-shape analysis: Evaluation of its logic and consistency and its systematic use in research. In I. Bartenieff, M. Davis, & F. Paulay, *Four adaptations of effort theory in research and teaching* (pp. 29–42). New York: Dance Notation Bureau Press.

Davis, M. (1982). *Body movement and nonverbal communication: An annotated bibliography, 1971–1980*. Bloomington: Indiana University Press.

Davis, M. (1983). An introduction to the Davis nonverbal communication analysis system (DaNCAS). *American Journal of Dance Therapy, 6*, 49–73.

DeGangi, G., Breinbauer, C., Roosevelt, J.D., Porges, S., & Greenspan, S. (2000). Prediction of childhood problems at three years in children experiencing disorders of regulation during infancy. *Infant Mental Health Journal, 21*(3), 156–175.

Dell, C. (1977). *A primer for movement description using effort-shape and supplementary concepts* (2nd ed.). New York: Dance Notation Bureau Press.

Dissanayake, E. (1995). *Homo aestheticus: Where art comes from and why*. Seattle: University of Washington Press.

Dowd, I. (1995). *Taking root to fly: Articles on functional anatomy*. New York: Author.

Downes, J. (1980). Movement therapy for the special child: Construct for the emerging self. In M. Leventhal (Ed.), *Movement and growth: Dance therapy for the special child* (pp. 13–17). New York: New York University.

Dulicai, D., & Silberstein, S. (1984). Expressive movement in children and mothers: Focus on individuation. *The Arts in Psychotherapy, 11,* 63–68.

Duncan, I. (1977). *The art of the dance* (3rd ed.). New York: Theatre Art Books. (Original work published 1928)

Egeland, B., & Erickson, M.F. (1999). Findings from the parent–child project and implications for early intervention. *Zero to Three, 20*(2), 3–16.

Emde, R. (1994). Individuation, context, and the search for meaning. *Child Development, 65,* 719–737.

Erfer, T. (1995). Treating children with autism in a public school system. In F.J. Levy (Ed.), *Dance and other expressive art therapies: When words are not enough* (pp. 191–211). New York: Routledge.

Eshkol, N., Shoshani, M., & Dagan, M. (1979). *Movement notations: A comparative study of Labanotation (Kinetography Laban) and Eshkol-Wachman movement notation.* Holon, Israel: The Movement Notation Society.

Eshkol, N., & Wachman, E. (1958). *Eshkol-Wachman movement notation.* Holon, Israel: Weidenfeld & Nicolson, The Movement Notation Society.

Fenichel, E. (2001). From neurons to neighborhoods: What's in it for you? *Zero to Three, 21*(5), 8–15.

Fraenkel, D. (1983). The relationship of empathy in movement to synchrony, echoing, and empathy in verbal interactions. *American Journal of Dance Therapy, 6,* 31–48.

Greenacre, P. (1960). Considerations regarding the parent–infant relationship. *The International Journal of Psychoanalysis, XLI,* 6.

Greenough, W., Gunnar, M., Emde, R., Massinga, R., & Shonkoff, J. (2001). The impact of the caregiving environment on young children's development: Different ways of knowing. *Zero to Three, 21*(5), 16–23.

Greenspan, S., & Lewis, D. (2002). *The affect-based language curriculum (ABLC): An intensive program for families, therapists, and teachers.* Bethesda, MD: Interdisciplinary Council on Developmental and Learning Disorders.

Greenspan, S., & Meisels, S. (1996). Toward a new vision for the developmental assessment of infants and young children. In S. Meisels & E. Fenichel (Eds.), *New visions for the developmental assessment of infants and young children* (pp. 11–26). Washington, DC: ZERO TO THREE.

Greenspan, S., & Salmon, J. (1993). *Playground politics: Understanding the emotional life of your school age child.* Reading, MA: Addison-Wesley.

Greenspan, S., & Salmon, J. (1995). *The challenging child: Understanding, raising and enjoying the five "difficult" types of children.* Reading, MA: Addison-Wesley.

Greenspan, S., & Wieder, S. (1993). Regulatory disorders. In C.H. Zeanah (Ed.),*Handbook of infant mental health.* New York: The Guilford Press.

Greenspan, S., & Wieder S. (2002). Editorial: A developmental model for research on interventions for autistic spectrum disorders. *The Journal of Developmental and Learning Disorders, 6,* 1–5.

Gunnar, M., Larson, M., Hertsgaard, L., Harris, M., & Brodersen, L. (1992). The stressfulness of separation among 9-month-old infants: Effects of social context variables and infant temperament. *Child Development, 16,* 290–303.

Gunnar, M., Tout, K., de Haan, M., Pierce, S., & Stansbury, K. (1997). Temperament, social competence, and adrenocortical activity in preschoolers. *Developmental Psychobiology, 31*(1), 65–85.

Hartley, L. (1995). *Wisdom of the body moving: An introduction to body–mind centering.* Berkeley, CA: North Atlantic Books.

Harvey, S. (1990). Creating a family: An integrated expressive arts approach to the family therapy of young children. *The Arts in Psychotherapy, 18,* 213–222.

Harvey, S. (1994). Dynamic play therapy: An integrated expressive arts approach to the family treatment of infants and toddlers. *Zero to Three, 15*(1), 11–17.

Harvey, S. (1995). Sandra: The case of an adopted sexually abused child. In F.J. Levy (Ed.), *Dance and other expressive art therapies: When words are not enough* (pp. 167–180). New York: Routledge.

Individualized Education Program Team, 34 C.F.R. §§ 300.16 (2004).

Individualized Family Service Plan, 34 C.F.R. §§ 300.17 (2004).

Levy, F.J. (Ed.). (1995). *Dance and other expressive art therapies: When words are not enough.* New York: Routledge.

Lockman, J., & Thelen, E. (1993). Developmental biodynamics: Brain, body, behavior connections. *Child Development, 64,* 953–959.

Mazo, J. (2000). *Prime movers: The makers of modern dance in America* (2nd ed.). Pennington, NJ: Princeton Book Co.

Nachmanovitch, S. (1990). *Free play: Improvisation in life and art.* New York: Tarcher/Putnam.

National Research Council and Institute of Medicine. (2000). *From neurons to neighborhoods: The science of early childhood development.* Washington, DC: National Academies Press.

Perry, B. (2003, October). *Bonding and attachment in maltreated children: Consequences of emotional neglect in childhood.* Retrieved December 15, 2004, from http://teacher.scholastic.com/Professional/bruceperry/bonding.htm

Ruttenberg, B.A., Kalish, B.I., Wenar, C., & Wolf, E. (1978). *BRIAAC: Behavior rating instrument for autistic and other atypical children.* Chicago: Stoelting.

Sandel, S., Chailin, S., & Lohn, A. (Eds.). *Foundations of dance/movement therapy: The life and work of Marian Chace.* Columbia, MD: The Marian Chace Memorial Fund of the American Dance Therapy Association.

Schmoelz-Schappin, N. (1997, November). The FAM Scale (Functional assessment of movement scale): Assessment tool and outcome monitor of treatment responses. *American Dance Therapy Association Proceedings, 195.*

Schneer, G. (1994). *Movement improvisation: In the words of a teacher and her students.* Champaign, IL: Human Kinetics.

Thelen, E. (1996). The improvising infant: Learning about learning to move. In M. Merrens & G. Brannigan (Eds.), *The developmental psychologists: Research adventures across the life span* (pp. 21–35). New York: McGraw-Hill.

Todd, M. (1937). *The thinking body.* New York: Dance Horizons.

Tortora, S. (1992–93). A toddler experiences joint custody. *Zero to Three, 13*(3), 22–26.

Van Meel, J., Verburgh, H., & DeMeijer, M. (1993). Children's interpretation of dance expressions. *Empirical Studies of the Arts, 11,* 117–133.

Wieder, S. (1996). Climbing the "symbolic ladder": Assessing young children's symbolic and representational capacities through observation of free play interaction. In S. Meisels & E. Fenichel (Eds.), *New visions for the developmental assessment of infants and young children* (pp. 267–289). Washington, DC: ZERO TO THREE.

Williamson, G.G. (1989). Coping behavior: Implications for disabled infants and toddlers. *Infant Mental Health Journal, 10,* 1.

Williamson, G.G. (1996). Assessment of adaptive coping. In S. Meisels & E. Fenichel (Eds.), *New visions for the developmental assessment of infants and young children* (pp. 193–206). Washington, DC: ZERO TO THREE.

Young, B. (1996–1997). Pain and creativity: The complex interplay. *Zero to Three, 17*(3), 26–34.

Zeanah, C.H. (Ed.). (1993). *Handbook of infant mental health.* New York: The Guilford Press.

Zeitlin, S., Williamson, G.G., & Szczepanski, M. (1988). *The Early Coping Inventory: A measurement of adaptive behavior.* Bensonville, IL: Scholastic Testing Service.

Resources for Dance Movement Therapy Props and Instruments

Dancing Colors
(*source for colorful floating silk and nylon scarves, available in a variety of sizes*)
Post Offices Box 61
Langley, WA 98260-5989
http://www.dancingcolors.com
emilyday@dancingcolors.com

Dyenamic Movement Products
(*source for items such as Elastablast, a large stretch band fabric; Airwalker, a stretch hanging bag; and CoOperBlanket, a large, circular, wideband stretch fabric*)
http://www.dyenamicmovement.com
dyenamicmovement@comcast.net

Mud Pie Productions
(*source for a wide variety of good quality instruments*)
http://www.mudpiemusic.com
tplimp@valinet.com

Appendix C
Glossary

acceleration Effort   *See* quick Effort.

activate (activating)   The second step in the *Ways of Seeing* process, used to help a child explore the environment through self-discovery, during which the therapist pays close attention to the child's response, body, and vocal cues and encourages the child to take a leadership role in the expanded interaction.

arrhythmic   Pertaining to a Phrasing pattern or sequencing of actions in which the pulsing accent occurs at irregular intervals.

arrhythmic rhythm   A rhythm that occurs when the timing between each emphasized action does not follow a consistent beat. *See also* regular rhythm.

assessment   An information-gathering process for the purpose of making evaluative decisions.

attunement   A person's matching of a particular quality of another person's movement, which does not completely depict the entire shape, form, attitude, or rhythmic aspects simultaneously, as occurs in mirroring. *See also* experiencing, mirroring.

authentic movement   A type of meditation through movement that includes a mover and a witness. The witness observes the mover from a place of open receptivity as the mover (with eyes closed) listens to his body as movement spontaneously unfolds rather than moves from consciously directed thoughts. In this discipline each participant discovers his or her own inner experience through this profoundly simple process involving movement and stillness.

Body Describes how and what aspects of the body are used to execute an action creating a posture, gesture, or sequence of movements. The specific ways in which a person uses her whole body and parts of the body to move creates expressivity, as the mover's body makes shapes in her surroundings.

body boundaries The awareness that one's body is contained, integrated, and physically separate from others; the sense that enables a mover to judge how close to place his or her body next to someone else during interactions.

body image The mental representation of body referred to in psychoanalytic literature.

bound flow The quality within the motion factor spectrum of flow Effort that describes the feeling tone or inner attitude of a movement; involves actions that create a sense of precision, resistance, restraint, control, and holding back, emanating the sense that the actions might stop at any moment. *See also* free flow.

breath flow The Phrasing pattern that resembles and is often directed by the rise and release of the breath.

cognitive focus Focus relating to a child's perceptions of his or her surroundings; what a child understands and how this understanding affects the child's actions, behaviors, and ability to learn.

communication plane All of the space an infant can see in the front, to the left, and to the right when lying prone or supine in a horizontal orientation.

continuous Pertaining to the Phrasing pattern in which movements flow from one action to the next without a noticeable stopping or starting.

core self Term used by Stern (1985) to describe one of the earliest senses of self that has a physical basis and enables a young infant to compare and differentiate experiences of self from other.

dance The emotionally expressive phenomenon that is created when movements are put together in a lyrical way.

dance-play All of the movement-oriented activities that occur during a *Ways of Seeing* session, including dance, movement, creative play, and storytelling; the term *dance* defines the embodied, improvisational, and choreographic elements, whereas the term *play* defines the active, pretend, and creative playful nature of the activity.

deceleration   *See* sustainment.

declarative memory   *See* explicit memory.

deictic gesture   A gesture that establishes reference by drawing attention to an activity, event, or object through pointing, reaching toward, holding up, or showing an object.

direct Effort   Pertaining to the Effort quality within the motion factor spectrum of Space Effort that describes the feeling tone or inner attitude of a movement; describes actions that create a sense of specific direction and intention in the body and produce a pinpointing, single-focused concentration.

directional movements   In the Shape category of movement analysis, movements or actions consisting of arcing and spoke-like actions that reach out from a person's center (torso) making clear lines in space; often interpreted as a person's efforts to reach out into space and connect with the people in the surroundings and the environment while still maintaining a clear relationship to self.

directive memory   *See* explicit memory.

distal (distally)   Pertaining to the parts of the body located at the end of the limbs, far away from the center and torso. *See also* proximal (proximally).

dyad   Two individuals regarded as a pair.

dyadic rhythmicity   The presence of a steady and consistent beat of interaction between a caregiver and a child.

dynamic   Referring to the nonlinear order of processes that emerges from an interplay of influences, with no implication of hierarchical or stage level relationships between the processes.

Effort   The term used in movement analysis to define the qualitative accents and specific characteristics of a movement; the feeling tone or inner attitude of the movement in four motion factors: space, weight, time, and flow.

embodied (embodying)   Pertaining to the expression and sensation of emotional, physical, and sensorial feelings through the body and body actions.

embodied experience   For a mover, the felt-sense qualities of the moving experience; for a witness/observer, being present in the moment, observing, and trying on the mover's actions through experiencing, mirroring, and attunement. *See also* attunement, experiencing, mirroring.

embodied experience focus   The focus that explores the interrelationship between both movement and physical/motor development and a sense of self from the perspective of a mover's spontaneous felt-sense experience.

embodied witness   A term developed in the discipline of Authentic Movement to describe a witness who is actually moving with a mover as opposed to sitting off to the side and observing the mover without moving.

emergent self   Term used by Stern (1985) to describe the experiential organization of a person concerned with establishing the sense of a core self.

emotional regulation   The ability to stay calm and focused; the ability to problem solve, maintain social engagement, communicate effectively, and benefit from the rich learning opportunities in everyday experiences.

energy level   The physical feelings created by a child or children's action(s); depicts the actual body and movement behaviors the child or children are exhibiting. When used in an analysis of the overall classroom curriculum, the *energy level* refers to the amount of concentration a task demands in relation to the resulting mental and physical activity exuded from the group (as a whole or as individuals), categorized as high, neutral or calm, low, or lethargic.

experiencing   A key word in dance movement psychotherapy that involves gaining an awareness of individual adults and children by following their lead and actually trying on their actions. *See also* attunement, mirroring.

explicit memory   Also known as directive or declarative memory; describes the active conscious awareness of personal occurrences and facts; narrative memory.

feeling self   The self created from the inner sensations occurring through bodily felt experiences.

feeling tone   The tone of the emotions depicted in a child or group's actions; refers to the overall mood of a child or a group.

felt-sense   Feeling an emotional and/or physical experience on a physical, visceral, sensorial, or body level.

flexible Effort   *See* indirect Effort.

flow Effort   One of the four Effort motion factors that describe the feeling tone or inner attitude of a movement, characterized by creating a movement attitude along the spectrum of free to bound tension; associated with a sense of progression, precision, and continuity; referring to how a person maintains or interrupts the flux or normal continuation of his or her movements. Although all movements require a degree of muscular tension, the quality of that tension is what differentiates between free and bound flow.

free flow   The quality within the motion factor spectrum of flow Effort that describes the feeling tone or inner attitude of a movement, involving actions that have a carefree, alive, and fluid feeling. *See also* bound flow.

general space   The term in the Space category of movement analysis referring to the space that lies outside of an individual's personal kinesphere. *See also* kinesphere.

hidden regulators   The term used by Hofer (1995) to describe the regulatory effects of a mother's sensorimotor, thermal-metabolic, and nutrient-based behaviors that shape multiple developing physiological and behavioral systems of her very young offspring; the term *hidden* emphasizes that these regulatory effects of the mother's behavior are not readily evident in first observing a mother–infant interaction, whereas the term *regulators* describes how the level, rate, or rhythm of each system is controlled by specific components of the continuing maternal social engagement.

implicit memory   Also known as procedural or nondeclarative memory; memories that are nonsymbolic, involving perceptual, sensory, reflexive actions that are remembered without full conscious awareness.

indirect Effort   Also known as flexible Effort. Pertaining to the quality within the motion factor spectrum of Space Effort that describes the feeling tone or inner attitude of a movement, involving actions that are all encompassing, with an attitude of flexibility created by sweeping, scanning gestures; full body actions; and overlapping shifts of body focus.

intentional nonverbal communication   Communication by intent or design generally thought to require more advanced bodily control and regulation as well as higher communicative and cognitive skills involving symbolic understanding.

interactive regulation   The concurrent and reciprocal influences each partner's behaviors have on the other.

interpersonal space   In the Space category of movement analysis, the area of space shared when two individuals are engaged; the interactive, changing spatial distances between people in a given environment.

kinesphere   In the Space category of movement analysis, the personal space around each individual that is reachable while the individual stays in one spot.

kinesthetic empathy   The component of the *Ways of Seeing* self-observation process involving becoming aware of and reflecting on personal emotional reactions being experienced and actually trying on the actions observed.

kinesthetic seeing   The component of the *Ways of Seeing* self-observation process involving becoming aware of and reflecting on personal sensorially based reactions.

Laban Movement Analysis (LMA)   The system of nonverbal movement analysis developed by Rudolf Laban that provides a detailed description of the qualitative aspects of an action.

light Effort   The Effort quality within the motion factor spectrum of weight Effort that describes the feeling tone or inner attitude of a movement, involving actions that create a slight body tension, buoyant, fine, or airy sensation of body weight.

LMA   *See* Laban Movement Analysis.

mirroring   A process that involves a therapist literally embodying the exact shape, form, movement qualities, and feeling tone of another person's actions, as if the therapist were creating an emotional and physical mirror image. *See also* attunement, experiencing.

mirroring diminished   As described in the *Ways of Seeing* approach, a type of mirroring in which some aspect of the movement quality is reduced, but the overall sense and style of the movement is left intact.

mirroring exaggerated   As described in the *Ways of Seeing* approach, a type of mirroring in which the embodied movement qualities are enlarged, but the overall sense and style of the movement is retained.

mirroring modified   As described in the *Ways of Seeing* program, a type of mirroring in which the overall style and quality of the movement is left intact, but some aspect is changed.

mobilize (mobilizing)   The third step in the *Ways of Seeing* process, used to help a child explore the environment through self-discovery, during which actions are developed into deeper expression and/or are developed physically and emotionally.

molding actions   *See* Shaping (molding) actions.

motor development   A child's progressive mastery of fine and gross motor skills following a developmental progression.

movement development   A child's developmental process of acquiring different movement qualities involving muscular tension, strength, timing, and spatial orientation.

movement melody   The harmonic composition of actions sequenced together that often exude a lyrical quality.

movement metaphor   A specific, personally stylized, nonverbal, qualitative element, posture, or sequence of movements that frequently recurs within an individual's movement repertoire and may have personal meaning.

movement phrase   Similar to a musical phrase, a phrase that is created when a series of movements is performed in sequence that creates a complete action or expresses a feeling; composed of qualitative dynamics and lasting for any duration; has a beginning, middle, and ending.

movement repertoire   The range of movement qualities and elements that an individual uses to express him- or herself.

movement signature   The specific qualitative actions used most frequently in an individual's movement repertoire; that is, the actions that most characterize or define an individual's style of moving.

mover   The person whose movements are being observed to determine specific nonverbal movement qualities.

narrating   As described in the *Ways of Seeing* approach, the act of providing an objective description of the events of an interaction as they are occurring.

nondeclarative memory   *See* implicit memory.

nonrhythmic   Phrasing that occurs when a clear rhythmic sense is not observable.

nonverbal dance   The relationship between self and other in which each member uses his or her body to relate and express.

nonverbal intentional acts   Gestural communication that is specifically performed with the goal of communicating.

perception–action level   As discussed by Bucci (1993), Appelman (2000), and Beebe et al. (2000), one of the two levels of representation that organizes social behavior; a level in which sensorimotor forms are presymbolic representations, encoded nonsymbolically, in which memory is implicit, procedural, and emotionally based, and may be out of conscious awareness. Perception–action levels of representation are dynamically created through an infant's experiential relationship with the environment that is continually being reorganized moment to moment. *See also* symbolic level.

perceptual images   Nonverbal symbols, independent of language, that become the basis from which nonverbal experiences connect to linguistic expression.

phase   The individual components of a movement phrase; the phases that define a complete phrase unit consist of a beginning action, a middle or main action, and an ending or recovery action.

Phrasing   The clustering actions together over a period of time, creating a flow, pulse, and rhythm as the actions start, continue, pause, and stop; Phrasing marks the unfolding flow of the movement sequence.

potential communicative acts   According to the *Ways of Seeing* approach, all actions are to be regarded as having the potential to be communicative; therefore, practitioners should pay attention to the qualitative aspects of nonverbal expression that provide valuable information about a child's intent.

presymbolic categorical mode   As discussed by Bucci (1993) and Appelman (2000), the nonverbal mode that occurs before symbolization that enables infants to categorize events, objects, and experiences into groups of discrete prototypic images.

procedural memory   *See* implicit memory.

proprioceptive   The system responsible for the muscular and joint sensations felt during active full body, body part, or limb movements, enabling people to sense the movement and position of their bodies in space; the system that establishes motor control and motor planning as the explorative movements of the muscles and joints become instinctive learned-movement patterns.

proximal (proximally)   The parts of the body located at the joints, close to the torso, or center. *See also* distal (distally).

psychophysiological responses   The term used by Lipsitt (1976) to describe body responses such as heart-rate reactions, biological and culturally based differences and influences, genetic determinants on development, the role of reflexes as precursors for behaviors, and emotional responses that effect autonomic responses to stimulation.

qualitative movement elements   The specific details of an action that affect how an action is performed, which can be used to construct a nonverbal language of movement.

quick Effort (sudden, acceleration)   Pertaining to the Effort quality within the motion factor spectrum of time Effort that describes the feeling tone or inner attitude of a movement, involving actions that have a sense of urgency, vivaciousness, or haste in regard to time.

reflexes   Early automatic movements controlled by the spine and brain stem that create the fundamental gross functional patterns that lie beneath all movements.

regular rhythm   A predictable, steady beat. *See also* arrhythmic rhythm.

relational movement metaphors The term developed in the *Ways of Seeing* program to describe the recurring nonverbal patterns that become established between two members of a particular dyadic relationship, are specific to the dynamics of the dyad, and often define the relational qualities of the dyad.

rhythm Created by the sequential flow between sound and silence in a distinctive, temporal patterning; marks the passage of time emphasized through marked or accented pulses, sequencing, and phrasing of a series of movements; the observable shift at some point in a movement phrase, which creates a demarcation or accent within the course of the action. Rhythm can be regular or arrhythmic (irregular) and creates the emphasis in a movement phrase. *See also* arrhythmic rhythm, regular rhythm.

rhythmic accents Accents that occur within a melodic tone, adding structure and emphasis to the quality of a movement phrase.

rhythmic Phrasing Phrasing in which the movement action has a pulsing, definite accent.

sagittal plane The longitudinal plane that divides the body into right and left sections; moving in the sagittal orientation enables a mover to enter and advance or to withdraw and retreat from the world.

self-focus actions Actions involving self-touch that can initially serve as a cognitive self-organizing function.

self-regulation The organization of internal and external sensory input, affecting how infants are affected by their own behaviors.

sense of body The sense of one's own body as well as the body of another or others; developed in a child by somatic, sensorial, and nonverbally based early childhood experiences; a concept used by the *Ways of Seeing* approach to suggest that body sensations significantly contribute to, inform, and continually influence one's experiences in the formation of the emotional, social, communicative, cognitive, and physical aspects of self.

sense of self Created by interactions that enable a child to learn about self as being different and yet still in relationship to others.

sensory integration The ability to perceive and process sensory information from the body and the environment in an organized way.

sensory integration dysfunction A dysfunction in which some or multiple aspects of an individual's sensory systems contribute to difficulties in modulating internal and/or external input.

sensory photograph The *Ways of Seeing* term referring to the felt-sense kinesthetic nature of memories (including those of trauma and abuse) recorded on a multisensory level that may be revealed through the observation of a child's unique movement metaphors. Analogous to the image of a photographic snapshot, sensory photographs are taken to register sensations, to create physical and visual images, to gain conscious awareness of difficult sensations, and to exert feeling control over these bodily felt impressions, as well as to retrieve and recreate positive sensory-based feelings when a pleasing physical state has been achieved.

Shape One of the five categories in nonverbal movement analysis that describes the forms that the body and movements make in space in response to objects or people in the surrounding space; shape flow, shaping, and directional movements are the elements within Shape that describe the changing forms the body makes in relation to self and the environment.

shape-flow actions The term in the Shape category of movement analysis describing movements such as breath movements that occur within the boundaries of the body and an individual's internal body space that create internal movement fluidity.

shape form The visible patterns the body makes as it moves in space that reflect each individual's unique style and manner.

shaping (molding) actions The term in the Shape category of movement analysis referring to actions of a mover that form his or her body around an object or another person, creating a sense of the mover's adapting to the contours in a space, be it a person, object, or the form the mover is creating.

shared dance-play Two-way communication occurring through playful movement exchanges.

slow Effort *See* sustainment.

Space One of the five categories in nonverbal movement analysis that describes the area where actions occur in reference to others and the surrounding spatial environment.

space Effort One of the four Effort motion factors that describe the feeling tone or inner attitude of the movement; characterized by movement along the spectrum of a direct to indirect or flexible attitude, focus, concentration, or attention toward space.

spatial directness An attitude that is single focused and specific, in which a person goes straight to a destination with precision and without distraction.

spatial pathways The floor patterns a mover makes as he or she traverses a room.

special needs   Used broadly to encompass issues in relating and communicating, developmental delays, learning challenges, and parent–child attachment disorders.

spontaneous choreographies   Interactions between self and others.

sporadic   A movement Phrase in which actions have clear stopping and starting points but may or may not have a regular rhythm.

stationary action   The term used when an individual's activities are confined to his or her current placement (i.e., lying down, sitting, standing) without moving away from the center or changing the full body spatial orientation either up or down, rolling, or moving around the room.

still movement   A state in which a child is not moving at all, regardless of the child's focus; stillness is a component of the movement spectrum despite any lack of active motion.

stimulate (stimulation)   The initial step in the *Ways of Seeing* process used to help a child explore the environment through self-discovery, during which the child is brought to an awareness of some aspect of behavior.

stress cues   Cues that reflect a person's coping style in dealing with struggles that present a deep personal threat or psychological conflict.

strong Effort   Pertaining to the Effort quality within the motion factor spectrum of weight Effort that describes the feeling tone or inner attitude of a movement, involving actions that create a forceful and firm use of body weight.

subsymbolic processing mode   As discussed by Bucci (1993) and Appelman (2000), the processing mode based on visceral, sensory, somatic experiences that have infinite gradations and variations.

sudden Effort   *See* quick Effort.

sustainment Effort (slow, deceleration)   The Effort quality within the motion factor spectrum of time Effort that describes the feeling tone or inner attitude of a movement, involving actions in which the attitude toward time is directed toward indulgence, drawing it out slowly and leisurely while keeping an active awareness of it.

symbolic level   The discrete, categorical, and explicit level of representation, such as words and intentional nonverbal gestures; one of the two levels of representation that organizes social behavior. *See also* perception–action level.

synchrony   A phenomenon in which the participants of a movement activity are moving in relationship to each other without needing to copy each other's actions exactly.

tempo The speed of music; can be constant or varied.

tension flow fluctuations Shifts between free and bound flow observed through the changes in a baby's breath; the muscular tension shifts from free to tense; and the sporadic actions of the limbs jutting out into space, created through joint flexion and extension. *See also* bound flow, free flow.

time Effort One of the four Effort motion factors that describe the feeling tone or inner attitude of a movement; time is characterized by movement along the spectrum of a sudden quickness or accelerating to a sustained or decelerating attitude toward time. The attitude associated with time relates to decision making and intuitive readiness. The term *when* is associated with the Effort attitude of time, referring to the person's approach toward time rather than the actual duration, pace, or tempo taken to execute the actions.

verbal processing A phenomenon that takes place when a therapist defines a nonverbal experience to explain or interpret its meaning as it is occurring.

vestibular system The body system that supports the senses of balance and equilibrium; the regulation of muscle tone and coordination; the control of visual steadiness; the sustaining or shifting through different arousal and emotional states; and the ability to discriminate, select, and maintain attention during an action. The vestibular system is engaged through head and body movements in response to gravity, such as swinging, spinning, and rocking.

Ways of Seeing A program of dance movement psychotherapy that combines the principles of child development, dance movement psychotherapy, the Authentic Movement discipline, and the system of Laban Movement Analysis (LMA) to create a complete assessment, intervention, and educational approach for infants, children, and their families.

weight Effort One of the four Effort motion factors that describe the feeling tone or inner attitude of the movement. An attitude of weight creates a strong or light physical body intention when executing an action, which provides the *what* quality to a movement because it reveals what level of body weight exertion is used to perform the action. Weight brings into awareness how the person is using body weight to affect the environment; mastery of this motion factor creates the feeling that the person has a clear body consciousness exhibited in his or her abilities to demonstrate responsive intent in the control of muscular engagement.

witnessing   Originating from the discipline of Authentic Movement and a component of the *Ways of Seeing* self-observation process, the monitoring of personal multisensory and nonverbal reactions by objectively mapping the details of the observed actions.

REFERENCES

Hofer, M.A. (1995). Hidden regulators: Implications for a new understanding of attachment, separation, and loss. In S. Goldberg, R. Muir, & J. Kerr (Eds.), *Attachment theory: Social, developmental, and clinical perspectives* (pp. 203–230). Hillsdale, NJ: The Analytic Press.

Laban, R. (1968). *Modern educational dance* (2nd ed.). London: MacDonald & Evans, LTD.

Lipsitt, L. (Ed.). (1976). *Developmental psychobiology.* Mahwah, NJ: Lawrence Erlbaum Associates.

Stern, D. (1977). *The first relationship: Infant and mother.* Cambridge, MA: Harvard University Press.

Index

Page numbers followed by *t* and *f* indicate tables and figures, respectively.